M000115261

THE CHAMPIONSHIP

David Henry Lucas

Col. Robley Robinson,
a pleasure to meet you.
Best Wishes,

David Hry Lucas

May 8, 2015

© Copyright 2013 by David Henry Lucas. All rights reserved.

No part of this book may be reproduced in any written, electronic, recording, or photocopying without written permission of the publisher or author. The exception would be in the case of brief quotations embodied in the critical articles or reviews and pages were commission is specifically granted by the publisher or author.

Although every precaution has been taken to verify the accuracy of the information contained herein, the author and publisher assume no responsibility for any errors or omissions. No liability is assumed for damages that may result from the use of information contained within. Books may be purchased in bulk or otherwise by contacting the publisher and author at:

Available at createspace.com/4385210

or

TELL Publishing, LLC
PO Box 247
Bishopville, SC 29010

lucas@thechampionship.biz
tellpublishing.com
thechampionship.biz

Design: Ken Maginnis
Publisher: Tell Publishing, LLC
Editor: Martha Black-Lucas

Library of Congress Catalog Number:
ISBN (paper): 978-0-9895730-0-9
ISBN (e-book): 978-0-9895730-1-6
First Edition Printed in the U. S. A

THE CHAMPIONSHIP

The Story of the 1969
University of South Carolina
Football Team

By David Henry Lucas

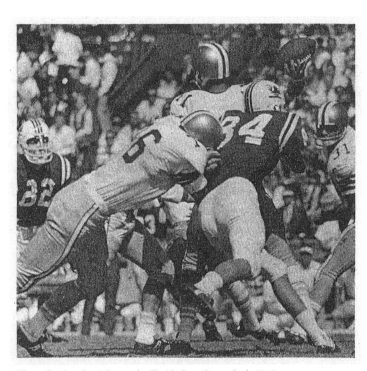

The author (number 84) goes after Florida State Quarterback, 1968.

Foreword

"In life, as in a football game, the principle to follow is:
Hit the line hard."

--- *Teddy Roosevelt*

David Henry Lucas heeded the words of Roosevelt on and off the field.

After a stellar football career at the University of South Carolina, the sack-artist defensive end --- a skinnier, mid-1960s version of current pass-rushing Gamecock star Jadaveon Clowney --- hit the business world hard and fast.

Lucas became an entrepreneur. He started in banking and moved on to real estate sales, building contractor, resort developer, land planning, cell phone investor, Arabian horse breeder, activist, consultant, bluegrass musician, writer and movie producer. He successfully pursued a private property rights lawsuit to the United States Supreme Court (Lucas vs. South Carolina Coastal Council), wrote a book about the experience ("Lucas vs. the Green Machine"), and founded the National Council on Property Rights.

His rollicking days as a cross-country traveler to Alaska as a student, fraternity life at the University of South Carolina and, of course, his insight into his USC teammates and coaches can all be found on the pages of The Championship.

--- *Ernie Trubiano*

Author Ernie Trubiano is a University of South Carolina Journalism graduate and retired sports writer at the State Newspaper in Columbia. Mr. Trubiano has authored two books: "The Carolina Cup: 50 Years of Steeplechasing and Socializing" and "South Carolina Sports Legends", and is the contributing author on a book on antique prints. He has written numerous freelance articles on sports and antiques and serves on the board of the South Carolina Athletic Hall of Fame.

Contents

Introduction   The game of American Football is in its 144th year. The modern-day game of football took its present form about 100 years ago when the NCAA was formed. It is not my intention to give a history of the game, but to give you, my reader a glimpse into what life was like for a college football player at the University of South Carolina in the second half of the 1960s. The game of football is genius, and although there have been some minor rule changes, the game we played then, is the same game played today. Only the strategies have evolved along with the popularity of the sport.

Life as a college football player in the 1960's did afford time for other endeavors and fun, so also within these pages are tales of fraternity life that are straight out of the movie "Animal House" and travel adventures that spanned this great country all the way to the 'Last Frontier'.

The 60's were a time of generational and cultural transformation. We, as student athletes, were dealing with this transformation as was everyone else. In football at South Carolina, there was a major coaching change that complicated life at the same time. But we did come together as players and coaches and we accomplished something that had never been achieved before at South Carolina. The 1969 South Carolina Football team went undefeated in conference play and won the ACC Championship. I was fortunate to have played on the team.While life as a student-athlete wasn't always easy, I am grateful for the opportunity to compete as a Gamecock and to have received a stellar education. I am equally grateful for the people I have met along the way, many who have become lifelong friends.

We were able to capture our first Conference Championship together and I think all of us-fans, coaches, staff and players, cherish those memories more each day. I feel certain that very soon, another team of South Carolina athletes, coaches and staff will not only win Conference Championships, but will create memories, they too can cherish for a lifetime.

I hope you enjoy this journey from the gridiron at the University of South Carolina to the wilds of Southeastern Alaska almost as much as I did taking it.

Go Cocks!

Dedication 'The Championship' is dedicated to the 1969 ACC Championship Team,
Coaches and Staff and to my Alma Mater, The University of South Carolina.

We hail thee, Carolina, and sing thy high praise

With loyal devotion, remembering the days

When proudly we sought thee, thy children to be:

Here's a health, Carolina, forever to thee!

Acknowledgements

I would like to express my gratitude to all who provided support, offered comments, assisted in proofreading, editing and design. Many thanks to my wife, Martha and my children, Carey, Jonathan and Lydia who supported and encouraged me throughout this process. To Ken Maginnis, I offer my eternal gratitude for all of his hard work as graphic designer. Special thanks to Julia Fisher and again Ken Maginnis who encouraged me to write 'The Championship' and to my friends and former teammates, Robert Miranda, George McCarthy, Jimmy Pope, Allen Brown, Candler Boyd, John D. Coleman who reviewed my story and offered their advice and inspiration. To Ernie Trubiano, former State Newspaper Sportswriter and author, thank you for your generous gift of time and wise council and to my friend and fraternity brother, Harry Brooks, please accept my gratitude for all of your efforts on my behalf.

There have been so many who have influenced, and enlightened me during the years of my life found within these pages. From my Dad, William Dollard Lucas, I received a determination to never quit. My Mother, Helen Wood Lucas, gave me my love for reading, my athletic ability and sense of adventure. My Uncle, Darby Fulton Lucas, gave me my love of the great outdoors that led me on my escapades in the Northland. There are many others from my early years that influenced me in positive ways but they are too numerous to name here.

To an athlete, his coaches make the difference in success and failure. I have been blessed with good coaches who were also good men throughout my athletic career. A special thanks to Coach Marvin Bass and Coach Ed Pitts for offering me the opportunity to play for the Gamecocks. The new coaches, Paul Dietzel and Larry Jones, found other talents on the defensive side of the ball and gave me the opportunity to employ them. Coach Dietzel showed us how to do things in a first class manner and for that I think all of his players are grateful. Most of all, I want to acknowledge the contributions of each character, named and unnamed, between the covers of THE CHAMPIONSHIP. You know who you are!

Go Cocks!

CHAPTER 1

'The Biddies'

The blue and white two-toned 1965 Chevrolet Impala drove slowly through the Columbia traffic. It was mid-August and the summer heat was adding a shimmering haze to the view. It's called the dog days of summer. The afternoon temperatures reached 100° and the humidity wasn't far behind. We had driven west on No.1 Highway passing through Camden, then Lugoff, which was just on the other side of the Wateree River. We kept westward until we reached the outskirts of Columbia. I had been to Columbia many times before to visit my great uncle, Clyde Dexter Galloway. Uncle Clyde lived just off of Two Notch Road in a small cottage that is behind present-day Pulliam Ford. He worked for the city of Columbia. His job back then was as a "smoke abatement officer." Today, his job would be considered environmental control, a precursor of things to come.

But today's trip was different. We weren't going to visit Uncle Clyde and his wife Aunt Leila Mae. Instead, my parents were taking me to the University of South Carolina's athletic dorms to begin my academic and athletic collegiate career. In the distance on that Sunday afternoon, the Statehouse loomed ahead like some huge cathedral.

The South Carolina Statehouse complex is one of the most beautiful in the nation. And to a country boy from the Turkey Creek section of Lee County, South Carolina, it sure was an impressive sight. It was also the largest building I had ever seen up until then. We pulled up right in front of the Statehouse and my Dad put on the left blinker. He turned onto Gervais Street and took a right at the first intersection which was Sumter Street. Up

(AP Wirephoto)

Two More Gamecocks
USC Head Coach Marvin Bass Talks With (L to R) David Lucas and Bob Teal and the Boys' Fathers, David Lucas Sr. and C. E. Teal.

Bishopville, Greenville Stars

USC Signs 3 Linemen

By BOB SPEAR
State Sports Writer

Three linemen, two from Bishopville and another from Greenville, announced Friday that they had signed football grant-in-aids with the University of South Carolina.

Tackle Bob Teal and end, David Lucas, the Bishopville duo, signed with Head Coach Marvin Bass at the USC Athletic Center and Wade Hampton High's Gordon Gibson signed with assistant coach Ed Pitts.

Teal, who stands 6-foot-1 and weighs 235, was on the second team Class A all-state and was a member of the Shrine Bowl squad that whipped North Carolina 20-6 two weeks ago.

"South Carolina had what I wanted, both academically and football-wise," disclosed Teal. "All the coaches have really impressed me.

"I don't know what I'll study yet, but I'm leaning toward law."

"I'm sort of like Bob," said Lucas, a 6-foot-5, 180 pounder. "South Carolina has an excellent all-around program, both academically and athletic.

"From an ends' point of view, I like their style of play. I have been impressed by all the coaches and am looking forward to playing for USC."

The pair led Bishopville to a 9-1-1 record, the school's best in years. Only a loss to Lower Richland and a tie with Darlington marred the record.

Gibson, a 6-foot-2, 210 pounder, is the brother of former Gamecock star Tom Gibson. The younger Gibson was a top-notch tackle of Coach Steve Satterfield's team.

The trio moved the number to 21 who have signed grants with South Carolina. All but three played their high school ball in the state.

12

An 1872 illustration of the Horseshoe, USC's original campus.

ahead about two blocks, the University of South Carolina came into view.

The core of the campus is called the Horseshoe and it appeared on our left as we drove south on Sumter Street. The Horseshoe is the original campus of The South Carolina College that was founded in December of 1801 by an Act of the General Assembly, initiated by Governor John Drayton, in an effort to promote harmony between the low country and the backcountry. The Horseshoe is listed on the National Registry of Historic Places, and most of its buildings reflect the federal style of architecture in vogue in the early days of the nineteenth century. Among them is the Caroliniana Library, which was designed by Architect Robert Mills and is the first freestanding academic library in the United States.

The elegant building known as The Longstreet Theater came into view as Daddy took his time driving. Just behind this beautiful old building, that was

currently being used as a gymnasium, stood our destination. Just to the rear and right side of Longstreet Theater was the complex of dormitories called the Honeycombs. There were six buildings of six stories each. One of these was nicknamed the "jock" dorm or J dorm, my new home.

SE Horseshoe gate

Dad slowed down as we approached Divine Street and put on his right hand blinker. The street was a beehive of activity. There were cars and people taking up the whole street. People were walking toward the dorms with suitcases, duffle bags and all sorts of sheets, blankets and towels in their arms. It was my first time moving into a college dormitory and while it was confusing, it was also very exciting.

We got lucky and found a parking place not too far from J dorm. Stepping out of the car, I looked around for anyone that I knew, but only saw strangers huffing and puffing in the August heat. J dorm was up on my right and that was where the letter from the athletic department said I was to be housed.

I had signed my grant-in-aid scholarship that spring at The Roundhouse, which was not located on the main campus. I hadn't been heavily recruited. As a matter of fact, the one scholarship offer I had received was from the University of South Carolina. My high school team, the Bishopville Dragons, had had a good year. We ended my final year with a 9-1-1 record. We had beaten a much bigger school, the Hartsville Red Foxes, two years in a row and tied the powerful Darlington Falcons. During my summers I had worked at the Lee County

Highway Department for Mr. Brownie Brown. He was connected to the University Athletic Department and had lobbied the Gamecock coaching staff for my scholarship. I am still grateful for his efforts on my behalf. Our high school principal, Pug Teal, had also been instrumental in getting a scholarship for me to play for the Gamecocks.

We had been given a tour of the athletic facilities then, but not of the campus, so I was unfamiliar with my new surroundings. The Rex Enright Athletic Center, commonly called The Roundhouse, was the center for football and was a multistory round brick building. The ground-level floor contained the offices for the football staff. Downstairs were the training facilities, equipment room and locker rooms. Kenny Lester, a former football player who was in law school and working as a graduate assistant coach, showed our group around. The group consisted of my Father, William Dollard Lucas, my high school principal, Pug Teal and his son, Bob Teal. Mr. Teal had played football for the Furman Paladins back in the 30's and was well known and respected around the state as an educator and former athlete.

Marvin Bass

His son, Bob and I had been teammates growing up in Bishopville. I played left end and Bob played left tackle right beside me. We had made a pretty good pair for the Bishopville High School Dragons. Bob had gotten most of the honors our senior year. He had been named to the All-State team as a tackle and also had been chosen to play in the annual Shrine Bowl Game held each year between high school all-stars from South Carolina and North Carolina. Bob also played in the North South All-Star game for South Carolina. All I had received were a few speeding tickets from our local highway patrolman.

The day we signed our grant-in-aid at The Roundhouse, I had met Coach Marvin Bass, Head Coach for the Gamecocks, for the first time. The Moose, as he was nicknamed, certainly lived up to that moniker. He stood about 6'2" and it seemed like he must've weighed 500 pounds. Everything about the man was big. His head was big. His shoulders were big. His arms were big. But the most impressive thing about him was the size of his hands. I felt like I was shaking hands with a ham. About six or seven years later, I had the pleasure of meeting and shaking hands with the World Heavyweight Champion boxer, Jack Dempsey, at his restaurant in New York. Now the champ had big hands, but after shaking hands with both of them, Coach Bass won, you might say, hands down. I took an immediate liking to Coach Bass. He was as warm and friendly as he was big and I was excited about becoming a Gamecock. I also knew that if I wanted a college education, this was probably the only way to get it.

So here I was on a hot, muggy Sunday afternoon getting ready to move into the athletic dorm to start my Gamecock career. Although I was excited, I did have some trepidation. I had played against one or two of my soon-to-be teammates, but I didn't know anyone well except Bob. During the summer I received a letter from the Athletic Department. In the letter I was given my dorm room assignment and the name of my new roommate.

I don't know what I expected, but as a naïve country boy, I was surprised when I found that my roommate was a damn Yankee. He was an offensive lineman and his name was George Waldo McCarthy. It was bad enough to have to room with a stranger, but to have to room with a Yankee was not appealing, to say the least.

We got out of the car, stretched and opened the trunk. We had all of the items that the letter suggested we bring. My Mother and Father grabbed a few bundles and I grabbed a couple more. It looked like it would take at least two trips for us to move all of the things we had brought. As we walked toward the building, we were constantly smiling and saying hello to other student athletes and their parents, who were doing the same thing. I think my room was number 605, which was on the top floor of J dorm. When we got to the room, I knocked, but got no answer so I opened the door to my new life.

Honeycomb Dorms

The room was about twelve feet wide and was laid out like most dorm rooms across the country. The floor was hard vinyl. There were single beds on each side of the room with a desk at the head of the bed and a closet at the foot. A couple of feet of floor space separated the closet from the bed. A sliding glass door at the opposite end of the room opened onto a small balcony. The outside of the building was covered with concrete latticework from which the building got its name, "The Honeycomb" dorms. This latticework ran from the ground floor to the roof. Looking out you couldn't see much, but it did let in the light. The veil blocks were probably in place to keep students from falling or throwing stuff out when they'd had a little too much to drink. The corner rooms, however, did have partial openings with a set of iron railings. The room looked pretty good to me. After depositing my luggage, we started out to get the final load. As we left, I locked the door behind me.

Typical Honeycomb dorm room

After grabbing the final bundles and dropping them off in my room, my Mother gave me a big hug and told me to be a good boy. My Dad gave me a hardy handshake and said how proud he was of me and reminded me to do my best. I walked them back to the car where we said a few more goodbyes and I watched them drive off, leaving me in my new world. I turned around and walked back to the dorm, deep in thought. I got off the elevator and started to my room. Standing there was a big guy with a shaved head. He was naked except for a towel wrapped around his bottom and wore a pair of flip-flops on his feet. I swallowed hard and took a deep breath as I walked in his direction. Reaching my room, I pulled my key out and started to open the door as the naked guy said with a pronounced Northern accent "Are you Lucas?"

"Yeah, I sure am."

"Well, hurry up and get the damn door open. I've been stranded in the shower for the last twenty minutes. You locked the door and I didn't have my key!"

"Man, I'm sorry."

"Yeah, you should be. I've been dodging mothers, sisters, girlfriends and fathers for the last half-hour."

What a way to start my relationship with this big Yankee. As it turned out, after George was able to get safely back in the room, he relaxed and started laughing.

"I think I gave some of those mothers and sisters a little shock."

"That's what they get for nosing around in the shower areas. I got here a day early and I didn't expect all these people to show up at the same time."

"Well George, I guess you just spiced up the afternoon for some folks," I replied.

"You're from Washington, DC aren't you?"

"Yeah, I am. But I went to high school in Maryland at a Catholic school called DeMatha High. You ever heard of it?" He asked.

"No, it's a little bit out of my territory."

"Yeah, my nickname in high school was Big G from DC."

George McCarthy
(Big G from DC)

George talked out of the corner of his mouth, just like an old 1930's era gangster. I thought I was talking to Edward G. Robinson. I knew right away that I was going to be rooming with a character. I also took an immediate liking to this guy. If I could get past his northern heritage, I felt we could even become pretty good friends.

We chatted awhile, asking each other about our families. George Waldo McCarthy was Irish Catholic. His father and mother were originally from Boston, Massachusetts. His father was a Colonel in the Air Force and worked some sort of government job in Washington. As Irish Catholics, they had about twenty three kids or at least, after he rattled off all the names, it seemed like that many. George had a twin sister, Helen, who was also attending the University of South Carolina and a brother named Brendan, who was a fullback, playing for Boston College. I eventually got to meet all of his brothers and sisters and there wasn't one in the bunch I didn't like.

Over the next few hours, all the freshmen arrived. This was back in the good old days when they recruited fifty or sixty athletes in one class. We met the athletes who were rooming close to us and they all seemed like nice guys. By then, it was around nine o'clock which was my usual bedtime at home. I crawled into bed thinking I might be able to get to sleep, but before I knew it there were about seven guys sitting around the room listening to Big G from DC talk about life in the big city. Most of our new friends were from small towns or rural areas, so a guy like Big G had tales most of us couldn't match. After a while though, 'sweet bumbo land' pulled me in and I drifted off to sleep.

The next morning, the coaching staff got us up bright and early, around six o'clock. It was off by bus to The Roundhouse to get fitted for our equipment and uniforms. Then we were bussed back to campus where we had our first workout as Gamecocks. Well, that's not quite right. Back in the 60's the NCAA didn't allow freshmen to participate in varsity competition, so we had our own freshman team. We were the 'Biddies', not Gamecocks quite yet. We had our own coaching staff and our head coach was one tough guy named Ed Pitts. Coach Pitts had been a great college player for the Gamecocks, in fact, an All-American. He had been drafted by the pros and seemed to have a very promising future ahead of him before a knee injury ended his NFL career. The man loved football and he loved the South Carolina Gamecocks. He was no-nonsense, determined and very intense.

Ed Pitts lettered in football at USC from 1957-59. He was the team captain on the 1959 team.

The first practice field we used in 1965 for the freshman team was located one building over from our dorms. It was called Davis Field. Just a year or two later, Davis Field became a beautiful reflection pool to enhance the then new, Thomas Cooper Library. It was bound on the west by Longstreet Theater. To the south of the practice field was the Library. To the east stood the student center, The Russell House and the north side of the practice field was flanked by Green Street.

The varsity practiced at the athletic facilities right behind The Roundhouse. There were a couple of practice football fields, the track and field facilities and at the far end, a baseball field. We had to work out on campus the first few practices when the varsity was using The Roundhouse Complex. As we got off the bus at Davis Field that morning, the coaching staff called us all together. Coach Pitts told us what he expected of us and then the coaches explained what our warm-ups would be like. In football it seems that every coach has a little bit different take on what warm-ups should be. Ours were pretty standard. First, we did some stretching exercises. We'd do the old reach for the grass between your legs followed by stretching of hamstrings and calves. After stretching for a while, it was time to start warming up with jumping jacks, running in place, jumping on the ground, getting back up and then jumping on the ground again. This would continue for ten to fifteen minutes.

After warm-ups, we broke up into our various positions with our position coaches. I had been recruited as an offensive end. Coach Pitts later told me the reason they recruited me was that I could catch the ball and ran well after the catch. The Coaches took us over to the side of the field where they gave us a few simple pass routes to run. Nothing fancy, we just began with 15-yard down and out patterns. I watched closely as several guys ran their routes. Now it was my turn. Back in Bishopville, I had been catching passes from the same quarterback for my entire football career, starting in grammar school. Harold Galloway had thrown ninety per cent of the passes I had caught, up until that morning. Harold had a firm passing touch and he had been a very successful quarterback at home, but Harold was not on the field that day. Instead, up stepped a brand-new quarterback named Ron Zukowski.

Ron Zukowski

Ron was 6' 1" and weighed about 190 pounds and hailed from New Jersey. He called the signal and I took off on my route. The adrenaline was pumping and I felt like I was flying. At the 12-yard mark I made a little head fake to the inside as I usually did on this route, and then made my turn. As designed, Zukowski threw the pass before I made my cut. The only problem was that he threw the ball really hard. I raised my hands to make the catch and the ball went right through my fingers. It felt like it took the first layer of my skin off with it. I thought to myself, "What in the hell was that?" I had missed the first pass thrown to me in my collegiate career. Things were not going the way I had hoped. Welcome to college football.

As I soon learned, you only got a few chances to prove yourself in practice because there were so many players on the team. If you made a mistake, it was tough to get back in the good graces of the coaches. I think we had ten to twelve ends all trying for the same two positions. This was going to be more of a 'weeding out' process than it was a "coaching you up to your potential" process. I would have to knuckle down if I was going to make the team. Little did I know worse was yet to come.

Coach Ed Pitts

We practiced in helmets, shoulder pads and shorts for the first few days. There was no contact, but we ran an awful lot. I thought our coaches in high school were pretty tough on conditioning, but that was before I met Coach Ed Pitts. I don't think I've ever run as much as we ran those first few days. Then the fun really began. Our first day of contact started. I was a tall, skinny kid. At 6'4", I weighed a whopping 175 pounds. I had pretty good speed and quickness, and I was going to need every bit of it. Most of the guys who played my position outweighed me by at least 20 to 25 pounds.

After the light workouts in shorts, it was time to get down to the real thing. We moved to the practice facilities at The Roundhouse. The first full pad contact drill I remember was something I had never done before. It was called "bull in the ring". Well, I guess we had done a version of this in high school, but we didn't use our helmets to butt each other or our forearms to deliver a blow. We just used our shoulders to block and that was the extent of the drill. This was going to be different. They expected you to use your forearm as a weapon and hit your opponent before he hit you. My high school coaches had always taught us to use our hands behind straight arms to keep blockers away from our bodies. It was the old fashion way of doing things. My high school coaches played their college football in the 1930's and 40's. This straight arm or hand "shiver" as it was called in the past was not what the college coaches wanted us to do. They wanted us to be mean and hostile and try to knock people down. It was tougher than I was used to, but I thought I was getting the hang of it.

That was before I ran into a guy from Tennessee named Butch Johnson. I still couldn't grow a full beard at nineteen, but Butch had a full five o'clock shadow fifteen minutes after he shaved. I remember stepping into Butch to trade blows and caught his big old hairy forearm right under my chin. He didn't completely dislocate my jaw, but he certainly loosened it up on the right side for me.

That lick lead to a real gut check. I wasn't hurt badly enough to need treatment. I just had to tough it out until after practice. The next morning we were up early, had breakfast and went to The Roundhouse for morning drills. I had just finished getting dressed in the locker room. I had all my pads on and was sitting on the bench with my helmet in hand. My jaw was sore and my muscles ached from the running and drills. I had bruises everywhere from the first day of contact. Everyone else had hit the field and I was still sitting in front of my locker feeling sorry for myself. I remember thinking; "This is too tough for me. Why didn't I play baseball or basketball or run track, anything but football."

My father had drummed into my head since I was a little boy in short pants, that to get ahead in life, you needed a college education. He had a few years of college at South Carolina, but did not earn a degree. Life with a wife and two children was too much of a load for him, so he left college behind and moved back to the old family farm in Turkey Creek. He tried a few different things, like selling produce door to door, but finally took a job as an instrument mechanic at the new DuPont May Plant in Camden, SC. He made a pretty good living there, but he certainly wasn't going to become rich working for wages.

My parents, like so many other parents of the time, wanted a better life for their children and my Dad saw a college education as the way to get it. I knew that if I quit and dropped out, his hopes for my future would be dashed. I had hopes and dreams too, so I stood up, took a deep breath and put on my helmet. My jaw was still sore and so was the rest of me, but I had to "suck it up" and get back down to business. I knew that if the coaches would give me a chance, I could play. After all, I had gone through a similar, less stressful experience just four years earlier.

I had been fortunate enough to earn a varsity high school letter as a ninth grader. That was very unusual for a freshman, but I got bored with the sport toward the end of the season and when the last game against Timmonsville came around, I decided that I wasn't going to play, so I stayed home. Bishopville lost the game and our Head Coach Max Dubose scolded me the next week at school.

He asked "Son, where were you?"

"Coach, I couldn't get a ride to town," I lied.

"Son, we would have sent somebody to get you if you had only called."

"I didn't think about that," was my excuse.

"You know if you had played, I think we would have won the game."

"They started running around your end and we just couldn't stop them and you been stoppin' people all year. We needed you and counted on you being there, so I guess you know that you let a lot of people down Friday night."

All I could do was come up with a lame apology, "Yes sir, I'm sorry."

I was young and had not realized fully the concept of being accountable to my team or the importance of football in the lives of most Southerners. Heading into my sophomore year of high school, I decided that hunting in the fall was more important than playing football, so I was thinking about hanging up my cleats. But then Fatty showed up. We had a neighbor who lived about a mile away named Fatty Clyburn. Mr. Clyburn was a bigger than life, genuine, southern character. He was a very successful farmer as well as one of my Dad's best friends. Fatty liked to drink and carouse and my father was often asked to accompany him on some of his "ride abouts" around the state. He and "Billy", as he called my Dad, would leave on a Saturday morning and visit friends while having a few toddies on their travels. They would also attend political gatherings and stump speeches all over South Carolina. They generally returned home late at night after we were all in bed.

One Saturday afternoon, Fatty pulled up in our backyard as he often did. That day he had another man in the car with him that I did not recognize. I called for Daddy, but "Mr. Fatty", as younger people called him, said, "Son, Hell come here, it's you I've come to see."

Now that surprised me. Mr. Fatty usually didn't take much time with kids my age, so somewhat taken aback I said, "Yes sir," and tentatively approached his big white Cadillac. The two men got out of the car just as my Dad came out of the house.

"Hey Fatty, How ya' doing today?" he said in greeting.

"Billy, you know my brother-in-law Coach Goat McMillan from Clemson, don't you?"

"Yeah, I've met you a couple of times before, Goat. Good to see you again."

"Billy, I been telling Goat about that boy there of yours and his football playin' and Goat says if he's going to be as good as I say he is, then Goat wants him to go up to Clemson and play ball for ole Frank Howard when he gets out of high school."

"Yeah Billy, Fatty tells me your boy is a damn good athlete. He looks tall enough and if he fills out some, then he could make a good college ball player," Goat said.

Turning to me he asked, "Are you interested son?"

I was astounded. Frank Howard was a legend in the state. I remembered watching Clemson play Paul Dietzel's LSU Bengal Tigers in the 1958 Sugar Bowl on television. We had only had a TV for a couple of years and it was still magical for most people. If you were important enough to make it on television, then you had to be important.

LSU had the "Chinese Bandits", LSU Stripes on their uniforms and Heisman Trophy winner, Billy Cannon. I think they were popular just because of that Chinese Bandit stuff. It was cool and unique. Clemson lost the game, but it was close. The final score was LSU 7, Clemson 0. Although LSU had won the National Championship that year, Clemson and Frank Howard had been on national TV and now, here in Turkey Creek was a big time college coach saying that he would be watching me. If I played well I could possibly get a scholarship to Clemson. I might even play on TV one day! I decided I needed to rethink the decision to give up playing football. There would be no more visions of imitating Daniel Boone or Davy Crockett who were frontier hunters, and American folk heroes. I realized that football was becoming popular and it was something I did pretty well. I didn't have to dream about it. I was a real live football player. So with a big ole grin on my face, I said "Yes sir that would be great." So football it was. Exploits in the wilderness would have to go. But, little did I know that one day I would get the chance to fulfill my abandoned dreams of adventure in "The Last Frontier."

Two weeks later, I showed up for two-a-day practices at the Dragon's football field right beside Bishopville High School. I had made the right decision.

Over the next three years of high school I grew a couple more inches and gained a few pounds. My football skills improved and I anxiously waited for a call from the Clemson Tigers and Coach McMillan. It never came, but I did receive the offer from South Carolina. They had always been my favorite team anyway. It was ironic that I was spurned by the Tigers, but encouraged by them to continue playing football.

Here for the second time in my football career, I was thinking about hanging up my cleats. But I decided to suck it up and get back to practice. Hoping that it was the right thing to do again, I trotted out to the practice field behind The Roundhouse with my sore jaw, sore muscles, bruises and battered ego.

Football was the same game as it is now. Teams played offense and teams played defense. They ran the football and they passed the football. You had to block and you had to tackle to play the game. In those days, there was no such thing as a water break during practice. When you hit the field you were out in the hot sun for two hours plus. The only water available was in the morning when there were still dew drops on the grass. When the coaches weren't looking, you could drag your helmet through the grass and if moisture stuck to it, you could lick it off. That was our water break, that and sucking the moisture out of old dirty sweat rags.

The Roundhouse 1960

The coaching we received was also very limited. That was partially because there were so many of us to coach. They did teach us basics such as not rounding off our pass routes. That took too long and gave the defensive man in coverage time to react. So the idea was to square off your routes and make sharp quick turns. They also put a great emphasis on staying square to the line of scrimmage. Whether you were on offense or defense, your shoulders were always supposed to be parallel to the line of scrimmage and your body, in good football position.

The freshman team started practicing at the far end of the complex and the varsity practiced closer to The Roundhouse. One day the varsity coaches came down to the freshmen practice field and asked for some volunteers. Since I was low on the depth chart and didn't even get to practice much, I raised my hand. About six other guys who weren't doing much either volunteered too. Volunteered for what, we hadn't a clue. We were told to follow one of the graduate assistants, Sonny Dickinson. Sonny waved his arm in a 'follow me' gesture and off went our merry little band of freshmen. We ran all the way to the varsity playing field and over toward some equipment trunks sitting on the side lines. Sonny opened the trunks and pulled out what I can only describe as full length baseball catchers' pads. In baseball, the catcher is protected on his upper-body by ribbed padding that covers his torso, shoulders and crotch. These pads were made out of the same material, only they covered the entire body from the upper arms and neck, to the ankles. It took a second or two to sink in, but it looked as if we were going to be 'live' dummies for the varsity. We were instructed to don the apparel and meet on the field in front of the varsity.

As we went about the task of suiting up, we could see the big boys loosening up by bumping each other. When I say big, most of these guys were huge and they were mean looking too. Dressed in our "catchers" pads, we moved over toward the ball and Coach Sonny. I have never felt or looked as awkward as I did then. Coach Sonny started to line us up as the varsity broke the huddle and headed to the line of scrimmage. The closer they came, the bigger they looked. Sonny lined us up and told us what to do. And guess what? We were going to be 'live' dummies for the varsity defensive line.

Syndicated Comic Strip
"Li'l Abner" by Al Cap

The padding was for our protection, but I wasn't convinced that the pads would work. I looked at the guy they had placed across from me and started praying. What a shock! It was Steve Cox. Steve was nick-named "Li'l Abner" after the newspaper comic strip character. He had a 58" chest and a 36" waist. He was about 6' 5" and weighed in at 250 pounds. That isn't impressive by today's standards, but in the 1960's, that was BIG! Already drafted by the pros, he was all muscle with a mean football reputation to go with it. But I was game even though he outweighed me by eighty pounds. I remember thinking, "What good is a college degree if you're dead?"

Oh well, it was too late to back out. They showed us what to do when the ball was snapped and the quarterback started the count. On the second hut here they came. Smack, crunch, I was on the ground being trampled. The whistle blew and the play was over. I felt around and nothing was broken and I was still coherent. OK, maybe this wasn't going to be so bad after all. Cox came over on his way back to the huddle and said, "Don't worry kid, you'll do fine."

Man what a pick me up. The famous Steve Cox had spoken to me, a skinny lowly freshman. That meant that I was almost a teammate! The rest of the practice went fine and I learned a few things. I learned some names and plays and had gained some varsity experience and "Little Abner" had asked my name. This was the first positive moment of my short career and it came at just the right time.

Our two weeks of practices were coming to a close and the varsity season was coming up. Once again, the coaches asked for volunteers to play against the varsity in a game type environment and I volunteered again. Don't ask me why! We got ready to scrimmage the varsity for real this time. No baseball catchers' suits. It was going to be real football. This game type scrimmage was held on the playing field in Carolina Stadium. It was under the lights and would be my first live contact in that venue. Even though it was still practice, because of the game conditions, (the varsity wore game uniforms, they had real referees and no coaches on the field) I was excited about the chance to play. Things did not go so well, however. We kicked off to the varsity and I was playing right end on the kickoff team.

The kickoff was taken by a sophomore running back named Benny Galloway. He started up the middle, got a couple of blocks, and darted toward the sideline I was guarding. Suddenly, there he was right in front of me. Benny was short and stocky. At about 5'9" and 190 pounds, he ran with power and speed. I drew a bead and hit him hard, or so I thought. I had made a mistake. I had hit him high, shoulder pad to shoulder pad. That was the wrong strategy and I just bounced off and hit the ground on my knees. I looked up to see Mr. Galloway continue down the sidelines for a touchdown. This college game was a little bit different from high school ball and it was going to require a lot more concentration and determination.

Soon the regular student body returned to campus and classes started. There were several good things about this. Number one, it meant that two-a-days were over and I was still around. Secondly, there were girls, lots of girls and some were really gorgeous. It was different than going to class in high school. In high school, all of our classes were in the same building. But here, classes were scattered throughout the campus which took some getting used to. We got to class like everyone else. We walked and we walked, but at least it added to my conditioning.

The football team occupied about four floors of J dorm. As I mentioned before, there were six of them altogether. Most of the other dorms were occupied by regular male students. There was no cohabitation in those days and if you tried it and were caught, that was a sure ticket home for all parties involved.

We had been given special meal cards. Most of the students were on student meals plans, if they could afford it. Our meal cards entitled us to extra helpings since we burned calories a lot faster than most of the other students. The central dining room was located in The Russell House, a

couple of hundred yards from J dorm and was the center of campus life back then. The campus post office and bookstore were also located there.

In the mid-60s, the University of South Carolina had about 12,000 students. If you sat in the hallway of The Russell House long enough, you would see just about every student pass by. The athletes didn't have a special dining room, but ate meals with the other students. Generally, however, football players hung with football players, because you knew them best. Occasionally, I met up with hometown friends and introduced them to my teammates. Making friends with my new teammates and other students my freshman year, was one of the most enjoyable things about being at South Carolina.

As we got to know each other better, I was pleased to find that other than talking funny, some of those damned Yankees were pretty good fellows. I became good friends with my roommate, Big G from DC. In addition, there was a quarterback from Scottsdale, Pennsylvania, named Bill Zarrella, who I liked a lot. This college stuff was changing my perception of the world.

W.D. Lucas

Helen Wood Lucas

I had never thought much about what I wanted to do after college, so I had no idea what to declare as a major. My faculty adviser, an athletic department member, advised me not to worry about it the first year. Most of the first year classes were required by all students, no matter their major, so I didn't have to make a decision right away. My Father had been a World War II Marine and so had my Mother. I had thought about joining the Naval ROTC, but football was taking all of my spare time. Practices were hard and tiring. By the time you finished practice and had supper at The Russell House, there wasn't much time left in the day. It was hard to call family if you were homesick, or talk to a girlfriend, since there were no phones in the rooms. There was only a hall pay phone for everyone to use. So most of the freshman ball players that first semester went to practice, ate, studied and slept. The ones who failed to keep a lid on their daily lives were soon out of school.

As the year wore on, our ranks thinned. Some of the guys got homesick almost as soon as they arrived. Some of them missed their high school sweethearts. A few would go to the coaches and discuss their situation and the coaches could sometimes talk them out of making the wrong decision. Others would pack their bags and leave in the middle of the night without saying anything to anyone. A few got hurt and needed surgery which would often end their football careers. I can't remember the numbers, but we lost twenty to thirty per cent of our freshman team by the end of the first semester.

I remember going to freshman orientation the first day of classes. The administrator conducting the orientation instructed us to look to our left and look to our right. He stated that two out of three students would not graduate from the University and he was right. If you added the lifestyle of a football player to the rigors of student life, the percentages went up for athletes.

Two-a-day practices were finally over. In the two weeks prior, we had gotten to know quite a few of the guys and some of these friendships would last a lifetime.

The personalities of the players ran the gamut. We had the choirboy types who wanted to be preachers and one that became a cat burglar. There were poor guys, rich guys, city boys, country boys, smart students, 'dumb as post' types, ladies men, guys who were shy and bashful, dedicated athletes, talented athletes and athletes that weren't talented at all. We also had a guy who was one of the funniest people I have ever met and that includes comics in Las Vegas Comedy Clubs I saw in my later years. There was a real kaleidoscope of characters on our team that freshman year.

The Biddie's opening game was with Gordon Military College located in Barnesville, Georgia. We took a Greyhound bus and traveled down for our opening freshman game. I had hopes of getting to play, but my number was not called. Instead, I sat there and watched us get whooped. Our starting quarterback, Allen Brown, was from Hinesville Georgia. Allen was a good quarterback, but our ends weren't adept at catching his passes. Blocking was poor and Allen spent most of the game running for his life. Coach Pitts was not very pleased, to say the least.

Allen Brown

The rest of the games went pretty much the same way. I don't remember a lot about the five games the 'Biddies' played that year. There wasn't much you would want to remember. I think our record was one win and four losses. As I recall, I got to play on the kickoff team in two or three of those games, but that was it. I never even made it to the substitution level, much less a starting position. It was very demoralizing. I had always been a starter on every football team that I played on, beginning with the midget football program when I was about eight years old, right through the twelfth grade. I had even started as a freshman in high school. It wouldn't have been so bad if I had been given an opportunity, but the coaches just didn't let me in. I knew that I had not been highly recruited. I hadn't received any postseason awards or played in any postseason All-Star games. Most of the guys who were playing ahead of me were more highly recruited and so the coaches gave them the opportunity. Looking back from today's vantage point, I suppose that was the right thing to do. Give the more highly recruited players the first chance to play. At the time, however, it was disheartening. If we had been winning games, it would have been easier to take. But we weren't. I had to sit there knowing that I could play better than some who were out on the field. Of course, every ball player sitting on the bench thinks the same way.

Toward the end of the season, I tore a hamstring muscle in my right leg. I do remember that it was a pretty painful experience. I was on crutches for a couple of weeks, so that pretty much ended my first year of football at the University of South Carolina. Our team trainer was a man named Jim Price. Jim gave me some good advice. He had been with the program for a few years and I respected Jim. He said, "Remember, good things come to those who wait. You'll get your chance sooner or later, just hang in there."

I met Jim while I was still in high school. One of my high school teammates was Ricky Traub. Ricky was a great high school running back. He was big for the running back position at 6 feet tall and 185 pounds and he was fast. His best in the hundred yard dash was a state record of 9.8 seconds. He was a year older and we were on the track team together, as well. He had injured his knee while running track and Jim Price had treated his injury at a state track meet. Ricky was a highly recruited high school athlete. I believe he had over a hundred scholarship offers. He decided not to play college football and enrolled at the University of Georgia. Looking back, if Ricky had played, I believe he could've been a great running back. But that is speculation. What was not speculation was that I had not accomplished much on the football field as a freshman. I appreciated the advice from Jim Price and I dealt with my disappointment, reminding myself that I was still getting a college education.

The Varsity played very well that year. Although their record was not that impressive, five wins and five losses, it was enough to give the University of South Carolina a chance to share the ACC Championship. It all came down to the final game of the season. That game was against our in-state arch rival, the Clemson Tigers. The game was played at Carolina Stadium that year and the stands were full with over 50,000 fans attending. I was sitting in the south end zone with my date, a beautiful girl from Fort Mill, South Carolina. I had met her at the beach the summer before I came to school. Our seats were down close to the field and as it turned out, a great spot for the climactic play of the game. Clemson had just scored a touchdown and the Tigers had a decision to make. If they kicked the extra point, the game would be tied. If they tried to go for two, they would win the game. If they tried for two and didn't make it, the Carolina Gamecocks would have a share of the ACC Conference Championship for the first time in school history.

Coach Frank Howard made his decision. The Clemson Tigers trotted back to the goal line. They were going to go for the two point conversion and the win. Excitement grew to a fever pitch as the teams lined up. Everybody in the stadium was standing and yelling as loud as they could. The tension was palatable. The Tigers were tough and the outcome of the game hung in the balance. Carolina had its back to the wall, literally, and the whole season was coming down to this last two-point play. It's been forty eight years, but I still remember the excitement and electricity as Clemson snapped the ball.

Our end zone seats were about five rows up, directly behind the goalpost, so we were up close and personal. In fact, it was as close to being on the field as I had gotten all season. The Clemson quarterback, Tommy Addison, dropped back to pass and threw toward his tight end, Bo Ruffner in the end zone. Carolina's linebacker, Bob Gunnells, stuck out his big right hand and batted the pass down. The Gamecocks had beaten the Tigers and for the first time in school history, the football team had a portion of the ACC Football Championship. And while the Gamecocks had to share the championship with the Duke Blue Devils, Coach Marvin Bass and the team were proud of their season. It was major college football at its best. Oh yes, and the date went very well that evening too.

This game also led to one of the all-time great football quotes. When asked by a member of the press, after the game, why the Clemson Tigers didn't go for the tie, Clemson Coach, Frank Howard's famous reply was, "Why hell fellows, a tie is just like kissing your sister. And that ain't much fun!"

After football was over, I turned my efforts to the books. Classes were a little more difficult than they had been at Bishopville High School, although our teachers and the faculty at Bishopville had prepared us very well. I believe that in the late 60's, our high school had one of the highest percentages of students, who upon entering college, graduated.

I did have one small problem that was interfering with college life. Lack of cash. Though better off than some, I didn't have any extra money to spend on dates or anything else for that matter. I met plenty of gorgeous girls, but there was no money to do more than meet them. I didn't have a car either, so dating would have to wait. The NCAA allowed the University to give the student athletes $15 a month to pay for their laundry. My parents couldn't afford to send money on a regular basis, so, all I had was the laundry money from the University and a little money saved from my summer job at the Lee County Highway Department.

Very few of us had automobiles. I think there were probably three or four cars between the fifty or sixty freshman football players. We walked or hitched rides everywhere. Most of the trips home my freshman year were hitchhiking expeditions. The only interstate highway in South Carolina at the time was I-26, which ran from Asheville, North Carolina, down through Columbia to Charleston, South Carolina. I-95 ran from the North Carolina border down through Georgia to Florida. Interstate I-20 was just under construction in our area. Upon completion, it would run east and connect to I-95 in Florence, South Carolina. Heading west to Columbia, I-20 would go through Georgia and on to the west coast. If I wanted to go home, I had to stick out my thumb and catch rides on No.1 Highway. It was about sixty miles to Turkey Creek from Columbia. Normally, the ride would take an hour to an hour and a half depending on traffic. Hitchhiking, it usually took double or triple that time. I usually took a couple of guys home with me for the weekend and people were reluctant to give rides to big ole guys like us. I suppose we looked a little intimidating.

Since there weren't any football workouts, our excess energy had to be spent on something and that something was generally mischief. There were several guys on the team who were big practical jokers. We had a freshman named Ron Cibick who was from the Pittsburgh area. He had his little quirks as most of us did, but one of his was pretty interesting. He was annoyed by the sound of bells. In those days, we still had the old-style alarm clocks that had bells. A couple of the guys went around and got about seven or eight of the clocks and carefully went around setting alarms for different times, hiding them throughout Ron's room. One or two were hidden under the bed. Another one was placed in a desk drawer and they hid a few under his dirty clothes. None of us got much sleep that night, because we all wanted to watch the action. Sure enough, the first alarm clock went off. Ron leapt out of bed and came storming out into the hall wanting to know who the smart ass was that had hidden the clock in his room. Of course, none of us had a clue. The fun lasted for hours as each alarm went off before we all got tired and went to sleep.

These kinds of pranks were almost a nightly occurrence. When it got too boisterous, someone would call the hall counselor who would come with his notepad ready to turn you in to the coaching staff or Dean Cooper (the Dean of men for Carolina with a reputation for enjoying handing out punishment), for discipline. One of our guys had another trick he loved to pull on people. He would fill his mouth full of lighter fluid and knock on your door. When you opened it, he would spray a fine mist of fluid onto an open flame from a cigarette lighter he was holding at arm's length and mouth high. Opening your door to a flame in your face would scare the tar out of you.

Some of the guys found a way to take three pennies and wedge them into the door locks from the outside. This would lock you into your room and everybody thought it was amusing to make you late for class.

One of the funniest, but most dangerous practical jokes morphed out of the lighter fluid trick. The floors were hard tile, laid on concrete, which made them impervious to flames. Two or three cans of lighter fluid were squeezed under the door while the occupants were sound asleep. The liquid expectorant would run down the middle of the room, and puddle between the two beds. When lit, it was just like a scene in a movie where the villain lights the gunpowder and tries to blow up the heroine in the mine. The flames would follow the flow of lighter fluid and rise up two or three feet high. Then the perpetrator would rap on the door yelling fire, fire! He would disappear around the corner and duck into his room. The startled sleepers thought it was a real emergency and that their lives were in danger. This was college hijinks at its best. Too bad we didn't have digital cameras to record it all.

Thanksgiving holidays came and my roommate George McCarthy invited me to go home with him to Washington DC. I had always been interested in history and had never traveled so far. We had been to Atlanta for weddings and to Greensboro, North Carolina to visit my Mother's family. We had been to the Blue Ridge Mountains for vacation, but this was going to be a real trip. I scraped together a little money and George and I took the train from Columbia to Washington DC, our nation's capital. I really liked history and Washington is jam-packed with it.

When we arrived, George's Dad picked us up at the station and took us to their multi-storied townhouse on Reservoir Road, located in the Georgetown section of Washington. Now my house was small. My dad had gotten a Veterans Administration loan in 1958 and we had built a 1000-square foot, three bedroom, one bath, brick house. When we walked up to George's door, I was amazed. The townhouse was half as wide as our small house. How in the world could all of George's family fit in this little box? What I didn't know until I entered and explored, was that the house had four levels. It was a three-story town house with a full basement. The living room, dining room and kitchen were on the entry-level. George's Mom and Dad had a bedroom on the second floor and all the girls lived on the third floor. The boys all slept in the basement, barracks style.

Two of George's older brothers, Mike and Tracy, were in the military. Brendan was the star running back for Boston College. As an All-American, he was later drafted by the Green Bay Packers. Fortunately, he was home for the weekend. He was the kind of guy you automatically liked. Brendan was big for a running back. He was 6'2" and weighed about two hundred pounds. He was a good-looking Irish guy and he certainly had the gift of gab. When we entered, Brendan was showing his mother a full-length portrait of himself in his Boston College football uniform painted by a famous Boston artist. After being introduced to Brendan, he turned back to his Mom and said, "Mom, this is a very valuable painting and I'm going to leave it here in your care while I take this Lucas kid and George out for a few beers. While we're gone, I guess it's all right if you want to lounge around the painting and look at it, but remember, don't touch it."

Brendan McCarthy, Boston College

I was totally blown away by his remark to his mother. If I had spoken to my mother in that manner, I would've been getting up off the floor, even if I was joking. But, I guess life up North was different. George's Mom just laughed and said, "Brendan, I think you are getting a little too big for your britches."

I stowed my gear in the basement under a bunk and George and I got dressed to go out. Brendan was excited about showing me "The Avenue." It was on Wisconsin Avenue where George and Brendan's favorite bars were lined up. Impatiently, he ordered, "Hurry up you guys. They're gonna' run out of beer!"

I protested to George, "Big G, I've been looking forward to seeing some of the historical sites like the Washington Monument, Capital Building and the Library of Congress. Why don't we go play tourist and meet Brendan later?"

George replied, "We ain't got but one car and Brendan's driving."

We got in the car and George said to Brendan "Hey, Lucas wants to go see the historical sights." Brendan replied, "Is that right?"

"Yeah Brendan, this is my first trip to Washington and I'd like to see some of the landmarks I've read about," I said.

"Okay, okay, if you want to see the sights, see the sights we will," replied Brendan.

I was excited as he pulled up close to the Washington Monument. He got out of the car and said, "Come on. Come on, let's go."

We followed Brendan to the elevator and we rode to the top of the Washington Monument. When we reached the viewing platform, Brendan grabbed me by the arm and took me to the first window. "Look over there, that's the f'ing capital. Look over there, that's the f'ing White House.

We walked to a different window, "There's the f'ing Jefferson Memorial. Now you've seen the f'ing sites of our nation's capital. It's time to hit the Avenue and drink some beer."

Down the elevator we went, crawled into the car and went to a succession of bars on Wisconsin Avenue. In a fashion, I suppose, I did get to see some of the sights on my first trip to Washington.

John D. Coleman

After the start of the next semester, I was invited to go home for the weekend with John D. Coleman. John D, as he was called, roomed next door to George and me. His roommate was a guy from Rocky Mount, North Carolina named Darrell Johnson. Since they were our next-door neighbors, we got to know the two of them very well. John D was from Latta, South Carolina, a small town near Dillon, which is another small town near Florence. John D lived out in the country about three miles outside of Latta. His father was a big time cotton farmer. We knew his father was pretty successful because John D was one of those guys that had an automobile his freshman year. As a matter of fact, it was a pretty sporty muscle car, a black GTO. We called it "the goat." John D's roommate, Darrell, only played with us for a year. Sadly, Darrell was drafted and went to Vietnam and is still missing in action.

I remembered my first impression of John D's home. We drove in through the front entrance to his house and there were about three acres of long-leaf pines. Beautiful moss draped oak trees led to a manicured lawn. Over two hundred azaleas were interspersed around the trees and the yard. The house was modern for the 60's, built in the antebellum style. We were greeted by his parents and shown to our rooms. I looked out of a window at the back of the house to see a large patio and a four acre fishpond about twenty yards away.

It was Saturday night and we decided to go to Myrtle Beach for some college fun (girls and beer). I remember taking a shower and marveling at the towels in their bathroom. Our towels at home were just regular sized towels and sometimes it took two to completely dry off, but those Coleman towels were thick and soft. I had never seen that kind of luxury before. A simple thing, I guess, but it has stuck with me for a long time.

We drove the forty-five minutes to Ocean Drive Beach. 'OD' is about twenty miles north of Myrtle Beach and was the place to go in those days. The most popular college hangout in 'OD' was a beer joint called "The Pad." It was easy to find, just across the road from the beach. It had a pool table, a jukebox and a patio for shagging. Not the English version of shagging, although that did occur from time to time, but the Carolina Shag dance. We partied hardy and came back to Latta tardy. It was about four in the morning when we finally returned to John D's home.

In the South, we had an unwritten rule. No matter what you had done on Saturday night, on Sunday morning you got up early, ate a big breakfast and went to church. Only a hospital stay could change that routine. My sister called it, 'Mother's Revenge'. Sure enough, after only about three or four hours of sleep, we were summoned for breakfast. Mrs. Coleman was excited about entertaining her son's friend and had really put out a great spread. There were creamy, buttery grits, biscuits and toast with all kinds of jams and jellies, piles of crispy bacon, savory sausage and country ham piled high on a platter and placed on a lazy susan. Under normal circumstances, this would have been a feast I would have really enjoyed, but this was not a normal set of circumstances. John D and I were suffering from a very severe case of the 'Honkey Tonk Flu'. We had caught a bad case of it after our night at The Pad and there was no cure for this illness but time.

With Mrs. Coleman's urging and under the watchful eye of Mr. Coleman, we loaded up our plates as if it were our last meal. After a few mouthfuls, we realized that we were in trouble. Unable to do more than stir the grits around the plate, Mrs. Coleman was concerned that something was wrong with her cooking. In those days, there was no admitting the truth, so we made up some sort of awkward story and asked permission to be excused. Embarrassed and feeling a little queasy, we finished getting dressed for church. The First Methodist Church of Latta was a beautiful, brick church. We entered the sanctuary and moved to the center pew near the front and sat down. There was no air-conditioning back then and the day was warm and humid. I am a Methodist and I knew that the service would last about an hour, more or less.

After a couple of hymns and prayers and a lot of standing up and sitting down, the preacher finally began his sermon. I think the sermon was about the wages of sin, a rather appropriate subject after our night at The Pad. The 'Honky-Tonk Flu' began to work its evil magic and I started to get queasy and my vision blurred. The deeper into the sermon the preacher delved, the worse I felt. I was sitting in the middle of the church with John D's family on each side of me, leaving no way to exit without causing a commotion. Suddenly, I knew I was getting ready to lose what little breakfast I had eaten. I remember thinking to myself, "There's no way I'm going to embarrass the Coleman Family in this church." Nice thought, but the 'Honky Tonk Flu' erupted and up came breakfast. I was determined not

31

to make a complete jerk out of myself, so with supreme effort I re-chewed my breakfast and swallowed hard. It worked. I didn't throw up, but I broke out into a sweat and it started running off my chin as if someone had turned on a water spigot. A stream about the size of my little finger was pouring off my chin into my lap. John D looked at me and broke into a grin. I thought he was going to hyperventilate!

Finally, church was over and I didn't die. But, I wanted to! We got out of church and drove over to the Florence Country Club for lunch. I didn't even know what a country club was back then, but it was nice. It was Mr. Coleman's turn to play the host. He ordered the biggest steaks the place served. Normally, I could eat half a cow, but I ate about three bites before I headed to the restroom, where I spent the rest of lunch. John D has never mentioned anything about that weekend, but I'm sure the Coleman's thought I was a very strange young man. That was an experience that I do not, would not, nor probably could, duplicate.

After the holidays we took exams and our first semester of college ended. My grade-point ratio was a 2.8. It wasn't the best grade on the team, but it wasn't bad. I wasn't going be on probation or lose my scholarship. Some of the guys weren't so lucky. There was another wave of players who decided that college was not for them. One was my friend, Bill Zarrella, who decided to go back home to Scottsdale, PA and work on the railroad.

It was time to get ready for spring practice. The year had rolled over into 1966 and I had made it through my first fall practice and my first semester of college and that, in itself, was an accomplishment.

1965 had been a very eventful year in my life. I had graduated from high school. I had received a football grant-in-aid from the University of South Carolina. I had stuck it out and adjusted, in spite of a tough, demanding regimen. I kept my spirits up, despite not getting any meaningful playing time. I was still on the team and had managed to get some decent grades, but most importantly, I had made new friends from all over the country.

We were moving into the second half of the 1960's and there was a great deal of news in the world around us. In 1965 President Lyndon Johnson had initiated a push toward socialism with his "Great Society" proclamation during his State of the Union address back in January. Sir Winston Churchill, one of the greatest Englishmen of all time, passed away that year and was buried with much pomp and ceremony. His funeral boasted the largest gathering of statesmen ever assembled in the world at that time. Up in Canada, they replaced the old Union flag with the now familiar red and white Maple leaf flag we see today. We crash landed a vehicle into the moon, marking the end of a successful mission to photograph possible landing sites for the upcoming Apollo Program. President Johnson continued to ratchet up the Vietnam War by sending more American Troops to South Vietnam throughout the year. It seemed that each week there was an announcement of more deployments to that war theater. The Civil Rights Movement was in full stride, and the news was focused on the State of Alabama. Clashes with police and large demonstrations by masses of people resulted in the passage of the Voting Rights Act of 1965.

Cosmonaut Aleksei Leonov became the first person to walk in space, stepping out of his capsule for twelve minutes. In Houston, Texas, the Astrodome opened for sporting events. In July, President Lyndon B. Johnson signed the Social Security Act of 1965 into law, creating Medicare and Medicaid. In Los Angeles, in August, the Watts Riots began. India and Pakistan went to war over Kashmir and also in 1965 Hurricane Betsy came ashore near New Orleans, Louisiana with winds of 145 mph. It caused 76 deaths and was the first storm to result in over $1 billion in damages. The storm was nicknamed 'Billon Dollar Betsy'. In October, the Gateway to the West Arch was completed in St. Louis, Missouri.

The music in 1965 was a mixture of rock 'n roll, rhythm and blues and country and I liked all three. Some of the top songs that made their debut in 1965 were: *(I Can't Get No) Satisfaction* by the Rolling Stones, *In the Midnight Hour* by Wilson Pickett, *Papa's Got a Brand-New Bag* sung by James Brown, *Yesterday*, a Beatles song, *California Dreamin'* by The Mamas and the Pappas, *I Fought the Law* by Bobby Fuller Four, *California Girls* by the Beach Boys, *For Your Love* sung by the Yardbirds and *Shotgun* by Junior Walker and the All-Stars.

 Gordon Gibson and I attended a concert at Columbia's Township Auditorium where we saw The Righteous Brothers and Dion Warwick perform. The Righteous Brothers had a big hit that year, *Unchained Melody*. And Dion Warwick was fabulous singing songs such as, *Do You Know the Way to San Jose*. Otis Redding was particularly popular around the Carolina campus with a top 25 song, *I've Been Loving You Too Long*. Sam the Sham and the Pharaohs had their one big hit, *Wooly Bully*.

Roger Miller had a country crossover hit, *King of the Road*. Miller actually dominated the country music charts. He had three tunes in the top 10. His other two songs were both crossover hits, *England Swings* and Engine, *Engine Number Nine*. Eddie Arnold also had a crossover song, *Make the World Go Away*. It seemed as if country music was moving closer to popular music and away from the traditional country style. But Little Jimmy Dickens stuck to traditional with *May the Bird of Paradise Fly up Your Nose*. Buck Owens was still singing with, *I've Got a Tiger by the Tail*. Johnny Cash sang *The Orange Blossom Special* and Marty Robbins had a hit with *Ribbon of Darkness Over Me*. Billy Walker's song, *Cross the Brazos at Waco*, was one of my favorites and George Jones had a good tune in *The Race Is On*.

There were also several good movies in 1965. The top grossing movie for the year, with ticket sales of over $163 million, was *The Sound of Music* starring Julie Andrews and Christopher Plummer. *Doctor Zhivago* was one of my favorite movies and still is. It starred Omar Sharif and the beautiful Julie Christie. The James Bond movies continued to rise in popularity.

Thunderball with my favorite James Bond, Sean Connery, was released. Clint Eastwood and Lee Van Cleef teamed up for another spaghetti Western, *For A Few Dollars More*. John Wayne starred with Dean Martin in the Western adventure tale *The Sons of Katie Elder*.

In football, Mike Garrett from USC (the Trojans of Southern California) won the Heisman Trophy.

It was a day of upsets as #2 Arkansas lost to LSU in the Cotton Bowl. Then came an even bigger stunner when #1 Michigan State lost to 13 point underdog UCLA in the Rose Bowl, 14-12. Trailing 14-6 in the final minute, Michigan State scored and went for a tying 2-point conversion but was stopped just short of the goal line. With #2 Arkansas and #1 Michigan State losing, the Orange Bowl game between #3 Nebraska and #4 Alabama would determine the national champion. Alabama, led by QB Steve Sloan, beat Nebraska 39-28 to claim the national title. The final AP poll was #1 Alabama, #2 Michigan State, #3 Arkansas, #4 UCLA and #5 Nebraska.

Bowl Games Played

BOWL				
ROSE	#4 UCLA Bruins	14	#1 Michigan State Spartans	12
COTTON	LSU Tigers	14	#2 Arkansas Razorbacks	7
ORANGE	#5 Alabama Crimson Tide	39	#3 Nebraska Cornhuskers	28
SUGAR	#7 Missouri	20	Florida Gators	18
BLUEBONNET	#9 Tennessee	27	Tulsa	6
GATOR	Georgia Tech	31	#10 Texas Tech	21

CHAPTER 2

'Change in the Wind'

In 1966 unbeknownst to the football squad, a major change was about to take place that would affect all of us. Coach Bass left South Carolina. There was no warning, no team meeting, it was just announced that he had resigned. He had gone to the Continental Football League and was the new head coach of the Montréal Beavers. The University moved quickly for a replacement. It only took a few days to make the hire. But who was it?

Soon the news was out. Our new head coach would be none other than Coach Paul F. Dietzel of LSU fame. He was the coach that I had been so impressed with when I saw his team on television winning the 1958 National Championship. This announcement certainly had the team talking. Other than Bear Bryant, the head coach at Alabama, Coach Dietzel was probably the most famous college football coach in the nation. He had won his National Championship with flair. The squad had three main teams, the White Team, the Go Team and the one that everybody remembered, the Chinese Bandits. We couldn't believe it, but this famous man was going to be our new leader. We were all excited and waited in anticipation to meet our head football coach.

The day arrived and a team meeting was called. We were all expected at The Roundhouse to meet our legendary new coach. On the main floor of The Roundhouse was a large auditorium that we used for team meetings and watching game film. The team filed into the room and milled about for a while, talking about our hopes for many great seasons ahead under Coach Dietzel. As we settled into our seats, the door opened from the side entrance at the bottom of the auditorium and in strode a tall, blond haired blue-eyed man. The head coach's office was just off the doorway and it was soon to become the inner sanctum, the holy of holies.

Coach Dietzel walked toward the podium, looking neither to the right or left. He placed a notebook down on the podium, looked up, smiled that big smile of his (he was nicknamed Pepsodent Paul after the popular toothpaste) and slowly looked around at the assembled football team. It was an electric moment for everyone. We, of course, had heard coaches talk before, but this was different. This was special. The other men were normal everyday coaches, but this guy had actually done it. He had won a National Championship and not only had he won it, he had won it with style. Ask any football fan from that era about the LSU team and they'll mention Coach Paul Dietzel, Billy Cannon, the Heisman Trophy running back, and the Chinese bandits. And here we were, about to hear the golden words that would make us into champions, as well.

Coach Dietzel cleared his throat and spoke, "I am pleased to be here at the University of Southern Carolina."

"*Southern Carolina*, where the hell is that," I thought to myself.

I looked around the room and realized I wasn't the only one. Coach Dietzel never even realized that he had made a mistake and continued with his opening comments to the team. After that first meeting, the team broke up into groups. Coach Dietzel's faux pas had dampened our enthusiasm, but we were still excited about the opportunity to learn all of the coaching secrets that were behind that brilliant 'Pepsodent Paul' smile.

We had our first spring practice under the new coaching staff. At the time, all of our athletic facilities were still in The Roundhouse complex. Davis Field, where our first practice was held, back on campus, was no longer available since the construction of a reflection pool on that site. Our locker rooms, training rooms, equipment rooms, meeting rooms, practice fields and film rooms were all located in The Roundhouse. Out the back and to the right of The Roundhouse was the track and field facility. To the left was our football practice field and at the end, was an additional football field. It was a pretty long complex going on for about four hundred yards. All of it was surrounded by a ten foot chain-link fence topped with barbed wire. To the left of the football

practice facilities just outside of the chain-link fence were railroad tracks. On the right-hand side of the complex behind the track facility was a hill that ran down the entire right side of the compound. There were houses that backed up to the chain-link fence, mostly duplexes leased by students. The hill was twenty to thirty feet high running down the entire eastern side of the complex. At the lower end the hill extended down into our practice area. It had its uses, mainly running punishment wind sprints which would wear

you out in a hurry. If you screwed up, an aggravated assistant coach would meet you at 6 AM to make you run the hills. Trust me; he didn't want to be there either. It wasn't fun for anyone.

The first day of spring practice under Coach Dietzel was uneventful except for a thunderstorm. It came up so quickly that we were still on the practice field when all of a sudden a bolt of lightning crashed down and was actually captured on film with Coach Dietzel in the foreground. He kept a copy of that photo in his office the entire time he was at South Carolina.

There was nothing really new or different about that spring practice except that it was, perhaps, a little more organized. No one on the coaching staff was looking my way, either for offense or defense. I guess they thought that I was too light to play college football. I was mostly used as filler wherever the coaches needed a body. Disappointed, I reminded myself that I was also at South Carolina to get an education, so if I couldn't play football, I decided I would concentrate on the books and hopefully have a little fun in my spare time.

Spring practice ended after the requisite twenty days. The semester drew to a close and I took exams and finished the year with another 2.8 GPR. I had made it through an entire year. I didn't have any major injuries, had not gotten into trouble with the coaches or teachers and had kept my grades above average for athletes. The 2.8 would keep me in school and eligible to play, if I ever got the chance.

My freshman year was over and I would return in the fall as a sophomore. I would be spending the summer back home in Turkey Creek, where I had a job working for Mr. Brownie Brown at the Lee County Highway Department. About five or six of my high school classmates worked alongside of me in the ditches and roadsides of the county. George Cummerlander was one of my good friends and teammates from high school. He was always fun and kept us entertained. We spent most of that summer clearing ditches of underbrush. With bush axe in hand, we would crawl into a deep ditch along the highway, spread out and start chopping bushes. Since it was summer in South Carolina, our uniforms consisted of tennis shoes, bermuda shorts and a baseball cap. Skin cancer was not on the radar during that time.

We found plenty of hazards down in those ditches in the form of snakes, wasps and worst of all, yellow jackets. The snakes were numerous and varied, but the ones that got your heart pumping were the water moccasins and rattlesnakes. I have seen people jump out of a five-foot deep ditch flat-footed. The wasps would build nests in the trees and if you struck the tree with a bush ax, they didn't mind letting you know you had disturbed their home. But the worst of the lot were the yellow jackets. Wasps sting and it hurts, but you could get away from them. Yellow jackets built nests in the ground and when they stung you, it felt like someone had hit you with a hammer. They would swarm you and chase you for quite a distance. Those were some mean little critters.

George and I were not above playing practical jokes. One of the permanent employees of the Highway Department was a very small man by the name of Bubba Matoose. Bubba was a country philosopher and could opine on just about any subject under the sun. The Highway Department issued shovels to all of its employees and they were all the same size, usually a number one. Bubba had purchased his own shovel from the hardware store. It was a number three shovel and about a third the size of a number one. It was a small shovel for a small man. If you brought it up, Bubba would get angry and tell you to mind your own business.

Bubba enjoyed dipping snuff. He used to take a little pinch between his cheek and his gum at least five or six times a day. George and I were riding with Bubba one day when he stepped out of his truck and left his snuff box unattended. We slipped out of the truck, grabbed a handful of sand and mixed in a generous amount of the grit into Bubba's snuff and waited. Needless to say, when he put the mixture into his cheek it wasn't pleasant, but we thought it was great fun watching him spit, stutter and cuss all at the same time.

The South Carolina Highway Department didn't pay very well, but we got enough to buy some beer for the weekends. It was hard to save any money to take back to school at the end of the summer.

We had to report back for fall practice around August 15th. I started spending some time after work at my old high school football field trying to get into some kind of shape. Our high school team had already started practice, so I worked out with them for a while. I would get out and run a few wind sprints and do a few agility and conditioning drills and the high school coaches even let me show the team some of the newfangled college stuff that I learned in my freshman year.

In that summer of 1966, all who loved Carolina Football heard some disturbing news. The ACC Championship the Gamecocks shared with Duke was stripped because of an eligibility blunder. While the details still are somewhat murky, below is an article from the State Newspaper that serves as an explanation. In addition are interviews with Coach Bass and players about the 1965 season.

In 1965, South Carolina tied Duke for the ACC title. An eligibility scandal stripped the Gamecocks of the title. Even worse, one of the teams named co-champs was rival Clemson. Few fans remember that season. For the players and coaches, the memories remain.

This is their story.

There are few reminders of what happened to the 1965 USC football team. Its record is listed at 5-5 in the media guide. A few players are recognized for All-ACC and other postseason honors.

But a glimpse at page 91 of the ACC media guide shows what transpired that season. The page includes a list of all-time conference champions. At the bottom right is a box entitled "1965."

It reads: "Duke and South Carolina finished the 1965 regular season tied for conference leadership with identical 4-2 league marks before ACC Commissioner Jim Weaver ruled that the Gamecocks had violated league rules in regards to the eligibility of two players and were required to forfeit all conference games in which the two players had participated. Due to the forfeit wins they received, N.C. State and Clemson, which had both lost to South Carolina, were declared ACC co-champions with 5-2 records in league play."

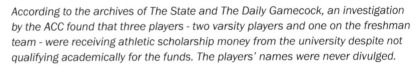

According to the archives of The State and The Daily Gamecock, an investigation by the ACC found that three players - two varsity players and one on the freshman team - were receiving athletic scholarship money from the university despite not qualifying academically for the funds. The players' names were never divulged.

In a column by former State sports writer Herman Helms, a source in the athletic department said each player received between $75-$100 for meals and textbooks.

While the scandal of having a championship taken away has faded over the years, the memories of the men who lived it have not.

MIKE FAIR: A LEADER UNDER CONSTRUCTION

When Mike Fair began his sophomore season in 1965, there was a lot of uncertainty in the USC program. The Gamecocks were beginning their first season without Dan Reeves at quarterback, and experience under center was limited.

So it came as a surprise to the Greenville native when the coaching staff asked if he would take a redshirt season.

"The first game of the year was The Citadel, and I found out - I guess it was in the next couple of days - that they wanted me to redshirt. They didn't tell me to redshirt; they asked me if I wanted to redshirt," Fair said. "It probably would have been a much better thing to do, but I didn't want to. I said, 'No, I'd rather not.'"

The result? Fair put together the best statistical season by a quarterback in program history at the time.

Fair replaced starter Ted Wingard at halftime of the second game, against Duke, with South Carolina trailing 14-0. Fair led the Gamecocks on touchdown drives of 51 and 64 yards in the second half of a 20-15 loss.

"There was nobody. It was just a good situation for me to step right in," Fair said. "There were no real experienced quarterbacks, and the one who had experience was a bit gimpy."

Fair led the Gamecocks into some of the South's most storied football cathedrals that season, including SEC powers LSU, Tennessee and eventual national champion Alabama. The Gamecocks lost all three games, but Fair carries plenty of fond memories.

Against LSU, the Gamecocks were the victims of a Tigers defense that bent but did not break in 21-7 loss.

"We actually could have won that game, but we didn't. A pass was dropped at the end zone that would have tied the game, if I remember, but that was early (in the contest)," Fair said. "(LSU) was a fascinating place to play football."

The next-to-last game of the season pitted the Gamecocks against Bear Bryant's Alabama team, which was in search of its second consecutive national championship.

Fair had his best game of the season with 243 passing yards, including two that went for more than 45 yards, in a 35-14 defeat.

But he was more impressed with the opponent.

"We should've scored four touchdowns. We lost the ball twice inside the 10 (-yard line), but they just scored when they needed to," Fair said. "They were so good."

Fair ended the season with a single-season record 1,049 passing yards on 89 completions. J.R. Wilburn, Fair's top target, caught 38 passes for what was then a school-record 562 yards.

"He had great, great hands, and he ran terrific routes," Fair said. "It was like throwing to a coach. It increased my confidence exponentially. If I'm throwing to J.R., somehow he's going to catch it."

After his playing career, Fair eventually got into politics. From 1984-95, he represented Greenville as a member of the state House of Representatives. Since 1995, he has been a member of the state Senate. Fair credits football, in part, for his successes as a politician.

"The whole thing about making your successes and failures public and learning that you don't die when you fumble or throw an interception, that's pretty hard stuff when you're 18 and 19 years old," he said. "That's a character builder."

As for the team having its championship taken away, Fair chooses to remember the good times.

"That feeling of achievement, that feeling of excitement that went along with it, it's in the memory bank," he said. "It can't be taken away."

MARVIN BASS: THE COACH

Marvin Bass had watched his USC team struggle in a 13-3 victory against The Citadel in the first game of the 1965 season. The team followed that with a poor first-half performance against Duke, which is when Bass benched Wingard and inserted Fair.

"I can't tell you why I put him in. It's those hunches you play, that's all," Bass said.

That hunch created the spark that led to the best season in Bass' five-year tenure. "I thought we were on the rise," he said.

So why did Bass, who also served as athletics director, leave for the Continental Professional Football League team in Montreal?

The former coach believed it was in his best interest, and that of the university. With a 17-29-4 record at USC, Bass had not been offered an extension on his contract, which was set to expire after the 1966 season.

"I knew I couldn't recruit very successfully just having one year left on my contract, and they wouldn't have fired me here; I'm convinced of that," Bass said. "But I told them when I left the meeting with them, if I don't get an extension on my contract, the first job that comes along, I'm taking it."

That job came after the 1965 season, and after the program was docked five scholarships and fined $2,500 for violations involving three players receiving improper benefits.

On April 1, 1966, Bass resigned and headed to Canada. But the real shock came when NCAA investigators showed up across the border to speak with Bass almost three months after he left the Palmetto State.

The details of what went wrong have become clouded to the old coach in 40-plus years.

"I wish I could get this thing cleared up myself," Bass said. "It's bothered me all these years because I wasn't sure what the real story was."

Despite how things ended for Bass, the soon-to-be 89-year old said Columbia was his favorite stop during his coaching career, and he moved back to the area when he retired. He cites his inability to establish a consistent winner at USC as his biggest disappointment.

While his time at USC could be seen as ending with a black mark, his hope is his players do not view that season as a negative moment.

"I still claim sharing the conference (championship) with Duke," Bass said. "They took it away from us, but I still share it in my own mind, and I hope all those players share it their mind, too."

BOBBY BRYANT: THE SUPERSTAR

Bass will not take credit for Bobby Bryant's success. The man who recruited the eventual All-ACC performer as both a defensive back and left-handed pitcher called Bryant a "self-made player."

But Bryant admits he had an ulterior motive to play baseball.

"Spring (football) practice was the worst thing you had to do. For me to able to get out of it was great. I didn't mind at all," Bryant said.

On the football field, Bryant finished 1965 with 11 punt returns for 161 yards, making him the ACC leader. His three interceptions were tops on the team.

After 20-plus seasons of playing football, Bryant admits the plays have begun to blur together a bit.

"I've probably been hit so much in the head that I don't remember all the stuff, but certain plays I remember," said Bryant, who is a salesman with Quacked Glass in Lancaster. "Some of the guys I played with, when we get together they talk about certain games we played in back then and they say, 'Bobby, you remember that game you fumbled three punts?' And I say, 'I never fumbled three punts. What are you talking about?'"

None of Bryant's interceptions were bigger than the one against Clemson. For the first time in their 70-year rivalry, the teams were meeting with the possibility of the winner receiving a share of the ACC title.

During Clemson's potential game-tying drive in the fourth quarter, Bryant picked off a pass at the USC 12-yard line.

Clemson scored on its next possession with 40 seconds remaining to close the deficit to 17-16. Tiger coach Frank Howard lined up his team for the point-after attempt but instead went for a two-point conversion, the win and the conference crown. USC's Bob Gunnels deflected the pass and sealed the title for USC.

The win also cemented Bryant's place in the rivalry's history.

"My freshman team beat Clemson, my sophomore year we beat Clemson, my junior year we beat Clemson and my senior we played them here and they killed us," Bryant said. "At least I had that to say when they say, 'Bobby, what was your record (against Clemson) when you played there?' It was 3-1, as a matter of fact."

After the ACC ruled the co-championship would be awarded to Clemson and N.C. State, Howard said, "the score was 17-16 as far as I'm concerned" and seemingly refused to accept the title. The Tigers and Wolfpack both recognize 1965 as championship seasons.

What happened after the Clemson game remains a bit of mystery to Bryant. He said he was surprised when Bass left the program for the job in Montreal.

"I don't recall whether there was any controversy or what the general opinion of him was or why he was leaving," Bryant said. "We had certain players that they knew everything that was going on, and it really didn't concern me."

The loss of the ACC title also surprised Bryant, who said players were never formally told why the league was vacating the championship they had been celebrating for almost eight months.

"When you look at the guy or guys that caused us to have it taken away, I don't think any of them were such superstars that if you had taken their part of the equation away that it would have changed anything," Bryant said. "We did win and were co-champions. Our record proved that."

Bryant believes what happened that season is another point of discussion in the search for reasons the program never has achieved elite status.

"The history of South Carolina, football especially, is just 'shoulda, coulda, woulda,' 'if only,' or 'what if' or 'man, we were so close.' It's not a real glorious past," Bryant said. "That's just another chapter on how we screwed something up that should have been, could have been a good chapter."

Bryant went on to play 14 seasons in the NFL as part of the heralded "Purple People Eater" defense with the Minnesota Vikings. During that time, the team appeared in four Super Bowls, each of which Bryant received a championship ring for.

But the piece of championship jewelry that has befuddled him was the little, gold football charm given to the players to commemorate the 1965 ACC championship. Bryant still is not sure what he was supposed to do with it.

"I wasn't sure if I was supposed to put it on a charm bracelet or put it on a gold chain and wear it around my neck or give it to my girlfriend," Bryant said. "I wasn't one for a lot of jewelry and stuff. I look at it once in a while when I go in there to get something out, and I say, 'My little co-championship football that no longer represents what happened.'"

Ben Garnto, Paul Dietzel and Benny Galloway pose for the Redbook cover.

BENNY GALLOWAY: THE B.G. BOYS TAKE THE STAGE

All athletes claim to believe the upcoming season will be a special one. But Benny Galloway had reason to believe the 1965 USC team was destined to do great things.

Galloway played on the 1964 freshman team, which lost one game. The previous season, the freshman squad had gone undefeated. So the team appeared to have plenty of talent in 1965.

In Galloway, the coaches found a stocky and powerful running back. Then there was Ben Garnto, a quicker and multi-faceted runner who could complement Galloway.

The pair were placed in the backfield together and became one of the first great running back tandems at USC.

It also made for a great nickname.

"I don't know (how it happened), because we had a lot of great running backs that came in '64," Galloway said. "And it was ironic that we had the same initials, and I think the press picked up on it and said, 'Hey, we may have something here.' Let's do this and see if that happens, and that became the B.G. Boys back then. And it worked good."

Galloway and Garnto each averaged more than 4 yards per carry that season, with Garnto's 437 yards leading the team. Galloway was not far behind with 415.

The pair's biggest day came in a 38-7 victory against Wake Forest. Garnto broke loose for an 89-yard run to the Demon Deacons' 5-yard line for what at the time was the longest non-scoring play in ACC history. Galloway capped the drive with one of his two rushing scores.

Galloway attributes much of the team's success to the connection between the players and coaches.

"The (coaches) we had then, it just seemed like you wanted to do things more for them because they were the ones that recruited you and was taking care of you and, really, other than you mother and father, your coaches raise you," Galloway said.

Nearly 45 years removed from that season, Galloway still cannot put his finger on what caused the Gamecocks to forfeit the championship. He believes the story of what happened has not been talked about or well documented since because of the upheaval in the program at the time, specifically the transition in coaches from Bass to Paul Dietzel and the school's hope that the change might put the issue behind it.

Yet Galloway emphasizes that he and his teammates share the idea that they were the first true championship football team at South Carolina.

(By ALEX RILEY – Special to The State)

To finally win, at least a share of the conference championship, was undeniably an accomplishment for the team and staff. To have it stripped was painful. The only solace is to know that the players won those games and for a time, were ACC Co-Champs.

Just before returning to school I had a little talk with my Dad about transportation. I had been able to save up a little bit of money, about $300, and I wanted to know if that would be enough for a down payment on a car. A friend of Dad's, Mr. Jack Gardner, ran a car lot about two miles from our house. Jack dealt in all kinds of used vehicles and I wondered if Dad thought he might have something that would work for me.

"Son there's only one way to find out. Let's go see what Jack's got for sale," he said unexpectedly.

We rode up to Jack's and got out to look around. The car lot was at a crossroad known locally as the Devil's Elbow. I have never been able to find out how it got that name. Jack was a small, wiry, former Marine with red hair and bright blue eyes. During World War II, Jack had been a champion lightweight boxer in the Corps. His face was covered in freckles and he generally had a chew of tobacco in his jaw. Jack turned his head sideways, spit out a brown stream of tobacco juice on the ground and said, "Hey Billy, what 'er ya'll doing up here today?"

"Jack, my boy here needs a car. He's got about $200 or $300 to spend and we were wondering if you might have something in that price range?"

Jack looked at me and grinned, "You looking for something to chase those college women with?"

Jack had a fondness for the ladies. He had married a girl from up north while in the Marine Corps and they didn't get along, so Jack wanted a divorce. She was a Catholic and didn't believe in divorce. I remember my father telling me several times, "Don't marry a Catholic, boy. If it don't work out you'll be stuck, just like Jack."

Jack had about fifteen to twenty cars lined up on his small lot.

"Billy, you know you can't get much of a car for $300," Jack proffered.

"I know Jack."

Just about then I saw it, a red convertible. I knew this was the car I wanted.

"How much is this one Mr. Jack?"

"Son, that car is a Buick Special, and it's in pretty good shape. I just traded for it yesterday. It's gonna cost you about $600, son."

Disappointed, we moved on and Jack showed me a few others that he said he could let go for $350 or $400. They were pretty rough looking vehicles, but I really needed a car.

My Dad said, "Jack, I doubt any of those cars will even get him back to Columbia."

"Billy, they don't look like much, but they run good."

"Yeah, but any girl he asks out will be too scared to get in it," Dad said, shaking his head.

He looked at me and smiled and then turned back to Jack and asked, "How much did you say you wanted for that little red car up there?"

"Billy, I really need about $750, but I'll sell it to you for $600 for friendship's sake."

"Jack, I might be able to scrape together a couple hundred dollars of my own to throw in. David really does need an automobile that can get him back and forth to Columbia. What do ya' say, Jack?"

I was stunned. For years, my Dad was an instrument mechanic at the DuPont plant in Lugoff. It was about eighteen miles from our home in Turkey Creek. I knew there wasn't a lot of extra money; we lived from week to week, so I was really surprised when Daddy offered to part with what little savings he had on my behalf.

"Well, if you take it the way it is, I'll do it for you this time on one condition," Jack said as he turned to look at me.

"What's that Mr. Jack?" I asked.

"You boys whip Clemson this year," he replied as he grinned from ear to ear.

"You can bet we'll give it our best shot," I said.

So I had a set of wheels. It was a red 1962 Buick Special ragtop. The upholstery was a little worn and you couldn't see out of the plastic window in the back. But it ran good and the tires were pretty fair, so I think I got a pretty good deal out of Mr. Jack Gardner that day.

CHAPTER 3

'Dietzel's Debut'

The time came to load up my Buick Special with the things I would need for the school year and head back to Columbia. This time the trip wasn't nearly as exciting as the year before, except for having a car of my own. Girls, look out! I was a sophomore now and knew all there was to know about college life. And I had a set of wheels. That 'excitement stuff' was only for freshman. By the time you completed your first year as a student athlete, most of the excitement had been knocked out of you by the Varsity football team. I had become a typical "know it all" college sophomore.

I had been assigned a new roommate. It was none other than Allen Brown. He was the quarterback that started our first game as a freshman. Allen was 6' tall and weighed about 180 pounds. He was redheaded and hailed from Hinesville, Georgia. Allen was one of those guys that had never met a stranger. Everybody liked Allen and I was no exception. My roommate from our freshman year, Big G from DC, lived down the hall with his new roommate, David Meadows. David was from Aiken, South Carolina and played linebacker. Over the summer, we had lost a few more of our freshman class for various and sundry reasons. We never found out why some of them left. They just didn't show up and we never heard from them again. Others kept in touch. We settled into our new environment, this time, on the fifth floor of J dorm.

I asked Allen what he thought his chances were of making the team. I knew that after the first freshman game Allen had not played very much. Allen's reply was that he didn't even know what position he was gonna be playing. It seems that the week after the Gordon Military College freshman game in '65, a coach had come over to the freshman team and picked out about five or six freshman backs. Allen happened to be one of them. He asked them if they had played defense before and in those days, most everyone had played both ways. So Allen was placed at the safety position to scrimmage against the varsity. Sure enough, the same back that I had tried to tackle in my first live scrimmage, Benny Galloway, broke through the line into the secondary and Allen set himself up to make the tackle. He slammed his right shoulder into Benny and crunch, his right throwing shoulder was dislocated. Unable to throw for a couple of weeks, he joined me on the bench. In another game that year, we played the Wake Forest freshman team. They had a running back named "Jimmy the Jet Johnson," who was a pretty good back. Allen was once again put on defense at the safety position and the same thing happened. He tried to tackle Jimmy with the same shoulder and got the same results. "The Jet" got a touchdown and Allen got his shoulder dislocated for the second time. That was effectively the end of Allen's freshman football career. It seemed we had a lot in common.

In those days, progressive coaches felt that athletes should all room together. Coach Dietzel was no exception, so all the football players occupied about four floors of J dorm. The idea was that the closer we became as teammates, the better our teamwork would be, and our chances of winning would be enhanced. It certainly did make for a close knit group and many of us are still friends after over 45 years. We were together for almost twenty four hours a day for nine months. The only time we weren't hanging out together was when we had a class or a date.

We had returned to J dorm on a weekend in the middle of August. Our first team meeting was set for early morning on Monday. Coach Dietzel had been busy during that summer fund-raising and making plans to improve our athletic facilities at the University. He showed us some architectural renderings of a new athletic complex. The complex was going to be located at the far end of our practice fields opposite The Roundhouse and it was to be called "The Roost". I had never seen an architectural rendering before and it was impressive. It seemed as if Coach Dietzel was getting ready to take us places. That was the good news. Then he unloaded the bad news on us.

Coach Paul Dietzel

Normally, during the first two weeks back, we would practice twice a day. It was the normal routine for every college team in the United States. Two-a-days were tough, particularly in the South, where we had so much humidity and heat. But they were absolutely necessary to get a team conditioned and ready to play in a two week time period. Generally, we would practice in the morning in helmets, shoulder pads and shorts. There wasn't much contact, but we ran a lot. In the afternoon, we suited up in full gear and after a few days we started contact drills. Coach Dietzel announced we would be having three-a-day practices! Three-a-day practices! I had never heard of such a thing. We were going to have a normal morning practice. Our afternoon practice would be moved up from 4 o'clock in the afternoon to 3 o'clock. Man! That was the hottest time of the day! Our third practice would be held from 7 o'clock until 8:30. The first two practices would be in shoulder pads, helmets and shorts. The 7 o'clock practice would be in full pads.

Coach Dietzel had been talking to us about getting tougher. Well, these three-a-day practices were certainly going to make us something. Tougher might be the result, but exhausted was a certainty. It was hard enough to get up in the morning after a two-a-day practice. Every muscle in your body ached. And after we started contact drills in full pads you could add bruises and cuts to the sore muscles. After about a week, your body would start getting into condition and the soreness would go away. We were about to find out how well we could withstand three practices a day.

We suited up for the first three-a-day practice session. Our normal practice routine consisted of warm-up calisthenics. Under Coach Bass, we started off with stretching exercises, and then moved to normal calisthenics like jumping jacks, picking the grass between your legs and rockers. Rockers were done in this way. First you would lean over and touch your toes. Still touching your toes, you would squat all the way down. Placing your hands on your hips, you would stand back up and lean back as far as you could. Then you would start all over again. We also did running in place and when the coach blew the whistle, we had to jump flat on the ground and get back up as quickly as possible.

Under Coach Dietzel, we also started with stretching exercises, but then we were taught to do "quick-cals". With quick-cals speed and quickness were emphasized. One of the assistant coaches would lead the drills and you had to follow him. Whatever he did, you were supposed to do. We would run in place with the coach, always remaining in good football position, which meant shoulders square, knees bent and a slight forward bend at the waist. The coach would take his hands and quickly bring them up to his ears. We would follow, then he would hit his hips and we would follow. Back to his head with his hands and then quickly reach down and slap his knees and we would follow, all the while, still running in place. Then the coach would hop to his right and we would follow. He would jump on the ground and back up again and we would follow. In the beginning this looks sort of silly, but after you got used to doing it, we understood that it had its uses. Quickness is a trait that every football player needs. The quicker the better and this drill helped develop that quickness. Ah ha, we thought, here's some of that secret stuff that wins National Championships. None of us had ever heard of quick-cals, but before long we could do them in our sleep. A few of the guys even made up dances using quick-cals. Unfortunately, it never caught on as a national craze.

After we finished with the calisthenics, we broke up into positions. The offense went to one field and the defense to the other. Offensively, the linemen were in one group, the running backs and quarterbacks were in another and the ends and wideouts did their own drills. Defensively, the interior linemen, the linebackers and the perimeter backs all worked in individual groups while the defensive ends practiced with the interior lineman part of the time and at other times, with the linebackers.

There were blocking drills, tackling drills, and one of my old favorites from my freshman year called "bull in the ring". This bull in the ring drill was a little different and went like this. One guy would get in the middle surrounded by five or six of his teammates. Coach would blow the whistle and we would all start running in place, while taking a good football stance with arms up, ready to receive a hit or deliver a blow to the opponent. Once the drill commenced, the coach would call out a name of one of the circling players. That player would charge forward with the intent of knocking the guy in the middle on his keister. The coaches wanted you to be aggressive and if you could get to the guy and hit him in the back, that was considered okay. The point of the drill was agility, quickness and toughness. If the coaches called someone's name behind you, you had to be agile and quick enough to turn in time to defend yourself. If you were successful at fending off the opponent's lick, then coach called another name. By this time, most people had become disoriented and couldn't remember where the next guy was lined up. So, you had to turn and find your next opponent before he got to you. This process was repeated five or six times or until someone got to you and knocked you down. When that happened at the beginning of the drill, it would start over. Some of the guys really enjoyed this kind of contact, especially if they could hit you before you reacted to their attack. Others like to give you a fair shake. It was almost like the cowboy in the movies who refused to draw his six guns until the bad guy was ready.

We did another drill called monkey rolls. Three guys would get down on the ground lying flat on their stomachs facing the coach. When the whistle blew, the guy on the right jumped left, using his hands and feet, over the guy in the middle. The one in the middle rolled to his right underneath the guy jumping to the middle. The third guy on the left now jumped to his right, over the guy, who had started from the right. The one who had jumped to the middle, as quickly as he touched the ground again, had to roll to his left to make room for the left-hand guy. This was repeated several times, jump and roll, jump and roll and then jump and roll again. It took place very quickly and when done correctly, it looked like a ballet. But if you forgot to roll, then you would get pounded by the other guy who was jumping your way. We had a few guys who never could get the hang of that drill. Trying to describe it, I'm not surprised!

After a few more drills, we would do our 'basics'; blocking, shedding blocks and tackling. This is where experience, skill and talent began to show up. It wasn't everything, however, as some guys who were very good, one on one, could not remember plays well enough to use their talent. They would go the wrong way, block the wrong person or just 'freeze' with indecision. We had some exceptional physical specimens that "looked good in the shower" but they just didn't have the innate ability to play the game well. These 'basics' would usually take up about the first thirty to forty five minutes of a practice.

For the next thirty to forty minutes the entire offense grouped together and the defense would gather on the opposite practice field. The first two teams on both offense and defense would run through plays using scout squad members as the opposition. The scout squad was made up of guys who weren't on the first or second teams. That's where I found myself, on the scout squad. As the season grew near, the evening practices were spent mostly scrimmaging. Scrimmages would generally pit the first-team offense against the second-team defense and vice versa. If you weren't playing, you gathered around on the sidelines and watched.

We had some real talent coming back. With these adept lettermen, the season looked very promising. Coach Dietzel, however, had talked to us about cleaning up our football team. He had decided, for whatever reason, that most of the team members, not all but most, were bad apples. He was not concerned with talent, but with attitude and perhaps morals. I never could figure out precisely what he was talking about. Today, that type of coaching is called 'changing the culture'. It all amounts to the same thing, only some coaches approach 'changing the culture' differently. That fall Coach Dietzel had decided to weed out as many bad apples as possible. The method he chose was the three-a- day practices. As those practices wore on, it became apparent to us that this was his plan. He even said as much in several of the team meetings. He informed us that he was trying to get rid of the "rape and run boys" as he called them. To this day, I have never figured out exactly what he meant by that.

As the opening game of the season approached, everybody expected the three-a-days would end so there would be time to get 'our legs back'. For those of you who have not engaged in three-a-day practices, if you continue to push too hard, instead of building a body up, it begins to have the opposite effect. It's simple science. If you don't give your muscles time to recover, you get diminishing returns on your workouts. A couple of the guys asked the coaches about stopping the three-a-days, but got no answer and we continued to have practice three times a day until about two days before the first game. We had a bunch of worn out players, who were not in peak condition to play.

I mentioned earlier that we had all types of people on our freshman football team, including one who was a great humorist. He told us a story about those three-a-day practices that illustrates my point and it's hilarious. His name is Dennis Fraser. We had nicknamed Dennis 'Big Dink'. He was 6'5", 250 pounds. His hometown of Walhalla is in the North Western corner of the state. It's located in the foothills of the beautiful Blue Ridge Mountains and according to Dennis, full of characters. It's true because I've met a lot of them, but one of the biggest characters of all was Dennis.

We gathered around 'Big Dink' one night after the season started and we were discussing how tough those three-a-days were.

Parking spaces at USC were hard to come by. J dorm was on the corner of South Main and Devine. Directly across Main Street was a laundromat and on the other corner was the University Bookstore. There was a steep hill that fell about seventy five feet all the way down to Assembly Street which was a block away. Underneath the back of the laundromat was a pool hall named "The Varsity Billiards". It was run by a guy named Big Al and was a favorite hangout of students and players. We shot pool and played pinball machines in rare moments of spare time. In back of the Varsity Billiards, there was a parking lot and there were parking spaces all along the street, most without parking meters. Parking here was about as close as you could get to the dorm without having to feed the meters.

Dennis began his tale.

"Boys, I'll tell you it was tough finding a parking spot last night. I had to park way down the hill almost to Assembly Street."

"I never realized how long and steep that hill is."

"It took me about thirty minutes to get from my car up that hill."

"I had to stop three or four times to rest. Boy I was tired."

"When I finally got to the dorm, it took me ten minutes before I had enough strength to push the elevator button to go up."

"I fell asleep in the corner of the elevator and had to ride that thing up and down about three times before I woke up and it stopped on my floor."

"I got off the elevator and leaned against the wall for about five minutes before I finally had the strength to walk to my door. I'm telling you, I ain't ever been that tired before."

"The door was open, thank goodness, so I got in the room, closed the door and fell into my bed."

"I was so tired; I didn't even undress or pull the covers over me. I didn't even pull my shoes off. Within two minutes I was sound asleep."

"I'm telling you, boys, I was tired."

"Then, just as I was dreaming about my girlfriend, I thought I heard something outside of my dream."

"I don't know how long I laid there, but I kept hearing this noise."

"It was somebody knocking on the door."

"After about fifteen knocks, I got aggravated enough to get out of bed and open the door."

"Y'all will never guess who it was knocking."

We all looked at each other with our mouths open, turned back to Dennis and said in unison, "Come on Dennis, who was it?"

Dennis smiled, looked around as if he didn't want anybody else to hear and said, "It was my ass just draggin' in!"

With the punch line delivered, as only Dennis could deliver it, we laughed until we cried. That wouldn't be the only time Dennis came up with one of his tales that left us bent double.

I had not made the team that fall, nor had many of my close friends. This was not unexpected, because of the number of lettermen who were returning from the ACC Co-Championship team of 1965. Coach Bass had been a lineman in his college days and it showed in his recruiting. We all thought we were going to have a good year. After all we had Coach Dietzel to lead us and Mike Fair, who had quarterbacked the 1965 team to its championship, had returned for his junior year.

Our expectations were not realized. We opened the season by traveling to LSU. It was ironic that the first game that Coach Dietzel commanded at South Carolina would be against his old team, the LSU Bengal Tigers. Irony on top of irony, it was Coach Dietzel himself, who had scheduled the game. The game was played in Baton Rouge in the stadium nicknamed "Death Valley". The Gamecocks scored first when Jimmy Killen, a great running back for us, dove over the goal line for a touchdown. The extra point was good and Carolina led 7-0. As the game wore on, we wore down and the final score was LSU 21-South Carolina 7. Those three-a-day practices caught up with us that night.

I had finally been officially placed on the 'Bohunk' team. That was the semi-derogatory term for the scout squad. We practiced with the varsity

every day, but did not dress out or travel to games. It was not unusual for a sophomore to be red shirted, but I didn't see it that way. I was disappointed. I wasn't going to make the varsity team just as I hadn't played on the freshman squad. The Bohunk team actually had its own coaching staff. The head coach of the Bohunks was an energetic, excitable little guy. He stayed on us all the time. He was so competitive, that he wanted to beat the varsity each time we scrimmaged against them. He was probably the smallest person on the field. I don't think he was much over 5' 8" and looked like he only weighed about 145 pounds dripping wet. He had sandy hair, spoke with a slight lisp and had blue eyes that looked huge through his glasses. We couldn't believe he had played linebacker and center in college. But he had, he had played for Kent State. His name was Lou Holtz.

Jimmy Killen scores 1st touchdown of Dietzel era

Jimmy Killen

He had me playing right defensive end and my friend Dennis Fraser, playing right defensive tackle beside me. It was actually a lot of fun, because Dennis was a damn good tackle. Not only was he big and strong, he was as quick as a cat and when he put out the effort, nobody on the varsity team could block him. There was probably a pretty good reason for that. Most of those big, mean linemen from the 1965 championship team weren't starters. Coach Dietzel had decided to start a few of our classmates along with some other players, instead of the lettermen. That had not gone over too well in the first game. It didn't work out very well in the next two, either. We lost to Memphis 16 to 7 and then lost a close one to Georgia at Carolina Stadium, 7 to 0.

A freshman teammate, who was a good friend of mine, had made the starting team as a sophomore at middle guard. His name was David Cy Grant. There was a major league pitcher for the New York Yankees named 'Mudcat' Grant at about that same time and our David Grant picked up the nickname of 'Mudcat' and it stuck. 'Mudcat' was a pretty tough customer. He was quick and strong and was known to be a hard hitter. He tells a funny story about that Georgia game. It was late in the fourth quarter and Georgia was driving toward its winning touchdown. They had moved the ball down to about our 3-or 4-yard line, after a long punishing drive. It was really hot and very humid that night. 'Mudcat' made the tackle at the 3-yard

56

line. Georgia went back to the huddle and the humidity got the better of 'Mudcat'. As he got into his stance right in front of the football, he threw up. He said he didn't get any on the football, but his 'supper' was in a pile right beside it. Georgia broke the huddle and came up to the line of scrimmage. The Georgia center leaned down to grab the football and spied the big pile of Mudcat's semi-digested meal. With eyes wide, he jumped back, looked at the refs and pointed. Then he stammered "what, what, what is that?" The refs came running up to see what he was pointing to, but the closer they got the slower they moved.

"Oh my God," the ref exclaimed, "Somebody get me a towel." A ball boy brought him a towel and they cleaned it up the best they could, but inevitably there was a sticky substance still on the field. The ref took the ball and moved it to the other hash mark as 'Mudcat' worked hard to regain his composure. I'm not sure that the referee consulted the rulebook, but he decided to move the ball anyway, rulebook or not. I don't know if it was audibled, but the next play went right over Mudcat's position for the winning touchdown. Those three-a-days were still not working out well.

The one bright spot of the season happened on the road the next weekend. The game was played in Raleigh, North Carolina against the North Carolina State Wolfpack. It was a seesaw affair until the game was put away on a punt return by Carolina's star, Bobby Bryant. I think it was a 98-yard touchdown run that salted the game away for us late. We had lost three fairly close games. But that day, we beat the Wolfpack by ten points. Bobby Bryant went on to play for the Minnesota Vikings for many years and had a great NFL career.

Meanwhile, back at the ranch, my bohunk career was in full swing. One of the things that we had to do as bohunks was scrimmage the freshman team each Monday afternoon. It was bad enough not to make the team, and to scrimmage the varsity, but scrimmaging the freshmen was just downright distasteful and demeaning. We were so low on the totem pole; we were even below the freshman. It was humiliating. After our warm-ups, Coach Holtz walked over. He was always giving us tips and trying to get as much effort out of us as possible. Sometimes, he was funny, sometimes, he tried to be fatherly, and a lot of the times, he was just plain aggravating.

We had nicknamed this Monday afternoon scrimmage with the freshman "The toilet bowl". The Coaches called it the "Dust Bowl", but we knew better. Our disdain for this assignment usually manifested itself in a lack of effort on our part. This lackadaisical attitude used to drive Coach Holtz crazy. But deep down inside, he understood the reason for our behavior. One day, after playing in two or three of these 'toilet bowl' scrimmages, a freshman running back, named Rudy Holloman, ran a sweep going away from my position around the opposite end. It was a nice day and for some reason I was feeling energetic and decided to actually try to play some football. I did something that was unheard of for a bohunk playing in the 'toilet bowl', I actually hustled. I took an angle and ran Rudy down from behind.

All of a sudden, out of nowhere came Coach Holtz. He jumped up and grabbed my facemask (he was famous for doing that). He pulled my head down and slapped me on the back of the helmet. "Son," he said, "I really appreciate your effort on that play. All you have to do is give me effort like that. If you do, I promise you that you won't always be a bohunk. You'll play and play a lot. And I'll tell you something else; I'm not always going to be a bohunk coach, either. One of these days, I'm going to be a head coach at a major program." I remember thinking to myself, "You're right in that I'm going to play, I'm gonna' be a starter. But there ain't no way you're going to be a head coach of anything, except bohunks. Well, I was half right.

Bohunks generally didn't attend team meetings during practice. The varsity would watch game films of their upcoming opponent, usually before practice. They also watched film of the past games and were graded by the coaching staff on their performance. As bohunks, we would usually have fifteen or twenty minutes to wait before practice began. All linemen secretly wanted to be star running backs and steal some headlines. To kill the time, while we were waiting on practice to begin, four of us started practicing running plays. I would be the quarterback, and 'Big Dink', Dennis Fraser, 'Big Daddy', Glen Thompson and 'Gourd Head', Gordon Gibson, would be the running backs. I would hold the ball, slap it with my free hand, (simulating the ball being snapped) then turn and hand off to 'Big Dink' who would run the ball off-tackle behind blocking by the other two.

We practiced the play over and over until we had it down to a 'T'. We scrimmaged the freshmen one night in a game type rehearsal. The scrimmage was even held in Carolina Stadium under the lights. Our offense was getting ready to score and we were ahead by three or four touchdowns. Now was our chance for glory. Coach Holtz had watched us practice our running plays and had even made some sarcastic remarks about monkeys trying to teach algebra. We came over and tried to talk him into letting us run our play on the next extra point attempt. To our surprise, he agreed and we got ready. Sure enough on the next play we scored and it was time for the extra point.

Excited, we ran onto the field and took over the huddle. The center was my old roommate George McCarthy. We called the play and broke the huddle. There was one problem. I had never taken a snap in my life from the center. In all the years that I had played football, I had never handled a direct snap in a 'T' formation. I was the punter on my high school team and an offensive end, so I was used to handling the football. I had seen it done and it looked easy. I stuck my hands down under the center and started the snap count. I yelled out," hut one, hut two, go."

George slammed the ball into my hands and I wasn't prepared for the force he delivered. The ball sailed up and over my head about ten feet. I had fumbled the snap and ruined everybody's chances for glory. Who knows, perhaps all of us could have been offensive superstars, if we could have just made that extra point. My big running backs did plow into the end zone, but without the football. It took about four days before they would speak to me again.

The varsity season continued and we continued to lose. After the win at North Carolina State, we hosted Wake Forest in Columbia. The Demon Deacons had a great team that year and we played another close game, but lost by a score of 10 to 6. The season was dragging on and although we were playing close games, we weren't having much success in winning them. What no one could understand was that most of those guys, who had lettered the year before, weren't starting. Not only were they not starting, they weren't getting much playing time at all, even as backups. There were some mighty unhappy guys riding the bench most of that season.

The next week, the Gamecocks traveled to Knoxville, Tennessee to play the Volunteers. They were ranked in the top 10 and playing them on the road was a tough 'Rocky Top' mountain to climb. Once again, we put up a good showing, but succumbed to the Vols by a score of 29 to 17. It seemed that Coach Dietzel was keeping his secrets of winning football games to himself for some reason.

Dennis and I were doing pretty well on the right side of the bohunk defensive line, when we scrimmaged the varsity. Dennis was whipping the offensive tackle in front of him soundly on a regular basis. I was pretty quick and had a knack for stringing out sweeps. When Dennis and I decided that we wanted to play, we generally had our way with the varsity offense. At the defensive end position, the pulling guards and fullbacks normally had the responsibility of blocking me when the play came to my side. The techniques for fighting off blockers that were taught by Coach Dietzel's staff consisted of staying square to the line of scrimmage and using a forearm to deliver a blow to the blocker. The idea was to get the forearm underneath the shoulders of the blocker and stop his forward progress. This worked, if you were strong enough and big enough, but even then, it wasn't easy. It was called a 'forearm shiver'. In high school as mentioned earlier, I had been taught another method. That method was called the 'hand shiver'. From the time I played midget football all the way through high school, my Bishopville coaches preached, "Never let a blocker get to your body." Instead of using your forearm like a club to bang on the helmet and shoulder pads of your opponent like we were being taught to do here, I had been taught to extend stiff arms and use your hands to nullify your opponent's block, thereby keeping him away from your body. I had found that in the open field this worked particularly well, if you used the opponent's kinetic energy against him. By that, I mean that you pushed your opponent to a slightly different angle and he would miss you all together.

Our starting fullback that year was a short stocky guy with a bull neck named Jim Mulvihill. Jim was a tough customer from up north who went full speed all the time. He was fast and he loved to hit. At practices, I made Jim's life miserable. They would call a play that came my way and they would break the huddle and lineup. I generally knew when they were coming toward me, because Mulvihill would always look sideways at me. I knew I was going to be his target. I was 6'5", but only weighed around 190. Jim was absolutely positive that he could break me in half and he tried to do that very thing time after time. But, I was always able to get my hands on his

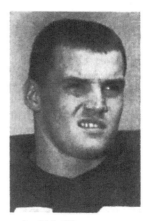

Jim Mulvihill

shoulders and leaning to one side or the other, I would use his momentum to carry him by me on either side. This would leave me free to either take on the next blocker or to make the tackle.

After several weeks of this, Jim had had enough. On his way back to the huddle one afternoon, Jim said to me," Lucas, you're making me look bad."

I replied, "Don't worry Jim, I'll make you look good from here on out."

The next play, Jim came charging my way. I stuck my hands out as usual, but instead of moving him to one side or the other, I used my hands to push backwards and I hit the ground on my back. The coaches yelled, "That a way Mulvihill, that's what you're supposed to do."

The next time they came my way, the same thing happened. This time I held on to his pads and allowed him to push me out of the way, before rolling on the ground. "Now you've got the hang of it Jim," yelled the coaches.

Lou Holtz did not buy it. He figured out what was happening. Before the next play, he strolled up to me, grabbed my facemask again and pulled my head down. He said, "If I catch you doing that again, you're gonna start running wind sprints and run until the end of practice, do you understand?"

"Coach, I don't know what you're talking about?" was my innocent reply.

"I know what you're doing, Lucas, it's a pretty ballet that you and Mulvihill have going, but I'm telling you, it better not happen again. Now, I'm going to ask you again, do you understand me now?"

"Yes Sir." My deal with Jim was off. I wasn't about to run extra wind sprints for anybody.

I started to enjoy those full contact scrimmages. I was gaining confidence with each practice. I had even caught the notice of some of the varsity coaches. There was a time or two, when they came up to me and asked me to allow the offense to run a couple of plays. They needed to practice the plays without me throwing a monkey-wrench into it. It looked as though I might get a chance to play the next year.

Jimmy Gobble

The varsity also practiced special-teams several times a week. The special teams' drills consisted of kickoffs, kickoff returns, punts and punt returns. That was when I really started having some fun. When the team lined up to practice their punts, I noticed that our starting center would arch his shoulders upward, just before he snapped the ball back to the punter. Jimmy Gobble was a good football player and his long snaps to the punter were one hundred percent of the time, right on the mark. It didn't take me long to realize, that if I took off when he lifted his shoulders, I could get the jump on my blockers. I was able to block almost every punt they attempted. I never mentioned my secret to anybody. After all, each time I did something good in practice, the varsity coaches were noticing. I got so good at this, that the coaches no longer let me rush the punter.

We were in the middle of the season and things weren't looking so hot for the varsity. The Gamecocks had won only one game out of six. The next week, we played the Maryland Terrapins in Maryland. All we could manage was a two-point safety. We lost 14 to 2. Things only got worse, as Florida State came to town the next week and routed us 32 to 10. This was not what we expected, when Coach Dietzel took over the coaching reins. Most of the team had truly been excited about the opportunity to play for a coach with his reputation and credentials. What we did not expect, was that Coach Dietzel was intent on cleaning house of, "morally undesirable players." He never pointed out any one individual, but it began to add up. We believed that the three-a-day practices were meant to weed out any weak individuals who couldn't take the grueling regimen. I don't recall anyone leaving the team during those three–a-days, but if you couple the practice sessions with the fact that there were clearly more talented older players from a championship team who weren't playing much, it added up. Resentment started to build among the team. It might've been all right for him to use the season to clear spots for his new recruits, but the feeling was that he was throwing away the season to do it.

We traveled to Alabama the next week and got shutout 24 to 0. That left one last game. We were on the road and traveled north to our in-state rival, the Clemson Tigers. They were still smarting from the close game they had lost to us the year before. Coach Howard had no intention of getting in a position to have to 'kiss his sister' again. The Tigers put it on us pretty good. They beat us 35 to 10. That turned out to be the largest point margin of the year. Even mighty Alabama had only beaten us by 24 points. Our team morale was not very good at the end of the season.

When the NFL draft came along that next spring, the Gamecocks had six or seven players drafted by the pros. Four or five of them had not started. Whether it was true or not, most of the guys on the 1966 team felt that Coach Dietzel had not played his most talented players. It seemed that he liked certain types of personalities and if you didn't fall into that category, you wouldn't get a fair shake and the chance to play.

There is an organization that has been around for a long time and is still very active today. It's called the Fellowship of Christian Athletes or the FCA. This is a fine organization and does many commendable things. I can remember in high school, we had the opportunity to hear one of my heroes, Raymond Barry, testify to his faith. Raymond Barry was the favorite target of Johnny Unites of Baltimore Colts fame. I was brought up going to our country church just about every Sunday. The St. Matthew Methodist Church was full of some of the most Christian and loving people I have ever known. When I was sixteen, I even preached a sermon I had written. Most of the songs that I had learned by heart were hymns I used to sing in that church. Two of our preachers at St. Matthew, were young men that played sports with us in church leagues. They were all good Christian people, but were not the type to wear their faith like a badge for all to see and admire. They led lives that spoke of their faith. Being a member of a Christian organization doesn't make you a Christian, any more than standing in a garage, makes you a car. All of my high school coaches were men of strong faith. During all of the years I played football in the little town of Bishopville, I do not recall hearing one coach use one word of profanity. Now, I don't know who 'John Brown' was, but his name was taken in vain often by one of our high school coaches. 'Dadgumit', was about as intense as it got. I tell the reader about this to illustrate that you can be a good Christian without having to show it off. But it seemed that becoming a member of the FCA was something that was almost required to be in the good graces with the coaching staff under Coach Dietzel. I'm not saying all of the coaches felt that way, but if you let it be known that you were a member, your chances of playing were much better. I remember thinking, "Just acting religious and going through the motions, is this what it takes, to play for this crowd?"

There were some momentous events in the news in 1966. In January, Pres. Lyndon Johnson made a speech stating that America should stay in South Vietnam until the Communist menace was eradicated. Robert C. Weaver became the first African American Cabinet member when he was appointed United States Secretary of Housing and Urban Development. Pres. Charles de Gaulle pulled France out of NATO. The Texas Western Miners defeated the Kentucky Wildcats with five African-American starters. This ushered in desegregation in athletic recruiting. Scheduled hovercraft ferries began service between Britain and France. In Communist China, the Cultural Revolution began, resulting in the murder of millions of Chinese. The last episode of the Dick Van Dyke show was aired.

In June of that year, the Supreme Court ruled that the police must inform suspects of their rights before questioning. This was the famous Miranda Ruling. The United States bombed the North Vietnamese cities of Haiphong and Hanoi. This sparked widespread antiwar protests across the United States. Pres. Johnson also signed the Freedom of Information Act. Richard Speck murdered eight nurses in Chicago and was captured on July 17. Construction began on the two World Trade Center buildings in New York.

The Beatles ended their US tour with a concert at Candlestick Park in San Francisco, California. It was their last-ever live performance, except for the short "rooftop concert" at the Apple Corps offices in January 1969. The first *Star Trek* episode aired on NBC. The United States added yet another department to government, the Department of Transportation. Dr. Sam Sheppard was acquitted in the second trial for the murder of his pregnant wife. This real life drama was the basis for the TV Series and movie, *The Fugitive*. The Washington Redskins outscored the New York Giants 72 to 41, in the highest scoring NFL game. Walt Disney died while producing *The Jungle Book*, the last animated feature to be produced under his direct guidance.

The top grossing movie of 1966 was *The Bible: In the Beginning.* It grossed almost $35 million and starred Ava Gardner and Richard Harris. Steve McQueen and Candace Bergen starred in *The Sand Pebbles. A Man for All Seasons* starring Paul Scofield, Wendy Hiller and Robert Shaw was a great flick. Clint Eastwood continued with his spaghetti Westerns starring in The *Good, the Bad and the Ugly.* One of my all-time favorite Westerns was *The Professionals,* starring Burt Lancaster and Lee Marvin along with the beautiful Italian actress, Claudia Cardinale. George Peppard was sensational in *The Blue Max* and *The Fantastic Voyage* was a great film starring Raquel Welch.

Believe it or not, the top song for the year of 1966 was *The Ballad of the Green Berets* sung by Sgt. Barry Sandler. Some of the other songs that I enjoyed that year were: *Cherish* by The Association, *You're My Soul and My Inspiration* by the Righteous Brothers, *The Poor Side of Town* by one of my favorite artists, Johnny Rivers, *Strangers in the Night* by Frank Sinatra, Somewhere, *My Love (Lara's Theme from "Doctor Zhivago")* by Ray Conniff and The Singers, Wild Thing by the Troggs and there was even a country song in the top 100, A*lmost Persuaded,* sung by David Houston. In looking back over the list of the top 100, I enjoyed almost all of them. It was a good year for music.

Country music had some great hits that year, as well. Buck Owens told us that he was *Waitin' in Your Welfare Line.* And Johnny Cash sang that, The *One on the Right Is on the Left.* Loretta Lynn warned her husband, *Don't Come Home a Drinkin' (With Loving on Your Mind).* Bobby Bare was one of my favorite country artists and he had a hit that year singing about his baby, who walked *The Streets of Baltimore.*

The NCAA college football season ended with a strong finish by several teams. In the final regular poll, Notre Dame, Michigan State and Alabama were first, second and third, with Georgia 4th and UCLA 5th. On December 3, #3 Alabama closed its season with a 31-0 win at Birmingham over Auburn, for its fourth straight shutout and a 10-0-0 record.

The bowl season went like this:

BOWL	Winner		Loser	
Sugar	#3 Alabama Crimson Tide	34	#6 Nebraska Cornhuskers	7
Cotton	#4 Georgia Bulldogs	24	#10 SMU Mustangs	9
Rose	#7 Purdue Boilermakers	14	USC Trojans	13
Orange	Florida Gators	27	#8 Georgia Tech Yellowjackets	12

other bowls

BOWL	Location	Winner		Loser	
SUN	El Paso, TX	Wyoming	28	Florida State	20
GATOR	Jacksonville, FL	Tennessee	18	Syracuse	12
TANGERINE	Orlando, FL	Morgan State	14	West Chester	6
BLUEBONNET	Houston, TX	Texas	19	Mississippi	0
LIBERTY	Memphis, TN	#9 Miami Hurricanes	14	Virginia Tech Hokies	7

The American Broadcasting Company began showing college football in color in 1966. By the NCAA rules, only 8 national and 5 regional telecasts were allowed during the season. The college football season was marked by controversy as the year of "The Tie", a November 19 game between the two top-ranked teams, Michigan State and Notre Dame. Neither team participated in a post-season bowl game.

Florida Gator, Steve Spurrier, won The Heisman Trophy. Spurrier finished his three-year, thirty-one-game career as Florida's starting quarterback completing 392 of 692 attempts, with 4,848 passing yards, thirty-seven touchdowns and 442 yards rushing.

The year was capped off by another trip to Washington, DC. A high school teammate of mine, Travis Windham, and I decided that it would be fun to visit Big G between Christmas and the New Year. We borrowed my dad's car and drove the five hundred miles to the Capital. As soon as we got there a blizzard hit the city. Well, it was more like a small snow-storm, but to me it was a blizzard. I had never seen so much white-stuff. Travis had received an athletic grant-in-aid scholarship to play football at Appalachian State and had gotten used to the snow in the mountains of North Carolina, so he wasn't impressed. We arrived in DC without mishap and George provided dates for the weekend so we went out drinking on the now familiar Wisconsin Ave. Because I wasn't used to driving on the slippery roads, George drove my dad's Chevy to avoid a potential accident. It almost worked. We were in the process of taking the girls home when we pulled up in front of the townhouse belonging to George's date. The windows were fogged up as "Big G" parked the car. Wham! George had backed into a Washington, DC Police car.

"What the hell was that?" George snapped as he opened the car door. He jumped out and spotted the cruiser. As the officer opened the door and got out, so did George's date. "Call me later", she purred and quickly headed to her place. The police officer walked up to the car with his ticket book in hand.

"Have you boys been drinking?"

"We might have had one or two," George replied.

"Who's in the car?" the officer asked as he opened the back door. He peered in at Travis who was trying to take a nap.

"Close that damned door, It's cold!" snapped Travis.

The officer politely closed the door and turned to George, "Some of you have had more than one or two."

George, in an effort to disarm the policeman, turned on the charm and asked, "Do you know Officer Pacorney? I worked with him as a patrol boy in the sixth grade."

"You were in that program?"

"Yes Sir, for three years." In fact, when Nixon was Vice President, he passed by the intersection I was patrolling every morning and Officer Pacorney and I would wave.

"OK son, get in that car and go home. And the next time you see a police officer, you smile and say hello."

"Yes sir!" George replied as he got in the car. Big "G" says he still smiles at policemen forty years later.

And so ended the year 1966.

CHAPTER 4

'Finally a Chance to Play'

Spring 1967

When we returned to campus in January, it was time to sign up for the next semester. At the time, the NCAA had strict rules as to the number of practices and workouts a football team could have. We were told in no uncertain terms, that one of the classes we were going to take was a conditioning class taught by some of the coaching staff. These conditioning classes were dubbed "physical fitness 207". It was open to all students, but only the football team showed up. The classes consisted of the usual wind sprints and agility drills.

During one of our 'non-mandatory mandatory' workouts, one of the infamous stories about 'Big Dink' (Dennis Frazier) took place in Longstreet Theater, which at the time was serving as a gymnasium. It was just before spring practice started and the afternoons had warmed up. Conditioning drills with lots of running and agility exercises were on that day's agenda. The coaches decided that 'Big Dink' needed to lose some weight and they insisted he wear a wetsuit. It was about three o'clock in the afternoon and the sunlight was streaming in through the high windows, heating up the gym. We were running sprints from one end of the gym to the other and each time the coach blew the whistle we had to reach down, touch the floor, turn around and sprint back. Sweating profusely, Dennis decided he had run just about enough in that wetsuit and he wasn't putting in a lot of effort since it was toward the end of the practice session. Coach Bill Rowe was conducting the drills and started in on Dennis in an attempt to get more effort out of him.

"Come on Fraser, move it." He blew the whistle again. Dennis continued to move, but not fast enough for Coach Rowe. "If you get any slower you'll be backin' up," yelled coach. In one last attempt to motivate Dennis he shouted, "Move it Fraser, your ass is as big as a piano!"

Dennis stopped and turned to the coach and shouted, "It might be coach, but when I shit, I don't hear no music." With that Dennis turned and trotted back to the other end of the gym leaving Coach Rowe stunned and stammering, while the rest of us broke out into laughing fits.

During these classes, the coaches also introduced us to stick wrestling. Two players would get down on a mat facing each other. The short stick was about the thickness of the big end of a pool cue. It was wrapped in adhesive tape to insure a good grip. The stick was just long enough so that each player could get both hands on it. The idea was for one player to take the stick away from the other player. It was supposed to promote strength and aggressiveness. A few of the players got into it pretty good, but most of us thought it was kinda silly. These were your teammates, your friends and sometimes a roommate. So, it became pretty common to do the hand stick ballet. They would usually go best two out of three. The players established a system where they either flipped a coin or did paper, scissors, rock to see who would win. There was much grunting, pulling, flipping and yanking, until the stick was taken from the losing wrestler. In a way, I guess it did breed camaraderie and team spirit, but not the way the coaches had envisioned.

'Big G from DC' and I remained good friends even though we were no longer rooming together. One of his big brothers had been in a fraternity at South Carolina, Pi Kappa Alpha. George decided it was time to become a fraternity man. I didn't know much about the fraternity scene. But I knew that the frat guys had great parties and the girls loved it. So I decided to tag along with George and go through fraternity rush. George and I knew that we would wind up with the Pi Ka's, but during rush week, prospective new fraternity members were required to visit each fraternity on campus.

The fraternity houses were located directly behind the Thomas Cooper Library. They were arranged in a U-shape with a quadrangle between them and the library. Each house consisted of a meeting room, a small room with a TV and usually a record player on the first floor. There were dorm rooms and a community bathroom on the top floor. An upstairs doorway connected the different houses on the second story. Each fraternity house was generally arranged the same way. So, when rush night came, George and I started at one end of the quadrangle and went from fraternity house to fraternity house. It was formal in those days. Everybody who was "rushing" wore a coat and tie. If you were pretty sure that you weren't going to, "pledge," a certain fraternity, you would spend only a few minutes with them so they would sign your rush card. This would let the Dean of Students know that you had fulfilled the requirement.

George and I were making pretty good time heading toward the Pi Ka House. We had spent some time with the Sigma Nu's because we saw a few of the football players who were members. About three doors down, we stopped by the Phi Kappa Sigma house. These guys seemed to be having a great time. Then I saw someone that I recognized. His name was Peter Fuge. George and I had ridden the train home from Washington DC and Pete had ridden back with us on the ten hour trip. I had gotten to know this character and a character he was. He wasn't from Washington, DC, but from a town in Maryland. One of the funniest stories Pete recounted for us on our journey was hilarious, but shocking. Pete and one of his high school friends didn't get along with Pete's neighbor, who lived across the street and down a couple of houses. They had evidently been chased off his property more than once.

To get even, the two of them went up to Pete's room with the Washington phonebook. They could see the neighbor's house clearly from his window. Pete and his friend opened the phone book to the Yellow Pages. First, they ordered pizza and had it sent to the neighbor's house. Next, they ordered Chinese food. They ordered anything that had takeout or delivery. After a couple of hours, Pete watched a stream of delivery vehicles pulling up in front of the man's house. There were even five taxis waiting to pick him up. The last straw was when a dump truck unloaded a huge pile of sand in his front yard. With that, Pete's neighbor grabbed a lawn chair, put a white towel on the end of a broomstick and just started waving the delivery vehicles away. I would've been petrified to have done anything like that, but Pete thought it was the funniest thing he'd ever seen.

Pete introduced me to several of his brothers and I immediately took a liking to most of them. Harry Brooks from West Virginia would become one of my best friends and the godfather of one of my children. Pete told us a few more stories and introduced us to several beautiful girls that were helping the fraternity with rush night. So far, these guys had the best looking women, so George and I stayed a while. Then we moved on to the Pi Ka's who had the last house on the quadrangle. Most of them knew George and we received a very warm welcome. We stayed and helped empty a few kegs of beer. Then it was back to J dorm which was just across the street from the fraternity quadrangle. There was one thing for sure about this fraternity business. They had great parties and attracted beautiful girls. The next day, all the fraternities sent out invitations to join or to "pledge" their fraternity. As expected, George and I received our invitation to become Pi Ka's. I also received an invitation to become a member of the Phi Kappa Sigma fraternity. In a move that surprised even me, I accepted the Phi Kappa Sigma invitation, instead of the one from Pi Ka. George and his friends at the Pi Ka house were a little disappointed. I apologized to 'Big G', but I had made my decision.

Johnny Glass

There were a couple of teammates who were already Phi Kappa Sigma's. One, whom I had gotten to know pretty well, was Johnny Glass from Kingsport, Tennessee. Johnny was a great guy. Each pledge selected a big brother to sort of show him the ropes and Johnny became my big brother. Each pledge class also had a pledge master and it just so happen that Johnny Glass was also the pledge master for my group. Two other football players were brothers. One was the star of our football team at the time, Bobby Bryant. The other was a guy from Reavesville, South Carolina named Donnie Myers. I also discovered that our head basketball coach, the legendary Frank McGuire, was an honorary brother of the Alpha Eta chapter of Phi Kappa Sigma at the University of South Carolina.

Frank McGuire had become the basketball coach at South Carolina in 1964. He was an Irishman from New York and had won a National Championship while coaching the North Carolina Tar Heels in 1957. He had finished that season with a perfect 32 and 0 record beating the Wilt Chamberlain led Kansas Jayhawks for the championship. After leaving North Carolina, he had gone on to coach the Philadelphia Warriors. When the Warriors moved to San Francisco, Coach McGuire resigned rather than move west with the team. He had a pipeline of great basketball players coming down from New York to South Carolina. So, during the mid-60's, the University of South Carolina had a basketball coach and a football coach who had both won a National Championship.

Basketball had not been my best sport in high school. I didn't start playing basketball until I was in the tenth grade. My skills were less than impressive. I was tall and quick and understood how to play defense, but my offensive skills were almost nonexistent. I didn't shoot very well, missed most of my layups and couldn't dribble more than five steps without losing control of the basketball. My senior year in high school, we were playing in our conference basketball tournament, when I stepped in front of an opponent's pass and intercepted it. It was a tight game and I started up the court with the basketball. With each step I took, I had less control of the ball. I heard laughter coming from the stands and I thought, "What are they laughing about?" Then I glanced around, and my own teammate, Heyward Stuckey, was attempting to steal the basketball from me so I wouldn't lose it. I really enjoyed playing the game, but it was embarrassing that I was the tallest guy on the team and couldn't help very much, especially on offense. Since coming to South Carolina and getting to know several of the basketball players and hearing all the hype about the sport, I was becoming a big fan.

I was presently, not only a sophomore and football player, but I was also a fraternity man. Until I came to the University of South Carolina, I'd never even heard of a fraternity, much less thought of joining one. But here I was a "Frat Cat" as some preferred to call us. Some of my 'country boy' teammates like Dennis Frazier and Mudcat Grant had a great time teasing me about 'country come to town'. Nevertheless, I was excited about this new opportunity to make friends outside of athletics.

Spring practice returned. Our freshman team had had a damn good year. They had gone undefeated and there were quite a few freshmen athletes that joined us for spring practice. I had already played against them in the fall during our 'toilet bowl' appearances. Spring practice went well for me. I had proven that I was pretty good at playing defense during the past year, scrimmaging against the varsity. Jim Mulvihill, our starting fullback, was very encouraging and had let me know he was sure I would get a chance to play. In those days, each starter from each team in the ACC was allowed to vote for All-ACC honors. Because of Jim's difficulties blocking me during practice, he claimed he had voted for me for all-ACC.

As spring practice wore on, I moved up on the depth chart to the number two position at right defensive end. A classmate of mine, Ron Zukowski was the starter. I was finally moving up the ladder and Coach Holtz was too. He was doing some coaching on the varsity level. The defensive coaching staff felt that I was too thin to be any good, even though I had showed what I could do in practice. The offensive coaches had watched me disrupt their offense all year, but not the defensive coaches. People were always cracking jokes about how thin I was. 'Mudcat' Grant was fond of telling people that I twisted my ankle while wading in a Pepsi-Cola bottle. Dennis accused me of being so thin, that I had to run around in the shower to get wet. Outwardly, I smiled and tried to give back as good as I got. One thing about your teammates in the 60's, you never let them know if something bothered you. If they found out that you were sensitive about anything, that's exactly what they would rag you about. There was no mercy and if you were smart, you'd better not ask for any. I think 'Mudcat' was probably the best at picking on people. He took great pleasure in finding something that aggravated you and loved to see how big of a rise he could get from his victim. But I was out to prove that I was just as strong and just as tough as anybody on that team.

When spring practice ended, I was logged in as the number two, right defensive end. This was certainly a step up from the bohunk team. At the end of spring practice, for those who had made the team for the first time, they issued jerseys. I was given number 84. For a bohunk to have a jersey number assigned was a major leap from playing in the 'toilet bowl' each Monday afternoon. Coach Dietzel warned us about staying out of trouble and staying away from unsavory characters. He wasn't a big fan of fraternities and said as much.

After spring practice, our fraternity was having a big beach bash, so I was off to Myrtle Beach to party and have some fun.

We arrived at the Ocean Forest Hotel on Friday and the party was already well underway. The only other football player there was Donnie Myers. There were several TV series about superheroes at that time. There was Batman and Robin, of course Superman and also Capt. America. That Saturday afternoon the fraternity and their dates were gathered around the swimming pool taking good care of a keg of beer. When what to our wondering eyes should appear, but Captain Rabbit, all dressed up in Superman gear. He had on a pair of white long John underwear with a pair of red shorts pulled over them. On his chest was emblazoned in red letters, "Captain Rabbit". He had a blue cape on his shoulders and a black mask covered his eyes. Captain Rabbit made his appearance holding a beer in each hand and dove into the pool. With this stunt, Captain Rabbit passed into the superhero hall of fame and spawned other superheroes that were yet to come. Donnie Myer's new official nickname was Rabbit, a name he still carries to this day.

We all survived and I don't think anyone from our fraternity went to jail that weekend. We got back to Columbia late Sunday night without too much incident. I don't think Coach Dietzel would've approved, but I liked this new fraternity life.

An event that happened on one of the last Saturday nights of school, illustrates both the fun we had and the concern Coach Dietzel had about fraternities. It seems that a fraternity brother of mine, Burkie Fields, lived off campus about two miles away. He and two or three of his fraternity brothers were renting a house together. The house had a large living room, kitchen and dining room combination. This part of the house didn't have an attic, but the ceiling was spanned by several large, dark colored rafters. For some reason, it reminded Burkie of the mead halls from the Beowulf epics, so they named the house, The Mead Hall.

That particular Saturday night they decided to have a farewell party before heading home for the summer. When the party was at its loudest, Burkie and his date slipped upstairs to Burkie's bedroom for a little private romancing. One of the other guys saw them slip away and enlisted the rest of his brothers in a typical college prank. They decided to strip down naked and creep up the stairs to Burkie's bedroom, where they would throw the door open and jump in a pile on top of Burkie and his date.

Burkie was a little suspicious when all of the noise died out from the party below. Guessing what was at hand, Burkie grabbed a .45 caliber pistol that he always kept in his dresser and threw back the door, stepping out of the bedroom. He was stark naked, holding a pistol across his arm. There, lined up in the stairwell were five of his fraternity brothers staring up at him, also naked. Burkie had a reputation for being hotheaded and the pistol was not taken as a joke. Someone yelled, "Burkie's got a gun, let's get the hell out 'a here." At that very moment, there was a loud banging on the front door and they heard a loud voice yell, "Police! Open up in there." In a panic, the guys ran out the back door or dived out of a window. In their panicked attempt to escape, they ran through the neighbors' backyards, still naked. From that party, the Columbia City Police Department received numerous calls of naked young men running and hiding in the bushes.

It just so happened that at the same time across town, closer to campus there was a group of football players who decided after a few beers, to have some fun as well. The main street running through the Carolina Campus all the way down to the Five Points area of Columbia was Green Street. Green Street was lined with apartments, duplexes and rental houses for students. Just before entering the Five Points area, there was a stoplight and a small hill. Several of the senior lineman thought that it would be funny to startle some of the motorists traveling Green Street. There were four of them, who will remain nameless. They also stripped down and were buck-ass naked. They hid in the bushes and waited for the stoplight to turn red. When the traffic stopped, these four huge guys would run out and line up in front of the cars. They would start doing calisthenics as if they were warming up for a game. When the light changed, they would trot back into the bushes and wait for the next opportunity to perform their warm-up dance. So, in addition to the naked frat boys running through yards on one side of Five Points, there were naked football players on the other side of Five Points. The police were sure there had to be a full moon or someone had opened the state mental ward down on Bull Street. None of the naked participants were apprehended, so the old adage that all is well that 'ends' well was appropriate!

At lunch one day, soon after my beach trip, Gordon Gibson and I sat down with Benny Galloway. Benny was the star running back for the Gamecocks that had injured Allen Brown's shoulder and the guy I had tried to tackle with no success, on my first try my freshman year. He was a year ahead of us and everybody looked up to Benny as a star halfback. Gordon was a freshman teammate of mine. The three of us talked about what we were doing for the summer and I said I would probably be heading back

Gordon Gibson

73

to Bishopville to work with the Lee County Highway Department. Benny started telling us about his summer job the previous year. He and his cousin, Rutt Galloway, had decided to go out to Walla Walla, Washington to pick peas. It was supposed to pay great money even though it was difficult work. While there, they met a guy doing the same backbreaking pea pickin' who told them about a better job. He had a cousin who was a game warden in southeast Alaska and he could get a job for all of them with the Alaska Fish and Game Department guarding salmon streams.

One of the main industries in Southeastern Alaska is the salmon fishery. Each year five different species of Pacific Salmon leave the Pacific Ocean and migrate up the rivers of Alaska, where they spawn and then die. The physiology of the fish has to change during this migratory process. While in the Pacific Ocean the salmon have to expel salt to survive. When they return to the Alaskan coastline to spawn in freshwater streams, they adapt to freshwater conditions. To accomplish this, they follow the high tide up into the mouths of the rivers where the salt and freshwater mingle. With each trip, the fish become more and more accustomed to freshwater. Each time, they move a little further up the river into freshwater, until finally their bodies have adapted and they can move all the way up into the river.

This process can take anywhere from two or three days to a week. During this time the salmon school together in huge groups. Sometimes up to 50,000 fish will gather in an area no bigger than a football field. Many people living on the coast of Alaska make their living by catching salmon. They use purse-seine boats to catch oceangoing salmon and a purse-seine operator has the ability to capture 50,000 fish at one time. The way a purse seine vessel works is quite interesting. The seine net has floats attached to the top of the net and anchor ring weights attached to the bottom, with a line running through the rings. The net is stacked on the back deck of a powerful diesel fishing boat.

Alaskan Purse-Siener boat

The end of the seine net is attached to a separate boat, called a seine-skiff. The seine net itself can be up to a half a mile in length or longer and about ten feet wide. When a school of salmon is cited, a crewman jumps into the seine skiff. The seine skiff is a small, strong boat, with a very flat propeller.

This flat propeller doesn't produce much speed, but is very powerful and that's what is needed next. The end of the seine net is attached to the seine skiff while the other end remains piled on the main vessel's back deck. The big seining boat takes off to make a big circle around the school of salmon. The seine skiff holds its position as an anchor for the net, as the larger boat goes after the fish.

As the main vessel moves, the seine net is pulled off the back of the vessel by the seine skiff in its holding position. The main vessel makes a circle and this puts the seine net around the salmon, trapping them. The larger vessel returns to the seine skiff and using a motorized pulley, attaches a line that runs through all the bottom weighted rings to the pulley. They turn on the pulley and draw the line in. This causes the seine net to be pulled together at the bottom or "pursed." Thus, the term, purse-seiner. Once the bottom purse is closed, they start bringing the top of the net closer to the main vessel. This bunches the fish up close enough to the purse seining vessel, so the fisherman can use a large braille net, also on an electric pulley, to scoop the fish out of the water and drop them into the hold of the boat.

These Pacific salmon all return to the same river or stream where they were born. It is important that enough of these fish are allowed to return upstream to spawn, so that the stream or river will continue to produce salmon for future generations yet unborn. Back in the 60's, these fish were selling for $3-5 a piece or more. If a commercial purse seiner was able to catch 50,000 fish in one set, it could mean as much as a quarter of a million dollars and secure an entire season. The Alaska Department of Fish and Game's job was to enforce the laws that were in place, to protect the salmon preparing to spawn. It was forbidden to fish for salmon with a purse seining operation within certain areas where the salmon congregated before traveling upriver. If a purse seiner caught the salmon in these restricted areas, they could conceivably wipe out an entire salmon spawning run. This would result in that river or stream losing salmon for the future.

In theory, this was an easy law to enforce. But Alaska has thousands of rivers that produce salmon. These rivers and streams are laid out along tens of thousands of miles of coastline and it would be impossible to police each and every stream. So after research by biologists, a prediction when and where salmon would be schooling was determined. The Alaska Department of Fish and Game would hire temporary wardens to guard the salmon streams. In the beginning they tried erecting a small cabin by the streams and putting one man out for several weeks to guard restricted areas. There was so much money involved in the salmon trade, that some of the men actually disappeared.

Whether the disappearance of the stream guards was due to bribery, foul play, wild animals or accidents, was never ascertained. So the wildlife department decided to use stakeout teams to do the job. They would take a pair of temporary agents and fly them out to a stream or river when all the fishing boats were back in port at the close of the season. A crew was flown out in a seaplane and dropped somewhere on the bank of the area to be protected. They set up a camp well back from the shoreline and camouflaged it. That way, the fishermen wouldn't know if a stream was guarded or not, thus establishing a deterrent for anyone who would consider fishing in restricted waters.

The State of Alaska required the Alaska Department of Fish and Game to hire residents for these temporary jobs. Sounds reasonable, but those who applied for the temporary jobs were often the sons, brothers, cousins or friends of the commercial fisherman. Since they weren't likely to arrest their family and/or friends, the law created quite a quandary. The solution was that after a suitable two or three week period, if no "suitable" in-state applicants came forward, the state of Alaska could offer the jobs to nonresident candidates. This solved the dilemma because it was unlikely the out-of-state candidates had any connections to the locals.

So Benny and his cousin, Rutt, decided to give it a try and traveled to Juneau, the Alaska State Capital. They were hired and spent the summer as temporary game wardens. Benny could certainly spin the yarns about his stay in Alaska. Amazing wildlife, majestic mountain scenery, and the wonders he discovered on the Pacific Ocean were just a sliver of all Benny had experienced. The news set Gordon and me on fire. The John Wayne classic, *North to Alaska,* with the theme song written and sung by Johnny Horton, was one of my favorite movies. When I watched that film back in 1960, Alaska seemed like it was at the ends of the earth. I never thought I would ever get to see that mythical land which was almost four thousand miles from Turkey Creek. But with Benny's encouragement, we began to think about going and getting a job as game wardens for the summer. With our imaginations running wild, we asked Benny if he was returning to Alaska. He had other plans for the summer, but he said he would give us some names and phone numbers of contacts there. Gordon and I talked it over and decided we were going. I was so excited. I couldn't wait for the semester to be over.

Soon exams were behind me and my grades held up yet again. My GPR was around 2.5 or 2.6. They weren't quite as good as the year before, but I chalked it up to my new social life with the fraternity. Gordon and I spoke to several of the other ballplayers who were good friends, to see if anyone else was interested in joining us on our great adventure. One of our friends, Ron Palmer, said that he might go. Ron was a running back from Morristown, Tennessee. Ron had been highly recruited and Dennis Fraser seized on that fact. Every time Ron was introduced Dennis would say, "Why people used to come from miles and miles around to watch Ronnie Palmer play football." Gordon and I told Ron that if the trip materialized, we would drop by Morristown to pick him up.

I got back home to Turkey Creek and after a night or two found the courage to speak to my Father about the proposed trip. My Dad was not impressed. "Boy, where did you come up with that harebrained scheme?" he thundered.

"Dad, this is something I want to do."

"Boy, that car will never make it all the way to Alaska."

"Yes it will Dad. It's been working great all year. I haven't had any trouble with it," I fibbed.

"Besides, Benny said they made over $500 a month plus room and board. We should be able to save almost $1000 for school next year."

"How much did you say?"

"Benny said that they paid them $485 a month take-home plus room and board. Benny and Rutt brought back about $1,200 apiece at the end of the summer. Working around here last summer I only saved about $300 and we spent all of that on the car. It sure would be nice to have a little money in my pocket next year and I don't want to ask you for help."

That seemed to soften him up. But the reason I finally got his permission to go was from my Mother. She was the one in our family who had the greatest sense of adventure. She said, "You know Bill, I've always wanted to go to Alaska. If I had the chance, I'd already be on the road."

"Yeah, and that's where he gets these harebrained schemes of his, from you!"

"When are you planning to leave and how much money will you need?" This was Dad's way of giving in and letting me go.

"I'll head out to Greenville to pick up Gordon tomorrow," I said.

"Tomorrow! Damn boy, if you leave tomorrow, all I can afford to give you is $75. I don't get paid until Friday. Can you make it on that?"

"Oh yes sir, that should be plenty," I replied with more hope than knowledge.

"Gasoline has gone up to $.30 a gallon, boy. Mrs. Gibson's boy gonna help put some gas in the car?"

"Yes Sir, we've agreed to split the cost of gasoline."

"I'm going to let you take that .22 caliber pistol of mine. It will come in handy if you get in a jam. And take my old Marine Corps duffel bag. You can pack a lot of stuff in there and it's easy to carry. Just promise me that you'll be careful. "

"I will, I promise. Thanks for letting me go, Papa," I said as I turned to start packing for Alaska.

CHAPTER 5

'North to Alaska'

I left early the next morning and drove to Gordon's house in Greenville. Gordon's Mom and Dad were also less than enthused about the prospects of our summer in Alaska. I remember Mr. Gibson was concerned about crossing the wide open prairies and not having enough water. He insisted that we carry a bucket and keep it full of water at all times in case we broke down somewhere out on the prairie. Gordon's Dad gave him about $300 for the trip. We left Greenville, and headed up to Asheville, North Carolina on our way to Morristown, Tennessee to pick up Ron. I had always loved the mountains and the trip took us right over the highest part of the Blue Ridge. We arrived at Ron's late in the afternoon, just in time for supper. After eating, we were anxious to get back on the road and wanted to travel as many miles as we could that night. Ron took us outside and told us he had decided not to go.

Ron's younger brother had been killed in an automobile accident earlier that year. Ron was now an only child and his mother and father weren't anxious for him to join us. They had not forbidden him to go, but being the dutiful son that he was, he didn't want to place any more stress on his Mother and Father, who were grief stricken over his brother's fatal accident. We were disappointed, but of course understood. We decided to spend the night and head out early the next morning.

We got up to the smell of bacon frying. Mrs. Palmer had fixed a wonderful breakfast. Along with eggs and bacon, she cooked some of the best biscuits and sawmill gravy I have ever eaten. We stuffed ourselves and headed back out to the "Special" as we had nicknamed my car. We said our goodbyes to the Palmer family, cranked up the car and headed west toward Nashville.

The United States interstate system was still under construction, so we traveled mostly on back roads. We drove the length of Tennessee, but it took us most of the day to do it. Gordon and I decided to swing north and headed up to Cairo, Illinois. Cairo is located near where the Ohio River and Missouri River come together to form the mighty Mississippi. I had seen the Mississippi River in lots of movies and we were actually going actually going thereAs I recall, it was about eleven at night and pitch black dark when we reached the bridge crossing over to Cairo. We could've driven a few more miles, because we still were on an adrenaline rush, but we decided it would be fun to spend the night camping on the banks of the Mississippi. We looked around for some side roads that headed toward the river and finally found one. We followed a little winding dirt road down through some woods and came out on a level plane. We could see the glint of lights up ahead reflecting off the water. This had to be it. We drove as close as we could toward the river, but the road was beginning to get muddy, so we decided to stop. We pulled our sleeping gear out and found a big Oak tree that was situated on a little knoll that was relatively dry. After checking out the area, we crawled under our blankets and drifted off to sleep. Before long, for some reason I was dreaming about dog fighting in WWII airplanes. I could hear fighter planes' engines whining as I dove after a German Messerschmitt fighter. Suddenly, I was awakened by a loud buzzing sound.

Growing up in the South, I was used to the sonorous drone of a mosquito. This sound was similar, but louder and angrier. Our heads, shoulders and necks were sticking outside of our blankets and were covered with hungry bloodsuckers. It wasn't a WWII aerial dog fight but I was definitely under attack by hordes of Mississippi River mosquitoes. Gordon and I scrunched into a ball under the covers. That worked pretty well for Gordon, but at 6'6", I had to really contort my body.

Our sleeping gear consisted of the following items: one sheet of plastic to place on the ground underneath us, a couple of old woolen army blankets for cover and we each had brought a pillow from our bedrooms. We covered up the best we could and just left our eyes peeping out from under the blankets and tried to get back to sleep. We did manage to drift in and out of sleep for an hour or two, but I woke up and spied some movement.

There, in the field in front of us, were lots and lots of rabbits. I had hunted rabbits all my life, but I had never been close enough to reach out and grab one. That night we got to watch the mating habits of the American rabbit up close and personal. They would mate and then the female would hop off around the Oak tree with the male rabbit hopping after her. As soon as she got back around the tree, the mating would begin again. I don't know how long we watched the mating ritual, but finally the rabbits and the mosquitoes proved too much. As we were lying there, we actually overheard a mosquito say to a buddy, "Do we eat 'em here or take 'em home?" With that, his buddy replied, "We better eat 'em here. If we take 'em home the biggins'll 'get 'em." With that, Gordon and I looked at each other and exclaimed at the exact moment, "Let's get out of here!" Tired and still sleepy, we left the misty Mississippi floodplain to the rabbits and the 'skeeters'.

We headed northwestward through Missouri. This was Jesse James country and sure enough we came by a place purported to be the house where Jesse James grew up. We kept driving and soon passed from Missouri into Nebraska. Missouri is a beautiful hilly state. There were picturesque farms, beautiful country roads and great cities like Kansas City, St. Louis and St. Joe, but we didn't have time for sightseeing. We were on a mission. The second day we made it as far as Valentine, Nebraska. There was a small creek just off the highway surrounded by Cottonwood trees. There were no Cottonwood trees in South Carolina, so we knew we were in the real West. We bedded down near Valentine that night along the little creek, by the Cottonwoods and camping was a little better. There were a few mosquitoes, but no X-rated rabbit escapades. We were pretty exhausted from lack of rest from the night before, so we slept through until the sun woke us up.

We found a small restaurant and stopped for breakfast. Gordon ordered some bacon, two eggs over easy, toast, coffee and grits. The waitress looked puzzled. She asked Gordon to repeat his order. Then she asked him to repeat it again. Agitated, Gordon asked the waitress, "What's the matter, don't you people speak the King's English out here?" The waitress replied, "Darlin' I just haven't heard many southern accents and I like to hear you talk. I'm sorry, but we don't have grits here," she said with a giggle. Gordon was incensed, "Accent, what accent!?" Gordon was truly mystified and hell, I understood him just fine.

General George Armstrong Custer

Leaving Nebraska behind, we angled northwest toward the Badlands of South Dakota, one of the highlights of our trip. We entered the Badlands National Monument and decided to stop at the headquarters. The terrain was rugged but beautiful. We spent a few minutes looking around and reading the plaques that told us all about the geology and history of the Badlands. This National Monument encompassed 242,756 acres of sharply eroded buttes, pinnacles, and spires, blended with the largest protected mixed grass prairie in the United States. It was designated by Congress as a national monument in 1929. We had never seen anything back home as spectacular. We could have stayed for a while to explore, but decided to move on and headed north by west into the Black Hills.

We reached Deadwood, South Dakota and were right in the middle of the beautiful Black Hills, sacred to the Sioux Indians who had destroyed Custer's legendary 7th Calvary. I had seen lots of movies about Wild Bill Hickok, Calamity Jane and George Armstrong Custer. We even took the time to find Wild Bill Hickok's grave. Deadwood had become a tourist destination and there were little shops selling keepsakes and souvenirs everywhere. One shop we came across caught our attention. They had fake publications purporting to be the Deadwood Newspaper. They would print fake headlines and for a fee, insert your name on the front page and mail it for you to family and friends. Gordon and I couldn't resist.

James Butler "Wild Bill" Hickok

My headlines were:

EXTRA!   **EXTRA!**

DAVE LUCAS
LIVES THROUGH BUFFALO STAMPEDE
RESTING COMFORTABLY AT BLUE BELL LODGE

THE BLACK HILLS NUGGET

VOL. XL, NO. 9   DEADWOOD, S. D.

Ranger Reprimands Tourist for Not Observing Warning Signs

BLUE BELL LODGE, Custer, S. Dak.—"Buffaloes are dangerous" says the signs in Custer State Park, and one tourist learned his lesson the hard way. The victim is resting comfortably at beautiful Blue Bell Lodge which is located on U.S. 87 in Custer State Park where the wild Buffalo of yesterday still graze in...
(Continued on Page 8).

Famous Sitting Bull Falls Before Bullets While Resisting Arrest

GRAND RIVER, Dec. 15, 1890 — Sitting Bull, famed Hunkpapa Sioux who masterminded Custer's massacre, died today while resisting arrest by Indian police.

Led from the house where he had been found asleep, Sitting Bull asked on his way out...

high priest of Wovoka, Nevada Paiute, who told the Indians that their dead were to rise up and aid them in defeating the whites. It was at this point that the Indian police were forced to intervene and the death of Sitting Bull fol-

Potato Creek Johnny Discovers Largest Gold Nugget in Hills

DEADWOOD (Special) — John (Potato Creek Johnny) Perrett

There were other articles that were actual historical news stories about Deadwood and the surrounding area, included in the fake newspaper. It was usually about Indian raids, stagecoach robberies, shootouts, gold strikes and bank robberies. It was the first time we had spent money on anything except food and fuel.

The next state we entered was Wyoming. The Devils Tower was the first landmark we saw in the Cowboy State. It is an impressive hunk of rock. It rises dramatically 1,267 feet above the surrounding terrain. We could see it for miles as we approached. Devils Tower was made a national monument in 1906 by President Teddy Roosevelt. The monument's boundary area encloses 1,347 acres. It was a breathtaking sight to a couple of lowland southern boys like us. Gordon and I wanted to take a closer look, but we decided we better push on westward. If we stopped to see everything that interested us, we would never reach Alaska. We arrived in the small town of Gillette, Wyoming, late in the afternoon.

The grandeur of Eastern Wyoming's high prairies was equally impressive. With the changing of environment, something new and wonderful appeared to us through the windshield. Heading into the setting sun, in the distance we could see mountains outlined against the horizon. We stopped to get gas and asked one of the attendants if it was the Rocky Mountains and he chuckled and said, "No sir, those are the Big Horn Mountains."

We got back in the 'Special' and continued on our way. A beautiful sight loomed ahead of us that June afternoon. The mountains in the distance were still covered in snow and the setting sun reflected colors of deep reds, oranges, yellows, and gold. I thought it was as pretty a sight as I had ever seen. It was a magnificent panoramic painting and we were determined to drive long enough to reach the snowcapped peaks.

After a couple of hours, we finally began the climb up into the Big Horn Mountains. It was dark and we were getting pretty tired. We wanted to pull over and get some sleep, but the road was closed in by snow banks. It was June 5th, 1967 and we couldn't believe there was still so much snow. We drove until we started nodding off and finally, we found a spot that was clear enough to park the car. We pulled out the sleeping gear and got some sleep.

It was around three or four o'clock in the morning when I awoke cold and shivering. We hadn't packed enough blankets for mountainous conditions and I decided to crawl back in the car to warm up. Finding it hard to get comfortable with my long body in the short car seat, I reached over and cut on the radio. Since we were on top of the mountains, it was pretty easy to pick up stations. I stopped on one broadcasting the news. The announcer was reporting that Israel had launched a preemptive strike against Egyptian forces in response to Egypt's closing of the Straits of Tiran. The Arab-Israeli War had begun.

The sun rose behind us in the East. I was still lying in the car, listening to the news about the Arab-Israeli War, when Gordon finally got up. It was time to get on the road again. I knew we were low on fuel, but back home there was a gas station at least every ten to twenty miles. Out here we only passed a few stations as we began our climb into the mountains, and they had been closed. The good news was that we had crested the mountains and were headed down on the western side of the Big Horns. We kept looking for a station, but there were none in sight. About halfway down, the car started sputtering. We were out of gas. Rather than pull off to the side of the road, we just decided to coast on down the mountain. It was fairly slow going, but we made progress and we finally saw the down slope of the mountain turn into a broad plain. I took my foot off the brakes and let the car roll as fast it would go to the foot of the mountain. We coasted about three miles to flatter land before we rolled to a stop.

There was nothing to do now but wait and hope someone would come by and stop to help. It wasn't long before we saw a red pickup truck turn on to the main highway from a dirt road. We were standing by the car and stuck our thumbs out. Sure enough the driver pulled over just in front of my Buick Special.

"You fellers havin' some troubles?" He asked as he walked up to the front of our car.

"Yes Sir. I'm afraid we ran out of gas."

"Run out a gas? How in the world did you manage to do a thing like that?" He asked with a sideways glance that said, "How could you be so stupid?"

"Well, we're from South Carolina headin' to the West Coast. We didn't realize how far it was between filling stations in this part of the country."

"Well boys, I reckon I can tow you," he said as he grabbed a logging chain out of the back of his pickup.

He leaned down at the back of his truck and hooked the chain to a tow bar he had rigged under his bumper. Turning to me, he handed me the other end of the chain and said, "See if you can find a good solid place to hook this."

"Yes Sir. I sure do appreciate this." I said as I hooked the chain around part of the frame. "We apologize for being so much trouble."

"It ain't no trouble, boys." He told us that he had a ranch back down the dirt road. He said he was heading into the small town of Greybull anyway, which was only about eight miles up the road. We got back in our car and he got in his pickup. Here we were, just a couple of 'tenderfeet' being towed by a Wyoming rancher down Wyoming Highway 14 to Greybull. Things seemed to be working out OK. Little did we know, the shit was about to hit the fan...or the...well, you'll find out.

We had gone about two miles when our progress was stalled. There was a small bridge crossing a stream up ahead and the bridge was blocked by a large herd of sheep. It was just like in the movies. I was surprised to see that sheep were allowed in Wyoming, but here they were. There were two sheepherders and three or four sheepdogs rounding up maverick sheep that tried to go their own way. There was nothing to do but wait. It was a beautiful morning, we were in some beautiful country and we were seeing something we had only seen on Walt Disney Presents. The pickup moved along slowly behind the sheep but after the herd crossed the bridge and moved down the road a couple of hundred yards, the dogs and herders moved them off the highway. It took twenty to thirty minutes for the entire herd to move over the bridge and eventually off the road.

The rancher stuck his head out the window and said, "Are you ready boys?"

"Yes sir, let her go."

I think our rancher friend was a little aggravated at this unexpected delay, so as soon as the chain tightened, he started picking up speed quickly. I was driving with my right arm steering the car, and my left arm resting out of the window. Gordon had his right arm out on the passenger side. As we accelerated, we noticed that the pickup's back tires started slinging something all over our car. At first we had no idea what it was. Initially, we assumed it was mud, but a split-second later our sense of smell enlightened us. We were being coated in sheep shit. We both jerked our arms inside the car at the same time and rolled up the windows pronto. Then we realized we were locking in the stench. We gagged, but since we hadn't eaten breakfast, we didn't lose anything. It took about a minute to move through all the droppings that large herd of sheep had left on the road. When we saw that the truck wasn't slinging sheep 'scat' any longer, we hurriedly rolled down the windows and gulped in three or four long breaths of fresh air.

We turned on the windshield wipers, but all it did was smear sheep shit across the windshield. It formed a thick layer and I couldn't see a thing. I had my whole head out the window so I could see to steer. The ole 'Special' wasn't looking too special. It only took us another five or ten minutes to reach the picturesque town of Greybull, Wyoming. The rancher turned into a gas station and pulled us up close to the gas pumps. In 1967, most service stations were still full service. Out of the door stepped the service attendant. He was dressed in a Texaco uniform that looked brand-new. We got out of the car as he approached and I made the common request of the times, "Fill 'er up, please, sir." He replied with the equally common question, "Regular or high test?"

"Regular."

The attendant went to the back of the car which was relatively free of sheep shit and removed the gas cap, which he put on the trunk of the car. He set the lever on the nozzle to automatic and began filling up our tank. Next, he reached over and grabbed his squeegee, his windshield-cleaning solution and some blue paper towels. He moved to the front of the car and began to clean our windshield. He sprayed on a generous portion of window cleaning solution and passed over the area with his squeegee. I was watching his face and could see that it was dawning on him that this was not mud. As he drew the squeegee back toward his body, he reached out with the paper towel to clean its edge. He hesitated, and eyed the squeegee, suspiciously. He wrinkled his nose and brought the yellowish brown substance a little closer to his nose. He took a small whiff and exclaimed, "Hell, that's sheep shit!" At the same time, he jumped back, as if he had stepped on a rattlesnake. The rancher doubled over with laughter. Gordon and I were too embarrassed to do or say much of anything. After the car was full, we did manage to find a do-it-yourself car wash. It took a lot of water and soap, but we finally left Greybull and a bunch of sheep manure behind. And that's no (Grey) bull shit!

We continued down Wyoming Highway 14 toward Cody. As you may know by now, growing up I was a big fan of Western movies. That love for cowboy movies had been instilled in me by my Father and his brother, my Uncle Darby. Cody was named after Wild Bill Cody and I had seen several people portray Wild Bill in movies. The actor, Joel McRae, was my favorite. There was a Buffalo Bill Museum in Cody, but I couldn't talk Gordon into stopping, so we kept driving.

Joel McRae as Buffalo Bill Cody

From Cody we continued on Highway 14 heading toward Yellowstone National Park. When I was little, each Sunday we watched the "Wonderful World of Disney." I remember several segments had included programs on this wonderful place called Yellowstone National Park. And I was about to enter this fabled land of geysers and buffalo. We had decided to stop and ask if perhaps there were any jobs available with the National Park Service. We asked a park ranger at the entrance to Yellowstone where we should go to apply. He directed us to their personnel office located in the middle of the park. The beauty of the park when seen for the first time is indescribable. We saw bears, moose and elk as we drove deeper into the park. I felt like I was beginning to fulfill my dream of wilderness adventure just like Daniel Boone and Davy Crockett.

Darby F. Lucas

It was a little after lunch when we arrived at the personnel office. The head of personnel was only a little older than Gordon and I. He told us there were plenty of jobs available and he encouraged us to stay and work at Yellowstone for the summer. Gordon spoke up and asked what they paid. Our young park ranger smiled and said, "We don't pay much. You earn enough to buy a couple cases of beer a week, but that's about it." He smiled at us and said, "However we do have an advantage here at the park when it comes to hiring. The ratio of girls to guys is about 9 to 1. The guys that wind up working here usually have a pretty good time."

Gordon and I looked at one another and replied, "Let us think about it and we'll get back to you by tomorrow if that's okay?"

"Sure, I'll be here and so will the jobs."

Sure enough, as we walked out into the parking lot two Greyhound busses pulled up. Looking out of each window were great looking girls. We could see them pointing in our direction, turning to look at each other and giggling. We watched as the two buses unloaded and they were all girls! As they filed past us we saw some really nice looking blondes, brunettes and redheads. They all smiled and we watched as they walked slowly into the main office. The last girl stopped and waved. Like two gumps, we just stood there and waved back and then looked at each other.

"Let's get something to eat." was all I could say.

"We've got some talking to do." Gordon replied. I just nodded my head in agreement.

We ducked into a nearby restaurant. The restaurant was in a large building made of logs which could probably seat about three hundred people. The place was packed with tourists, but we found an empty table and sat down. We struck up a conversation with a pretty waitress who was very friendly. After we ordered, we told her about our predicament. We had to decide either to press on to Alaska and make good money or to stay in Yellowstone National Park and have a fun filled summer. She told us that her shift ended around 6 PM and that she and a group of her friends were going up to a spot by a lake for a small party. We were invited to join her.

We met our waitress at the appointed time and place. She crawled in the car with us and we drove up a service road that said 'employees only'. We reached the camp site just as the sun was going down. It was really a picturesque place. We were introduced to three or four guys and about fifteen girls. The job at Yellowstone was going to be hard to turn down. There was plenty of beer and they were roasting hotdogs over an open fire. Our hostess was from Oregon and she told us she hoped we would stay. We spread our camping gear out nearby and as the party wound down, we finally got some sleep.

The next morning, Gordon and I decided we were going to stick to the original plan. We packed up our sleeping gear, loaded it in the Buick Special and headed north out of Yellowstone. About every ten miles or so, we passed another Greyhound bus loaded with girls headed to the Park. We were really tempted to turn around, but we had made our decision and kept on driving.

We headed up toward Missoula, Montana. It just seemed like there was more beautiful scenery just over the next mountain pass or across the next river. Ron Palmer had told us about his uncle who lived in a little town called Cut Bank, Montana. It was located in northwest Montana just below the Canadian border. We decided to make a side trip to say hello. Ron's Uncle was surprised to see us but was glad to hear from his family back in Tennessee. We didn't stay long, but he did insist on feeding us lunch. After visiting for a while, we pushed off toward the Rocky Mountains once again.

We left Montana and crossed into Idaho. Our route took us through Cour d'Alene, Idaho. Cour d'Alene has got to be one of the prettiest places on the face of the earth. The town sits by a lake of the same name surrounded by beautiful snowcapped mountains. We kept motoring west, admiring the magnificent scenery that appeared all around us. We crossed over into Washington State and passed through Spokane. Our destination, Seattle's Sea-Tac airport, wasn't far away.

Before we left South Carolina, Gordon's Dad had checked with a local travel agency. It seemed that the cheapest way to get to Juneau was to drive to Sea-Tac Airport, and catch a flight on Alaskan Airlines from Seattle to Juneau. We had crossed most of the United States and only had Washington State left to traverse. South Carolina is a very small state. You can drive in just about any direction and cross it in no longer than two or three hours. We had hoped to reach Seattle by going through Washington in one day. We made it up into the Cascade Mountain range, only about halfway through the state, before fatigue and darkness forced us to stop once more. We pulled over and spread our sleeping gear on the cold hard ground.

The next morning, bright and early, we woke with the sun and began the last leg of our journey to Seattle. To the south was the towering panoramic view of snowcapped Mount Rainier. We had seen a lot of mountains but nothing was as magnificent as that slumbering volcano in the distance. Its immense size dominated the horizon and we were awestruck to think that it was several hundred miles away and still looked so colossal. We came down out of the Cascade Mountains and saw signs directing us to Sea-Tac Airport. Arriving at the airport, we parked our car in front of the terminal and went inside to find the Alaskan Airline ticket counter. Tickets didn't cost much back then, it was only about $30 or $40 for a one-way ticket from Seattle to Juneau. Our flight was scheduled to leave at 8 o'clock the next morning. With our tickets in hand we exited the terminal and suddenly realized we hadn't considered what to do with the car for the sixty days we were going to be away.

When we checked around the airport, it was going to cost more to store the car than to fly to Juneau. That would break the bank, so we had to come up with a new plan. There was another Texaco filling station nearby. We pulled in and asked the attendant if they would store our car for thirty bucks cash. We offered to pay half up front and the other half when we returned. He talked to his boss and they agreed. We were set. We found a cheap motel for the night and bright and early the next morning, we dropped the car off at the station. One of the attendants drove us to the airport. It was time for our flight to Alaska.

Times were certainly different back then. Gordon and I had both dressed for the great outdoors. We both wore blue jeans, cowboy boots, plaid shirts and blue jean jackets. Before we left South Carolina, I had gone to the Army surplus store and bought two Marine Corps commando knives. I believe they were called KA bar fighting knives. They were pretty impressive. The overall length was 11 7/8 inches. It had a 7 inch black epoxy powder coated carbon steel blade. The knife weighed about .68 pounds. The handle was polished stacked leather with a carbon steel guard and butt. They had both come with brown leather sheaths. I had taken mine home and practiced throwing. It looked easy when Jim Bowie did it on TV. I was determined to learn how to throw a knife like Bowie, so every chance I got I would spend time practicing and got pretty good at accuracy and distance.

We handed our duffel bags to the baggage guys behind the counter at Alaskan Airlines. Security wasn't nearly as tough in those innocent days. I had my Dad's .22 pistol wrapped in some clothes inside my duffel bag and Gordon and I both had our commando knives strapped on our belts. So armed with weapons, we walked down the covered airway to board our flight.

We were greeted at the door by two beautiful women. Neither Gordon nor I had ever flown before and we didn't know what to expect, so we followed the crowd. The two young women were dressed funny. They were beautiful, but there was nothing sexy about their outfits. We thought maybe we had gotten onto an airline owned by some sort of religious cult. The 'stews' had long sleeve blouses with high collars buttoned tight around the neck. They also had on full-length skirts. This was not what we had seen on TV or in the movies. Stewardesses had short skirts that were tight fitting and sexy. It was just our luck to fly on an airplane that was crewed by Amish people. We found our seats and I had the seat by the window.

The captain's voice came on the intercom and cleared up the mystery. It was the 100th Anniversary of the Alaska Purchase and in celebration; the crew was wearing costumes from 1867. For those of you who are not familiar with this part of American history, Alaska was purchased from the Russian Empire in the year 1867. Russia had originally claimed Alaska and to make money, the native Alaskans were forced to hunt for furs. The Russian Orthodox Church also was doing missionary work in an effort to convert the natives to Orthodox Christianity. From 1853-1856 Russia fought the Crimean War with the British Empire. What drove the sale of Alaska to the United States was a foreboding by the Russians that the British in any future war would try to take Alaska by force. Gold had recently been discovered in nearby British Columbia and the population there started to increase rapidly. This prompted the British to create a crown colony right next to Alaska. The Russians decided it would be better to sell Alaska to the Americans than have to fight the British to keep it. So on March 30, 1867 the United States bought Alaska with a purchase price of $7.2 million or about two cents per acre.

After the captain told us about the celebration, he asked us to fasten our seat belts in preparation for the flight. Gordon and I fumbled around with ours as seatbelts weren't required in automobiles then, and we didn't have a clue how to buckle up. After a few cross buckles, we finally got it right. The plane pushed back from the gate and turned toward the runway.

KA-Bar knife, standard military issue for many years.

This was going to be a new experience for both of us. We were getting ready to blast off into the wild blue yonder. The plane had moved along for quite a while but had not picked up speed. I was getting worried. I looked out of the window and could see how much runway we had left. Nearing the end of the runway I said," Gordon, it looks to me like we're coming up on the end of the runway."

"You're right," Gordon said with a worried look on his face.

We paused and looked at each other, and then both of us looked out the window again, contorting our heads to try to get a better view. Sure enough, we could clearly see that the end of the runway was coming up.

Gordon settled back a little bit and with a shaky voice said, "Ain't this thing got to get going a little faster before it can take off?"

"Yeah Gordon, I think you're right, something must be wrong."

Neither one of us realized that we were just taxiing in preparation for takeoff. We thought that the plane just backed from the gate, turned around, put the pedal to the medal and took off. Finally, the plane turned into the wind and jet powered acceleration began. We were impressed and slightly anxious. Our first takeoff had been a real thrill for more reasons than one.

The flight up the west coast of British Columbia was beautiful. The stewardesses were fantastic. They gave us free mixed drinks and didn't even ask for an ID. South Carolina law only allowed beer to be served in bars, so this was something new to us.

As the Air Alaska plane flew northward along the rugged Canadian coastline, the poems of Robert Service were recited over the intercom throughout the passenger cabin. I had read a few of Robert Services' poems in high school, but now, winging my way to the very land that he described, I was much more attuned to the words he had written. This is one of his poems we heard that day on the flight to Juneau:

The Shooting of Dan McGrew

A bunch of the boys were whooping it up in the Malamute saloon;

The kid that handles the music-box was hitting a jag-time tune;

Back of the bar, in a solo game, sat Dangerous Dan McGrew,

And watching his luck was his light-o'-love, the lady that's known as Lou.

When out of the night, which was fifty below, and into the din and the glare,

There stumbled a miner fresh from the creeks, dog-dirty, and loaded for bear.

He looked like a man with a foot in the grave and scarcely the strength of a louse,

Yet he tilted a poke of dust on the bar, and he called for drinks for the house.

There was none could place the stranger's face, though we searched ourselves for a clue;

But we drank his health, and the last to drink was Dangerous Dan McGrew.

There's men that somehow just grip your eyes, and hold them hard like a spell;

And such was he, and he looked to me like a man who had lived in hell;

With a face most hair, and the dreary stare of a dog whose day is done,

As he watered the green stuff in his glass, and the drops fell one by one.

Then I got to figgering who he was, and wondering what he'd do,

And I turned my head — and there watching him was the lady that's known as Lou.

His eyes went rubbering round the room, and he seemed in a kind of daze,

Till at last that old piano fell in the way of his wandering gaze.

The rag-time kid was having a drink; there was no one else on the stool,

So the stranger stumbles across the room, and flops down there like a fool.

In a buckskin shirt that was glazed with dirt he sat, and I saw him sway;

Then he clutched the keys with his talon hands — my God! But that man could play.

Were you ever out in the Great Alone, when the moon was awful clear,

And the icy mountains hemmed you in with a silence you most could hear;

With only the howl of a timber wolf, and you camped there in the cold,

A half-dead thing in a stark, dead world, clean mad for the muck called gold;

While high overhead, green, yellow and red, the North Lights swept in bars? —

Then you've a hunch what the music meant . . . hunger and night and the stars.

And hunger not of the belly kind, that's banished with bacon and beans,

But the gnawing hunger of lonely men for a home and all that it means;

For a fireside far from the cares that are, four walls and a roof above;

But oh! so cramful of cozy joy, and crowned with a woman's love –

A woman dearer than all the world, and true as Heaven is true –

(God! how ghastly she looks through her rouge, – the lady that's known as Lou).

Then on a sudden the music changed, so soft that you scarce could hear;

But you felt that your life had been looted clean of all that it once held dear;

That someone had stolen the woman you loved; that her love was a devil's lie;

That your guts were gone, and the best for you was to crawl away and die.

'Twas the crowning cry of a heart's despair, and it thrilled you through and through –

"I guess I'll make it a spread misere", said Dangerous Dan McGrew.

The music almost died away. . . then it burst like a pent-up flood;

And it seemed to say, "Repay, repay", and my eyes were blind with blood.

The thought came back of an ancient wrong, and it stung like a frozen lash,

And the lust awoke to kill, to kill. . . then the music stopped with a crash,

And the stranger turned, and his eyes they burned in a most peculiar way;

In a buckskin shirt that was glazed with dirt he sat, and I saw him sway;

Then his lips went in in a kind of grin, and he spoke, and his voice was calm,

And "Boys," says he, "you don't know me, and none of you care a damn;

But I want to state, and my words are straight, and I'll bet my poke they're true,

That one of you is a hound of hell. . .and that one is Dan McGrew."

Then I ducked my head, and the lights went out, and two guns blazed in the dark,

And a woman screamed, and the lights went up, and two men lay stiff and stark.

Pitched on his head, and pumped full of lead, was Dangerous Dan McGrew,

While the man from the creeks lay clutched to the breast of the lady that's known as Lou.

These are the simple facts of the case, and I guess I ought to know.

They say the stranger was crazed with "hooch", and I'm not denying it's so.

I'm not so wise as the lawyer guys, but strictly between us two –

The woman that kissed him and – pinched his poke – was the lady that's known as Lou.

Our excitement was building as we flew closer to Juneau. After a couple more poems and a couple more drinks, the captain announced that we were getting ready to land. As we circled in for our approach, I spied something else I had never seen before, except in pictures. There, off the right wing tip of the airplane, was the blue ice river known as Mendenhall Glacier. We were finally about to touch down in 'The Last Frontier'. As I recall, it was a very smooth landing. We were glad to be safely back on terra firma.

We deplaned and took in our first lung full of intoxicating Alaskan air. We claimed our gear and asked someone outside the terminal how far it was into Juneau and he told us it was seven miles. Seven miles! Something else we hadn't thought about. We shook our heads and walked over to a taxi and asked the cabbie, "How much to downtown Juneau?"

"That'll run you around $15."

 We had just landed and I was about out of money. We needed a job quickly. We hopped in the cab and took the $15 ride into Juneau. He took us right up to the Alaska Department of Fish and Game. Their offices were located near the dock overlooking Gastineau Channel. We got out of the cab, grabbed our duffel bags and looked around. We were both hungry, so we decided to get a hamburger, so our stomachs wouldn't growl when we applied for the job. We walked into a restaurant, sat down at the counter and grabbed a menu. We opened the menu and were shocked. Back in South Carolina, a hamburger was $.50. Here they were five dollars! I only had about $15 left. Gordon had a little over $100, but even if we pooled our money, at this rate, we weren't going to last very long. Calling home and asking for money was not an option. We were determined to see this through on our own. And now that we had gotten this far without any help, there was no turning back or begging for help from our parents.

We ordered our five dollar cheeseburgers and they didn't taste any better than the $.50 cheeseburgers back home. As a matter of fact, at that price, it was sort of hard to swallow it. But eat'em we did. We were hungry. I'm afraid the waitress didn't get much of a tip. After we finished eating, we hoisted our duffel bags on our shoulders and returned to the office of the Fish and Game Department. We met the game warden who was over the entire district of Southeastern Alaska. We had been given his name by Benny Galloway. We had to wait about an hour before we got in to see him but he greeted us warmly and assured us that we would be hired. That was the good news. The bad news was the required time period for hiring in-state residents wouldn't expire for two weeks. He said, "Don't worry fellas. You've got a job, but you'll just have to wait a couple weeks for us to hire you legally."

Shaken by the news, we walked out to the parking lot.

"What in the hell are we going to do now, Gordon? We're almost out of money. With the prices so high around here, we won't last a week."

"You're right, Luke. We had better call the people Benny said would help us if we got into trouble. And I think we're in trouble."

Benny had given us the name of a young couple that he and Rutt had become friends with when they were in Juneau. They had spent a good bit of time with the family and had helped make repairs on their home.

We found the number and made the call. A lady answered the phone and she was excited to hear from friends of Benny's and offered to come pick us up right away. She drove up after only about ten minutes. She was young and very pretty. There were a couple of kids in the car with her. We put our duffel bags in the trunk and she drove us to her home three or four blocks away. We explained our situation and she was very sympathetic. However, she explained, "My husband is down in the lower 48 and won't be back for about a week. I'm sorry, but under those conditions I can't let you stay here."

Of course we were disappointed but understood. She suggested that we camp out until the job opened up. We explained that we weren't prepared for that. We didn't have a tent or cooking utensils or supplies. She thought a long moment and said, "Going south out of town about fifteen to twenty miles, is the old DuPont gunpowder warehouse. It's abandoned, but still in pretty good shape. I can take you down to the end of Thane Road. It's about a four to five-mile hike from there to the warehouse. There's a good trail that leads from the end of the road to that spot. It's got a great dock where they used to offload ships. There's good fishing off the end of that dock. You can use your remaining money to buy supplies and you should be able to last for a couple weeks."

It seemed like a good plan to us. She drove us down to a small grocery store. Neither of us had done any camping other than an occasional overnight stay in the backyard. But we were determined to see this through, so we spent our remaining money buying camping supplies. We didn't want to show our ignorance, so we didn't ask for help. We stocked up on cans of spaghetti and meatballs, peas, butter beans, bread and sandwich meat. We had brought along a couple of casting rods and reels and did ask for the best bait to use for fishing. We didn't have anything to cook on, but spied a small three-legged black kettle that we decided to buy. We bundled all of the supplies into a big cloth bag, purchased at the same store, and got back in the car for the ride to Thane Road.

About a half a mile outside of the city limits of Juneau, the pavement ended and the next twelve miles were gravel. It was mid-June by then and it was warm enough, but the road sure was dusty. She dropped us off at the end of the road and pointed out the path we would take through the woods to the warehouse. She told us to watch out for bears and I told her not to worry, that I had my father's pistol with me. After wishing us good luck, she got back in the car, turned around and started back to Juneau. Gordon and I stood there and watched until she was out of sight.

We turned and started our trek through the forest. The trail was well traveled and easy to follow. Our supplies were heavy and that three-legged black iron kettle was awkward to carry. We had to stop about every half mile to rest and after about two or three hours of walking, we reached our destination. The warehouse sat up on the edge of the forest and looked out over a beach at the south end of Gastineau Channel. There was a good roof on the building and the floors were solid wood. Off the front was an overhang facing the beach. The beach was small, compared to the beaches in South Carolina. To the left was a small freshwater stream that cut the beach in half. It would provide good drinking water while we were there. To our right was a huge dock that had been built to accommodate oceangoing vessels. This was a pretty good setup or so it seemed.

photo: Bob Mattson - Ruins of the DuPont dock, Gastineau Channel.

We decided to store our supplies in the warehouse where we could close the doors and keep everything safe from any critters that might wonder into camp. The wooden floors in the building were hard, so we decided to sleep on the softer sand under the overhang. We looked around and found plenty of firewood lying about. We gathered some rocks and formed a circle to contain our fire. We set our cooking pot on three fairly flat stones and it worked very well. Soon we had a nice fire going and decided to open a can of spaghetti and meatballs. After we got our little pot nice and hot, we opened our first two cans and emptied the contents into the black kettle. We brought out a couple of tin plates along with a couple of forks. There was only one problem. We hadn't thought to bring any cooking oil or butter. So the spaghetti and meatballs stuck to the bottom of the pot. Not only did the food stick, but it was burnt since we couldn't regulate the heat of the campfire.

We were hungry after our hike in, so we ate it anyway. When we finished eating, we realized we had forgotten to buy detergent to clean the utensils. So, in Scarlett O'Hara fashion, we decided we'd worry about that tomorrow. We lay down to sleep and dozed off. All through the night, I woke up hearing strange, unfamiliar sounds emanating from the woods. There was also an odd feeling that little fingers were running across my body. It took me two days to figure out what it was. The warehouse was full of mice and they would scurry right over us in the middle of the night. It was scary at first, and then it was just aggravating, as we got used to the little guys.

The next morning, we looked at the dirty plates and food caked kettle, and realized we had to figure out some way to clean them. I remembered reading somewhere or seeing on TV, that the pioneers used sand and water to wash things. So we grabbed our dirty dishes and went over to the stream, where we scrubbed them with the sand and water and it did a pretty good job. At the time, we didn't realize what a dangerous position our ignorance of this country had put us in. Leaving food out overnight was an invitation for native brown bears. We found later, that we had no concept of what a brown bear was really like. That little .22 pistol of my father's would've only been good as a noisemaker. If I had been dumb enough to shoot a brown bear with that small caliber pistol, it would have just made him mad. Thankfully, our luck held and we encountered no bears.

Our food supply dwindled down much quicker than anticipated. After three days, we only had two cans of ravioli and one box of instant mashed potatoes left. Another item we had failed to buy was salt. That night we made a pot of mashed potatoes and they turned out so runny, you could pour them like water. We tried a spoonful, but without salt it tasted like wallpaper paste. We were so hungry by that point, we just dumped a can of ravioli into the pot and ate it all mixed together. The fishing was good off the end of the pier and we pulled in all kinds of fish but we had no idea what they were. We just knew they weren't bass or brim. Several of the ones we reeled in looked edible, but we didn't have a practical way to cook them. Each time we tried to cook fish in our pot they would just fall apart and stick to the sides of the kettle. We even tried skewering them with sticks and roasting them over the open fire, but that didn't work out too well either. Without salt they tasted pretty awful. We were just about totally out of food, when up walked a man and his son with their fishing gear. The warehouse dock was renowned for its fishing and he and his son had come to give it a try.

We spent some time talking and found the gentleman and his family had moved up to Juneau a couple of years earlier from California. I told him that I thought this would be a great place to raise children, but he wasn't so sure. "It's a long way from everything else in this country. In Alaska, you learn to live a certain kind of life and if you ever moved to the lower 48, the culture is so different that I don't think you would be prepared for normal American society."

I've often thought about that statement over the years and I can see his point. Perhaps today, Alaska is not as isolated as it once was. But I was fascinated at the time with the chance to taste the wilderness life and I still thought living in Alaska would be one great big adventure.

As we talked, the man reached into his knapsack and pulled out sandwiches, sodas, and a couple of bags of chips. We were still hungry and it was hard to sit there and watch them eat their lunch. I don't remember drooling, but we did salivate. They started casting off the end of the dock once more and had a successful day fishing. They decided to head home before it got dark. As they packed their gear, I noticed the man was wearing what looked to be a 45 automatic pistol on his hip.

"Boy, that's a big pistol you've got there."

"Well, anytime anyone up here goes off into the woods, they wear pistols or carry rifles. You don't want to be caught without one if you run into a brown bear."

"Are there any around here?"

"You bet cha'."

He added, "I hope you boys have some protection"

"Sure, I've got a gun over there in camp."

"Well, you better keep it with you. It won't do you any good if a bear shows up between you and your weapon. Come on son, we've got to get back to the car."

We said our goodbyes and thanked him for his advice. We tried to cook fish again, but were only able to get a few mouthfuls that were fit to eat. I had never been hungry before. If you got hungry back home, you just walked into a little store and bought a snack or grabbed something out of the refrigerator at home. What were we to do? We still had ten days before the jobs opened up. We went to bed with a lot on our minds.

The next morning, we talked it over and decided we weren't going to stay at the warehouse and starve to death. The best course of action seemed to be for us to get back to Juneau and find some temporary work. So, we packed up all of our gear and started the long hike back through the forest toward Thane Road. I had cut a small pole and tied the black kettle on to one end. I slung my duffel bag over one shoulder and carried the pot on the other. Weakened by hunger, we had to stop about every hundred yards to rest. After about four or five hours, we finally reached Thane Road. There was nothing to do but keep on trudging down the long gravel road.

We had gone about two miles when we saw a small car approaching in front of a cloud of dust. As the car got closer, we saw that it was a little blue Fiat. It was about the size of a big sardine can. There were two people in the car, a man with a cowboy hat and a female. They waved at us and we waved back as they drove past toward the end of Thane Road. We were pretty tired by this time and assumed they would be heading back shortly, so we decided to try and hitch a ride. Sure enough, a few minutes later, here came that same little Fiat trailing another cloud of dust that rose up about fifty feet in the air behind them. We put on our best boyish grins and stuck out our thumbs. Sure enough, the car stopped just past us. The man in the cowboy hat got out and said, "You boys need a ride into town?"

"Yes sir, we sure do." We replied in unison.

"Well, I think we can give you boys a lift."

He opened up the tiny trunk and we were barely able to stuff in our duffel bags. About that time, the passenger door opened and out stepped the woman. She said, "My name's Juanita and this old cowboy here, is my husband, Bud. What you boys gonna do with that three legged pea pot you got there?"

"I'm not sure ma'am. We hadn't thought much about it." I answered as I put the kettle into the trunk.

"Well, I've been looking for a pea pot like that ever since we got up here to Alaska. I need it to cook me some beans. Would you be willing to trade a ride into Juneau and maybe some supper for that old pea pot?"

I looked at Gordon and he looked at me and we turned and simultaneously said, "Yes ma'am, we can do that."

Deal done, Gordon and I tried to fit ourselves into the backseat of that little Fiat. It was difficult to get my 6' 6" frame crunched into the back and Gordon had a similar problem. He was 6' 2" and weighed about 210. So between the two of us and the three legged pea pot, we literally filled up the entire back seat. Bud got into the driver's seat, reached down into the floor and grabbed a beer. He turned his head back toward the rear seat and grinned at us.

"You boys comfy back there?"

"Yes Sir, we're just fine."

"Yeah, you look like a couple of packed sardines without the oil back there," and then he chuckled and drove toward Juneau.

The shock-absorbers on the Fiat were just about worn out. With all the extra weight, each time we rolled over a rock, it jarred us clear from our rear ends up through the top of our heads. When we hit a big bump, both of our heads slammed into the roof. As we approached a small store, Bud turned in so quickly we thought the Fiat was gonna roll over. He slammed on brakes and we skidded to a quick halt.

"Bud, what the hell are you doing?" demanded Juanita.

Bud turned around again with a sly grin and asked us, "You boys drink beer?"

"Yes sir, we drink beer."

"Well, I figured you did and so we're gonna take you home and feed you and you've got to have some beer to drink with supper. Does that suit?"

"Oh yes sir! That'll be fine."

"Juanita, don't cha' think I better get a couple of cases?"

"Yeah Bud, that aughta hold 'em for a few hours."

Bud got out of the car and headed into the store. Juanita was in her mid-40s. She was about the same age as our mothers. Neither Gordon nor I had ever heard an older woman or a younger one, for that matter, say a curse word. As we watched from the cramped back seat, Bud walked toward the store and Juanita turned to us and said, "Boys, old Bud there, he's like a sore peter, you can't beat him!"

"Yes ma'am," we stammered. We were so shocked we couldn't think of anything else to say. It was funny though and as we soon found out, true.

Bud returned with a couple of cases of Rainier beer. In those days, that brand and most other west coast brands could not be lawfully sold east of the Mississippi River. Bud handed us a couple of cold ones to try. Man, it tasted good. It was light and had a great flavor. Bud climbed into the driver's seat once again and drove us the five or six remaining miles back into Juneau. We pulled up in front of a five-story apartment building. Bud grabbed the cases of beer from our laps and he and Juanita started for the building. We extracted ourselves from the back seat and grabbed our gear out of the trunk. I think the little Fiat actually let out a sigh of relief as we got out. With Juanita carrying her new "pea pot", we went up to the third floor to their flat. Bud and Juanita Parsons shared a one-bedroom efficiency apartment. Bud loaded the refrigerator with the newly purchased Rainer beer, asked how we liked it and handed us a couple more. They sure did go down smooth and on an empty stomach the effect of the alcohol was almost immediate. Juanita started cooking our supper while Bud kept handing us beer.

It wasn't long before Juanita had supper ready. She was used to cooking for two and not for a couple of 19-year old football players. I think it only took me about four mouthfuls to finish the entire meal. Gordon inhaled his in a couple of bites. There was no more food, but rather than complain, we thanked Juanita profusely for the delicious meal. When Bud finished eating, he went over to the refrigerator and opened the freezer door. He reached for a chilled shot glass and a bottle of Old Grand-Dad bourbon. He poured a shot for himself and offered us a drink. We said, "No sir, beer will be just fine."

"You boys from South Carolina?"

"Yes Sir, we got here about five days ago. We thought we had a job lined up with the fish and game department, but we have to wait two weeks before they'll hire us. They have to offer the jobs to native Alaskans first. If the jobs aren't taken within two weeks, then we're in. We didn't bring much money with us and we've spent most of it on camping supplies. So, we've got about ten days to go and no money and no place to stay."

"Well boys, Juanita and I ran into a situation like that when we first got here. I'm from Oklahoma. I rode the rodeo circuit for about twenty years. I even won a national championship in roping once. I wasn't doin' much rodeo'n so to earned a little money I was bartending in Oklahoma City. Juanita pulled in there one night and sat down at my bar. She got to flirting with me so I flirted back. She bought a drink, I bought her a drink and then I bought her a few more. I couldn't let a lady drink alone, so I got to drink'n with'er. The next thing I know, I sobered up in Seattle." I asked, "Juanita, how the hell did we get way up here?" She said, "Bud, I told you I was on my way to Alaska and you said you wanted to come along. She told me, "But Bud, this ain'a gonna be no regular shack job, so if you're going on to Alaska with me, we're going to get hitched today."

"Well, I didn't have any money; I had only the clothes on my back. There wasn't nothin' left for me in Oklahoma City, so I said, what the hell, let's find a preacher. That's how we got hitched and ended up here."

"We took the ferry from Seattle to Juneau. It was the middle of winter and my God, it was cold. Then the same thing happened to us that happened to you boys. That job Juanita thought she had fell through. We were in one hell of a mess. Our money ran out pretty fast and we spent about three weeks living in her car. Don't get me wrong, it was a nice car, a Cadillac. We finally had to sell the Cadillac to get money for food. We lived in a cheap motel and things were looking pretty grim. I finally got a job with a transfer company and Juanita got a job about a week later. Since then we've done pretty good for ourselves. It ain't wintertime, but it ain't no fun to be broke up here with no place to stay. I can tell you that we ain't gonna let that happen to you boys. Ya'll are going to stay right here with us until we can find you a job. How's that sound to ya'?"

"Well Mr. Parsons," I started in reply.

"Now, let's get one thing straight. My name's Bud and I don't want no argument from you two boys. You're staying with us and that's the end of it."

That was the end of that conversation. We had a few more beers and Bud had several more shots of Old Grand-Dad as we watched Juanita make a pallet on the floor. Bud insisted that we were to take the bed and they were going to sleep on the pallet. I tried to argue with him, but to no avail. So, sometime around eleven or twelve, we drifted off to sleep. I think that was the first sound sleep we'd had since we left home. It was probably a combination of beer, hunger and fatigue. Whatever it was, we slept soundly, but for only about four hours.

Bud, it seems, was a very early riser. He started drinking Old Granddad the moment his feet hit the floor. We weren't going to get a full night's sleep anytime soon. Bud continually sipped on his Old Granddad and chased it with a Rainier beer, so he had a pretty good buzz by seven or eight that morning. He wanted to arm wrestle us. Then he'd tell a joke and slap you hard on the back as he laughed. The next thing I knew, he had grabbed Gordon and challenged him to a full wrestling match. I could tell that Gordon was about to lose it.

"Gordon, quit fooling around with Bud. You know we've got to go check on that job again this morning," I piped in.

"But its Saturday morning," Bud observed.

"I know, Bud, but the head warden told us to check back as soon as we got into town. Those game wardens work on the weekends, you know."

"You boys want me to run you down there?"

"No sir, we're gonna walk so we can stay in shape."

Gordon and I hit the street and began walking down the hillside toward Gastineau Channel. From our vantage point up on the hill, we could see the fish and game department in the distance. There were no cars in the parking lot.

"Luke, I don't know how much of this I can take. He sure does drink a lot."

"Yeah he does and he's aggravating, but I think he means well and after all, we don't have many options here."

"Yeah, I guess you're right. I guess we'll stay away from Bud as long as we can. I can take it for a few hours before he goes to sleep."

It wasn't too long before we reached the fish and game department offices. We hung around there for a while and decided to walk the waterfronts of Juneau. It got to be pretty boring, so after two of three hours, we decided to go back to Bud's. When we got there, Bud was sound asleep. Juanita said to us, "Sometimes old Bud drinks too much, but he don't mean nothin' by it."

That weekend went by pretty quickly. Bud and Juanita took us to one of their favorite bars. It was the Taku Bar and Grill over across Gastineau Channel in Douglas, Alaska, the sister town to Juneau. The music they played was country and western which was right up my alley. They had a big crowd on Saturday night and I asked Bud how they did during the week. He said, "Not bad, but most bars in Alaska do real well all the time."

"You know Bud, I pick and sing a little country myself. Do you think they would be interested in having some live entertainment in exchange for a little food money?"

"Well, I don't know, but I sure can ask."

Bud walked over to the owner and they spoke for a minute or two. They were both looking my way when Bud nodded and motioned for me.

"This is the boy from South Carolina I was telling you about, David Lucas. He says he can provide some live entertainment cheap if you're interested."

"Well, hi there young fellow, are you any good?"

"I don't know how good I am sir, but I've sung in my school and in church and I was in a country band. We played for several local events over the past three or four years and nobody threw anything at us, so I guess we did okay."

"Okay son, I'll give you a try and if they don't boo you off stage, I'll pay you $30 a night. That'll be for Thursday, Friday and Saturday nights. Wha'da'ya say to that?"

"It's a deal."

There was only one problem. I didn't have my guitar with me. Bud told me we'd fix that Monday morning. He knew we'd be able to find a guitar in the local pawnshop. I could pay him back either out of what I earned or when I left, I could sell the guitar back to the pawnshop. It seemed like a good arrangement to me. Monday morning when Bud finally got up, we found a pretty nice guitar. I bought a couple of sets of strings and a pick or two.

My Dad had sung on the radio in the early 50's in Columbia. He had his own radio show and his theme song was "Heartaches". My brother and I had often been lullabied to sleep, as my father sat at the foot of the bed with a songbook open in front of him. I knew the words to a lot of Hank Williams, Ernest Tubb and Hank Snow tunes I had learned from my Dad. I could sing songs from my own favorite country music artist, Johnny Cash and my Dad and Uncle Darby had taught me to play the guitar.

About the middle of the next week, Gordon and I stopped in to see the game warden. He was very encouraging and said there hadn't been very many in-state applicants for the jobs. Even though they were paying almost $600 a month, that was low pay compared to working on a fishing boat. He told us to check in with him the next Monday. He also told us that we would have to attend a training school that was required for all new temporary employees. The training school was scheduled to start the next Wednesday.

Bud, Gordon and I went over the bridge to the Taku Bar and Grill on Thursday night and I got my chance to pick and sing. It's pretty tough playing for a bunch of drunks. But I got through the weekend and nobody threw anything at me, so I guess I did okay.

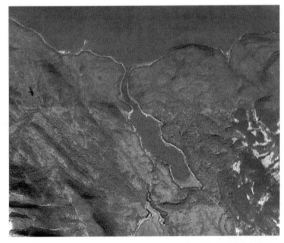

Oliver's Inlet

Monday morning we became employees of the state of Alaska. The game warden training camp was to be held nineteen miles south of Juneau in a secluded bay on Admiralty Island called Oliver's Inlet. There would be about thirty temporary trainees at the camp, and after our training, we would be assigned to different districts throughout Southeastern Alaska. We were told to be ready to go the next day. We said our goodbyes to Bud and Juanita and thanked them for their kindness and told them we would keep in touch.

When we arrived at the Alaska Department of Fish and Game offices, we met several other temporary employees headed for the same Oliver's Inlet training camp. They herded us all outside and pointed to an orange seaplane that was tied to the dock. It was a good sized aircraft called the Grumman Goose that held about fifteen people. We stowed our gear and crawled into the plane. Our second flight was going to be in a seaplane piloted by one of those famous Alaskan bush pilots. I don't know how famous he really was, but to us any bush pilot was famous. We taxied out to the middle of Gastineau Channel and before we knew it, we were skimming south between the surrounding mountaintops. The scenery that spread out below us was absolutely stunning. We quickly covered the nineteen miles to our destination and started in for our first seaplane landing. It looked like our pontoons were brushing the tops of the Sitka Pine trees as we approached the water of Oliver's Inlet, but without mishap we touched down firmly and coasted up to a small wooden cabin.

Grumman Goose ca. 1942

The door opened on the Grumman Goose and the copilot got out and tied the seaplane up to a dock. On the dock was a building called a wanagan. The house-like structure was on the floating dock and was held in place by an anchor. I had never seen anything like it, but I found out that wanagans were very common in Alaska. It could take several forms and is defined as a small house, bunkhouse or shed, mounted on skids or a floating dock and towed behind a tractor or boat. The wanagan was used as the eating and sleeping quarters for a work crew. This particular wanagan had a full kitchen, bathroom facilities, a small meeting room and bunks for six people. This is where we were told the game wardens, who would be conducting the training sessions, would stay.

As part of our training, we would be shown how to build camps and camouflage them on the nearby shore. The shoreline was about fifty yards away from the wanagan. This wanagan even had running water. The builders had taken plastic piping and run it through the fifty yards of water to the shore. The pipes were run up into a stream where a small dam was built out of rocks, so the freshwater formed a deep pool behind the dam. The pipe was set at the bottom of the pool and gravity did the rest. The fresh water from the stream was put into a tank on board. The 150 gallon tank held pure mountain water and warmed it enough so that if you were the real brave type, you could take a shower without freezing.

A Wanagan waiting for the tide to come in.
photo: gillfoto

As soon as we got off the airplane, we were given our camping gear. We loaded our new gear onto a skiff and were ferried to shore. The game warden who deposited us told us to pick out a campsite. We were instructed to choose a site that could be camouflaged well. If we selected a spot that was not suitable, we would have to tear it down and start over.

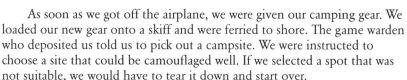

Our equipment consisted of a pop-up tent for two, a Coleman stove for cooking, propane bottles, entrenching tools, hatchets and cooking and eating utensils. In addition, there was a big package that took two of us to carry. We found out later it was a portable kayak. It took about three trips to get everything up to our chosen campsite. To find a good spot, Gordon and I moved about thirty yards further inland than anyone else and erected our camp behind a fallen tree. It was more work hauling equipment the additional distance, but a lot less work trying to camouflage the camp. It seemed like the right thing to do.

Bald Eagle
photo: Mike Scoltt
mikescottphotos.com

Standing on shore for the first time, I remember looking around and counting twelve bald eagles fishing in Oliver's Inlet. After a few days, I asked one of the game wardens about all the wildlife. He told me that just about a half mile from the end of Oliver's Inlet over a narrow portage was Seymour Canal. Seymour Canal had the greatest known concentration of nesting bald eagles in the world. The average was more than one eagle's nest per mile of coastline. The area teamed with Sitka black tailed deer, harbor seals, whales, and sea lions. All of this wildlife utilized Seymour Canal throughout the year. Trumpeter swans, whistling swans, and other migrating waterfowl also used Admiralty Island as a layover. He also warned me that Admiralty Island National Monument, which is adjacent to Oliver's Inlet, was noted for having one of the largest brown bear populations in Southeastern Alaska.

We didn't have much time to enjoy the views or the wildlife. The game wardens were a lot like drill sergeants. There were about fifteen groups of temporaries and the training started immediately. After they approved the site we had chosen, we were pretty well on our own to make the camp as comfortable as possible. Once that was accomplished, they taught us how to use our hatchets and entrenching tools to improve the camouflage around camp, so we couldn't be seen from the water. Several of the other teams were not as lucky and the game wardens forced them to relocate their sites. That caused a lot of grumbling.

The next day we learned how to put the kayak together. The kit consisted of a rubberized skin and sections of collapsible wooden frames. One section was for the front and another section for the aft. The wooden frames were held together by metal hinges. You expanded one section to its full width and then inserted the frame into the skin and repeated the process with the other frame. Once the two sections were in place, you locked them together and had a very sturdy kayak. After we had assembled and disassembled it several times, we learned how to use the kayak in the water.

We all gathered around the shoreline and watched one of the wardens put his kayak through its paces. These boats were fast in the water, but they also capsized easily. They showed us a neat trick with the double bladed oar. If your kayak tipped over, you could right yourself by pushing down on the water at a right angle with the paddle. The boat, when upside down, would not take on water because of an air pocket that formed. If you were really good at using the double bladed paddle, you could twirl around continuously. Only problem with that was the freezing water.

Each team was also issued a .30-06 bolt action rifle. The main purpose for the rifle was for protection from bears. It was a sobering experience to learn how dangerous brown bears were, and a .30-06 rifle was considered almost too small to stop a charging bear. My dad's .22 caliber pistol would've only gotten me into a lot of trouble out at the warehouse. We spent most of the next day target practicing and were instructed what to do when encountering Alaska's bears. The Kodiak bear also known as the Kodiak brown bear or the Alaskan grizzly bear occupies the islands of the Kodiak Archipelago in Southwestern Alaska. It's the largest subspecies of brown bear and one of the two largest members of the bear family, the other being the polar bear. They can be as tall as 9 feet and weigh over 1000 pounds.

They taught us that one of the biggest mistakes you could make with a charging bear was to try to shoot him in the head. Bullets literally bounce off the head of those huge carnivores. Their foreheads are sloped backward and their skulls are very thick. Shot in the head, the bullets just glance off the angled skull. They taught us not to try to kill the bear with the first few shots, but to aim for the shoulders. Once the bear had been broken down by a wound to the shoulder and could no longer run, then was the time to apply the coup de grace. After a day or two of more practical lessons on campsites, safety and practicality out in the Alaskan wilderness, they taught us the legal aspects of our job.

Each temporary stakeout team consisted of two men. If and when we saw a violation of the salmon fishery laws, we were to make an arrest. We were also supposed to keep notes of all fishing vessels in the area. If a fishing vessel was sighted, it had to be notated, whether they were fishing illegally or not. Areas near the mouths of salmon streams had been posted. There were 'NO COMMERCIAL FISHING' signs clearly posted on either side of the stream. Depending upon the terrain, the signs could be as much as a mile apart. This was the area where the salmon schooled to acclimate themselves to a freshwater environment before traveling up the salmon stream to spawn. At this point, the fish were vulnerable to being wiped out by large purse seiners. It was going to be our job to make certain that the commercial fishermen didn't seine inside of these prohibited areas.

Upon seeing an illegal set, the two members of the stakeout team were to step out into plain view of the fishing vessel. One member remained on shore with the rifle. The other would get in the kayak and row out to the offender. Before boarding the vessel, you were to identify yourself as a member of the Alaska Department of Fish and Game. Then you were to board the vessel and place everyone under arrest. After taking charge of the vessel, you orderd the captain to radio the Department of Fish and Game on the department's frequency and report that you had a certain vessel and its crew in custody. You would instruct the captain of the vessel to return to the game warden's office in the nearest town.

Napping Harbor Seals

The training camp lasted for a week. During that time, along with the eagle sightings, we saw plenty of bears and deer. Paddling the kayaks, we also encountered lots of harbor seals and a few sea lions. At first, I wasn't sure what the difference was between seals and sea lions. The harbor (or harbour) seal, also known as the common seal, is a true seal found along temperate and Arctic marine coastlines of the Northern Hemisphere. Harbor seals are brown, tan, or gray, with distinctive V-shaped nostrils. An adult can attain a length of 6.1 feet and a mass of 290 pounds. Females outlive males (30–35 years versus 20–25 years). Sea lions are pinnipeds characterized by external ear flaps, long fore flippers, the ability to walk on all fours, and short, thick hair. Their range extends from the subarctic to tropical waters of the global ocean in both the Northern and Southern Hemispheres, with the notable exception of the northern Atlantic Ocean. They have an average life span of 20–30 years. A male California sea lion weighs on an average about 660 pounds and is about 8 feet long, while the female sea lion weighs 220 pounds and is 6 feet long.

During summertime in Southeast Alaska, the days are very long. The sun rises around three AM and doesn't set before eleven o'clock. We generally ended our instruction by five or six o'clock in the afternoon and had a lot of fun taking the kayaks and exploring Oliver's Inlet. The kayaks could even easily be paddled up the streams that entered the salt water. If you were quiet, you could sneak right up on any of the wildlife, but it wasn't wise to get too close to the bears. The bear's eyesight is not very good, but they have a keen sense of smell. If you were downwind, you could approach even a bear and bump it with the kayak. That is, if you were real stupid. They also taught us that a bear could run a horse down in forty yards, so it paid to be careful.

Some of the trainees were pretty colorful characters. One was a native Alaskan by the name of Ed. Ed smelled bad when we first met him, but after a week you couldn't get within ten feet of Ed without gagging. Most of us would heat water up on the Coleman stove and at least take sponge baths. Deodorant was plentiful, but it seemed that Ed was allergic to soap, water and deodorant.

One day after class that was held on the wanagan, we had reached the tipping point with Ed. Five or six of the guys grabbed dirty Ed and stripped most of his clothes off. Holding him by his arms and feet, they swung him back and forth over the water. With each swing they would say, "Dirty water, dirty dishes, dirty dogs" and tossed Ed as far as they could out into the inlet. Everyone yelled in unison, "Dirty Ed!" He came up sputtering and spitting water and cussing at the top of his lungs. He swam back to the wanagan and tried to climb aboard, but was shoved back into the water and given a bar of soap. After a half-hearted attempt at washing himself in the cold water, Ed was finally allowed back on the dock.

The game wardens had a pretty good set up on the wanagan. As I mentioned earlier, there was water for cooking and bathing. One trainee was an Army veteran and he decided that we deserved some time off from the grueling training schedule. So he took a plastic bottle of dish washing detergent and went over to the pipe in the stream that fed the freshwater to the wanagan. He pulled the end of the pipe up out of the water and emptied an entire bottle of dish soap into the water supply. The idea was that the game wardens would drink the soap laced water and get a bad case of diarrhea and we would have a 'Soap Holiday'. His scheme might have worked except that one of the game wardens, Fred Schulz, was taking a shower at the time. He was rinsing off, but the more he tried, the more he lathered up. He was an Army veteran too and he knew what was happening. The game wardens turned the trick on us by making a batch of 'soapy' Kool-Aid and served it for lunch. Most of the trainees spent the rest of the day in the woods digging latrines.

The last day of camp, they gave us our assignments. Gordon and I were being sent to the Sitka office. That office was run by none other than our 'soapy' game warden, Fred Schulz. The temporary agents were assigned to four game warden districts in Southeast Alaska; Juneau, Ketchikan, Wrangle and Sitka. I had never even heard of Sitka, Alaska, but it was going to be my home for the next sixty days, or better described, my home base.

Gordon and I flew with Fred Schultz on the Grumman Goose southward from Oliver's Inlet to Sitka. We arrived about midday and unloaded our gear at the game warden's office. Fred took us downtown to the Sitka hotel where we would stay when we weren't on stake out. He told us it would be a couple of days before he would have an assignment ready for us. Fred's assistant, who was originally from Arkansas, went by the nickname of 'Arky'. We immediately liked him especially because he spoke 'Southern English' and that was hard to find in Southeast Alaska. We were given vouchers for our meals and hotel rooms. The first day or two all we had to do was report to Fred. He was waiting on the biologist to tell him where the largest concentrations of salmon would be.

With time on our hands, we got a chance to explore Sitka and found it to be a very interesting place. It was founded by the Russians in 1799 under the name "Redoubt Saint Michael". The local natives were members of a warlike tribe call the Tlingits. They destroyed the first Russian settlement, but the Russians returned in 1804 led by Governor Alexander Baranov. They established the town again as New Archangel and made it the capital of Russian Alaska. They built a fort for protection from the Tlingits and also erected The Cathedral of St. Michael a little later, in 1848. This small town of around five thousand people was once known as the "Paris of the Pacific" in the first part of the 19th century and was one of the most important ports on the West Coast. In 1867, when the United States bought Alaska from the Russians, Sitka, the capital of Russian Alaska, was the site of the transfer of sovereignty. The Russian flag was lowered and the American flag was raised on Friday, October 18, 1867. There were some great historical buildings, but it seemed that every other structure in Sitka was a bar.

Each district was assigned a field biologist to assist the game wardens in discovering where to concentrate their efforts. They spent most of their days during the fishing season spotting by air, schools of salmon that were entering coastal waters. Schools of salmon were referred to as a "run" in reference to a group of salmon running up a freshwater stream to spawn. They had a very effective method for counting the fish and if the salmon run was too small, the surrounding area would be closed to commercial

Basket Bay looking northwest

fishing. When a healthy salmon run was discovered, the biologist would allow commercial fishing to coincide with the returning salmons' arrival. So the game wardens knew in advance where the largest salmon concentrations of fish were and where the biologist was going to open the season for commercial fishermen. The season might only last three or four days before it was closed again but areas could be opened and closed several times during the summer months. This allowed the fishermen to catch some fish, but it also allowed a good portion of the salmon to reach their spawning grounds. They were trying to be fair to both the salmon and the fisherman.

After about two days, Fred told us to be ready to leave at five the next morning. We loaded our gear on to a local seaplane and crawled in. Fred instructed the pilot to take us to Basket Bay. Basket Bay is located on Chichagof Island, which is north of Sitka. The bay opens on to a very large body of water, Chatham Straits, which leads north toward Juneau.

We landed on the bay very close to the head where the salmon stream came down and emptied into the northwestern corner of Basket Bay. Most of the shoreline was rocky and mountainous. There was one small, sandy beach that looked like a good place for the floatplane to run up on and put us ashore. It was close to the 'NO FISHING' signs that had been posted on our side of the bay. If you took field glasses, you could see the other 'NO FISHING' signs on the opposite shore. Fred helped us unload our equipment and wished us good luck. He pointed out a good place to locate our camp and hurriedly said goodbye. He didn't want a passing vessel to see the plane either land or take off, because it would give away the location of our stakeout team and ruin the mission. We stood on the shore and watched as the plane headed down the bay. The sound of the engine was amplified off the sides of the mountain on each side and could be heard for quite some time even after it disappeared from sight. I understood why Fred had to take precautions coming in and out of a stakeout site.

Gordon and I looked at each other and it dawned on us that this was the real deal. There was no one within seventy miles and we had no way to contact anyone if we had trouble. With some trepidation, we walked back to the campsite and began erecting our new home. It didn't take long before we had our camp in a reasonably comfortable situation, but we still had to put up the camouflage. We worked for a couple of hours and actually did a pretty good job. We assembled the kayak and found a suitable spot close to the water to hide it. The kayak was fairly heavy. Light weight material had not been invented, so we hid it close to the water. We found a large log on the beach that was high enough above the tide, so the kayak wouldn't float away. Unlike South Carolina, where the tides are only three to five feet high, in Alaska, the average tide was nineteen feet. We utilized the log along with some driftwood and branches for camouflage.

By that time, it was late afternoon, so we decided to fix supper. We moved back up into camp and sorted through our rations. Everything we had was freeze-dried. We had freeze-dried peas, freeze-dried pork chops, freeze-dried Salisbury steak and freeze-dried mashed potatoes. We had been smart enough to stock up on some extras and had purchased about ten packages of Oreo cookies. We ate our meal and finished off a package of Oreos and decided it was time to get a little shut eye. One of us was supposed to stay awake at all times. Gordon was of the opinion that any boat coming into Basket Bay would put up such a racket, we would wake up immediately. I couldn't find fault with his reasoning, so starting the first night, we disobeyed orders and both of us went to sleep. Little did we know at the time, that instead of a five day stakeout, we would be marooned on Basket Bay for three weeks.

After sleeping for about eighteen hours, we got up to fix our next freeze-dried meal. After eating, we decided to do a little exploring. We had noticed while setting up the camp, that a game trail ran alongside the bay. It was on a small ridge that ran about thirty yards back from the shoreline. We walked two hundred yards toward Chatham Strait before we turned back to camp. One of the smartest things we had done in addition to buying those Oreos was to stop at a little bookstore to purchase used paperbacks. The next few days were spent catching up on our reading. I remember reading John Steinbeck's novel "Travels with Charley". It was one of my favorite books that summer. And Alexander Pushkin, the Russian novelist and poet, became one of my favorite authors.

After six days, we were getting anxious. Fred had told us that he would return to pick us up in four. It was now six, going on seven, and our supplies were running low. Both of us were getting a little rank. We had finished our reading material and boredom was setting in. It had rained every day, all day long. Other than the small walk we had taken, we had been forced to stay in the tent or under the canopy that served as the front porch. Just at sunrise the next morning, we heard an engine gunning. We sprang up out of a dead sleep and Gordon slammed on his boots, grabbed the field glasses and ran toward the beach. We didn't want Fred to catch us both sleeping. Gordon stumbled just as he got close to the tree line and slid down a bank about thirty feet to the rocky shore behind a clump of bushes. Just as he straightened up and stepped out on the beach, there was Fred, not more than fifteen yards away, walking up to our camp.

"Mornin' Fred, boy are we glad you made it back. We were thinking you'd forgotten about us."

"Yeah, well we've extended the season. It seems there are a lot of fish out there headed this way and you guys are going to have to stay here a little bit longer."

"But Fred, were about to run out of food."

"Don't worry, I've brought you at least another ten days' worth of supplies."

I climbed down to the beach about that time carrying the .30-06 rifle.

"You mean we're not going back with you?" I asked.

"Nope, the season's been extended. The fishing is good around here and more salmon are coming in. The bay will be loaded with salmon in a few days. This will be one of the prime fishing locations and we've decided this is one of the places we have to guard more closely. Have you guys seen anybody?"

"No sir, there have been no signs of humanity until you showed up."

"Well, I was glad to find you guys awake this morning. You just keep doing your job out here and we'll get you back into town soon. Here, help me unload your stuff."

We did as we were instructed and got all the supplies back up to the tent. Fred was, as usual, in a hurry to get in and out without being seen. So, in the blink of an eye, for the second time, we stood on the beach and watched as the plane disappeared into the misting rain. With absolutely nothing to do, we had another five or six days to sit around camp and look at each other. Our nerves were beginning to fray a little around the edges.

Another week passed and Fred and the seaplane arrived again. This time, we were watching the plane as it made its landing approach into the bay. Unfortunately the news was the same. The season was closed, but only for a day or two and then it would be opened again. Several seining vessels had been spotted working inlets and bays close by. We were told that we had at least another week before we would be pulled out. By way of consolation, Fred did bring out several more packages of Oreos and a few books for us to read. But the one thing Fred couldn't alter was the weather. We had been there fourteen days and it had rained fourteen days. The temperature stayed in the 50's during the day with a constant mist that often turned into a hard rain. Our clothes were damp and smelled so bad that they would've probably gagged a buzzard off a gut wagon.

We were beginning to really get on each other's nerves. I had continued to practice throwing my Marine Corp knife for hours on end. The constant sound of the knife thudding into trees was just about to drive Gordon crazy. He even threatened to use the rifle and shoot me if I did it one more time. Of course I looked at him, and deliberately moved in slow motion and threw the knife again. We finally got a break in the weather. By this time we would have tried just about anything to get away from each other, so I decided to go exploring. I followed the game trail, determined this time to go all the way to the end of the bay, bears or no bears, I grabbed the rifle and went looking for some solitude.

After a mile or two, I came upon a large white sandy beach. This was where the salmon stream we were guarding emptied into the upper end of Basket Bay. It was a fairly good size stream, about fifty yards wide at

its mouth. There was a wide sandy beach on both sides and the stream was jam-packed with salmon. I believe they were Sockeye and are described as follows: A Sockeye Salmon can be as long as 33 inches (84 cm) and weigh 6 to 8 pounds (2.5 to 3.5 kilos). It has an elongated, torpedo shaped body, with an adipose fin, and a bluntly pointed snout. The gill rakers located just behind the head are long and closely spaced. Its coloration changes as it migrates from saltwater to freshwater in preparation for spawning. In freshwater, its color is bright red with a pale green head; females may have green and yellow marks or stains. Its color in saltwater is bluish-green on top, silvery on the bottom, with uniform shiny skin.

They almost filled the entire stream. They were just treading water, not moving forward or backward. They just sat in the water, pointed upstream against the current, with their tails moving from side to side. It was the first time I had seen such a sight. I finally understood why we were here. With a big net, you could've caught 50,000 fish right there.

The trees and brush came down to within thirty or forty yards on either side of the water where I was standing. I decided since it was wide open for a good way back towards the woods that I would follow the stream to see how far the salmon had gone. After I had walked about a hundred yards upstream, the open sandy beach began to narrow and the forest was closer and closer. After another hundred yards, the beach was gone and the trees and brush came up to the water's age. I stopped and looked up at the snowcapped mountains and was in awe. There were no more salmon this far up, but it was beautiful here. At that moment, I felt like a true frontiersman. I turned back toward the bay and happened to notice a set of tracks just to my right. I knelt down and upon closer inspection, realized they were bear tracks, big bear tracks. The hair on the back of my neck literally stood up. I gazed around carefully, but didn't see anything. I interlocked my thumbs and stretching my little fingers as far apart as I could, I was barely able to cover one paw print with both of my hands.

I slowly backed away looking over my shoulder. I took the safety off the rifle and walked away from the stream where the beach widened out. I turned and headed quickly back to camp. I had my neck on a swivel looking for any signs of danger. About fifty yards back downstream, I saw more bear tracks. I hadn't spotted any tracks on my way in. As I looked closer, I realized that some of the bear's tracks were superimposed over my shoe prints. This could only mean one thing. The bear had seen me approaching and had moved off into the brush and was circling behind me. He had stalked me for about fifty yards and gotten within thirty or forty yards of my back, before I had stopped to look at the stream and found his tracks. When I stood up and turned to look around, he had silently slipped back into the brush. I was more than a little apprehensive as I quickened my pace and moved back toward camp. Gordon didn't believe my story until we returned and I showed him the paw prints. We only saw the first few tracks, because neither one of us were interested in tangling with a thousand pound brown bear, rifle or no rifle.

We spent the remaining week snarling at each other and arguing over who got the last of the Oreo cookies and who smelled the worst. Twenty one days without a bath or a change of clothes and we were making 'Dirty Ed' look pristine. Late one night on about the twentieth day, we were awakened by the sound of a purse seiner entering our bay. It was about two thirty in the morning and it was very dark and cloudy that night. All we could see were the running lights. It was too dark to make out the name of the vessel and we couldn't see if they were fishing. They came close to the 'NO FISHING' signs, but as dawn began to break, they moved on back down Basket Bay toward Chatham Straits without putting out a net. We were finally able to get the name of the boat and wrote it down. It was our first entry in our stakeout logbook.

A day or two after spotting the purse seiner, Fred arrived for the fourth time. He told us to pack our gear. We were headed back to Sitka. We had been camped for three weeks straight on the shores of Basket Bay and it had rained every single day.

It was late in the evening when the seaplane touched down in Sitka. We stowed our camping gear and the kayak at the nearby fish and game warehouse and put our duffel bags in the back of Fred's station wagon. Fred had already booked a room for us at the Sitka Hotel. We checked in and climbed the stairs to our quarters. By this time neither one of us was too fond of the other. We took a look at the bathroom and decided to flip a coin to see who got to shower first. Gordon won. That was some shower. He used all the hot water and I had to wait for it to heat up again. Gordon thought that was funny. I was not amused. I had never been three weeks without a bath or shower and when I finally had my turn; it was the best feeling in the world!

Refreshed and somewhat rejuvenated, we headed downstairs for a real meal. The hotel restaurant had a nice steak on its menu with all the trimmings. We ordered steak with baked potato, sour cream, bacon bits, butter and a nice garden salad with (appropriately) Russian dressing. We savored our dinner like a wolf feasting on a freshly killed rabbit. We inhaled every bite in about five minutes. Leaving the restaurant, we decided to check out the nightlife of downtown Sitka.

As we walked along the street, we happened to glance down at a rack holding a bundle of newspapers. The headlines read, "Detroit In Flames". We had been out in the woods so long we hadn't heard any news since the report about the Arab-Israeli War. That conflict had only lasted six days, so by the time we reached Juneau, the war was over. The 1967 race riots were well underway. It seemed that with each return trip to Sitka that summer, another American city had partially gone up in flames. There were over one hundred and fifty cities that experienced partial destruction by its own citizens. We didn't realize it then, but the 60's counterculture was hitting its stride.

We were hoping to find some girls our age, but after checking into about four or five bars it became apparent they didn't hang out there. If there were girls in Sitka, they were not in those erstwhile drinking establishments. We found a bar that played country music, so we stuck around a while to listen and even chatted with the owner. I mentioned to him that I had played over at the Taku Bar and Grill in Douglas. He told me he was familiar with the place and if I was willing, he would put me on stage as well.

We had the next few days off and did manage to run into a couple of nursing students that worked at the Sitka Hospital. One of the girls was from Oregon and the other was from California and they agreed to go to dinner with us. We discovered there was a pretty big cultural divide. The blonde from California, asked Gordon, "What do you think of hard rock?" In all sincerity Gordon innocently asked, "I don't know, what does he sing?" Neither one of us had a clue what she was talking about. The girls looked at us incredulously and explained that hard rock was a type of music, not a musician. Our chances of a second date with the nursing students were 'Slim and None' and with Gordon's comment, 'Slim had left town'.

A day later we boarded the seaplane once again and headed out into the wilds of Southeastern Alaska for our next tour of duty. The stakeout lasted only five days and was uneventful. There was a lot more activity by the purse seiners, but they stayed well away from the 'NO FISHING' zones.

We returned to Sitka and did some sightseeing. We visited St. Michael's Russian Orthodox Church and the Sitka Lutheran Church which was built in 1840 and the first protestant church on the Pacific coast. It seems that the Russian-American Company employed a lot of Swedes, Finns and other Lutherans to work their fur trade.

During this stay in Sitka the sun finally came out. The clouds evaporated and for the first time in over a month the skies were clear. We looked across Sitka Sound out into the Pacific Ocean. Just a little to the northwest across Sitka Sound was the stunningly beautiful Mount Edgecumbe, an extinct volcano sitting on the southern end of Kruzof Island which is about two miles across Sitka Sound.

Mount Edgecumbe

The night before we were to return to our duties, we stopped by the country music bar. After the house band completed its first set, the owner decided to put me on stage. After asking permission, the guitar player agreed to lend me his guitar. On stage I glanced out at a smoky room full of fishermen, lumberjacks and assorted heavy drinkers. This wasn't going to be easy. I started with a rendition of the Hank Williams song, *Your Cheating Heart*. A couple of people looked around to see what the noise was and turned back to their drinks. It was disheartening, but I got a lift from a most unexpected source. There was a loud mixture of applause and shouts coming from a table near the back of the room. Being the ham that I was, I started playing to that table. I loved the applause, but the shouts were unintelligible. My eyes finally grew accustomed to the dim barroom lights. As I finished the song, I could see a table of Japanese fishermen giving me a standing ovation. They loved it. I sang a few more Hank Williams tunes for them before the house band came back for their second set. I wondered, "Should I travel to Japan and try my hand at country music?" Naaaah!

We were deployed once more to stakeout another salmon stream. When we returned to Sitka, it was the first week of August and time to return to South Carolina and get ready for practice. We said our goodbyes to Fred and caught a ferry boat from Sitka to Juneau. Although Gordon wasn't too thrilled, I insisted that we spend the night with Bud and Juanita. They were happy to see us and the next morning they drove us to the airport for the return flight to Seattle. I told them I would stay in touch and that we hoped to return the next summer. We boarded the Air Alaska jet and had an uneventful flight back to Seattle.

Arriving late in the afternoon, we gathered our gear and hiked from the terminal to the station that had agreed to keep my car for the summer. We reached the station about sundown and surveyed all the cars parked there. My red Buick Special convertible was nowhere to be seen. I had written down the guy's name we had dealt with and approached one of the attendants. He said, "Oh yeah, Ed likes that car. He's been driving it all summer."

"Well, where is Ed now?" I asked with irritation.

"Oh, he just left. He went to get something to eat and should be back in about thirty minutes."

"We'll wait," I replied.

We found a comfortable curb to sit on and waited for about forty five minutes. Sure enough Ole Ed pulled into the station in my Buick. He got out and started walking toward the station just as Gordon and I crossed out of the shadows into the light.

"Hey, Ed," I yelled as we moved toward him.

Ed didn't recognize us. Startled, he jumped away and was crouching down, getting ready to run. In a more friendly voice I said, "Ed, relax, we're the guys who left the car here back in June."

Ed, somewhat reassured, stopped and turned to look at us. He moved closer and I could see the light of recognition appear in his eyes. He straightened and came up with an outstretched hand.

"Yeah, I recognize you guys now. You gave me a start there for a minute. This can be a pretty rough neighborhood sometimes. The station's been robbed twice this summer."

"Yeah, we didn't think about that. Sorry, those kinds of things don't happen very often back in Turkey Creek where I'm from."

I asked him how the car was doing and he told us that he drove it once in a while to "keep the battery charged." That was his story and he was sticking to it and I wasn't about to argue with him at that point. I handed him the $15 we owed and he gave us the keys. We got in the car and headed for home.

We decided to drive north to Vancouver, Canada. The plan was to pick up the Trans-Canada Highway in Vancouver and see Canada on our return trip. We had saved a good bit of money, around $1,300 apiece, so we got a cheap motel for the night. We figured we could share motel rooms and split the cost without doing too much damage to our bankrolls. The next day we made it to Vancouver and stopped at a pretty nice looking hotel for the night.

Bright and early the next morning, we started eastward on the Trans-Canada Highway. We continued until we reached Abbotsford, British Columbia. Just outside of Abbotsford, the highway started to swing north. The country was fairly flat, although there were mountains in the distance. Just outside of Greensdale, we reached the Fraser River. It's a fast-moving silt laden river, the color of dirty milk, running to Vancouver and the sea. We followed the Fraser north and the terrain became more rugged. The ride beside the Fraser River was one of the most memorable I have ever taken. The water smashed its way through rapids and down steep canyons. It reminded me of the 1954 movie and song, *The River of No Return* starring Robert Mitchum and Marilyn Monroe. At the Town of Hope, British Columbia, we moved away from the Fraser River Valley and into rugged terrain. The highway continued northward along a ridge crest surrounded by some of the highest mountains in North America.

The journey was dreamlike. With each bend in the road, it seemed like a new vista opened up in front of us with a view more dramatic and beautiful than the last. Gordon had grown up in Greenville which sits in the foothills of the Appalachian Mountains and as a child; I had enjoyed our frequent trips up into the Smokey Mountains. But even our Alaskan experience had not prepared us for a landscape this magnificent. In Alaska, we had seen a different kind of beauty. The mountains surrounded us and of course, large bays, inlets, channels and straights. But the mountains of Southeastern Alaska were all forested. In fact, Southeastern Alaska is covered with the largest rain forest in North America.

This terrain was different. There were jagged granite peaks, deep ravines and river valleys. We continued north until we reached the city of Kamloops, British Columbia. It felt as if we had reached the roof of the world. Our journey carried us into some high mountain lake country. Shuswap Lake, one of the first large Alpine lakes we saw took our breath away. We made camp just outside of the small town of Revelstroke. This little town was situated on a crossing of the headwaters of the Columbia River.

Mt. Eisenhower

The next morning, we continued our northward climb to beautiful Lake Kinbasket. It was inconceivable that the country could be any more majestic, but ahead of us was indescribable Lake Louise and Banff National Park. As we turned south, moving away from Lake Louise, we stopped to gaze at a mountain, at the time, named Mount Eisenhower, after our 34th President, so named in honor of Eishenhower for his role as Supreme Allied Commander in World War II. In 1976 due to intense public pressure from the Canadians, the name reverted back to 'Castle Mountain'.

Our progress through the Canadian Rockies was generally east by southeast. After we passed through Banff, it was all downhill until we hit the prairies. We left the Rocky Mountains behind and 'stampeded' into Calgary, Alberta Province. Slowly the scenery changed from rugged mountain terrain to beautiful more level farmland. We pushed on to the East and camped out once again near the town of Medicine Hat.

Spoiled by the scenery in British Columbia, we decided to take turns driving and push on as hard as we could. We drove on through Moose Jaw, Saskatchewan and then into Manitoba province. We passed through Regina at night and reached Winnipeg and our route dropped southward toward the Great Lakes. We hit the Canadian side of Lake Superior and skirted its edge all the way to Sault Ste. Marie, Ontario Province. We made the decision to cross back into the United States at this point. The journey was interesting and we debated whether or not to stay on the Canadian side, but the route down through Michigan seemed to be the quickest way back to South Carolina. So we crossed the international bridge into the Upper Peninsula of Michigan. It didn't take long before we passed over the Mackinac Bridge into Lower Michigan. We drove through acres and acres of beautiful farmland until we hit the industrial area around Detroit. From Detroit, we cruised through Ohio, reaching Cincinnati.

We crossed The Ohio River and then into Kentucky, the Bluegrass State. We drove through the beautiful rolling hills around Lexington, which were almost soothing after seeing the jagged peaks of the Canadian Rockies. Near the little town of Corbin, Kentucky, we stopped to get something to eat. When we returned to the car, it wouldn't start. Luckily, just across the street was a garage. The words modern, clean and professional could not be applied. It was an old wooden building, weather stained and surrounded by junk cars, piles of tires, car parts, engine parts, barrels full of some sort of black oily liquid and a heavy timbered scaffolding complete with a logging chain and pulley with a dangling engine block. We pushed the car across the road without too much effort. A man in old grease stained coveralls came out with a wrench in one hand and a dirty rag in the other. As he walked up, he was polishing the wrench with his greasy rag. He turned his head to one side, spit a stream of brown tobacco juice into a bucket and said, "What can I do for you fellers?"

"We can't get the car to start," I replied.

"All right boys, just push her on into the shop. Stick it over there by that Ford I'm busy working on. I'll get "Polecat" to take a look at your vehicle. Polecat, where the hell are ya?"

"I'm coming Mr. Jeff," a muffled voice replied from behind a door. The door opened and out strolled a young man of about twenty. As he came walking up, we discovered that his nickname was not a fanciful moniker given to him by some childhood friends. He had earned it. He had reached the highest level achievable for body odor. If Dirty Ed was the 'B. O.' Champ of Alaska, then we were privileged to have come across Mr. Universe! After we got over the initial shock to our olfactory nerves and explained our dilemma he turned out to be a good mechanic. He diagnosed the problem as a bad fuel pump, and he did it without our help, because we were standing out on the street as far away from "Polecat" as we could get without leaving the property. There was a parts store close by, so we purchased a new fuel pump and within an hour my car was running again. For those of you who aren't from the South, a polecat is the same as a skunk. All I can say is that if you want to truly understand what a unique experience we had that day, you must find a skunk, pick it up, lift its tail and get him to spray you right in the face. Only then, can you imagine what it was like that day in August of 1967 when Gordon and I met 'Polecat'.

The charges for the repair were around $50. We had agreed to split any cost for possible repairs on my vehicle and Gordon fussed the entire three hundred miles back to his home in Greenville. He told me he hoped the 'Special' didn't break down again until after I dropped him off. Gordon had the reputation for being tight with money. He handled a nickel like it was a manhole cover. Thankfully, we made it to Gordon's house without any further problems and I said goodbye and immediately headed for home. I reached Turkey Creek and spent days describing all the things we had seen and done on the trip. I was especially glad to see my Grandfather, Henry Lucas, whose health was not the best. But soon my time at home had come to an end and once again, I packed my bags and returned to school and the J Dorm.

CHAPTER 6

'Time to Step Up'

Candler Boyd

Coach Dick Weldon

I arrived on campus in mid-August. Columbia had not changed, nor had the weather. It was still hot and humid. It was going to take time for my body to adjust from the cool dampness of southeastern Alaska to the scorching, muggy South Carolina heat. Reporting to J dorm once more, I found that I had a new roommate. I had played against him many times the year before while he was on the freshman team. His name was Candler Boyd. He was from the same hometown as my previous roommate, Allen Brown, and had attended the same high school, Bradwell Institute. Allen's team was good his senior year, but Candler's team the following year had won the state championship for their high school classification in Georgia. Candler had been a great running back in high school, but he had been moved to the defensive side of the ball for the upcoming season.

The one incident I remembered about Candler from the year before happened during one of our 'Toilet Bowl' games when we kicked off to the freshman team. Candler took the kickoff near the goal line and started up field. One of our favorite assistant coaches was Coach Dick Weldon. Coach Weldon was known throughout South Carolina because of his stent as a very successful high school football coach in the small town of Bamberg. His teams had won several state championships in the class B division and he had sent a lot of his high school players from Bamberg to Carolina to play for the Gamecocks. He was the ultimate enthusiastic coach. At practice, he was always sky-high and wanted you to play that way.

Coach Weldon was standing right behind Candler when he caught the kickoff. With his usual amount of enthusiasm, he ran up behind Candler shouting, "Take that ball and go son! Let me see some moves, boy!"

Candler put on a little shake-and-bake exhibition and eluded the first tackler or two. Coach Weldon continued to run alongside Candler yelling, "That's it, give 'em some more of that!" Suddenly Candler broke free and had a clear path toward the opposite end zone. Coach Weldon ran the whole length of the field, step for step with Candler, shouting the whole time. It was hard not to like Coach Weldon and you could see why he had been successful as a high school coach.

At the end of spring practice, I had moved up to second team right defensive end on the depth chart. The starter who had been moved from quarterback to defensive end, was Ron Zukowski, who had thrown me the hot football my freshman year. That summer while I was in Alaska, a girl I had been dating from Sumter wrote me a few letters. In the last one I received from her, just before we left to come home, she had enclosed a clipping from The State Newspaper. The article stated that Ron Zukowski had left school and would not return. When I came back to practice that fall, I would be listed as a potential starter at right defensive end for the University of South Carolina.

Gamecocks Lose End Ron Zukowski

Ron Zukowski, who had been counted on as one of South Carolina's starting defensive ends for the 1967 football season, will not be available due to academic deficiencies, Coach Paul Dietzel said Friday.

Zukowski, 6-1, 196, attended the first session of summer school, but his grades were not high enough to make up grade-point deficiencies, Dietzel said.

A former high school quarterback star from Trenton, N. J., Zukowski took over the starting right defensive end spot in spring practice when Lyn Hodge, the starter there last year, suffered a compound fracture of his right leg.

Zukowski was a "redshirt" in 1966 and was expected to have three seasons of elegibility with the Gamecocks. Dietzel called his loss "a tough blow," especially since Hodge will not be recovered from his broken leg in time to play this fall.

"Losing your first two right ends would be tough to overcome any time," Dietzel said. "But, we were thin to begin with and the loss of Zukowski cuts even deeper into our depth."

Dave Lucas, a 6-5, 184 pound sophomore from Bishopville, who had been expected to be the Gamecocks' "third end", backing up both Zukowski and left end Gene Schwarting, likely will move up to the starting lineup.

With all of my Alaskan adventures and the picturesque trip home, I hadn't thought much about football. But it was time to get back to work. I was determined to hang on to that starting position. I had to show the coaching staff and the doubters that even though they thought I was too thin to play major college football, I had something to contribute to my team. Our first game was against the Iowa State Cyclones, but that game was still three weeks away and fall practice loomed before us.

Coach Dietzel had evidently learned his lesson about the three-a-day practices. The team had performed so poorly the year before that the Gamecocks had rolled up their worst record ever, one win against nine losses. We started our fall two-a-day practices and they went very well. The team's enthusiasm was high. We believed we could play with anyone considering the starting talent we had. If there was a weakness, it was lack of depth. We had lost a lot of athletes that chose to leave after our losing season the year before. Coach Dietzel had also been very demanding and strict. It was all part of his agenda to "clean up the program." I guess from his point of view, it had worked. A lot of eligible players had left college or transferred to other schools.

We loved playing practical jokes on some of the more naïve team members. Some of our shenanigans were simple and innocent. Others were a little more complex, but definitely entertaining. There were a lot of country boys on the team who loved to hunt and fish and there was a large wildlife area below Columbia where they often hunted. Several of the guys had traveled down Bluff Road toward the Santee Cooper wildlife area and about four miles below the stadium discovered a dirt road that led to an abandoned home about a mile from the main road.

John D and I decided it would be a lot of fun to play a prank on some of our less savvy teammates. We let it be known around the dorm that there was a girl who enjoyed the company of the football team and soon we had a carload of suckers who wanted to enjoy some female company. John D drove out to the house about thirty minutes before we were scheduled to arrive. He parked his car at the rear of the house so that it couldn't be seen from the road. He took his shotgun and a lantern and set himself up inside the house.

Minutes later, I turned down the road with a load of freshmen and bohunk players. We had been talking up the charms of a girl named Mary for at least a couple of weeks. Just before we reached the house I pulled the car over to the side of the road. They asked why I was stopping and I told them that her husband was a truck driver and I wanted to be sure he wasn't there.

"You didn't tell us she was married!" came back an alarmed reply.

"Don't worry, he's always away on trips. I called Mary and the coast is clear. I just wanted to make sure. We walked up to the front porch. The light was on in the window. Just before I stepped onto the porch, I turned and said to the five love-starved young men, "Y'all wait here."

I turned and knocked softly on the door while calling out in a soft voice, "Mary, Mary, are you there?"

John D was waiting on the other side of the door. He kicked the door wide open and stepped out onto the porch carrying his shotgun. It was dark, so all anyone could see was a huge frame standing in the doorway holding what looked like a shotgun. John D said in a very loud voice, "I finally caught you SOB's. You're the ones who been messing with my wife!"

I turned and yelled, "It's her husband and he's got a gun!"

John D fired his shotgun up into the air. I jumped on the ground, crumpled over and yelled, "Oh my God, I've been shot!"

Those five 'wanna be' lovers turned on their heels and I believe could have set Olympic records in the hundred yard dash. Some ran all the way back out to Bluff Road. Others ran out and hid in the woods tearing their clothes on the barbed wire fence that ran down the side of the dirt lane. When we got back to the car, we heard a voice calling "Help, help me get out of here." We could hear our teammate from Marietta, Georgia but couldn't find him. He said, "Here I am, get me out of here." At 6'5" he had wedged himself underneath the back bumper of the car in a squatting position. It took two of us to lift up the back end of the car high enough to get him untangled and out from underneath the bumper.

The two guys that ran deep into the woods got lost. One was a city boy from up North and the other was a Southern boy from a small town down in Georgia. We had retrieved the first three and told them about the hoax, but it took an hour to finally get those two out of the woods. It all turned out to be so much fun, that we did it a couple of times during the year. One group we took to 'see Mary' was comprised of some players who became respectable members of the legal community in later years. When the shotgun went off that night, one particular 'lover' was smoking a cigarette. John D and I had run to the road to watch as they fled from the vicious husband with the shotgun. Our teammate never dropped his cigarette. As he ran, the pumping action of his arms made the cigarette move in a circle and it was all you could see. The red tip of his cigarette was going round and round as he put distance between himself and his tormentor. It was hilarious!

All was going well back on the football field until about halfway through fall practice. I was hit on a blind side block and injured my knee. After waiting two years, it looked like once again, I was going to be relegated to the bench. Even worse, I possibly needed surgery. Our team surgeon, Dr. Lunceford, examined my knee after practice that day. He could tell I was nervous. He smiled at me and said, "Lucas, don't worry. It's just a minor strain. You'll be out for three or four days and then you'll be released for full contact again."

I was relieved, but still concerned. How was this going to affect my chances of starting? After a few days the coaching staff made the decision to move a teammate, Don E. Buckner, over from linebacker to defensive end. At my next examination, Dr. Lunceford said, "Lucas, I'm going to hold you out of this first game. I don't want to take any chances. These knee injuries are tricky and I'd rather be safe than sorry."

This was not the news I wanted to hear. I had worked hard to obtain that starting position and I wasn't going to get the chance to play in the first game of the season. Iowa State came into Carolina Stadium on September 16, 1967 for a night game. Coach Dietzel had played most of his home games at LSU under the lights. We were going to continue that tradition, now that he was at South Carolina.

Iowa's linemen outweighed us by about twenty pounds per man. When they came out on the field, they looked like they were the size of a professional team. The evening was hot and humid and the corn fed boys from Iowa didn't last long on that sultry Carolina night. With Mike Fair, our senior quarterback, leading, our offense put up 34 points. The defense played well too and held the Iowa State offense to just 3. It was a great win and a good way to start the 1967 season. The final score was Gamecocks 34, Cyclones 3.

Monday at practice, Dr. Lunceford released me and I was ok'd to play. I started practicing again, but since we had won the first game so handily, the coaches saw no immediate need to change the depth chart. Don E. Buckner had done a good job against Iowa State and he was going to be the starting end for our next game. It was another home game against the North Carolina Tar Heels.

USC Alters Game Plans

The South Carolina Gamecocks spent two hours running through drills Wednesday in preparation for the upcoming North Carolina game Saturday night in Carolina Stadium.

"North Carolina is a difficult team to prepare for," stated coach Paul Dietzel following the Gamecocks' practice. "They have a lot of variation and motion in their attack and this requires somewhat of a defensive adjustment for us."

"We feel that North Carolina has two fine quarterbacks in Gayle Bomar and Jeff Beaver. Both are good runners."

Dietzel said that South Carolina has had to make some changes in its game plan because of the variations that North Carolina uses.

"North Carolina is a good team. They have some good line personnel. This should be a great game."

Business manager Ralph Floyd reports that there are still plenty of good seats left for the game. Due to the band night commitments, there will be no knothole tickets sold for the game. Season knothole tickets will be honored however.

* * *

CHAPEL HILL, N.C. (AP) —Despite rain, North Carolina's Tar Heels went through another strenuous practice Wednesday, working on blocking and tackling to get ready for Saturday's test with South Carolina.

Drawing praise from Coach Bill Dooley was linebacker Mark Massa, who was shifted from a starting fullback last season to his defensive post.

Headquarters for

Hi-Roll Collar SHIRTS

Seven button in sizes 14½ to 17. Colors . . . Blue, Yellow, plaids and Stripes.

Select Yours Now!

The Debonair Shop
1516 Pine Street   AL 3-0919
(Next to Allen's Gym)

123

Gail Bomar

Their starting quarterback was a left-hander named Gail Bomar. North Carolina was reputed to have a very good passing attack. The passing game was not as wide open then as it is today. Most teams ran a five-two-four defense. There were five defensive linemen, backed up by two linebackers and two corner-backs. Behind the linebackers were two safeties, a free safety and strong safety or rover. As always, your job was to play your assignment. As a defensive end, my assignment consisted of keeping the football to the inside of my body. Once that was accomplished, you tried to make the tackle. The ultimate responsibility was containment. Containment simply meant you always kept the football to your inside. The theory was, there were more players on the inside that could help make the tackle. If a runner got outside you with the football, his chances of a long run were much enhanced, due to the simple fact that there were fewer players on the outside of the defense to get past.

It felt good to be back practicing at full speed. We generally had light workouts on Monday, and watched game film on our opponents in the afternoon. On Tuesdays and Wednesdays, we usually had full speed scrimmages. Thursdays we lightened up and again watched game films. On Fridays we had a very light workout, usually just a walk-through and then got a good night's sleep. We were up early on Saturday mornings and had breakfast as a team. We would break into positions and go over our game plan with the coaching staff and then it was lunch time. We really looked forward to lunchtime on game day, because we were served steak and potatoes. Then, it was back to our rooms for a little rest and reflection. Around five o'clock we boarded the bus and headed out to the stadium.

The University of South Carolina is located in a downtown urban environment about three blocks from the Statehouse. The downtown commercial area of Columbia is just on the other side of the Capitol and Carolina is hemmed in on all sides by either commercial development or residential neighborhoods. The stadium is located about four miles away from campus out on Bluff Road. On Saturday night, September 23, 1967, I took my first bus ride with the team out to Carolina Stadium. My level of excitement and anticipation was high.

The game against the Tar Heels began and during the first half, it became apparent that North Carolina wasn't going to be easy to beat. They moved the ball very well against us that first half. Their great running back, Don McCauley, was having success running sweeps and getting to the corner. Don E. Buckner, my replacement, was trying his best, but he was a linebacker and not a defensive end. The game was tied at halftime 10 to 10 and we were lucky that we weren't behind. Our head defensive coach, Larry Jones, came up to me at halftime.

"Luke, do you think you can stop that sweep?"

"Yes Sir, Coach, I think I can."

"Well, you're gonna' get the chance. I'm movin' Buckner back to linebacker and we'll give you a chance to show us what you can do."

Coach Dietzel called the team together. He gave us one of his small pep talks. His theme was, "The Fourth Quarter Is Ours". The idea was that we had worked harder at conditioning than our opponents. Hopefully, this would result in our opponent wearing down during the fourth quarter and we would win the game due to our superior conditioning. With that, we ran back on the field to loosen up and prepare for the second half. I was finally going to be in a college football game. I was so excited that I think I floated on to the field. I've been asked in the years since if I was nervous or scared? Hell no, I wasn't scared. You've got to remember, I'd been up against 'Lil Abner'.

Don Buckner

We kicked a couple of field goals and took a 16-10 lead into the fourth quarter. I was successfully able to string out sweeps and stop McCauley from having any more long gains. Then, late in the fourth quarter, Bomar started slinging the football all over the field. North Carolina's passing was effective. Then, our offense made a huge mistake. They fumbled the ball on our 26-yard line. The way the Tar Heels had been moving the ball, it looked as if they were going to pull out a win by scoring late in the fourth quarter.

North Carolina had the ball in excellent scoring position when Bomar dropped straight back and set up to throw. I was able to shake my blocker and moved in cleanly toward the quarterback. He saw me coming, but before he could recover, I had him on the ground. It was my first sack in college football. It was second down and long. This time instead of 10 yards or less for the first and ten, they had to go 15.

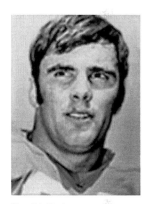

Don McCauley

We lined up again, the ref blew the whistle and they ran a roll out pass play. It was coming right at me. In today's terminology, they 'moved the pocket' to give the quarterback more time to throw. There were two blockers after me this time, but I tried my 'Jimmy Mulvihill trick' and shed their blocks using their own momentum against them. After the second blocker missed me, I grabbed Mr. Bomar again and had my second college career sack. This was fun!

North Carolina was facing a third and more than 20 yards to go. They broke the huddle and reached the line of scrimmage. I had the short side of the field for this play. North Carolina was lined up strong to the wide side, away from my position. The ball was snapped and they called another roll-out pass play to the opposite side. Their backside guard had dropped back to block me. I gave him an inside move and drove to the outside. He missed his block and before Bomar could get the pass off, I caught him from behind. Down he went and to my amazement, I had the third sack of my college career.

Now, North Carolina was facing fourth down and infinity for a first and ten. With less than two minutes on the clock, they had no option but to go for the TD. South Carolina fans were all standing, stamping their feet, clapping their hands and yelling their lungs out. North Carolina came to the line of scrimmage and snapped the ball. They had called another straight drop back pass. It was a Hail Mary. I wish I could remember the details, but I can't. All I remember is moving in toward the quarterback, getting around a blocker or two and suddenly I was hugging Mr. Bomar again. Down he went and I had my fourth sack on four consecutive plays. Four sacks in a row in my first game.

I didn't think much about it all then. But what I do remember is how happy we were winning the game. We took over the ball, ran the clock out and the game ended. The final score was, The South Carolina Gamecocks 16, The University of North Carolina Tar Heels, 10. Our record was 2 wins and 0 losses. It was a very happy locker room. All Coach Jones could say to me after the game was, "Luke where in the world did that come from?"

Our next game was at Duke. It was my first road trip and we were traveling to Durham, NC. Away games are always more difficult. Monday afternoon, we went through our light workout, as usual, and watched game film on the Blue Devils. As we could see from the film, Duke played a different style of football than North Carolina. Where North Carolina had mixed the pass with a run, this Duke team was a ground pounding team of hard-hitting players. They had a stud for a fullback, who liked to run over people. His name was Jay Calabrese and at 6'1" and over 200 pounds, he was almost as big as some of our linemen.

Jay Calarese

We spent our scrimmaging days, Tuesday and Wednesday, working on what our coaching staff called the 50-short defense. This meant that everybody on our defensive line got spaced a little closer together and the linebackers, cornerbacks and safeties, all moved up closer to the line of scrimmage. After viewing the game films we had anticipated that most plays would be running plays. For defensive ends, the difference was small, but significant. We would normally line up against our opponent with our nose located on the outside shoulder of the blocker. In a 50-short, we lined up against the blocker with our nose opposite his outside ear. This may not seem like much of a difference but it constituted one step either way. If you were right and it was a running play, a 50-short defense got you to the ball carrier one step quicker. If they ran outside or passed the football, then you would be one step in the wrong direction. In football, quickness is the key to success. If you are one step quicker than your opponent, all other things being equal, the quicker player wins the battle.

So all that week, we practiced the 50-short defense, sensing the Blue Devils tendencies by studying game film. The film revealed that they would run between the tackles about 80% of the time. If this became reality during our game, we should have a good chance of pulling off a win. If they decided not to stay with their tendencies and passed or ran wide, we would have to return to the normal 50 defense. We saw from the game films that they liked to take the football and run it down your throat. So it was our 50-short defense against their power running offense.

HERMAN HELMS

Executive Sports Editor

Muir

USC's Warren Muir Bursts Thruogh Gaping

This Team Is Committed

THE SEASON is just two games old, and it is true that South Carolina has not yet played the teams that are thought to be the strongest on its schedule.

But even this early, there is one enthralling fact about these 1967 Gamecocks, one thing so visible that no eye can miss it. This is a team committed. These kids of Paul Dietzel play their hearts out, come hell or high water, and no more can be asked of any athletes.

Sunday, Dietzel was looking back with relish on the second conquest in as many weeks, a 16-10 decision over North Carolina in a barn-burner at Carolina Stadium Saturday night.

"Our boys played a heck of a game," praised the tall leader. "It was probably the best game we've played since I've been here.

"We have a grading system in which a score in the sixties is considered good. Our offensive grading score Saturday night was 82 per cent and our defensive mark was 77 per cent. In other words, we think our kids did a real fine job and we're proud of them.

"But few games are perfect and we made some mistakes. We had breakdowns on our first three offensive plays in which we completely left a defensive man open. That could have been disastrous.

"Our defense also looked awfully soft at one stage."

The Tar Heels, a lively, aggressive group that has obviously responded to Bill Dooley's teachings, had the upper hand in the first half and did considerable damage to USC's defense with a power sweep and option play.

The Tar Heels picked up a whopping 168 yards rushing in the first half, but were held to 33 yards in the final half.

"They had us confused for a while because they changed their game plan," reflected Dietzel. "We were playing them to run the wide side of the field and instead they went to the short side. They also were using ball carriers that we didn't anticipate. They simply changed things and it worked well for them for a while.

"North Carolina has good personnel. We knew we were going to have a tough time with them. We knew it would

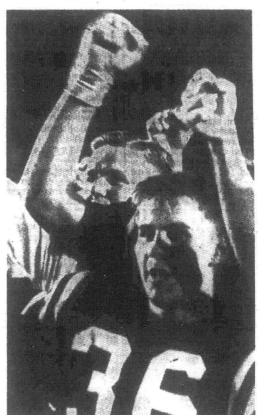

Warren Muir...Happy Warrior

be a war, just as it was. It was a wild game for the coaches, but I don't imagine any of the spectators had any complaints."

127

'They Found It Could Be Done'

TREMENDOUS running by sophomore sensation Warren Muir and a USC defense that bowed its back, drew the line and wouldn't budge pulled the victory out for the Gamecock in the second half.

The comeback, a repetition of sorts of the previous week's 34-3 rout of Iowa State, had to please Dietzel. "They've had a taste of winning," he said. "They've come back from destruction. They've found out it can be done."

Muir carried the ball an incredible 35 times and also ripped off an incredible 164 yards.

"North Carolina forced us to run inside," said Dietzel. "Their ends and their tackles were cutting off the outside, so we had to go inside. I didn't realize we were giving Warren the ball that much, but I'd have to say that he responded quite well. He's just one heck of a football player."

Judgment, perhaps, should not be passed on any player too soon. Muir has played just two games. But if this explosive bull of a kid keeps up the pace he's set so far, before he's finished his career he will have made the All-American team or they should burn the ballots and forget it.

"Mike Fair did a great job, Muir was superb and we graded our halfbacks, Ben Garnto and Butch Reeves, at 89 per cent. That's excellent football," said Dietzel. "But our offensive line is making a heck of a difference. They're taking people on, giving Mike time to throw and giving Warren, Butch and Ben some room to run."

* * *

Wild And Exciting And Proud

There were many standouts in the tough USC defense. Mudcat Grant and Tim Bice each had 12 tackles, Bob Cole had nine, Joe Komoroski and Don Somma each had five and three assists, Gene Schwarting had eight. Dave Lucas, who played less than half the game, still had four tackles, three assists and recovered a fumble.

It was this kind of a game. The tide and the complexion seemed to change almost with every series of downs. But the team that was down kept getting up off the rug and coming back swinging. The persons who made up a turnout of 39,136 — largest crowd ever to view any game other than a Carolina-Clemson battle at Carolina Stadium — had to go home with admiration for what they had seen, a real matchup between two football teams that kept the faith.

Saturday afternoon, George Terry, the kindly and knowledgeable coach who has been Dietzel's right arm for so long, sat down for a moment with the anxious USC head mentor.

"Paul," he said, "I know it's going to be a tough game. North Carolina wants to win very badly, just as we do. But if we could beat them, I believe this town would go wild."

And that's just about what Columbia was like this weekend — wild and excited and proud. The last time the Gamecocks won the first two games of the season was back in 1959. Success after so long can be intoxicating.

It is true that the Gamecocks go to Duke next Saturday, the first leg on a rugged three-week road trip that finds them facing the Blue Devils, Georgia and Florida State. That's the way it is in football, today's glory can be buried under tomorrow's disaster.

But the heck with tomorrow or next week. A town and a team that has waited and suffered so long can be forgiven for breaking down and enjoying just for the moment a present that is so different and nice.

We boarded Greyhound buses that Friday morning and headed up to Durham. We went out to the Duke stadium and had a light workout. Duke's Wallace Wade Stadium was an old facility, even back in those days. Our high school in the little town of Bishopville had better dressing room facilities than they had at Duke. Coach Dietzel had the team all dressed in our school colors of garnet and black. Our sport coats were garnet, we wore white shirts, Gamecock colored ties of alternating stripes of garnet and black, black slacks and black shoes. Coach was determined we'd go first class, dress first class and act first class. These were the nicest clothes that I had ever worn and to me, all of this was first class.

An afternoon game, kickoff was at 1:00 o'clock. Durham was no cooler than Columbia that day. The humidity was a little lower, but not much. The sun was out and it was blazing hot. We were thirsty before we even started to run. Duke won the coin toss and elected to receive. The only two choices you had were to either receive the football if you won the toss, or choose which end zone you wanted to defend. In those days, ninety nine per cent of the time, the team that won the coin toss elected to receive the football.

Lucas Wins Starting Spot For USC

SOUTH CAROLINA'S Gamecocks began preparations Monday for their upcoming game with Duke Saturday afternoon in Durham. Coach Paul Dietzel referred to the Duke game as "the biggest challenge of the year for us."

Dietzel made several changes in the lineup. Sophomore end Dave Lucas of Bishopville, has returned to the starting defensive unit, replacing Don Buckner of Cleveland, Tenn., also a sophomore.

"Lucas' return is a great break for us", stated Dietzel. "With Dave out, we had to bring Buckner in from the defensive secondary to fill the gap. Don did a great job for us at end, and we can move him back to the secondary where he is better suited, now that Lucas is back. We were very pleased with the way Don played against North Carolina."

Buckner has moved back to the rover back position behind junior Wally Medlin.

"We were very fortunate to come out of the North Carolina game in the fine condition that we did," commented Dietzel.

Sophomore rover back Candler Boyd of Hinesville, Ga., sprained an ankle, but should be back by the end of the week. Junior safety Wally Orrel of Savannah bruised a leg Saturday night, but should be ready for action by Saturday also.

Tickets for the Duke game are on sale at the Roundhouse ticket office on Rosewood Drive.

* * *

CLEMSON — Clemson players who saw most of the action Saturday against Wake Forest worked out in sweat clothes Monday, but the rest of the squad held a 25-minute scrimmage.

The first 44 players earlier got a look at what to expect Saturday when the Georgia Bulldogs invade Death Valley. The entire squad worked on this for 35 minutes before going into the scrimmage.

Since we elected to kickoff, our defensive team took the field ready to go. Our placekicker, Jimmy Poole, ran up and boom, the game was on. I sprinted as hard as I could down field, careful to stay in my lane as the runner caught the ball. We started to converge on the ball carrier, when our linebacker, Tim Bice, lowered his shoulder to make the tackle. His helmet slipped to one side and just as he made contact with his shoulder, his head knocked the ball out of the runner's arms. The ball squirted back into the end zone. Another teammate, Allen "Goat" Owens hit the runner and put him on the ground. I continued to sprint after the football and fell on it. I had recovered the fumble in the end zone and had scored the first and only touchdown of my college football career. I looked up at the scoreboard and there was only six seconds off the clock. The game had barely begun and I had scored a touchdown and we were ahead 6-0.

Man, did I love college football! The fun, however soon developed into hard work. Duke recovered from that opening blow and made it into a real football game. True to the scouting reports, they began to hammer us with their big fullback, Jay Calabrese. Their philosophy consisted of; run the football off-tackle left, run the football off-tackle right, run the football up the middle and they would throw a pass about every tenth play. That type of football is designed to wear a defense down. The defensive end's assignment on those off-tackle running plays was pretty simple. Duke generally ran with two tight ends, so I always had to contend with a tight end on my side. The

Don Somma

Gene Schwarting

Joe Komoroski

blocking scheme they used was also simple. Their tight end and tackle would double-team our defensive tackle, Don Somma, who was right beside me. Gene Schwarting was the other defensive end and Joseph Komoroski was the other defensive tackle. Our first job, as ends, was to hit the tight end in an effort to disrupt his block on the defensive tackle. The halfback would move at full speed in an effort to knock the defensive end away from the tight end and out toward the sideline. If successful, he would open up a hole between the defensive end and the tackle. The fullback would lead through the open hole and try to block the linebacker and after that, the runner would sweep by with the football. The defensive end's job was to jam up the hole by holding his ground, taking on the block from the halfback and/or pulling guard. The DE had to do this at all times, while keeping the outside arm free, so if they tried to go wide, the DE could prevent that from happening by bouncing outside.

Duke must have looked at the North Carolina film from the previous week and decided I was too light to be a serious impediment to their inside running game. It felt like much of the first three quarters, they spent running that off-tackle play to my side of the field. I was determined to hold my ground and do my assignment, no matter the size of my opponents. It was late in the fourth quarter and Coach Dietzel's theme came to the fore again. 'The Fourth Quarter Is Ours.' Mike Fair and the offense had added a couple of touchdowns to the one that Tim Bice, Allen Owens and I had teamed up to produce on the opening kickoff. Duke had powered in two touchdowns and added a field goal. The score was Carolina 21 and Duke 17.

With time running out, Duke decided to change tactics. They went to the air and started passing the ball. It went back and forth for a while and I added three more sacks during the interim, but Duke continued to move the football through the air. They moved down to about our 25-yard line and the Duke quarterback dropped back to pass. I didn't get the sack, but I did hit him just as he released the ball. The pass was off target for the Duke receiver, but Bobby Cole, one of the best Gamecock linebackers of all time, plucked it out of the air, to end the threat and clinch the victory. Our offense ran the clock out and we had our third victory in a row.

I was happy with the outcome as were we all. My most lasting memory, however, was that I was as tired as I've ever been in my life. It took all of the energy I had left to walk off the field and back into the dressing room. It was one tough day and Duke was one tough football team. But on that day, the Gamecocks were four points tougher than the Blue Devils. The final score was *South Carolina 21, Duke 17*.

Coach Lou Holtz had been promoted from the scout squad coach to varsity defensive back coach that year. His earlier prediction during the 'Toilet Bowl' that he would someday be a head coach and I would someday be able to play, was well on its way to becoming a reality. Coach Holtz was always entertaining and when he wasn't yelling at you, he could be very funny. He was responsible for hanging me with a unique nickname.

At the time, there was an English model named Leslie Lawson. By 1967, she had become famous as 'Twiggy'. Twiggy was known for her pencil thin build and good looks. She had large eyes, long eyelashes, and short hair. By 1967, Twiggy had modeled in France, Japan and the US and landed on the covers of "Vogue" and "The Tatler", a publication focusing on the glamorous lifestyles of the upper class in Great Britain. Coach Holtz spouted off to the press that the Gamecocks had their own "Twiggy", and unfortunately, the name stuck pretty much throughout my career.

Our next game was against the Georgia Bulldogs, in Athens, Georgia. We were going to play between the famous 'hedges'. We had hedges at either end of Carolina Stadium and I recall hedges were located in several of the other stadiums we played in over the years. But tradition gives that distinction to the University of Georgia. If you use the term, "playing between the hedges," every football fan in America knows you're playing in Athens, Georgia.

Monday rolled around and South Carolina was ranked in the top 25 for the first time since 1958. We were an excited bunch of Gamecocks and looking forward to taking on the Georgia Bulldogs. The Duke game had taken its toll, however, and we had several injuries to some of our backup players. This we couldn't afford. We just didn't have the depth. The Bulldogs had a great football reputation with many successful seasons under their belts. The state of Georgia had twice the population of South Carolina and I think at the time, the only two schools that played football were the Bulldogs and the Rambling Wrecks from Georgia Tech.

South Carolina with less than half the population had seven schools with football programs. They were: the South Carolina Gamecocks, the Clemson Tigers, the Furman Paladins, the Citadel Bulldogs, the Presbyterian Blue Hose, the Wofford Terriers and the Newberry Indians. The scholarship limits in the 1960's for major college teams was 120 players per school. South Carolina's high school football talent was diluted mightily by this fact. We also lost some of our best talent to out of state programs with stronger winning traditions. This is a fact of life and not an excuse and Georgia, our next opponent, for whatever reason, had a great football tradition. And they had a very good coach in Vince Dooley.

We arrived in Athens, again by Greyhound bus, on Friday, October 6th. Dressed in our sport coats, we went to the movies and later, at the hotel, we huddled around Coach Dietzel for his Friday night talk. It was the usual kind of talk for underdogs like us, "Men, we all put on our pants the same way."

One of the team members mumbled under his breath, "Yeah, but their pants are a lot bigger." The year before, in Columbia, we had given Georgia a fit. They were lucky to come away with a 7 to 0 win. We felt we had a fair shot to take home a win. Then our trainers handed out our snacks. We each

The Splinter,

the Pencil,

the Blade,

Twiggy

and Twiggy

131

USC Hits Late, Then Halts Duke Bid For 21-17 Victory

By JOE WHITLOCK
State Sports Writer

DURHAM — South Carolina, an underdog on paper but a winner in the guts department, scored a touchdown with 40 seconds left in the game and withstood a last-gasp aerial assault to dump Duke, 21-17, in the weekend's stellar Atlantic Coast Conference battle here Saturday afternoon before 25,000 stunned fans.

Paul Dietzel's Gamecocks, stymied on offense in the first half, collected two touchdowns in the second half and snuffed out a determined drive in the final few seconds to collect their third victory in three games this season.

USC, defying what should have been, just would not give up and its final TD march, with less than two minutes left in the game was one of Dietzel's patented—and abbreviated—victory marches.

The Blue Devil throng, watching its first match in Wallace Wade Stadium (it changed from Duke Stadium eight minutes before the game), didn't have time to digest the goings on.

The Gamecocks scored their first touchdown on the game's opening kickoff, its second shortly after the final half started,

and its third when it was too late for the Blue Devils to retaliate.

Statistically, Duke walloped

Dietzel's gutty hardfits, 333 yards to 206 in total offense and 20 first downs to 11.

The Gamecocks, however,

didn't know how bad the paper work was going...They simply decided to win themselves another

(See GAMECOCKS, 3-C, Col. 1)

. . . Jars Ball Loose . . .
. . . And The Gamecock Linebacker Goes Down As Hepler Wheels To Chase The Escaped Ball . . .
Staff Photo by Vic Tutte

A Fierce Tackle . . .
South Carolina's Tim Bice Latches On To Duke's Bob Hepler And The Ball Pops Loose . . .
Staff Photo by Vic Tutte

. . . And USC Nabs It For TD
. . . But USC's Dave Lucas Gets There First And Falls On Ball In End Zone For Touchdown On Opening Kickoff.
Staff Photo by Vic Tutte

ball game.

Duke was behind three times (7-0, 14-10 and 21-17) and it had to be a heart - ripping loss for a Tom Harp club that played well enough to win under normal circumstances.

The victory was South Carolina's first over the Blue Devils since 1930 and the first here in 37 years.

South Carolina, only a one - touchdown underdog to Duke, alleviated the deficiency on the first play of the game when the Blue Devils made the error of receiving.

USC's Jimmy Poole kicked to Bob Hepler at the Duke four yard line and in six seconds South Carolina was ahead, 7-0. Hepler was pursued by Dave Grant, Gene Schwaring and Tim Bice when he caught the ball.

Bice, the tough little linebacker, knocked the ball loose with a jarring tackle and onrushing sophomore Dave Lucas, a youngster from Bishopville who hasn't done too many things wrong yet, pounded on Poole booted the point after before the game had barely started.

Duke, offensively potent with fullback Jay Calabrese and quarterback Al Woodall handling the chores, promptly rallied for ten points in the second quarter and a 10-7 intermission lead.

The Blue Devils TD came on a one-yard plunge by workhorse Calabrese with 11:50 left in the half and the three pointer was the product of a perfect 27-yard field goal by Bob Riesenfeld with two minutes left in the half.

Duke's first - half dominance was so methodical it seemed almost obvious that Harp's charges were heading for an easy victory. The Blue Devils held USC to 44 yards rushing and one passing in the first two quarters while accumulating 130 and 64.

It was Duke 11 to two in first downs and the home club had also intercepted two of the three passes Gamecock Mike Fair had thrown.

South Carolina, which has developed the desirable habit of getting down to business in the second half, came out of its offensive shell after intermission and with 3:30 gone in the third period the Dietzel

express was in the lead.

Duke, which faux pas when it received in the first half, was in error again in the second. It took eight plays and

an eight - yard bootleg by Fair to make the difference.

Warren Muir, the league's top rusher, had 42 yard run in the 67-yard drive.

The Blue Devils, using Calabrese for all he was worth, crunched out an 68-yard TD drive on the first series in the fourth quarter and the husky fullback scored his 22nd career touchdown from the one with 5:45 left in the game. Calabrese rushed nine times in the 18-play march.

The Gamecocks, very much down but surprisingly not out, held Duke on its next series and took over with less than three minutes left when Fair engineered a nine - play march with Muir plunging from the one. Forty seconds were left in the game when Poole made it 2-17.

Duke moved all the way back to the USC 22 when linebacker Bob Cole intercepted for the Gamecocks on the last play of the game.

	SO. CAR.	DUKE
First downs	11	20
Rushing yardage	119	242
Passing yardage	141	91
Return yardage	14	
Passes	7-13-2	10-16-2
Punts	5-39	6-30
Fumbles lost		1
Yards penalized	55	10

South Carolina	7	0	7	7—21
Duke	0	10	0	7—17

SC — Lucas recovered fumble end zone (Poole kick)
Duke — (Calabrese 1 run (Riesenfeld kick)
Duke — FG Riesenfeld 27
SC — Fair 8 run (Poole kick)
Duke — Calabrese 11 run (Riesenfeld kick)
SC — Muir 1 run (Poole kick)
Attendance 25,000.

DUKE
RUSHING

Player	Att.	Gain	Loss	Net
Calabrese	22	95		94
Ryan	7	92		92
Schafer	13	48	2	46
Bagilan	10	22		22
Davis	3	11		11
Woodall	4	14	13	3
Courtillet	3	2	4	2

PASSING

Player	Att.	Compl.	Intc.	Yds.
Woodall	10	4	91	2

PASS RECEIVING

Player	No.	Yds.	TD
Schafer		18	
Ryan		9	0
Calabrese		7	0
Dearth		30	0
Cottle		27	

SOUTH CAROLINA
RUSHING

Player	Att.	Gain	Loss	Net
Muir	19	88	1	87
Garnto	13	35	3	32
Fair	8	15	19	-4
Reeves	3	10		10

PASSING

Player	Att.	Compl.	Intc.	Yds.
Fair				

PASS RECEIVING

Player	No.	Yds.	TD
Garnto		1	0
Gregory		9	
Seigler		47	0

got a carton of milk, an apple and two chocolate chip cookies. Milk and cookies! Oh well, Coach wanted us to be good boys.

It was another afternoon game and 1 o'clock kickoff. It was still hot, but thankfully, not as bad as it had been up in Durham the week before. We won the toss and Georgia kicked off to us. Toy McCord, a Carolina teammate, had played high school ball in Manning, South Carolina and they were in the same 6-A conference as my old Bishopville Dragons. Toy was a great high athlete. He was highly recruited from all over the country and as I recall, had over 100 scholarship offers to play college football. Toy was actually even better as a baseball player and played professional baseball after leaving Carolina.

Dietzel Piles Praise On USC's Komoroski, Somma

By JOE WHITLOCK
State Sports Writer

South Carolina's Gamecocks, after scoring in the game's first and last minute Saturday afternoon to whip Duke, 21-17, won special praise from Head Coach Paul Dietzel for the defensive work against the Blue Devils.

"Duke is a mighty big and very strong football team," Dietzel said Sunday afternoon, "and they really overpowered us in the first part of the game.

"We didn't block their middle guard (Bob Foyle) very much. He's just a tremendous football player. And it looked like they kinda toyed with us for a while until our defense went to work."

The Gamecocks, now unbeaten after

Komoroski

"We got the best defensive tackle play in this game that I've seen since coming to South Carolina," Paul Dietzel said. "Joe Komoroski was the game captain and he had eight individual tackles and two assists and that's very high for a tackle. Then we graded Don Somma and found out he had 12 individual tackles and five assists. Any time you get twenty tackles and seven assists from just two boys, you've really had an effort."

Somma

three games and leading the Atlantic Coast Conference with a 2-0-0 mark, scored their first TD when the game was only six seconds old and their final TD with 40 seconds left in the game.

The first USC score was a defensive gem. The Gamecocks kicked off to Bob Hepler at the Duke four and Dave Lucas recovered Hepler's fumble in the end zone for the tally.

"Tim Bice actually knocked Hepler loose from the ball," Dietzel said, "but Allen Owen saved us on the play. Owen rushed down and knocked Hepler out of the play and that's how Lucas was able to go in and make the TD.

"I don't know how you could improve the start of a football game," the USC coach. "Somebody said right after it was over that we really did dominate the first six seconds of the game."

Dietzel, after watching the game films, heaped praise on defensive tackles Joe Komoroski and Don Somma.

"We got the best defensive tackle play in this game that I've seen since coming to South Carolina," he said. "Komoroski was the game captain and he had eight individual tackles and two assists and that's very high for a tackle, more like a linebacker's score.

"Then we started grading Somma and found out he had twelve individual tackles and five assists. Of course, those two played every play of the game and they made some real key plays. But any time you get twenty tackles and seven assists from just two boys you've really had an effort.

"The linebackers did a heck of a job, too," Dietzel said. "Bice went out of the game in middle of the second quarter and Ron Bunch came in and played a tremendous game. He finished with nine tackles and five assists. Bice, and he only played a quarter and a half, also had nine tackles and five assists.

"Ol' Bob Cole, as always, just played a tremendous game at linebacker for us, too. Warren Muir did a very fine job and Ben Garnto really put us in business when he made a spectacular kickoff return that let us go in and score. And ol' Garnto hadn't even returned kickoffs before. He didn't even know where to

Staff Photo by Dave Underwood

Closes In (3), But Fred Zeigler Knocks Out The Duke Defender (4) . . .

Things started off well for us as Toy took the opening kickoff and with a few key blocks, broke free. It looked like he was heading for a touchdown when one of the Georgia linemen ran Toy down from behind and caught him at about the 20-yard line. This Georgia football team was not just big, they were pretty fast, as well. We couldn't stick the ball in the end zone on that drive or any other, that day. But we were playing pretty good defense and the score was still 0 to 0 into the 2nd period. We had Georgia backed up on the 13-yard line and it was third and eight.

We expected Georgia to be conservative in their play calling so close to their goal line. We had gotten into a 50-short defense and it had worked twice to stop Georgia from advancing the football. Two running plays off-tackle had resulted in only a couple of yards for the Bulldogs. Our defensive captain called another 50-short defensive alignment as Georgia broke the huddle and lined up in the same formation they had been using to try to punch it out from the shadow of their own goalpost. The ball was snapped and it was the off-tackle power-play that Duke had run so often the week before. I pushed down on the tight end, took on the halfback, got rid of his block, and saw the quarterback hand the ball to the fullback. I went for the tackle and grabbed the fullback. The only problem was that the fullback didn't have the football. He had fumbled the handoff, and the ball

line up on the play.

"Something even better happened after the game, though," Dietzel said. "About a thousand South Carolina fans lined up outside the dressing room and cheered every player when they came out.

"Then when we got about ten miles out of Columbia on the way home, a state patrolman stopped us and told us to go to the Russell House. We came down Sumter street and the Horseshoe on the campus was absolutely deserted. Then we turned down Green and it was so dark we couldn't see a thing.

"Then all of a sudden there must have been over a thousand students standing there cheering the team. I'm telling you, the squad really appreciated it, too.

"It was a pretty delightful trip coming home," Dietzel smiled. "It's always a mighty short ride home after one like that.

"Honestly, it's so much better this way," he said. "I like this winning business. I'd much rather have a team that's in there fighting like this one is. They're fun to coach. This team has a fantastic amount of enthusiasm and it rubs off on the fans and the coaches and everybody. They're wild."

had bounced back to the quarterback. The Georgia quarterback was now outside of me. I had lost containment. Toy McCord, who was playing the cornerback position behind me, also thought the fullback had the ball. By the time we realized our mistake, it was too late. That Georgia quarterback was already at the 40-yard line and there was no one within 20 yards of him. Unlike the Georgia team, our linemen weren't able to run down backs from behind. So after two weeks of pretty positive play, I had participated in a Georgia record. It was the longest run from scrimmage in Georgia football history at that time. And I had let it happen right around my end.

Toy McCord

They scored two more touchdowns that day. None of them were as spectacular as the first and we lost the game 21 to zip and the loss was not the end of our troubles. Adding insult to injury, when we went back to our dressing room and started showering, there was no hot water. Whether lack of hot water was some sort of joke or a maintenance problem, we never found out. All of us were ready to leave Athens and get back to Columbia.

It seemed that things weren't going to get any easier for us. The next week we had to travel down to Tallahassee, Florida to take on the Florida State Seminoles. Our travel routines were all the same, except this trip was twice as long. The Seminole fans were loud and aggressive, but the Seminoles did treat us a little better in that they only scored 17 points on us. They also provided hot water for showers. Our offense had another tough day and just couldn't score against a tough Seminole defense. The result was the second shutout in a row. The final score was Florida State Seminoles 17, South Carolina Gamecocks 0.

We were at the midpoint of the season. We had played five games and won three. I was learning quite a few lessons. The most important lesson was that the game required complete concentration, if you wanted to be successful at this level. I felt I had proven that I deserved the scholarship that the University had given me and it was a good feeling. My teammates were fast becoming good friends and they were beginning to believe I could get the job done even though I was rail thin. The 'skinny' jokes continued, but nobody complained about my play. The coaches even complimented my play once in a while. I graded pretty well when they rated my performance on the game films. Even Coach Dietzel got in on the fun and added another nickname to the growing list. He dubbed me "The Splendid Splinter". I thought to myself, "cute."

The week of October 21, we returned home to Columbia against the University of Virginia Cavaliers. The Cavaliers came into town with a record very similar to ours. They had a talented group of athletes and it was going to be another one of those, "if we play well, we should win," games. It was one hell of a game. We wound up winning on a punt return by our sophomore corner back, Pat Watson. Pat took a punt late in the fourth quarter and ran it back for a touchdown. We outscored the Virginia Cavaliers by one point when Candler Boyd intercepted the Cavalier's two point conversion try. The final score was the South Carolina Gamecocks 24, the Virginia Cavaliers 23.

The next week, the Maryland Terrapins traveled to Columbia. We played our best game that Saturday night, since the opening win against the Iowa State Cyclones. Maryland was not a very strong team that year. Their record was 0 and 6. We scored almost at will and didn't allow Maryland a touchdown or a field goal. Two plays stand out in my memory from that game. The first one was a tremendous hit on a safety blitz, by Candler Boyd, on the Maryland quarterback. Candler timed it perfectly. He hit the quarterback just as he was about to release the football. The ball popped up into the air about five feet and wobbled around. Big G from DC was in the right place at the right time and plucked the errant football out of the air. George streaked into the end zone from 17 yards out for a defensive touchdown. Well, that's the way Big G described it. Others claimed that he lumbered into the end zone, panting and wheezing. There are no game films so I guess we will never know, but a touchdown is a touchdown! The other play was one in which I was involved along with Big G.

Gamecocks Violated 'Sound Principles'

By HAROLD MARTIN
State Sports Writer

TALLAHASSEE, Fla. —"We'll start the season all over again next week," said University of South Carolina Coach Paul Dietzel late Saturday afternoon.

"We're going to regroup and get after Virginia next Saturday," Dietzel continued. "I'm pretty sure of that. I can guarantee one thing. I'm not going to be easy on them in practice next week."

Dietzel, never an easy loser, had just watched his Gamecocks drop a 17-0 decision to Florida State—the second straight year ex-aide Bill Peterson has beaten him badly — and the big man from Ohio was not in the happiest of moods.

"We violated some sound football principles today," said Dietzel, "and when you do that, you don't win.

"We didn't do a good job of getting the ball in the end zone when we got close. We threatened, but we couldn't get it in and that always takes the spark out of an offense.

"That's happened to us for two straight weeks and we've got to start getting something on the board when we get close."

Although he declined to use it as an excuse, Dietzel pointed out that loss of several key South Carolina performers played a big part in the final result.

"We got caught in a chain reaction again," said Dietzel. "When you lose your right hand man (fullback Warren Muir), it

does cost you. Muir went out with a bruised hip early in the second quarter, and we had to go to our third fullback because our second was playing right half.

"Safety Wally Orrell twisted a knee getting off a bus after a movie and defensive halfback Toy McCord was left home with an injury. Linebacker Bob Cole sprained an ankle on the third play of the game and Candler Boyd, another member of the defensive secondary, was knocked silly and missed almost a half.

"That's the way it is when you're as thin as we are," said Dietzel. "You borrow someone from another position and get into trouble at two or three spots.

(See DIETZEL, 8-C, Col. 4)

George was playing right defensive tackle beside me that night. Maryland ran a play off-tackle and George made a great hit on the ball-carrier. He caused the back to fumble and the ball popped right up into my hands. I was behind everyone and just knew I had my second touchdown of the year. All I had to do was turn around and run to the end zone. As I turned to make a cut, my foot came down directly on the foot of the referee. He was startled and so was I. The ref fell down backwards and tripped me.

135

Poole's 45-Yard Field Goal Caps Brilliant Gamecock Comeback, Sinks Virginia, 24-23

By HERMAN HELMS
Executive Sports Editor

A 45-yard field goal by little Jimmy Poole with 5:14 left in the game climaxed a sensational rally and carried South Carolina to a thrilling 24-23 decision over Virginia at Carolina Stadium Saturday night.

A Homecoming crowd of 34,150 saw the Cavaliers, who led 17-0 at the end of the first half, fail to pull it out when Braxton Hill kicked short on a 45-yard field goal attempt with 1:08 left in the see-saw struggle.

The Gamecocks, completely outplayed during the first half got back into the ball game by scoring two touchdowns in less than two minutes in the third period.

A 67-yard punt return by Pat Watson and a 13-yard pass from Mike Fair to Ben Garnto produced the scores.

Poole converted after the first score and Fair hurled a two-point conversion pass to Garnto after the second tally.

Then after a 90-yard kickoff return by the Cavaliers' Frank Quayle had built a 23-15 Virginia lead, Carolina struck back with a long fourth period march that was climaxed by a 14-yard touchdown run by Warren Muir.

Fair attempted to run for a two point conversion, but was stopped a yard short by linebacker Boyd Page of the Cavaliers and Virginia clung to a 23-21 lead.

That put the pressure on little Poole, who pulled it out with his long kick that barely cleared the crossbar.

The first half was strictly no contest as the sharp Cavaliers moved the ball almost at will.

Kicking special Braxton Hill put Virginia on the scoreboard for the first time when he booted a 30-yard field goal with 6:51 left in the opening quarter.

His boot kept a drive that had begun at the Virginia 49 and came to a stop at the USC 12.

The Cavaliers scampered 77 yards in 10 plays for their first touchdown.

Quayle and Arnet carried the load in the long advance, and Quayle climaxed it with a brilliant six yard dash around left end for the score.

The brilliant halfback broke several tackles on his trip in. Hill kicked point for a 10-0 Virginia lead with 1:21 gone in the second quarter.

A fumble recovery at the USC 42 set the stage for Virginia's second touchdown. The Cavaliers covered the distance in seven plays. Arnet hurdling the line to score from one yard out with 9:39. Hill converted and the Cavalier lead was now 17-0.

That's the way it stood at halftime, but only late kept the Virginia margin from being larger.

The Cavaliers had one touchdown called back — a beautiful 42 yard pass from Arnet to end Jeff Calimmos — on a motion penalty early in the second period and were denied another score when Arnet fumbled in the end zone on a sweep around right end and USC's Don Somma recovered the ball for a touchback.

This last break against the Cavaliers came in the closing seconds of the half and stopped a drive that had begun at the Virginia 24.

The Cavaliers collected 298 yards in total offense during the half against a mere 83 for USC. The Cavaliers led in first downs, 16-3.

USC came to life to jam across two touchdowns in a space of less than two minutes in the third quarter.

Safety Pat Watson returned a Virginia punt 67 yards for the first score with eight minutes left in the period.

Fair passed to Garnto for a two-point conversion, but the play was called back on an offside penalty against the Gamecocks. Poole then kicked the extra point, shaving the Virginia lead to 17-7.

Moments later and Gene Schwarting of the Gamecocks recovered a fumble at the Virginia 21 and four plays later Fair passed to Garnto for 13 yards and a touchdown.

Six minutes and three seconds were left in the period when Fair hit Garnto on a pass for a two point conversion and Virginia lead 17-15.

Quayle electrified the crowd by returning the kickoff 90 yards to a touchdown to widen the Virginia lead to 23-15. An Arnett pass for a two-point conversion was intercepted by the Gamecocks' Candler Boyd.

A Big Gain: Virginia's Bob Serino Snags Pass (R), Meets Pat Watson (C) And USC Back Stops Play (L)

Down on the turf I went, ending the play in true 'Keystone Cops' fashion. That ended my chance for a touchdown, but it did give us great field position. The final score was South Carolina 31, University of Maryland 0.

As you know by now, I liked to play the guitar and sing. One day after practice, I was playing a tune when Coach Dietzel entered the room at J Dorm. "Lucas, why aren't you studying?"

"Coach, I was just finishing up this song."

"I want you to put that guitar down and pick those books up. What were your grades last semester?"

"Coach, I had a 3.2 GPR."

"Well, you can do better. Put that guitar away and get those books out!"

"Like I said coach, I will, as soon as I finish the song."

Several nights later a similar event occurred. I was playing and singing a little country tune, when the door opened and Coach Lou Holtz walked in. He looked at me with a surprised expression on his face and said, "Lucas, I didn't know you played the guitar?"

"Yes Sir, I play and sing a little bit".

"Do you know *Red River Valley*?"

"Yes Sir. I can play that one."

"Well let's hear it!"

I played *Red River Valley*, *You Are My Sunshine* and several more songs and Coach Holtz sang right along with me. A crowd of ballplayers gathered

136

The Marvelous Moves Of Muir.....

USC's Warren Muir (36) Follows Jimmy Gobble (50) On 11-Yard Burst Through Maryland Line . . .

Muir, Fair And Defense Key 5th Win

By JOE WHITLOCK
State Sports Writer

South Carolina's high-stepping Gamecocks, mounting a newly-found first-half offense and a bone-crushing defense, shut out Maryland, 31-0, before 34,427 Carolina Stadium fans Saturday night to remain unbeaten in Atlantic Coast Conference action.

The Gamecocks, who trailed by 17 points against Virginia last week, led by the same margin Saturday night over the winless Terrapins and pushed their league record to 4-0. Paul Dietzel's club has lost only to Georgia and Florida State, and now owns a 5-2 mark, assuring it of only the second .500 season since 1959.

South Carolina produced a bone-shattering rushing attack all the way and complemented it with a devastating defense that yielded only 53 yards all evening on the ground and only 113 through the air.

The shutout was the first for USC since the last game of the 1960 season against Virginia, and marked the first time in the last 67 games that an opponent hasn't crossed the South Carolina goal line.

Sophomore fullback Warren Muir, healthy for the first time in three weeks, was in top form throughout the contest and picked up 115 of the 287 yards the Gamecocks collected on the ground.

Muir, a 5-10, 197-pounder from Fitchburg, Mass., scored the game's first TD on an 11-yard dazzler for his sixth touchdown of the season.

Senior fullback Curtis Williams of Bamberg, subbing for Muir, tacked on USC's second first-quarter touchdown and placement specialist Jimmy Poole threw in a 30-yard field goal in the second quarter to give the Gamecocks their commanding lead at intermission.

Quarterback Mike Fair, who completed five of eight passes for 68 yards and rushed for 24 more, kicked in with a four-yard scoring dash in the third quarter.

The final South Carolina touchdown, with three minutes left in the game and a sophomore-heavy unit on the field, was a defensive gem.

Staff Photo by Maxie Roberts

....Produce A Touchdown

And Speeds Into End Zone For First Period Score.

around us and we had a regular 'sing along'. After about four songs, Coach Holtz stood up and looked around the room.

"Fellas, how are your grades?" Coach Holtz went around the room asking each individual how they were doing. Then he said, "The books come first, football second and after that, it's your choice."

There was definitely a different approach in the styles of those two coaches.

Our next two games were on the road. We were to travel the next weekend to Wake Forest. The summer race riots had abated somewhat but there was still tension in much of the country. We arrived in Wake Forest to find a very tense racial situation. The Friday night before the game, our

History Of Concussions Ends Career Of USC's Wingard

By ADD PENFIELD, JR.
State Sports Writer

"Before the season started, I felt that Wake Forest would be one of the hardest teams for us to prepare for," said South Carolina Coach Paul Dietzel Tuesday. "I felt that with the possible exception of Clemson they had the best personnel in the Atlantic Coast Conference and it's still true."

Dietzel's Gamecocks face Bill Tate's Wake Forest Club in an important ACC test in Winston-Salem Saturday night and the Deacons' 1-6 record does not bring any comforting thoughts to the USC staff.

"They have played some of the hottest teams around — teams like Houston, N. C. State, and Memphis State — and still haven't been c o m p l e t e l y stopped by anyone."

"No one stops this Freddie Summers boy at quarterback. We are startled by his quickness and that's something we don't even like to dream about — playing against real quick quarterbacks. They also have some big, strong backs who can fly.

"We feel that this is one we have to win. We haven't taken anyone more seriously than we take Wake Forest.

Injuries, which have struck key personnel for the Gamecocks all season, have lopped another Gamecock from the ranks. Offensive guard Tom Wingard has been forced to drop from squad.

"Wingard is a tremendous loss for us," said Dietzel. "He is a boy who has had a history of concussions. He got blind-sided and knocked unconscious in the Maryland game. After discussing it with Tom, we decided it would be best not to take any more chances with the boy's health.

"He was our best offensive lineman last year and one of our best this year. There are just some things more important than football."

Wingard's spot will be filled by Jack James, who filled in for Bob Morris as a starter against the Terrapins.

Assistant coach Bill Rowe, who scouted the Deacons in their 20-10 victory over North Carolina last week, came away impressed by Wake Forest's improved showing.

"They had a little difficulty at the beginning of the season," said Rowe, "but they have been improving each week. They seemed to have gotten on the right track against North Carolina and they are moving the ball well.

"The defense has been much better lately. They now seem to have confidence that they can move the ball and stop people as well. It's just unfortunate for us that they picked now to get started."

Rowe praised the defensive play of

(See WAKE, 3-B, Col. 1)

(Continued From 2-B)

Grant and linebacker Carlyle Pate. "Grant," said Rowe, "is one of the best in the country. He's a real tough, rugged boy. They flip-flop him to where they think the action is going to be. It's best to stay away from his side.

"Pate is an outstanding linebacker who has done a fine job as a sophomore. He could be a real star for anyone.

"The biggest improvement in their defense came last week when they moved Butch Henry, the outstanding split end, to defensive safety. He has fine hands, good speed and helped them tremendously last week.

"Their defense can now shut people off. The sophomores (six start on defense) have taken their licks and they have now arrived."

In earlier games, Rowe explained, the Deacons have been their own worst enemy, halting drives with fumbles, pass interceptions and penalties. They eliminated most of these problems against the Tar Heels.

Ron Jurewicz is the power back of the offense and will team with either Jimmy Johnson or Jack Dolbin as the running backs. Johnson did not play in the UNC game. Dolbin was in for only two plays, one a 39-yard kickoff return and the other a 51-yard touchdown run which put the Deacs on top.

"The real key to the Wake Forest offense is Summers," said Rowe. "He has everyone fits. He runs extremely well and has thrown for 671 yards.

"We'll have a real problem containing this young man. Our main job will be to stop Summers and Johnson."

---

coaches kept us in our motel rooms, because there were riots all around us that night. You could hear the sirens and lots of noise in the distance and we didn't get much sleep. The next night, we played the Demon Deacons and it was very cold. The ground was hard and so was the game. Our offense scored three touchdowns, but Wake Forest scored five. I don't remember much about that game except the cold, but I did have a couple of sacks and made some solo tackles. I was surprised to learn on Monday morning that I had been chosen the ACC Defensive Player of the Week. It didn't mean much since we had lost the game. But it made my Father happy as he added the article to his collection of newspaper clippings.

This was a tough loss for us. It was one of those games we thought we could win and we were even favored. Whether it was the riots that kept us up or the cold weather, we just weren't ready to play and it showed up in the loss.

The next Monday morning after class, I dropped by the fraternity house. My fraternity brother and good friend, Harry Brooks, told me not to be too downcast about the game. He asked me if I had heard about the great party the fraternity had had that weekend. I said I hadn't talked to anybody, so Harry told me they had had a big keg party over at the Virginia Court Apartments in West Columbia. In those days, very few games were on television, so the fraternity had decided to get a keg and listen to the Gamecocks on the radio. South Carolina had a Hall of Fame radio announcer, Bob Fulton. Bob was known as, "the Voice of the Gamecocks." His voice was deep and booming, but with a lilt. He could make the simplest play sound like the most amazing moment in the history of the sport.

The keg for the party arrived around five o'clock that afternoon and with good intentions, Harry announced they weren't going to tap the keg until eight o'clock. He was greeted with a chorus of, "Yeah Harry, whatever you say." Harry said that by eight o'clock the keg was almost empty. The party was getting a little rowdy and some of the neighbors complained about the noise. Not to be intimidated, the partiers continued to ratchet up the intensity so the neighbors called the cops.

It may have been because of all the riots storming across the country that summer, but the West Columbia police force wasn't about to let a fraternity party get out of hand. No less than five squad cars arrived and half of the police were dressed in riot gear. The partiers inside were oblivious to the flashing blue lights and the growling police dogs about to descend on them. One fraternity brother was outside taking a leak and spotted the policemen lining up and heading in the direction of the party. Alarmed, he started up the stairs, but was delayed by a stream of beer flowing down the steps.

He tried to sound the alarm, but no one would listen. One of the brothers was completely naked and as the cops came through the door this future judge asked them if they wanted to play with his nipples. There were lots of scantily clad students looking for someplace to hide. It was only a two-bedroom apartment and suitable hiding places were scarce. One fraternity brother and his date were aux-naturel doing what you probably shouldn't do up in one of the bedrooms. Hearing the commotion outside and realizing that the cops were raiding the apartment, they grabbed their clothes and hid in the closet under some dirty laundry that had been piled on the floor. Sure enough, in came the policemen and hurriedly looked through the room. They looked under the bed and opened the sliding closet door. Jim and his date had hidden so well that the cop didn't spot them. The window was open and Jim heard one policeman say, "They must've gone out the window."

The closet for the other bedroom was separated from Jim's by only a thin piece of sheet rock and Harry was attempting to hide in the other closet. He had emptied a golf bag of all the clubs, and placed the bag over his head. When the cop opened the closet door he was greeted by a body with a golf bag on its head. The cop was not amused. "Okay son, I see you. You're under

Inspired Deacons Stun South Carolina, 35-21

By HERMAN HELMS
Executive Sports Editor

WINSTON-SALEM — Wake Forest's inspired Deacons, finally jelling into the offensive machine that they were thought to be in pre-season prognosis, raced for two late fourth quarter touchdowns to break a 21-21 tie and upset South Carolina, 35-21, here Saturday night.

Quarterback Fred Summers darted 17 yards through right tackle on a keeper play to tally the touchdown which actually wrapped up the victory for Coach Bill Tate's fiery Deacons. Two minutes and 45 seconds were left in the wild offensive struggle when Summers dashed into pay dirt to climax an advance of 55 yards.

The Deacons tacked on an insurance touchdown in the dying seconds of play after USC, gambling on fourth down, surrendered the ball to Wake at the Gamecocks' 30-yard line. Halfback Buz Leavitt tallied with just 14 seconds left on the clock.

The Deacons, who entered the game seven-point underdogs, used a powerful ground attack to send USC to its first Atlantic Coast Conference defeat after four victories.

Wake, which scored the first two times it had possession to open a 14-0 lead, crashed out 323 yards on the ground in an awesome display of speed and muscle that delighted a homecoming turnout of 13,000 persons, who braved racial disturbance in this city and cold November weather to see the battle.

Halfback Jac Dolbin, who sprinted 60 yards in the opening minutes of play to set up Wake's first touchdown, led the powerful Deacon infantry with 122 yards in 12 carries. Leavitt, who scored two touchdowns, contributed 103 yards in 19 trips.

Summers, who also tallied two touchdowns, got 63 yards in 15 rushes and completed six of 10 passes for 54 more yards.

Summers went one yard for Wake's first touchdown. Fullback Ron Jurewicz charged two yards for the second tally and Leavitt stormed four yards for the third.

Quarterback Mike Fair scored two of USC's touchdowns on runs of five and one yards. Halfback Ben Garnto got the other tally on a one-yard smash.

The Deacons, who were winning their second straight game after absorbing six defeats to open the season, swept 72 yards in seven plays for their first touchdown before some of the spectators had reached their seats.

Dolbins 60-yard scamper to the USC four set up a one-yard slash off left tackle by Summers for the score with 3:12 gone in the game.

Chick George kicked the first of five conversons to put Wake out front, 7-0.

The next time they had possession the Deacons roared 69 yards in 10 plays for another tally, and it began to appear that a rout was in the making. Jurewicz scored from the two with 5:52 remaining in the first period and George kicked the point.

But USC, which is famed for its comebacks, came off the floor to get on the scoreboard early in the second period. The Gamecocks moved 55 yards in 11 plays, Fair scoring from the five with 3:10 gone in the second quarter. Jimmy Poole's conversion cut Wake's margin to 14-7.

Midway of the quarter, the Gamecocks surged 63 yards in eight plays to tie it up. A 33-yard pass from Fair to Johnny Gregory highlighted the march, and Garnto finally went in from the one with 6:26 left in the half. Poole's kick tied it at 14-all.

A pass interception by the Deacon's Digit Laughridge an dthree-yard return to the USC 42 set up Wake's third touchdown late in the half. A 35-yard burst by Dolbin led the march. George's kick gave Wake a 21-14 halftime advantage.

USC took the third quarter kickoff and drove 80 yards in 18 plays to tie it again. Warren Muir, who turned in a tremendous performance in defeat, carried on nine of the plays, and crashed for 43 yards. Fair sneaked one yard for the touchdown, and Poole's conversion brought a 21-21 tie with 6:33 left in the third quarter.

That's how it stood until Wake's late burst which broke up the thriller.

USC missed one scoring opportunity in the fourth period. The Gamecocks drove from their 37 to the Wake 11 where Poole kicked wide to the left on a 27-yard field goal attempt.

Muir picked up 122 yards in 31 carries to lead USC's rushing. Fair gained 76 yards in 18 trips and completed seven of 13 passes for 87 yards.

139

arrest. Get out of there and come with me!" With that he took his baton and knocked the golf bag off of Harry's head.

Harry exclaimed,

"YOU CAN'T ARREST ME, I'M A FOUR WOOD!"

With only a piece of sheet rock separating Harry from Jim, Jim and his date heard Harry and started laughing. The Police nabbed Jim and his date and put them under arrest. Jim paid a fine and was released later that night, but his poor date who attended the all girls' school, Columbia College, was not so lucky. She was suspended from school, as further punishment, after being released by the police.

Another fraternity brother, Frank Whitten, had taken up where Capt. Rabbit had left off at the Ocean Forest Hotel party back in the spring. He was dressed up as the "Wonder Wizard" and had on long Johns that had been dyed a deep blue under a pair of red gym shorts. On his chest, in big bold red letters was his name, Wonder Wizard. There were beer tabs clamped on his ears for earrings and several more pop tops on his fingers. He had a green cape draped over his shoulders and a black mask covering his face.

Frank had avoided the police by jumping out of one of the back windows. Acting like a superhero, he stayed well into the shadows and was able to slip down the street. After a few blocks, he decided to come out of hiding and just strolled along down the sidewalk back toward campus, which was about seven miles away. A patrol car spotted Frank and pulled up beside him throwing a searchlight right in his face. Frank responded by yelling at the police car, "Get that light out of my eyes." Two police officers leapt out of the car and grabbed Frank by the arms. One of the officers asked, "Son, why didn't you hide?"

Frank, still in character, responded "This is impossible. How did you see me? I'm invisible!"

"Well, now you're arrested!" said the officer as he tried his best not to break out laughing.

About fifteen or twenty of the party goers were taken to the booking area of the West Columbia Police Department. Several of the guys were thrown into the drunk tank which was already full of Saturday night's regular winos. The door to the station opened and in walked two officers with the Wonder Wizard. The desk sergeant took one look and started laughing. "Well Joe, I guess we've just about seen it all."

Frank was brought up before the desk sergeant by the two officers, one on each side tightly gripping his arm. After the laughter subsided, the desk sergeant lifted his pen and look down at his paperwork and with a big grin on his face said, "Okay Wonder Wizard, what's your name?"

Playing his role to the end, Frank replied in a loud voice that echoed throughout the station, "I must warn you, sergeant, if you learn my true identity, I'll have to kill you!"

Playing 'Bama Is Like Heading For An Uprising

By JOE WHITLOCK
State Sports Writer

"When you play football against Alabama in Tuscaloosa you are not faced with a game," Paul Dietzel said Tuesday. "You're heading for an uprising."

Dietzel and his Gamecocks head to the Alabama midlands Saturday for a dance with Bear Bryant and his Crimson Tide and South Carolina will certainly be faced with one of its toughest games of the season.

"Alabama may not have a great Alabama football team this year," Dietzel said, "but it's a great one by most any other standard. They have a tremendous football team and have beaten some exceptionally fine clubs.

"Bryant and the folks in Alabama think they're having a terrible year because their record is only 7-1-1, and I know it makes 'em mad because they're not rated in the top ten.

"To beat Alabama is to gain your place in the sun," the USC coach added. "Florida State tied 'em and that was an accomplishment that few achieve.

"I think Alabama will definitely go to a bowl this year and they're after national recognition right now," he said, "so it's no secret that we have a tremendous challenge coming up.

"Fortunately, I like to play a great team and our athletes do, too. Good athletes seem to perform better against good

(See STABLER, 5-B, Col. 1)

(Continued From Page 2-B)
competition and we're looking forward to the game."

South Carolina, now 5-3 and coming off an idle weekend, faces a club that has lost only to second ranked Tennessee and is hot on a three-game winning skein that includes a 7-6 triumph over LSU last weekend.

"Normally, I don't like open dates," Dietzel said, "but in this case I think the layoff has helped us.

"We were pretty bruised up coming out of the Wake Forest game and we'll be in pretty good physical condition for Alabama.

"Actually, they're going to be favored by 20 or 25 points and it's going to be hard to convince them they've even got a game Saturday," Dietzel said. "But even if they have an 'off' day they're not going to play bad. They just have too much depth."

Assistant coach Johnny Menger, who scouted the Crimson Tide for the past few weeks, said that stopping quarterback Ken Stabler and flanker Dennis Homan will be the key to USC's fortunes.

Stabler has connected on 91 of 158 passes for 1,089 yards and eight touchdowns. Homan, who caught all eight TD tosses, is the leading Tide receiver with 47 catches for 718 yards.

"Stabler is the best long ball passer I've ever seen," Menger said, "and he's a fantastic option player. Homan's not a good receiver. He's great. He can outrun anybody on our team."

"Somebody asked me this morning if we were looking ahead to the Clemson game," Dietzel said with a grin. "How in the world can you overlook Alabama?"

The desk sergeant and cops holding Frank didn't think it was too funny anymore. (Harry and I thought it was hilarious!) The sergeant ordered, "Throw that smart ass in the drunk tank with the rest of the idiots."

The two officers half dragging the Wonder Wizard approached the drunk tank. The jailer slid back the door as they got ready to shove Frank inside. The Wonder Wizard however, was not finished with his theatrics and took a flying leap into the middle of the drunk tank and landed à la Superman, with his hands on his hips. Several of the old alcoholics watched incredulously through their drunken haze. Most of them jumped back against the wall and pleaded with the officers, "Get me out of here. Don't put that thing in here with me!" It was rumored that the police officers continued to recount the scene that night for years.

Our next opponent was the Alabama Crimson Tide. We were traveling down to Tuscaloosa for our next to last ballgame of the 1967 season. Alabama was a strong team that year and at one point had been ranked number one in the nation. Our record was five wins, three losses. We had a good week of practice and had confidence, as we boarded our chartered plane and headed southwest toward Tuscaloosa. We arrived around midday and on our way to the motel, Coach Dietzel took us on a detour. Alabama had some of the first athletic dorms that were built in the United States and Coach Dietzel wanted to show us their athletic facilities, to let us know that ours were going to be even better. Our athletic dorms were under construction in Columbia, located at the far end of our practice complex at The Roundhouse. We had watched the construction every day during practice.

We drove up to their athletic complex in two Greyhound buses. As Coach Dietzel was telling how our facilities were going to be superior, one of the doors to the dorms opened and out stepped the legendary Coach Paul Bear Bryant, hounds-tooth hat and all. Every player on our bus and every player on the bus behind us jumped up and moved to the window to get a closer look at this icon of college football. Coach Dietzel was not impressed and ordered us to get back in our seats. I have realized since that time, that it's pretty hard to beat a legend.

We kicked off to the Crimson Tide the next day at one o'clock. Defensively, we played a pretty good game. But, offensively, we didn't complete a pass until the fourth quarter. Alabama's quarterback at the time was the future NFL Hall of Famer, Kenny "the Snake" Stabler. The final score of the game was Crimson Tide 17, Gamecocks 0. For years I had three solid memories from that encounter. The first one was getting to see the legendary Coach Bryant. The second memory was the final score 17-0. And the third memory was of one particular play that took place in the second quarter of the game. Alabama had the football on their own 35-yard line. It was third down and 9 yards to go for a 1st and 10. Alabama came up to the line and the ball was snapped and Ken Stabler moved to my side of the line with the football. It was a simple option play. The quarterback had two choices. He could keep the ball and turn up field or he could pitch it out to the halfback. My job was to hold my ground and force him to either pitch the ball or tackle him if he kept it and tried to run. The ideal situation was to make the quarterback pitch the football to the halfback and to force the halfback out of bounds or make the tackle before he could get back to the line of scrimmage.

Ken Stabler

I was in good position, ready for either alternative. My eyes locked on to Stablers' eyes and then it happened. Stabler glanced over at the halfback without moving his head. He just moved his eyes. I looked to see where the halfback was and when I looked back, Stabler had disappeared. The SOB had tricked me! I turned my head to the left and sure enough, he had given me the slip. I tried to make a dive for him, but it was too late. He was quick and had made a great play fake. He gained 12 yards on that play for a first and 10. We managed to stop the drive after a couple of first and tens and Alabama was forced to kick a field goal. Through the years, I always wondered if the game might have turned out differently if I had stopped Stabler from making that first and 10. That was Alabama's first score and I felt personally responsible for losing the game.

Bear Bryant being carried off after another Alabama victory

Many years later, I ran into Don Somma, who played defensive tackle right beside me for the entire 1967 season. After graduating, Don had coached high school football. The day we saw each other, Don said, "Luke, I've got a present for you. It's one of our games. I happened to be in Tuscaloosa visiting the "Bear Bryant Museum. They had our 1967 game film and I got a copy of the DVD for you." Then he said something puzzling to me. "You played a pretty good game."

My first thought was of all the games that I had played during those three years as a Gamecock, why was this the only one I would be able to show my grandkids. That busted play that led to their first score was all I remembered. After viewing the DVD a few times, I discovered that memories can be selective. It was probably one of the best games I played in my Gamecock career. I had made 11 individual tackles, sacked Stabler four times, forced a fumble that we recovered, tipped a pass, and made Kenny hurry a throw on another. Other than the one play I remembered, it had been a pretty good day's work. I also recalled that I was the ACC Defensive Player of the Week for the second time that year for that effort against Alabama.

Alabama's next score was just plain lucky. They had an All-American receiver named Dennis Holman. Wally Medlin, our safety had him covered deep. Holman got one step on Wally and Stabler threw the football. My roommate, Candler Boyd, was playing the other safety. He came over and was in perfect position to bat away the pass. Candler hit the ball, but he hit it on the nose. Instead of knocking the ball away, it just spun around and went right into the hands of Dennis Holman. The result was an Alabama touchdown.

Offensively, we struggled against the Crimson Tide. Our running game was good between the 20 yard lines. We could move the ball inside and gained good yardage each time. Unfortunately for us, our pass protection was almost nonexistent. Instead of staying with the running game, when we got behind, we attempted to catch up by throwing the football. It didn't work and we lost again. It was a long flight back to Columbia. The final score was, Alabama Crimson Tide 17, South Carolina Gamecocks 0. It was the third time that year that we had been shutout.

We had one game remaining. To play in a bowl, a minimum of seven games was required. Even if we won our last game, we would miss the mark by one. Our last opponent was the Clemson Tigers. They were coming to Columbia the next weekend with the same record we had garnered, five wins, and four losses. The winner of the game would finish the year with a solid six and four record.

Coach Holtz as the defensive backs' coach was livid at the mistake my roommate, Candler Boyd, had made on the first touchdown drive of the Alabama game. After watching and grading the game films, Coach Holtz raked Candler over the coals. He pulled him off the first team and told him he would never play again. Candler's ego was bruised by what he considered harsh and unjust criticism.

On November 23, 1967, I played in my first Carolina-Clemson rivalry game. Carolina Stadium was packed to the rafters and beyond. It was a one o'clock starting time and Clemson won the toss. We lined up for the kickoff and down the field I ran. Clemson had an All-American guard named Harry Olszewski. At 230 pounds and under 6 feet tall, he was short but stocky. He came over to block me and his helmet came up and caught me under the chin strap. He stretched me out flat on my back in front of all the fans. That was the hardest lick I had gotten all year. As a matter fact, that was the hardest lick I had gotten playing college football.

Buddy Gore

They beat us pretty soundly that day. I recovered a fumble behind the line of scrimmage, but the rules in '67 wouldn't allow you to advance the ball. Clemson's great running back, Buddy Gore, needed 189 yards to break the ACC's rushing record and by the beginning of the second quarter, he was well on his way. Most of his yards were coming on the same off-tackle play. He was being hit at the line of scrimmage, but poor tackling was allowing him to gain more and more yardage. Candler wasn't playing. He had taken Coach Holtz at his word and though he had dressed out and was on the side lines, Candler hadn't bothered to put on his hip pads, knee pads or thigh pads and hadn't even fastened his shoulder pads. Candler was kneeling down on the sidelines leaning with his hand on his helmet in an early form of "T-Bowing".

Coach Jones came over to Candler and said, "Candler, Coach Holtz wants to talk to you on the phone." Candler reached out and took the headset. Candler was an emotional type player and wasn't happy about

144

being benched. "Hello," Candler spoke into the microphone. "Son, can you stop that off-tackle play Gore is running?"

Without hesitation Candler shot back," I've been stopping it all f'ing year, coach!"

Coach Jones overhearing the conversation was astonished. "What did you say?" "I said I've been stopping that play all f'ing year, coach," Candler repeated without hesitation. Coach Holtz said, "Well, get in there and stop it now!"

"Coach, you told me that I wasn't going to play anymore this year, so I don't have any knee pads, hip pads or thigh pads and my shoulder pad straps aren't even buckled."

"I don't give a damn if you're naked. I said get in there and stop that play!"

With that Candler trotted on the field and stopped the big gainers for the rest of the game. Gore gained exactly 189 yards that afternoon to break the record.

It was very unusual to have much conversation on the field with your opponents. The coaches kept a tight rein on that sort of thing. They didn't want a player to do or say anything that might inspire the opposition. Clemson had a tight end that day who threw away that unwritten rule. On one play near the goal line, he tried to block me and remarked after the play was over in a very sarcastic manner, "Ah, Twiggy, is that the best you can do?" Of course, he said it at the close of the game when the outcome had already been decided. At least he knew who I was. The final score was Clemson 23, South Carolina 12. Living with the loss by Clemson for an entire year wasn't fun for the team or the fans but we were all just going to have to suck it up until we could hopefully redeem ourselves the following year.

David "Mudcat" Grant decided to get married the very next weekend. The date of his wedding was December the 2nd, 1967. He was marrying his high school sweetheart, Nell. The wedding was going to be in Mudcat's hometown of Clarksville, Georgia. Clarksville is located in the foothills of the Blue Ridge Mountains and some of us decided to go and join in the festivities. Allen Brown, Candler Boyd and I left Columbia about twelve o'clock that Friday in possession of several cases of beer. John Tomanack, Ron Palmer and his roommate, Joseph Kommoroski, also were going. Allen, Candler and I arrived at the Grant home at about four o'clock in the afternoon. We pulled up in the front yard after consuming a case and a half of beer with our bladders full to bursting. No one was around, so we jumped out of the car to relieve ourselves just as David and his Mother stepped out onto the front porch to greet

Coach Larry Jones

Candler Boyd

Coach Lou Holtz

David (Mudcat) Grant

145

us. Mudcat saw what was taking place and advised his mother to step back inside. She replied, "After raising you four Grant boys, I'm used to this kind of thing."

We finished our business and walked up to the front door and Mrs. Grant gave us all a great big hug and kiss of welcome. She fed us supper and that helped us speak without slurring our words. Mudcat's father had been an All-American at Georgia back in the 1930s. He was the principal of Clarksville High School. Later that evening Mr. Grant and some of his friends took us all up on a mountaintop just outside of town. We were going to have the bachelor party for Mud there and it consisted of a fox hunt and some good old-fashioned Georgia whiskey drinking. We built a nice bonfire and piled up some dead limbs to feed the fire. After the fire was up and roaring, all of us started passing the bottle around and listening to each other's stories. The bonded whiskey ran out and Mudcat and Candler visited a local moonshiner and brought back some real Georgia moonshine.

Joe Komoroski

We continued to drink and tell stories while we listened to the hounds run the fox. As the night wore on, the fire began to die down and the store of wood had run low. Mr. Grant picked up the axe that was lying by the fire and said that he was going to get more wood. Our teammate, Joe Kommoroski, had grown up in New Jersey. This was his first hunting trip and he was enthusiastic about everything he was experiencing on the mountainside. He jumped up and took the axe from Mr. Grant's hand saying, "I'll chop the wood, Mr. Grant."

Joe and the axe disappeared into the darkness. We continued listening to the hounds and stories while we sipped. Out in the darkness, we could hear the axe make contact with wood…Chop-chop-chop. All of a sudden Joe's deep New Jersey voice rang out, "TIMBER!" We turned toward the woods and watched as a big Georgia pine tree came smashing down to within ten feet of the fire. Joe had not been chopping up fallen limbs. He had cut down a pine tree three feet in diameter! We all jumped back as the tree came crashing down. Joe, now aka, 'Joe Bunyan', walked into the light of the fire with a proud look on his face. We didn't let Joe go for more firewood that night.

My first football season as a starter for the University of South Carolina Gamecocks had ended. Our five and five record was certainly an improvement on the one win and nine loss season of the year before. Coach Dietzel had been recruiting hard the past couple of seasons and we had a really good freshman team in 1967. That team was led by future South Carolina Hall of Fame quarterback, Tommy Suggs. Tommy was from Lamar, South Carolina and I had played against him in high school. The freshman team had rolled up some impressive scores in its undefeated season. Coach Dietzel had also been telling us that after his LSU squad went five and five, they had turned things around and had their undefeated National Championship season. We felt as if we were getting ready to turn the corner.

With the season over, it was time to concentrate on academics and also to have some fun. The counterculture of the 1960's was in full swing. All of us were following the hippie movement and the antiwar demonstrations. The drug culture was beginning to rear its ugly head, even at our conservative University. The music was also changing. Most of us in the South had grown up listening to rhythm and blues. Some of the hits that year were: *Respect*, by Aretha Franklin, *Soul Man* by Sam and Dave, *I Was Made to Love Her* by Stevie wonder, *Reflections* by Diana Ross, *I Second That Emotion* by Smokey Robinson & the Miracles, *Your Love Keeps Lifting Me Higher and Higher* by Jackie Robinson, *Ain't No Mountain High Enough* by Marvin Gaye and Tammi Tarrell, *Shake a Tail Feather* by James and Bobby Purify and one of my favorites, *Try a Little Tenderness* by Otis Redding.

Psychedelic and hard rock music was emerging but personally, I despised that kind of music. I was not into the drug culture or the hippie movement that seemed to go along with it. Not everybody in the sixties was into drugs and alternate life styles, but I think all of us as red-blooded American guys were definitely in favor of the 'free love' idea. The radio was broadcasting songs such as *Incense and Peppermint* by Strawberry Alarm Clock, *Sgt. Pepper's Lonely Hearts Band* and *Magical Mystery Tour* by the Beatles. Eric Burton and the Animals came out with *Winds of Change*, the Doors with their albums, *Doors* and *Strange Days*, and *Are You Experienced* by the Jimi Hendrix Experience.

Staff Photos by Vic Tutts

...Put Tigers In A Hole

...USC's Dave Lucas (84) Races In And Beats Cain To The Ball To Set Up Gamecocks' First Touchdown.

There was some really good pop music on the airwaves. There were songs like *To Sir with Love*, by Lulu, *Ode to Billie Joe* sung by Bobbie Gentry, *Light My Fire* popularized by the Doors. Even Frank's Sinatra and his daughter Nancy got in on the act with *Something Stupid*. I was dating a pretty brown-eyed girl from Orangeburg at the time and *Brown Eyed Girl* by Van Morrison was a favorite song of mine. I also really liked Johnny River's rendition of *Baby, I Need Your Loving*.

Johnny Cash was becoming my all-time favorite artist and his hit, *Jackson* with June Carter, was big that year. I listened to artists like Buck Owens, Ray Price, Meryle Haggard, Charlie Pride, Lynn Anderson, Glen Campbell, Don Gibson, Charlie Walker, Marty Robbins, Billy Walker, Waylon Jennings, Skeeter Davis, and Lester Flatt and Earl Scruggs. Flatt and Scruggs had a hit with *The Foggy Mountain Breakdown*, from the movie, *Bonnie and Clyde*.

It was about this time that our fraternity split right down the middle. Half of the guys listened to Country, R&B and pop songs, while the other half were all into the hard rock and psychedelic music. We still had toga parties and the traditional social gatherings, but some drank less beer and used other methods of intoxication. I convinced some football players to

147

Bobby Miranda, Gamecock

Bobby Miranda, Actor;
here playing 'Blake Raines'
in 'Virgini's Run

pledge our fraternity. My roommate of the year before, Allen Brown, and my present roommate, Candler Boyd, both became members of Phi Kappa Sigma. They weren't really interested in fraternity life, but it made it easier to entertain girlfriends with the regularly scheduled parties.

The practical jokes continued. We had a great running back from Connecticut named Robert Guy Miranda. Today, Bobby lives in California and has been a character actor for years. He has acted in movies such as *The Rat Pack*, *Sister Act*, *Gotti* and *The Untouchables*, and co-starred in a movie that I wrote called *Virginia's Run*, just to name a few. As an Italian kid and originally from a city up north, Bobby wasn't up to speed on all things Southern. He was very excitable and became a target for a couple of practical jokes by Benny Galloway and me. I came back to school one weekend, late in the fall, with about fifteen persimmons. Persimmons grow in the wild all throughout the southern countryside. When the fruit is ripe and soft, it tastes good, and in Asia, persimmons are considered a delicacy. But if you bite into one when it's green, it is highly astringent and it tastes like alum. It will turn your mouth inside out. I had laid the persimmons out on my desk. There were only two fully ripened. Bobby walked into my room and asked, "Hey Luke, what is that?"

"They're fall plums, Bobby," I replied.

"Fall plums. I've never heard of those."

"Oh yeah, we love these things down here. They're really good, you should try one." I reached down and grabbed one of the ripe persimmons and made the biggest show enjoying the fruit. Bobby decided to try one and I watched closely as he reached down and picked a green persimmon. He brought the green fruit up to his mouth and took a big ole bite. The astringent juices flowed into his mouth and his eyes widened with surprise. "Jesus Christ, you've poisoned me, you've f'ing poisoned me!" he sputtered through puckered lips. We could have won 'America's Funniest Home Videos' hands down if we'd had a recorder back in those days.

That same fall, Bobby would return from class at a certain time every day. There were usually two or three guys sitting around in his room shooting the breeze. His routine was always the same. He would walk into the room, say hello to everybody, sit down at his desk and open the top drawer to get his cigarettes. Benny had caught a foot long green snake and just before Bobby returned, Benny removed the pack of cigarettes and replaced them with the snake. Word about the hoax had gotten out and there were probably ten or fifteen guys jammed into Bobby's room to watch the fun. Sure enough, right on time, in came Bobby. First, he looked around the room and asked, "What the f##k are all of you guys doing in here?" "Oh, we just got a good 'BS' session going," was the reply. Bobby plopped down into his chair, purposely left open for him. Everybody grinned as Bobby reached for his desk drawer. He opened it and stuck his hand in to grab his cigarettes. By now everyone in the room was giggling out loud. About that time, he jerked his hand out of the drawer and looked in alarm as the little green snake bit him between his thumb and index finger. That snake had latched on to Bobby's hand and was hanging on for dear life. Bobby snapped his hand up and down quickly and the snake flew off and so did Bobby. With one flying leap, he was out of the room and didn't return for three days.

I was hitting the books and had taken a class that I really enjoyed. The class was offered by the Department of International Relations. It was a small department at the time, located in the World War I Memorial building. The building was just off the Horseshoe, at the corner of Sumter and Pendleton Streets. My major, initially, was in business, but I discovered that accounting was not for me. I was drawn to history and politics and the course I had taken was a combination of the two. I talked to a few of the professors and I liked all of them, so I changed my major from business to international relations. The fall semester ended and I had a 3.2 GPR.

World War I Memorial building on Horseshoe

photo: Ramon Gomis

Basketball season was in full swing and the entire University was behind Coach Frank McGuire's guys. They weren't champions yet, but they were winning a lot of games and beating teams they weren't supposed to beat. Frank McGuire had brought in some colorful athletes. He had recruited mostly from up North, but they all seemed to be pretty good guys. The leaders were Skip Harlicka and Gary Gregor. Jack Thompson wowed us all with his behind the back, full court passes. My first year roommate, Big G from DC anointed Jackie, "The Mayor of Carolina" because somehow Jackie Thompson knew every student on campus by their first name. Frank Standard was another good basketball player. During a trip up to play Kentucky in Lexington, Standard was late for a team meeting. An angry Coach McGuire greeted Frank with, "Standard, where the hell have you been?" "Coach, I was just about to get on the elevator when I ran into a Kentucky fan. He informed me that Adolph Rupp was a much better coach than you are. Well, I couldn't pass that up so I stood there and argued the point with him and that's why I'm late." Standard was 'quick' on AND off the court! The whole team and Coach McGuire had a good laugh at what was clearly a concocted excuse.

Other team members that year were Al Salvadori, Tom Farrell, Lynn Burkholder, Bob Felter, Bob Gorgrant, Larry Womack, Skip Kickey and Earl Lovelace. Lynn Burkholder had the biggest hands, with the longest fingers I have ever seen. Different from Coach Bass's hands; not as thick, but his fingers were much longer. It seemed as if he could throw a basketball as if it were a baseball. Larry Womack had an older brother named Dooley that had played baseball at the University of South Carolina and after graduation had moved on to the pros and was playing for the New York Yankees. The basketball team was still playing games in the old Carolina Field House which only held about 4000 fans. If you were lucky enough to get a ticket, you saw some great basketball. 1967 was the last year the team would play in the old Field House as construction was nearing completion on the new Carolina Coliseum which would hold over 12,000 fans.

There were some good movies released that year and the highest grossing film, earning over $104,000,000, was *The Graduate*, starring Dustin Hoffman and Ann Bancroft. Some of the most memorable for me were: *Bonnie and Clyde* starring Warren Beatty and Faye Dunaway, *The Dirty Dozen* starring Lee Marvin, Robert Ryan and Ernest Borgnine. The James Bond franchise continued with *You Only Live Twice* starring Sean Connery. I really enjoyed the musical *Camelot* starring Richard Harris and Vanessa Redgrave. The college crowd would've probably voted *Cool Hand Luke* starring Paul Newman and George Kennedy as the best movie of the year and In the *Heat of the Night* starring Sidney Poitier and Rod Steiger delved into race relations.

When I attended classes in my new major, I found that the International Relations' professors and students debated current events often and with lots of gusto. News from home and around the world that year never failed to provide us with critical issues that were ripe for lively discussion. The Vietnam War continued to dominate the headlines. The Parliament of the United Kingdom nationalized ninety per cent of its industry in Great Britain. Joseph Stalin's daughter, Svetlana Alliluyeva, defected to the United States. Large groups of demonstrators protested the Vietnam War in cities throughout our country. Elvis Presley married Priscilla Beaulieu. The People's Republic of China detonated their first hydrogen bomb and Dr. Christiaan Barnard performed the first heart transplant operation in Cape Town, South Africa.

In college football Gary Beban, the quarterback for UCLA, won the Heisman trophy. It was the last season in which the National Championship was awarded before bowl games were played. The Associated Press would award the championship to the team that received the most votes by sportswriters using a point system of ten points to the first-place team, down to one point for the ninth placed team and the National Championship would go to the team that garnered the most points. The final regular season Associated Press poll was: 1.USC 2.Tennessee 3.Oklahoma 4.Indiana 5.Notre Dame 6.Wyoming 7.Oregon State 8.Alabama 9.Purdue 10.UCLA.

The bowl games that year were:

BOWL	Winner		Loser	
ROSE	#1 USC Trojans	14	#4 Indiana Hoosiers	3
ORANGE	#3 Oklahoma	26	#2 Tennessee Volunteers	24
SUGAR	LSU Tigers	20	#6 Wyoming Cowboys	13
COTTON	Texas A & M Aggies	20	#8 Alabama Crimson Tide	16

Other bowls:

BOWL	Location	Winner		Loser	
SUN	El Paso, TX	Texas Western	14	Mississippi	7
GATOR	Jacksonville, FL	Penn State	17	Florida State	17
TANGERINE	Orlando, FL	UT-Martin	25	West Chester	8
BLUEBONNET	Houston, TX	Colorado	31	Miami (Fla.)	21
LIBERTY	Memphis, TN	N.C. State	14	Georgia	7

152

CHAPTER 7

'Great Expectations'

After our winter workouts were over, spring practice arrived and the coaching staff began to work some of the promising freshman into the varsity program. There was going to be some pretty interesting competition for a lot of positions. Hopefully, that would help remedy the depth problem from the year before. I was able to keep my place on the roster as the number one right defensive end, although Joe Wingard and Jimmy Pope were pushing hard for playing time. Coach Dietzel, in an effort to improve our offensive output, opened up practice and let players try out for positions. I still had visions of becoming a wide receiver, so I went over to the offensive side of the ball to try out for split end. My defensive head coach, Larry Jones, discouraged me from moving over to offense and I knew I'd have to do something pretty spectacular to be allowed to make the change. The coaching staff pretty well had me slated for the defensive side of the ball.

My time came to catch a pass and the rising sophomore, Thomas Suggs, was the quarterback who would make the throw. The Coach called a pass play to me in the huddle and I was ready. The route I ran was a 15-yard curl-in pattern. I ran the 15 yards, made a move as if I was going to the inside and stopped, turned around and looked back at the quarterback. I was open and Suggs threw the ball. The pass was high and the nose of the football was still climbing. I jumped as high as I could, but only my fingertips touched the bottom of the ball. When I came back down to the ground, the wide receiver's coach smiled at me and said, "Coach Jones said to get back on defense, Lucas." So I turned and trotted back over to the defensive side of the field. That was my last shot at playing offense.

Spring practice ended and I held on to my starting position. Gene Schwarting, a classmate of mine, who played left defensive end, was moved over to offense and became the new tight end. Some guys have all the luck, or so I thought at the time. Lynn Hodge, another good defensive end, who had lettered in 1966, was returning after sitting out the previous season with a broken leg. I wasn't really too disappointed with the outcome of my offensive trial. I was grateful for the chance to play and the defensive end position had been good to me in '67. Plus, I genuinely liked all of my defensive coaches.

Coach Lou Holtz was no longer with us. He had accepted the job as assistant coach under Woody Hayes, at Ohio State. Most of us really liked Coach Holtz. He was funny and was always entertaining us with his magic tricks, but I'm not sure if he and Candler Boyd's relationship ever recovered from the last two games of the '67 season.

It was time for a break from football. Allen Brown and I decided to take a couple of dates and head down to Ocean Drive Beach for the weekend. In those days, the DUI laws weren't nearly as severe as they are today and we

The Pad

decided to party all the way from Columbia to OD. Allen and I had been to the Knights of Columbus bar for one of our fraternity parties. Since it was a private club, it was one of the few places in Columbia where you could buy a mixed drink. Both of us had had a couple of whiskey sours and we decided that was the drink of choice for our trip. We found a glass gallon jug and decided to mix up a batch of whiskey sours. We had packets of whiskey sour mix and the Bourbon to go with it. Armed with what we thought was going to be our 'love juice', we started our journey to Ocean Drive.

Those whiskey sours were really sour and after an hour of drinking the concoction, our lips and mouths were so puckered we decided we had a classic case of too much of a good thing. We ditched the whiskey sours and switched to beer. We had had quite a bit to drink by the time we reached OD. When we got to the beach, we found a parking place right across the street from the Pad. The Pad was still the gathering spot for the college crowd from all over the Carolinas. Still in the car drinking beer, I tilted my head back for a swig when my door opened. An arm reached in and jerked the beer out of my hand. I looked over and saw a police officer. He lifted the cup to his nose, smelled the contents, turned to his partner and said, "Its beer. Get out boy, you're under arrest."

"Well this is it," I thought to myself, "I'm done for. I don't think I'll even head back to Carolina and give Coach Dietzel the pleasure of throwing me off the team."

My date wasn't quite as drunk as I was and she jumped out of her side of the car and ran up to the policeman. "May I speak to you, officer?"

"Yeah, what is it?"

"Officer, this guy is the starting defensive end for South Carolina. If Paul Dietzel gets wind of this, he'll be kicked off scholarship."

"Is that true, son?"

"Yes Sir it is, and I sure don't want to lose my scholarship."

Sports Clip

by JACOB SHUFORD

Hometown Boy Makes Good

Thirty-nine thousand people were on their feet in Carolina Stadium. Their eyes were glued near the goal line at the north end of the field. Just minutes ago they had seen Carolina fight back from a 7-3 halftime deficit to lead North Carolina 16-10. But now the excitement had droned the fans' jubilance into silence: somehow the Tarheels were only a few yards from a touchdown and victory. There was just enough time left for them to score and they had four plays to do it in.

Just as remarkably as the Gamecocks got into trouble, they got out. North Carolina's quarterback Gayle Bomar, on the first down play of this crucial series, was thrown for a loss by a tall, skinny defensive end. When his name came over the public address, few people took much notice because North Carolina still had 3 more downs to score. On the next play, the same skinny end threw the same quarterback for another loss. The fans were beginning to believe that the Gamecocks could possibly hold the last ditch Tarheel effort. It was third down. Bomar dropped back to pass, but before he could get rid of the ball, the same defensive end that had plagued him the two previous plays hit him again—for another loss. The crowd hardly believed it! Who was this remarkable end? This time they heard his name, and it wasn't the last time they heard it, because on the very next play, North Carolina's last chance, the tall skinny fellow threw Bomar for another loss and by doing it saved his team from losing a game that it had fought so hard to win.

"Thank God for Dave Lucas!" These emotion filled words came from U.S.C. head football coach Paul Dietzel at the beginning of his post-game comments. And to everyone else that saw the game it certainly did seem that Lucas was heaven sent.

**Dave Lucas
U.S.C.**

From Dragon To Gamecock

After his sudden initiation into stardom after the North Carolina game, Lucas went on to show everyone that his sparkling defensive play wasn't just a flash-in-the-pan. In the very next game at Durham against Duke, he picked up a fumbled ball in the end zone for a touchdown early in the first period to boost U.S.C. to a quick lead.

Lucas became quite skilled at recovering fumbles. At the end of the season he had picked up no less than four loose balls to lead his team in that category.

Lucas also had his share of tackles. He participated in a total of 61. Of these 61, he made 44 unassisted. He was seventh on his team in this department. His efficiency in the Carolina-Clemson game, as coach Frank Howard said on his Sunday program, prompted Clemson to run their sweeps and quick pitches away from Lucas, around the other end.

The most striking thing about Lucas is his build. He is almost six and a half feet tall and weighs only 189 pounds. This physique has earned him nicknames such as "The Pencil," "The Blade," and "Twiggy." But Dave is far from being fragile. A U.S.C. assistant coach compares him with leather — you can't break it: it only bends.

On the 21st of this month the fighting Gamecocks open their season against Duke in Columbia. Dave Lucas, a tall, skinny end from Bishopville will be there, too.

155

"It's illegal to have an open container of alcohol in public. You can walk across the street to The Pad and drink all you want as long as you don't bring it outside. I'm going to drop this charge on one condition."

"Yes Sir, what condition is that?"

"The condition is that you beat Clemson this year," he smiled.

"Yes Sir! And Sir, I promise I won't drink any more in public and we'll whip Clemson."

"All right son, stay out of trouble."

We crossed the road and went into The Pad. Just inside the door I grabbed my date and gave her a long kiss. Her quick thinking had saved my behind. That was a lesson learned and we had a great weekend with no further mishaps.

After returning to Columbia, my teammates and friends were talking about what they were going to do over the summer. I was definitely headed back to Alaska. They were increasing salaries of the temporary game wardens to just over $800 a month and my boss, Fred Schultz and I had gotten along very well the year before. Gordon had something to do and was going to be delayed, but he planned to join us a couple weeks after I was scheduled to arrive in Sitka. Ron Palmer had decided that he was going. He had pledged Pi Ka fraternity and one of his fraternity brothers had decided to go as well. He was older and a US Navy veteran and seemed to be a good guy.

The school semester ended and I returned home. I was getting ready to pack my bags for the return trip to Alaska when my grandfather approached me. We were very close and he was getting on in years. H.S. Lucas, my Grandfather, had just turned eighty earlier that May. He said to me, "Son, I don't want you to go."

"Why not Granddaddy, I need to make some money this summer for school. Jobs around here don't pay nearly as much as they do up in Alaska. Besides, I won't be gone but a couple of months."

"If you go, I'll never see you again, son."

Stunned, I looked at my grandfather. He seemed healthy. There was nothing particularly wrong with him and he was able to get around well. I said, "Ah, Granddaddy you'll be fine. Is there something wrong that I don't know about?"

"No son, nothing in particular. I just have a feeling that if you leave I won't see you again."

"Granddaddy, I need to make money for school and I'm sure you'll be okay."

"Okay son. I guess it'll be alright, it's just a feeling I have."

With that I got into the Buick Special and started out of the yard. I glanced back and noticed a tear rolling down his cheek.

I went through Columbia and picked up Ron's fraternity brother. We drove through to Morristown, Tennessee and picked up Ron. We followed pretty much the same route we had taken the year before. We did make a detour to the Little Big Horn Monument in South Dakota. We arrived about midnight and camped out right beside the car. There wasn't a lot to see other than some rolling brown hills and a little stream off in the distance. There were grave stones and a large monument, but that was about it. After spending about ten minutes looking around, we continued on our journey.

It became apparent that this fraternity brother of Ron's was going to be more trouble than he was worth. We seriously considered leaving him at a truck stop in South Dakota. That would have been one of the longest 'road trips' anyone had taken from the University of South Carolina.

A 'road trip' was a prank generally pulled off by fraternities. One of the funniest ones that I took part in took place after our formal dance that spring. The entire fraternity had rented tuxedos and the girls were all in evening gowns. After the party was over, the girls were taken home. One of our fraternity brothers had passed out in the back seat of the car. We cleaned out his pockets and left him with a quarter and a dime and drove down to the railroad tracks that bisect Columbia and waited. After about twenty minutes an empty coal train came by right on schedule. It rumbled to a stop and we grabbed our fraternity brother, still dressed in his tuxedo and laid him down in the bottom of a coal car. He woke up about fifty miles away in Augusta, Georgia. He was lying in the bottom of the coal car with tree branches flying by overhead. After the shock wore off, he was able to climb out of the car and jumped off the train as it slowed down going through Augusta. He used his thirty five cents to call his fraternity brothers and they drove to Georgia to pick him up.

Ron's fraternity brother was constantly complaining about everything. He talked incessantly about the girlfriend he had left in Columbia. We reached Seattle without incident and dropped my car off at the same station. They agreed, once again, to store the car for the summer. The three of us boarded the flight to Sitka.

Arriving in Sitka, we reported to Fred Schultz and I was hired immediately. Ron and his fraternity brother filled out an application, but the job had become so popular that there were several people ahead of them. Fred invited us to stay at his house for a couple of days until we found out if Ron and his buddy were hired. I was about to have my first and only experience as a potential alcoholic.

Fred pulled out a bottle of bourbon. After that bottle was gone, we opened another. I don't know how many more we went through. I do know that none of us could remember anything about the following three days. When I finally came out of my drunken stupor, I was lying on a bear skin rug on Fred's floor. I don't believe I ever want to experience that feeling again. It seems that during his alcoholic stupor, our game warden had gone out and taken some potshots at airplanes as they landed on the water near his home. The state troopers arrived and he had been, "taken to the hospital for treatment". Ron and I came to our senses pretty quickly after realizing what had happened. Ron's friend was still looking for more booze to drink. When he had turned the place upside down to no avail, he said, "I'm heading into town to get another bottle."

"What are you going to use for money?"

"Hell, I can steal some." was his reply.

With that, he pushed past us and headed for the street. Almost as tall as me and weighing around 250 pounds, he was a big man. I looked at Ron and he looked at me and he said, "Luke, what are we going to do?"

I clenched my fist, held it up and pointed to it. Then I pointed it at our drunken friend. Ron nodded in agreement. We couldn't afford to let Ron's friend go into town in that condition. We caught up with him and tried to persuade him to go back to the house. He wouldn't listen and started to push past us. I looked at Palmer and he looked at me and we both nodded. Reluctantly, I gave the big guy a sock on the jaw. He stumbled backward toward Ron. Ron grabbed his shirt and threw him down in a ditch. He wasn't hurt and we were finally able to persuade him to go back to Fred's. It took most of the day, but he eventually sobered up.

After drying out for a couple of days in the hospital, Fred made it home. He told Ron and his friend they needed to go to Juneau to find work. All the spots in Sitka had been taken. I gave Ron, Bud and Juanita's phone number and said goodbye as they boarded the plane for the short flight to Juneau. They never did get hired by the Department of Fish and Game, but they did find work with a construction crew that was doing salvage work in an old gold mine and it actually paid much better wages than I was receiving as a game warden.

Fred's assistant 'Arky' had left Alaska and so Fred hired me to fill in. Different than the stakeout job, I would be in town more often and would have use of the department's patrol boat. I was sent out from Sitka in all directions on rounds. Sometimes I would go north through the Narrow Passage straits. I learned to use charts and to respect the rocks

and underwater reefs located throughout the watery world of southeastern Alaska. Generally, I was alone on patrols and if I had any trouble there would be no one to help. I did have a radio on the boat and could talk to the base fishing game unit located in Juneau. They had placed relay towers on strategic mountaintops throughout the coastal area, but there were dead areas where the radio signals couldn't get across the mountains.

A favorite spot of mine was Peril Straight. There were usually whales galore every time I took the patrol boat through the waterway. My first encounter with one happened just after I had entered Peril Straight. I heard a noise like a cannon shot coming from farther down the Straight. It was a repetitive boom, boom, boom. I rode up to the noise and found a huge humpback whale lying on its back. He was rolling over and slapping the water with one huge flipper and then rolling over and striking the water with his other flipper. It was amazing to be so close to such a magnificent creature.

My new duties also allowed some time for fishing. Fred had recommended several streams for trout and salmon and the first stream I tried reaped a strike on every cast. I would have pulled a fish in each time, but some were so big, they broke my line. It was quite a fishing experience and the only reason I stopped that afternoon was because of a large brown bear that seemed too interested in inspecting my catch of the day. I boarded my boat and quickly moved out into deeper water.

One of the other recently hired wardens left early due to a family emergency and there was a large group of salmon fisheries getting ready to open up. I was drafted to go on stakeout to take his place, so back in the boonies I headed with a new partner from California. After a couple of days of inactivity, my partner who had been watching the bay while I slept woke me up. "They're making a set inside the posted area," he said.

"Are you sure?"

"I'm sure. They started inside the point where the sign is located."

"Okay, if you're sure about this, let's go check it out."

We grabbed the rifle and started to the beach. Still well hidden behind the brush and rocks, my partner pointed out a large purse seiner that had already completed the circle around a school of salmon. The tide was taking the boat outside of the restricted area, but we could see that they were clearly in the process of making an illegal set. I decided to move. Both of us stepped out onto the beach in full view of the fishing vessel and went over to the kayak. Since I was his senior, I was the one that was going to make the arrest. It was like an opening-day kickoff. My adrenaline was already pumping as we carried the boat toward the water. My partner stayed on the beach in plain view, holding his rifle while I got into the kayak and started paddling out the mile that separated us from the purse seiner. It didn't take very long to cover the distance and as I approached the boat, the crew members all came over to the railing. In training, there was no purse seiner available for practice and I wasn't prepared for the distance from the kayak to the top of the vessel's sidewalls. I'm tall but I couldn't reach up high enough to get a grip on the side. One of the crew members offered me a hand up. It was also pretty tricky trying to stand in a floating kayak.

The crewman pulled me aboard and I found myself surrounded by five or six pretty rough looking fisherman. A tall well-dressed man stepped forward and extended his hand, "What can we do for you officer? Do you require some help?" I swallowed hard. This was going to be more difficult than I had expected. They acted as if they had no idea what I wanted. To this day, I'm still not sure if it was an act to throw me off, or if they really didn't understand why I was there. I looked toward the shore and tried to line up the two posted signs on the opposite banks. Once I had done that, I found that we were still barely inside the restricted area. I turned back to the well-dressed man who obviously was the captain of the vessel and exclaimed,

159

"You're under arrest!" The words didn't come out quite right. My voice cracked when I said, "You-u-ur under arrest." I sounded more like Barney Fife than John Wayne.

This pronouncement stirred up the crew. Comments began to fly.

"You ain't no Alaskan! I bet you don't know a salmon from a halibut." The captain held up his hand and looked at me for a second. "And just why are you arresting us?"

"You're under arrest for making an illegal set in restricted waters."

"We are not in restricted waters!" He pointed to the signs and lined himself up so that both arms pointed in opposite directions. I looked at the positioning again and he was correct. The vessel had drifted back out into legal waters.

"It doesn't matter where we are now," I replied. "We've been watching where you made the initial set and it was well inside prohibited areas."

"Let's take a look at your catch." I walked over to the open hole and looked down at a measly twenty five or thirty salmon.

"He's a dumb ass captain," offered up one of the crew members from behind my back.

This had a very positive effect on my attitude. I slowly turned around as my jitters turned into a slow burning anger. This time my voice did not crack. "Let me explain something to you. I am a duly appointed officer of the state of Alaska and if I were you, I would cooperate. Let's get this over with as quickly as possible. Captain, would you please take me to your radio room?"

The captain escorted me up to the bridge and I followed the training instructions I had been given by the wardens in training camp the year before. It took me several tries to raise anyone on the game warden frequency but I finally got in touch with the Juneau office and described the situation. They told me to take the vessel and crew back to Sitka and they would reach Fred and have him meet us at the docks. The captain had overheard the conversation and realized this was a serious problem for him. The fines could be as high as $25,000 and one year in jail, but the most costly outcome could be the loss of his fishing license for five years. These types of penalties could also be assessed against his crew members.

The captain asked, "Well, what do we do now?"

"Pull my kayak on board, finish loading what fish you've caught and take the seine skiff over to pick up my partner on shore." It took about an hour and then, with my partner on board, we turned and headed back to Sitka.

It was late, about one or two o'clock in the morning when we finally arrived in Sitka. As promised, Fred Schulz met us at the dock and took charge of the investigation. The next morning, my California partner and I had a debriefing session with Fred. After we described what had happened, Fred decided not to press charges for several reasons. First, only one of us had seen the vessel make a set inside the prohibited waters. That weakened our case. Secondly, my partner had left the beach to wake me up. A good lawyer would have them say they released all of the fish from the posted area. Finally, by the time we both saw them it could be argued that they weren't really inside of the signs. By my own admission, just after I climbed on the boat, we had drifted outside of the markers.

I was pretty disappointed with the decision not to prosecute, but it had been a thrilling experience. Fred, however, was not disappointed at all. He said that even though we couldn't make the case stick, the word would get around soon enough through the entire fishing industry that the Alaskan Department of Fish and Game was on the job. It would give pause to others who might think about breaking the law.

The next day a different type of law enforcement officer stopped by the department to visit with Fred. As a college student, I thought this guy had the coolest job in the world. He worked for the Alcohol and Beverage Control Commission for the state of Alaska. I'm sure the name of the agency isn't correct, but suffice it to say, that he worked for the people who regulated the sale of alcoholic beverages in Alaska. His job was to travel throughout the state, incognito and visit as many bars as possible. He would go into a bar and casually have a drink or two while he made certain the establishments were obeying the state's liquor laws.

The two of us hit it off pretty well and he asked me if I would like to accompany him that evening. He said the drinks would be on the state, so I agreed. He wasn't wearing any sort of uniform which, of course, would blow his cover. My uniform consisted of a pair of khaki pants and a khaki shirt with a game warden's badge pinned on my chest and the Alaska Department of Fish and Game patch on my shoulder. We hit a few bars, but didn't stay long, as all seemed well. At the third bar we visited, things picked up. We were sitting in the back booth sipping on our drinks when a fight broke out near the front door. My new friend pulled out his wallet and opened it to reveal his badge. He looked at me and said, "Let's go!"

The two of us jumped up and started toward the two combatants. Although I was behind him I could see over his head and what I saw gave me a start. The two guys fighting had pulled out large hunting knives. It looked like something in the movies. They were circling each other warily and were alternately trying to stab or slash each other. My new partner shouted, "Police, drop your weapons! You're both under arrest."

With that the two men turned and ran out the door. One took off down the left-hand side of the street and the other took off to the right. My partner pointed to the right and told me, "You get him. I'll get the other one."

With no time to think, I took off. My suspect quickly turned down an alley way and I slammed into the corner of the building with my hands. Just like taking on a blocker during a football game, I used my hands to push off and change directions down the alleyway. I was easily gaining on the guy and I saw him toss his knife under a building as he passed by. He looked back over his shoulder and realized that I was gaining on him, so in an effort to shake me off, he dove under a building and started crawling. I got to him just as he was disappearing and grabbed him by an ankle and yanked him out. He was a short guy with a slight build. He couldn't have weighed more than a hundred and forty pounds so I was able to pull him out without much difficulty. I gave him the obligatory, "You're under arrest."

I didn't have any handcuffs to secure him so I put him in a hammerlock. Even though he was caught red handed, he innocently asked, "What were you chasing me for?"

"You know why! It's illegal to fight with knives. As a matter of fact, it's illegal to fight in public at all."

"What knife?" He asked as we passed near the spot where he had thrown it away.

"Hold it," I said. I could see the knife sticking in the ground, so I reached down and snatched it up. "This knife! I saw you throw it away."

We returned to the front of the bar where a couple of local deputies had pulled up in a squad car. My partner was standing there with his suspect who was already handcuffed. The officers took charge of my prisoner, handcuffed him and stuffed him into the back of the squad car. The two of them sat still eyeing each other angrily.

A couple of days later when I had had a chance to reflect on what I had done, it dawned on me that it could've turned out very differently. Instead of running, the guy that I was chasing could've turned on me with that knife. My law enforcement training had taught me what to do in case I was attacked by a bear but it was presumed that I had enough sense to have a .30-06 rifle with me. I had not been trained to handle an armed human. But I had seen enough Western movies to know that the good guy usually wins and I had played enough football to know that the bigger and stronger guy usually wins as well. However, the operative word here is 'usually'!

Ron had sent me a letter from Juneau. He was doing very well in his new salvage job and had made friends with Bud and Juanita. It seems his fraternity brother had lost heart and headed back to Columbia to see his girlfriend. The money Ron was making working for the salvage company was double what he would've made working for the Wildlife Department. They didn't pay for his room and board, but he lived in a cheap trailer located on the company's lot. It was mid-July and Ron had already made more money than I would make the entire summer. I really enjoyed my work however, and I got to see quite a bit of Southeastern Alaska by boat and seaplane.

My patrols took me to the small fishing and logging villages of Hoonah and Angoon. Hoonah was a Tlingit Indian community just on the other side of Chichagof Island from Sitka. It's thirty miles west of Juneau, across the Alaskan Inland Passage used by the ferryboat system of Alaska. Hoonah is the only town on Chichagof Island. It was little more than a village with a population of less than 500. In Tlingit Indian, the name means "village by the cliff" or "place protected from the north wind." It was well worth the detour to spend a few hours walking around that little village.

Angoon is the other small village I visited while on patrol. This little town of less than 300 Tlingit Indians was very picturesque. There were no automobiles and no roads. There was a boardwalk built out over the water and some of the folks used scooters and bicycles to get around. It's a very isolated place to live but it has its charms. Angoon was the largest settlement on Admiralty Island and the only permanent one and lies about sixty miles southwest of Juneau.

It was nearing the end of July, when I heard a knock on my hotel room door. I opened the door to see Fred Schultz standing there. I greeted Fred with my usual, "Good morning Fred. What in the world are you doing here at this hour?"

"David, I've got some very bad news for you. I got a call this morning and your Grandfather has passed away."

I was stunned. The memory of our last conversation came flooding back. My grandfather had told me he would be gone when I returned. His exact words were, "Son, I will never see you again."

"Fred, can I use the office telephone to call home?"

"Sure you can. Get dressed and will go to the office right now."

I felt the guilt welling up inside of me for leaving my Grandfather and not staying home with him those last couple of months. I couldn't understand it. He was in good health when I left. I dressed and walked with Fred into the office to make the call home. My Dad answered the phone and told me that my Grandfather was doing fine until about a week before when he suffered a small stroke. He was in the hospital and seemed to be improving when all of a sudden, had a massive stroke. He only lasted a few hours after that before he passed away. I asked my Dad when the funeral would be. I knew that normally people in our little community waited no more than three days to have a funeral. It would be very difficult for me to get all the way back to South Carolina that quickly. My Dad said to catch a flight home as soon as possible.

Saddened by my loss, I explained to Fred that I would be leaving immediately. Fred understood completely, offered his condolences and helped arrange my trip home. I could make it to Juneau that same afternoon and catch a plane out the next day back to the lower 48. I called Bud and Juanita and they picked me up at the Juneau Airport. I spent the night with them and also visited with Ron Palmer. I gave him the keys to my car and he offered to pick it up and drive it back at least to Tennessee. He would have to drive by himself, but I had to get home. The next morning I said my goodbyes and boarded the plane from Juneau to Seattle.

When I landed in Seattle, I caught the red-eye that would eventually take me into Columbia. I had connections in Chicago and Atlanta. Before I left Seattle, I called Dad to let him know when I would arrive. He told me that he would plan to have the funeral the day after I returned. I think delaying the services caused some problems with other family members but my Father told me, "Don't worry son, you were always one of his favorite grandchildren and he would approve."

Columbia was hot and steamy as usual. I was a tired cowboy after the long trip and I went to sleep as soon as I got home. It took several conversations with my Dad to shake off the guilt I was feeling. I often wonder, even today, how he knew that the end was so near. I had been very close to Granddaddy as a young boy and learned quite a bit about life from him. I still miss him every day.

CHAPTER 8

'An Inspirational Block'

Willie T and the Magnificents are shown performing at Coachman and Four on Christmas Eve, 1967.
photo: Olivia Webb

From 1964 through 1974, the Coachman and Four Club, in Bennettsville, S.C., was a place for teens and twenty-somethings to dance, drink, fall in love (or something like it) and listen to their favorite music.

"It was more than the Temptations, the Four Tops, Smoky Robinson and the Miracles, Jr. Walker, the Tams, Jimmy Ruffin, Mary Wells and a host of other Beach Music all-stars," wrote "Fessa" John Hook, historical consultant to the club's reunion committee. "It was also the cradle and proving ground for dozens of bands who grew from regional obscurity to headliner status."

Olivia Webb
Richmond County Daily Journal

The Gamecock football season didn't open in 1968 until the 21st of September. That meant we didn't have to report to fall camp for our two-a-day practices until the last week in August. I had about three weeks of free time to get myself into some sort of shape and to catch up on the latest news in Bishopville. I had met a girl from Hartsville. She was tall with a great figure, black hair and a set of piercing blue eyes. I had asked her for a date and she seemed excited, but she said I would have to give her a call because she had to ask her parents. This was the 1960's. I found it rather unusual that she would be sensitive enough to ask her parents for permission to go on a date. She was extraordinarily pretty and seemed very sweet, so I called her the next day.

She said after much discussion with her parents, she would be glad to go out with me. I drove to Hartsville and picked her up that Saturday evening about 7 o'clock. The most popular spot around for college-age kids was The Coachman and Four Club in Bennettsville, about thirty miles away. We started our drive toward Bennettsville and my date told me about herself and her family. Both of her parents were Baptist missionaries and she had lived in several different places around the world. They had only been back in Hartsville for a couple of years and I was the first person she had dated outside her circle of church friends. She was her parent's only child and she was very religious and very Baptist.

The club was jam packed that night. Jerry Butler, "The Iceman," was the featured attraction. The only parking place available was out by the highway. My date gazed out warily and asked, "Are they drinking in there?"

"Yes, some of them are, but we don't have to, if you're not comfortable." I opened the door and got out, walked around the car and opened her door. She swung her legs out but then stopped and stared at the building. You could hear the music and a happy throng of college kids partying outside. I extended my hand, which she took, and we started toward the entrance. There were several couples standing around outside drinking beer and making out. When she saw them, she stopped abruptly and said to me, "I can't do it. I can't go in that place."

No matter how much I tried, no matter what I said, she was going to have none of it. Finally, she got a little angry and said, "I'm sorry, but my father was right. You are the worst person I've ever dated." Stunned, I stood there with my mouth open as she turned on her heels and marched back to the car. She glanced over her shoulder and said, "Please David, take me away from here."

I glanced back at the packed club, sighed, shrugged my shoulders and obeyed. On the way back to Hartsville we didn't say much to each other. She did explain her comment. She had never dated anyone that offered to take her to such a terrible place. All I could think was what a waste of a beautiful girl. That was the last time I saw her but sometimes I wonder how her life turned out.

Architectual rendering of the athletic facility called "The Roost"

The weeks passed and it was time to report for fall camp. We no longer reported to J dorm. Our new home was the "Roost". The Roost was located on the opposite end of the athletic complex from The Roundhouse and about a mile away from the main campus. Coach Dietzel and the administration had built a first class facility for the athletes. The room layouts were the same as most dorm rooms of the time. The room was set up for two student-athletes with a window in the middle and two desks on either side of the window facing the wall. Connected to the side of the desk was a single bed but these beds were 7 feet long and 12 inches wider than normal. It was the first time in years that I was able to sleep in a bed where my feet didn't hang off the end. There was a little floor space between the foot of the bed and a small double closet that completed the room. We also had garnet carpet on the floor instead of the usual hard tile. The carpet was a perk that Coach Dietzel gave to the starting offensive and defensive teams. His philosophy was that people would try harder to gain the little extra perks that come with being a starter. In point of fact, all it really accomplished was to supply fodder for jokes by the rest of the team.

A community bathroom and a weight room were in the middle of the building. There were three of these buildings set up the same way. The first team offense and defense lived in the first one story building. There were two other two story buildings that housed not only the rest of the football team, but the basketball team as well. Just outside the first dorm was a recreational room with a pool table, ping pong table and a lounge with a nice color TV. Next to that building was the dining hall. All of the buildings were connected by covered walkways. My roommate that year was going to be one of my best friends, "John D" Coleman. John D was slated to be the starting left defensive tackle.

Mrs. Sue Kurpiewski (Mrs. K)

Our new home was opened for our arrival and check-in on the weekend and by Sunday we were all moved in. We were introduced to Mrs. K, so called because she had a long Polish name that none of us could pronounce. She ran the dining room and the food was really good and there was lots of it. The team's enthusiasm was high. As I mentioned before, the previous season ended with five wins and five losses and we felt we should have won at least one or two of those games we let slip past us. There were a good many Letterman returning and with an undefeated freshman squad, it looked as if all the stars were beginning to line up in our favor.

Coach Dietzel called a team meeting for noon on Monday. We were anxious to hear our Coach outline how he planned to build us into a

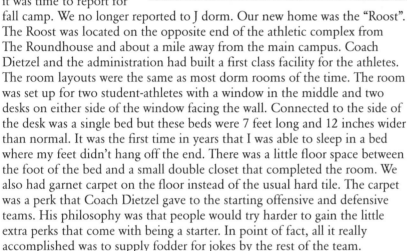

real powerhouse. We assembled in the auditorium at The Roundhouse in expectation of an inspiring speech that would rival the famous Knute Rockne's "Let's go out and win one for the Gipper" speech. Coach Dietzel walked into the auditorium, sporting his dazzling 'Pepsodent Paul' smile.

He looked around the room and held up his hand for quiet. The smile slowly evaporated as he took on a much more somber look. Here it was; the inspirational speech that would lead us on to heights of football glory we had all dreamed about since we were little kids. Then Coach began.

"Men, I've got a story that I want to relate to you."

"There was a fine young Christian man that had just graduated from high school with honors. His parents reluctantly sent him off into the world. He was going to a fine university close to his home. His first year, he excelled academically and his parents were very proud of him. The next year however, he made friends with some of those frivolous fraternity types. They asked him to join their fraternity but he was reluctant. They constantly cajoled him and kept insisting he was missing out on college life if he didn't join that fraternity. The young man relented. And as these fraternity boys are wont to do, they soon gave him his first taste of alcohol."

I was sitting with George McCarthy, and we glanced at one another and I whispered under my breath, "Where's he going with this?"

"I have no idea," was Big G's reply.

Coach Dietzel continued. "One night the fraternity decided to have a party at one of those drive-in theaters. They told their young pledge that this was going to be a special night for him. They said they were going to introduce him to a girl and he would no longer be a virgin. The young man wanted to run away but those men got him to drink some of their alcohol. Soon the young man was feeling no pain. He had watched as several members of his fraternity spent time in the backseat of a nearby parked car. Then it was his turn. They dragged him to the back of the car. He opened the back door and crawled in to see a half-naked girl lying there waiting on him. He started to take off his clothes and looked down at this fallen girl and to his horror, realized it was his sister."

Big G turned his head to me and said, "Don't laugh. You'll be kicked off scholarship." With that one speech, all of the air had been let out of our balloon. Or should I say the air had been let out of our football season. We had been expecting a rousing, inspirational football-based story that would prepare us for the campaign ahead. Instead, we got a warning about what happens to wonderful young people when they fall prey to those terrible fraternity men. Half of the football team belonged to fraternities. From that point on, all of the excitement and anticipation drained out of the team.

Our first opponent in 1968, were the Duke Blue Devils. As we prepared for the opening game, we watched a lot of film from the previous year. We had beaten Duke in '67 but it had been a hard-fought battle. Duke's power offense pounded the ball between the tackles for most of that very hot afternoon. Our coaching staff reminded us that last year's victory hadn't been easy and they expected the Blue Devils to do more of the same. All of us kept up with the sports section in the State Newspaper and we had been reading articles about the new Duke quarterback. His name was Leo Hart and he had set several records in high school for passing, both in numbers of pass completions and yards gained. Some of us questioned our coaching staff about whether this new quarterback would change Duke's offensive approach. The articles led one to believe that Duke was going to be a passing team instead of a power running team.

Leo Hart

"Don't you fall for what they say in the newspaper. That's what Duke's coaching staff wants us to believe. You remember those guys from last year? They came at us hard and fast. That coaching staff isn't going to change what it does with the football. But we are going to be ready for them. We're going to open the game with our 50-short defense and we're going to stop that running game."

The 50-short defense, if you remember, was where all of the defense lined up one step closer together and the linebackers and defensive backs moved up closer to the football. It was designed specifically to stop the run. The 50-short defense would NOT be good against a passing attack.

Duke rolled into town on the 21st of September. The game was slated for an 8 o'clock kickoff. Sure enough Duke's new quarterback came out slinging the football. It seemed like he was throwing a pass on every play. It was like he had more than one football in his hands. It just rained footballs that night. We went up to our coaches and pleaded with them to get out of the 50-short. If we could loosen up, it would make it easier to rush the passer. The answer was, "No. As soon as we do, they'll go back to the run." We found ourselves behind 14 to 7 late in the fourth quarter. Finally, the coaches relented and we got out of the 50-short defense. We were able to stop the Blue Devil's passing game stone cold. We had one chance to tie the game late in the 4th quarter when we drove the ball down inside their 2-yard line. A touchdown and an extra point would tie the game and perhaps give us the opportunity to win. It was first and goal, South Carolina's ball, when disaster struck. One of our really good young running backs fumbled the football just before crossing the goal line. We had a few more opportunities to score, but it didn't work out for us. The game ended in a loss for the Gamecocks. Duke had won 14 to 7.

Doc Blanchard, 1945

The next week we were scheduled to play the North Carolina Tar Heels in Chapel Hill. One of the North Carolina tight ends I would be pitted against was Tony Blanchard. His father was the famous Doc Blanchard who had won the Heisman Trophy in 1945. I knew all about Doc Blanchard, because he was originally from my home town of Bishopville. This didn't mean anything to anyone else, but I thought it was pretty cool to be playing opposite Doc's Son.

Up-And-Coming Gamecocks Battle Blue Battle Blue Devils

By HERMAN HELMS
Executive Sports Editor

Duke, an old football giant that some think is about to run into bad times, and South Carolina, a longtime also-ran that dreams of moving up in this world under Paul Dietzel, launch the college football season at Carolina Stadium tonight.

Most forecasters — apparently believing that Duke, despite its great football history, is on the way down and South Carolina, despite its horrendous past, is about to get something going — have installed the Gamecocks as better than one touchdown favorites. The kickoff is scheduled for 7:30.

The favorite's role in a clash with Duke is a strange sensation for USC, and Dietzel, the coaching dynamo who is starting his third season here, does not buy the forecasters' appraisal of the match.

"Our coaches thought Duke was one of the finest squads they saw during the spring," the Gamecock boss said Friday on the eve of the opener. "As a matter of fact, Tom Harp, their coach, said this was going to be the best team he has had during his three years at Duke.

"Then, in an unfortunate incident, they lost two ball players,

Tickets Available

Priority for University of South Carolina students expired Friday afternoon and USC officials announced that there will be approximately 1,000 tickets available for tonight's Duke-South Carolina game.

These tickets will be available at the ticket office at the North End of Carolina Stadium starting at 8 a.m.

and now some people seem to be selling them down the river. Well, anyone knows that two ball players cannot wreck a team.

"I have great respect for Duke. I know that this is going to be a very tough game."

Finding a replacement for quarterback Al Woodall, who left school because of academic

Rusty Ganas

The game was a disaster for us for three quarters that afternoon. At the beginning of the fourth quarter, we were behind 29 to 3. Even some of the fans who had followed us all the way to Chapel Hill gave up hope and boarded their charter bus to head back to Columbia. But the Gamecocks weren't finished. Tommy Suggs hooked up with my classmate, Freddie Ziegler, for a touchdown to begin the 4th quarter. It was up to the defense to get the ball back as quickly as possible for our offense. Rusty Ganas, a sophomore, was playing right defensive tackle beside me and had replaced Don Somma who had graduated. At the line of scrimmage, I started slapping Rusty on the shoulder pads trying to get him fired up. It worked. Rusty started playing like a man possessed. I moved over to some of the other guys on the line and tried to get them energized. Our defensive unit started flying around on the field and playing with emotion and we stopped North Carolina in their tracks. Their All-American halfback, Don McCauley, had run all over us the first three quarters, but no more. We stopped him cold.

Our offense responded with another touchdown. It was 29 to 17. The busload of fans who had abandoned our cause was still following the game on the radio. When they heard that we had scored again, they ordered their bus driver to turn around and head back to the stadium. By the time they arrived, we had scored again and now the score was 29-24. All but one of those fans had thrown their ticket stubs away and the gate attendants wouldn't let them back in the stadium, so they missed the rest of the game.

Our defense fought back once again and stopped the Tar Heels, forcing a punt. Our offense had the ball. The combination of quarterback, Suggs and split end, Freddie Ziegler, worked their magic once more, along with some tough running by Warren Muir and our halfback, Rudy Holloman. We punched in the go-ahead score and successfully kicked the extra point. The final score was South Carolina Gamecocks 31, North Carolina Tar Heels 29.

It was the biggest comeback in South Carolina history. It may have even tied a record nationally at the time. That was one nice bus ride back to Columbia. There were plenty of heroes in that game and it was fun to talk about it on the way home. We didn't celebrate long though, because our next opponent was Georgia. They would be in Columbia the next weekend.

The win over North Carolina had given our confidence a boost. Georgia was always a tough game for us but we felt good about playing them at home. It was going to be another night game in front of a good size crowd of mostly Carolina fans. The game was the reverse of the game against the Tar Heels. We got ahead early. Our running back, Warren Muir was the offensive star of the evening. He ran over, around and through the Georgia bulldog defense that night. Defensively, we played a pretty good game too. Georgia was backed up on its 15-yard line. They tried a quick-

HERMAN HELMS

Executive Sports Editor

Wilder Finishes May Have Existed

...But Who Would Want To See One?

YOU KNOW the kind of a game. You've read about it many times . . . in fiction. The good guys are nine miles behind, getting the tar beat out of them and the game is getting old.

Just when things are darkest, the hero — who's big and strong and talented — paces the sidelines like a tiger and says, "Don't worry, gang, we're going to win this game."

And the good guys do win with a fantastic rally, just like the hero said. You know the story. You've read about such a game many times, a piece of fiction born of the wild imagination of a writer.

But Saturday at Chapel Hill, it was not a piece of fiction. It happened in real life. Real, live football players, human beings, played such a game, and South Carolina won, 32-27, with an incredible finish.

South Carolina that had its pants beaten off for three quarters, South Carolina that was trailing, 27-3, with 15 minutes of football left, South Carolina that didn't have a ghost of a chance.

Just before it all happened . . . the most fantastic comeback in the history of Atlantic Coast Conference football and one of the most fantastic in the history of football period . . . a player walked the sidelines and said the sort of thing that the hero always says in fiction.

But his player wasn't a big, strong fellow. He was just a little drip of a guy, a 168-pound end named Johnny Gregory, and if he believed what he was saying he was about the only person in the place who did.

"C'mon," shouted Johnny to his red-shirted teammates, "we can still win this game."

Twenty-four hours later, on Sunday afternoon, it was incredible to believe, fantastic to think, but delightful to know that the Gamecocks did, indeed, win that ball game, that storybook ball game.

USC Was Suddenly The Complete Team.

IT IS beyond Paul Dietzel, beyond Bill Dooley, beyond any sports writer or any sports fan to say what it is that can dramatically turn a football game the way that one was turned at Chapel Hill Saturday.

South Carolina was badly beaten for three quarters, North Carolina, a victory-starved team, had a convincing win in the sack. And then it happened.

South Carolina was suddenly a complete football team, a machine with all the parts . . . a defense that stopped the Tar Heels cold, an offense that hit like lightning. The Gamecocks scored 29 points in ten minutes and one second, getting 22 of them in the remarkable time of four minutes and five seconds.

One of the Gamecock touchdowns was helped by a North Carolina fumble. But the other three touchdowns were not at all "cheap," coming after drives of 46, 61, and 66 yards.

Such a turnabout of a game, such a rally is difficult to explain, but magnificent to see. The defense that kept forcing North Carolina to give up the football was tremendous. Little Tommy Suggs and Randy Yoakum were two beautiful quarterbacks in that last quarter. Warren Muir was what he always is . . . one of the premier ball carriers in college football.

Rudy Holloman made some big plays, so did Doug Hamrick and Eddie Bolton. So did they all. A comeback such as this one had to be a team accomplishment.

It is difficult to explain why it happened, but it did and perhaps the answer lies in Johnny Gregory's words, in the origin of his words, in his heart. The comeback can only be described as a tremendous testimonial to the courage of some young men.

'Are We Going To Wait For The Plane?'

AS HE left a motel at Chapel Hill late Saturday afternoon, USC Coach Dietzel was approached by a jubilant Gamecock fan.

"How are you going back to Columbia, Coach?" the fan asked. "We're flying," replied Dietzel.

"What time is your plane due?" asked the fan. "Oh, are we going to wait for the plane?" said Dietzel.

Later in the air and on the way home, the proud coach tried to unwind. Beside him sat his pretty wife, Ann, who had become ill at the game, her nerves simply shattered. Sue Floyd, the attractive blonde wife of USC business manager Ralph Floyd, also had become ill at the game.

Dietzel, quite concerned about his wife, confessed, "I've never come so close to collapsing at a football game in my life. I just didn't feel that I could take any more . . . I mean I felt that way in the third quarter. The fourth quarter I'd like to live over and over and over and over . . . did you ever see a more beautiful offense, did you in your whole life?"

He will live it over in his memory for only as long as he lives.

"There is one thing we must remember," reflected Dietzel. "This is a young team. One time I looked out on the field and seven of the 11 players we had in the game were sophomores. We are giving a lot of fine young players some experience and this is a good thing. They are going to make some spectacular mistakes, but they're also going to make some spectacular gains. Wouldn't you say they were spectacular today?"

Just out of Columbia, Dietzel looked out the window of the plane and said, "Look at that moon, what a beautiful moon."

It wasn't much of a moon, just a piece of a moon, a quarter moon maybe. But it looked beautiful to Dietzel. The world looked beautiful to Dietzel. The Gamecocks were, indeed, flying home.

For South Carolina, it was a fabulous victory. But poor North Carolina. Poor Bill Dooley. They had it won until the Gamecocks took it away from them. Maybe sometime, somewhere there has been a more incredible finish, but who would want to see it?

171

Schwarting Rejoins Gamecocks

South Carolina Monday reviewed the many mistakes that hurt the Gamecocks in the 14-7 opening football loss of Duke and then began preparations for Saturday's Atlantic Coast Conference game at Chapel Hill.

Senior Gene Schwarting, who missed the Duke game with an ankle injury, rejoined the squad at tight end with the first team and senior Johnny Gregory, who filled in for Schwarting in the opener, moved back to his regular split end spot. This bumped sophomore Eddie Bolton, the split end starter against Duke, back to the second team.

The Gamecocks, who were inside the Duke 20 yard line five times without scoring Saturday night, including once when they had first and goal at the four, worked on their power drill from the 10 yard line Monday, following a kicking review under pressure against North Carolina defenses run by the jayvees.

Prior to the brief Monday varsity practice, the jayvees played the freshmen in an abbreviated "Dust Bowl" game on the practice field with a frosh winning 7-0 on Jim Mitchell's four yard fourth down run after the Biddies had recovered a jayvee fumble at the 25 yard line.

The University Ticket Office reported about 1,400 tickets remained for the next home game, Oct. 5, against Georgia. The ticket office has about 1,200 tickets for Saturday's game at North Carolina. These will be on sale from 8 A.M., until 6 P.M., through Wednesday and all remaining will be returned to North Carolina Thursday.

'Most Unbelievable Comeback I've Ever Seen'——Dietzel

By BOB SPEAR
Special To The State

CHAPEL HILL—"The score gets to be 27-3 and it's pretty easy for the team with the three to give up and go home. But our kids wouldn't quit and came up with the most unbelievable comeback I've ever seen or hope to see."

Paul Dietzel stood on a locker in the corner of the South Carolina dressing room, explaining the 29-point explosion that brought his Gamecocks to a 32-27 triumph over North Carolina here Saturday, and the words "magnificent, brilliant, fantastic" kept popping up into the conversation.

And with good reason. The Gamecocks experienced difficulty in even looking like a football team for three quarters and then could do no wrong in the final period.

"I thought the best a team of mine could ever do came against Virginia last year (USC wiped out a 17-0 halftime deficit in a 24-23 victory)" said Dietzel. "But this one makes the Virginia game look tame.

"This victory is a real tribute to our squad. We did everything wrong for so long and then we came to life. I think Don Bailey's long kickoff return (90 yards to the UNC 10) late in the half gave us our first gasp of breath and the fumble we recovered after our first touchdown got us rolling."

The Tar Heels overcame four fumbles in the first half to take a 10-3 lead and wasted little time in building the advantage to a quite comfortable 27-3 in the third period.

But then the roof fell in on the Tar Heels.

"There is no word or no way to describe the way we feel," offered North Carolina coach Bill Dooley. "To say we are extremely disappointed is simply not adequate.

"I take the blame for this loss. I haven't done the job of conditioning my squad mentally. With a lead like we had, we should have been thinking positively. Instead, it was almost like we were standing around wondering how it was happening.

"South Carolina certainly deserves a lot of credit. Under any circumstances it is hard to come from that far behind. Coach Dietzel and his team did a fine job."

Despite the huge deficit South Carolina faced, the Gamecock players contended that losing never crossed their mind.

"We were getting knocked around pretty good for a long time, sorta like we were in a daze," said Tim Bice, the Gamecocks' All-Atlantic Coast Conference middle guard. "But we finally got going. We knew we could do it."

"This one beats the Virginia game a mile. It took us an entire half to catch up, and we didn't have that much time today. North Carolina came at us real good an Coach kept telling us that somehow something would happen. And, by golly, it did."

Quarterback Tommy Suggs, who provided the spark, expressed the same feelings.

"I never felt the game was lost," he said. "Still, it's a little hard to believe. We got the breaks in the first half and couldn't do a thing. But it was different in the second half."

Warren Muir, USC's All-Conference fullback who gained 83 yards in 18 carries, echoed his teammates.

"I never had any doubts about our getting that last touchdown," he said. "We really had the momentum going in the final quarter.

"I think physical condition played a big part in the comeback. North Carolina didn't seem to be coming at us quite as hard late in the game."

---

out pass in the flat over on the opposite side of my position. The other defensive end, Lynn Hodge, was about my height, but outweighed me by ten pounds. Reacting to the pass attempt, Lynn jumped up and grabbed the ball out of the air. He had clear sailing to the end zone and just like that, the Gamecocks were ahead by a score of 7 to 0. We added another touchdown and two more field goals for a half time score of 20 to 0.

In the third quarter, Georgia threw another quick-out pass to my side of the field. Taking a cue from Lynn, I jumped up and intercepted the pass. Unfortunately, Georgia wasn't backed up in their territory, but deep inside of ours, so I didn't have a walk-in touchdown. As a matter of fact, I got tackled pretty quickly. It was still unusual that both defensive ends intercepted passes that night. Our coaching staff must've been a little overconfident with the lead. We started playing prevent defenses and ran conservative plays on offense. Sure enough, Georgia caught up with us late in the fourth quarter. They had moved the ball down to our 20-yard line but we were holding them. It was third-down with 10 yards to go. Georgia called a pass play. I did

Story-Book 29-Point Rally In 4th Period Revives Punchless Gamecocks To 32-27 Win

By HERMAN HELMS
Executive Sports Editor

CHAPEL HILL. — South Carolina, listless and punchless and apparently a badly-beaten football team after three quarters, reached 'way down some place and found the courage to stage a fantastic fourth period rally that edged North Carolina, 32-27, in an unreal game here Saturday afternoon.

The Tar Heels, looking considerably unlike the team that got walloped by N. C. State a week ago, ran up a bulging 27-3 lead in the first three periods. And, as the sun began to sink in the west and the final period rolled around, school appeared out for sure for the Gamecocks. But somebody forgot to tell the Gamecocks.

Suddenly, a USC team that had been so ineffective that it could score only three points out of four fumbles that the Tar Heels turned over to them deep in UNC territory, hitched its belt and began playing football.

And what happened in that final, tell-tale fourth quarter was strictly from a storybook.

The Gamecocks poured across 29 points in a space of ten minutes and one second, racking up 22 of them in just four minutes.

Little Tommy Suggs, a miniature Fran Tarkenton, rolled out to the right and stepped four yards for the touchdown that decided a wild, wild ball game with just 4:54 left to play.

Suggs' score came at the end of a 61-yard USC advance. Butch Genoble kicked a meaningless 32nd point for the unreal Red Shirts of Coach Paul Dietzel.

A Suggs to Fred Zeigler touchdown pass of 18 yards with just five minutes gone in the final quarter launched the unbelievable USC rally. This tally climaxed a drive of 46 yards, but Warren Muir was stopped short on an attempted run for a two-point conversion. UNC was out front 27-9, but it was still a ho-hum ball game, all over but the shouting.

North Carolina, which was to lose five fumbles during the day, coughed it up on the kickoff and USC was back in business at the Tar Heel 24-yard line where Pat Watson scooped up the loose ball.

In two plays — 21 seconds later — the Gamecocks had a-

nother touchdown on a four-yard burst by Muir. Suggs ran a two-point conversion, the score had been cut to 27-17 and the partisan Tar Heel crowd of 28,000 began to get nervous.

USC, smelling blood now, stormed 66 yards in eight plays for another tally. Muir shot in for this score from the two and Suggs fed Rudy Holloman a two-point pass. The Tar Heels were sitting on a shaky 27-25 advantage, and there was still ten minutes and 50 seconds to play—more than enough for this suddenly alive USC crowd.

The game-winning Gamecock drive covered 61 yards in nine plays. The big gainer was a 37-yard pass from Randy Yoakum to end Eddie Bolton, who ran like a bull to the Tar Heel four after he caught it.

Yoakum was hurt on the play, but Suggs came back in to finish off the remarkable comeback with his four-yard ramble.

The first three quarters were unbelievably one-sided with North Carolina, the underdog, dishing it out and the Gamecocks playing the role of punching bags.

The Tar Heels moved 68 yards in 13 plays for their first touchdown the first time they had possession of the ball. Ken Borries scored from the one and Don Hartig kicked the point.

Hartig increased the UNC cad to 10-0 with a 45-yard field goal with 3:24 left in the half. In between those UNC scores, the Gamecocks were blowing three scoring chances that were offered them by Tar Heel fumbles. USC couldn't make a first down after getting the ball at the Tar Heel 29, couldn't make a first down after getting possession at the UNC 38 and also uldn't get anything started after nabbing another fumble at their own 39.

Don Bailey almost put USC in business by returning the kickoff following Hartig's field goal 90 yards to the Tar Heel ten, but would you believe, that they didn't get anything out of this threat either?

Genoble terminated the advance by missing a 22-yard field goal try. Moments later, UNC fumbled again, Wally Orrel got it for the Gamecocks at the Tar Heel 34, and the Gamecocks finally scored. Genoble kicked a wobbly 24-yard field goal that barely made it over the bar with 12 seconds left in the half.

North Carolina increased its lead to 17-3 on a 77-yard march, climaxed by a one-yard shot off tackle by Don McCauley with 9:03 left in the third quarter. Hartig kicked a 39-yard field goal to make it 20-3 with 6:28 remaining in the third period.

Benny Galloway Seeks Running Room In UNC Line

State Photo By Vic Tutte

173

Gamecocks' Lyn Hodge Rambles Into End Zone For 1st TD On Interception

'Boy, Oh Boy, What A Tragedy'—Dietzel

By RANDY LANEY
State Sports Writer

South Carolina's Gamecocks, after playing the come-from-behind role to perfection a week ago, saw the tables reversed on them here Saturday night as Georgia rallied from a 20-7 halftime deficit to claim a thrilling 21-20 victory.

"Boy, oh boy, what a tragedy," lamented USC Coach Paul Dietzel after watching South Carolina's courageous upset bid fail before the nationally ranked Bulldogs.

"You can't rationalize a great effort into a victory — we still lost — but I'm awfully proud of our team," Dietzel continued. "Our boys did everything we asked them to do, and I guess we played about as well as we could."

Coach Vince Dooley's Bulldogs, startled by two early interceptions which the Gamecocks converted into a 14-0 advantage only four minutes into the battle, rallied in the second half behind brilliant sophomore quarterback Mike Cavan for two long sustained scoring drives. A week ago, USC scored 29 points in the last quarter to down UNC, 32-27.

"It was a tremendous comeback," the delighted Dooley shouted at midfield. "South Carolina's small, but they're quick and aggressive and they came at us like we thought they would."

"They were better prepared and better coached. We were just spunky enough to capitalize on second-half breaks like South

(See FUMBLES, 11-F, Col. 2)

Staff Photo By Vic Tuttle
Warren Muir Bangs Into Bulldog Line 2nd TD

Staff Photo By Vic Tuttle
Tough Bulldog Defense Halts Tommy Suggs

(Continued From Page 1-F)

Carolina did in the first half."

End Lyn Hodge picked off Cavan's first pass attempt and rambled 22 yards only 54 seconds into the game and Butch Reeves intercepted the Thomaston, Ga., native's second attempt to set up another score.

Georgia regrouped to drive 55 yards in seven plays to slice the gap in half midway the quarter, but second-quarter field goals of 42 and 23 yards by soccer-style sophomore Billy DuPre upped the lead.

Another Reeves interception, his second of the half and USC's fourth, and a 54-yard runback gave the Gamecocks a golden opportunity to pull away just before intermission as USC went to work at Georgia's 31.

Workhorse fullback Warren Muir blasted 28 yards to the Bulldog seven, but the bruising junior suffered a hip-pointer on the play and did not return to action. DuPre's 22-yarder ended the drive, but all eyes were on the stretcher which bore Muir to the dressing room. With it, realistically, went USC hopes for a fantastic upset.

"Losing Warren didn't help at all," Dietzel reflected. "With Benny Galloway hurt, we built our game plan completely around Muir. Benny went in after Warren was hurt, but we only used him as a decoy.

"I have to congratulate Georgia on a marvelous comeback — a compliment to their determination and courage. There were all kinds of breaks in the game — they got some and we got some — but we couldn't capitalize when we really needed to."

The Gamecocks led, 20-14, when Reeves — the game's defensive standout — broke

through to block a Georgia punt and give USC control 23 yards from paydirt. But Rudy Holloman was hit hard at the 13 seconds later and fumbled.

After Georgia drove 95 yards in 11 plays to take the lead on Cavan's perfect 15-yard toss to Kent Lawrence and Jim McCollough's placement, the Gamecocks again gained control. But Bob Miranda fumbled at the USC 11 with seven minutes left and Georgia had clinched its second straight victory following an opening tie with Tennessee.

"The fumbles killed us," Dietzel explained. "Holloman did a great job all night, especially after Warren got hurt, but Georgia was keying on him and he really got smacked and the ball popped loose.

"That killed our chance for a near-certain field goal which would have carried the momentum back to us.

"We gave such a great effort," said Dietzel. "Now it feels like someone has taken the insides out of you. That Cavan boy is a terrific athlete — he hurt us more than anyone — but we had our bright spots, too, even though they've lost a little of their luster now."

Sophomore signal-caller Tommy Suggs, starting in only his second varsity contest, connected on nine of 16 passes for 76 yards. Junior flanker Fred Zeigler was on the receiving end of all nine as he tied a Gamecock record for receptions set by J. R. Wilburn.

"They brought the fight to us," Dooley commented, "and made us work for everything we got. I'm sure it hurt South Carolina to lose Muir — it would hurt anybody to lose a back like him — but I'm awfully proud of our comeback.

"We met an inspired ball club, and it took a great second-half effort for us to win."

a good job on my blocker, but reached the quarterback a split second too late. He had already released the ball and so I used my hands to push off of his shoulders to turn to see what was going to happen. Their fine receiver, who was from South Carolina, Kent Lawrence, made a move to the inside, but broke back to the sideline. The ball was right on target and he caught it just before he stepped out of bounds. It was an 11-yard gain, good enough for a first and goal at the 9-yard line. They scored a couple of plays later. The Bulldogs left Columbia that night with a 21 to 20 victory. We all felt we should have won that game. We had played too conservatively and it had cost us dearly.

Our next opponent was North Carolina State. Coach Dietzel had said in his Friday night pep talk we were going to sneak into town, win the game and then sneak out of town. It didn't work out that way as North Carolina State routed us by a score of 36 to 12. For some reason, instead of leaving for Raleigh the night before our match against NC State, we departed the morning of the game. Whether this decision affected our performance I cannot say, but it sure didn't help. On the trip home late that same night the bus carrying the 'Brown' team lagged behind our Greyhound. Coming

Wolfpack Jumps On Opportunity

USC Shows Other Side After UNC, Georgia Showing

BY HAROLD MARTIN
State Sports Writer

North Carolina State caught South Carolina with its guard down and Earle Edwards' Wolfpack took every advantage of the letdown to apply a knockout to the Gamecocks' hopes for an upset Saturday night.

But the Gamecocks, although bruised and battered and their pride ruffled by the 36-12 whipping Saturday night, are not dead and buried yet.

Paul Dieftzel's yougish troops demonstrated during an incredible fourth quarter against North Carolina a couple of weeks ago and against nationally-ranked Georgia that they possess courage and some degree of talent.

Saturday night, the Gamecocks showed another side. South Carolina left no doubt that if it does not play close to its potential, a good football team can run the Gamecocks off the field.

North Carolina State did not surprise the Gamecocks with a bag full of tricks Saturday. Instead, the Wolfpack simply had better blocking, harder running and superior execution than the Gamecocks and took charge

EARLE EDWARDS
Had Emotional Edge

early to post a convincing triumph.

Dietzel is not one to offer excuses after a debacle such as his team took over the weekend and this was no exception.

"State literally beat the fire out of us," he said after the game and that appeared to be a true statement of fact.

Looking back, however, it

seems almost inevitable that the final outcome, although not by such a margin, was bound to occur.

Dietzel was willing to shoulder most of the blame for Saturday's showing, saying that he failed to get his squad ready to play. But the feeling is that the USC coach might be a little hard on himself for emotion and psychology, which play such a large part in football, were all on the side of N. C. State.

South Carolina, whose lineup is sprinkled with sophomores in several positions, was probably due for a letdown after the tremendous winning rally against North Carolina and a magnificent performance against Georgia in a narrow loss which could have gone either way.

State, on the other hand, was playing before the friendly home folk for the first time in nine games and the 'Pack was determined to make up for two straight humiliations suffered in the Southwest.

Perhaps the most important psychological factor, however, was that South Carolina two years ago had abused the Wolfpack's hospitality in the first game ever played at Carter Stadium, 31-21 — a defeat that

PAUL DIETZEL
'Team Wasn't Ready'

still rankles State's coaching staff and players.

During the course of the contest, there were two vital plays and both of them went against South Carolina. Those two plays, no doubt, were largely responsible for the final one-sided count.

The first came just before halftime with State holding a

17-3 lead. But South Carolina had finally gained momentum and with a little more than two minutes remaining, Tommy Suggs passed 14 yards to Fred Zeigler for what looked like a touchdown.

Zeigler, however, was charged with offensive pass interference, the play was nullified and the Gamecocks were set back from the 14 to the 29.

The second was an 86-yard punt return for a touchdown by State's Jack Whitley in the third quarter.

"Both those plays hurt us badly," said Dietzel. "The offensive interference penalty killed our momentum by taking away a score that we really needed. Had the score stood, we were planning to go for two and I believe we would have made it since we had the momentum right then.

"That would have made it 17-11 at halftime instead of 17-6 and that's a lot of difference.

"But the punt return really broke our backs," said Dietzel. "Our punt coverage was not good against State, but on that one, we really covered it too well. We were covering so well that we just over-ran the man with the ball."

up over a rise, the bus bumped into a car driven by an elderly woman who had slowed to a crawl. Her vehicle slid off the road into a small ditch but thankfully, no one was hurt. As the fender bender occurred, Jimmy Pope stood up in the aisle way of the bus and exclaimed, "Damn! That's the hardest lick we've delivered all night!" We had lost three games and won only the one come-from-behind victory over the Tar Heels.

At one of the practices the following week, we were doing some pretty tough hitting. Our tight end, Johnny Gregory, had gone out for a pass and was returning to the huddle. One of the defensive linemen had a bad head cold. His head was really stopped up and he didn't have a handkerchief with him at practice. He reached way down and snorted up a huge 'loogie'. He turned his head and let it fly away from all the other players toward the

175

sideline. His timing was perfect. Just as he let it go, Johnny came trotting by. The nasty thing hit Johnny on the leg just right under his pants. He looked down just as the green goop flipped over and started to slide down his leg. We heard a loud scream as if someone had been shot. All heads turned toward Johnny. If you've ever seen a dog dragging his rear end on the ground, then you've got a picture of what Johnny looked like. He hit the ground and started going round and round in circles dragging his leg through the grass trying to rid himself of the disgusting attachment. He was yelling the entire time, "Get it off me, get it off me!" At first we weren't sure what had happened and just watched as the trainers ran over to Johnny. It is still one of the funniest things I've ever seen on the football field.

Next, we traveled up to Maryland to play the Terrapins. Coach Dietzel gave us a mini tour of Washington, DC. We visited the Tomb of the Unknown Soldier and watched the Changing of the Guard. This was the most impressive, most enjoyable thing about the trip. We lost to a very poor Maryland team (they were only two and eight that year) by a final score of 21 to 19. We felt we should have won all but one of the four we had let slip through our hands. It was disheartening to come so close to winning games without being able to pull out victories.

Things weren't getting any better as we prepared for our next opponent, Florida State. Another night game, they were coming to Columbia and were ranked in the top 10. Florida State had an All-American end that year named Ron Sellers. Sellers was about my size and played split end. He was a very prolific receiver. In his Friday night talk, Coach Dietzel made a decision. "Most teams that play Florida State double-team this Sellers guy. We're not going to give them the satisfaction. We're going to play single coverage on him." Bad decision! Mr. Sellers caught five touchdown passes that night. He picked on Pat Watson, the cornerback, who played right behind me. Sellers was 6'6" and quick. Pat was 5'11" and weighed about 160 pounds. It was the classic mismatch and Pat had no help. Our offense kept it close, however, and the final score was Florida State 35, South Carolina 28. There was a lot of second guessing going on.

Terps Cash In Chances, Clip Gamecocks, 21-19

By HAROLD MARTIN
State Sports Writer

COLLEGE PARK, Md. - Opportunist Maryland took full advantage of a couple of South Carolina errors and made homecoming a happy affair for 28,200 fans at Byrd Stadium Saturday afternoon with a thrilling 21-19 triumph.

It was a dark and dreary day at College Park and a day-long rain left the field treacherous and the fans uncomfortable.

Most of them, however, went home happy as the Terps, who broke a 16-game losing streak a week ago against North Carolina, made it two in a row and their second Atlantic Coast Conference victory against one loss.

For the Gamecocks, who were able to move the ball very well on occasion, it was another bitter loss, their fourth in five starts this season.

	S. Carolina	Md.
First downs	22	12
Rushing yardage	97	213
Passing yardage	273	60
Return yardage	12	65
Passes	17-46	5-15
Punts	6-19	6-45
Fumbles lost	2	0
Yards penalized	25	35

South Carolina	6-7-0-13—19
Maryland	7-7-0-7—21

Md. — Torain 33 pass from Pastrano (Carlson kick)
MD — Lovett 4 run (Carlson kick)
SC — Galloway 3 run (DuPre kick)
SC — Zeigler 47 pass from Yoakum (pass failed)
Md — Landolt 26 pass interception (Carlson kick)
SC — Zeigler 26 pass from Yoakum (run failed)
A - 28,200

Maryland jumped off to a 14-0 advantage early in the game were tough in the clutch situations.

deep in his own territory, was hit from the blind side while trying to pass, the ball popped into the hands of Maryland's Dean Landolt and the Terp linebacker romped unmolested into the end zone for what proved to be the clincher.

Earlier, Maryland quarterback Alan Pastrano had thrown to tailback Ernie Torain on a screen for 33 yards and Terp fullback Billy Lovett, who had a tremendous day, had bulled four yards for touchdowns.

Randy Yoakum, who was in for all three USC touchdowns, connected on a pair of brilliant plays to flanker Fred Zeigler for six pointers and fullback Benny Galloway got the other on a four-yard effort.

Yoakum, who hit on 12 of 31 passing attempts, passed 47 yards to Zeigler early in the fourth quarter to pull South Carolina within a point. But Yoakum's pass to Galloway for a two-point conversion and the lead was no good.

Yoakum found Zeigler, who had seven receptions in the game for 161 yards, on a 26-yard touchdown play with 3:36 remaining, but again the conversion was no good when Yoakum was halted short of the goal on a roll out.

South Carolina wound up with 22 first downs to 12 for the Terps, but Maryland defenders

(See MARYLAND'S, 4-F, Col. 5)

Lovett, a brutish inside runner, carried the ball 39 times for the Terps and finished the day with 153 net yards.

South Carolina proved to be its own worst enemy, losing the ball five times on pass interceptions and twice more on fumbles.

The Gamecocks used the forward pass as its chief weapon Saturday, putting the ball in the air 46 times for a school record and connecting on 17 of them for 273 yards.

Maryland, gambling on a pair of fourth down situations with the game barely under way, drove 49 yards in eight plays to snatch the lead with just over five and a half minutes gone.

The Terps gained possession when Galloway fumbled the wet football after a five-yard burst and John Gebhardt gathered it in at the USC 49.

Three plays after the Terps got the football for the first time, Maryland faced a fourth and one at the USC 40 and despite the wet field, coach Bob Ward sent Lovett into the line

and the crunching fullback responded by picking up the first down to keep the drive alive.

Three more plays gained only six yards, but again the Terps went for broke and Pastrana hit Torain on a screen to the short side of the field.

Torain, who had not handled the ball in almost two years for the Gamecocks finally got on the board with a 62-yard drive which took 13 plays.

The following Monday afternoon the defense was gathered in the film room watching the Florida State game film. The coaches were grading us and showing us what we could have done differently. We were watching one play when Jimmy Pope who played defensive left end was centered in the camera lens. All of a sudden Jimmy disappeared. It was as if someone had taken a chalk eraser and erased a figure from a blackboard. He was there and then he was just gone. The coaches ran the film back and replayed the sequence in slow motion. It seems Jimmy had been the victim of a crack back block by one of Florida State's linemen. Jimmy said he saw the guy approaching out of the corner of his eye. He had just enough time to tense up for the impact. The lick dazed him and when his vision cleared he said he thought the hit had caused tunnel vision. But, Jimmy had taken such a wallop that he realized he was looking through the ear hole in his helmet. After turning his helmet back into the right position, he saw the Florida State blocker staring down at him. The guard grinned. All of his front teeth were missing. He said to Jimmy, "That was a pretty good lick whut'n'it?" Jimmy replied, "Yes it was," as he got up and trotted back to the Carolina sidelines.

Jimmy Pope

This loss was the fourth in a row. Our record was one win, five losses. It was the low point of the season. We had gone from a team that was looking forward to playing football and competing for a conference championship to a team that was hoping the season would end quickly. The magical formula that would turn our program around had not materialized and we had four more games to play.

We traveled to Charlottesville, Virginia, to take on the Virginia Cavaliers. Their record was four and two. They had a fine running back named Frank Quayle who was setting records for the school in rushing. Virginia was vying for the conference championship, so we knew this was an important game for them. It was not the time for us to roll over and play dead. Coach Dietzel always advocated going first class and he tried to make these road trips enjoyable. He took the team to see Thomas Jefferson's Monticello. Since I was very interested in history, this was one of the most memorable side trips our football team took during my career. What a beautiful and interesting place.

The next day we had a 1 o'clock kickoff with the Cavaliers. The most popular television show in 1968 was probably the sketch comedy show, "Roland & Martin's Laugh-In." What made the show so popular with the young guys were all the gags that contained sexual innuendos. In their rapid-fire jokes they would often use the term, "sock it to me, sock it to me, sock it to me." The line was usually delivered by a very pretty girl, such as a scantily clad Goldie Hawn, but once even Richard Nixon said it on the show. Just before kickoff we were gathered in the locker room around Coach Dietzel. We had been waiting for two and a half years to hear a pep talk that would inspire us. That day he delivered. He was speaking about Virginia and he told us to, "go out and sock the pine to them." He wasn't Goldie Hawn in more ways than one, but the line was his attempt to clone the famous "Sock it to me." The line was conveyed with an up thrust arm, a clenched fist and a very determined expression. I'll have to give him credit, he really was trying to relate.

Goldie Hawn from 1968 TV show, "Laugh-In"

'Suggs, Offensive Line Have Made Change,' Declares Happy Dietzel

By HERMAN HELMS
Executive Sports Editor

CHARLOTTESVILLE, Va.
Five weeks had passed since they had last tasted victory. The breakthrough for South Carolina's Gamecocks came here Saturday in a resounding 49-28 wrecking of Virginia, and it was ever so sweet.

Late Saturday afternoon, Coach Paul Dietzel savored the big win and said the sort of things you'd expect a coach to say after a splendid performance against a strong, favored opponent.

"That Tommy Suggs is something," beamed Dietzel, "he's just like a flea running around out there, but what an arm he has.

"Fred Zeigler made some catches that I still can't believe . . . How sweet it was to see ole Benny Galloway romp in there for two big touchdowns . . . Our offensive line was great, they never once let Virginia throw Suggs for a loss . . . Rusty Ganas and Wally Orrel were just great on defense."

It was a big, big win for a victory-starved and deserving team and Dietzel was enjoying the great moment to the fullest.

"Suggs and our offensive line have made a great change in us during the last two weeks. Tommy just scrambles around back there until Zeigler or somebody gets open and he hits them. For a little man, he has one heck of an arm.

"One play that he made was absolutely fantastic. He went back to pass, dropped the ball, picked it up, got hit and still fired a completion to Zeigler on his way to the ground.

"I was thinking just the other day about Zeigler, trying to remember when I've coached a boy who had hands to compare with his. The answer is that I never have. He's the best catcher we've ever had.

"Our offensive line was put to a test today, Virginia had been throwing people for big losses all season, but not once were they able to get Suggs for a loss. That line of ours has come a long way."

The Gamecocks broke a batch of records in the smashing win over a team that had been a ten-point favorite to take them.

The 311 yards that they gained in passing gave them a season's mark of 1,491, shattering a previous USC season's record of 1,334 set in 1953.

The 15 pass completions Saturday gave the Gamecocks 102 for this season and that's another USC record.

The five touchdown passes that Suggs hurled were both a USC and Atlantic Coast Conference record for one game. Zeigler caught 12 passes for another USC mark and became the Gamecocks' top pass receiver in history with a career total of 84 catches for 1,080 yards.

Billy DuPre's seven extra points were an ACC record.

Suggs and Galloway hooked up on two long scoring passes in the last half, the first covering 43 yards and the second 62 yards. Both times Galloway made the catch in a wide open field and dashed in for the score.

"It's what we call a waggle play," said Dietzel. "Most of our receivers go left and Benny just sorta drifts out to the right. He told us at the half that he was getting wide open. 'They're losing me out there,' he said.

"We took his advice and threw to him. Two plays covered 105 yards and two touchdowns. That's pretty good, isn't it?"

"I think the statistics speak for themselves," continued Dietzel. "When you hold an explosive team like Virginia to 67 yards rushing, when you limit a great back like Frank Quayle to 29 yards in 15 carries, a lot of people are playing defense.

"The story of this game is pretty simple. We just finally put it all together."

That line was so innocently funny that the entire team started laughing as we trotted out onto the field. We had been so uptight and depressed because of the way the season was going and Coach Dietzel's pep talk had been somehow therapeutic. It worked a wacky sort of magic on the team. We huddled on the sideline, without any coaches and agreed that it was time to play football. We decided to just go out and play and have some fun. We weren't going to worry about all of the pressure to win anymore. So we all extended arms and hands into the huddle and pledged to just enjoy playing the game.

Coach Dietzel generally called the plays from the sideline. He called a certain pass play and Benny Galloway, one of our running backs, was assigned to protect our quarterback's weakside. When he set up to block, Benny noticed that the defenders rotated away from him and left the backside flat wide open. So in the huddle Benny told Suggs to call the same play but after a short delay, to throw it to him in the flat. Coach Dietzel called another play and Tommy was afraid to go against his coach. A short argument ensued and Benny, who was older and stronger and had the support of the rest of the team, won out.

The team broke the huddle. Coach Dietzel realized that this was not the formation he had sent in and started yelling from the sidelines, "What are you doing?! That's not it, that's not the play I called!" The ball was snapped and Tommy dropped back to pass. "No, no, that's not----" Just then, Benny released into the flat and caught the pass from Tommy. Turning up field Benny saw nothing but daylight. Coach Dietzel's shout went from "that's not what I called, to *run Galloway, run*!"

It was a 60-yard touchdown play. This scenario was repeated at least two other times where the play that was sent in was countered by the players on the field. The result was a win for the Gamecocks and a final score of 49-28.

That win sure felt special. It changed a pretty miserable bunch of guys into a group who believed they could play the game successfully and have fun to boot! The trip back to Columbia was a happy one for a change.

The Demon Deacons were our next adversary so we traveled to Wake Forest the following Friday. Our practices had been very good that week. We were a loose group once again and had decided that we were going to play football for the fun of it, as it should be. The team was tired of losing and Wake Forest paid the price. When the dust settled, we had defeated the Demon Deacons 34-21.

While we were in Wake Forest that weekend my fraternities' antics were in full swing. It seems Frank Whitten, had decided that it would be a good idea to have some photographs taken while posing as a super hero.

Dietzel: 'We've Got Some Real Athletes'

By HERMAN HELMS
Executive Sports Writer

WINSTON-SALEM — "Gosh, what a remarkable recovery this team has made," said a delighted Paul Dietzel here late Saturday afternoon.

The University of South Carolina coach had just come in from the rain and cold of Groves Stadium where his Gamecocks had wrecked favored Wake Forest, 34-21.

Dietzel couldn't have been happier if he had been sunning on a Florida beach.

"That was a great victory," he said. "This team is now what I had maintained it was earlier in the season — a real good ball club.

"You don't go to Virginia and Wake Forest and beat the kind of teams they have this year with a bunch of trash. We've got athletes, real athletes on this team.

"We're going to have other days like this one," continued the beaming USC coach. "Days like today remind you of the future we have ahead of us."

Dietzel credited the superlative performance by the Gamecock defense as a big factor in Saturday's demolishing of the Deacons.

"The most encouraging thing about our team," he said, "is that the defense is getting so much better. When you set your sights to stop an explosive player like Freddie Summers and you do stop him, you have reason to be quite proud.

"We made up our minds we couldn't let Summers run and I don't believe he made a good run all day," declared Dietzel.

Summers, who had accounted for over 1,400 yards in total offense prior to Saturday's game,

was put through a painful afternoon by the fired-up Carolina defense. He completed six of 17 passes for only 71 yards and had five intercepted. He finished with minus 22 yards rushing, giving him a day's work of 49 yards.

Dietzel cited cornerback Pat Watson, who intercepted an At-

Gamecocks' Rudy Holloman Spots Opening In Wake Forest Line ...

lantic Coast Conference record four passes, linebacker Al Usher, and end Lynn Hodge as standouts in the fierce Gamecock defense.

USC coach analyzed. "I thought all our ends played exceptionally well and Hodge seems to be getting better with every game."

Tiny quarterback Tommy Suggs, who had another great day, completed nine of 17 passes for 139 yards and four touchdowns. That gave him nine scoring passes in the last

"Last year, they (Wake Forest) killed our ends, but it was a different story today," the two weeks and he received this high compliment from his coach.

"I've run out of things to say about him," said Dietzel. "He's just an amazing little ball player."

Suggs, crossing up the Wake Forest defense, used split end Johnny Gregory as his pet receiver Saturday instead of flanker Fred Zeigler, who had been his favorite target in earlier games. Gregory caught three passes, all for touchdowns, and Zeigler, the ACC's leading pass receiver before Saturday, caught only two for 31 yards.

"This was not anything that we had planned before the game," Dietzel explained. "They were simply double-teaming Fred and Gregory got open and we certainly don't mind throwing the football to him. He is an excellent catcher."

Dietzel also had high praise for tailback Rudy Holloman, who was the Gamecocks' leading rusher with 91 yards.

"He makes fantastic moves," said the coach. "A couple of runs he made today were very much like that great dash he made against Virginia last week.

"Of course, we would like to have won all our games, but I would rather be a late bloomer than an early bloomer. And I'd have to say that our team has really begun to bloom."

Gregory's three touchdown catches tied Zeigler's school record that was one week old.

His costume was the usual long johns, mask and cape but this time he was "The Blue Bat" instead of "Wonder Wizard". His game plan was to have a fraternity brother follow him with a Polaroid camera down to the train tracks just below campus. Standing in front of the stopped locomotive, he would pose with his hands out as if he was stopping the train. They arrived and found the train sitting idle on the tracks and Frank assumed "the stronger than a locomotive" Superman pose. Just about that time the train started to roll. The engineer looked out of the compartment and saw Frank frantically trying to get out of the way of the moving train. The engineer slammed on the brakes and brought the train to a halt. Unfortunately for Frank, there was a federal railroad agent with the engineer who jumped down and arrested Frank charging him with interfering with interstate commerce which is a federal crime. This time they took him to the Columbia Police Department. It took Frank thirty years to have that incident expunged from his record.

A strong Virginia Tech Hokie's team was coming to Columbia the next weekend. They were a very good running team and their favorite play was what we dubbed, "student body left, and student body right". As a defensive end this is what I would be facing. First, the offensive end would try to hook me to the inside. If this failed the tackle would try to block me. After the tackle, came the pulling guard, the two halfbacks and the fullback. At the end of this blocking train came the quarterback with the football under his arm. It was the ultimate power sweep and Virginia Tech ran that play to perfection.

George Constananitas fights for yardage

Late in the game, VT called that sweep to my side again. I got away from the end who was trying to hook me. Next, the tackle and guard both missed me but I still had to take on both the halfbacks. I got by the first blocker but the second guy got to my body and threw me off balance. I was in the process of straightening up when I glanced up to see their fullback bearing down on me. The fullback's name was George Constananitas. He was about 5' 8" and weighed 240 pounds. He looked like a cannonball coming at me. He hit me right on the point of my shoulder before I could get my arms extended. I had committed the cardinal sin by allowing a blocker to get to my body. I felt something snap as he crashed into my left shoulder. After the whistle, I ran to the sidelines and found Jim Price, our team trainer. He examined the shoulder and called over Dr. Lunceford. I was done for the night. The Hokies beat the Gamecocks by a score of 17 to 6.

On Monday instead of going to practice I went to the doctor and they took x-rays. It was determined that I had a slight tear in the cartilage that held my arm to my shoulder. Dr. Lunceford didn't think at the time it would require surgery, but he told me my season was over. We only had one more game to play and it was against the Clemson Tigers in 'The Kitty Litter Box', known to some as "Death Vally". Since it was the last game of the year, Allen Brown, Candler Boyd, Allen Owen and I decided to rent a mountain

Gamecocks Fear Tigers' Running
Lucas, Reeves, Orrel Praise Ground Offense

By HAROLD MARTIN
State Sports Writer

The University of South Carolina Gamecocks started to get ready for their annual showdown with arch-enemy Clemson Monday and a trio of veteran USC defensive performers feel they know what to expect.

The three — end Dave Lucas, rover Wally Orrel and halfback Butch Reeves — think that Frank Howard's Tigers will attempt to establish their ground game which has proved so successful against the Gamecocks for the past two years.

"I think Clemson has the same sort of team as N. C.

Butch Reeves:: Expects Close One

State and Virginia Tech," said Lucas, a stringbean who looks much too frail to withstand the punishment a defensive end must undergo. "By that," continued Lucas, "I mean Clemson is the type of team that likes to run right at you.

"I remember last year," said Lucas, "when they'd just keep hitting off tackle, hitting off tackle. And then, when you tighten up to stop that, they'd come with a quick pitch to the outside.

"They have good blocking and their offense is pretty tough to stop the way they run it.

"I really haven't seen too much of this year's team," said Lucas. "This is the first day we've seen any film of their games. But from last year, I would expect them to be a sound team — one that won't

Wally Orrel: 'Gore Is Trouble'

make too many mistakes."

Reeves, who has participated in two Clemson games, but has never played at Death Valley, expects the Tigers to be tough on the ground, and at the same time feels they might go to the air.

"The two times I played against Clemson, they ran the ball much of the time," said Reeves, who was in on a winning effort at Carolina Stadium three years ago and was on the losing side last fall. Reeves missed the 1966 season because of an injured knee.

"Clemson may have changed a little this season," Reeves said. "I understand (Billy) Ammons is a real good passer.

"Clemson is very good at running outside," said Reeves. "They are especially strong on the sweep and quick pitches to both sides. They make it pretty tough on the defensive secondary because you can't come up too fast because of the pass threat.

"I expect it will be just like all the other Carolina-Clemson games," Reeves allowed, "hard-fought and probably pretty close."

Orrel, another Gamecock senior, will see the Tigers from a different position this time, having been switched from safety to rover in the USC defensive alignment.

"From what Clemson has done to the rest of the teams in the Atlantic Coast Conference," said Orrel, "you'd have to say they have a real fine football team.

"They're the type of team, I think, that just comes out and plays a real solid game — the kind of team that will force you into making mistakes. On offense, they just come right at you with good blocking and hard running.

"I think the man who has made them into a much better team than they were at the start of the season is Charlie Waters. I think he has developed into a very fine flanker and I expect he'll give us a lot of trouble.

"And Ammons does a real fine job of getting the ball to him," added Orrel.

"Buddy Gore is just great at tailback," said Orrel. "Of course, he's been injured and we really don't know if he'll play or not.

"But from what I've seen of him the past two years, he has to be a tremendous competitor and I expect he'll play. I'd be very surprised if he didn't.

"When you consider what he's done against us in the last two years, I'd have to say he's just about the best running back we've seen since I've been here.

"Playing rover is a little different from safety," said Orrel. "As a rover, I can get to the action a little sooner, unless I get knocked down.

"I think Clemson does the best job of running the sweeps and running off tackle. That's because they block so well."

cabin for the weekend. Clemson has a beautiful campus located in the foothills of the Blue Ridge Mountains. And since we weren't going to a bowl game, as soon as the Clemson game ended our season was over.

I didn't practice that week, but attended all of the film critiques on the Clemson Tigers and all of the team meetings. Friday morning I got a call from Coach Jones and he told me that I would be making the trip with the team. This threw a monkey-wrench into the plans we had made, but I certainly wasn't going to argue with my coach. The game against the Tigers was an afternoon game so just after an early lunch of steak and potatoes; we went to the stadium to get dressed. I was sitting on a dressing table while our equipment manager taped some extra padding to my shoulder pads to cushion my injury. I looked over and saw Dr. Lunceford approaching. He had a hypodermic needle in his hand and my Lord, it was the largest,

181

meanest, looking thing I had ever seen. I saw him take that huge needle, turn it up and squeeze out a little bit of the liquid. I swallowed hard, and asked, "wha-wha- what isssss that?"

"It's Novocain. I don't think you're gonna play today, but you never know what might happen, so the coaches wanted me to numb your shoulder just in case they need you."

"Yes Sir, if you think it'll be okay."

"Yeah, even if you have to play, the extra padding should protect your shoulder." And with that he injected the needle into my skinny shoulder. The injection hurt worse than the lick that caused the injury!

We ran out onto the field and went through our warm-up drills. It was a cold gray day, just right for football. I was pretty relaxed since my friend Joe Wingard was taking my place on the kickoff team. Clemson had won the coin toss and elected to receive the football. The whistle blew and Clemson took the ball and turned up field. We made the tackle and I turned to look in the stands to see if I could find our dates. I heard someone yelling, "Lucas, Lucas, get your butt over here." I turned around to see Coach Jones motion for me to get over to him. I ran up and asked, "Coach, what is it?"

"Joe's down."

I looked and sure enough, there was my replacement, stretched out on the field. He had been knocked out cold and was being carried off the field on a stretcher.

"Get in there and hold 'em Luke!"

Out on the Tiger's field I ran. Things weren't working out the way I had anticipated. But as the saying goes 'the best laid plans of mice and men.' The game turned into a defensive battle. Clemson had the same great running back, Buddy Gore. Gore's right knee had been giving him some problems late in the season and that day it seemed to work in my favor. Each time he tried to run to my side of the line, his knee would give out when he tried to make a cut and he would fall down. I would jump on top of him every time he slipped, seemingly making the tackle. I did have to make other tackles and fend off blockers so my shoulder did take a beating.

Joe Wingard

Clemson took a 3-0 lead on a field goal late in the first half. Our offense was moving the ball well, but they just couldn't get the ball in the end zone. We had the ball four times inside the Clemson 10-yard line but couldn't score. Somebody would fumble or Clemson would intercept a pass. Our offense seemed jinxed that day. Defensively we held them pretty well and other than the field goal, they didn't get close to our goal line. We dominated them on offense and defense but the score was still 3-0. No matter how well we had played, we were still losing.

The hero of the game was our defensive safety and punt return man, Tyler Hellams from Greenwood, SC. Clemson was punting to us and a return to the right side was called. My job on the play was to take a few steps toward the punter and then peel back to help set up a wall of blockers for the ball carrier. It worked to perfection. I got back just in time to block the first defender that had a crack at Tyler. Along with three or four other good blocks, Tyler had clear sailing into the end zone. The extra point was good and we were up 7 to 3. After two or three

Tyler Hellams

possession changes, the game was over. We had upset the Clemson Tigers in their home stadium. It was my first taste of sweet victory over the Tigers.

After the game, we joined our dates and headed to the mountains for the balance of the weekend. I was dating a girl from Virginia and had been dating her pretty much the entire fall. We had such a good time that I asked her to wear my pin. Each fraternity had its own insignia made into a small pin that was worn on a shirt or sweater. The image for my fraternity, Phi Kappa Sigma, was a skull set into a cross, with the Greek letters, Phi,

183

Hellams' Brilliant Punt Return By Clemson, 7-3, Kills Tigers'

By HERMAN HELMS
Executive Sports Editor

CLEMSON — Persistent and determined South Carolina, refusing to be discouraged by a series of magnificent clutch stands by Clemson's defense, used an electrifying 73-yard punt return by Tyler Hellams for a third-quarter touchdown and squeaked by the Tigers, 7-3, in a tension-filled thriller here Saturday.

The incredible Clemson defense stopped the Gamecocks seven times inside the Tiger 25-yard line, once holding them for three downs at the one-yard line.

Six times in a dramatic second quarter the Gamecocks charged to within the shadows of the Clemson goal and six times the gutty Tiger defenders threw them back.

The breaking point in the 66th meeting between the old foes came early in the second half as Hellams, sophomore safety from Greenwood, scooped in a Tiger punt at the USC 27, bolted with great speed up the middle of the field, then suddenly turned to the right sideline and scampered 73 yards to the only

Dash To Glory: Gamecocks' Tyler Hellams Avoids Joe Lhotsky (L), Breaks Clear (C), Heads To

(Continued From Page 1-F)

walkaway for the Gamecocks were tucking away their fourth victory against six losses this season.

Warren Muir led Carolina's ground attack with 82 yards in 28 trips. Quarterback Tommy Suggs accounted for 248 yards in total offense, getting 193 of the yards on 17 pass completions in 36 attempts.

Suggs' Saturday theatrics left him with a passel of South Carolina school records. For the year, he completed 110 of 207 passes for a 53.1 percentage and 1,544 yards. He hit for 13 touchdowns through the air and rolled up 1,658 yards in total offense. All these figures were USC school records.

Tailback Buddy Gore, closing out a sensational career at Clemson, fought through a tough USC defense for 92 yards in 32 carries to key the Tigers offense.

While it was Clemson's tough clutch defense that kept the game a contest, Carolina's defenders were also having themselves quite a day in never allowing the Tigers to get up much offensive steam.

Linebackers Al Usher and Tim Bice and defensive backs Pat Watson and Butch Reeves were other standouts besides Hellams in the inspired Gamecock defense.

The defense gave Clemson one last big chance to pull out the victory late in the game, and it looked for a while as if Gore might take the Tigers to paydirt and really leave the Clemson people with something to remember him by.

But Carolina's defense would not allow it, rising up to halt the Tigers at the USC 20 with just 3:42 left on the clock.

The day was growing old when linebacker Jimmy Catoe intercepted a Suggs pass at the Carolina 43-yard line. Six minutes and 29 seconds were left and the Tigers started out as if they meant business.

Gore ran the ball six consecutive times for a first down at the 20, but Clemson could get no further and Carolina was home free.

The action-filled second period went like this.

Late in the first quarter, Carolina moved to a first down at the Tiger four. Muir went to the one-foot line on first down, but he could gain not an inch on third down and on fourth down Suggs was pinned for a slight loss at the one.

The Tigers took over there on the first play of the second period and spent the rest of the quarter denying the Gamecocks entrance to scoring territory.

A Carolina drive that began at the USC 42 carried to the Tiger 13, but Fulmer intercepted a third down pass by Suggs in the end zone.

Hellams' diving interception of a Billy Ammons pass at the Clemson 46 had the Gamecocks back knocking at the door moments later.

This time they got as far as the 18 where Craig came up with his first interception of the day and returned 19 yards to the Tiger 36.

Clemson had to punt and Carolina surged from its 24 to the Tiger 11. This bid died when Craig took a Suggs pass away from Gamecock Rudy Holloman in the end zone.

A fumble recovery by Watson at the Clemson 22 gave USC another shot. But the Tigers stopped them on another interception by Craig at the four.

One more time the Gamecocks tried and one more time they failed. A Watson recovery of a Gore fumble at the Tiger nine gave USC its last first half chance. But the threat ended as Clemson tackle Mike Locklair grabbed Suggs on a sweep of right end at the two-yard line.

That's what kind of battle it was until Hellams broke it up with his brilliant dash early in the second half.

SOUTH CAROLINA

Rushing

	Att	Gain	Loss	Net	LG
Muir	28	83	1	82	13
Suggs	12	70	15	55	27
Galloway	8	23	1	22	4
Holloman	4	12	1	11	4
Walkup	4	13	0	13	4

Passing

	Comp	Att	Intc	Yds	LG
Suggs	36	17	5	193	25
Galloway	1	1	0	20	20

Pass Receiving

	No.	Yds	TD	LG
Holloman	7	82	0	22
Muir	4	33	0	10
Galloway	3	77	0	25
Hamrick	2	24	0	18
Suggs	1	20	0	20
Bolton	1	11	0	11
Schwarting	1	4	0	4

Punting

	No.	Avg.	LP
Parker	6	44.2	54

Punt Returns

	No.	Yds	LP
Hellams	4	88	73

Kickoff Returns

	No.	Avg.	LP
Bailey	2	18.0	20

Pass Interceptions

	No.	Yds.	LP
Hellams	2	0	0
Reeves	1	0	0
Watson	1	0	0

CLEMSON

Rushing

	Att.	Gain	Loss	Net	LG
Gore	32	99	7	92	9
Michael	4	5	1	4	2
Hook	1	4	0	4	4

Passing

	Comp	Att	Intc	Yds	LG
Ammons	22	5	3	56	
English	1	0	0	0	0

Passing Receiving

	No.	Yds.	Td.	LG
Waters	2	36	0	31
Anderson	1	19	0	19
Gore	1	0	0	0
Sursavage	1	0	0	0

Punting

	No.	Avg.	LP
Cain	7	39.1	46

Punt Returns

	No.	Yds	LP
Luzzi	2	30	16
Funderburk	1	3	3

Kickoff Returns

	No.	Avg.	LP
Anderson	1	72.0	77
Shields	1	31.0	31

Pass Interceptions

	No.	Yds.	LP
Craig	2	19	19
Fulmer	2	0	0
Catoe	1	0	0

. Brushes Aside Sammy Cain (L), Turns

184

Pulls USC Title Bid

touchdown of a throbbing football war.

The only Tiger who had a good chance at him was punter Sammy Cain. But Hellams broke out of Cain's grip at the Clemson 25 and went in for the

score with only 3:38 gone in the second half.

Hellams, proving that there is a chance for glory for defensive players in this day of wild offensive football, was a super hero for the charged-up and persistent Gamecocks.

The soph safety came up with two big pass interceptions, — one on a gorgeous diving catch — and made a flock of tackles in addition to his touchdown run.

A crowd of 53,000 — largest turnout ever for an Atlantic Coast Conference game — saw the Gamecocks hand the league title to N. C. State with their upset of the favored Tigers.

A victory Saturday would have carried Clemson to its third straight crown, but it didn't happen.

•   •   •

	So. Carolina	Clemson
First downs	23	6
Rushing yardage	185	100
Passing yardage	213	56
Return yardage	88	51
Passes	18-37-5	5-23-4
Punts	6-26	7-27
Fumbles lost	0	2
Yards penalized	38	56

S. Carolina   0   0   7   0—7
Clemson   3   0   0   0—3

Clemson—FG Barnette 21
SC—Hellams, 73 punt return (Duora kick).
A—53,000 (estimated).

•   •   •

Clemson moved into quick command as Jack Anderson returned the game's opening kickoff 72 yards to the USC 28 where that man Hellams saved disaster for the Gamecocks by riding him out of bounds.

The Tigers drove to the USC five-yard line where on fourth down, kicking specialist Jimmy Barnette gave Clemson its only points of the day with a 21-yard field goal.

Only three minutes and 53 seconds had passed in the game. Clemson had a quick 3-0 advantage, but the Tigers were to spend most of the rest of the chilly afternoon fighting off Gamecock scoring threats.

The Gamecocks kept coming, and the Tigers kept rising up and stopping them as emotion spilled over the top of Clemson Memorial Stadium.

Clemson's soldiers up front halted them at the one, at the two, at the 11, 13, 18 and 22 yard lines in a nerve-chilling second quarter. Pass interceptions — two by left safety Bob Craig and two by cornerback John Fulmer — stopped four of the Gamecock bids.

South Carolina's seventh deep penetration of Clemson soil died at the Tiger seven yard line in the early moments of the fourth period.

The statistics underscored South Carolina's dominance of the battle. The Gamecocks racked up 23 first downs to only six for the Tigers, led 185 to 100 in rushing yardage and piled up a 213 to 56 advantage in passing yardage.

If it had not been for Clemson's defensive strength in the clutch, this might have been a

Sidelines (R) ...

Staff Photos By Dave Underwood And Ed Andreski

Toward Goal (R) ... (See GAMECOCKS, 11-F, Col. 1)

Kappa and Sigma, on the bottom three arms of the cross. A star was on the fourth bar above the skull. Originally, the fraternity emblem was a gold skull on a gold cross but when the War Between the States ended, the southern branches of this fraternity replaced the gold skull with a silver one. I offered my pin to my date and she accepted.

We returned to campus and settled back into normal college life. I found that the Department of International Relations offered courses I really liked. My new major was so enjoyable I even liked to study. I got along well with the professors and with the head of the department. He sat

Staff Photos By Dave Underwood And Ed Andreski

...Rambles Alone (L) As Fred Zeigler Applauds (C), Completes TD Journey (R)

down with me one day and asked what I wanted to do with my International Relations degree. I admitted that I hadn't thought much about it and he told me that it was time to seriously consider what I wanted to do with my life. I had always wanted to travel and see the world, so I asked him if this degree could lead to a job with the Foreign Service. He answered in the affirmative and I also mentioned that I might be interested in a career in the military. This pleased him greatly since he was a retired colonel in the Army.

185

I'm So Proud I Don't Know What To Say: Dietzel

BY HAROLD MARTIN
State Sports Writer

CLEMSON — "The football team just gave me the game ball and I'm so proud, I don't know what to say."

"The football team just made up their minds to win this football game, and that's exactly what they did."

South Carolina Coach Paul Dietzel was doing the talking and he was flushed with the drama and happiness of his Gamecocks' 7-3 triumph over Clemson as he could possibly be.

At the moment, defensive back Pat Watson, an impish sort who is always in the thick of any action, interrupted with:

"Hey, the Boss hasn't been in the showers yet. Come on. Come on, let's get him."

"You can put me anywhere you want right now," Dietzel replied with a laugh as his players grabbed him and carted him off, fully clothed, to the showers.

A few minutes later, Dietzel, "Actually, I thought our defense won it for us," he said.

"We moved the ball a lot. I can't remember having it so many times in scoring position in such a short time as we did in the second quarter—but Clem-

son is pretty big and tough when you get in there close.

"I've had some great wins in my day, but I have a short memory. This one has to be the greatest.

"I thought (Fred) Zeigler was going to whip me at halftime," Dietzel recalled with a laugh. His ace flanker was out of action with a broken collarbone.

"He told me during the half that he was going to suit up and play the second half," said Dietzel, "and when I wouldn't let him, he was ready to fight."

During the game, South Carolina kicked off to Clemson twice and the Tigers ran both back much too far for Dietzel's comfort.

"I don't know what in the world happened on those kickoffs," he said. "They almost broke clean both times and the first one was almost a disaster.

"You've got to give Clemson credit for playing great defense," Dietzel said. "When you get down there toe to toe, they are mighty big and strong.

"The first time we got it down there, we tried to ram it in. We almost made it, but not quite. The next time, we tried to go wide and that didn't work either.

"It seemed like every time we got it down there, we forgot the plays that had gotten us there. But after the first time, I was calling the plays.

"But when you get it down that close, you kind of hate to throw it and take the chance of giving it up on an interception.

"Tyler Hellams has played well for us all year," Dietzel remarked, "and he's a real fine athlete. But this has to be his best game. He was just tremendous out there today."

Tigers' Michael Fumbles After Being Hit By 3 Gamecocks (L) And USC's Watson Recovers (R)
Staff Photo By Dave Underwood

By CHARLES HILL
State Sports Writer

CLEMSON — "Of all the ones I've ever wanted to win, that one was it."

Frank Howard, veteran coach of Clemson's Tigers, had just seen his team drop a 7-3 decision to South Carolina, and with it went a third straight Atlantic Coast Conference title, a chance at a winning season, and a third consecutive victory over the arch-foe Gamecocks.

"About all I can say is, they just outplayed us," Howard went on. "I thought we were ready to play a good game, but we didn't do it, and that's a shame."

The contest, full of heart-stopping climaxes that are belied in a 7-3 score, was a bitter paradox for Clemson. The Tiger defensive unit, a bulwark when backed to the wall, stopped USC six times inside the Clemson 25 in the second quarter, only to see the yeoman effort erased in the next period by Tyler Hellams' sparkling 73-yard punt return.

"That's just football, gentlemen," was Howard's reaction. "That's why 53,000 people were out there this afternoon — you just never know what to expect.

"The defense stopped 'em pretty good — the defense was real fine," Howard praised. "Course, if they had stopped 'em farther up the field they wouldn't have had to stop 'em so many times at the goal line."

The offense, which could manage only a 31-yard field goal, scored the first time the Tigers had the ball for their afternoon's work, had to be the cloudy day's most disappointing feature for Clemson partisans.

Usually roaming with ease in friendly Death Valley, the offensive unit could manage only six first downs and 156 yards total offense.

"We had bad field position all day and the offense just couldn't get going. You can't blame it all on the backs, 'cause they can't run when there ain't no holes," said Howard.

"You can't say it was because Yauger was out either," Howard said of sophomore fullback Ray Yauger who missed the game with a broken arm. "They lost a good one too (flanker Fred Zeigler), so that wasn't it.

"The way they were catching the ball, I don't think they missed him much.

"We tried to adjust to Suggs' passing at halftime," Howard said after USC quarterback Tommy Suggs had passed for 178 yards in the first half. "I think we did better the second half, but they didn't throw the

ball that much either," Clemson had intercepted four Suggs passes in the second quarter.

"But that Suggs was a fine quarterback, I'll say that," Howard added.

Howard was asked about the effect of emotion on the 66th renewal of the spirited rivalry.

"The Gamecocks were up to play, and we weren't," Howard said.

"For the last two years, we've had the emotion on our side," Howard recalled the 35-10 and 23-12 Tiger triumphs of the last two seasons. "But this year, they had it.

"Mebbe we just went too long without scrimmaging," Howard said. "But I just had so many boys bummed up this week I hated to scrimmage. I practiced for them just like we always do.

"But I guess it just wasn't enough this time."

John Fullmer Intercepts In Front Of Johnny Gregory
Staff Photo By Dave Underwood

The very next weekend following the Gamecock victory over Clemson, South Carolina's basketball team opened their season in the brand-new Carolina Coliseum against another Tiger team. The Auburn Tigers. The Carolina Coliseum had a seating capacity of 12,401 and it was packed to the rafters for the game. We watched as the Gamecocks won its opener 51 to 49. John Roche put on a show that night and hit some running jump shots that I have never seen equaled. A new group of players and some of Frank Maguire's best recruits were: Bobby Cremins, John Roche, Tom Owens, Corky Carnevale, Hank Martin, Dennis Powell, John Ribock, Gene Spencer, Tommy Terry, Charlie Vacca and Billy Walsh. They posted an overall 27-7 season and finished second in the powerful ACC to North Carolina with an 11-3 record. It was a great year for our basketball team, and the best was yet to come.

Dr. Lunceford's office called and an appointment was scheduled to check my shoulder. It had never caused any pain but there was just a nagging feeling that my left arm wasn't connected to my shoulder as well as the right one. They took x-rays and Dr. Lunceford came in to show me the problem. I don't remember the medical term but there is a piece of cartilage that connects the shoulder to the arm and the end that ties into the shoulder had been torn loose. Dr. Lunceford was going to perform surgery.

During surgery the frayed end of the damaged cartilage was shaved back, and stitched into the shoulder. I re-injured the same shoulder a couple of years later but never had it repaired again. The only lasting affects I've had is that if I stand around for over thirty minutes it feels like I'm carrying a ten pound weight with my left arm.

1968 was a year full of news relevant to my course of study. In January, the war in Vietnam was really heating up. The battle of Khe Sanh erupted and lasted into April. At the end of January, the Vietcong started the Tet Offensive that continued through the end of August, costing many American lives. In March, the My Lai Massacre occurred and added more fuel to the growing antiwar movement. Under pressure from antiwar demonstrators, President Lyndon Johnson announced that he would not run for another term as Commander in Chief.

In April of that year the movie, "*2001 a Space Odyssey*" was released. Coach Dietzel had taken us to see it on a Friday prior to one of our away games. It definitely got mixed reviews. Some of the guys thought it was the dumbest thing they had ever seen but I really enjoyed the film. Another movie released that spring was the original *Planet of the Apes* starring Charlton Heston. I still can't decide if I liked it, even today. Those two movies were certainly thought provoking pieces of cinema, especially for college kids.

Also in April Martin Luther King was assassinated. He was shot while giving a speech on the balcony of the Lorraine Motel, in Memphis Tennessee. It caused riots all across America that lasted for days. Race relations continued to disintegrate when the Black Panthers and the Oakland police shot it out just a few days later. President Johnson, that same month, signed the 1968 Civil Rights Legislation in an effort to improve life for minorities in the United States.

1968 was also a presidential election year. The Republicans held their national convention in Miami in August and nominated Richard Nixon for President and Spiro Agnew for Vice President. Later that same month, riots broke out at the Democratic National Convention which took place in Chicago, Illinois. They nominated Hubert Humphrey for President and Edmund Muskie for Vice President. In the midst of those two events, the Russians sent troops and tanks into Czechoslovakia and ended that brave country's bid for freedom. In the November 5th presidential elections, Richard Nixon and Spiro Agnew defeated their Democratic opponents.

The semester ended and I did pretty well. Genuine interest in my studies in International Relations had paid off and my GPR was 3.8, one of the best I had turned in so far. That semester one of my classes had, as required reading, a book by a little-known Harvard professor, Henry Kissinger. The book was entitled, *Nuclear Weapons and Foreign Policy*. The very next year Kissinger became the National Security Adviser and eventually Secretary of State under Richard Nixon. Dr. Kissinger was in the news continuously for the next ten years.

Over the New Year's break, I visited my girlfriend in Newport News, Virginia. I met her two older brothers for the first time and we had some very interesting conversations. Her older brother was an attorney and the entire family was very liberal. During my classes, debates had continued between the students and faculty, both formal and informal. The student body, just like my fraternity, was split evenly among those who were pro-war and those who are anti-war. There had been some rather sharp exchanges during the debates and at the time, most of the professors leaned to the conservative side of most issues.

When my girlfriend's older brother attempted to explain to me why I was mistaken about my support of the war in Vietnam, I was prepared to defend my position with finely tuned arguments honed by some pretty sharp minds. I think he was surprised to find that I could hold my own in a debate with a lawyer. After we had exhausted our opinions on the Vietnamese war, we discussed race relations. Our viewpoints weren't far apart on the topic and instead of debating who was right or wrong we discussed the best way to achieve certain goals. We both agreed that every individual was entitled to basic civil rights.

Popular music that year had about the same mix of R&B, psychedelic hard rock, popular and country. The top-selling song for the year was Hey Jude, by the Beatles. One of my all-time favorites was Otis Redding's, *(Sittin' On) The Dock of the Bay*. *Those Were the Days,* by Mary Hopkins and the instrumental theme song from Clint Eastwood's second spaghetti Western, *The Good, the Bad and the Ugly* were also popular in my circle and Simon and Garfunkel had their *Scarborough Fair hit*. If you wanted to listen to country music you had to leave campus. My fraternity brother, Harry Brooks, enjoyed the country sounds as much as I did and sometimes Harry and I would drive out to a nearby truck stop. We dubbed it, "going trucking". The country music was great and the rib sticking truck stop food wasn't bad either. We would put a quarter in the jukebox and listen to songs like *Folsom Prison Blues* by Johnny Cash, *Mama Tried* and *Sing Me Back Home* by Merle Haggard, *Another Place, Another Time* by Jerry Lee Lewis and *The Easy Part's Over* by Charlie Pride. There were other songs that year by Roger Miller, Connie Smith and of course, Tammy Wynette and Loretta Lynn.

During the 1968 college football season, the system of "polls and bowls" was modified. The Associated Press returned to its pre-1961 system of ranking the Top 20 rather than the Top 10, and voted on the National Champion after the bowl games rather than before. The AP poll in 1968 consisted of the votes of as many as 49 sportswriters, though not all of them voted in every poll. With a Top 20, it resulted in more matchups between ranked teams. Those who cast votes would give their opinion of the ten best teams. Under a point system of 20 points for first place, 19 for second, etc., the "overall" ranking was determined.

The Heisman Trophy

O.J. Simpson, running back for the USC Trojans, was the overwhelming choice for the Heisman, with 2,853 points. Second was Leroy Keyes, running back for Purdue, with 1,103 points, followed by Terry Hanratty (QB-Notre Dame), Ted Kwalick (TE-Penn State) and Ted Hendricks (DE-Miami).

The Bowl Games of 1968

Because #1 Ohio State and #2 USC were the champions of the Big Ten and Pac-8 conferences, respectively, they were automatically set to meet in the Rose Bowl. #3 Penn State accepted an invite to the Orange Bowl. Kansas, which shared the Big 8 crown with Oklahoma (even after losing to the Sooners) got the other bid. The Sugar Bowl featured the #1 SEC team against the #2 SWC team (Georgia vs. Arkansas) while the Cotton Bowl pitted the #1 SWC against the #2 SEC (Texas vs. Tennessee)

When the sportswriters voted for the Top 20 after the bowl games, Rose Bowl winner Ohio State won the AP Trophy and the unofficial national championship, taking all but five of the 49 first place votes. Penn State, which had narrowly won the Orange Bowl, was second. The final poll was 1.Ohio State 2.Penn State 3.Texas 4.USC 5.Notre Dame 6.Arkansas 7.Kansas 8.Georgia 9.Missouri 10.Purdue 11.Oklahoma 12.Michigan 13.Tennessee 14.SMU 15.Oregon State 16.Auburn 17.Alabama 18.Houston 19.LSU and 20.Ohio University.

Bowl games:

BOWL				
ROSE	#1 Ohio State Buckeyes	27	#4 USC Trojans	16
ORANGE	#2 Penn State Nittany Lions	15	#7 Kansas Jayhawks	14
SUGAR	#6 Arkansas Razorbacks	16	#8 Georgia Bulldogs	2
COTTON	#3 Texas Longhorns	36	#13 Tennessee Volunteers	13

Other bowls:

BOWL	Location	Winner		Loser	
SUN	El Paso, TX	Auburn	34	Arizona	10
GATOR	Jacksonville, FL	Missouri	35	Alabama	10
TANGERINE	Orlando, FL	Richmond	49	Ohio	42
ASTRO-BLUEBONNET	Houston, TX	SMU	28	Oklahoma	27
PEACH	Atlanta, GA	LSU	31	Florida State	27
LIBERTY	Memphis, TN	Ole Miss	34	Virginia Tech	17

CHAPTER 9

'The Year of the Rooster'

Spring 1969

1969 YEAR OF THE ROOSTER

According to the ancient Chinese lunar calendar, the YEAR OF THE ROOSTER, began Feb. 17, 1969. The 4,667th recorded year on the Chinese calendar began with fireworks, parades, decorated homes and feasting.

The rooster ranks as one of the 12 symbolic beasts of the Chinese zodiacal order and will rule the roost, astrologically speaking, until Feb. 6, 1970. This will take the Gamecocks through football season and most of basketball before the YEAR OF THE ROOSTER gives way to the Year of the Dog.

The ancient Chinese referred to the cock as "the domestic animal which knows how to tell time" and characterized him as courageous, commanding and warlike.

The cock was credited by the Chinese with driving away Demons. Hopefully, he will do the same this fall with Blue Devils, Tar Heels, Bulldogs, Wolves, etc.

The second semester began and I was required to take a senior thesis course to graduate. Spring was the only time the course was offered which worked for me. I would have more time to study, do my research and write in the spring, than in the fall during football season. The class met twice a week, on Tuesday and Thursday afternoons at 2 o'clock. Practice began at 3 o'clock. The coaches weren't very happy because it knocked me out of half of my spring practice sessions. I had to have the course to graduate so there was nothing anyone could do. Although I couldn't participate in any physical drills or scrimmages because of my shoulder, I would miss skull sessions. I was a fifth year senior and had already been through four spring practices, so there really weren't a lot of new techniques and methods to learn.

When spring practice began, there were quite a few classmates of mine who didn't return. It had become apparent during the last season that Coach Dietzel was intent on playing the people he had recruited. If you were one of the Marvin Bass recruits still on the team, you had better be head and shoulders above any competition, if your competition had been recruited by Coach Dietzel. Coach Dietzel had preached to us about getting the right kind of players to come to the University of South Carolina and we all agreed that we wanted the best athletes, but we watched very good athletes replaced by players who were either less experienced, not quite as good, or in some instances, not very good at all. Also, to further complicate issues, there were even players favored within the classes recruited by Dietzel and his staff. It just didn't seem to matter about athletic ability. The 'favored sons' played. This truth was evident in the one and nine record in Coach Dietzel's first season as head coach in 1966. The next season, 1967, my first season as a starter, a lot of athletes just left which resulted in a team with very few reserves. Then the process that took place in 1966 was repeated in 1968, when Coach Dietzel's first full recruiting class was eligible to play. The older players remaining on the team who were recruited by Coach Bass felt like second-class citizens. Many of them were moved to different, unfamiliar positions to make room for more favored players. The Bass recruits were referred to in private as "Marvin's Men" and Coach Dietzel's recruits were referred to as "Paul's Prisses." Sometimes a certain part of the female anatomy was substituted for "Prisses".

Knowing it would cause problems for the team, we didn't let our feelings carry over into our relationships with our newer teammates. Nothing was held against them. It wasn't their fault that they were recruited by one coach and not another. But it did raise problems for the team overall. Good players chose to transfer to other schools or to just stop playing football, because they felt the process was unfair. With all of the transfers and dropouts, it looked as if there were only going to be six or seven of Marvin's Men left for the upcoming 1969 season. Most of these guys were either starters or very solid backups.

Not all of the coaches were blamed for what seemed unfair. There were still some holdovers from the Marvin Bass coaching staff. We liked most all of our coaches and had gotten close to some. Those of us who were left were determined to make the upcoming season one of the best in our history. We were going to prove that a few of the Marvin Bass recruits could help lead this team just as well as Coach Dietzel's recruits.

Our coaching staff that year consisted of a capable group of men. Along with Coach Dietzel, one of his former players at LSU, Larry Jones, was the head defensive coach. Coach Jones also trained the defensive ends, so I spent a lot of time getting to know him. He was a fair and competent coach and had the respect of the guys who played for him. Coach Bill Rowe instructed the linebackers and did a fine job and Coach Johnny Menger was in charge of the defensive backs.

Coach Dietzel spent most of his time on the offensive side of the ball. Bill Shalosky coached the offensive line and Dick Weldon did a great job coaching the running backs. Coach Scooter Purvis was in charge of our receivers. Coach Pride Ratterree was the assistant head coach and was very popular with everyone on the team. Coach Jackie Powers trained the kickers and special teams.

Spring practice went well and ended with no major injuries. I retained my starting position at right defensive end and most of the players recruited by Coach Bass retained their spots on the roster as well. It was time to finish my senior thesis and make plans for the summer.

Taking novices out to see Mary had become very popular. Coach Dietzel had brought in the first African-American athlete on scholarship. His name was Carlton Haywood and he hailed from South Georgia. He was persuaded to go with some of his teammates to visit the popular young woman who lived out on Bluff Road. Many on the team had experienced the rush of excitement as they walked up to the cabin to meet Mary. And when the shotgun blast rang in their ears, they really did 'rush'. It's a shame that we couldn't use official times on some of those races out to Bluff Road as the perpetrators tried to elude their potential assassin.

In preparation for the next chapter in the Mary story, previous participants came early to find a nice vantage point to watch the drama unfold. They took up positions on both sides of the dirt road and waited for

From The
Gamecock Roost

VOL. 4, No. 2   COLUMBIA, S. C.   MAY 1969

"COCKFIGHT '69"

Intra-Squad Game Climaxes Spring Football

BY TOM PRICE
Sports Information Director

"Cockfight '69," in Carolina Stadium Friday night, May 9 will give Carolina fans a preview of the 1969 Fighting Gamecock football squad.

The annual intra-squad game will climax spring football practice prior to Coach Paul Dietzel's fourth season at the Gamecock Roost. Kickoff time is 7:30 P.M., and admission is $2 for adults and $1 for students.

ONE OF THE LARGEST CROWDS

The football game will be preceded by the annual barbecue sponsored by the USC Association of Lettermen. Barbecue will be served in the stadium beginning at 4 P. M. The serving line will be beneath the West stands and barbecue prices are $2 for adults and $1.50 for children.

DAVIES   **VASGAARD**   **MOONEY**

Heading into the home stretch of spring practice, it appeared that two redshirt sophomores and one true sophomore may be in the starting lineup this fall. Otherwise, the starting 22 on offense and defense should be lettermen, including 17 who were starters at least part of the time last year.

There are 30 lettermen among the 91 candidates out for spring practice.

SOPH STARTERS

Redshirt sophomores Steve Vasgaard at center with the offense and Kevin Mooney at middle guard with the defense were operating with the first team as spring drills headed into the final few days. Bo Davies, a standout with last fall's unbeaten freshman team, was starting at rover back in the defensive secondary.

Vasgaard, 6-3, 218, was waging a close battle with letterman Ken Ross for the center spot until Ross suffered a shoulder injury in practice that kept him out of action two weeks. He was expected to be ready for the spring game. Vasgaard has been backed up by rising sophomore Mack Stone since Ross was injured.

The middle guard position, where there is no returning

experience from last year, has been a see-saw battle all spring among Mooney and two rising sophomores, Pat Kohout and Greg Crabb. Mooney, 6-4, 218, who became a redshirt last fall after suffering a pre-season knee injury, was slightly ahead in the race during the next-to-last week of practice.

Offensively, the Gamecocks will again be a multiple team this fall wtih a couple of new formations expected to be added to the repertoire. The squad has been working a great deal this spring with the "Texas Y" formation, an alignment with the flanker brought into the backfield as a second halfback and the fullback lineup a yard closer to the line of scrimmage than the two halfbacks.

With this alignment, Fred Zeigler—last year's flanker who caught a school record 59 passes—has been shifted back to the split end position that he played as a sophomore, and rising junior Ken Walkup, who lettered as a reserve halfback last fall, has moved into the starting lineup at right halfback or flanker.

COCKFIGHT '69
USC SPRING FOOTBALL
MAY 9   CAROLINA STADIUM

Otherwise, the veterans have been working at the same positions they played last fall. An ankle injury has slowed defensive end Lynn Hodge somewhat and Dave Lucas, the other starting defensive end last fall, is skipping spring practice to recover from shoulder surgery. As a result, rising juniors Jimmy Pope and Joe Wingard, who played a great deal last fall, have been operating with the first team at the defensive ends.

Jimmy Poston, last year's starter at left tackle with the defense, has missed a considerable amount of spring work due to illness and the coaching staff has been looking at redshirt sophomore Jake Wright (6-5, 220) at that position.

INJURIES

Dave DeCamilla, starting offensive left tackle last fall,

(Continued on Page 2)

(Continued From Page 1)

pulled a hamstring muscle after spring drills were more than halfway completed, and is a doubtful performer in the spring game. Rising junior Rick Hipkins (6-4, 230), backed up by rising sophomore Bill Boyte (6-2, 225), moved up.

Flanker Jimmy Mitchell, leading pass receiver with last year's freshman team, pulled a hamstring early in spring drills and hasn't practiced since. He is a doubtful spring game participant. Definitely out are rising sophomore defensive back Gary Campbell who underwent knee surgery, and redshirt sophomore flanker Jimmy Cleckler who suffered a dislocated shoulder.

Coach Dietzel expressed general satisfaction with the squad in spring practice, saying, "We have more football players than we have had in the past and also have more size. In fact, we are a reasonably big football team now while in the past we have been on the small side."

| SUGGS | WALKUP | ZEIGLER |

BETTER DEPTH

The Gamecocks appear to have considerably better depth with 30 lettermen and a number of good young prospects up from the freshman team. There are only nine seniors among the lettermen so it is still a relatively young football squad.

The squad is especially deep at quarterback with juniors Tommy Suggs and Randy Yoakum, the top two last fall, challenged by rising sophomores Glenn Morris and Tommy Rhodes.

At tailback, senior Rudy Holloman has a strong challenger and backup man in sophomore Billy Ray Rice and the same is true at fullback where All-America candidate Warren Muir has an outstanding sophomore behind him in Tommy Simmons.

| LUCAS | DECAMILLA | HODGE |

At defensive safety, rising sophomore Jimmy Nash has gotten a chance to work with the first team this spring since last year's starter—Tyler Hellams—was excused from spring practice to participate in track.

With some last-minute changes still possible and anticipating the full recovery of those on the injury list, the depth chart could look something like this (lettermen in caps):

OFFENSE

Split end—FRED ZEIGLER, Bill Duffle, Jimmy Mitchell
Left tackle—DAVE DECAMILLA, Rick Hipkins, Bill Boyte
Left guard—DON BUCKNER, Ken Wheat

From The
Gamecock Roost

Published weekly during football season and periodically throughout the year by the University of South Carolina GAMECOCK CLUB. Sent to members of the GAMECOCK CLUB in the interest of better education through athletics at Carolina. Republication of any of the contents is invited.

PAUL F. DIETZEL
Head Football Coach & Athletic Director

ED PITTS
Director, The Gamecock Club

Edited by TOM PRICE, Sports Information Director

Center—Steve Vasgaard, KEN ROSS, Mack Stone
Right guard—CHRIS BANK, Richie Moye, Tim Beans
Right tackle—TONY FUSARO, DANNY DYCHES
Tight end—DOUG HAMRICK, Billy Freeman
Quarterback—TOMMY SUGGS, RANDY YOAKUM, Glenn Morris, Tommy Rhodes
Tailback—RUDY HOLLOMAN, Billy Ray Rice
Fullback—WARREN MUIR, Tommy Simmons
Flanker—KEN WALKUP, Tom Trevillian

| POSTON | HOLLOMAN | MUIR |

DEFENSE

Left end—LYNN HODGE, JIMMY POPE
Left tackle—JIMMY POSTON, Jake Wright
Strong linebacker—BENNY PADGETT, MACK LEE THARPE
Middle guard—Kevin Mooney, Pat Kohout, Greg Crabb
Weak linebacker—AL USHER, Chan Beasley, BILL PARKER
Right tackle—RUSTY GANAS, George McCarthy
Right end—DAVE LUCAS, JOE WINGARD
Left halfback—DON BAILEY, Jake Stone
Rover—Bo Davies, Carroll Jones
Safety—TYLER HELLAMS, Jimmy Nash, ANDY CHAVOUS
Right halfback—PAT WATSON, Bob O'Harra

Roche Makes Three All-America Teams

The naming of John Roche to The Basketball News first team All-America team brought to three the number of post-season All-America squads made by the Gamecock sophomore who earlier had made a clean sweep of Atlantic Coast Conference honors.

Earlier, Roche had been named to the 36-member Helms Foundation All-America and to the second team All-America selected by basketball expert Chuck Taylor for the Converse Rubber Co. The Helms selections were not divided into first, second teams, etc., but named all 36 selectees to equal stature as All-Americans.

One other Atlantic Coast Conference player, junior forward Charlie Scott of North Carolina, was named to the 10-

(Continued On Page 3)

ED SAYS
By ED PITTS

FOOTBALL TICKET APPLICATIONS HAVE BEEN MAILED TO ALL 1969 MEMBERS, paid or pledged. If you have joined for 1969 and have not received your ticket application or if you received your application and misplaced it, let us know and we will be happy to send you an application.

Please remember, all priority expires May 15. The Ticket Office must receive your ticket application and payment by May 15 if you have had season tickets in the past and would like to retain priority on your seats. We request that you place your order on an official ticket application. Please do not try to place your order over the phone.

If this is your first year as a Gamecock Club contributor, or if you have been a Gamecock Club member in the past but this is your first year as a season ticket purchaser, you will be able to obtain tickets to all five of Carolina's home games; however, your seat for the Carolina-Clemson game will be located in Carolina Coliseum and the game will be on black and white Eidiphor large screen projection.

COLISEUM

After our supply of tickets for the Carolina-Clemson game in Carolina Stadium has been exhausted, you will automatically be assigned seats in Carolina Coliseum unless you notify the Ticket Office in writing that you would rather be refunded. This includes anyone who did not purchase season tickets last year, anyone who increases the number of season tickets over last year, even though you increase your contribution for this year, and anyone who purchased more season tickets last year than his contribution retains priority on, and we are forced to recall some of his seats as outlined on page 6 in our brochure.

Contributions are showing a considerable increase over last year, and this is very essential to the progress of the University's entire athletic program. If you have increased your contribution for 1969, we will do everything possible to improve your seats, but at this time it looks as if it will be impossible to improve anyone's seats over 1968, regardless of contribution. If you have a request, we suggest that you write it on the ticket application itself rather than writing a letter or calling the Ticket Office.

If you increase your order over 1968, please make it clear on the ticket application if you would like the same location that you had last year and your additional seats in another location.

AREA MEETINGS

Coach Dietzel will attend the following **area** Gamecock Club dinner meetings. All Gamecock fans and their wives are invited. In most cases there is a very limited amount of space available. Plan now to attend by ordering your tickets from one of the addresses listed below. Please enclose a self-addressed envelope with your check.

May 13
Georgetown, S. C. — Holiday Inn
$4.00 per plate
Order tickets — Mr. Arthur Flowers
P. O. Box 418
Georgetown, S. C. 29440

May 16
Greenville, S. C. — Eppes Eating Place
$2.50 adults per plate
$1.25 children per plate
Order tickets — Calhoun H. Turner
Suite 2000, Lawyers Bldg.
Greenville, S. C. 29601

May 20
Saluda, S. C. — Saluda Recreation Center
$2.50 per plate
Order tickets — Dr. R. C. Rollings
P. O. Box 308
Saluda, S. C.

(Continued From Page 2)

man first team All-America selected by The Basketball News, a nationally circulated basketball newspaper published in Coral Gables, Fla.

Joining Roche and Scott on the first team were Terry Driscoll of Boston College, Bud Ogden of Santa Clara, Rudy Tomjanovich of Michigan, Lou Alcindor of UCLA, Spencer Haywood of Detroit, Pete Maravich of LSU, Rick Mount of Purdue, and Jo Jo White of Kansas.

The Basketball News, in announcing the selection, had this to say about Roche:

Roche launched his varsity career with a virtual sweep of all top honors available including first soph to ever win player of the year award in the ACC, MVP in the Quaker City Classic, unanimous all-ACC team, unanimous all-ACC tournament team and the squad's own MVP award . . . In Quaker City Classic he scored 26 points as the Gamecocks handed LaSalle their only loss of the year . . . In leading South Carolina to its first-ever 20-game winning season (21-7), he topped the team in scoring with a 23.6 average off a fine 47.1 field goal percentage and 81.4 at the free throw line . . . Also led the team in assists and logged most playing time (an average of 39 minutes a game) of any member of the squad . . . Led USC in scoring in 23 of the 28 games and was seven times over the 30-point mark . . . High games were 38 in 68-66 win over North Carolina, 37 against Duke and 35 against Virginia . . . Scores with complete assortment of shots, from outside jumpers to driving layups, and rates as an standout defensive performer.

May 21
Anderson, S. C. — Holiday Inn
$3.00 per plate
Order tickets — Mr. Doug Gray
P. O. Box 1745, Station A.
Anderson, S. C. 29621

May 23
Charleston, S. C. — Francis Marion Hotel
$6.00 per plate
Order tickets — Mr. Edward Pritchard, Jr.
P. O. Box 250
Charleston, S. C. 29402

the action to commence. This particular evening, Jimmy Pope, was posted down the dirt road with a policeman's flashlight. As the frightened runners came pounding toward him, Jimmy jumped out from behind a tree and hit them in the eyes with the bright beam and ordered them to, "Hold it boys! You been out here messing with this man's wife?" The victims looked like deer in headlights as they stopped and raised their hands in the air.

"You're all going to jail! We've been hearing complaints about you boys for weeks now and we've finally got you."

Carlton and Jimmy were good friends and Carlton thought he recognized Jimmy's voice. As Jimmy continued making threats, Carlton was trying to look around the beam of the flashlight. "Hold it right there son, you're in enough trouble already!" Carlton was able to get close enough to see Jimmy and grabbed him around the neck crying, "Jimmy, thank God it's you, thank God it's you." After they returned to the dorm, Carlton was interrogated by some of his teammates and asked, "Carlton, what were you thinking when that shotgun went off?"

"I was thinking that if they were going to shoot those white boys for being out there with that man's wife, what would they do to this poor black boy from South Georgia?"

Another one of our teammates was from Pennsylvania. His name was Bob White. Bob's fraternity had a large pledge class that was unaware of what went on at Mary's place. The 20+ members were taken out to see Mary and her two cousins. This time there were almost 200 people hiding in prime viewing positions on both sides of the dirt road. We had added a new wrinkle to the hoax that night. When the shotgun went off and the pledges bolted for safety, our star halfback, Benny Galloway started chasing them. Benny could growl just like a rabid bulldog. He could outrun even the fastest pledge, so it wasn't long before he overtook them, snarling and growling, as he reached down to grab a pledge's calf. When his fingers closed on the pledge's leg, the poor guy screamed as he fell to the ground ready to be devoured. It was an experience they would never forget. A great time, but between all the hijinks and football, we did actually try to get a college education.

The Department of International Relations sent a representative every year up to West Point, the United States Military Academy, to participate in a student conference. I was chosen to represent the University of South Carolina. This was quite an honor as the SCUSA Conference is considered the most prestigious of its kind in the country. The following excerpt is taken from the United States Military Academy's website.

"SCUSA is the largest and most prestigious conference of its kind in the world, held here at West Point every fall."

"The Student Conference on US Affairs is an annual four day conference hosted at The United States Military Academy at West Point. The purpose of the conference is to facilitate interaction and constructive discussion between student delegates in order for them to better understand

Lucas goes to West Point

Dave Lucas, is one of two University of South Carolina students selected to attend the 21st annual Student Conference on United States Affairs at West Point, N.Y.

Lucas, a starting defensive end for the ACC Champs and student government officer, Charles Dallara of Spartanburg, were nominated by Dr. Thomas F Jones to represent South Carolina during the four day conference at the U.S. Military Academy Dec. 3-6.

"Foreign policy Directions for the Seventies" will be the theme of the student conference at West Point. Lucas will serve on the South and Southeast Asia Roundtable. He is writing his Senior Thesis on Thailand.

Last year, 186 students representing 81 institutions from throughout the North American continent attended the 20th annual student conference.

the intricacies of the challenges that the United States faces in a global society. SCUSA delegates attend panel discussions, hear keynotes speakers, and participate in roundtable sessions. Roundtable sessions such as Strategic Asia, and Transnational Crime, and Human Security in the Developing World are designed to produce thought provoking conversations between participants. The result of discussions is policy proposal papers, the best of which are published in the Undergraduate Journal of Social Sciences. "

The four-day conference was quite an experience. The Vietnam War was the most popular topic, but race relations in the United States were also explored by the students from many different schools. There were passionate proponents of ideas on both sides of many controversies. The experience was a great lesson for me in debating ideas and attempting to sway others to my side of the issues. It was sometimes a difficult thing to do, because attitudes had hardened across the country particularly on the war in Vietnam.

Traveling to the conference was my first trip to New York City. It was a real eye-opener for a small town boy from Turkey Creek, South Carolina. Seeing New York on television or in the movies was impressive, but actually being in the "city that never sleeps" was amazing. Upon my return to Carolina, I gave a full report to the faculty and students gathered in a special class for that purpose.

My fraternity brother, Harry Brooks, also had quite an experience at the end of the semester. He had signed up for a very difficult math course. When he arrived for his first day of class, he found he was one of about one hundred and fifty students in a large auditorium. The professor teaching the class was Chinese and had only been in the USA for a few years. His English was progressing but Harry couldn't understand what he was saying. Harry also found it difficult to understand the mysteries of mathematics. The combination of broken English and math terminology seemed to be too high a hurdle for Harry. He needed the class to graduate but he knew it would be unlikely that the semester would end with a satisfactory grade.

Harry made the decision to drop the math course and try again the next semester, but unfortunately Harry was too busy. He was so busy with Blue Ribbon beers at Doc's Rosewood Lounge, helping to plan the next fraternity party, studying the best looking girls in the sororities and attending the afternoon entertainment sessions at the rapids of the Congaree River that he forgot to officially drop the course. Time passed and Harry never attended another math class. One day he received notification of his final exam.

Harry was alarmed by the news and turned to his fraternity brothers for advice. He couldn't afford a failing grade much less a zero. That would put his hope of graduating at risk. After much discussion it was recommended that since he had only been to class once, the professor couldn't possibly recognize him, so it only made sense to find someone proficient in math to take the exam in his place. Our fraternity advisor, Dr Charles Cooledge, was a history professor and had taught us in one of his classes that during the War Between the States a draftee could avoid military service by paying someone to serve in his place. The replacement was called a 'substitute' and it was perfectly legal. This seemed to be a logical solution to the problem and we all agreed that hiring a substitute was Harry's only hope. But who did we know that could pass an advanced math exam? At just about that time, in walked another fraternity brother who lived off-campus. His name was Johnny Johnston. Johnny was an engineering major and actually studied and earned good grades. Without telling him anything about the situation he was questioned about the math courses he had taken. Sure enough he had aced the same course. After hearing of Harry's dilemma, Johnny was asked if he could help. Although he was reluctant at first, after the offer of a modest payment of $20, he agreed to take the exam in Harry's stead. The substitute agreement that would have made Civil War veterans proud was in place.

The day of the exam arrived and Johnny walked into the auditorium. The exams were placed on the corner of the Chinese professor's desk and each student walked up, took an exam and found an empty seat. It didn't take Johnny long to breeze through the test. He looked around the room and realized he was the first student to finish as he got up and walked down to the professor's desk in the front corner of the auditorium. The professor was reading a book as Johnny approached. Johnny started to lay his work on the desk when all of a sudden the professor laid his book down, dropped his head and peered up at Johnny over his glasses. Smiling, the math professor reached out and took the paper from Johnny. He glanced down and the smile vanished. Johnny had signed the exam, Harry D. Brooks. The professor looked up at Johnny and then back at the signature. With a very puzzled look on his face he said to Johnny, "Misser Brew? You no Misser Brew!" (Chinese for Mr. Brooks)

Knowing the gig was up, Johnny reached down and quickly snatched the test from the professor's hands. He turned and skedaddled out of the auditorium. The professor was calling to him as he vacated the premises but Johnny couldn't understand a word of Chinese.

Afraid of being followed, Johnny took a circuitous route back to the fraternity house where Harry was anxiously waiting. When Johnny arrived, he gave Harry the news. This could spell trouble for not only Harry and Johnny but the entire fraternity. Harry's father had always told him to be cool under fire. There was nothing left to do but bluff his way out.

Harry had an ace in the hole. A fraternity brother, who was a bit older, was a doctor in West Columbia. Off Harry raced to see Dr. Bunny and get an excuse for missing the exam. Happy to comply with a fraternity brother's request, the doctor's excuse was issued and properly documented. The next day, with the demeanor of James Bond, Harry strolled into the professor's office and handed him the excuse. The Chinese professor stared for a few seconds at the paper as Harry held his breath. Finally looking up and gazing directly at Harry, the professor pulled his glasses off his nose and tilted his head to the side. "Misser Brew, some ting strange going on here. Someone else try to take exam using your name yesterday."

With an innocent look Harry replied, "Is that a fact?"

"Yes, that is fact!"

"I agree. That is really strange. I am ready to take my exam now."

"Okay," the professor said as he paused with a suspicious look on his face.

Harry sat down and took the same exam that he had gotten from Johnny the night before. The results were satisfactory and Harry received a good grade in his required course.

The semester ended and another summer vacation was about to begin.

CHAPTER 10

'Return to Juneau'

Several of my fraternity brothers had enjoyed the tales of my two summers in Alaska and they decided to make the trip with me. We had two carloads ready to travel and left in late May from Columbia headed for the West Coast of Washington State. We had rendezvoused in Morristown, Tennessee at Ron Palmer's home. The morning we left, Harry Brooks, Ron Palmer and I were in the lead car. John Tominack was driving the second car and his two passengers were my fraternity brother, Pete Fuge, and teammate and frat brother, Allen Owens.

After traveling about thirty miles we noticed that John had his wipers on behind us. We thought he was just cleaning his dirty windshield but Harry noticed that the wipers continued to run for another ten to fifteen miles. Curious, we finally pulled over into a gas station. We asked him why he had the wipers going and he said that there was a liquid spraying all over his windshield. Harry reached down and grabbed some of the liquid on his fingers and it was motor oil. We checked Harry's car and sure enough it had been spraying oil for the past fifty miles. John and Allen had been listening to Pete's stories and weren't paying attention. Thankfully, we caught the problem before it caused major damage to Harry's car. At a nearby garage we had it repaired and were soon back on the road heading west.

It was a fairly uneventful trip until we reached Deadwood, South Dakota. There was a saloon known as 'Number 10', a famous tourist attraction. Its draw was that it was reputed to be the saloon in which the famous Wild Bill Hickok met his end. We decided to stop and have a look around and get a drink. The story of Wild Bill had been told dozens of times in different movies and on television shows and this was too good a chance to pass up.

James Butler (Wild Bill) Hickock

The story is that Hickok, the famous gunfighter, entered what was then Nuttall & Mann's Saloon and while drinking at the bar, was invited to join a poker game. Hickock always preferred to sit with his back against the wall to avoid being vulnerable to attack from an adversary. However, the only seat available at the table had its back to the door of the saloon. Hickok asked one of the players, Charlie Rich, to switch seats, but he refused so he reluctantly took the vacant seat. Subsequently, Jack McCall, who had lost money in a poker game to Hickok the day before, entered the saloon and calmly walked up behind Hickok and shouted, "Damn you! Take that!" and shot him in the back of the head with a .45 caliber double-action revolver. The bullet exited through Hickok's cheek and hit Capt. Massie, another poker player, in the wrist. McCall fled, while a few people tried to revive Hickok. Their attempts were futile as he died instantly. The poker hand Hickok was holding when he was shot was reportedly a pair of eights and a pair of aces–all black, which has become known as the "dead man's hand".

The bar had a famous local bartender. In the brochures we picked up and read, he was noted for his ability to tell some of the tallest tales in the West. It was all delivered with a straight face as if his stories had been recited straight from the Bible. When Pete read the brochure, it was like waving a red flag in front of a bull; 'Bull' being the operative word because Pete was full of it. Pete walked up to the bar and settled down in front of the bartender. He held up the brochure and asked if he was the barkeep described in the brochure. The bartender replied in the affirmative and proceeded to tell a tall tale. The rest of us gathered around and when he delivered the punch line of his story, we all had a hardy laugh, except for Pete, whose face remained impassive. Pete immediately launched into a story that wasn't set in the West, but was just as absurd. We sat there for the next thirty minutes watching them duel it out with their tall tales. Neither one cracked a smile or made a comment about the opponent's story.

The No. 10 saloon

The tales got taller and we were laughing so hard, tears were rolling down our cheeks. The bartender finally brought out his killer story that had never been bested. He hadn't ever met such tough competition, but he had never met Pete Fuge. The bartender began by telling about a local character who was very obese and who liked to get drunk on Saturday night. As always, he wound up in the Deadwood city jail and stayed there until he sobered up which was usually on Sunday. It seems that this particular Saturday night he was more intoxicated than usual and the next day he was still wasted. In fact, he seemed even drunker than the night before. This continued for several days and the jailers couldn't figure out how he was getting more booze. They stripped him and took his clothes as they looked for a hidden bottle but found nothing. Days passed and he was still inebriated. The authorities finally discovered his secret. The guy was so fat that he was hiding half pint bottles of whisky in the rolls of extra skin and fat that covered his body.

We looked at Pete and there was no sign of emotion on his face. He started by saying, "That story reminds me of a guy I knew back home in Washington." Pete's tale was about a guy that became so obese that the doctor had told him that if he didn't lose weight he would die an early death. The fat young man went on a crash diet and lost 300 pounds in only three months. He dropped the weight so fast that he lost the natural elasticity of his skin and while he had succeeded in losing the weight, it wasn't long before he gained it all back and more. Because of the sudden weight gain and lack of elasticity in his skin, he burst and died.

203

The bartender cracked a smile at Pete and looked around at the rest of us and said, "You guys have a drink on me." Match won! After finishing our victory drinks, we grabbed Pete and hustled him out the door. We congratulated him for besting the best tall tale teller in the United States.

Our journey continued until we reached the town of Cody, Wyoming and Harry's poor car quit on us. We found a garage and the repairs were going to cost several hundred dollars. We didn't have enough money between us so Harry decided to sell the car and take a flight to Seattle and on to Juneau. But there was a problem. The nearest airport with commercial flights was located in Billings, Montana. Billings was several hundred miles from Cody so we found a Trailways bus going from Cody to Billings with a stop in Deaver, Wyoming.

Buffalo Bill Cody, 1886

Ron would travel in the car with Pete and the guys and Harry and I would take the bus up to Billings and catch the flight to Seattle and rendezvous with the others there. We said our goodbyes and shook hands all around. Harry and I stood at the bus station and watched as the four intrepid travelers drove off into the sunset. We boarded our bus to Deaver and after a couple hours on the road reached the Trailways Café in downtown Deaver, Wyoming. We had about a three-hour wait before our bus to Billings arrived so we stowed our gear in a corner and looked around for something to do to pass the time. There was one pinball machine at the end of the bar so Harry and I started playing.

Not much was happening in Deaver and I mean not much. We had been there over an hour and hadn't seen one car pass by. Finally, in the distance, came the sound of an approaching vehicle. The waitress and the cook started placing bets on what type of vehicle it was going to be, a Ford or a Chevy. As the car got closer, they ran to the window and the waitress started yelling excitedly, "It's a Ford, it's a Ford. Jack you owe me a dollar."

"Melba, this is the third time this week you beat me. I ain't gonna' play no more. I done lost three dollars to you."

Just after the exchange, one of their regular customers came in. He was a grizzled old cowboy and he sauntered into the café and glanced over at Harry and me. "Whada you say Fellers?" The cook offered up, "Howdy Fred." Then the waitress chimed in and asked, "Where you been the last few days, Fred?"

"Oh I been up in the hills chasing cows. Melba, I think I'll have a cup of coffee and a piece of that cherry pie yonder."

"Coming right up Fred."

Fred started drinking his coffee and eating his cherry pie as we stayed in the corner shooting pinball. Every now and then Fred would look over at us as if we were a pair of aliens. He finished his first and second cups of coffee and placed his right elbow on the bar just beside his cup, propped his head up on his hand and within thirty seconds was fast asleep. Not only was he fast asleep but he was snoring loud enough to cover the sound of the pen balls banging into the sides of the machine. After about fifteen minutes another regular came into the Trailways Café. Clearly, another ole cowboy, he looked around, said hello to us and spotted Fred napping at the counter. He walked over to Fred and placed his hand on his shoulder and gave Fred a vigorous shake. Fred cocked his head around to the left and opened one eye and said, "Oh, Buck, it's you. Sit down and have a cup of coffee and a piece of pie. That cherry pie there's real good."

"Nah, I ain't hungry. I saw your truck and stopped in to see what you're planning to do tonight."

"Well Buck, I don't know whether to stay here and have another piece of pie or go home and go to bed." Harry and I decided that the life of a cowboy was not quite as exciting as it was portrayed in the movies.

Our bus to Billings arrived and we figured when we left, the 'excitement' was going to die down in Deaver. The driver put our duffel bags under the bus in the storage compartment and we got on board. As I climbed on the bus I glanced around at the passengers and lo and behold, I saw a very nice-looking girl sitting by herself near the front of the bus. I decided to take a chance and ask her if the seat next to hers was taken. The bus was only half full and she was a little surprised by my request and looked around as if to let me know there were plenty of other seats available. But she smiled demurely and invited me to sit down.

The ever-present Deaver, Wyoming hotbed of excitment; the Trailways Café.

I settled into my seat next to her and Harry sat across the aisle. The diesel roared to life, the bus driver closed the door, checked his rear view mirror, engaged the clutch and shifted into first gear and we headed up Highway 310 toward Billings, Montana. I introduced myself and asked her where she was going. She told me that she was on her way to White Plains, New York. She had volunteered to go into the ghettos to work with minorities. She told me how much guilt she had for the way white folks had treated the blacks. She smiled sweetly and asked where I was from. When I told her I was from South Carolina, she immediately assumed I was a racist and began to rail on and on about the terrible way black people were treated in the South.

Things weren't going in the direction I had hoped. I asked her where she was from and she told me she had grown up in Wyoming and that this was going to be her first trip east. She wouldn't allow me to change the subject and kept rattling on about racism and the awful people down South. I asked her a simple question. "Tell me, what do you think about the Indians?"

"Those filthy savages, they're nothing but a bunch of drunks and loafers. They wouldn't work to save their lives. They're useless!"

"Well lady, you're talking about my great-grandmother's people. She was a full blooded Cherokee Indian and you are the biggest hypocrite I've ever met."

With that, I got up and changed seats while Harry laughed. Harry wasn't just laughing. It was more like a guffaw. As a young red-blooded American boy, it took a lot to drive me away from an opportunity like that, but I decided that it just wasn't worth the effort. Looking back, I realized I learned a lot of lessons about different cultures during those intervening years and hopefully my lady friend learned about the world outside of her comfort zone too.

We rolled into Billings after another hour of traveling and got off the bus. We found a cheap motel for the night and went to the airport the next day to catch our flight to Seattle. Harry looked very sad and I asked him,

"Why the sad look?"

"Luke, I'm headin' back East. Maybe I'll try again next year."

"Ah, come on Harry."

"Nah, I've made up my mind. This 'car thing' has screwed up my summer. I'm going back to New Jersey and make sure I can earn enough money to replace my car."

"Well, okay, but you know you're gonna take a lot of ribbing. Everybody's going to be calling you 'Billings Brooks'.

"I can't help it Luke, my mind's made up."

So with that, I bought a ticket to Seattle and Harry bought one to New York. My flight to Seattle and on to Juneau was uneventful. Bud and Juanita were waiting for me up at the airport and we headed to their apartment and I spent the rest of the evening trying to keep up with Bud's drinking which was impossible. Ron arrived and we applied for a job with his old construction crew. I had decided to try something different for the summer.

The company we went to work for was salvaging metal from the old Juneau gold mine. My first day on the job was my last. I have a natural fear of heights since falling out of the top of a big pecan tree when I was eight years old. The gold mine was on the side of Mt. Juneau and there was a large sheet of iron perched on the edge of a cliff. My job was to crawl out on the sheet of metal and hook a chain to the iron plate so the crane could drag it up higher on the mountain. I walked out on the sheet of metal. It was about 30' x 15' and I had to attach a chain to an iron rod sticking up in the middle. About one third of the way, the iron sheet started sliding to the edge of the cliff. There was nowhere to go so I rode it for about ten feet before it finally stopped. Five feet of it was hanging over the edge of the cliff. That was too much for me and I decided that working for the Alaskan Fish and Game Department, although it didn't pay as well, wasn't as dangerous as climbing around on a cliff face.

Allen Owens and Pete Fuge arrived in Juneau. They had lost John Tomanack who had turned back for home as well. I had already gone to work for the Juneau branch of the Alaskan Department of Fish and Game as an assistant game warden. Pete and Allen had to wait a couple of weeks, before they were hired and then attended the same training camp I had two years earlier in Oliver's Inlet. After camp, they were assigned to the Hoonah district to guard the salmon runs there.

As described earlier, Hoonah is a small fishing village with a population of less than 500. Allen and Pete were staying in a small hotel in Hoonah when they weren't out guarding salmon streams. Since this was a commercial fishing village and Pete and Allen worked for the Alaska Department of Fish and Game which regulated commercial fishing, the locals weren't particularly friendly to my two fraternity brothers. The hotel was very small with only four or five rooms that were located upstairs over a restaurant/bar. One of their stays in Hoonah coincided with the first day of the month when most of the villagers received their checks. Allen said the line at the only liquor store in Hoonah wound down the entire boardwalk and that for the next three days there wasn't a sober person in the village.

The harbor of the idyllic and serene town of Hoonah, Alaska

I arrived earlier in Alaska that year and had decided to return to South Carolina in mid-July so I would have extra time to get in shape for my last year of football. I spent my days in Juneau, patrolling the coastal waters by boat and freshwater trout streams by auto and foot. I not only enforced commercial regulations but all fish and game laws, including sport fishing and hunting for the first time. I gave out several citations to tourists for fishing without a license and I was one of the officers who arrested an Italian Prince for shooting a brown bear out of season. He had a permit to take one brown bear a year and then he bought a second permit. He got his dates mixed up and shot the second bear during the same hunting season. The law required that he wait until the next fall before taking his second bear. Although the kill had taken place in a different calendar year, one hunting season spanned the winter and spring of two separate years. He was not happy about the arrest, nevertheless he paid his big fat fine without comment. He was really angry, however, when we confiscated the beautiful bear skin rug he'd had made from that second bear.

207

Concorde was the first civil aircraft to utilize the 'Fly by Wire' system. The first copy, called 001 and was manufactured in Toulouse on March 2, 1969.

These and other features permitted Concorde to attain an average speed of Mach 2.02 cruise (about 2140 km/h or 1330 mph) with a maximum altitude of 60,000 feet flying over twice the speed of conventional aircraft. It had a relatively high landing speed: 298 km/h (185 mph). Since engineers have used hard-aluminum (aluminum alloy) for the entire plane, due to low cost and ease of processing; the maximum temperature of aluminum supported was 127°C (260°F), limiting the maximum speed of Mach 2.02.

Photo: David Parker
BWP Media/Getty Images

I said goodbye to Bud and Juanita who, as always, had treated me as if I was their son. Ron had decided to transfer to Carson Newman, a small college in Tennessee to play football and Allen Owens transferred to Troy State University in Alabama. It was the last time I would see either of them for a while. I was still dating the girl from Virginia, so on my way home I took a detour to visit her. It was great seeing her and arguing with her brothers about politics again. From Virginia, I grabbed a Greyhound bus and arrived in Turkey Creek after a long twelve hour bus ride.

I got back to the lower 48 just in time to see the news about the incident at Chappaquiddick involving Ted Kennedy in which Mary Joe Kopechne died. The event that I was anxious to see was the Apollo 11 landing on the moon. My whole family sat up that night along with 500 million other people to watch Neil Armstrong take his first step from the Eagle Lander onto the moon; "One small step for man, one giant leap for mankind." There was other news, of course, in 1969. In January, Richard Nixon took office as the 37th President of the United States. President Dwight D Eisenhower passed away in March. The novel, "The Godfather" was published that year.

The Boeing 747 was put into service for the 1st time and the French-British supersonic jet, the Concorde, made its 1st flight at the Paris Air Show. The Concorde was an amazing flying machine. It flew at an altitude of 60,000 feet. From that height, passengers could see the curvature of the earth. The flight between New York and Paris took less than half the time of normal jet flights, three hours versus eight. The Concorde reached speeds of Mach 2.2 or around 1,354 miles per hour. I was fortunate enough to travel on it several times during the late 1980's.

Later that year, the government held the 1st draft lottery in the United States since World War II. I remember that day. The numbers, with accompanying birthdays were read over the radio as they were drawn. A low number meant you would be drafted. The higher your number, the lower your chance was of being drafted. As the numbers were announce over the radio, screams of anguish could be heard coming from the dorms and fraternity houses. " Oh my God, I'm number 23" was a common sound that day. My draft lottery number was 364. No draft for me.

Wal-Mart was incorporated as Wal-Mart Stores, Inc. The anti-war demonstrations were picking up speed all around the country and there was a second flight to the moon by Apollo 12. Although not as exciting as the 1st manned moon landing, it was still amazing to watch those guys strolling around up there.

The movie, *Midnight Cowboy*, was released and launched the careers of John Voight and Dustin Hoffman. I thought the movie was disgusting, but I did enjoy, *Butch Cassidy and the Sundance Kid* that starred Paul Newman and Robert Redford as two famous Western desperadoes. Music was still a big thing for kids in college and we paid close attention to what was on the radios and jukeboxes around town. The top seller for 1969 was *Whole Lotta Love*, by Led Zeppelin followed by *Proud Mary* and *Bad Moon Rising* by Credence Clearwater Revival. We listened to *Honky-Tonk Women* and *You Can't Always Get What You Want* by the Rolling Stones. Frank Sinatra sang a beautiful song, *My Way*. Politically we had to listen to, *He Ain't Heavy, He's My Brother*, by the Hollies and the melancholy, *A Rainy Night in Georgia*, sung by Brook Benton. Elvis was making a comeback and he hit the charts with his version of, *In the Ghetto*. Joe Cocker had a lot of imitators singing his hit, *She Came in through the Bathroom Window* at fraternity parties. There was a lot of so-called, "crossover artists". Bob Dylan came out with a country and western album and did a good job on the song, *Lay Lady Lay*. Johnny Cash made us all smile with his song, *A Boy Named Sue*. Roberta Flack sang the romantic, *The First Time Ever I Saw Your Face*. BJ Thomas had a hit theme song from the movie *Butch Cassidy and the Sundance Kid*, *Raindrops Keep Falling on My Head*. Glen Campbell made the charts with *Galveston*. The band Chicago released, *Nobody Really Knows What Time It Is*, Blood Sweat and Tears sang, *And When I Die*.

I was still listening to country music but my country music was changing. Affected by the crossover artists such as Elvis Presley, Glen Campbell, Bobbie Gentry, Kenny Rogers and Bobby Goldsboro, I felt their sounds were moving away from what I considered true country music. Merle Haggard's style was more to my liking and he had the smash hit, *Okie from Muskogee*. Charlie Pride had a string of hits, *Afraid of Losing You* and *All I Have To Offer You Is Me* and Buck Owens sang his version of *Johnny B Goode*. Tom T Hall continued to tell stories with his songs as in *A Week in a County Jail*. I enjoyed hearing Jerry Lee Lewis sing just about anything and I loved the lyrics of his song, *She Even Woke Me up to Say Goodbye*. Roger Miller put out his version of *Me and Bobby McGee* and Marty Robbins released, *It's a Sin*.

CHAPTER 11

'The Championship
Comes Home to Roost'

The team reported back to The Roost on a hot day, August 20, 1969. Our first game was a month away against Duke. In the two preceding years the Gamecocks had been just a couple of steps away from vying for a conference championship, but success had eluded us for various reasons. The 1967 team had played very well against tough opposition, but we had no reserves. When any of the starters were injured it really hurt our chances of winning. We still had an opportunity to win the ACC Championship by beating a Wake Forest team that had won only one game, but that victory slipped away from us. We had another chance to win, at least, a share of the championship by beating Clemson, but the fates were not kind and neither were the Tigers, as we lost that game in Columbia and wound up with a five and five record.

Our '68 team came into fall camp expecting to improve on the '67 record and perhaps take the ACC Championship for the first time. But the team didn't gel for reasons previously cited until the end of the season. By then it was too late for a championship run. We did have the satisfaction of beating Clemson 7 to 3 and we had a sensational comeback game against North Carolina earlier that year. To speculate on what could have been is interesting, but '67 and '68 were in the record books.

Coaching transitions are often tumultuous and a lot of talented players had left for various reasons. The new coaching staff had to make evaluations of the program they had inherited but as players recruited by the previous coaching staff, we had sometimes been treated like redheaded stepchildren. Those of us who were left from the Bass years decided we weren't going away quietly. As seniors, we were playing not only for our current team, but also for all of those departed stepchildren. Motivation is one of the most important keys to winning football games, wherever it comes from.

Open and fair competition for playing time is essential for success. This is especially true for football teams. It is also true that you must have a close-knit team to be successful. The key is to have good competition for starting roles, balanced with respect and friendship among the team. When some players felt cheated out of their opportunity to play because of favoritism, it made the other component of the equation, molding a team, much more difficult. In my opinion, that is what makes a handful of football coaches successful year after year. They have the knack of fitting the two pieces together. They can build a team that puts the best athletes on the field while maintaining a tight-knit group. Those teammates look out for each other, on and off the field.

For the most part, attrition had taken care of the competition component of the winning formula. The job of molding us into a championship team now fell to the coaches and the seniors. Coach Dietzel and his staff had done a great job of recruiting some very good athletes. To

THE 1969 GAMECOCKS

Coach Paul Dietzel predicts the Fighting Gamecocks will be a stronger football squad in 1969, but "perhaps not as strong as some of our alumni think."

Coach Dietzel enters his fourth season at Carolina better stocked with players than at any time since he arrived in April 1966. There are 30 lettermen on hand plus sophomores up from a second straight unbeaten freshman squad.

"We have more athletes, more experience and more depth," Dietzel says, "but we are not without some question mark areas. We worked hard to solve these problems in spring practice."

TROUBLE SPOTS

The biggest trouble spots appear to be offensive center, defensive rover and middle guard, primarily due to inexperience at these spots.

Wally Orrel, who has graduated, was an All-Atlantic Coast Conference choice at rover last year and Dietzel said of his departure "you don't lose a football player like Wally Orrel without creating some problems. He was like a coach on the field; one of the smartest football players we have ever coached." Heir-apparent to the spot in the Gamecock secondary is sophomore Bo Davies, a former high school all-state quarterback in Pennsylvania who is a fine athlete and outclassed all other candidates in spring practice.

At middle guard, the Gamecocks lost Tim Bice, a 1967 All-ACC choice who was hampered by injuries last year, and Dave (Mudcat) Grant, a hard-nosed three-year letterman who was as tough as they come. Kevin Mooney, who was injured shortly before the 1968 season began, underwent knee surgery and wound up a redshirt, was the top middle guard at the end of spring practice. He is big (6-4, 218), quick and aggressive, and has fine potential.

Last year's most valuable player was center Bob Mauro, a converted tackle, who took over the pivot his senior year and did a great job. There are two lettermen listed as potential successors to Mauro but the position is not as experienced as it seems. Danny Dyches—a giant

213

at 6-5, 260—was shifted to center the final week of spring practice due to injuries to other personnel after lettering as a reserve offensive tackle last fall. He adjusted well in the short period and was number one at the end of spring drills. Ken Ross, a senior, earned a letter last fall, primarily in a specialty role of snapping the football for punts, field goals and extra points. Steve Vasgaard, a redshirt, was number one center until he underwent knee surgery just prior to the shift of Dyches and he will be in the picture if his injury heals in time.

STRONG SPOTS

Elsewhere, the Gamecocks can start a veteran at every position with the most depth at defensive end—where there are two lettermen on each side—and quarterback where Tommy Suggs and Randy Yoakum return from last year to face a challenge from sophomores Glenn Morris and Tommy Rhodes.

Offensively, all-time Gamecock pass receiving champion Fred Zeigler returns to split end for his senior season after a year at flanker. Tackles Dave DeCamilla and Tony Fusaro return as do guards Don Buckner and Chris Bank; and Doug Hamrick is back at tight end. In the backfield, Warren Muir is healthy again at fullback, Rudy Holloman was last year's leading rusher at tailback, and as previously mentioned, there is depth at quarterback. With Zeigler returned to split end, the flanker spot has gone to Ken Walkup, who lettered as a sophomore halfback last fall, with competition from non-letterman junior Tom Trevillian, a former fullback.

Defensively, four ends of near equal ability —Dave Lucas, Lynn Hodge, Jimmy Pope and Joe Wingard—make this the strongest area on the Gamecock squad. At tackle, Rusty Ganas (6-5, 238) and Jimmy Poston (6-4, 258), started as sophomores last year and are now seasoned veterans. Both are big, strong and good football players. The middle guard and rover back situations were discussed earlier and at linebacker there are three lettermen led by Al Usher, who established himself as a sophomore as one of the finest athletes on the squad. He's the starter at the weak side linebacker position with Benny Padgett, who started part of the

214

time as a sophomore, at the strong side. Mack Lee Tharpe also lettered as a sophomore at linebacker. Pat Watson, who set a conference pass interception record, is back for his third season as starting right halfback. Roy Don Reeves is gone on the left side, but Don Bailey who lettered as swing man last fall takes over. Sophomore speedster Dick Harris also figures in the halfback picture. At safety, Tyler Hellams is one of the top athletes in the ACC, starring in both football and track. His 73-yard punt return was the winning edge in last fall's Clemson game.

The kicking game will be about the same with soccer-style little Billy DuPre handling extra point and field goal attempts and Bill Parker the punting. Last year's kickoff man, Richard Genoble, is gone and it's not yet certain who will do the kicking off this fall.

LOSSES

Chief losses from last year include captain Johnny Gregory at split end; alternate captain Benny Galloway, a top performer at halfback or fullback; most valuable player Bob Mauro at center; All-ACC Wally Orrel at rover; three-year starter Roy Don Reeves at defensive halfback; 1967 All-ACC Tim Bice, Dave Grant and Ron Bunch at middle guard and linebacker; and Wally Medlin from the defensive secondary.

SOPHOMORES

Sophomores up from last year's second straight unbeaten freshman team who may break into the dressout squad include Bo Davies at rover back, Jim Mitchell at split end, Ken Wheat and Richie Moye at offensive guard; Bill Boyte, offensive tackle; Billy Freeman, tight end; Glenn Morris and Tommy Rhodes at quarterback; Billy Ray Rice at tailback; Tommy Simmons at fullback; Jake Wright at defensive tackle; Pat Kohout at middle guard; and Dick Harris, Jake Stone and Jimmy Nash in the secondary.

Kevin Mooney at middle guard and Steve Vasgaard at center, if his knee surgery is healed, are the top redshirts.

LETTERMEN

RETURNING

OFFENSE

SPLIT END—Fred Zeigler (2), Eddie Bolton (1)
TIGHT END—Doug Hamrick (1)
TACKLES—Tony Fusaro (2), Dave DeCamilla (1)
GUARDS—Don Buckner (2), Chris Bank (1)
CENTER—Danny Dyches (1), Ken Ross (1)
QUARTERBACK—T o m m y Suggs (1), Randy
    Yoakum (1)
TAILBACK—Rudy Holloman (2)
FULLBACK—Warren Muir (2)
FLANKER—Ken Walkup (1)

LOST

SPLIT END—Johnny Gregory (3)
TIGHT END—Gene Schwarting (3)
GUARD—Bob Morris (2)
CENTER—Bob Mauro (2)
TAILBACK—Benny Galloway (3)

RETURNING

DEFENSE

END—Dave Lucas (2), Lynn Hodge (2), Jimmy
    Pope (1), Joe Wingard (1)
TACKLE—Rusty Ganas (1), Jimmy Poston (1)
LINEBACKER—Al Usher (1), Benny Padgett (1),
    Mack Lee Tharpe (1)
HALFBACK—Pat Watson (2), Don Bailey (1)
ROVER—Candler Boyd (1)*
SAFETY—Tyler Hellams (1), Andy Chavous (1)*

LOST

TACKLE—John Coleman (1)
MIDDLE GUARD—Tim Bice (3), Dave Grant (3)
LINEBACKER—Ron Bunch (2)
HALFBACK—Roy Don Reeves (3)
ROVER—Wally Orrel (3), Wally Medlin (2)

RETURNING

SPECIALISTS

PLACEKICKER—Billy DuPre (1)
PUNTER—Bill Parker (1)

LOST

PLACEKICKER—Richard Genoble (1)

Note: Number in parentheses is the number of letters earned. Asterisk indicates last lettered in 1967.

DEPTH CHART

Although revisions are certain before the Fighting Gamecocks line up for the season opener, a tentative depth chart based on spring practice, last season's performances, etc., is listed at right. Lettermen in all caps, spring practice weights in parentheses.

OFFENSE

Split end—
  80 FRED ZEIGLER (183)
  90 EDDIE BOLTON (205)
  20 Jim Mitchell (156)
Left tackle—
  DAVE DECAMILLA (230)
  Rick Hipkins (254)
Left guard—
  DON BUCKNER (196)
  Ken Wheat (236)
Center—
  DANNY DYCHES (260)
  KEN ROSS (200)
  Steve Vasgaard (217)
Right guard—
  CHRIS BANK (233)
  Richie Moye (200)
Right tackle—
  TONY FUSARO (238)
  Bill Boyte (234)
Tight end—
  DOUG HAMRICK (214)
  Billy Freeman (198)
Quarterback—
  TOMMY SUGGS (180)
  RANDY YOAKUM (197)
  Glenn Morris (193)
  Tommy Rhodes (197)
Tailback—
  RUDY HOLLOMAN (172)
  Billy Ray Rice (188)
  Bob Miranda (191)
Fullback—
  WARREN MUIR (197)
  Tommy Simmons (202)
Flanker—
  KEN WALKUP (189)
  Tom Trevillian (196)

DEFENSE

Left end—
  LYNN HODGE (206)
  JIMMY POPE (209)
Left tackle—
  JIMMY POSTON (258)
  Jake Wright (219)
Strong linebacker—
  BENNY PADGETT (194)
  MACK LEE THARPE (219)
Middle guard
  Kevin Mooney (218)
  Pat Kohout (214)
  Greg Crabb (194)
Weak linebacker—
  AL USHER (211)
  Randy Williams (205)
Right tackle—
  RUSTY GANAS (238)
  George McCarthy (216)
Right end—
  DAVE LUCAS (189)
  JOE WINGARD (209)
Left halfback—
  DON BAILEY (182)
  Dick Harris (156)
Rover—
  Bo Davies (181)
  Jake Stone (178)
  Carroll Jones (178)
Safety—
  TYLER HELLAMS (158)
  ANDY CHAVOUS (183)
Right halfback—
  PAT WATSON (152)
  Bob O'Harra (181)

15

my knowledge, both the older players and the new players seemed to get along just fine. The players recruited by the new coaching staff were the same mix of personalities and talent that had been recruited by the old staff. It was the usual ménage of characters.

Our offensive line was bigger than it had been in the four years prior. We also had depth at most positions. At the center position were Danny Dykes and Ken Ross, both juniors. At tackle, were David Decamilla and Rick Hipkins, both juniors. At the guard positions Chris Bank, a junior and Tony Fasaro, a senior, were ready to play and the tight end position was filled by two capable guys in Tom Trevillian and Doug Hamrick. Our wide receiver position was led by the record-setting hands of Freddy Zeigler, another senior classmate of mine, along with Jimmy Mitchell, a sophomore. The running back corps was led by the All-American candidate Warren Muir, a senior, Rudy Holloman, a senior, Bobby Miranda, a junior, along with capable backups, Tommy Simmons, a sophomore, Billy Ray Rice, and Ken Walkup, both juniors. They were joined in the backfield by star quarterback Tommy Suggs, a junior and also Randy Yoakum, a junior, who always seem to shine when given the chance.

Our defensive line was going to be good, particularly with juniors, Rusty Ganas and big Jimmy Poston as tackles backed up by Big G and Jake right. Lynn Hodge, a senior, was a starter at the left defensive end position and I was the right defensive end. Additionally, we had Jimmy Pope and Joe Wingard who were both lettermen. It was going to be a solid, if not very good defensive unit. We had Donnie Buckner, a senior, at nose guard. Our linebackers were Benny Padgett, a junior, Pat Kohout, Byron Sistare and Greg Crabb, all sophomores. Playing behind me at right cornerback was Pat Watson, a senior. The other cornerback position was played by Dicky Harris, a sophomore and future All American.

ATLANTIC COAST CONFERENCE FAMILY PORTRAIT

Candler Boyd, a junior, Don Bailey, a junior along with Jimmy Nash and Bo Davies, both sophomores, were very talented, in the defensive secondary.

In an attempt to foster competition for starting positions, it was Coach Dietzel's policy to give the starting team some additional perks. Coach Dietzel always rode with the starting offensive and defensive units in the lead bus. The starting players received four game tickets and the second-team only received two. The starters lived in a one story dorm closest to the dining facility and in team meetings and film reviews, the first-team sat in the front and the second-team sat in the rear.

Yoakum Fires Two TD Passes

USC 'Wilted' In Drills

Paul Dietzel: Team 'Wilted'

Two long touchdown passes from quarterback Randy Yoakum to split end Fred Zeigler highlighted an otherwise lackluster South Carolina scrimmage Saturday.

After more than a week of cool, rainy weather, it was hot and humid at the Rex Enright Athletic Center and in the words of head coach Paul Dietzel, "we wilted."

"It wasn't a very good game," Dietzel said of the scrimmage which saw three touchdowns scored, all on passes, plus a 36-yard field goal by specialist Billy Du Pre.

First team quarterback Tommy Suggs was held out of the workout with a sore arm and Yoakum, running the first team, hit Zeigler in the clear on the third play of the day for a 60-yard touchdown bomb.

Later, the same combination clicked for 47 yards.

In between, sophomore Glen Morris — aided by a 15-yard penalty on a fourth down situation — directed the second offensive team 80 yards for a touchdown. Morris passed 12 yards to fullback Tommy Simmons for the score.

The defense was hampered by the absence of both its starting tackles. Jimmy Poston was called home to Can-

ton, N. C., due to illness in his family and Rusty Ganas was in the University infirmary with a temperature. Starting offensive tackle Rick Hipkins also missed the scrimmage with a temperature.

Dietzel used fullback Warren Muir and tailback Rudy Holloman sparingly, preferring to take a long look at his younger backs, Billy Ray Rice at tailback and Simmons at fullback.

"We didn't get much done running the football," Dietzel said. "It wasn't a very good exhibition of football. I thought Yoakum did a good job except for one interception he threw and Morris showed promise in the touchdown drive he called. Otherwise, I didn't see anybody that looked great."

The University ticket office will begin the week with less than 1,500 tickets remaining

for the Oct. 11 game with N. C. State, 2500 for the Sept. 27 meeting with North Carolina, and about 4,000 for the Oct. 25 homecoming game with Maryland. The Sept. 20 opener with Duke is already a sellout as is the Nov. 22 game with Clemson, although fans can still see the Clemson game on closed circuit television in Carolina Coliseum.

JUST ARRIVED For FALL
- SUITS
- SPORTCOATS
- SLACKS

Wright Johnston

Fred Zeigler . . . Snares 2 TD Tosses

The second-team players declared that they were being treated like shit. Shit was brown, so instead of being called the second-team, they became known as the 'Brown' team. I'm not sure if the coaching staff ever figured out the derivation of the name because they began to use the terminology informally, as well. The Brown team also developed a nickname for the starting team. As starters we were called the "Sporty Top 40." The Brown team had its own mystique. If a player was demoted to the 2nd team, there was an initiation ceremony held to induct them into the ways of the Brown Team. They had their own captains and took every opportunity to prove they had more fun than the starters. It was because they felt they had less scrutiny by the coaching staff in general and Coach Dietzel in particular.

Dietzel—USC Defense 'Best We'

Offensive Line Is Question Mark

By HERMAN HELMS
Executive Sports Editor

"We should have the best defensive team we've had here. . .if Warren Muir doesn't make the All-America team, there's something wrong with the system. . .we're still unsettled in the offensive line. . .this is my fourth year of watching Fred Zeigler and I still don't believe him."

These were some of the comments that University of South Carolina Coach Paul Dietzel made during an interview here Tuesday morning with writers and broadcasters making the annual tour of Atlantic Coast Conference football camps.

It has been a sad start to this season for Dietzel. A few days before practice began, George Terry, his longtime coaching associate, died. Early Monday morning, death came to a freshman football player, Steve Sisk.

There was heartbreak in Dietzel's face and in his voice when he faced the writers Tuesday. He prefaced his remarks on the football team with some personal thoughts about the young player and the veteran coach who are gone.

"I've never served a season as a head football coach without George Terry at my side," he said. "He was a tremendous professional as well as a personal loss to me.

"As to the loss of that fine young man on Monday morning. . .well, there's no way to express how I feel about that, no way at all. Sometimes grief is too deep for words."

But life must go on and there is a football season approaching. The men of the news media had come to town for some football talk and Dietzel obliged them with the lowdown on the Gamecocks.

"Probably the strongest position on our team is defensive end," the lanky coach observed. "We have four lettermen there, and they're all good ball players. I think in Rusty Ganas and Jimmy Poston we have potentially the best pair of tackles we've had here, and I don't believe there is a linebacker in this part of the country who's better than Al Usher.

"We've got the best set of athletes we've had in our secondary. The only two sophomores that we'll start on defense — Bo Davies and Dick Harris — are part of our secondary. They will make some sophomore mistakes, but they're so quick that they'll make up for them."

Dietzel turned to the USC offense and cited the offensive line as a question mark of the club. "When we moved Don Buckner from offensive guard to middle guard on defense, we had to juggle our offensive line," he said. "The situation is still not settled. We may change again before the

Fred Zeigler . . . Dietzel's Finest

220

The Brown team kept it very low key and accepted it all as great fun. The captain of the Brown team was my old roommate, Big G from DC.

Our fall camp went very well. The excitement grew. Our offense was really clicking and defensively, we were ready to get the season started. Our opening game was on September 20th, at home against Duke. We remembered that Duke had beaten us the year before in Columbia. That loss had been hard to take. It was close, but it had started us on a downward slope at the beginning of the season and it had been difficult to recover. We reminded the coaching staff that the 50-short defense might have cost us the game. The same quarterback for Duke, Leo Hart, was back again with another year's experience under his belt and a lot of ACC passing records to his credit. He had thrown the ball all around Carolina Stadium the year before and we expected him to do the same in our opening ball game.

On Fridays, before our home games, we would go to The Roundhouse, get dressed in our game uniforms, board the bus and head to the stadium. We would take to the field, walk through our assignments and go over our game plan. After forty-five minutes or so, we would head back to The Roundhouse and put on our street clothes. This time, when we return to The Roundhouse, we were told to assemble in our auditorium upstairs. This was unusual. Normally we would just get dressed and go back to The Roost. As we gathered, everyone was questioning the reason for the special meeting. Maybe, after waiting three years, we were finally going to get the pregame address that would kindle extra enthusiasm and give us the winning edge.

ve Had Here'

season opens. We've got the biggest offensive line we've had here, but I don't know how good it is.

"We're in fine shape at quarterback with Tommy Suggs, who has a knack for getting the football into the end zone, backed up by Randy Yoakum and two fine sophomores in Tommy Rhodes and Glenn Morris. The tipoff to our backfield is that even Warren Muir must look over his shoulder at some competition this year.

"Warren is the finest inside runner in college football in my book. If he doesn't make the All-America team there's something wrong with the system. I've coached All-Americans. I believe I know one when I see one, and Warren is one.

"But we've got a sophomore, Tommy Simmons, who is a fine replacement. With Tommy available, we can take Warren out of the game and rest him some and not mess up our offense. The same goes for Rudy Holloman at tailback; Rudy is our best open field runner, but he's got a sophomore, Billy Ray Rice, breathing down his neck.

"Our passing game should be strong, if for no other reason than that we have Tom-

my Suggs and Fred Zeigler. Tommy can throw it, and Zeigler can catch it — how he can catch it! He's the finest receiver I've ever coached. He has poor vision and must wear contact lens. He can't see the football, but he sure catches it. I think he must smell it coming. I've seen him make catches in practice for four years that I just don't believe."

The coach had a lot on his mind Tuesday. A lot of sadness was sealed up inside him, but the world must go on. Men from the news media had come to town to hear some football talk, and he gave them the lowdown on the Gamecocks.

We heard the door open that led to Coach Dietzel's office and two striking men entered the auditorium. As Coach Dietzel addressed the team, it was hard to take your eyes off the imposing figure that stood near the podium. He was dressed immaculately in a tailored suit with monograms on the cuffs and his gold cufflinks sparkled in the auditorium lights. Each hair on his head was meticulously in place and his blue eyes were shining with an intensity that we weren't used to seeing.

Coach Frank McGuire looked around and said, "Boys, Coach Dietzel has asked me to speak to you this evening and I am proud to have the chance to address this team."

Coach Frank McGuire

221

tion E   Columbia, South Carolina, Sunday, September 14, 1969   Page One

...And Grown Men Turn Into Kids

College Football—It's Only A Game!

ute Rockne...Master Coach

A hundred years to produce. A cast of tens of thousands. A cost of millions. That's College Football, 1969 — a show that begins its annual three-month stand around the nation in full force Saturday afternoon.

It's only a game, of course. But what a game! A rich heritage. An unlimited future. Action that turns grown men into school kids. A chance for a youngster from the wrong side of the tracks to win the hearts of millions. An opportunity that throws race, color and creed out the window and puts man against man.

The Four Horsemen. The Seven Blocks of Granite. Mr. Inside and Mr. Outside. Knute Rockne. Jim Thorpe. The Gipper. The Galloping Ghost. O. J. Mighty Mo. And more, many more.

All carved their niche in college football's history. All helped to make it what it is today. But so did others. The lowliest scrub. The guy who never played. He's not remembered, but

College football reaches a milestone when it begins its 100th season Saturday. Special writer Bob Spear takes a nostalgic look at the past both in South Carolina and across the nation—and a brief glance into the future of the college game.

he did his part, too. He helped.

Rutgers and Princeton tangled in the first game in New Brunswick, N. J., November 6, 1869. This season, 612 colleges and universities will put teams on the field.

The game started in the East and did not spread rapidly. The West Coast got its first

taste in 1892, but Eastern influence prevailed into the 20th century.

The date football fever put its initial germs in South Carolina is a mystery. Wofford records reveal a 5-1 victory over Furman in 1889. Furman records don't go back that far. At any rate, it's safe to call the situation disorganized until the turn of the century.

But the late start, no matter when, has not stunted the game's growth in the Palmetto State. The fans flock to the stadium these days, whether its Carolina-Clemson or Furman-Citadel.

And Red Grange, the Four Horsemen and O. J. Simpson don't have a doggone thing on the athletes who displayed their skills for South Carolina schools. From Erskine's Dode Phillips to Clemson's Buddy Gore, Wofford's Ted Phelps and South Carolina's Warren Muir, the performers have sparkled like the

(See FOOTBALL, Page 9-E, Col. 1)

(Continued From 1-E)

stars on a clear night.

The greatest game? The greatest player? Who can say? Who can pick one performance or one player over another from such a multitude of great ones?

Dode Phillips. The old-timers say he could do it all. But is he better than a Buddy Gore or a Ted Phelps? Look at their records. Check out Steve Wadiak or Banks McFadden or Bobby Pate or Clyde Hewell or Billy Matsy or Paul Maguire or any of a bushel more.

Rivalries? Fierce and tremendous is the best description, Carolina-Clemson. Furman-Citadel. Presbyterian-Newberry. Wofford-Presbyterian. Newberry-Wofford. None take a back seat to the Army-Navy clash.

Big Thursday, the name hung on the Carolina-Clemson showdown until it became an end-of-the-season, due-to-the-death affair after the 1959 game, brought the state a mountain of publicity and some of the state's fondest football memories. That the Thursday - afternoon - during-Fair-Week date is only a relic has not altered the situation.

Great games? Another bushel basketful. Dick Christy's one-man show — all his team's 29 points, including the tie-breaking field goal after the clock expired — in leading N. C. State to a 29-26 victory over South Carolina in Carolina Stadium in 1957 will do for a starter. Either in this state or on the moon.

But what about South Carolina's 17-16 victory over Clemson in '65 or Presbyterian's 26-6 conquest of Newberry in '59 or Clemson's near-miss

against national champion LSU in the '59 Sugar Bowl or Wofford's 35-27 triumph over Lenoir Rhyne a few years back or Clemson's 24-23 Gator Bowl win over Missouri? The list is endless.

Coaches? Lonnie McMillian and Walter Johnson at Presbyterian, Rex Enright at South Carolina, Phil Dickens at Wofford, Billy Laval at Furman, Laval, Fred MacLean and Harvey Kirkland at Newberry. And, of course, Frank Howard at Clemson, who is the dean of the nation's college coaches today.

Oddities? It's hard to top Wofford's unbelievable five ties during 1948. The Terriers won four that season and finished with perhaps the weirdest record ever posted—4-0-5.

Individual performances? Like the rest of the other categories, it's impossible to

choose one over a bunch of others. Steve Wadiak's 256-yards rushing that helped South Carolina to a 14-14 tie against Clemson's 10-0-1 team in 1950 might be a good place to start. But Don King's 234-yards rushing in Clemson's 12-12 draw with Fordham in 1952 would be hard to overlook.

There's really no place to stop.

Maybe Red Grange's 402-yard afternoon that produced five touchdowns in Illinois' 39-14 romp over Michigan in 1924 or the Four Horsemen "outlined against the blue-gray October sky" riding again or Jim Thorpe going wild for the Carlisle Indians o u t s h i n e performances by South Carolina athletes. Maybe.

No matter. South Carolina's heritage can stand with the

rest. No ifs, ands, or buts.

Now, the big show is getting ready to raise the curtain for its centennial year. It's a vastly improved game from the one Rutgers and Princeton played a century ago and it's getting better all the time.

We were astonished. There had been a rumor circulating that Coach Dietzel and Coach McGuire did not always see eye to eye. Just the fact that he was there was enough to hold our attention. The entire team slid forward in their seats in anticipation.

"You fellows are opening up with those bastards from Duke. I've hated the sons of bitches since 1936. I was a starting pitcher for St. John's when we played Duke and they ran a ringer in on me. I was just a kid, but I knew what they were doing and those people do it every chance they get. They sure screwed up your season last year and I hope you're not going to let them get away with it again. You fellows have a great team here and it sure would be a terrible shame to let those assholes from Durham ruin another season."

The more Coach McGuire talked, the lower our jaws dropped and the higher the adrenaline rose in our veins. By the time he was finished we were ready to play the game right then and there. It was one of those kick-ass kinds of talks that came at just the right time. We were ready to kick some butt. There was no way we were going to lose to the 'despised' Blue Devils. That would've disappointed Coach McGuire, whom we all admired. He had an amazing style, a winning tradition and obviously an innate ability to motivate. It was an honor to have Frank McGuire talk to us and a smart move by Coach Dietzel.

Football Kickoff

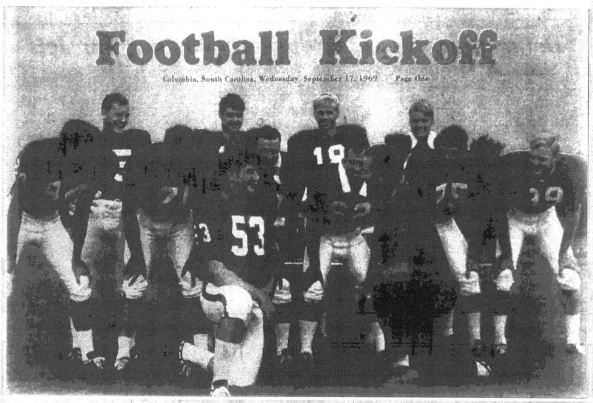

Dietzel And His Defenders

Coach Paul Dietzel Huddles With The Defensive Team That He Calls His Best At USC. Back Row (Left To Right) Are Pat Watson, Tyler Hellams, Bo Davies And Dick Harris. Middle Row (L. To R.) Are Dave Lucas, Rusty Ganas, Al Usher, Don Buckner, Jim Poston And Lynn Hodge. Kneeling With Dietzel Is Benny Padgett.

Staff Photo by Vic Tutte

'69 Gamecocks Should Be Dietzel's Best

Clemson Strength Is Passing Attack

By HAROLD MARTIN
State Sports Writer

In the not-too-distant past, Clemson could be expected each and every fall to exhibit some of the finest-looking football beef in the country and woe betide any foe who tried to butt heads with the muscular Tigers.

Those who chose not to wrestle, though, found that quick-striking offenses and defenses could neutralize Clemson's massive linemen and some Tiger foes experienced considerable success over the past couple of seasons.

This fall, though inexperienced and somewhat of a question mark in the Atlantic Coast Conference, Clemson has discarded its old-time muscle and Frank Howard's 30th edition of the Tigers has taken on a "lean-'n-mean" posture.

Not that the Tigers have given up on muscle altogether. You still have no trouble finding tackles in the 240-260 range. But these days, the Tiger linemen stretch up rather than sideways and in general they are more agile than their stocky predecessors.

All this means that Howard, certainly one of the youngest 60-year-olds in the country, is likely to put forth one of the most explosive attacks in a long and glory-laden career in the South Carolina foothills.

"I think we're going to have a pretty fair running attack," Howard drawls, "and a heckuva passing game."

Giving the statement added emphasis is the fact that it was made so close to the opening game this weekend at Virginia. Howard was speaking as football coach rather than athletic director, a position which Howard also holds at Clemson.

Clemson, which has won more outright league championships (5) than any other school since the Atlantic Coast Conference was formed, lost heavily from the offensive and defensive lines of a year ago.

The Tigers, who could have won their sixth conference crown last fall by beating arch-foe South Carolina in the final game, had five All-ACC performers in 1968. All were lost to graduation. Five starters from each of the lines have also departed.

Graduation also took workhorse Buddy Gore, the Tigers' brilliant halfback who is the school's all-time rushing leader.

Gamecock Express

USC Fullback Warren Muir Blasts For Yardage Against Clemson In Gamecocks' Upset Victory Last Season.

(Staff photo by Dave Underwood)

It goes without saying, then, that Howard has a lot of holes to fill. First and foremost, however, he had to find a quarterback and he came up with two, both untested sophomores.

Baby-faced Tommy Kendrick, an unheralded six-footer from Stone Mountain, Ga., had taken a back seat to Easley's Rick Gilstrap during most of the preseason speculation, but has handled the first unit slightly more than half the practice time and may be

(See SOPHS, 3-C, Col. 4)

Sophs Will Start In USC Secondary

(Continued From Page 1-B)

breathing down his neck.

But the one position that undercores the Gamecock depth better than any other is the fullback slot. Warren Muir, prime candidate for All-America honors, one of the most explosive ball carriers in USC history, "the best inside runner in college football" in Dietzel's words, has competition. Yes, even Warren Muir.

Sophomore Tommy Simmons looks like a most capable understudy to the renowned Gamecock senior. "For the first time since Warren has played here, we can take him out of a game and give him some rest and not mess up our offense," says Dietzel. "We have that much confidence in Simmons."

Ken Walkup and Tom Trevillian, two juniors, are contesting for the flanker back slot. Walkup will start there, and—Dietzel expects good things from him. "Kenny is a better football player than he showed last season," argues the coach.

In addition to Suggs and Muir and Holloman, the Gamecocks have some other outstanding individuals — one in particular. Split end Fred Zeigler is almost in a class of

PAUL DIETZEL
Expects Improved Squad

his own as a pass receiver. Dietzel calls him "the finest receiver I've ever coached."

Linebacker Al Usher, a junior, is one of the best in the ACC, junior defensive tackles Rusty Ganas and Jimmy Poston glitter with potential and defensive safety Tyler Hellams proved in the Clemson game last season that he is a special kind of player.

Two sophomores will start in Saturday's opener with Duke, both in the defensive

secondary. Bo Davies, a brilliant high school quarterback and a superior athlete, will be the rover back and Dick Harris, a swift and tough little man, will open at left half.

Dietzel has no qualms, no qualms at all, about using these two newcomers. "Davies is just a fine athlete," the coach states. "Harris will make some sophomore mistakes, but he's so fast he can compensate for them."

"We're going to have the biggest offensive line we've had here," he states, "but I don't know how good it will be."

Dietzel appraises his squad in this manner: "We've got better people and more of them than we've had in past seasons here. We should be faster on defense, we should be bigger and stronger on offense. But how quick or fast we will be on offense remains to be seen. We will have better balance in our attack. Our passing game is sound. We have an excellent quarterback and an excellent receiver. Our running game hasn't been as good as we expected it to be in practices because we've had to shuffle our offensive line so much."

"In seasons past, we've had to take whoever was left over from offense and play them on defense," reflects Dietzel.

"But that is not the case at all with our present defensive team. We're playing then on defense because they're good defensive players."

The Gamecocks have an explosive backfield, one of college football's finest pass receivers and the best defensive team in Dietzel's term at USC. But the Gamecocks have a problem. The offensive line is in a state of flux, and on the eve of the season Dietzel is still not sure what the outcome will be.

The switching of Don Buckner, an established offensive

Clemson Foe Nov. 22

guard, to the defensive middle guard post to replace Kevin Mooney, an academic casualty, set off a series of changes in the planned interior offensive line.

The Gamecocks, in brief, will be better. They will be contenders for the Atlantic Coast Conference championship, admittedly one of several contenders, but how often has South Carolina been contender for anything in football?

Gamecocks Meet Challenge, In Dying Moments To Knock

By HERMAN HELMS
Executive Sports Editor

South Carolina's Gamecocks, displaying class and strength in a challenging moment, marched 75 yards to a late touchdown and edged Duke, 27-20, in a thunderous season's opener at Carolina Stadium Saturday night.

Only one minute and 25 seconds remained in the dramatic struggle of Atlantic Coast Conference powers when fullback Warren Muir slashed two yards through left tackle for the game-winning score.

With just 6:20 left, Dave Pugh, the Blue Devils' kicking specialist, had boomed a 43-yard field goal to forge a 20-20 tie and put the pressure on the Gamecock offensive unit. They were equal to it.

Muir's strong legs and the good right arm of quarterback Tommy Suggs were the prime weapons as USC covered the long distance to victory in 12 plays. Muir opened the drive, which began at the Gamecock 25 following a kickoff return by Dick Harris, with a 10-yard burst and later took in a 16-yard pass from Suggs.

A 24-yard shot from Suggs to Fred Zeigler, the 100th catch of the super Gamecock end's collegiate career, was the third big play in the advance.

On first down from the two, Muir charged into the end zone as a sellout crowd of 42,791 went wild.

The Gamecocks, thanks to a dramatic 60-yard touchdown flight by halfback Rudy Holloman and a 20-yard field goal by Billy DuPre, carried a 10-3 lead to the dressing room at halftime. For one half, the Gamecocks found the defense for the passing of Duke's great quarterback Leo Hart in a brutal line rush.

Hart was held to just five completions in 12 attempts for a meager 28 yards in the first half. But it was a vastly different story in the final half as Hart found the range on 15 of 22 passes for 164 yards.

With Hart hot in the air and the Gamecocks continuing to expose an explosive running game, the final half was a raging offensive show that drained the emotions of the huge crowd.

A 51-yard scoring march led by Hart's passing and capped by a three-yard toss from the quarterback to Marcell Courtillet pulled Duke into a 10-10 tie with 8:32 left in the third period.

DuPre booted his second field goal of the night, a 37-yarder in the early minutes of the final period to send USC back out front, 13-10, but Duke came storming back once more behind Hart.

The Duke marksman, completing four of five passes for 52 yards, moved his team 79 yards in eight plays to the touchdown which got the Blue Devils back out front, 17-13.

Eleven minutes and 57 seconds remained in the tense battle when Hart hit Wes Chesson with an 18-yard scoring flip.

A little over a minute later, the Gamecocks had regained the lead, 20-17, on a 48-yard scoot through the right side by Suggs. The little quarter-

Staff Photos by Ed Tilte

Tommy Suggs Cuts Into Hole (1), Breaks Clear (R)...

...Picks Up Speed (L), Scores (C) And Gets Hug From Paul

Sweep 75 Yards Off Duke, 27-20

back, in a gorgeous bit of witchcraft, faked a handoff, but he kept the ball and darted through right tackle and scampered into the end zone

the bitter duel between a powerful USC running game and Duke's passing, keyed by the brilliant Hart. For the game, Hart was true on 20 of 35 tosses for 194 yards. The Gamecocks, meanwhile, compiled 446 yards in total offense, 339 of them coming on the ground.

Holloman, who produced the first of the game's series of spectacular plays with his 60-yard touchdown gallop in the second period, was USC's leading rusher with 113 yards in 16 carries. Suggs gained 98 yards in 15 trips, alternate halfback Billy Ray Rice gained 65 yards in six attempts and Muir slashed off 47 yards in 12 carries.

Suggs was true on ten of 16 passes for 107 yards. Zeigler was his top target, taking in six passes for 73 yards.

Defensive ends Jimmy Pope, Dave Lucas and Joe Wingard led the angry USC defense which shut Hart off in the first half.

without a single Blue Devil placing a hand on him.

Duke came back to drive from its 23-yard line to the Gamecock 27 where Pugh tied

Lucas also came up with key tackles in the final half, the biggest one being a rush job on Hart which produced an 11-yard loss and forced the Blue Devils to settle on Pugh's field goal in the final period.

Each team was handicapped by the loss of a star defensive performer. USC safety Tyler Hellams suffered an ankle injury while returning a kick in the first period and was never able to return to duty.

Hellams was carried to the USC infirmary where his injury was diagnosed late Saturday night as a fracture of the left leg. The junior defensive back is expected to be lost to the team for from four to six weeks.

Duke's stellar linebacker Dick Biddle had to leave the game several times as a result of a knee injury which he had suffered in the Blue Devils' final pre-game scrimmage a week ago.

the game once more, 20-20, with his 43-yard field goal.

Statistics told the story of

A Suggs fumble, which was scooped up by Duke linebacker Mike Fitzpatrick at the USC 33, set the stage for the game's first score. Eleven plays later, with the ball in play at the USC seven, Pugh kicked a 24-yard field goal to send the Blue Devils out front, 3-0.

Holloman, getting a great block from tackle dave De-Camilla, put the Gamecocks on the board with his 60-yard sprint with just 2:05 having passed in the second period. DuPre's 30-yard field goal, with 5:32 left, closed out the scoring for the first half.

	DUKE	SO. CAR.
First Downs	21	21
Yards rushing	112	339
Yards passing	194	107
Return yardage	21	
Passes	20-35-0	10-16-0
Punts	5-33.3	4-40.3
Fumbles lost	0	1
Yards penalized	20	77

Duke 3 0 7 10—20
South Carolina 0 14 0 17—27

Duke—FG Pugh 24
SC—Holloman 60 run (Du-Pre kick)
SC—FG DuPre 30
Duke—Courtillet 3 pass from Hart (Pugh kick)
SC—FG DuPre 34
Duke—Chesson 18 pass from Heart (Pugh kick)
SC—Suggs 48 run (DuPre kick)
Duke—FG Pugh 43
SC—Muir 2 run (DuPre kick)
A—42,791

DUKE Rushing

Player	Att.	Gain	Loss	Net	L.G.
Asack	17	73	0	73	13
Baglian	5	18	0	18	9
Chesson	5	28	17	11	14
Hart	10	11	44	-33	9
Cappellano	4	39	0	39	21
Hepler	1	4	0	4	4

Passing

Player	Att.	Compl.	Int.	Yds.	L.G.
Hart	34	20	0	194	18
Chesson	1	0	0	0	0

Pass Receiving

Player	No.	Yds.	TD	L.G.
Courtillet	7	91	1	18
Chesson	7	69	1	18
Dearth	3	31	0	17
Baglian	2	3	0	4

SOUTH CAROLINA Rushing

Player	Att.	Gain	Loss	Net	L.G.
Muir	12	47	0	47	11
Holloman	16	125	12	113	60
Suggs	15	105	7	98	48
Rice	6	65	0	65	16
Simmons	4	11	0	11	4
Walkup	2	5	0	5	3

Passing

Player	Att.	Compl.	Int.	Yds.	L.G.
Suggs	16	10	0	107	24

Pass Receiving

Player	No.	Yds.	TD	L.G.
Zeigler	6	73	0	24
Muir	2	23	0	16
Muir	3	23	0	16
Holleman	4	4	0	4
Hamrick	1	7	0	7

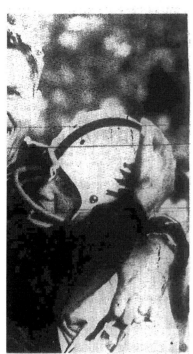

Staff Photo by Ed Tilley

Dietzel For 48-Yard Run

Students Form Line For Game Tickets

Football fever and a fierce rivalry combined Monday to put several hundred University of South Carolina students on the street in a pre-dawn lineup for Clemson game tickets.

Seniors, graduates and law students — many sitting on the ground wrapped in blankets — started forming a line shortly after midnight outside Carolina Coliseum to get tickets for the Nov. 22 game.

About two dozen spent the night. The number grew to more than 700 by the time the doors opened at 8 a.m. The situation will likely be repeated since juniors, sophomores and freshmen get tickets today through Thursday.

Breakers-in-line were almost non-existent, and any attempt to move forward was greeted by loud boos and taunts.

The crowd had a different reception, however, for food and coeds walking to early morning classes — cheers and whistles of appreciation.

About 5:30 a.m. students in the front of the line "engineered" an appearance by a doughnut truck. The salesman discharged a good portion of his cargo and roared off, accidentally dumping several boxes in the street. They didn't remain

long, however, as four students sprinted into the middle of the street to retrieve them.

The doughnut salesman returned a few minutes later with 10 cups of coffee which went immediately at a quarter a cup.

A milk truck passed shortly after the doughnut truck departed and was stopped by a group who lined up to buy quarts of milk for breakfast.

An even larger reception greeted a passing beer truck, but the driver declined to stop.

The crowd was for the most part good natured except when someone tried to break in line. "Red rover, red rover, send Jimmy Lee over," one group chanted to people across the street. Another shout arose, "I'd like to see somebody break this line."

A yearbook photographer braved the perils of his profession to get pictures of the front of the line where he was assaulted by a boxful of cookies thrown individually, some doughnuts and a dead squirrel.

Besides lining up for good seats, the students were seeking date tickets of which less than 400 were available. After the date ticket supply was exhausted, the line moved rapidly through the coliseum.

It was cool the night of the season opener and sure enough Leo Hart threw the football more often than he had the year before. Our coaching staff had learned its lesson, however, and we didn't play our 50-short defense except on goal line situations. Duke scored 20 points on us that night, but our offense played well and we hung 27 points on them for our first win. South Carolina Gamecocks 27, Duke Blue Devils 20.

The North Carolina Tar Heels came down to Carolina Stadium the next weekend. Our last contest in Chapel Hill was one of the greatest comeback games Carolina has ever played. We were determined not to let them get up a head of steam in Columbia. The year before, they had scored 29 points to our 3 during the first three quarters of the game. Defensively, we played much better. North Carolina only scored 6 points and South Carolina 14. It was another win for the Gamecocks. We were 2 and 0 and both wins were conference games.

16-C   THE STATE — Columbia, S.C., Wednesday, September 17, 1969

For Duke, Element Of Surprise Gone

By ADD PENFIELD, JR.
State Sports Writer

A year ago, few people knew of the existence of a rawboned Duke sophomore named Leo Hart. Everybody knew the Blue Devils had a problem at quarterback.

But it didn't take long for the young sophomore with the whiplash arm to make a dent in the Atlantic Coast Conference football scene. Calm under pressure, the sophomore "unknown" promptly led Duke to a surprising 14-7 upset of South Carolina.

In the weeks to follow, Leo Hart became a name to be feared and respected by all foes as he re-wrote the Duke and ACC passing record books in a dazzling display of passing wizardry.

Well, Hart is getting ready for "The Second Season" and the opposition has been plotting for months to see that the script is not re-written. Blue Devil Coach Tom Harp is well aware of what has been going through the minds of his foes.

"One thing we have lost with Leo," says Harp, "is the element of surprise. A year ago no one knew about him or what we meant about throwing the football. Now that the records are in, the films available to everyone and all the rest, other coaches are beginning to realize what the Duke pass offense is.

"They are all taking measures to combat it and we know that Leo won't have the openings that he had and he will be rushed harder," Harp continues. "This will force us into having check valves. The screens and draws are now much more important to our offense."

Hart's magical talents are obviously the keys to Duke's offensive success this fall, but the Blue Devil defense was often mutilated a year ago — so much so that Duke foes were often willing to let Hart have a fling or two just to get the opportunity to go against the porous Blue Devil defenders.

Yardage came by huge hunks in Blue Devil battles and seldom was there a chance for an opponent to come away without anything on the scoreboard.

"Our passing game," Harp relates, "has, of course, lost Henley Carter (an ACC-leading 65 pass receptions) and that undoubtedly will have an effect on us, although we still have a few good receivers

Clemson Foe
Nov. 8

left in Marcel Courtillet, Bob Hepler, Wes Chesson and Jim Dearth. And, of course, Leo is still throwing.

"We hope to generate a stronger running game (only 1,580 yards were produced on the ground last year as opposed to 2,653 through the air), but we haven't evidenced it yet."

But the pervading interest on the Gothic campus is the defensive situation.

"Defense is the area where we are needing the greatest improvement. It will remain a question mark until we get a couple of games under our

USC Foe
Sept. 20

belts," Harp maintains, "because so many of them are young players. We'll have six or seven sophomores starting on that unit.

"We think those sophomores are pretty good athletes, but being young, we don't know how they will do under pressure. We do have more speed and quickness defensively and this is a plus factor."

Harp is not about to forecast anything close to a banner season for his campaign and pegs the Blue Devils as perhaps the league's third or fourth club.

"If our offense can approach last year it might be even better if the defense also improves.

"While we are not favored to win the conference — I think South Carolina and N. C. State are the top clubs — we could have a say as to who does what, I don't feel that we will be outclassed as we have been in the past."

Staff Photo by Larry Cagle

...To Fred Zeigler, Who Goes Up And Claims Deflected Pass...

'North Carolina Outplayed Us,' Declares Dietzel

By BILL MITCHELL
State Sports Writer

"That's what I like. Put 'em away early and relax," joked South Carolina's Paul Dietzel after his team held on for a 14-6 triumph over North Carolina in a hectic Atlantic Coast Conference battle at Carolina Stadium Saturday.

The Gamecocks, who showed little sign of life in the first half, broke loose for a pair of third period touchdowns to erase a 6-0 Tar Heel lead.

But then the Gamecocks reverted into sluggish play and the Tar Heels roared down the field in the final minutes of play until Dick Harris intercepted a Paul Miller pass with 22 seconds left in the game.

"Harris' interception was one of the greatest sights of the night for me," said Dietzel. "Those quarterbacks are a pair of fine young players."

"North Carolina outplayed us tonight," said Dietzel. "We were awful lucky to win because we weren't ready to play. I could see it coming all week.

"We played about 15 minutes in the third period," said Dietzel. "The rest of the time it was kinda like one team playing football. It's a shame that people only got to see one team play.

"North Carolina was really prepared to play football and they came down to do that," added Dietzel. "They really came out after us."

The Tar Heels, prone to commit violations at critical times, carried the play to the Gamecocks for the entire first half, but managed only a pair of field goals by Don Hartig for their golden opportunities.

"Our defense played pretty well in the clutch," said Dietzel. "But North Carolina got a bunch of yards, particularly in the first half."

The Gamecocks, who managed only one first down in the first half, could do very little with the Tar Heel defense with the exception of the third period spurt.

Perhaps the key offensive play of the night for the Gamecocks came on a 26-yard pass from Tommy Suggs to Fred Zeigler with 1:05 left in the period.

Zeigler, guarded closely by a pair of Tar Heel de-

fenders dove to come up with the deflected ball which narrowly missed being knocked out of reach by Rusty Culbreth.

"That was a spectacular catch on Zeigler's part," said Dietzel. "We have come to expect something like that from him but it certainly came at a good time for us."

"We had a great deal of difficulty picking up their defenses," said Dietzel. "I don't know that we ever really did. We knew where they were and what they were going to do, but we didn't attack the defense well at all."

South Carolina, fending off North Carolina scoring efforts most of the first half, found itself deep in its own territory constantly.

"We started inside our own 20 several times," said Dietzel. "I don't much like to throw down there and we just weren't good enough to get the ball out on our own.

"Field position hurt us in the first half, but I would have to say that North Carolina's defense had more to do with our offense not functioning than the field position."

It was the second consecutive frustrating defeat for Coach Bill Dooley's team which dropped a 10-3 decision to tough N. C. State in the season's opener last week.

"I must say that we beat ourselves," said Dooley. "Everytime that we got close, we would jump offsides or have a motion call against us.

"I felt that we should have stuck it in there at least twice in the first half.

"But we're not going to quit," said Dooley. "We've got to keep getting after people and some things are going to come our way."

The next week we would have our work cut out for us. We had to travel over to Athens, Georgia for an afternoon game against the always tough Georgia Bulldogs. We had almost taken them the year before. We had been ahead at halftime 20 to 7 the year before and should have won that game. If it hadn't been for conservative play, and a late hit by a Georgia defender that took our running back, Warren Muir, out of the game with a hip pointer, it would've been a win. We had every confidence running out onto the field between the hedges that this was going to be a win for Carolina. It was a one o'clock game and it was hot. The Georgia Bulldogs were hot offensively, as well. It seemed like they had been in our defensive huddle all afternoon and they scored 41 points. It was the most points that had been scored on our defense during the three years I had been a starter. Our offense moved the ball well that day, but could only score 16 points due to interceptions and fumbles. It was a very disappointing afternoon all the way around as we were soundly beaten by the Bulldogs.

The next week in practice, we spent time licking our wounds and getting ready for the upcoming game. The North Carolina State Wolfpack was coming to Columbia. These guys were always tough. It was a conference game and even though the loss to Georgia hurt, if we won against North Carolina State, we would still be in the hunt for the conference crown. The Georgia debacle was forgotten by Tuesday and we all concentrated on the next battle. We were keeping our eyes on the ball and were determined to win.

The kickoff was scheduled for seven o'clock on the night of October 11th. In front of a packed stadium, we played a tight game against the Wolfpack. They had whipped us pretty good the year before up in Raleigh. That was the game where Coach Dietzel said we were going to "sneak into town, beat'em and sneak out". The final score of that 'sneaky' game was Wolfpack 36 Gamecocks 12. The Wolfpack was as tough as ever, but that Saturday night in Columbia, we finally pulled away in the 4th quarter and captured our 3rd victory against one loss. The final score was Gamecocks 27, Wolfpack 16, our third conference win.

The next weekend we traveled to Blacksburg, Virginia to take on the Virginia Tech Hokies. This is the same team that had come to Columbia the year before and scored 34 points against us and it was enough for a win against our 24. More importantly for me, that was the game in which I injured my shoulder. VT had graduated a lot of seniors and I was glad that I didn't have to face that same bunch of bulldozers. But they were still a very sound football team and watching the game film, we realized they were every bit as physical as they had been the year before. It was an afternoon game, played in a stadium surrounded by mountains draped with fall colors. I don't think I ever played in a more beautiful setting.

Our defense played better than it had the year before and we held them through the 4th quarter to just 16 points. There was one small problem, however. With about a minute to go, we had only scored 14 points. We

Long Mitchell, Harris Kick Returns Trigger Gamecocks To 21-16 Triumph Over State

BY HERMAN HELMS
Executive Sports Editor

A pair of spectacular kick returns by two sophomore pony backs set off a tremendous offensive charge that swept South Carolina to an exciting 21-16 victory over N. C. State at Carolina Stadium Saturday night.

The Gamecocks, popping off like gun powder, scored three touchdowns in the space of eight minutes and four seconds to surge from behind and win the critical Atlantic Coast Conference battle.

But if it had not been for those fast feet of Dickie Harris and Jimmy Mitchell, it might never have happened.

State had just struck for a third quarter touchdown to open a 10-0 lead and things were looking black when Harris took in the ensuing kickoff at the USC two-yard line and reeled off a 45-yard return to send the Gamecocks on the way to their first touchdown.

Moments later, Mitchell accepted a Wolfpack punt at the USC 28 and combined blazing speed with some good blocks to bolt 72 yards to the touchdown that put the Gamecocks out front for good.

Mitchell weighs 155 pounds and Harris tips the scales at 150 but the little folks must have looked as big as life itself to the partisan Gamecock crowd of 42,786 when they hailed the jack through one of the ACC's soundest defensive teams.

Following Harris' sensational kickoff return, the Gamecocks charged 53 yards in eight plays to get on the scoreboard for the first time in the bitter conference struggle.

Two Tommy Suggs-to-Rudy Holloman passes, covering 22 and 17 yards, were the big plays in the advance. On fourth down, alternate tailback Billy Ray Rice dived off left tackle to score from the one-foot line with 3:33 left in the third quarter, Billy Du-Pre's conversion sliced the State lead to 10-7.

The Wolfpack couldn't gain on the next series of downs and Gary Yount punted on fourth down to Mitchell, who took the ball in at the USC 28 and was a red streak as he dashed off 72 yards to paydirt. One minute and 36 seconds remained in the third period when Dupre again kicked the point to lift the Gamecocks into a 14-10 lead.

South Carolina rambled 60 yards in ten plays for the early fourth period touchdown that iced the big victory. A 20-yard run by Holloman, a 16-yard pass from Suggs to alternate flanker Tom Trevillian and two Suggs-to-Holloman passes, good for 13 and ten yards, keyed the surge.

P o w e r f u l Warren Muir cracked in for the score from three yards out with 4:39 having passed in the final period. DuPre again kicked the point.

State took a 3-0 lead into the dressing room at halftime following a 32-yard field goal by Mike C h a r r o n which capped the Wolfpack's first series of downs.

USC had several scoring chances in the half, but failed to muster the n e c e s s a r y punch in clutch situations. The Gamecocks were stopped after a drive to the Wolfpack seven-yard line early in the second period, and later in the half, DuPre failed on a pair of field goal attempts — the first from 43 yards out and the second from 39 yards.

State took the third quarter kickoff and used its bread and butter ground game to crunch out 73 yards in 16 plays for the touchdown that opened up a 10-0 lead. Wingback Leon Mason banged over from the two for the score and Charron kicked point with 7:05 left in the third quarter.

The Wolfpack had consumed seven minutes and 55 seconds in the long advance, but that was the end of the grunt and groan football for the night. Harris had the football a moment later and was sailing up the field to set off USC's game-winning explosion.

State drove 76 yards to its last touchdown in the last seconds of play. A 54-yard pass from quarterback Darrell Moody to Mason set the stage for a three-yard Moody to Wayne Lewis touchdown pass. A Moody pass on an attempted two-point conversion was intercepted by the Gamecocks' Pat Watson with 49 seconds left in the game.

The statistics underscored the area in which the game was decided. State led in first downs, 18 to 17, but USC had a 157 to 147 advantage in rushing yardage and a 188 to 131 edge in passing yardage. In the tell-tale kick return yardage, USC had 120 yards to 12 for the Wolfpack.

Suggs, the Gamecocks' brilliant little q u a r t e r b a c k, showed his true colors in a tremendous comeback following an "off" game against Georgia last week. The USC junior completed 14 of 21 passes for 188 yards and added 25 yards rushing in five carries for a fat 213 yards in total offense. His passing average would have been even more impressive but for the fact that at least four of his first half deliveries were dropped by receivers.

Muir led USC's rushers with 54 yards in 16 trips. Freddie Zeigler became the ACC's top pass receiver of all-time when he nabbed four Suggs tosses for 46 yards, giving him a career total of 109 receptions.

Halfback Charlie B o w e r s was a tremendous workhorse in defeat for State, carrying the ball 28 times and powering for 127 yards.

Moody, the State quarterback who is more noted for his running ability than his passing ability, drilled ten completions in 14 attempts for 131 yards.

USC's Jimmy Mitchell Takes Punt (L), Cuts Up Field (R)...

...Breaks Through Heart Of N.C. State's Coverage

Staff Photos By Vic Tutte
Staff Photo by Vic Tutte

Receiving

Player	NO.	Yds	TD	LG.
Mason				
Bowers				
Lewis				
McLean				

SOUTH CAROLINA
Rushing

Player	Att.	Gain	Lost	Net	L.G.
Muir					
Holloman					
Suggs					
Wakup					
Rice					
Trevillian					
Miranda					
Sisters					

Passing

Player	Att.	Compl.	Inte.	Yds.	L.G.
Suggs					

Receiving

Player	No.	Yds	TD	LG.
Muir				
Zeigler				
Holloman				
Hamrick				
Rice				
Trevillian				

FRED ZEIGLER
Sets ACC Record

The victory, USC's third straight in the conference against no losses, placed the Gamecocks further in the driver's seat in the ACC race. The loss left State with a 2-2 league record and may have put the Wolfpack out of the title running.

N.C. STATE   S. CAROLINA

First Downs	18	17
Rushing Yardage	147	157
Passing Yardage	131	188
Return Yardage	12	120
Passes	10-14-0	14-21-0
Punts	8-40.5	5-38.2
Fumbles Lost	0	0
Yards Penalized	0	35

N.C. State	3	0	7	6 — 16
S. Carolina	0	0	14	7 — 21

NCS—FG 32 Charron
NCS—Mason 2 run (Charron kick)
SC — Rice 1 run (DuPre kick)
SC — Mitchell 72 punt return (DuPre kick)
SC—Muir 3 run (DuPre kick)
NCS — Lewis 3 pass from Moody (pass failed)
Attendance 42,786

N. C. STATE
Rushing

Player	Att.	Gain	Loss	Net	L.G.
Bowers	28	127	0	127	14
Mason	11	37	4	33	14
Moody	7	30	7	23	9
Rodgers	2	9	0	9	5
Moor	1	2	0	2	2
Altman	1	3	0	3	3

Passing

Player	Att.	Compl.	Inte.	Yds.	L.G.
Moody	14	10	0	131	49

DuPre's FG In Closing Seconds Lifts USC Over Gobblers, 17-16

By HAROLD MARTIN
State Sports Writer

BLACKSBURG, Va. — Diminutive Billy DuPre, a five-foot-five package of determination, rammed home a 47-yard soccer-style field goal with only nine seconds remaining as South Carolina rallied from the brink of defeat to nip Virginia Tech, 17-6, in a Lane Stadium thriller here Saturday afternoon.

The whiplash arm of quarterback Tommy Suggs and the suction cup hands of split end Fred Zeigler set the stage for the heart-stopping finish as the Gamecocks ran their record to 4-1 in another cliffhanger.

The Gobblers, frustrated for the fifth straight week, had apparently pulled it out with a touchdown pass 1:13 from the end.

But the Gamecocks, beaten badly a year ago by the Gobblers, refused to stay whipped Saturday and most of the crowd of 28,000 stayed glued to their seats as Suggs moved USC down the field in a march against the clock and the traditionally-tough Tech defense.

Dick Harris returned the kickoff following Tech's second touchdown to the USC 32 and Suggs, who hit on 13 of 21 for 127 yards, took to the air.

The stubby scrambler from Lamar hit Zeigler for nine, and found his split end again for ten on the next play for a first at the Tech 49. Suggs then went to tight end Doug Hamrick for 14 yards and a first at the Tech 30 with 34 seconds to go.

Suggs missed two attempts and had to run when he couldn't find a receiver on third down, picking up one to the 29.

USC Head Coach Paul Dietzel then called on DuPre, who had missed two long distance shots earlier Saturday.

The ball started out low, looking as if it never had a chance to make it. But the ball stayed up and cleared the bar

But the former Flora ace, who once kicked one 50 yards in high school, didn't miss the one that counted.

Just before the winning drive, Tech had roared from behind on a beautiful 26-yard touchdown pass from third string quarterback Gil Schwabe to wingback Jimmy Quinn, who played a sensational game.

It was Schwabe's first appearance of the year, but Tech coach Jerry Claiborne had no choice when his first two signal callers, Bob German and Al Kincaid, were injured.

Before that, Tech had scored on a three-yard run by tailback Terry Smoot and a 43-yard field goal by Jack Simcsak. Simcsak, a sensational punter and placekicker, missed the extra point after the second touchdown and, as it turned out, that cost the snakebitten Gobblers a tie.

South Carolina held a 14-7 lead at halftime, led 14-10 after three quarters and apparently had the game under control until Tech's rally in the dying moments.

Zeigler, who had six catches for 49 yards, scored the first USC touchdown on a seven yard pitch from Suggs. Warren Muir, who gave Tech a touch of its own medicine with 95 rushing yards on 29 carries, got the other on a one-yard burst.

Tech dominated the opening minutes of play when the Gamecocks, who have not scored during the first quarter this

Diving For Touchdown
AP Wirephoto
USC Split End Fred Zeigler (80) Snags Pass From Tommy Suggs In Gobblers' End Zone In Front Of Tom Bosiack.

---

year, started slowly for the fifth straight game.

The Gobblers took the opening kick-off and rolled to three straight first downs, all on the ground, before the Gamecock defenders halted the advance. Simcsak, who has a 55-yarder to his credit, attempted a 50-yard field goal against the wind, but it was not close and the Gamecocks took over for three plays and a punt.

Bill Parker got off a poor 24-yard boot and the Gobblers moved 49 yards in ten plays to take the lead after a fair catch.

Wingback Quinn sent the Gobblers on their way with a magnificent 25-yard run on a counter in which he broke two tackles and gave Tech a first at the USC 24.

Four smashes into the USC line gave the Gobblers a first at the Gamecock 13. Linebacker Don Buckner caught Smoot for a three-yard loss, but on the next play German scrambled for ten after trying to throw.

Smoot, who tormented the Gamecocks a year ago, then slashed for three on the right side before knifing across from the three on fourth down. Simcsak's boot left Tech in front, 7-0 with 6:00 left in the period.

Defensive back Dick Harris gave the Gamecocks beautiful field position when he returned the ensuing kickoff 48 yards to the Tech 49, but USC

had to kick it away after making one first.

Middle guard Pat Kohout put the Gamecocks back in business, however, when German fumbled a handoff deep in Tech territory and the USC soph dropped on it at the Gobbler 26. It took the Gamecocks seven plays to tie it from there.

The key play in the short march was a third and nine pass from Suggs to Hamrick that covered 13 yards and gave USC a first at the Tech 12.

Three running plays moved the ball to the seven as the quarter ended and, on the first play of the second period, Suggs found Zeigler breaking clear in the corner of the end zone and hit for the score. DuPre's kick evened the count just five seconds into the period.

With six minutes left in the half, Tech's Donnie Cooke fumbled a fair catch and tackle Tony Fusaro recovered for the Gamecocks at the Tech 42. From there, USC moved it across in nine plays with the aid of a tremendous break.

Suggs threw for three to Holloman and then Hamrick made a great diving catch for eight yards and a first at the Tech 31. Two plays later,

Suggs threw into a host of Gobbler defenders and Ronnie Holsinger intercepted at the ten, returning to the Tech 24. A Tech defender, however, was charged with a face mask violation and the penalty allowed the Gamecocks to retain possession and gave them a first at the Tech 15.

Muir took over from there — pounding Tech's first line of defense with five hammer blows that shot the ball into the end zone. The payoff came with 2:32 remaining in the half from slightly more than a yard out on a smash at right end. DuPre's kick gave USC a 14-7 advantage at intermission.

The Gobblers narrowed the gap in the third period when Simcsak booted a 43-yard field goal with the wind, his seventh of the season. Later in the period, Simcsak attempted a 50-yarder that appeared to be long enough, but just outside the right upright.

First downs	SC.	VA. TECH
Rushing yardage	14	14
Passing yardage	147	196
Return yardage	127	42
Passes	15	43
Punts	13-21-1	3-12-1
Fumbles Lost	10-34	8-45
Yards penalized	0	4
	45	25

South Carolina   0 14 0 3 — 17
Virginia Tech   7 0 3 6 — 16

Tech — Smoot 3 run (Simcsak kick)
SC — Zeigler 7 pass from Suggs (DuPre kick)
SC — Muir 1 run (DuPre kick)
Tech — FG Simcsak 43
Tech — Quinn 26 pass from Schwabe (kick failed)
SC — FG DuPre 47
A — 28,000

SOUTH CAROLINA RUSHING

	Att	Yds	Td	L.G.
Suggs	9	95	0	9
Muir	29	95	1	9
Holloman	14	39	0	9
Watson	2	8	0	3
Rice	3	3	0	3
Simmons	4	-3	0	3

PASSING

	Att	Comp	Yds	Td	L.G.
Suggs	21	13	127	1	18

RECEIVING

	No.	Yds	Td	L.G.
Zeigler	6	49	1	16
Hamrick	4	53	0	18
Holloman	2	11	0	16
Freeman	1	14	0	14

PUNTING

	No.	Yds	Avg	L.G.
Parker	10	340	34	44

VA. TECH

	Att	Yds	TD	L.G.
German	5	37	0	10
Smoot	24	87	1	17
Edwards	3	9	0	9
Quinn	15	49	0	25
Russo	2	2	0	2
Tiberio	4	13	0	4
Matflevich	1	4	0	4
Kincaid	1	9	0	9
Kushner	1	4	0	4

PASSING

	Att	Comp	H.I.	Yds	TD	L.G.
German	3	1	0	11	0	11
Schwabe	2	1	0	26	1	26
Kincaid	2	1	1	11	0	11

RECEIVING

	No.	Yds	Td	L.G.
Quinn	2	31	1	26
Humphries	1	11	0	11

PUNTING

	No.	Yds	Avg	L.G.
Simcsak	5	225	45	55

WAKE FOREST-CLEMSON

First downs		16	21
Rushing yardage		129	301
Passing yardage		106	113
Return yardage		8	56
Passes		13-23-1	19-31-3
Punts		6-43	6-37
Fumbles lost		2	1
Yards penalized		20	10

Wake Forest   7 7 6 0 — 21
Clemson   7 7 14 0 — 28

Clem—Yauger 4 run (Barnette kick)
WF—Leavitt 4 run (Lousbury kick)
Clem — Tolley 12 run (Barnette kick)
WF — Russell 12 run (Lounsbury kick)
Clem — Yauger 1 run (Barnette kick)
Clem — Waters 6 run (Barnette kick)
A — 31,000.

WAKE FOREST RUSHING

Player	Att	Gain	Loss	Net	L.G.
Russell	19	57	14	43	14
Dalbin	8	41	4	44	11
Gavin	6	40	9	40	11
Leavitt	4	14	-12	4	4
Jurewicz	1	8	6	2	2

PASSING

Player	Comp	Att	Intc	Yds	L.G.
Russell	23	13	1	103	26
Leavitt	1	1	0	87	37

PASS RECEIVING

Player	No	Yds	TD	L.G.
Winrow	3	44	0	15
Bowden	2	35	0	25
Kobes	2	16	0	15

CLEMSON RUSHING

Player	Att	Gain	Loss	Net	L.G.
Yauger	36	202	19	19	39
Anderson	9	39	0	39	11
Medlin	3	37	0	37	14
Waters	7	16	0	16	13
Tolley	1	12	0	12	12
Shields	3	5	0	5	3
Gilstrp	2	5	10	-5	5

PASSING

Player	Comp	Att	Intc	Yds	L.G.
Kendrick	19	9	3	113	13
Gilstrap	2	1	0	15	15

PASS RECEIVING

Player	No	Yds	TD	L.G.
Waters	5	48	0	21
Anderson	3	20	0	14
Yauger	3	19	0	15
Suravage	1	18	0	18
Tolley	1	8	0	8

moved the ball pretty well, but a couple of bad breaks and penalties on our final drive had stalled our progress. Our hopes rested on the leg of our placekicker, Billy DuPre. Billy was going to attempt a 49-yard field goal. If he hit it, we would win. I remember standing on the sidelines and thinking how long the kick was going to be. A teammate said it would be 49 yards, but it looked more like 89 to me. The snap went back to the holder and Billy moved forward and made contact with the ball. I heard the 'thunk' of his foot, striking the ball and watched as it sailed toward the goalpost. It was straight and true and long enough. We won the game by a score of 17-16. Jubilation reigned on the Gamecock's sideline. Winning games like this made us believe 1969 could be our year.

The next weekend we played Maryland at home, another conference game. Even though Maryland's record at the time wasn't as good as ours, we remembered the loss to them the year before in their stadium. The only thing good about that trip was visiting the tomb of the Unknown Soldier. As impressive as that ceremony was, its poignancy was heightened by what was happening to our troops over in Vietnam. One of our teammates from the freshman team was Darrell Johnson. Darrell had dropped out after his first year and had been drafted. He was John D Coleman's roommate our freshman year and John D had kept in touch with him. Darrell had been drafted into the Army and sent to Vietnam. He had been missing in action for over a year. You couldn't help but think of our missing teammate while watching the Changing of the Guard.

We scored 17 points against the Terrapins that night and got our only other shutout of the 1960's. The final was South Carolina 17, Maryland 0. The first shutout since 1958 came in 1967 when we beat Maryland 31-0.

We were 4 and 0 in the Atlantic Coast Conference. With the season half over, we were getting closer to achieving our goal of winning the conference championship. We had some nonconference business to attend to for the next couple of weeks. Both were on the road. First, we traveled to Tallahassee, Florida to take on the Florida State Seminoles.

As usual the "Noles" had a very good football team. Thank goodness they had graduated Ron Sellers. He was the all American 6'5" wide receiver that had scored five touchdowns against us the year before in Columbia, when the coaching staff decided we weren't going to double cover him . We had helped make Sellers an All-American that year.

Unfortunately, we got the same results against Florida State as we did against Georgia, a loss. I recall thinking in the locker room before the game that we just weren't ready to play. The Florida State Seminoles scored 34 points and we could only muster 9. The only bright spot to this game was that I got to see an old high school sweetheart of mine, Becky Creighton. It was late in the game when I heard someone behind me calling my name. I had lost track of her after high school and was surprised when I turned around and saw her bright smile. It didn't help much, though, as we suffered our second loss of the season. Thankfully, it wasn't a conference loss.

'...Vandy Could Never Beat Alabama...'

★ ★ ★   ★ ★ ★   ★ ★ ★

Dietzel Warns Against Letdown Against Terrapins

Tom Miller...Terrapins' Fullback

By HAROLD MARTIN
State Sports Writer

"Just about anything is possible in college football these days," University of South Carolina Head Coach Paul Dietzel said at his weekly press luncheon Tuesday.

"Of course, a team such as Vanderbilt could never beat a team like Alabama," he continued tongue in cheek, "but just about anything else could happen."

The point of Dietzel's remarks is that his Gamecocks, leading the Atlantic Coast Conference with a 3-0 mark and 4-1 overall, can ill afford to let down against the Maryland Terps of Roy Lester Saturday night at Carolina Stadium when USC celebrates Homecoming at Carolina Stadium.

"One thing about it," observed Dietzel, "Maryland is just as capable of beating us as any team on our schedule. There are no lousy teams anymore — at least not on our schedule.

"No one could predict before the season started just what kind of a team Maryland would come up with this year under their new coaching staff," Dietzel said.

"But their young staff has really done a tremendous job. Maryland is a well-coached team that really gets your attention."

Earlier, USC assistant Jackie Powers, who gave a scouting report on the Terps, said Maryland, which ranks third in the conference with a 2-1 league record, is most impressive with its rushing offense.

"They use an unbalanced line with a lonesome end," said Powers, "and their entire front are powerful blockers. Syracuse, for example, has a big, strong defensive front and Maryland just knocked them off the line of scrimmage. They have blocked everybody they've played off the line.

"They like to run the football. (Dennis) O'Hara, their quarterback, had rather not run that pass. But he can throw. Against Duke last week, he passed four times and completed two, both for touchdowns."

"Their tailback, Al Thomas, ran against Duke like his coaches hoped he would and gained 170 yards. Tom Miller, their fullback, added 101 yards rushing.

"We expect them to run the football Saturday night and the things they like best are the power plays, options and option passes. If we expect to win," said Powers, "we must stop their runs and especially their fullback, Miller."

Dietzel, who urged ticket holders to leave early for Saturday night's contest because of the State Fair, in progress next door to Carolina Stadium, is still more than a little concerned about his defense.

"We have a little more depth on offense," Dietzel noted, "but it is a different story at certain positions on defense. And it is at the positions where we were thin that injuries have hurt us the most.

"We lost our two linebackers, Al Usher and Benny Padgett, and our middle guard, Don Buckner, for a couple of games. We also lost our safety, Tyler Hellams. That really took the guts out of our defense.

"Under the circumstances, I think the defense has done a heck of a job and they've been getting better. But they're going to get a good test this week.

"One thing I'm happy about," Dietzel said, "is that we don't have to play Maryland up there. They have beaten us twice in three years and both losses were at Maryland."

Holloman Spies Daylight
USC Tailback Rudy Holloman (24) Races Through N. C. State Defense For Gain In Gamecocks' 21-16 ACC Victory.

"Virginia Tech was a big victory for us. Virginia Tech is an outside team and we have to start beating some of those teams. We needed to win that game.

"But now we come back to the ACC. And to lose this one

would be just as bad as losing to N. C. State a couple of weeks ago. This one counts in the standings and is a very important game for the Gamecocks — the most important right now because it is this week.

"Maryland is going to bring a tough, hard-nosed football team to Columbia. They have a lot of talent and they're mature. They're not a bunch of young kids who are likely to get rattled by a big crowd.

"We haven't met a team like Maryland this year," Dietzel said. "Maryland does an excellent job of running the option and we're going to have to spend a lot of time trying to stop it. But then they get you conscious of the option and kill you with the

counter.

"And don't forget," Dietzel reminded, "the last ACC team to beat South Carolina was Maryland."

Not One Of Gamecocks Better Efforts...
...But Good Enough To Remain Atop ACC

By HAROLD MARTIN
State Sports Writer

It was still early in the Atlantic Coast Conference contest at Carolina Stadium Saturday night and Maryland and South Carolina were in the process of feeling each other out.

All of a sudden, South Carolina quarterback Tommy Suggs rifled a pass to split end Fred Zeigler and the sure-handed receiver turned it into a 15-yard gain. Suggs came right back with the same play to the other side and Zeigler gathered it in for an 11-yard advance.

That offensive spurt fizzled out when USC received a five-yard penalty and Suggs was caught behind the line, but the Gamecocks had just given Maryland a little taste of the poison that would later prove to be the Terps' downfall, 17-0.

Another full house, 42,756 this time, filled Carolina Stadium for the fourth straight time this season, many of them South Carolina alumni who were on hand to celebrate Homecoming.

The huge throng was not rewarded with one of the Gamecocks' top performances and the script was changed a little from earlier comeback victories in the Cockpit.

Gamecocks fans, however, are not about to look down their noses at any

kind of a victory. There have been too many times in recent years that South Carolina has played its heart out only to come out on the short end of the score.

For much of the contest, Roy Lester's Terps carried the battle to the Gamecocks with a bruising ground game that featured two tough runners in tail-

Sour Moment For Shugars
USC Defensive End Jimmy Pope Pounces On Maryland Quarterback Jeff Shugars.

back Al Thomas and fullback Tom Miller.

The Terps wound up with 205 yards rushing with Miller accounting for 94 and Thomas 92. That was not exactly a surprise for Maryland has been able to move on the ground against most of their opponents.

And after all, as South Carolina Coach Paul Dietzel said, "The purpose of defense is to keep the other team from scoring," and the Gamecocks did just that.

Dietzel was understandably disappointed that the South Carolina running game did not function better. South Carolina managed only 90 rushing yards for the game with Warren Muir (69) and Rudy Holloman (29) getting most of those.

For much of the way, South Carolina nursed a 3-0 advantage earned by little Billy DuPre's 40-yard field goal in the second period. But Maryland found out in the second half, as four previous teams had this season, that the Gamecock offense is too explosive to keep the cork in forever.

Suggs, a stumpy little junior from Lamar who has experienced some magnificent moments, again proved to be a master scrambler down the stretch

when it counted. In all, Suggs connected 12 times in 17 throws for 190 yards, setting up both touchdowns and passing for one.

As usual, Zeigler was sensational. The senior receiver who has been driving defensive secondaries crazy for three years, had seven receptions for 107 yards, including a tremendous, 51-yarder that set up the clincher in the fourth quarter.

A week ago, the Gamecocks were sky high at Blacksburg, Va., and they had to be to whip Virginia Tech, 17-16, in the final seconds on DuPre's 47-yard field goal.

They were not as sharp before the Friendly Homecoming crowd Saturday night. But it is nice to know that the South Carolina program has reached the point that the Gamecocks can win now and then without being at their peak.

But Dietzel, his coaching staff and the Gamecocks have little time to savor this one. Six games do not a season make — not even if you're 5-1 at that point.

Ahead of the Gamecocks are such outstanding outside foes as Florida State and Tennessee and Atlantic Coast Conference e n e m i e s Wake Forest and Clemson. Three of those, all except Clemson, are on the road and that makes it even tougher.

One has to go all the way back to 1946 to discover a

South Carolina team that was 5-1 after six games. And that year's edition of the Gamecocks lost the only two remaining games.

It will be interesting to see how South Carolina reacts to the challenge in 1969.

HOWARD JOHNSON'S

(CAYCE ONLY)

SANDWICH BAR

"Fastest Lunch In Town"

The State SPORTS

2-B Columbia, S. C., Wed., October 22, 1969

We knew the next week would be another hard fought battle. We would be traveling to Knoxville, Tennessee to take on the Volunteers. Tennessee was undefeated and ranked No. 3 in the nation, behind Ohio State and Texas. This was going to be my first trip to play in Knoxville and I was in for quite an experience. Neyland Stadium was built in 1921, had undergone sixteen major renovations and now held over 102,000 spectators. It was the third largest non-racing stadium in the United States and the only stadium with artificial turf. We worked hard all that week getting ready for the game and watched a lot of game film. Although Tennessee was good, we felt like we could play with them, crowd or no crowd.

The team flew up to Knoxville on an early afternoon flight. That morning just before I left campus, I stopped by a fraternity brother's apartment. Mike Craig lived in a second story apartment overlooking Green Street about two blocks from campus. Everyone was excited about the upcoming ballgame with number three ranked Tennessee and my fraternity was no exception. They were planning a huge party at Mike's for that Saturday afternoon. The alcohol would be flowing while they listened to the game. Mike had been making a batch of homemade wine for the occasion and asked me to come by and taste some of his special brew before I left for Tennessee. He was very proud of his wine-making skills and handed me a cup to try.

Mike, after all these years, I hate to tell you but it wasn't very good. But as a college student, having access to free alcohol was exceptional and taste wasn't the important thing. I managed to finish the cup. It was pretty strong stuff. I headed back out to the Roost and we loaded our gear and departed for the airport to board our flight to Knoxville. Everything went smoothly for the first part of the flight, but about half way there I suddenly got a bad case of the green apple quickstep. The lower part of my stomach felt as if it was about to explode, so I spent the rest of the flight sitting in the head.

Knoxville is a really pretty town surrounded by the Great Smoky Mountains. It was early November, so the peaks and ranges had not lost their colorful hues. As usual, we visited the stadium and did our walk-through. The artificial turf made you feel as if you were walking on a pool table. Just outside of the stadium, the Tennessee River flowed by and we saw the area where boats would be tying up for the game. Many of them were already there, although the partying had not started in earnest. The next day, kickoff was at one o'clock and for brunch, we had our usual steak and eggs and pep talk by Coach Dietzel. We were ready to play the Tennessee Volunteers in front of their hundred thousand plus fan base.

The game was pretty exciting and we stayed within striking range for most of the contest. Two plays come to my mind, when I think of the Tennessee game of 1969. The first was a fumble on a pitch play to the Tennessee halfback coming around my end. Their halfback dropped the pitch and I had an opportunity to recover the ball and stop the drive. I was a split-second too late and although I had the ball for a second, a volunteer managed to get control. When they say football is a game of inches and seconds, it's true. The next play I remember was late in the game. We had Tennessee backed up into their own territory and our offense had been moving the ball well the last few times we had possession. It was third and long and the Tennessee quarterback dropped back to pass. I got by the blockers and closed in on the quarterback. Once again I was a split-second too late. I hit the quarterback just as the ball was released and pushed off using momentum to turn to see the play. Looking down field, I could clearly see the intended receiver and was glad he was well covered by our defensive player. Then as if in slow motion, our defender left the receiver open by taking the inside fake. He played the receiver and not the ball and sure enough the pass was completed down the middle for a touchdown. That put the game out of reach. There just was too little time left for us to score twice. Those two plays are etched in my memory as clearly today as the moment they occurred. The opportunity to upset a top 10 team was foiled, but again, it was not a conference loss.

During the week of practice leading up to the Tennessee game, Joe Wingard and Jimmy Pope had been practicing kickoff returns. They had come up with a homemade reverse play they thought would work well. Each time they tried it at practice Coach Larry Jones would scold them severely and tell them to stick to the routine. As members of the 'Brown team', Joe and Jimmy didn't listen very well to the coaches sometimes. They decided during the Tennessee game it would be a good time to run their reverse play. It would be unexpected.

Tennessee had just scored a touchdown and prepared to kick off to us. Joe runs up to Jimmy and the two of them go over to Candler Boyd, who was lined up as the up back in the kickoff receive formation. They told Candler that if they caught the ball, they would give it to him and he could pitch it back to Dickie Harris, who was having a great year as a return man. Usually the ball was kicked deep, directly to Dickie. The kicker trotted up and booted the football. It wasn't a particularly long kick and it was sailing high over Joe's head. Joe turned and started sprinting down the field to get under the football. Sure enough, Joe made a tremendous over the shoulder catch. Since this was never to happen, it surprised everyone, including the other players on our team. Joe started back up the field and cut back toward the middle where Candler and Jimmy were standing. As Joe ran past them, he handed the ball off to Jimmy instead of Candler. Jimmy was surprised, but cut up field with the football. Catching Tennessee off guard, Jimmy was able to gain about 16 yards out to the 42-yard line. It was good field position, even though it was accomplished in an unorthodox manner.

Jimmy and Joe came trotting off the field with huge grins on their faces. They knew they were in trouble for doing something the coaches hadn't endorsed. When players were off the field, the team lined up with the defense on one end of the bench and the offense on the other. You were always expected to line up by position. The ends were together, the tackles together, the linebackers together. This way, if a coach needed to put a player in the game, he could find his man quickly. As the two unauthorized ball carriers

Facing Vols 'Matter Of Realism'

★ ★ ★ ★ ★ ★ ★ ★ ★

'Tennessee Overpowers The Opposition'—Dietzel

By HERMAN HELMS
Executive Sports Editor

The topic of discussion was the awesome challenge that awaits South Carolina's Gamecocks at Knoxville, Tenn. Saturday.

"We're approaching the game as a matter of realism," Coach Paul Dietzel told newsmen attending his weekly press conference Tuesday. "We know who we're playing, we know what a great team Tennessee has, we know what a real challenge this is for us.

"Tennessee just overpowers the opposition," declared Dietzel. "You can't find a film of any game in which they don't look great."

A capacity crowd of 64,000 is expected to fill Shields-Watkins Stadium at Knoxville Saturday to watch the unbeaten and third-ranked Vols take on the Gamecocks.

Although the game brings together teams that are leading their respective conferences—the Vols have a 3-0 record in the Southeastern while the Gamecocks sit atop the Atlantic Coast Conference standings with

a 4-0 record—Tennessee has been established as a heavy favorite.

Cam Lewis, a graduate assistant on the USC coaching staff who has scouted Tennessee in victories over Alabama and Georgia, told the newsmen that he feels defense is the key to Tennessee's success.

"Defense has accounted for many of Tennessee's touchdowns this season," Lewis pointed out. "Their first three touchdowns against Alabama were all made possible by the defense.

"Tennessee is winning and is such a fine team, because of its defense."

Lewis had particular praise for two of Tennessee's defensive players, calling linebackers Jack Reynolds and Steve Kiner "true All-Americans."

Lewis said he believes the Vols are "getting better each week on offense.

"Their coach, Doug Dickey, has been quoted as saying that he doesn't feel the team has reached its potential offensively. I hope they never do," commented Lewis.

"Their best back is the fullback, Curt Watson, who's just a sophomore but he averaged a little over ten yards per carry against a Georgia defense that is very much respected.

"Tennessee doesn't have breakaway type runners," said the USC scout. "They have power runners who run inside the tackles most of the time. They prefer

to run the ball, and then hit you with a pass."

Dietzel, reflecting on USC's disappointing 34-9 loss to Florida State last week, said, "We came out of that game with a lot of bruises. You get bruised anytime you stand around and let the other team take the fight to you.

"That was the kind of game you simply can't explain. A weird series of circumstances had a demoralizing effect on our team, and we simply never recovered.

"After the Tennessee game, we have two ultra-important games with Wake Forest and Clemson. I said after our game with Maryland that if we were lucky enough to beat Wake Forest, we would be playing Clemson for the conference title on November 22.

"Those two conference games are mighty important to us, but we aren't thinking about them this week."

Lewis pointed out that the kicking game is one of Tennessee's strong points.

"Their punter, Herman Weaver, had quite a duel with Spike Jones of Georgia."

Curt Watson . . . Vols' Top Runner

KINER

REYNOLDS

Glory, Grief At Knoxville
Gamecocks Played Vols To Standstill

By HERMAN HELMS
Executive Sports Editor

KNOXVILLE, TENN. — It was a superb effort that brought South Carolina's Gamecocks both glory and grief.

Glory because they played the nation's third-ranked college football team to a virtual standstill, and grief because they didn't win.

Coach Paul Dietzel told the story moments after the Gamecocks had lost a 29-14 decision to Tennessee here Saturday — a final score that was not at all indicative of the closeness of the fierce game watched by a crowd of 62,868.

"I just don't know how to say it," said the USC coach. "I'm so doggone proud of our boys for their great effort, but I'm so hurt that they lost.

"There's some consolation in playing well even though you've lost, but the sad part is that our kids played well enough to win."

PAUL DIETZEL
Proud And Hurt

"We're a good football team. I think we proved that to a lot of people today. I think the kids proved it to themselves."

Tennessee was a prohibitive favorite. South Carolina, so the forecasters said, didn't have a chance. But with five minutes and 40 seconds left to play in the tense thriller, Randy Yoakum fired a 22-yard touchdown pass to Rudy Holloman, the Gamecocks had cut Tennessee's lead to a thin 16-14, the Vols' unbeaten record and high national ranking were hanging in the balance and the big crowd of Tennessee partisans were nervous, very nervous.

But Tennessee came back then the way a good team is supposed to come back and charged 76 yards in seven plays for the touchdown that put them ahead 23-14 and ended the Gamecocks' dreams of an incredible upset.

That touchdown march that came in the last three minutes of play was tearing at Dietzel's heart in the aftermath of the exciting game.

"That drive killed us," he said. "I thought we had them stopped when we threw them for a loss back out to our 40-yard line. That brought up third down and 14, and if we held them then we would get the football and we had time to get into field goal range."

But the Gamecocks didn't stop the Vols. Quarterback Bobby Scott fired a 40-yard touchdown bomb to end Gary Kreis on the big third down play. The Vols were later to get still another touchdown, but it was the product of late, desperation gambles by the Gamecocks.

There were many heroes in defeat for the Gamecocks. Dietzel said "both our offensive and defensive lines played their best games of the season. Our offensive line just blew a great Tennessee defense out of there, and our defensive line contained one of the best running games in football better than it has been contained all season."

But the greatest of USC's heroes was fullback Warren Muir, who slashed through Tennessee's touted defense for 159 yards in 31 carries.

"I thought our whole team played well," praised Dietzel, "but Warren was super. You talk about a thoroughbred. When the chips are down, when it's a big game, he's just a wild thing. If he isn't an All-American, I've never seen one."

Tennessee coaches and players were lavish in their praise of the Gamecocks and Muir.

"South Carolina is a good football team, and they came here to play with a fine game plan," said Tennessee coach Doug Dickey. "They played their best and I want to compliment them."

"South Carolina was a lot tougher to throw over than anybody we've played this year," said Vol quarterback Scott.

"Muir is a good runner, about the best we've faced this year," declared defensive safety Bill Young. "They were as fine a defensive team as we've played against," stated offensive guard Don Denbo.

The Gamecocks used what Dietzel described as "an old chestnut" — a spread formation — to great success in the game. The USC coach explained that it was not the first time he has employed such a tactic.

"I've used it in the past on special occasions," he said. "The first time we ever used it was against Navy in 1964 and our Army team upset the Middies, 11-8. We also used it here at Carolina during my first year (in 1966) against Georgia in a game that we lost 7-0."

"I don't like moral victories," said Dietzel. "I don't want our players or our fans to get to thinking that there's anything great about a moral victory. But I can't fault the great effort that our kids made. I'm so proud of them for that. We're getting closer all the time, closer to where we want to be."

That was the story of a titanic struggle at Knoxville — close but not quite, glory and grief for the Gamecocks.

Dietzel . . . 'Can't Take Them Lightly'

By HERMAN HELMS
Executive Sports Editor

South Carolina has an important football date with Wake Forest at Winston-Salem Saturday.

Despite the fact that the Deacons' record is just the opposite of the 5-3 mark of the Gamecocks, this may be USC's biggest game of the season to date for two reasons:

(1) South Carolina can clinch at least a tie for the Atlantic Coast Conference championship by beating the Deacons. Should Clemson lose its Saturday match with North Carolina, the crown will go outright to

USC, and it would be the school's first football championship in 75 years of football.

(2) USC can post its first winning season in football in ten years by defeating Wake.

Both Head Coach Paul Dietzel and freshman Coach Pride Ratterree, who has scouted the Deacons, spoke with respect of Cal Stoll's team at the weekly press conference Tuesday.

Ratterree, who saw the Deacons lose in North Carolina and defeat Virginia, warned that the Gamecocks could have trouble defensing Wake's sophomore quarterback Larry Russell.

"Wake's attack is geared around him, and he has a lot of ability," said Ratterree. "He is both a fine runner and a fine passer."

Russell is one of the ACC's leaders in total offense with 1,091 yards. He has completed 63 of 139 passes for 691 yards and has rushed for 400 yards.

"I can remember Russell playing against us at Carolina Stadium as a freshman," said Ratterree, "and, frankly, I didn't expect him to turn out to be as fine a varsity player as he is. He apparently has great desire to go with his ability."

Ratterree noted that tight end Gary Winrow is Russell's pet receiver. They have combined on 19 completions for 208 yards.

"Wake is an experienced team with good size," said the USC scout. "They start only one sophomore in their offensive line, and Russell is surrounded by three seniors in the starting backfield."

Ratterree pointed out that Wake made an adjustment in its defense against Virginia last week, installing a five-man front, and limited the Cavaliers to a single yard rushing in the last half of a game that the Deacons won, 23-21.

"You don't under-estimate anybody in our league," Dietzel said, "especially not a team like Wake Forest which has made such tremendous comebacks this season."

Dietzel pointed out that the Deacons came from behind to rack up each of their three victories — over Virginia Tech, N. C. State and Virginia.

The State Sports

2-B Columbia, S. C., Wed., Nov. 12, 1969

The USC coach said that alternate fullback Tommy Simmons, who was injured in last Saturday's Tennessee game, "may be able to play this week."

"His injury was not as serious as we first thought, and there is a chance that he will play against Wake Forest."

Dietzel also revealed that roverback Bo Davies, who missed the Tennessee game, will return against the Deacons.

"I think Cal Stoll has done a fine job in his first season at Wake Forest," said Dietzel. "I have told our team that they must play their best to beat the Deacons. We're not kidding ourselves. We know we're in for a tough game."

Halfback Jack Dolbin, who starred as the Deacons smashed the Gamecocks, 35-21, two years ago, will miss Saturday's game due to a broken arm.

came off the field, instead of stopping where the defensive ends lined up, they kept going all the way to the opposite end and sat down with the offensive ends. They plopped on the ground at the end of the bench to make it even more difficult for the coaching staff to find them.

The Gamecocks moved the football deep into Tennessee territory and scored on that drive. The offense was bolstered with that 16-yard return by Jimmy Pope, so after the touchdown, Jimmy and Joe snuck behind the squad and finally returned to their proper places. To this day, the record book shows Joe Wingard with one return for 0 yards and Jimmy Pope with one return for 16.

The next day we were back in Columbia and went out to breakfast at the House of Pancakes, a popular restaurant with a lot of the team members. We had a Saturday night curfew, but a lot of us stayed at a fraternity brother's apartment instead of returning to The Roost. The coaches generally didn't check on Saturday nights or more than half the team would've been in a lot of trouble. One of my fraternity brothers joined me for breakfast and relayed the story of Mike's wine tasting party that Saturday during the game. The entire fraternity had shown up at Mike's apartment along with their dates. Other friends were also there, in hopes of a fun night and free wine.

From the time I drank Mike's wine Friday morning until I got hit with the green apple quickstep was about three hours. It took the exact amount of time for Mike's elixir to work on everyone at the shindig. There were over a hundred students at the party and only one bathroom upstairs to accommodate everyone. The wine affected both girls and guys all about the same time. With no time to find additional suitable accommodations, I was told that many were introduced to each other's most private moments. This novel experience lasted anywhere from half an hour to two hours. That was one fraternity party I didn't mind missing.

That same Sunday morning, while reading the sports section of the Sunday paper, we discovered a silver lining in the storm that we had encountered in Tennessee. Because of the wins and losses of other games in the ACC, we could clinch our first outright ACC Championship with a victory over the Wake Forest Demon Deacons the very next Saturday.

USC Names Tri-Captains

South Carolina will depart from its usual format and will have three game captains for its important Atlantic Coast Conference football game Saturday at Wake Forest.

In past games, Coach Paul Dietzel and his staff have selected two seniors — one from offense and one from defense — to lead the Gamecocks each Saturday with the permanent captains for the season to be selected the week of the final game with Clemson, scheduled next week.

For the Wake Forest game, however, ends Lynn Hodge and Dave Lucas will combine to lead the defense while guard Tony Fusaro will captain the offense.

Hodge, 6-4, 202, from Union, was a starter as a sophomore in 1966, missed the 1967 season with a broken leg, and snapped back to become a regular again in 1968 and 1969. A Management major, he was chosen Atlantic Coast Conference defensive line-

man of the week for his play against Maryland.

Lucas, a starter at defensive right end for the Gamecocks for three years, is generally considered the best pass rushing end in the ACC. From Bishopville, he is 6-5, 194 and majoring in International Studies with law school plans after graduation.

Fusaro, from Huntington, N. Y., moved to offensive left guard for his senior season after two years as the Gamecocks' starting right offensive tackle. A 6-2, 238 pound Physical Education major, he is married and recently became a father for the first time.

Advertise your Business with Magnetic Signs

Plasti-Magic of Columbia
101 Lexington Ave. West Columbia
Ph. 796-0583

CONSTIPATED?
DUE TO LACK OF FOOD BULK IN YOUR DIET
TRY
Kellogg's ALL-BRAN

Wake Forest had beaten us the year before pretty soundly in Winston-Salem and we had to travel there again. We had played Wake Forest three years in a row at home in Columbia; '64, '65 and '66 and then we had to play them for the next three years; '67, '68 and now 1969 in their stadium. They had a pretty good team, although their record for the year was 3 and 5. Their losses had been close games and could have gone either way.

Game Captain Tony Fusaro

Monday's practice was a spirited one. We were excited about the prospect of winning the ACC Championship. Coach Dietzel always appointed seniors as Game Day Captains. He would usually choose one from the offense and one from the defense. This time, however, he selected two from the defense. Lynn Hodge and

Game Captain Dave Lucas

I were chosen to represent the defensive side of the ball as captains for that game. It was pretty exciting to be the game day captain for one of the biggest football games in the history of the University. The other game captain, representing the offense, was Tony Fasaro. All three of us had been recruited by Coach Marvin Bass.

The team traveled by bus for the third year in a row to the Wake Forest campus. Along with a group of fans following us, was the greatest fan of all, R. J. Moore. R. J. is a retired Army Master Sergeant. He was a member of one of the Army units that replaced the Marines during the Battle of Guadalcanal. My father was one of the Marines relieved by that Army unit. Small world, isn't it?

Game Captain Lynn Hodge

R.J. was originally from Finger, Tennessee, but had chosen Columbia as his home after being stationed at Fort Jackson. In those days, having an automobile was a real privilege for most students but when you finally did get a car, it usually wasn't a new one. RJ, as everyone called him, had opened a filling station about four blocks from The Roundhouse, up on Rosewood Drive and took care of our cars. He would extend credit if you couldn't pay up front and RJ didn't just do it for athletes; he did it for any and all students at South Carolina. I can remember being broke and waiting

237

R.J. Moore

Small world: My dad was a Guadalcanal Veteran. When the Marines were relieved by the army, RJ More was part of the relieving force. When RJ's platoon marched into camp, he noticed a marine stirring something in a pot. He asked,"Hey buddy, what you got cooking?"

The gaunt marine laconically replied, "Jap" as he plucked a skull out of the boiling water with his knife for RJ to see.

for my next laundry check. RJ would cash a check for you without hesitation and hold it until you could cover it. He became a banker for thousands of students at Carolina.

Thirty years later, RJ showed me a file cabinet full from top to bottom and from back to front, with bounced checks. He never prosecuted one person for failing to honor the checks he had cashed. There are even checks from some athletes who went on to make millions playing pro sports. He is a fine man and remains a cherished friend and the greatest Gamecock fan. When my wife, Martha, was in labor with our first child, Carey, we stopped by R.J.'s station on the way to the hospital to share the news of the upcoming arrival.

The day of the Wake Forest game was cold and gray. The temperature at the opening kickoff was twenty two degrees. Our offense worked liked a well-oiled machine and by the end of the game, scored 24 points. Our defense played equally well allowing Wake Forest only 6. Two field goals were all they could muster. I recall that my counterpart, Lynn Hodge, played a great game. We met in the backfield often, chasing their fine quarterback. It was one of those games we dominated comfortably and were never in any real trouble after the first quarter. It was nice to be in command of the game with so much riding on it. When the gun sounded, the score was University of South Carolina Gamecocks 24 and Wake Forest Demon Deacons 6. We had won the ACC Championship. Candler Boyd, another Bass recruit was voted ACC defensive player of the week with 15 tackles and an interception.

As the game ended our offense had possession of the football so the Game Captain for the offense, Tony Fasaro, grabbed one of the game balls as a souvenir. Coach Dietzel got us into the huddle on the sideline to congratulate us. After the pep talk, I turned to my buddy Joe Wingard and said, "Joe, it's not fair that Tony got a game ball and I didn't."

Joe was always enthusiastic and in all of the excitement, he looked at me and said, "Luke, don't worry about it, I'm going to get you a game ball."

With that, Joe took off across the field. One of the Wake Forest assistant coaches was casually walking back toward the dressing room tossing one of the game balls up in the air. He was throwing the ball in a spiral about ten feet up and catching it. I watched as Joe crept up behind the coach and timed his move perfectly. As the ball came down, Joe swooped in just like a defensive back and made the interception. The coach yelled some sort of obscenity at Joe, and screamed, "Hey, come back here with that football!" Joe didn't turn around, but started sprinting across the field toward me. The coach was giving chase and had picked up some company. There were about ten people chasing Joe by the time he reached me. I was standing by the dressing room door as the 'grab' took place. Everyone else had gone in to shower. Joe came running at full speed, flipped the ball to me and said, "Here you go Luke, I gotcha one!" I ducked into the locker room behind Joe and closed the door.

Marion, Bishopville Coaches
Pleased With Playoff Wins
See Stories, Page 8-C

Section C — Columbia, South Carolina, Sunday, November 16, 1969 — Page One

Gamecocks Claim First ACC Championship With 24-6 Romp Over Mistake-Ridden Deacs

HERMAN HELMS
Executive Sports Editor

WINSTON-SALEM — The long, dry spell finally ended. The University of South Carolina won its first football championship in 75 years of playing the game Saturday.

The hustling Gamecocks, who came to Groves Stadium on a very cold day smelling roses, buried Wake Forest amid its own mistakes on the way to a 24-6 victory over the Deacons.

The USC win, coupled with Clemson's 32-15 loss to North Carolina, wrapped up the Atlantic Coast Conference championship for Paul Dietzel's spirited team.

The victory also assured South Carolina of its first winning season in ten years. The Gamecocks will take a 6-3 overall record and a 5-0 ACC mark into next Saturday's season finale with Clemson.

A raging USC defense which forced Wake Forest into countless turnovers and a quick-striking offense that knew what to do with the football once it got it collaborated to rack up the convincing win over the Deacons.

South Carolina's three touchdowns all followed fumble recoveries in Deacon territory.

It was a rewarding day, a day of plenty for Dietzel's smart team, and many people made it so . . . a lot of people on that hopped-up defensive team; quarterback Tommy Suggs, who passed for all of USC's touchdowns; tailback Rudy Holloman, who caught two of the scoring shots; and fullback Warren Muir, who charged in to the Wake line and left a debris of bodies behind him many, many times during the bitter cold afternoon.

These were just a few of the heroes on a day that will live long in the history of USC football.

Suggs drilled a ten-yard pass to Fred Zeigler for South Carolina's first touchdown with just six seconds gone in the second quarter. A fumble recovery by defensive end Lynn Hodge at the ten set the stage for the score.

Suggs popped a 13-yarder to Holloman for the second USC touchdown after offensive guard Chris Bank had recovered a Wake fumble following a Gamecock punt at the Deacon 26. The score came late in the first half.

Defensive end Jimmy Pope dropped on a Wake bobble at the Deacon 40 to set up USC's third TD. Suggs and Holloman hooked up on a 16-yard pass for

Clutch Plays Yield A Happy Ride

Gamecocks' Coach Paul Dietzel, With Game And ACC Title Locked Up, Gets Pleasant Victory Ride (R) — Thanks To Clutch Plays Like Mack Lee Tharpe Collaring Wake's Larry Russell (L) And Rudy Holloman Scoring In A Crowd (C).

Staff Photo By Dave Underwood

this tally which came in the early seconds of the last quarter.

Kicking specialist Billy DuPre booted a 34-yard field goal early in the third quarter after the Gamecocks, showing good muscle, had driven from their own 43 to the Deacon 17-yard line.

Running back Steve Bowden dived one-yard for Wake Forest's only touchdown with 45 seconds left in the half. But that fiery USC defense arose to mess up an attempted kick for the extra point. Little Pat Watson roared in to block Tracy Lounsbury's effort.

An estimated crowd of 25,000 braved 34-degree temperatures at kickoff time to sit in on the game. Gamecock fans in the gathering must have carried some warm thoughts home with them of that brilliant defense which took five fumbles away from the Deacons and intercepted four Deacon passes.

An interception by the ball-hawking little Watson stopped a Wake Forest drive that had reached the USC 21-yard line in the third quarter when USC was clinging to a not-too-solid 17-6 lead.

Defensive back Andy Chavous came up with another big save when he scooped up a Deacon fumble at the USC three in the final quarter.

Suggs fired eight completions in 15 passes for 96 yards and three scores. He thus becomes the leading passer in yardage to ever play for the Gamecocks. Suggs' current total of 2,581 yards breaks the old record held by Dan Reeves.

Muir slammed through the Deacons for 93 yards in 22 trips to become the second leading rusher in Gamecock history. His career total now stands at 2,055 yards.

Zeigler was Suggs' pet target, pulling in five of the Little Man's tosses for 51 yards.

To single out the heroes in the USC defense would be to merely call the roll. All of the Gamecock defenders were rugged soldiers in this very crucial game.

But Watson, Pope, Hodge, Chavous and Jimmy Poston came up with some especially big plays.

Quarterback Larry Russell led a strong Wake Forest ground game that moved the ball well — clicking off 340 yards rushing — but the Deacons simply didn't have the punch in the clutch and give the USC defense credit for that.

Russell gained 86 yards in 28 rushes. He also completed seven of 14 passes for 103 yards.

Suggs fired eight completions.

* * *

	USC	WF
First downs	14	26
Rushing yardage	148	340
Passing yardage	103	103
Return yardage	60	2
Passes	9-18-1	7-14-3
Punts	6-40	3-31
Fumbles Lost	1	5
Yards penalized	80	44

South Carolina	0 14 3 7	—	24	
Wake Forest	0 6 0 0	—	6	

SC — Zeigler 10 pass from Suggs (DuPre kick)
SC — Holloman 13 pass from Suggs (DuPre kick)
WF — Bowden 1 run (Kick blocked)
SC — FG DuPre 34
SC — Holloman 16 pass from Suggs (DuPre kick)
A — 25,000.

SOUTH CAROLINA
RUSHING

Player	Att.	Gain	Los	Net.	L.G.
Muir	22	101	8	93	14
Holloman	6	19	0	19	12
Suggs	4	42	6	36	24
Mirania	4	18	0	18	10
Yoakum	1	8	7	1	
Rice	2	1	5		
Sistare	2	1	5		

PASSING

Player	Comp.	Att.	Inc.	Yds.	L.G.
Suggs	8	15	1	96	

PASS RECEIVING

Player	No.	Yds.	TD	L.G.
Zeigler	5	51	1	
Holloman	2	28	2	
Hamrick	1	14	0	
Rice	1	3	0	

WAKE FOREST
RUSHING

Player	Att.	Gain	Los	Net.	L.G.
Lawill	17	63	4	59	11
Jurewicz	17	53	7	16	10
Bowden	13	33	7	16	10
Gavin	5	29	2	27	14
Russell	28	104	18	86	13

PASSING

Player	Comp.	Att.	Inc.	Yds.	L.G.
Russell	7	14	3	103	

PASS RECEIVING

Player	No.	Yds.	TD	L.G.
Winrow	3	58	0	
Bowden	1	27	0	
Gavin	1	15	0	
Jurewicz	1	17	0	

I kept that game ball for many years. It stayed in closets and on book shelves. My children finally bought a beautiful display case with an appropriate placard for the football. For several years we displayed it prominently in our home. On several different occasions I considered donating the football to the University but it didn't seem that many of the intervening head coaches were very interested in preserving the history of our championship. Several said that they would take the football and find something to do with it. It was not until Coach Steve Spurrier arrived, that I felt comfortable enough to give it up. He was the only coach who seemed to want to build a tradition at South Carolina and to make past lettermen feel welcomed around the football program. After speaking with him at one of the many team functions where the lettermen had been included under his direction, I told him the story about the game ball. He assured me that he was trying to build a tradition at South Carolina and would welcome this symbol of accomplishment, so I donated the football that had meant so much to me, my teammates and all Gamecock fans. Coach Spurrier has it prominently displayed in the trophy case next to the team meeting rooms, where it will hopefully inspire our football team to duplicate 'The Championship' in the SEC.

We were a pretty happy bunch as we rode the Greyhound bus back to Columbia. Coach Dietzel was rightly concerned that our determination to win might subside after the conference championship but he didn't need to worry because our next opponent was Clemson. We had beaten them 7 to 3 the year before, in the 'kitty litter box' and so we were back in Columbia in the Cockpit for the final regular season game. We had read in the newspaper that the legendry Tiger's Coach, Frank Howard, was retiring. If the Tigers could beat us, they could tarnish our championship season and end their year with a 5 and 5 record which would give Coach Howard a winning season and a befitting farewell. We were bound and determined not to let that happen.

Our practices were intense as we prepared to welcome the Tigers to Columbia. We were healthy and we were the ACC Champs. That week of preparation was the most fun I had ever had in college football. The significance of winning the ACC had not been completely realized, but we felt we had turned the corner and that many more championships were on the horizon. Our differences with the coaching staff had diminished by that week of practice. Winning championships cures a lot of bruised egos. As seniors, and as Marvin's Men, we had proven we deserved to be playing Division 1A football. We believed we were good enough to play if given the chance and we had confirmed it with the ACC Crown. It was a good year for our team, coaching staff, and Gamecock fans everywhere. With one more game to play, it was time to prove that we could persevere and complete the season with an impressive performance against our rivals. We weren't about to let the Tigers throw cold water on our parade, so we prepared to give Clemson a proper Carolina Gamecock welcome on Saturday, November 22, 1969.

HERMAN HELMS
Executive Sports Editor

A Moment Supreme In USC Football
THE GAMECOCKS were flying home at sunset from Winston-Salem Saturday, and the sky was some-

USC-Clemson Battle Is Key To Bowl Bid For Gamecocks

thing to see. Coach Paul Dietzel pointed out the window of the big airplane to some fiery streaks of red against a gorgeous backdrop of blue. "Isn't that beautiful?" said the admiring coach.

The whole world was beautiful to Dietzel late Saturday. He was flying home with a South Carolina team that was something no other USC athletic team has ever been. These Gamecocks were champions.

Cashing in on a bundle of Wake Forest mistakes with professional skill, the Gamecocks had wiped out the Deacons, 24-6, earlier in the day. This victory, coupled with Clemson's 32-14 loss to North Carolina, had brought the Atlantic Coast Conference race to a screeching halt and left the Gamecocks standing all alone as undisputed champions.

The players sang and threw water on each other in the dressing room at Groves Stadium in Winston-Salem. Riding by bus from the stadium to the Winston airport, they had some real fun.

"The varsity has earned the weekend off," announced one squad member. "The Brown (reserve) team will scrimmage tonight at eight."

"I'm gonna enjoy this while I can," confessed a certain member of the Brown team, "then tomorrow he (meaning Coach Dietzel) will grade the film."

Just before their chartered plane landed in Columbia to a big welcome from several hundred loyal fans Dietzel went on the intercom system and announced, "Gentlemen, you are now approaching Columbia, home of the ACC champions."

This was a heady hour, a moment supreme, the most momentous day in the history of USC football, the end of the long, dry spell.

Win Over Tigers Could Lead To Bowl

Saturday's victory marked a bunch of firsts for USC. It was the Gamecocks' first football title in 75 years of playing the game and the school's first out-

right championship ever in any sport. It also assured USC of its first winning football season in ten years, and it marked the first time that the Gamecocks have been able to rack up grid victories in one season over North Carolina's entire "Big Four."

Now that the ACC title is theirs, the question arises on this pleasant Monday morning . . . can there be something else for the Gamecocks this season, some other high plateau to be reached, say like a bowl?

The answer seems quite simple. The Clemson game is the key. If the Gamecocks dust off Clemson, their chances of going to a pre-New Year's bowl are good. If they lose to the Tigers, the chances are nil.

Three of the so-called "secondary" bowls have all shown an interest in the Gamecocks. Of the three, the Peach Bowl at Atlanta seems to be looking at the present time with the most favor upon USC. But the Liberty at Memphis and the Sun at El Paso, Tex., are also known to be keeping eyes on the Gamecocks.

As a matter of fact, the Liberty made the first advances when it dispatched representatives to scout USC against Maryland three weeks ago.

The Gamecocks can go bowling it seems possible . . . if they beat Clemson, but only if they beat Clemson.

This is a situation that Paul Dietzel, for obvious reasons, would just as soon forget about until after next Saturday. Bowl talk now can only cause the Tigers to bristle with desire for an upset, and it can only put a lot more pressure on the Gamecocks.

But in the shadows of the season, this is the way it is . . . the Gamecocks are a victory away from another possible plum. The possibility of a bowl merely adds a little more flavor to that Civil War that will be played at Carolina Stadium next Saturday, as if it needed any more flavor.

Not A Great Team, But A Good One

THE GAMECOCKS were not an overpowering machine against Wake Forest Saturday. They simply got the job done, as a fine defense which forced the Deacons into a mass of mistakes collaborated with a quick-striking offense that seized on its opportunities.

The ball-hawking defense, which offered many heroes — Dave Lucas, Candler Boyd, Benny Padgett

and Pat Watson, to name just a few — scooped up five fumbles by the Deacons and intercepted four Wake passes.

The USC offense, triggered by Tommy Suggs' good right arm, followed up three of the fumble recoveries with touchdowns. The very nature of this performance said something about these Gamecocks, these champion Gamecocks.

How many times in its unhappy football past has USC played give-away and seen an opponent profit from it? Now it is the Gamecocks who make their opportunities and know what to do with them.

This is a good football team, not a great one but a good one. The Gamecocks have had two bad breakdowns, against Georgia and Florida State. They have had some classic moments — the last quarter against Duke, several minutes against N. C. State and almost the whole game against Tennessee, to cite a few.

The team has not played a complete game all season because, in truth, the team has not yet advanced to that stage. The story in this rewarding season of 1969 is simply this: the Gamecocks are champions and they are a good football team. After so many disappointing years, USC football is very definitely on the rise.

The credit, of course, belongs primarily to one man, Paul Dietzel. This tall man is a lot of things. He is a good coach, a promoter, a cheerleader, an organizer and a master politician. If he were anything less than what he is, he might never have been able to lead the Gamecocks out of the woods.

Dietzel analyzed the situation accurately at the end of a long, rewarding Saturday. "Some people will say that it is no great thing to win the ACC championship because ACC football isn't that good," he said. "But I've never experienced a more thrilling day in my life because I see it for what it is — a beginning."

A Tennessee student was waving a big sign in front of the USC buses when the Gamecocks left Knoxville a week ago Saturday. It had been a frightening day for Tennessee, but the student was looking to the future. His sign said simply this: "We'll be greater later."

The message was intended for the Vols, but it might also apply to the Gamecocks.

WATSON
Jolted
Staff Photo by Dave Underwood
Ball Pops Free As Wake Forest Defender Smacks South Carolina's Doug Hamrick Saturday.

That Saturday dawned cold, clear and beautiful. The excitement and enthusiasm was apparent as we started the day with our usual Saturday morning brunch. The bus took us to the stadium as the stands were filling up for the big game. It was an odd feeling to know that this would be the last time I would play football in Carolina Stadium. If we could beat Clemson, we could end the regular season with a 7 and 3 record which would make it our best season since 1958. We had, that same week, accepted an invitation to play the West Virginia Mountaineers in the Peach Bowl. The Carolina Gamecocks had not been to a bowl game since before I was born, when we played in the 1946 Gator Bowl, 23 years before.

Offensively, we moved the ball at will. Tommy Suggs, Warren Muir and Freddie Zeigler put on an offensive show that day, as did all of the offense. When the game ended, our offense had racked up a total of over 500 yards on the ground and through the air. Our running backs ran effectively and our receivers caught the ball well. Coach Frank Howard, always the showman, tipped his hat every time the Gamecocks scored. It was bright and sunny during the course of the game and Coach Howard claimed afterward that he tipped his hat so often that he got sunburned on his bald head. Our offense tacked on 27 points in addition to the 500 yards of offense.

Defensively, we were able to hold the Tigers to 14 points. They had less than 300 yards in total offense and their two scores came late, after the game had already been decided. Both offensively and defensively, we dominated the Tigers and the final score was South Carolina Gamecocks 27, Clemson Tigers 14. This was our day, our season and our first conference championship. Not only had we won the ACC Championship outright, but we had done it by going undefeated in the ACC. There was a lot of joy in "Mudville" that night, because "Casey" had hit a home run to win the game. The victory over Clemson was icing on the cake.

241

USC Kept Hodge's Promise

★ ★ ★   ★ ★ ★

Dietzel: 'This Was Strange Game'

By HAROLD MARTIN
State Sports Writer

It was halftime at Carolina Stadium Saturday afternoon and South Carolina had squandered most of a 17-point lead against arch-foe Clemson and the Gamecocks were now sitting on a precarious, 17-13 edge.

But during the rest period, USC defensive end Lynn Hodge came to Paul Dietzel and told his coach:

"We messed things up, coach, but don't worry, we're going to make up for it."

Make up for it they did. Hodge and his defensive mates held the Tigers scoreless over the final 30 minutes while the offense was putting ten more points on the board for a 27-13 triumph.

When it was over and the Gamecocks were on their way back to the Rex Enright Athletic Center to shower and dress, Dietzel said, "That was a happy bunch of boys — and here is a happy coach.

"It was a great victory for us," Dietzel continued, "and I told the team after the game, 'now you can talk about the Peach Bowl.'"

South Carolina, champion of the Atlantic Coast Conference, will play West Virginia in the Peach Bowl at Atlanta Dec. 30.

"This was a strange game," Dietzel said, "one of the strangest I've seen. The Gamecocks were really cranked up for this one.

"We went out there and carried the battle to them. Then, doggone me, we relaxed out there and let them get back. And before we could turn around, it was 17-13.

"I thought there were two really big plays in the game," Dietzel said, "and our punter, Billy Parker, figured in both.

"The first was when Clemson blocked that punt in the second quarter. That kind of play always electrifies the team that is able to pull it off and it certainly did that for Clemson.

"The other," Dietzel continued, "was Parker's pass from punt formation to (Fred) Zeigler in the third quarter."

That pass, on a fourth down play from the Clemson 35, resulted in a 19-yard advance to the Tiger 16 and eventually resulted in the Gamecocks' final three points on Billy DuPre's second field goal.

"We though we could throw against

Staff Photo By Ed Andrieski

The Holloman Stretch
Rudy Holloman Stretches For Tommy Suggs Pass, Gathers It In.

Clemson," Dietzel said, "and we planned to open up our attack. We were going to let it all hang out because we felt Clemson was just too big for us to try to slug it out with them.

"And I thought we did a pretty good job with our attack. We got the ball down there a couple of times, but then we couldn't get it in.

"But I think our team was ready to play Clemson today. I'm as proud as I can be of all of them, and especially the 11 seniors who played their final game at Carolina Stadium."

Three of the Gamecocks' offensive aces, fullback Warren Muir, quarterback Tommy Suggs and flanker Fred Zeigler, received praise for outstanding performances. Muir rushed for 127 yards, Zeigler caught nine passes for 122 and Suggs hit on 15 throws for 211 yards.

Staff Photo By Ed Andrieski

The Pressure's On
USC's Lynn Hodge (89) Bursts Through Clemson's Offensive line And Heads For Quarterback Tommy Kendrick (14)

242

Our football season wasn't over. Bowl eligible; we were looking forward to playing the West Virginia Mountaineers at the Peach Bowl in Atlanta, Georgia on December 30th, a Tuesday night. But for a little while, we were going to enjoy our success. West Virginia had lost only one game that season, a 20 to 0 shutout against No.2 ranked Penn State. Penn State was undefeated and would remain in that slot behind top-ranked Texas. Both teams finished with identical 11-0 records. Obviously, West Virginia was another very good team. They were ranked 18th at the time, but their record proved they were even better. Because West Virginia was a school from a small state with respect to population, they didn't have the press for a higher ranking. Their Coach was a colorful character by the name of Jim Carlin. Jim would become a future South Carolina Head Coach, and a good friend and business partner of mine.

We studied a lot of game film on the Mountaineers and they were a tough looking crew that loved to run the football straight at you. Their offense reminded me of the Duke Blue Devil team we had played back in 1967. But instead of having one really good running back (Jay Calabrese), they had two, Jim Braxton and Bob Gresham. These two 240 pounders were tremendous running backs with great size and speed and both of them eventually had successful careers in the NFL. It was going to be the Gamecock's speed and finesse against the power and size of the Mountaineers.

The basketball season started that year on the same weekend as our win over Clemson. We were just as excited about basketball and their potential conference championship run as we had been about our season. Coach Frank McGuire and the Gamecocks had accomplished something no one had, before or since. The team was ranked preseason No.1. Our football program had achieved quite a feat, but we weren't even in the top 20. We all hoped our football team was on its way to also being ranked as one of the best in the nation, but Coach McGuire had done it with his basketball team. That was a lofty status, but sadly, it did not last long. We lost our first game and fell out of the top spot in the rankings but it didn't matter. We were playing with the best and beating them. Coach Maguire had assembled some of the finest talent in the country. At the time, the West Coast dominated basketball. UCLA's Coach, John Wooten, was in the midst of his reign in college basketball. So for us to be ranked ahead of his team, if only for a couple of weeks, was an honor, indeed and the future looked rosy.

The 1969 Carolina Basketball team was extraordinary. The big stars were All American Guard, John Roche and All American Center, Tom Owens. They averaged 40 points per game between the two of them. Other outstanding players were Tom Riker, future Georgia Tech head coach Bobby Cremins, Rick Aydelett, John Ribock, Bobby Carver, my fraternity brother, Gene Spencer, Corky Carnevale, Dennis Powell, Tommy Terry and Billy Grimes. After losing the first game, they duplicated the football team's record and went undefeated in the ACC and won the conference regular season championship. It was one of the rare instances where two athletic teams from the same school went

243

undefeated in conference play in the same season. It was a feather in our cap to have captured ACC Championships in football and basketball in 1969/1970 and John Roche was voted ACC Player of the Year.

In those days, only one team from each conference was invited to play in the NCAA Tournament and the team that moved on was the winner of the ACC Tournament, not the regular season conference champions. That year, our star John Roche, suffered a severe ankle sprain just before the ACC tournament championship game against the North Carolina State Wolfpack. In a heartbreaking development for the Gamecocks, we lost the game by three points in double overtime, eliminating us from NCAA tournament play. We did finish ranked No. 6 in the nation ending the year 25-3, and that team still holds the record for the best basketball season in school history. Coach McGuire went on to put together 6 back-to-back 20 win seasons.

The Peach Bowl was fast approaching and we began preparing after only a week off. At one of our team meetings, Coach Dietzel tried using a little psychology to spur us on. The ACC had presented each Carolina player with a golden coin emblazoned with the ACC Logo on each side. At the time that was all we had received for winning the conference crown. Coach Dietzel told us that if we won The Peach Bowl, we would be presented with championship rings by the South Carolina Athletic Department. In addition, we would receive extra money for our trip to Atlanta and would enjoy two additional days in the hotel. If we didn't win the game against West Virginia, there would be no ring, no extra money over the minimum required and only one extra day after the game, in the hotel.

We understood what he was trying to do. He was trying to motivate us by using the carrot and stick approach and while it might have worked for some, for others it was the wrong approach. If the South Carolina Gamecocks had been for years, a football powerhouse and had won other conference championships, I believe his approach may have worked. But most of the players felt that winning the first conference championship in school history, and going to the first Bowl game since 1946, should have been worth more than a coin as a token, so it took a little shine off our Gamecock helmets.

A couple of days before we were to leave for Atlanta, I decided it was time to upgrade my wardrobe for the trip. I had tried to get into the swing of the 60's, earlier in the year, when I dared to grow sideburns. When Coach Dietzel noticed my modest burns, he immediately ordered that I take a razor and destroy what I had been working on for about a week. I protested and told him that I wasn't trying to become a hippie, but that I was growing the sideburns in honor of my ancestors. I told him that my grandfather, great-grandfather, and great-great-grandfather had all worn sideburns. Coach Dietzel said it didn't matter why I was growing them; I wasn't going to be wearing sideburns on his football team. I complied with his wishes.

Coach Dietzel was a fine Athletic Director for South Carolina and was also a talented artist and poet. He designed the Gamecock Logo and wrote the lyrics to the Carolina Fight Song and both are still in use today. In

Those Gamecock Champions Are A Bunch Of Odd Birds

By BILL BALLENGER
News Sports Writer

WINSTON-SALEM — The University of South Carolina defeated Wake Forest 24-6 in Groves Stadium Saturday and thus won their first football championship in history. They won it easily although they were outgained heavily on the ground and matched in the air. That is an unusual way to win. This is an unusual football team.

South Carolina's Gamecocks are a football team led by a 5:9 quarterback who is forced to roll out on all of his passes because he cannot see over his center's rump. When this quarterback throws, he throws to a 5:11 end who wears a size 13 shoe and needs contact lenses because otherwise he is rated blind by the highway department.

And when Tommy Suggs and Fred Zeigler aren't doing their throw and catch act, a transplanted West Point dropout named Warren Muir plunges on the ground for yardage.

That's pretty unusual. But that's not the half of it. Saturday the defense was captained by Dave Lucas—try not to laugh. Lucas is a rough, tough 6:5 end who weighs 189 pounds and looks like something that ought to be in a line for food stamps.

His was the duty Saturday of putting the pressure on Wake Forest's sophomore quarterback Larry Russell. Lucas wound up the day winded and wheezing and with but four tackles to his credit, but he and all the other USC ends did a pretty good job. Russell drove all of them batty with his fish-in-a-bowl maneuvers, but he got away only once. Wake scored that one time when the little Deacon hurled the ball to Steve Bowden after the long chase.

THAT MADE the score 14-6

DAVE LUCAS
...Gaunt Gamecock

at halftime. Thereafter Lucas and Eddie Bolton and Jimmy Pope and Lynn Hodge and Rusty Ganas and Candler Boyd and Benny Padgett usually got the long end of Wake's Wishbone-T. Suggs hurled three touchdown passes and Billy Dupre kicked a field goal for the USC scores.

"I thought we'd never get the day over with," Lucas said afterwards. "I'm known for my ability at rushing the passer, but this was different.

"Most quarterbacks are righthanded and I've always liked to sneak up inside on them and hit them from the blind side.

"This guy was lefthanded. I had him four times on one play and he got away from me. It was pretty embarrassing.

"As for now, this has to be the happiest day of my life."

Lucas began his football playing in Bishopville, S. C. at age six. In all of his years of playing football, he has never played on a championship team before.

"My senior year at Bishopville we had a 9-1 record," he said. "We lost one game and that was to Lower Richland

High and it knocked us out of the state playoffs."

Going into that year, Lower Richland High had lost 47 athletic games of all kinds in a row.

Lucas' achievements were largely offensive. He and Bishopville's other end were the team's leading scorers, so he was invited to USC as an offensive operative.

WHEN he got there the staff discovered he had china hands and a high metabolism. Every effort they made to get him up in weight failed. He came at 6:4 and 175, which makes him look beefy today.

"I tried and tried," he said, "but all that worry just made me lose more weight. I just have to do it with what I have to do it with."

On the squad they laugh at him as he tapes up his socks to keep them from falling down. He is known as "Twiggy" and "The Splendid Splinter" and "The Blade." And nobody likes to be tackled by him, they say, because he leaves welts.

One way or the other, with what he has, Lucas has led a good part of the Gamecock defense. It gives up a lot, but has the knack of making the big play. Five Wake fumbles and four interceptions Saturday tell mutely of how well they do this.

"I like to keep talking to my sidekick in the line," Lucas says. "We kind of growl to each other. Keep each other alert, on the stick."

His sidekick is 6:5, 240-pound tackle Rusty Ganas. They are close buddies on and off the field, hanging around on campus together much of the time. Together they average out to two average fellows.

They are known by their buddies as "The Odd Couple" which is in keeping with what they are: teammates on the USC football champions of 1969—a pretty unusual team.

his retirement, he has made a new career as a water color artist. Coach Dietzel took great pleasure in posting drawings on our dressing room walls and sketched one of me with sideburns that same week. The posters were entitled "Rhett Butler Lucas." There was a definite likeness, except for the exaggerated sideburns added to my profile. We all had a good laugh about it and knowing what I know now, I wish I had grabbed the posters to keep for posterity.

Since I wasn't able to wear sideburns, I did the next best thing. I bought a "mod" ensemble; a pair of low cut, blue bell bottom trousers and a funky looking psychedelic shirt with an extra-long collar. I didn't want to go to the big city looking like country come to town. There were three modes of dress in those days; the conservative Country and Western look which consisted of blue jeans, cowboy boots and usually a Western-style shirt. The other was the 'Frat Cat' look of khaki pants, white or blue button-down collar, long sleeve shirt, alpaca sweater and penny loafers with no socks and the mod look I just described.

We were allowed to go home for Christmas for a couple of days, but we returned to The Roost and left for Atlanta the day after Christmas. Our Peach Bowl Game was going to be televised. It would be the first time that these Gamecocks had played on national television. My current girlfriend had gone home to California to spend Christmas with her brother and his family, so she wouldn't be able to join me in Atlanta, but could watch it on the tube. One of my teammates, Bill Duffel, rectified my situation. After the game, he had arranged a blind date for me.

Our hotel accommodations were first-class. We stayed in one of the downtown Atlanta high-rise hotels. It was much different than the usual motel accommodations and we had a magnificent view of the City of Atlanta. During the flight over from Columbia, the stewardess's had as much fun as we did flirting. It was the first time any of us had ever heard the cool nickname for Atlanta and our stewardesses made up a little poem about setting us down in "Hotlanta" where the girls were hotter than the weather.

The festivities leading up to the bowl game were great. We were entertained one afternoon by Billy Joe Royal who had one of the hottest hits of the year entitled, *Down in the Boondocks*. The Peach Bowl was a brand-new bowl and we were playing in only its second year. Atlanta and the State of Georgia were going all out to make this a first-class event. The new Governor of Georgia, Lester Maddox, even got into the act and officiated at one of our banquets. Lester was known for his stance in favor of segregation and the fact that West Virginia was a fully integrated team did not go unnoticed. At our banquet, we were entertained by Miss Georgia, a beautiful girl dressed as a Southern Belle. The team captains from both the Mountaineers and the Gamecocks were to present a bouquet of flowers to the lovely lady. Our Captain, Pat Watson, went first and ever the flirt, Pat decided to bestow a kiss on the cheek of Miss Georgia. That would not usually present a problem except that the captains for West Virginia were black. The crowd held its breath and watched one of the Captains from West Virginia bestow a kiss, as well. All of the people on stage, including the Governor, handled the situation with class. Gov. Maddox also would be part of the halftime entertainment. He was going to ride a bicycle backwards all the way around the field. Fortunately, or unfortunately, depending on your point of view, we would miss this feat of agility, since we would be in the dressing room trying to figure out how to win the football game.

Tuesday arrived and it was time to get down to business. West Virginia was bigger, with a strong running game. We passed more than we ran and did it well. Our quarterback, Tommy Suggs, was at the top of all of the stats of quarterbacks in the ACC. Warren Muir was first or second in most categories and Freddie Zeigler, our top-notch receiver, ranked high as well. Rudy Holloman, one of our fastest halfbacks also ranked in receiving for both yards and touchdowns. We believed we could hold the Mountaineers defensively. We were playing in the home stadium of the Georgia Tech Yellow Jackets, Grant Field

West Virginia Will Face USC In Peach Bowl

By BILL MITCHELL
State Sports Writer

Things have been pretty cold and damp up in the West Virginia mountains for the pride of the state — West Virginia's gridiron Mountaineers — but all that has changed now.

Coach Jim Carlen, in his fourth season as the head coach of the Mountaineers, has guided his club to an 8-1 record thus far this season

---

The University of South Carolina ticket office late Monday received 15,000 tickets to the second annual Peach Bowl football game in Atlanta, Ga., in which the Gamecocks will meet West Virginia University Dec. 30.

These tickets will go on sale at the University ticket office at the Rex Enright Athletic Center on Rosewood Drive at 8:30 A.M., Wednesday. Applications for Peach Bowl tickets will be mailed to all Gamecock Club members this week, probably by Thursday. Fans ordering by mail should include an extra 50 cents with each order to cover handling and insurance.

Tickets to the Peach Bowl are $6.50 each. Telephone orders will not be accepted.

JIM CARLEN
Pleased With Invitation

and the school has accepted a bid to oppose South Carolina's ACC champions in the Peach Bowl, Dec. 30th.

"We are very pleased to accept the Peach Bowl invitation," said Carlin. "We're about like South Carolina — we don't get to go very often.

"The only thing that we have on our minds right now is Syracuse," added the Mountaineer head coach. "You have to keep them the first thing in your mind or they'll knock you around."

Carlen, whose team has lost only to fourth-ranked and undefeated Penn State, suffered a losing season in 1966, his first year at the helm of the Mountaineers. But things have become increasingly brighter since.

The Mountaineers compiled a 5-4-1 mark in 1967 and a 7-3 record in 1968 before this year's season in which Carlen's team has scored less than 30 points only twice.

"We have won 11 out of our

1969 Record

Cincinnati	57-11
Maryland	31- 7
Tulane	35-17
VMI	32- 0
Penn St.	0-20
Pitt	49-18
Kentucky	7- 6
Will. & Mary	31- 0
Richmond	33-21
Syracuse	Nov. 22

which was located on the Georgia Tech campus with the Atlanta skyline as a backdrop. None of us had paid much attention to the weather report, but during warm-ups we noticed there were some dark clouds rolling in. Just after we finished our drills, the bottom fell out. It began to rain so hard that the frogs were jumping up on the goalpost to get out of the torrent. Because it was winter, all of the grass had died leaving only dirt on the field. It turned into a quagmire. When we ran back out to start the game, it was into a driving rain and the mud was up to our ankles.

Our quarterback, Tommy Suggs, is less than 6' tall, but most of our linemen were all over 6'3". Tommy was most effective when he was able to roll out or scramble. He could throw well on the run with Freddie Zeigler catching anything near him and it was usually a very successful combination. With the deluge and all the mud, we knew the planets weren't lining up in our favor. Defensively, we held them pretty well but after an interception which gave the Mountaineers a short field, they scored a touchdown. Their two big running backs just slammed it into the end zone using the 'old 3 yards and a cloud of dust', or in this case, 'the splash and slide'. We mustered

247

Alert Defense, Strong Mounties Over USC

By HERMAN HELMS
Executive Sports Editor

ATLANTA - West Virginia had just the right weapon for the weather — a quick, strong running game — and the Mounties used it to prance through the rain and mud to a 14-3 Peach Bowl victory over South Carolina here Monday night.

The Mountaineers, who entered the game as slight favorites, scored their touchdowns on the first and last times

Little General Directs

South Carolina Quarterback Tommy Suggs (12) Hands Off To Fullback Warren Muir (Left Photo) During First Half Of Peach Bowl

A crowd of 48,452 braved nasty weather to watch the battle. Over 54,000 tickets were sold for the nationally televised game, but some ticket holders obviously chose to watch it in the comforts of home.

Hard rain fell prior to the game and in its early stages, leaving the Grant Field turf a sloppy mess.

A fumble killed a Gamecock scoring threat at the West Virginia 12 in the first quarter. Fullback Warren Muir lost the slick ball, and the alert Crennel seized it for the Mounties.

USC reached the West Virginia 26 early in the third period, but the tough Mountaineer defense threw the Gamecocks back. It was the pesky Crennel who once again broke the drive, pinning quarterback Tommy Suggs for a six-yard loss on a fourth down and one play at the 26.

A pass interception by West Virginia defensive back Terry Snively stopped another USC drive that carried to the Mountaineer six-yard line in the fourth period.

The Gamecocks were held to 64 yards rushing and col-

Warren Muir: Top USC Rusher

lected 126 yards through the air.

Muir ripped off 52 yards in 18 carries to lead USC's rushing. Suggs, under a heavy rush and thrown for big losses many times, managed to complete nine of 17 passes for 98 yards. Alternate quarterback Randy Yoakum hit on two of six passes for 28 yards.

The game hero, Williams, was very much of a "secret weapon." Gresham and Braxton had been the celebrated ponies in West Virginia's powerful running game throughout the regular season, and each performed well in the bowl clash.

Gresham charged for 98 yards in 16 carries, while

Braxton picked up 60 yards in 20 trips.

But neither was in Williams' class Tuesday night. The soph flash had gained just 381 yards in 53 carries during the regular season, but the burden was placed on him in this blue chip battle and he responded sensationally.

West Virginia's Ron Pobolish fumbled a Gamecock punt late in the first half and USC offensive center Ken Ross fell

* * *

WEST VIRGINIA
RUSHING

	Att.	Yds.	For	TD	L.G.
E. Williams	35	208	0		37
Gresham	16	98	1		38
Braxton	20	60	1		9
Sherwood	8	10	0		3
TOTALS	79	356	2		38

PASSING

	Att.	Cpl.	Hi	Yds	TD	L.G.
Sherwood	2-1-0			3	0	3
TOTALS	2-1-0			3	0	3

PASS RECEIVING

	No.	Yds.	TD	L.G.
Braxton	1	3	0	3
TOTALS	1	3	0	3

SOUTH CAROLINA

	Att.	Yds.	TD	L.G.
RUSHING				
Muir	18	52	0	6
Helloman	7	18	0	6
Yoakum	2	10	0	11
Suggs	11	16	0	8
TOTALS	38	64	0	11

PASSING

	Att.	Cpl.	Hi	Yds.	TD	L.G.
Suggs	17	9	1	98	0	24
Yoakum	6	2	1	28	0	19
TOTALS	23	11	2	126	0	24

Ground Game Lift In Peach Bowl, 14-3

that they had possession of the football.

West Virginia marched 66 yards in ten plays for its first touchdown, tailback Bob Gresham going for the score for 11 yards out with just 5:36 having passed in the game.

The Mounties moved 61 yards in 11 plays for their sec-ond TD. Fullback Jim Braxton tallied this one from the one-yard line with 23 seconds remaining in the second annual classic.

Braxton kicked the point after each score.

In between their touchdown marches, the Mountaineers covered a lot of real estate as a sophomore running back Eddie Williams, turned in a near-incredible performance.

The Mounties, proving themselves to be excellent mudders, gained 356 yards rushing, and Williams, fittingly chosen as the game's most outstanding offensive player, ripped off 208 of them in 35 carries.

Middle guard Carl Crennel of the Mounties was voted the game's top defensive player.

The Gamecocks, who didn't have the punch to convert several scoring chances, averted a shutout on a 37-yard field goal by Billy DuPre late in the first half.

The Attack
Attempts Pass Despite Efforts Of West Virginia Defender.

Staff Wirephotos By Dave Underwood

	West Virginia	South Car.
First Downs	21	5
Rushing yardage	356	64
Passing yardage	3	136
Return yardage	53	0
Passes	1-2-0	11-23-2
Punts	4-26	6-39
Fumbles lost	3	1
Yards penalized	30	65
West Virginia	7 0 0 7—14	
South Carolina	0 3 0 0— 3	

WVA—Gresham 10 run (Braxton kick)
SC—FG DuPre 37
WVA—Braxton 1 run (Braxton kick)
A—48,452

PASS RECEIVING	No.	Yds.	TD	L.G.
Holloman	5	33	0	11
Hamrick	4	64	0	19
Muir	2	29	0	24
TOTALS	11	126	0	24

on the loose ball at the Mountaineer 41-yard line to set the stage for the Gamecocks' only points of the game.

USC moved as far as the Mountaineer ten-yard line, but Suggs was thrown for a big loss back to the 19 on third down and Dupre came on to kick his 37-yard field goal on fourth down.

His sinking kick barely cleared the crossbar and struck the post that supports the goal-posts.

But for some fine clutch play by USC's defensive team West Virginia's victory margin might have been much larger.

The Mounties were stopped at the USC one-yard line in the dying seconds of play in the first half, and Braxton missed a pair of field goal attempts in the third period after West Virginia drives had bogged down deep in Gamecock territory.

Running It Back
Gamecocks' Dick Harris Returns Kickoff Against West Virginia In Peach Bowl.

Staff Wirephoto By Dave Underwood

249

3 points on a field goal by Billy DuPre. I recovered a fumble in the backfield at one point, but in the 60's you couldn't advance a fumble. We might've been able to tie the game or take the lead, if we had had the same rules that are in effect today.

The rain kept coming down and other than the field goal; we didn't score again. We had the football with about a minute to go deep in our own territory and it was 4th and long. We had no choice but to go for it. Our attempt at a first down was unsuccessful, so West Virginia got the ball once again with a short field inside of our 10-yard line. They were able to punch in one more score and the game ended, West Virginia Mountaineers 14, South Carolina Gamecocks 3. We had lost our bowl game. We didn't get a championship ring for winning the ACC or additional money and extra days in our high-rise hotel.

The college football season ended in the following manner.

Bowl Games

BOWL	Winner		Loser	
COTTON	#1 Texas Longhorns	21	#9 Notre Dame Fighting Irish	17
ORANGE	#2 Penn State Nittany Lions	10	#6 Missouri Tigers	3
SUGAR	#13 Mississippi Rebels	27	#3 Arkansas Razorbacks	22
ROSE	#5 USC Trojans	10	#7 Michigan Wolverines	3

East Tennessee State went undefeated and beat Louisiana Tech, led by Terry Bradshaw, in the Grantland Rice Bowl in Baton Rouge, LA. At the Cotton Bowl in Dallas, the #1 Texas Longhorns were facing the end of their unbeaten streak before a crowd of 73,000. Trailing 17-14 with 2:26 left in the game, Texas was 10 yards from goal, but it was 4th down, and going for a tie was out of the question. Failing to convert would give Notre Dame the ball and the chance to run out the clock. Texas QB James Street managed to fire a pass over the head of the equally determined Notre Dame linebacker, Bob Olson. Cotton Speyrer came down with the ball on the 2-yard line, just before the ball hit the ground. The officials paused before ruling that the pass was indeed complete, giving Texas the first down, and two plays later, Billy Dale took the ball in for the winning points and, ultimately, the title .[7] In the final poll, the Texas Longhorns were the top choice for 36 of the 45 writers voting, and won the AP Trophy as the final #1. The Final Top 20 was: 1.Texas 2.Penn State 3.USC 4.Ohio State 5.Notre Dame 6.Missouri 7.Arkansas 8.Mississippi 9.Michigan 10.UCLA 11.Nebraska 12.Houston 13.LSU 14.Florida 15.Tennessee 16.Colorado 17.West Virginia 18.Purdue 19.Stanford and 20.Auburn.

Other bowls:

BOWL	Location	Winner		Loser	
SUN	El Paso	Nebraska	45	Georgia	6
GATOR	Jacksonville	Florida	14	Tennessee	13
TANGERINE	Orlando	Toledo	56	Davidson	33
ASTRO-BLUEBONNET	Houston	Houston	36	Auburn	7
LIBERTY	Memphis	Colorado	47	Alabama	33
PEACH	Atlanta	West Virginia	14	South Carolina	3
PASADENA	Pasadena	San Diego State	28	Boston U.	7
Rice Bowl	Baton Rouge	East Tennessee State	34	Louisiana Tech	14

The Heisman Trophy was won that year by Steve Owens of Oklahoma who had rushed for 3,867 yards and scored 56 touchdowns in three seasons with the Sooners. In 1969, he had 29 touchdowns and scored 138 points, and rushed for 248 yards against Iowa State. He later played for the Detroit Lions. Second in the voting was Mike Phipps, quarterback for Purdue.

My football career was over. It was a very strange feeling to know that this would be the last time I would play the game I had enjoyed since the age of nine. It was a bittersweet moment, but there was also a great feeling of accomplishment. To know that we had won the first conference championship in school history was huge. The 1965 team had been ACC Co-Champions and if you talked to members of that team, most of them will tell you, they still believe they won a share of that conference championship. I agree with Frank Howard's assessment. His comment when asked about his thoughts on the ACC Championship being stripped from South Carolina was, "They can take the championship away if they want to, but South Carolina still won it where it counted, on the football field."

Tailpiece

I hope you, my readers, have enjoyed this insider's look at college football and college life in the 1960's. As my teammates and I said goodbye to 'Our Carolina', we all felt the future was bright for South Carolina Athletics. There is an old saying that Rome wasn't built in a day, but forty four years is too much of a gap. I look forward with great expectation to the future of South Carolina Football and the championships I believe will come our way. Ray Tanner and the Gamecock Baseball Team have proven that lightning can strike twice. And now, with the ole Ball Coach, Steve Spurrier, leading the Gamecocks, I see big thunder clouds, full of "Garnet Lightning," building in the East.

Go Cocks!

CHAPTER 12

A compliation of
1965, '67, '68, and
'69 Redbooks,
and the 1969
Reports from the
Roost booklets

FIRST ROW: Ben Garnto, Benny Galloway, Jim Mulvihill, John Dyer, Curtis Williams, Bob Cole, Bob Wehmeyer, Mike Fair, Jimmy Gobble, Johnny Glass, Don Somma, Joe Komoroski, Hyrum Pierce, Scott Townsend, Jimmy Poole, SECOND ROW: Ray Edwards, Bob White, Bob Mauro, Roy Don Reeves, Gene Schwarting, Tim Bice, Dave Grant, Tom Wingard, Johnny Gregory, Toy McCord, Wally Orrel, Wally Medlin, Ron Bunch, Jack James, Carl Cowart. THIRD ROW: Don Buckner, Rudy Holloman, Dan Harbson, Allen Brown, Larry Royal, John Tominack, Richard Harrelson, Fred Zeigler, John Coleman, George McCarthy, Dave Lucas, Gordon Gibson, Ronnie Palmer, Warren Muir. FOURTH ROW: Clyde Smith, Tony Fusaro, Don Brant, Bob Morris, John King, Pat Watson, Candler Boyd, Billy Tharp, Andy Chavous, Frank Tetterton, Fletcher Spigner, Jim Ross, Don Dunning, Allen Owen. TOP ROW: Coach Don Purvis, Coach Dick Weldon, Coach Pride Ratterree, Coach Bill Shalosky, Head Coach Paul Dietzel, Coach Larry Jones, Coach Bill Rowe, Coach Johnny Menger, Coach Lou Holtz, Trainer Jim Price.

254

"Fighting Gamecocks"
1969

Front Row (L - R): Coach Larry Jones, Don Buckner, Eddie Whittington, John King, Lynn Hodge, Warren Muir, Rudy Holloman, Ken Ross, Pat Watson, Andy Chavous, George McCarthy, Dave Lucas, Clyde Smith, Fred Zeigler, Tony Fusaro, Head Coach Paul Dietzel. Second Row: Coach Bill Shalosky, Tommy Suggs, Ken Walkup, Al Usher, Bill Parker, Don Bailey, Benny Padgett, Candler Boyd, Randy Yoakum, Eddie Bolton, Tyler Hellams, Billy DuPre, Joe Wingard, Chris Bank, Dave DeCamilla, Jimmy Pope, Coach Bill Rowe. Third Row: Coach Dick Weldon, Doug Hamrick, Steve Vasgaard, Mike Stirling, Bob Miranda, Tom Trevillian, Rusty Ganas, Mack Lee Tharpe, Jimmy Poston, Danny Dyches, Don Brant, Rick Hipkins, Joe Regalis, Pete Unsworth, Mike Mobley, Coach Don Purvis. Fourth Row: Coach Pride Ratterree, Byron Sistare, Richie Moye, Steve Wade, Billy Freeman, Steve Dietzel, Lester Ballard, Randy Williams, Jimmy Johnson, Kevin Malone, Jimmy Cleckler, Bill Duffle, Don Montgomery, Carroll Jones, Glen Morris, Tommy Rhodes, Coach Johnny Menger. Fifth Row: Trainer Jim Price, Greg Crabb, Van McMillan, Greg Black, Dennis Ford, Tim Russell, Steve Lipscomb, Gary Latham, Jake Wright, Deane Hall, Steve Holstad, Butch Jones, Bob O'Harra, Charlie Jetton, Dick Harris, Coach Jack Powers. Back Row: Jake Stone, Jim Mitchell, Gary Campbell, Tommy Simmons, Billy Ray Rice, Jeff Tope, Steve Gruchacz, Terry Key, Jimmy Nash, Pat Kohout, Ken Wheat, Bill Boyte, Mack Stone, Chan Beasley, Manager Bill Anderson.

Another exciting play on the gridiron, commentary by Jimmy Pope; #84 Lucas, making sure no one hits him, #33 Usher, piling on to get an assist for his stats, #15 Watson, showing his "157lbs of heart" (Coach Dietzel), #86 Pope, looking at #15, trying to figure out what's going on, and #75 Poston, looking for a cigarette...

Selected pages fro the 1965 Redbook

FORMER GAMECOCK STARS

ALL-SOUTHERN

1929—Julian Beall, center
1933—Earl Clary, back
1938—Larry Craig, end
1941—Stan Stasica, back
1942—Louis Sossamon, center
1943—Louis Sossamon, center
1944—Dom Fusci, guard*
1943—Ernie Bauer, guard
1944—Skimp Harrison, end
1946—Pat Thrash, end
1950—Bryant Meeks, center
1951—Steve Wadiak, back
1950—Steve Wadiak, back
1951—Steve Wadiak, back
1952—Johnny Gramling, defensive center
Larry Smith, offensive center
Harry Jabbusch, defensive center
Leon Cunningham, defensive center
John Latorre, defensive end
Don Earley, defensive tackle
Norris Mullis, defensive halfback

ALL-ATLANTIC COAST

1953—Clyde Bennett, end
Leon Cunningham, center
Frank Mincevich, guard
Johnny Gramling, quarterback
1954—Leon Cunningham, center
Frank Mincevich, guard
1956—Buddy Frick, end
1958—Alex Hawkins, halfback
Ed Pitts, tackle
John Saunders, fullback
1959—Ed Pitts, tackle
Phil Lavoie, fullback
1960—Jake Bodkin, guard
1961—Jim Moss, tackle
Billy Gambrell, halfback
1962—Billy Gambrell, halfback
Jim Moss, tackle
John Caskey, end
1963—Tom Gibson, tackle

FUTURE GAMECOCK SCHEDULES

Athletic directors with major college football programs have to work years in advance in order to line up schedules with first class opponents and the schedules that athletic director Marvin Bass has booked for head coach Marvin Bass to play are no exceptions.

The Gamecocks open series this fall with Alabama, Tennessee and L. S. U. and have future games booked with Memphis State, Iowa State, Virginia Tech, Florida State and Georgia, in addition to other members of the Atlantic Coast Conference.

Schedules through 1971 include:

1966
Sept. 17 — at LSU
Sept. 24 — Memphis State
Oct. 1 — Georgia
Oct. 8 — at N. C. State
Oct. 15 — Wake Forest
Oct. 22 — at Tennessee
Oct. 29 — at Maryland
Nov. 5 — Florida State
Nov. 12 — at Alabama
Nov. 19 — at Clemson

1967
Sept. 16 — Iowa State
Sept. 23 — North Carolina
Sept. 30 — at Duke
Oct. 7 — at Georgia
Oct. 14 — at Florida State
Oct. 21 — Virginia
Oct. 28 — at Maryland
Nov. 4 — at Wake Forest
Nov. 18 — at Alabama
Nov. 25 — Clemson

1968
Sept. 21 — Duke
Sept. 28 — at North Carolina
Oct. 5 — Georgia
Oct. 12 — at N. C. State
Oct. 19 — at Maryland
Oct. 26 — Florida State
Nov. 2 — at Virginia
Nov. 9 — Wake Forest
Nov. 16 — Virginia Tech
Nov. 23 — at Clemson

1969
Sept. 20 — at Duke
Sept. 27 — North Carolina
Oct. 4 — at Georgia
Oct. 11 — N. C. State
Oct. 18 — at Virginia Tech
Oct. 25 — at Maryland
Nov. 1 — at Florida State
Nov. 8 — at Tennessee
Nov. 15 — at Wake Forest
Nov. 22 — Clemson

1970
Sept. 19 — Wake Forest
Sept. 26 — at N. C. State
Oct. 3 — Virginia Tech
Oct. 10 — at North Carolina
Oct. 17 — at Maryland
Oct. 24 — Florida State
Oct. 31 — at Georgia
Nov. 7 — Tennessee
Nov. 14 — Duke
Nov. 21 — at Clemson

1971
Sept. 18 — at Duke
Sept. 25 — N. C. State
Oct. 2 — at Memphis State
Oct. 9 — Virginia
Oct. 16 — Maryland
Oct. 23 — at Florida State
Oct. 30 — Georgia
Nov. 6 — at Tennessee
Nov. 20 — at Wake Forest
Nov. 27 — Clemson

42

FRESHMAN BULLETIN

The last two University of South Carolina freshman football teams have won eight games against only one loss and one tie. The coaching staff believes it has lined up a 1965 freshman squad that will compare favorably with the 4-0-1 1964 squad and the 4-0-1 1963 team.

The Biddies, under Coach Ed Pitts, will play the usual five-game schedule, which includes:

Sept. 25 — Gordon Military College at Barnesville, Ga., 8 P.M.
Oct. 8 — N. C. State Frosh in Carolina Stadium, 8 P.M.
Oct. 15 — Wake Forest Frosh in Carolina Stadium, 8 P.M.
Oct. 21 — The Citadel Frosh in Carolina Stadium, 8 P.M.
Nov. 5 — Clemson Frosh at Clemson, S. C., 3 P.M.

Candidates expected to report for the 1965 freshman squad include:

Name	Pos.	Hgt.	Wt.	Home Town
Billy Anderson	T	6-0	220	Ware Shoals, S. C.
Jack Bremen	G	6-2	210	Leechburg, Pa.
Allen Brown	QB	6-2	190	Hinesville, Ga.
Ronald Bunch	FB	5-11	190	Bamberg, S. C.
Luke Cannon	G	6-3	210	Conway, S. C.
John Coleman	E	6-5	195	Latta, S. C.
Tom Cooper	FB	6-0	190	Clemson, S. C.
Carl Cowart	FB	6-2	175	Jesup, Ga.
Henry Cusack	QB	6-0	175	Pittsburgh, Pa.
Ray Edwards	G	6-0	205	Chatham, N. J.
Tommy Fleming	G	6-2	190	Atlanta, Ga.
Dennis Frasier	G	6-0	210	Walhalla, S. C.
Gordon Gibson	T	6-4	225	Greenville, S. C.
David Grant	T	6-2	210	Clarkesville, Ga.
Richard Harrelson	FB	5-11	195	Barnwell, S. C.
Sonny Hendrix	HB	6-3	185	Vidalia, Ga.
Bill Higgs	E	6-3	175	Asheville, N. C.
Lynn Hodge	T	6-4	220	Union, S. C.
Billy Howard	HB	5-10	190	Aiken, S. C.
Badger Humphries	T	6-1	220	Johnston, S. C.
Leo Hunter	G	6-1	180	Atlanta, Ga.
Jack James	HB	6-0	180	Atlanta, Ga.
Darrell Johnson	HB	6-0	210	Rocky Mount, N. C.
William Klesch	G	6-1	185	Valley Grove, W. Va.
Harold Lane	HB	6-0	185	Columbus, Ga.
John Lee	FB	6-2	185	Moorhead City, N. C.
David Lucas	E	6-5	180	Bishopville, S. C.
George McCarthy	C	6-2	215	Hyattsville, Md.
Toy McCord	QB	5-11	170	Manning, S. C.
Nick Maycmont	E	6-1	195	Brunswick, Ga.
Dave Meadow	HB	6-1	180	Aiken, S. C.
Ed Moore	FB	6-2	205	Florence, S. C.
Monte Moore	HB	5-11	185	Spartanburg, S. C.
Tommy Nix	HB	6-0	170	Easley, S. C.
Wally Orrel	QB	6-0	160	Savannah, Ga.
Ronnie Palmer	HB	5-6	160	Morristown, Tenn.
Frank Poleski	C	6-1	205	Vandergrift, Pa.
Walter Poleski	G	6-0	210	Vandergrift, Pa.
Mike Rentz	HB	6-0	195	Bamberg, S. C.
Billy Reynolds	C-G	6-0	215	West Point, Ga.
Larry Royal	E	6-3	190	Virginia Beach, Va.
Gene Schwarting	T	6-3	220	Bamberg, S. C.
Jeff Skogen	T	6-3	210	Warner Robins, Ga.
Dennis Stevens	T	6-5	212	New Kensington, Pa.
Dennis Stons	FB	6-1	205	Bishopville, S. C.
Bob Teal	T	6-1	234	Bishopville, S. C.
Glynn Thompson		6-4	250	Triadelphia, W. Va.
John Tominack	G	6-0	195	Ocilla, Ga.
Thomas Wingard	HB	5-11	210	Greenwood, S. C.
Bob White	HB	5-11	175	Sharon, Pa.
Ron Znkowski	QB	6-1	195	Trenton, N. J.

43

RICHARD B. (DICK) WELDON

Dick Weldon didn't play football until his junior year at Presbyterian College, but he built an outstanding record in 13 years as head coach at Bamberg, S. C., High School before joining the South Carolina staff in December 1964.

His primary on-the-field duties are with the defensive guards and tackles.

Born April 29, 1929 at Latta, S. C., Weldon attended Bennettsville, S. C., High School where he earned four letters in baseball and three in basketball. He entered Presbyterian on a baseball scholarship and lettered four years as a shortstop. He also earned two letters in track as a sprinter and, coming out for football for the first time as a junior, lettered twice as a quarterback.

Weldon received the bachelor of arts degree from Presbyterian in 1952 and immediately became head coach at Bamberg. In 13 football seasons his teams won 104 games, lost 35 and tied five. He coached basketball 12 years, compiling a 216-87 record; and handled the baseball team nine years with a 118-32 mark. Thus, his won-loss record as a head coach in three sports is 438 wins, 154 losses and five ties, or nearly 75 per cent victories.

Weldon was selected to coach the South basketball team in 1956 in the annual South Carolina Coaches' Association North-South All-Star games; and coached the South football team in 1962.

A veteran of two years Marine Corps service, during which he reached the rank of corporal, Weldon married the former Mary Deane Currie of Loris, S. C., Aug. 10, 1951. They have three sons: Dicky, 11; Steve, 9; and John, 3.

Weldon says his hobbies are "all sports."

WEEMS OLIVER BASKIN, JR.

Although he doesn't actively coach football anymore, the influence of Weems Baskin on the Gamecock grid program is evident by the large number of Georgia boys on the roster.

A native of Carrollton, Ga., the veteran South Carolina head track coach and intramural director has long recruited football talent in his native state. Such stars as Leon Cunningham, Billy Gambrell, Dan Reeves and many others came to South Carolina at the urging of Weems Baskin. Undoubtedly, many others will follow.

Baskin has been head track coach 16 years and his teams have won 72 dual meets while losing 39. He served 13 seasons as a South Carolina football assistant.

He also previously coached football and track at Auburn, Georgia and Mississippi. Baskin was a national champion hurdler at Auburn, graduating in 1927, and also lettered in football as an end. All-America in outdoor track in 1926 and in indoor track in 1927, Baskin ran with the New York Athletic Club 1928-29. He is immediate past president of the National Collegiate Track Coaches Association and chairman of the NCAA Track & Field Rules Committee.

Married June 7, 1934 to the former Etta Mack May of Montezuma, Ga., Baskin has a 29-year-old son, Weems III, who was a star end and with South Carolina; and a 21-year-old daughter, Anne. A retired U. S. Naval Reserve Lieutenant commander, Baskin's hobby is golf.

JIMMIE IRVIN (JIM) PRICE

Jim Price is a Texan who has been on the athletic staff as a trainer at the University of South Carolina for five years, and head trainer the past two years.

Born Dec. 27, 1932 at Jefferson, Tex., he lettered in baseball two years in high school and graduated from Lon Morris Junior College at Jacksonville, Tex., in 1957 with an Associate of Arts degree. He attended the University of Texas, 1957-58, and served as a student trainer there before coming to South Carolina. He was coordinator of intramural activities at Lon Morris Junior College while a student there.

Price married the former Nancy Ann Killen of Kilgore, Tex., Aug. 24, 1958. They have three children: Scott Dickerson, 6; Nancy Celeste, 5; and William Christopher, 4. His hobbies are reading, fishing and golf.

WALTER (CHIEF) MACKOWSKI

Chief Mackowski, a retired chief boatswain's mate with 20 years of Naval service, has been South Carolina's equipment manager since February, 1956.

He was born Aug. 31, 1915 in Syracuse, N. Y., and lettered three years in football, two in track and one in baseball at Lincoln High School. He played service football on the West coast.

Mackowski married the former Beth Moody of Marshall, Mo., Feb. 8, 1944 and they have a daughter, Donna Mary, 17. His hobbies are golf and hunting.

WELDON B. (SARGE) FRYE

Sarge Frye, a retired master sergeant with 23 years of Army service, has been supervisor of athletic fields and other facilities since October, 1954. Last year his duties were expanded to place him in charge of maintaining all campus grounds.

Born May 7, 1913 at Medon, Tenn., Frye married the former Ruby Howard of Anniston, Ala., March 4, 1936. Their son, Jerry, 25, was a star end and football co-captain with the Gamecocks and is now head coach at Clover, S. C., High School. They also have a married daughter, Nancy, 22. Frye's hobbies are fishing and gardening.

RALPH NIXON FLOYD

Ralph Floyd has been a member of the South Carolina football staff since 1956, coming to the University with Marvin Bass from the University of North Carolina.

Floyd is Bass' administrative assistant, having charge of equipment purchases and other administrative duties. He has held a number of assignments in the past and for 1965 will be the chief scout of opponents and director of the demonstration team that runs opponents' offenses and defenses against the Gamecock varsity in practice.

A native of Washington, D. C., where he was born July 10 1925, Floyd attended Roosevelt High School and was graduated from Devitt Prep in 1942. He lettered in football, basketball and baseball, and enrolled at the College of William and Mary where he lettered three seasons in football as a lineman prior to graduation in 1949 with a B.S. degree in Physical Education. He also attended the U. S. Merchant Marine Academy for two years.

Floyd coached one season in high school (5-4-1); and prior collegiate coaching experience includes one season at William and Mary, two years at the University of Richmond, and two and one-half years at North Carolina.

Floyd married the former Susan Sara Trimble of Arlington, Va., June 11, 1953, and they have two children, Candice, 8, and Nicky, 5. His hobbies are fishing and handball.

JOHNNY MENGER

Johnny Menger, who coaches the offensive backs on Head Coach Marvin Bass' staff, played in four bowl games as a varsity halfback at Georgia Tech.

Born August 18, 1934 at Augusta, Ga., Menger received a bachelor of science degree from Georgia Tech in 1957. Freshmen were eligible for varsity competition due to the Korean War when Menger entered Tech in September 1953 and the following January 1 found Johnny and his Yellow Jacket teammates in the Sugar Bowl. Menger played in the Cotton Bowl as a sophomore, the Sugar Bowl again as a junior, and in the Gator Bowl as a senior.

Also a four-year letterman as a baseball third baseman, Menger played one season of professional baseball as an infielder with the Columbia Gems of the South Atlantic League in 1957.

Therefore, he was no stranger to Columbia when he joined the Gamecock staff March 1, 1965. Before coming to South Carolina, Menger was a student assistant at Georgia Tech in 1957; assistant freshman coach in 1958; head coach at Atlanta's Druid Hills High School in 1959 and '60 (11-7-2 record); an assistant at Furman University, 1961-62; and an assistant at Tulane University, 1963-64.

Johnny married the former Ann Coleman of Atlanta, Dec. 27, 1957, and they have three children: Bobby, 6; Billy, 4; and Kathy, 2. His hobby is golf.

10

EDWARD HOLLAND PITTS

Ed Pitts was one of the finest tackles ever to play for the University of South Carolina and he joined the coaching staff from the student body in 1962.

He is head freshman coach, recruiter and executive secretary of the Gamecock Club, the University's athletic booster organization. In three seasons as freshman coach, his Biddies have compiled a 10-4-1 record, including an unbeaten (4-0-1) mark in 1963 and 4-1-0 last year.

Born Jan. 26, 1938 at Clinton, S. C., Pitts starred in football and track at Clinton High School. He played in the Shrine Bowl All-Star game at Charlotte, N. C., and was a co-captain in the North-South game in Columbia.

He graduated from the University of South Carolina in 1961 with a B.S. degree in Education and since has done additional work in Business Administration. Pitts lettered three years as a football tackle, was co-captain his senior year and an All-Atlantic Coast Conference choice in 1958 and '59. He was named to Paul Williamson's All-America team in 1959 and served as co-captain in the North-South Shrine game at Miami, Fla.

Pitts signed with the Boston Patriots of the American Football League but his pro career was terminated by a knee injury and he returned to school to serve one season as a student assistant before becoming a full-time member of the Gamecock staff.

Pitts is single and his hobbies are hunting and fishing.

JAMES FRANKLIN (JIMMY) VICKERS

Jimmy Vickers, a former All-Southeastern Conference end at the University of Georgia, coaches the offensive ends and linemen for Head Coach Marvin Bass.

Born May 7, 1937 at Omega, Ga., Vickers graduated from Moultrie, Ga., Senior High School where he earned three letters each in football, basketball and track. He received the bachelor of science degree in education from the University of Georgia in 1960 after earning three varsity letters in football.

Vickers was a first team All-SEC selection in 1959 when the Bulldogs had a 9-1 record in regular season play and defeated Missouri 14-0 in the Orange Bowl. He was alternate captain of that team. He also played in the 1960 Hula Bowl All-Star game in Honolulu.

After graduation, Vickers remained at Georgia one season, 1960, helping coach the freshmen, and then played one season of professional football with the Edmonton Eskimos of the Canadian League.

He joined the Presbyterian College staff in 1962 and remained there three seasons before coming to the University of South Carolina Feb. 1, 1965.

A corporal in the Marine Corps Reserve, Vickers is single and his hobbies are hunting, boating and fishing.

11

259

FRANK JOHNSON
Assistant Athletic Director

Frank Johnson, oldest man in point of service in the athletic department at the University of South Carolina, is also one of the busiest.

For 16 years, interrupted by two years of Naval service during World War II, Frank served as the University's head basketball coach. Nine of his teams produced winning records and the 1957 Gamecocks, led by All-America and national scoring champion Grady Wallace, advanced to the finals of the Atlantic Coast Conference tournament before losing to North Carolina's NCAA champions.

Since retiring from active coaching in basketball, Frank has served four years as business manager of athletics and the past five years as assistant director of athletics. He relinquished his business manager's duties July 1, 1962 to devote full time to aiding Marvin Bass and Frank McGuire in directing the University's ever-growing athletic program.

A 1936 graduate of the University of Georgia where he was an All-Southeastern Conference athlete in three sports, Johnson came to South Carolina in 1940 after a brief coaching tenure at Georgia and Mississippi. In addition to basketball duties, Johnson coached the Gamecock freshman football team from 1940 through 1950. He now coaches the golf team.

A native of Rockford, Ill., Frank was a football guard, basketball forward, and a baseball pitcher at Georgia. In addition to All-SEC, he received All-America recognition in football and basketball.

Johnson played basketball at Georgia under Coach Rex Enright, and the late Gamecock head football coach and athletic director brought Frank to South Carolina in 1940. Johnson is married to the former Margaret Ann (Peg) Schoen of Rockford, Ill., and they have one son, Frank Jr. (Johnny), who is 15.

8

FOOTBALL STAFF

RICHARD L. (DICK) BESTWICK

Dick Bestwick, who coaches the defensive ends and linebackers for Head Coach Marvin Bass, is a Pennsylvanian with a master's degree and a studious approach to football.

Born Aug. 19, 1930 at Sharon, Pa., Bestwick lettered in football, basketball and baseball at Sharon High School before entering the University of North Carolina where he was a three-year football letterman as a guard and linebacker. He received the bachelor of arts degree in education from North Carolina in 1952 and the following year received the master of education degree from Pennsylvania State University. Bestwick has since completed 41 hours beyond the master's degree in counseling and administration.

Bestwick joined the South Carolina staff in March 1965 and his coaching background includes stints as freshman line coach at Penn State in 1952 while attending that institution on a graduate fellowship. He compiled a 47-30-5 record in eight years as a high school coach at Montoursville, Norwin and Grove City, all in Pennsylvania. He was an assistant at Oberlin College, 1962-63, and at Westminster College, 1963-65.

Dick played in the Cotton Bowl with the North Carolina team in 1950 and three times coached the Mercer County high school all star team in Pennsylvania.

He married the former Phyllis Jones of Sharon, Pa., March 18, 1950, and they have three children: Susan, 12; Rick, 11; and Kim, 2. Bestwick's hobbies are reading and music.

LEON (BUD) CARSON

Bud Carson, a former star defensive back at the University of North Carolina, heads up the defense on Head Coach Marvin Bass' staff.

Born April 28, 1931 at Freeport, Pa., Carson attended high school in Freeport, Pa., where he lettered in football, basketball and track.

He received a bachelor of arts degree in education at the University of North Carolina in 1952 and has since done graduate work toward a master's degree at the University of Pittsburgh.

Carson lettered in football three years at North Carolina as a halfback and a defensive safety. He was named to the All-Southern Conference defensive team in 1951.

A veteran of two years Marine Corps service during the Korean conflict, Carson played service football at Quantico, Va., and in Japan. He was named most valuable player in the Rice Bowl in Tokyo, Jan. 1, 1954.

Carson coached high school football two years, with a 14-2 record, and the North Carolina freshman team one season, with a 5-0 record, before spending seven years as a Tar Heel varsity assistant, first under Jim Tatum and then under Jim Hickey. He left North Carolina in March 1965 to join the South Carolina staff.

Carson participated in the Cotton Bowl Jan. 1, 1950 as a player and in the Gator Bowl in December 1963 as a coach.

He married the former Jean Hetrich in 1957 and they have two children: Dana, 6; and Clifford, 5.

9

260

GEORGE PICKARD HOGAN

George Hogan is one of the newest members of the University of South Carolina athletic family, joining the staff July 1, 1965 as athletic comptroller.

George is in charge of the business end of the athletic program. A 43-year-old native of Chapel Hill, N. C., he came to the University well qualified, having served 10 years, 1947-57, as executive secretary of the University of North Carolina's Educational Foundation.

A 1947 North Carolina graduate, Hogan was engaged in private business prior to joining the South Carolina staff. He is married to the former Frances Burns of Sumter, S. C., a graduate of Winthrop College who was an assistant professor of physical education at North Carolina. They have two children, Alwin Burns, 14, and Frances Buchanan, 12.

THOMAS HART (TOM) PRICE

Tom Price has been sports information director at the University of South Carolina since April, 1962, returning to his alma mater after nearly 11 years with United Press International, a worldwide newsgathering agency.

Born Nov. 28, 1926 at Augusta, Ga., Price grew up on Wadmalaw Island, S. C., and was graduated in 1943 from St. John's High School, Johns Island, S. C. He served four years in the Navy, 1943-47, before entering the University of South Carolina in February, 1948. He graduated in June 1951 with an A.B. degree in journalism.

Price was a reporter, sports editor, managing editor and editor-in-chief of *The Gamecock*, student weekly, while attending USC; and ran the University's News Service in a part-time capacity his senior year.

He married the former Margaret Fletcher of Charleston, S. C., June 10, 1950, and they have three children, Tommy, 14; Melissa, 11; and Rick, 10.

14

THE 1965 GAMECOCKS

The Fighting Gamecocks of Coach Marvin Bass enter the 1965 football season filled with confidence that the momentum built up by last year's season-ending winning streak will carry over into the new season.

South Carolina won its last three games after a frustration-filled seven weeks that produced only two ties and five losses and that portion of 1964 is viewed as a continuation of the nightmare that was 1963. Gamecock faithful prefer to recall only the final three weeks of the 1964 season, climaxed by the thrilling come-from-behind win over Clemson, with a confident look to the future.

To back up this enthusiasm, Bass and a nearly new staff of assistants have 28 lettermen and a promising group of sophomores, especially among the backs. On the other hand, the Gamecocks must replace quarterback Dan Reeves, South Carolina's all-time passing and total offense leader. The schedule includes last year's national champion, Alabama, always powerful LSU, and Tennessee among the non-conference opponents.

Reeves was one of only nine lettermen lost by graduation. However, two potential starters were lost when Mike Johnson became gravely ill last Christmas, ending his playing career, and Joe Komoroski withdrew from school at the end of the spring semester. Another letterman, Johnny King, also left school to bring to an even dozen the number of lettermen lost from 1964.

Johnson was the starting offensive center the final half of his sophomore season and was considered a great prospect by Bass. Komoroski played a great deal as a sophomore and recovered the fumble that started the Gamecocks on their 93-yard touchdown drive to beat Clemson. King would have been a senior this fall.

Despite these losses, South Carolina should be considerably stronger than last year with 20 letterman linemen giving experience up front and a fine crop of sophomore backs producing better team speed and depth.

Just how much stronger, however, depends upon a number of factors, among them adjustment to the new substitution rules that dictate the use of offensive and defensive platoons. The Gamecocks had an unusually large number of injuries during spring drills and the manner in which these players recover will affect play this fall.

On the other hand, injuries to experienced players gave some of the lesser known boys a chance to show the coaching staff what they could do and this possibly could help the depth factor this fall.

15

1963 and '64, Legat was primarily an interior lineman, and Dickens, as previously mentioned, played end last year.

Bass has five new assistant coaches, a three-game winning streak, 28 lettermen and some bright new faces. The Gamecocks also play five of their six conference games at home. The South Carolina faithful hope these factors add up to a successful autumn.

These lettermen have played out their eligibility with the Fighting Gamecocks and will be missed during the 1965 season: Guard Ed Hertwig; Quarterback Dan Reeves; Placekicker Jack McCathern; Halfbacks Ray Curtis, Sonny Dickinson, Larry Gill, Lide Huggins and Marty Rosen; and Fullback Pete DiVenere.

DEPTH CHART

Although some revisions are likely before the Sept. 18 season opener, and a few players will see action both ways, the offensive and defensive depth charts listed below are the approximate way the Gamecocks will line up when pre-season drills begin Sept. 1.

OFFENSE

SE—J. R. Wilburn**; Wayne Tucker*; Mac Perry
LT—Bob Collins**; Dennis Darling**
LG—Dave Berry*; John Dyer
C—Jon Linder**; Jimmy Gobble; Jimmy Warren
RG—Wilbur Hodge*; Phil Thornton; Donnie Rose
RT—Randy Harbour*; Billy Nelson*
TE—Mike Ragin*; Don Browne; John Breeden**
QB—Jim Rogers*; Ben Garnto; Ted Wingard; Mike Fair
TB—Julie Smith*; Benny Galloway; Buster Kimbrell; Jeff Jowers*
WB—Bobby Bryant*; Ronnie Lamb*; Cooter Williams; Bob Harris; Waly Medlin
FB—Phil Branson*; Jimmy Killen

DEFENSE

LE—Doug Senter*; Leroy Bailey, Ken Thornton
LT—Steve Cox**; Terry Harmon
MG—John Ewing*; Paul Phillips*; Don Somma
RT—Len Sears**; Jerry Soles**; Marcellus Gabryelski
RE—Butch Williams; Bob McCullough; Bob Wehmeyer
LLB—Bobby Gunnels**; Bob Cole; Johnny Glass
RLB—Dan Legart**; Bill Dickens*; Gene Lindsey
LCB—Benny Galloway; Gary Musgrove
RCB—Butch Reeves, Paul Harman, John Paul Chambliss
LS—Dave Truby*; Jim Mulvihill
RS—Stan Juk*; Perry Adkins; Donnie Myers

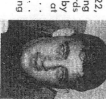

18

MEET THE GAMECOCKS

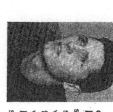

PERRY DANIEL ADKINS, 191, 6-0, 21, Junior, defensive back, Swansea, S. C. . . . Broken hand kept him from playing last year although he made several trips with the squad . . . plays defensive safety . . . quarterback at Swansea High School where he earned five football letters in addition to four in baseball and three in basketball . . . worked as file setter during summer vacations . . . Business Administration major . . . Baptist . . . single.

DAVID LEROY (LEROY) BAILEY, 205, 6-2, 21, Sophomore, defensive end, Gaffney, S. C. . . . Red-shirt last year after duty with '63 frosh . . . came along fast in spring drills and was number two defensive left end in pre-season depth chart . . . has worked as fireman during summer vacation . . . Management major . . . Baptist . . . single.

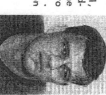

DAVID CLARK (DAVE) BERRY, 236, 6-1, 20, Junior, offensive guard, Warner Robins, Ga. . . . Lettered as soph interior lineman playing both ways and quickly earned offensive guard berth when Gamecocks went to two platoon in spring drills . . . exceptionally quick despite his size and a good blocker . . . Business Administration major . . . Methodist . . . single.

PHILLIP ALAN (PHIL) BRANSON, 211, 6-0, 22, Senior, fullback, Church Hill, Tenn. . . . Leading ground gainer on squad last season with 276 yards and 3.2 average despite being hampered by pinched neck nerve . . . lettered one season at Kentucky before transferring to South Carolina . . . considered a fine fullback by coaching staff . . . had summer job unloading trucks . . . Accounting major . . . Methodist . . . single.

19

JOHN LUTHER BREEDEN, 210, 6-3, 22, Senior, tight end, Columbia, S. C. . . . Two-year letterman but missed spring practice with back ailment and will have to win a spot in pre-season drills . . . caught one pass for 15 yards last year and caught three for 25 yards in 1963 . . . nephew of late Jim Tatum, Maryland and North Carolina coaching great . . . English major . . . Methodist . . . single.

DONALD V. (DON) BROWNE, 184, 6-1, 20, Sophomore, tight end, Toms River, N. J. . . . Redshirt in football last fall but lettered in track where he consistently threw javelin more than 200 feet and took first in state meet . . . number two tight end in pre-season depth chart and should see lots of action . . . summer job in construction work . . . Business Administration major . . . Christian Scientist . . . single.

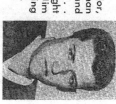

ROBERT EUGENE (BOBBY) COLLINS, 239, 6-6, 21, Senior, offensive tackle, Abbeville, S. C. . . . Two-year letterman and a starter last half of 1964 . . . fine blocker and should start as senior . . . tallest Gamecock and one of the biggest . . . had summer job cutting rights-of-way for electric utility . . . lettered in football, basketball and track at Abbeville High School . . . Business Administration major . . . Baptist . . . single.

STEPHEN H. (STEVE, LIL' ABNER) COX, 250, 6-4, 22, Senior, defensive tackle, Easley, S. C. . . . Was tri-captain of '64 Gamecocks but dislocated hip in season opener and granted additional season of eligibility by ACC . . . already drafted by both pro leagues . . . underwent minor heart surgery last winter but fully recovered from that and hip injury and expected to be top Gamecock lineman this fall . . . works in Dad's peach cannery summers . . . Education major . . . Baptist . . . a July 10 bridegroom.

BOBBY LEE (BONES) BRYANT, 175, 6-0, 20, Junior, wingback, Macon, Ga. . . . Caught three passes as soph, including sensational 69-yarder for touchdown against Wake Forest . . . also had several long punt returns, including 88-yarder against North Carolina that penalty nullified . . . missed spring drills due to wrist operation but took regular turn as southpaw pitcher with baseball team, posting 4-3 record despite cast on right arm . . . number one wingback on pre-season depth chart . . . Business Administration major . . . Baptist . . . single.

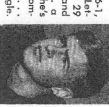

ROBERT BURNS (BOB) COLE, JR., 215, 6-3, 21, Sophomore, linebacker, Columbia, S. C. . . . Redshirt last year and was leading contender for starting linebacker spot in spring drills when broke wrist in scrimmage . . . should be fully healed by September . . . led 1963 frosh in rushing as fullback . . . four sports letterman at Eau Claire High School . . . Business Administration major . . . Presbyterian . . . married with daughter.

DENNIS ARTHUR DARLING, 218, 6-3, 22, Senior, offensive tackle, Burlington, N. C. . . . Two-year letterman as two-way tackle . . . wound up on offensive platoon at end of spring drills and likely number two man on left side . . . gives squad good experience and depth at tackle . . . Geography major . . . First Reformed Church . . . single.

WILLIAM PHILLIP (BILL) DICKENS, JR., 200, 6-1, 20, Junior, linebacker, Bloomington, Ind. . . . Lettered at end as soph, catching one pass for 29 yards . . . moved to linebacker in spring drills and should be one of the best on the squad . . . a hard-nosed competitor who gives it everything he's got . . . father was head coach at Indiana, Wyoming and Wofford and star tailback at Tennessee . . . Arts and Science major . . . single.

20

21

JOHN EVERETT EWING, 224, 6-0, 22, Senior, middle guard, Hartsville, S. C. . . . Two-year letterman who has played both guard and tackle . . . likely starter at middle guard spot this fall . . . three-year football letterman at Hartsville High School . . . hopes to teach and coach after graduation . . . Education major . . . Baptist . . . married.

MICHAEL LARRY (MIKE) FAIR, 197, 6-1, 19, Sophomore, quarterback, Greenville, S. C. . . . Three-sports star at Parker High School . . . number one QB on '64 frosh when he rushed for 225 yards and 5.5 average, passed for 187 yards, threw five TD passes and scored five himself . . . hit .333 as outfielder with frosh baseball team . . . one of four prime candidates for top QB job . . . Arts and Science major . . . Baptist . . . single.

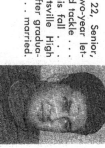

JAMES CLIFTON (JIMMY) GOBBLE, 239, 6-2, 21, Sophomore, offensive center, Spartanburg, S. C. . . . Redshirt last fall after attack of high blood pressure . . . okay in spring and had good off-season practice . . . number two offensive center in pre-season depth chart . . . Business Administration major . . . Lutheran . . . married with infant daughter.

DAVID BENNETT (BENNY) GALLOWAY, 187, 5-9, 19, Sophomore, defensive back-tailback, Easley, S. C. . . . One of few Gamecocks scheduled to play both ways . . . probable defensive cornerback starter and will see much action on offense at tailback . . . selected one of six top prep players in nation by national magazine . . . had 93-yard kickoff return with frosh and averaged 5.6 yards per rush . . . has potential to be a great one . . . Business Administration major . . . Protestant . . . single.

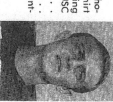

BENNIE EDMOND (BEN) GARNTO, 193, 5-10, 19, Sophomore, quarterback, Columbus, Ga. . . . Hero of spring drills climaxed by 108 yards rushing, 31 passing and two TDs scored in spring game . . . had 7.2 rushing average and scored three touchdowns with frosh teams and is in thick of battle for starting quarterback spot . . . summer job as lifeguard . . . Arts and Science major . . . Baptist . . . single.

SANDY BOB (BOBBY) GUNNELS, 203, 6-1, 22, Senior, linebacker, Clarkesville, Ga. . . . Two-year letterman at both offensive center and linebacker . . . came along fast as linebacker late in 1964 season and set for regular duty at that position this fall . . . Dad played football at Georgia . . . Marketing major . . . Baptist . . . single.

RANDALL VINSON (RANDY) HARBOUR, 220, 6-4, 20, Junior, offensive tackle, Greenville, S. C. . . . One of top sophomore linemen on squad last year and likely starter in '65 . . . father is Air Force officer and family now lives at Marietta, Ga. . . . three-sports letterman at Greenville High School . . . summer job in construction work . . . Management major . . . Methodist . . . single.

PAUL EVERETT HARMAN, 162, 5-10, 20, Sophomore, defensive back, Lexington, S. C. . . . Redshirt last year . . . looked good as cornerback in spring drills . . . high school quarterback . . . Dad is USC grad and superintendent of Lexington school . . . three-sports letterman at Lexington High School . . . summer job in brother's funeral home . . . Accounting major . . . Lutheran . . . single.

MICHAEL LEE (MIKE) RAGIN, 196, 6-1, 20, Junior, tight end, Columbia, S. C. . . . lettered as soph and caught one pass for seven yards . . . may be starting tight end this fall . . . played end, fullback, guard and center during three-year career at Flora High School . . . summer construction job . . . Business Administration major . . . Baptist . . . single.

ROY DON (BUTCH) REEVES, 180, 5-11, 19, Sophomore, defensive back, Americus, Ga. . . . Played wingback with frosh and caught nine passes for 233 yards and six TDs to lead frosh in scoring . . . fine defensive play impressed varsity coaches, however, and he was number one right cornerback at close of spring drills . . . younger brother of Deacon Dan Reeves, Gamecock quarterback great . . . summer job running asphalt spreader with Dad's construction company . . . Business Administration major . . . Baptist . . . single.

MANUEL JAMES (JIM) ROGERS, JR., 193, 6-0, 21, Senior, quarterback, Charlotte, N. C. . . . Hero of 7-3 win over Clemson last year when he guided 93-yard TD drive and scored himself . . . two-year letterman as understudy to Dan Reeves . . . one of top candidates for starting job . . . shoots in 70s on golf course . . . missed spring intra-squad game with knee injury . . . Business Administration major . . . Baptist . . . single.

LEONARD F. (LEN) SEARS, 236, 6-5, 22, Senior, defensive tackle, West Babylon, N. Y. . . . Two-year letterman, starter most of the time . . . may be starter defensively again this fall . . . already drafted by both pro leagues . . . has tools to be great . . . three-sports letterman at West Babylon High School . . . Business Administration major . . . single.

DOUGLAS M. (DOUG) SENTER, 177, 6-1, 22, Senior, defensive end, Marietta, Ga. . . . Two-year letterman and starter both ways last year when he caught seven passes for 98 yards and one TD . . . may still see some duty at tight end but main plans are for his defensive ability . . . may also punt some . . . outstanding cadet in Air Force ROTC unit and plans to become AF pilot . . . Business Administration major . . . Baptist . . . single.

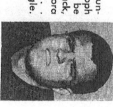

JULE GARRETH SMITH, 178, 5-1?, 22, Junior, tailback, Chesterfield, S. C. . . . Lettered last year and started some games when he rushed for 143 yards and 3.2 average and caught 13 passes for 188 yards . . . scored one TD . . . one of best hustlers on squad . . . number one tailback at close of spring drills . . . underwent springtime surgery to correct old ankle injury . . . Business Administration major . . . Methodist . . . single.

JERRY MITCHELL SOLES, 222, 6-2, 21, Senior, defensive tackle, Tabor City, N. C. . . . Two-year letterman harassed by injuries . . . hurt back in '64 Nebraska game and underwent knee surgery in spring . . . if fully recovered from latter, may be one of starting defensive tackles . . . in any event will play a lot . . . Marketing major . . . Baptist . . . married.

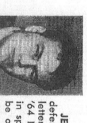

PHILIP B. (PHIL, RED) THORMAN, 235, 6-1, 23, Sophomore, offensive guard, Medford, Mass. . . . Service veteran and starting tackle on freshman team . . . moved to offensive guard in spring drills and started intra-squad game . . . certain to see lots of action as soph . . . lettered three years in hockey at Medford High School in addition to three in football . . . Physical Education major . . . Catholic . . . single.

28

29

DAVID CHARLES (DAVE) TRUBY, 186, 5-10, 22, Junior, defensive back, Atlanta, Ga. . . . Lettered as defensive specialist in '63 but dropped off team last fall . . . returned in spring and started spring game . . . could be starting safetyman . . . father played quarterback at Florida . . . family now lives in Rye, N. Y. . . . Business Administration major . . . Presbyterian . . . single.

WAYNE MARION TUCKER, 203, 6-2, 21, Senior, split end, Moultrie, Ga. . . . Top pass receiver on '62 frosh . . . saw some action in '63 but didn't letter . . . lettered last year when he caught one pass . . . should play quite a bit as senior . . . was breaststroker on age group swim team coached by current Gamecock assistant Jimmy Vickers some years ago . . . Business Administration major . . . Baptist . . . single.

JOHNNIE RICHARD (J. R.) WILBURN, 195, 6-2, Senior, split end, Portsmouth, Va. . . . One of finest athletes on USC campus . . . already lettered three times in track where he led '64 team in scoring while participating in javelin, broad jump, triple jump and high jump . . . two-year football letterman and leading '64 pass receiver with 21 for 236 yards . . . already drafted by both pro leagues . . . candidate for All-Star honors . . . Business Administration major . . . Baptist . . . single.

VERNON CRAIG (BUTCH) WILLIAMS, JR., 193, 6-1, 21, Junior, defensive end, Columbia, S. C. . . . Played briefly in 1963 but didn't letter . . . out of school last fall . . . returned in spring and started intra-squad game . . . excellent prospect as defensive end . . . Business Administration major . . . Baptist . . . single.

30

CURTIS EUGENE (COOTER) WILLIAMS, 194, 5-11, 19, Sophomore, wingback, Bamberg, S. C. . . . High school quarterback and fullback with frosh when he rushed for 137 yards and 3.9 average . . . moved to wingback in spring drills and started intra-squad game . . . high school coach was current Gamecock assistant Dick Weldon . . . Engineering major . . . Methodist . . . single.

JOSEPH THEODORE (TED) WINGARD, "199, 6-1, 20, Sophomore, quarterback, Greenwood, S. C. . . . Redshirt last fall after qua..erbacking unbeaten '63 frosh when he rushed for 118 yards and passed for 352 . . . should be in thick of battle for top QB spot although slowed in spring drills by shoulder injury . . . younger brother enrolled at USC in summer and will be candidate for frosh . . . outstanding student who plans to enter medical school . . . Biology major . . . Lutheran . . . married.

GAMECOCKS IN PROFESSIONAL FOOTBALL

Six former University of South Carolina football players in the National or American football leagues last season and a seventh was on the taxi squad of the AFL champion Buffalo Bills.

All seven are expected to be back this fall with several members of the 1965 graduating class also bidding to make the grade in professional football.

The Gamecocks had three alumni active in each league last year with two of the six serving as team captains and one as president of the AFL players association.

"CAPTAIN WHO"

The greybeard of the South Carolina pros is "Captain Who," Alex Hawkins, who will be starting his seventh season with the NFL Baltimore Colts. Coach Don Shula, impressed with the Hawk's leadership and on-the-field hustle, made him captain of the Colts' special teams last season. He leads the squad that runs back kickoffs and punts in addition to filling in at split end, flanker, running back or

31

266

SOUTH CAROLINA'S 1965 VARSITY SQUAD

NO.	NAME	POS.	HGT.	WGT.	AGE	CLASS	HOME TOWN
25	Perry Adkins	DB	6-0	191	21	Jr.	Swansea, S. C.
87	Leroy Bailey	DE	6-2	205	20	Jr.	Gaffney, S. C.
2	Martin Becker	PK	5-7	153	19	So.	Orangeburg, S. C.
65	Dave Berry*	OG	6-1	236	20	Jr.	Warner Robins, Ga.
30	Phil Bronson*	FB	6-0	211	22	Sr.	Church Hill, Tenn.
86	John Breeden**	TE	6-3	210	22	Sr.	Columbia, S. C.
24	Don Browne	WB	6-1	184	20	So.	Toms River, N. J.
46	Bobby Bryant*	WB	6-0	175	20	Jr.	Macon, Ga.
33	John Paul Chambliss	LB	6-0	185	20	So.	Americus, Ga.
71	Bob Collins**	LB	6-3	215	21	Sr.	Columbia, S. C.
78	Steve Cox**	DT	6-6	239	21	Sr.	Abbeville, S. C.
77	Dennis Darling**	OT	6-4	250	22	Sr.	Easley, S. C.
60	Bill Dickens*	OT	6-3	218	20	Jr.	Burlington, N. C.
69	John Dyer	OG	6-1	200	20	So.	Bloomington, Ind.
61	John Ewing**	MG	6-0	215	22	So.	Bloomington, Ind.
12	Mike Fair	QB	6-1	197	19	So.	Hartsville, S. C.
73	Marcellus Gabryelski	DT	6-2	235	19	So.	Greenville, S. C.
20	Benny Galloway	DB-TB	5-9	187	19	So.	Easley, S. C.
11	Ben Garnto	QB	5-10	193	19	So.	Columbus, Ga.
68	Johnny Glass	LB	5-11	192	19	So.	Kingsport, Tenn.
50	Jimmy Gobble	OC	6-2	239	21	So.	Spartanburg, S. C.
57	Bobby Gunnels**	LB	6-1	203	22	So.	Clarkesville, Ga.
67	Randy Harbour*	OT	6-4	220	20	Jr.	Greenville, S. C.
17	Paul Harmon	DB	5-10	162	20	So.	Lexington, S. C.
74	Terry Harmon	DT	6-5	245	19	So.	Cleveland, Tenn.
42	Bob Harris	WB	6-1	178	19	So.	Pt. Pleasant Beach, N. J.
63	Wilbur Hodge*	OG	6-4	234	22	So.	Greenville, S. C.
40	Jeff Jowers*	TB	6-0	195	21	Jr.	Union, S. C.
16	Stan Juk*	DB	6-2	205	20	Jr.	Bamberg, S. C.
31	Jimmy Killen	DB	6-0	202	20	So.	Georgetown, S. C.
41	Buster Kimbrell	TB	6-0	202	19	So.	Georgetown, S. C.
21	Ronnie Lamb**	WB	6-2	215	21	Sr.	Spartanburg, S. C.
64	Dan Legat**	LB	6-0	220	22	Sr.	McCormick, S. C.
52	Jon Linder**	OC-LB	6-2	220	21	So.	Hopewell, Va.
54	Gene Lindsey	OC-LB	6-2	207	20	So.	Union, S. C.
28	Bob McCullough	WB	5-11	174	19	So.	Columbia, S. C.
43	Wally Medlin	WB	5-9	198	20	So.	Kingsport, Tenn.
44	Jim Mulvihill	DB	6-0	186	20	So.	Ehrhardt, S. C.
14	Gary Musgrove	DB	6-1	180	20	So.	Atlanta, Ga.
62	Donnie Myers	OT	6-3	220	21	So.	Meigs, Ga.
45	Billy Nelson*	SE	6-0	185	20	Sr.	Reevesville, S. C.
79	Mac Perry	MG-DT	6-4	258	21	Jr.	Atlanta, Ga.
1	Paul Phillips*	PK	5-8	157	19	So.	Gaffney, S. C.
80	Jimmy Poole	TE	6-1	196	20	Jr.	Due West, S. C.
26	Mike Rogin*	DB	6-0	180	19	So.	Columbia, S. C.
53	Butch Reeves	OG	6-0	193	21	So.	Americus, Ga.
10	Jim Rogers**	LB	5-11	180	19	Sr.	Charlotte, N. C.
72	Donnie Rose	DT	6-1	236	22	So.	Charlotte, N. C.
83	Len Sears*	DE-TE	6-5	197	22	So.	Portsmouth, Va.
32	Doug Senter**	TB	5-10	178	22	Jr.	West Babylon, N. Y.
75	Jule Smith*	DT-MG	6-2	222	21	Jr.	Chesterfield, S. C.
66	Jerry Soles**	MG	6-0	223	19	Sr.	Tabor City, N. C.
66	Don Somma	MG	6-0	223	19	So.	Middlesex, N. J.

76	Phil Thornen	OG	6-1	235	23	So.	Medford, Mass.
84	Ken Thornton	DE	6-4	223	20	So.	Charlotte, N. C.
27	Dave Truby*	DE	5-10	186	22	Jr.	Atlanta, Ga.
88	Wayne Tucker*	SE	6-2	203	21	Sr.	Moultrie, Ga.
55	Jimmy Warren	OC	5-11	199	19	So.	Jesup, Ga.
89	Bob Wehmeyer	DE	6-2	210	20	So.	Hackettstown, N. J.
81	J. R. Wilburn**	SE	6-2	195	22	Sr.	Portsmouth, Va.
85	Burch Williams	DE	6-1	193	21	Jr.	Columbia, S. C.
22	Cooter Williams	WB	5-11	194	19	So.	Bamberg, S. C.
15	Ted Wingard	QB	6-1	199	20	So.	Greenwood, S. C.

* Denotes number of letters earned.

PK—Placekicker; QB—Quarterback; TB—Tailback; WB—Wingback; FB—Fullback; SE—Split end; TE—Tight end; DE—Defensive end; DT—Defensive tackle; OT—Offensive tackle; OG—Offensive guard; MG—Middle guard; LB—Linebacker; OC—Offensive center; DB—Defensive back.

NUMERICAL ROSTER

1 Jimmy Poole, PK
2 Martin Becker, PK
10 Jim Rogers, QB
11 Ben Garnto, QB
12 Mike Fair, QB
14 Donnie Myers, DB
15 Ted Wingard, QB
16 Stan Juk, DB
17 Paul Harmon, DB
20 Benny Galloway, DB-TB
21 Ronnie Lamb, WB
22 Cooter Williams, WB
24 Bobby Bryant, WB
25 Perry Adkins, DB
26 Butch Reeves, DB
27 Dave Truby, DB
28 Wally Medlin, WB
30 Phil Bronson, FB
31 Jimmy Killen, TB
32 Jule Smith, TB
33 Bob Cole, LB
40 Jeff Jowers, TB
41 Buster Kimbrell, TB
42 Bob Harris, WB
43 Bob Cole, LB
44 Gary Musgrove, DB
45 Mac Perry, SE
46 John Paul Chambliss, DB
50 Jimmy Gobble, OC
52 Jon Linder, OC-LB
53 Donnie Rose, OG
54 Gene Lindsey, OC-LB

55 Jimmy Warren, OC
57 Bobby Gunnels, LB-OC
60 Bill Dickens, LB
61 John Ewing, MG
62 Billy Nelson, OT
63 Wilbur Hodge, OG
64 Dan Legat, LB
65 Dave Berry, OG
66 Don Somma, MG
67 Randy Harbour, OT
68 Johnny Glass, LB
69 John Dyer, OG
71 Bob Collins, OT
72 Len Sears, DT
73 Marcellus Gabryelski, DT
74 Terry Harmon, DT
75 Jerry Soles, DT-MG
76 Phil Thornen, OG
77 Dennis Darling, OT
78 Steve Cox, DT-MG
79 Paul Phillips, DT-MG
80 Mike Rogin, TE
81 J. R. Wilburn, SE
82 John Breeden, DE-TE
83 Doug Senter, DE-TE
84 Ken Thornton, DE
85 Burch Williams, DE
86 Don Browne, TE
87 Leroy Bailey, DE-TE
88 Wayne Tucker, SE
89 Bob Wehmeyer, DE
Bob McCullough, DE

Punters — Mike Fair (12)
Donnie Myers (14)
Jeff Jowers (40)
Doug Senter (83)

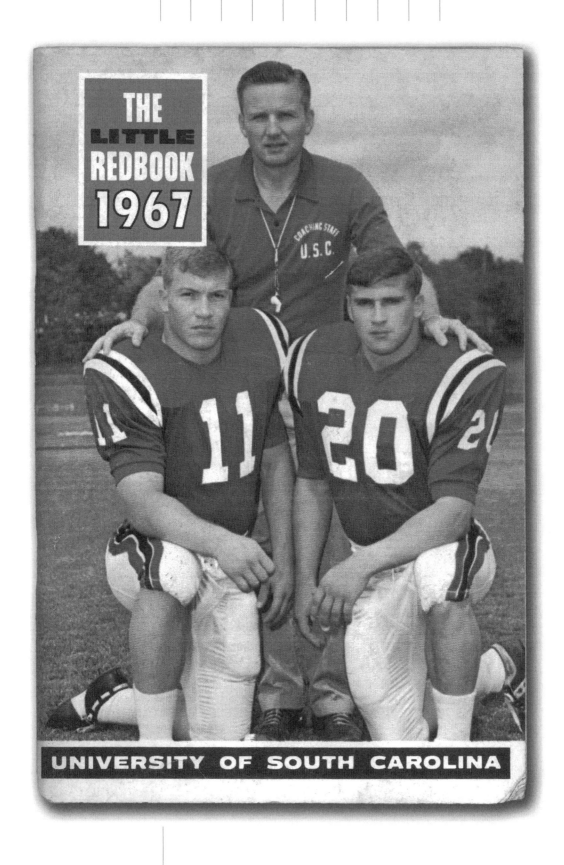

THE LITTLE REDBOOK 1967

UNIVERSITY OF SOUTH CAROLINA

THE LITTLE REDBOOK

Edited by TOM PRICE, Sports Information Director

This brochure of information on the 1967 University of South Carolina football squad is presented as a service to the press, radio and TV with copies also going to members of the Gamecock Club.

Additional information and pictures will be furnished to news media. Working press or scouting tickets to home games should be requested through the Office of Sports Information several days prior to the game date.

MISCELLANEOUS FACTS

Location	Columbia, S. C.
Colors	Garnet & Black
Mascot	Fighting Gamecock
Enrollment (including off campus centers)	14,000
President	Dr. Thomas F. Jones
Faculty Chairman of Athletics	Dr. James A. Morris
Head Football Coach and Athletic Director	Paul F. Dietzel
Football Office	765-4271
Sports Information Office	765-4277
Sports Information Director's Home Phone	787-2395
Ticket Office	765-4274
Gamecock Club	765-4276
Area Code	803
Zip Code	29208

TABLE OF CONTENTS

Printed by VOGUE PRESS

1967 GAMECOCK SCHEDULE

Sept. 16 — **IOWA STATE UNIVERSITY AT COLUMBIA—7:30 P.M., EDT— First meeting between two schools. Tickets $5.00.**

Sept. 23 — **UNIVERSITY OF NORTH CAROLINA AT COLUMBIA—7:30 P.M., EDT—Series record, 7-29-4. North Carolina won the last game, 24-6, in 1964 at Chapel Hill. Tickets $5.00. (Band Day.)**

Sept. 30 — DUKE UNIVERSITY AT DURHAM, N. C.—2:00 P.M., EDT—Series record, 5-17-2. Duke won the last game, 20-15, in 1965 at Columbia. Tickets $5.00.

Oct. 7 — UNIVERSITY OF GEORGIA AT ATHENS, GA.—2:00 P.M., EDT—Series record, 4-17-2. Georgia won the last game, 7-0, in 1966 at Columbia. Tickets $6.00.

Oct. 14 — FLORIDA STATE UNIVERSITY AT TALLAHASSEE, FLA.—2:00 P.M., EDT—Series record, 0-1-0. Florida State won the last game, 32-10, in 1966 at Columbia. Tickets $5.00.

Oct. 21 — **UNIVERSITY OF VIRGINIA AT COLUMBIA—7:30 P.M., EDT—Series record, 13-9-1. Gamecocks won the last game, 17-7, in 1965 at Charlottesville. Tickets $5.00. (Home-coming.)**

Oct. 28 — **UNIVERSITY OF MARYLAND AT COLUMBIA—7:30 P.M., EDT—Series record, 8-15-0. Maryland won the last game, 14-2, in 1966 at College Park. Tickets $5.00. (Scout Day.)**

Nov. 4 — WAKE FOREST UNIVERSITY AT WINSTON-SALEM, N. C. —7:30 P.M., EST—Series record, 19-18-2. Wake Forest won the last game, 10-6, in 1966 at Columbia. Tickets $5.00.

Nov. 18 — UNIVERSITY OF ALABAMA AT TUSCALOOSA, ALA.—1:15 P.M., CST—Series record, 0-6-0. Alabama won the last game, 24-0, in 1966 at Tuscaloosa. Tickets $5.00.

Nov. 25 — **CLEMSON UNIVERSITY AT COLUMBIA—2:00 P.M., EST—Series record, 24-37-3. Clemson won the last game, 35-10, in 1966 at Clemson. Tickets $6.00.**

1

Hundreds of student athletes have had their education at the University of South Carolina financed through contributions of Gamecock Club members.

The Gamecock Club is the University's official athletic booster organization. All contributions go directly to the University treasurer's office where they are expended for the educational needs of qualified students who have earned athletic grants-in-aid.

Grants-in-aid are awarded to student-athletes who qualify on the basis of prescribed levels of scholastic achievement established by the National Collegiate Athletic Association, the Atlantic Coast Conference and the scholarship committee of the University, in addition to meeting the standards of athletic ability and achievement set by the coaching staff.

Without the financial aid provided by the Gamecock Club, it would be impossible for the University of South Carolina to maintain an athletic program compatible with the level of competition that the Gamecocks meet.

Gamecock Club membership is open to any alumnus or friend of the University; anyone interested in the advancement of the University and its athletic program.

The minimum contribution is $25 with additional classifications for contributors of $100 (Century Club), $250 (Roundhouse Club), $500 (Half Scholarship Donor), and $1,000 or more (Scholarship Donor). Gamecock Clubbers receive membership cards, decals, regular newsletters, brochures, and priority on purchase of tickets. Contributors of $100 or more receive reserved parking privileges at Carolina Stadium.

The biggest benefit, however, is the member's knowledge that he is helping worthy young men receive an education at the University of South Carolina. Further information may be obtained by writing Ed Pitts, Gamecock Club Director, University of South Carolina, Columbia, S. C. 29208.

CAROLINA
1967
GAMECOCK CLUB
SCHOLARSHIP · LEADERSHIP

DR. THOMAS F. JONES
PRESIDENT

Dr. Thomas F. Jones became the 23rd president of the University of South Carolina July 1, 1962.

Under his guidance, Carolina has made gigantic strides in many areas. The graduate school program has more than doubled . . . research facilities have been strengthened . . . a giant building program is in full swing . . . enrollment is booming.

The athletic program has not been forgotten in this surge forward to meet the challenges of the space age. When the University needed a football coach, Dr. Jones went out and landed a national champion, Paul Dietzel. Under Dr. Jones' leadership the building program includes Carolina Coliseum, a multi-million dollar academic-athletic complex that will provide the University with a super coliseum for basketball and other events. Construction began last spring with completion in early 1969.

Dr. Jones has said many times "the Fighting Gamecocks are an integral part of the University. Our pride in our athletes shows respect for their scholarly work in the classrooms and laboratories fully as much as it acknowledges their spirited performance in sports competition."

Dr. Jones came to South Carolina from Purdue University at Lafayette, Ind., where he was head of the School of Electrical Engineering. A native of southwestern Tennessee, Dr. Jones received his bachelor's degree from Mississippi State College, and the master's and doctor of philosophy degree from Massachusets Institute of Technology.

3

PAUL F. DIETZEL

Director of Athletics and Head Football Coach

Throughout his more than 25 years in organized football, success and Paul Dietzel have been synonymous.

During his early years as an athlete, Paul Dietzel played on Mansfield, Ohio's first junior high football team. It was undefeated. In high school, young Dietzel maintained high grades, held down an after-school job as a butcher's helper, and received All-State honors in three sports. After graduation he chose Duke University as a recipient of a football scholarship. Like many others, his college career was interrupted by World War II, and he enlisted in the Army Air Corps. He received his wings in August of 1944 and married his high school sweetheart, Anne Wilson.

At 20-years of age, Lt. Dietzel was a B-29 co-pilot in the South Pacific, flying 12 missions over the Japanese Empire.

Paul Dietzel enrolled at Miami University at Oxford, Ohio following separation from the service, where he played football for two years. He was elected captain of the undefeated 1947 team, was chosen as Little All-America center, to the Coaches All-America team, and later to the All-Time Miami team.

While at Miami, he was the butcher in the veterans' store in addition to being the president of three national honorary societies and graduating with an average of 3.46 of a possible 4.00. An invitation to join the Plebe staff at West Point cancelled his plans to enter medical school.

For seven years, Coach Dietzel served as an apprentice to some of football's all-time great coaches. These included Col. Earl (Red) Blaik at the U.S. Military Academy in 1948 and again in 1953-54; Sid Gillman at the University of Cincinnati, 1949-50; and Paul (Bear) Bryant at the University of Kentucky, 1951-52.

In 1955, at the age of 31, Paul Dietzel became one of the youngest head coaches in the history of the powerful Southeastern

4

COACHING STAFF

271

Conference when he left Army for Louisiana State University. LSU had won but two conference games in the two previous years and for three rebuilding seasons, the Tigers won 11 while losing 17. But in his last four years at LSU, Coach Dietzel's Bayou Bengals won 35 and lost 7, and won two SEC championships. His teams participated in the Sugar Bowl twice and the Orange Bowl once, compiling a 2-1 bowl record.

In 1958, LSU was national champion and Coach Dietzel was voted National Coach of the Year by his fellow coaches. He was also coach of the Gray squad twice in the Blue-Gray classic, head coach of the victorious East team in the Hula Bowl in Hawaii, co-coach of the winning North squad in the 1964 North-South game in Miami, Fla., and on the staff of the victorious East team in the 1966 East-West Shrine game in San Francisco. He will again coach in the East-West game after the 1967 season as well as the Hula Bowl.

In 1962, Coach Dietzel left LSU to return to West Point as head coach. In four seasons, his teams had a 21-18-1 record. He was named heard coach and athletic director at the University of South Carolina in April 1966.

South Carolina's 42-year-old coach is undoubtedly one of America's most quoted coaches. He is author of the book, "Wing-T and the Chinese Bandits" and co-author more recently of "Go, Shorty, Go." Two of his best known writings are a treatise on "Why Play Football?" and his poem, "Sissy."

Coach Dietzel has appeared on many football clinics, including three to our armed forces in Europe. He appeared on bi-weekly television programs while at LSU, and for two years had national weekly radio shows from New York. At South Carolina he has a weekly television program on a statewide network during football season, a Monday night local show in Columbia, and a radio program.

Coach Dietzel's great demand as a speaker has taken him throughout the nation. He has served with many civic organizations. He is a former member of the ethics committee of the American Football Coaches Association and at present is the organization's second Vice-President, chairman of the National Program Committee and a member of the board of trustees.

Dietzel is an active member and immediate past president of the board of directors of the Fellowship of Christian Athletes. Anne and Paul Dietzel have been happily married for 22 years. They have two children, **Steve**, 18, and **Kathy**, 14.

6

FIGHTING GAMECOCKS
OF THE UNIVERSITY OF SOUTH CAROLINA

SCHOLARSHIP · LEADERSHIP

1967 FOOTBALL SCHEDULE

SEPT.16-IOWA STATE 7:30
SEPT.23-NORTH CAROLINA 7:30
SEPT.30 at DUKE 2:00
OCT.7 at GEORGIA 2:00
OCT.14 at FLORIDA STATE 2:00
OCT.12-VIRGINIA 7:30
OCT.28-MARYLAND 7:30
NOV.4 at WAKE FOREST 7:30
NOV.18 at ALABAMA 1:15
NOV.25-CLEMSON 2:00

REX ENRIGHT ATHLETIC CENTER

272

MEET THE STAFF

GEORGE TERRY, Assistant Director of Athletics

George Terry is called "my right arm" by Paul Dietzel. They have been together ever since Coach Dietzel landed his first head coaching job at LSU more than 12 years ago. As Assistant Director of Athletics, Terry performs many of the administrative duties of the athletic department, including scheduling. On the football field, he was in charge of defensive strategy until he retired from active coaching after the 1966 season to devote full time to administrative duties.

Born April 4, 1909 in Newport, Ark., Terry attended high school in Batesville, Ark., where he participated in football, basketball and baseball. He attended the George Washington University, and was graduated in 1933 from the College of the Ozarks with a Bachelor of Arts degree. He later earned the Master of Science degree from the University of Arkansas. In college, he participated in football, basketball and baseball.

Terry coached a number of years in high schools at Pine Bluff, Ark., and Greenville, Miss., and while in service was an assistant coach at Tufts College, Boston, Mass., in 1942. He joined the Louisiana State University staff in 1954 under Gus Tinsley, and remained at LSU when Paul Dietzel became head coach the following year.

Terry moved to the U.S. Military Academy with Coach Dietzel in 1962, and accompanied him to South Carolina in April 1966. During six summers, Terry coached with the Ottowa Roughriders of the Canadian Professional League during pre-season camp. He participated in two Sugar Bowl games and one Orange Bowl while coaching at LSU.

Serving in the U. S. Navy, 1942-46, Terry reached the rank of Lieutenant Commander. He married the former Frances Trevahan of Batesville, Ark., in 1937 and they have one son, Jeff, and two grandchildren.

8

LARRY BRUCE JONES
First Assistant; Defensive Line

Larry Jones joined the LSU staff immediately after graduation in 1954 and except for two years as a First Lieutenant in the U. S. Air Force, has been with Coach Paul Dietzel since, moving to the U. S. Military Academy in 1962 and to South Carolina in April 1966.

A native of Little Rock, Ark., Jones was born Dec. 18, 1933. He participated in football, basketball and baseball in high school, and was a standout football center at Louisiana State University where he earned the Bachelor of Science degree, and in 1961 the Master of Education degree.

Jones played in the 1954 Blue-Gray all-star football game and has been a coach in one Sugar Bowl and one Orange Bowl game.

He married the former Judy Bianchi of Dallas, Tex., Dec. 28, 1954 and they have three children, Bruce, 6, Kevin, 4, and Laura, 2.

WILLIAM ANDREW (SHAD) SHALOSKY
Offensive Coordinator; Offensive Line

Bill Shalosky is called "the finest lineman I ever coached" by Paul Dietzel. Shalosky was a star guard and linebacker at the University of Cincinnati while Coach Dietzel was an assistant there. Shalosky was All-Ohio, Honorable Mention All-America, and played in the East-West Shrine game and the College All-Star game. He also played in the Sun Bowl game with Cincinnati.

Born Sept. 23, 1931 at Louisville, Ohio, Shalosky participated in football and track in high school. He earned three football letters at Cincinnati and also participated in track, in the shot put and sprints. He received the Bachelor of Science degree in Education in 1953.

Shalosky was Plebe line coach at Army in 1954, and offensive line coach at Cincinnati, 1955-59; he joined Coach Dietzel at LSU in 1960, moved with him to Army in 1962, and to South Carolina in April 1966.

Shalosky served two years as a Second Lieutenant of Artillery in the U. S. Army. He married the former Rita Murrer of Cincinnati, Ohio Jan. 6, 1954, and they have two children, Mike, 11, and Kathy, 8.

9

RICHARD B. (DICK) WELDON
Offensive Backfield

Dick Weldon joined the Gamecock staff in January 1965. He worked with middle guards and linebackers in 1965 and as Director of High School Relations and chief recruiter in 1966. He returned to on-the-field coaching in 1967 as offensive backfield coach. Weldon also served one season, 1966, as head baseball coach, posting a 15-8 record.

Weldon didn't play football until his junior year at Presbyterian College, but he earned two letters as a quarterback. He also lettered four times as a baseball infielder and twice in track.

He received the Bachelor of Arts degree from Presbyterian in 1952 and spent the next 13 years coaching at Bamberg, S. C., High School where his record was 104-35-5 in football; 216-87 in basketball; and 118-32 in baseball.

Born April 29, 1929 at Latta, S. C., he played high school basketball and baseball at Bennettsville, S. C., and served two years as a Marine corporal.

He married the former Mary Deane Currie of Loris, S. C., Aug. 10, 1951 and they have three children, Dicky, 12, Steve, 10, and John, 4.

WILLIAM GERALD (BILL) ROWE
Defensive Linebackers, Middle Guards

Bill Rowe was an outstanding center and linebacker at the U.S. Military Academy where he received the Bachelor of Science degree in Engineering in 1959. He earned three varsity football letters, was an All-East and Honorable Mention All-America.

Born July 11, 1937 at Newville, Pa., Rowe attended high school in Carlisle, Pa., where he participated in football, baseball and basketball. He was Plebe coach at Army, 1960-62, while serving in the U. S. Army as a Captain of Artillery. He coached at the Manlius School, Manlius, N. Y., in 1963; and returned to West Point in 1964 as a varsity assistant. He accompanied Paul Dietzel to South Carolina in April 1966.

Rowe married the former Mary Lou Beithel of Carlisle, Pa., June 14, 1959, and they have three children, David 7, Peter, 5, and Sally, 3.

LOUIS LEO (LOU) HOLTZ, Defensive Perimeter

Lou Holtz came to Carolina in February 1966 as defensive backfield coach.

Born Jan. 6, 1937 in Follansbee, W. Va., Holtz grew up in East Liverpool, Ohio. He participated in football, basketball and baseball in high school and attended Kent State University where he lettered two years in football as a center and linebacker.

Holtz received the Bachelor of Science degree from Kent State in 1959 and the Master of Arts degree from the University of Iowa in 1962. He was freshman coach at Kent State, 1959, and an assistant at Iowa, 1960. He served three seasons as backfield coach at William and Mary, 1961-63, and was number one assistant at Connecticut, 1964-65, before joining the USC staff in February 1966.

A former First Lieutenant of Infantry in the Army, Holtz married the former Beth Barcus, July 22, 1961. They have three children, Luanne Rae, 5; Louis, Jr., 3; and Kevin Richard, 1.

DON (SCOOTER) PURVIS
Pass Receivers

Don Purvis was the "Go" team left halfback on Louisiana State University's national championship football team of 1958. He played in two Sugar Bowl games during his three varsity seasons under Coach Paul Dietzel, and also played in the Hula Bowl all-star game in Honolulu.

A native of Crystal Springs, Miss., Purvis received the Bachelor of Science degree in Education from LSU in 1960 and the Master of Education degree in 1964. He served one year on the staff at Murrah High School in Jackson, Miss., before joining the LSU staff in 1961. He was head freshman coach at LSU when he was named to the South Carolina staff in April 1967.

Purvis married the former Bunny Cobb of Jackson, Miss., Aug. 5, 1961, and they have two sons, Chris, 5, and Jeff, 1½. A third child was expected in late summer.

THOMAS HART (TOM) PRICE
Sports Information Director

Tom Price has been sports information director at the University of South Carolina since April 1962, returning to his alma mater after nearly 11 years with United Press International, a world-wide newsgathering agency.

Born Nov. 28, 1926 at Augusta, Ga., Price grew up on Wadmalaw Island, S. C. He served four years in the Navy, 1943-47, before entering the University of South Carolina in February 1948. He graduated in June 1951 with a Bachelor of Arts degree in Journalism.

Price was a reporter, sports editor, managing editor and editor-in-chief of The Gamecock, student weekly, while attending USC; and ran the University's News Service in a part-time capacity his senior year.

He married the former Margaret Fletcher of Charleston, S. C., June 10, 1950, and they have three children, Tommy 16; Melissa, 13; and Rick, 12.

PETER EVANS III
Sports Information Student Assistant

Pete Evans is a rising sophomore in the School of Journalism beginning his second year as student assistant in the sports information office. He works with statistics and travels with the freshman football and basketball teams as well as the varsity baseball squad.

THE 1967 GAMECOCKS

The 1967 Fighting Gamecocks will be the smallest football squad, both in size and numbers, at the University of South Carolina in many years.

There were only 71 squad members at the end of spring practice, the largest of which was 232-pound veteran center Jimmy Gobble. By contrast, the starting defensive right halfback — rising sophomore Pat Watson — weighed in at 152 pounds.

The first team offensive line averaged 201½ pounds. This was from 15 to 20 pounds lighter than Gamecock forward walls of recent years.

Coach Paul Dietzel and his staff have a fair amount of experience with 25 lettermen, 21 of whom earned monograms last year plus four who last lettered in 1965.

Most prominent among this four is Roy Don Reeves, a starting defensive halfback in 1965 who missed the entire 1966 season after suffering a knee injury just before the season opened. Shifted to split end in spring practice, Reeves was the starter there in the spring game.

Split end appears to be one of the best fortified positions with Fred Ziegler, a redshirt sophomore, giving Reeves a battle for the starting job. On the other hand, tight end was a trouble spot in the spring and Johnny Gregory, the regular split end as a sophomore, was shifted there despite his lack of size. Gregory weighs only 172 pounds, but as Coach Dietzel said, "John did the best job of anyone we tried at tight end, so he has the job until someone beats him out." Gregory caught 17 passes for 301 yards and two touchdowns as a split end last year.

Bob Mauro, a redshirt who came out for spring football after the baseball season ended (he was a regular outfielder), started the spring game and will battle letterman Bob Wehmeyer for the offensive left tackle spot. Senior Hyrum Pierce, who is a steady performer, will be at the other tackle spot.

Bob Morris, small at 187 pounds but quick and agile, nailed down the offensive left guard spot in spring practice and this rising sophomore looks like a comer. The other guard will be junior Tom Wingard, one of the better football players on the squad. Backing up Morris and Wingard will be sophomore Jack James and senior Johnny Glass.

Jimmy Gobble, a two-year starter who is one of the Gamecocks' most consistent players, is back at center, backed up by three sophomores.

Dietzel says he wouldn't trade his starting offensive backfield for any other in the Atlantic Coast Conference and if this quartet can

remain healthy, the ball carrying and passing departments will be in good hands.

Mike Fair, who had 1,127 yards total offense — 1,049 of it passing — as a sophomore, hopes to avoid the injuries that crippled him as a junior, cutting his offensive output to 657 yards. He passed for 184 yards and ran for 40 more in the spring game and appeared ready to duplicate his sophomore season.

"THE 'BG' BOYS"

The "BG Boys" — Benny Galloway and Ben Garnto — give the Gamecocks two of the finest halfbacks in the business. Galloway rushed for 580 yards and caught 16 passes for 211 more last year despite pesky injuries that either slowed him down or kept him out altogether in several games. Garnto rushed for 440 yards, caught 19 passes for 243 yards, and threw 15 passes, completing eight for 93 yards last year.

Complementing these three seniors will be transfer sophomore Warren Muir at fullback. A strong-legged runner, he was the top back on the U. S. Military Academy's Plebe team in 1965.

Fair is the Gamecocks' only letterman quarterback. Dan Harbison, up from the freshman team, could also figure in the picture this fall.

Curtis Williams, a senior two-time letterman who has played every backfield position, and sophomore Rudy Holloman back Galloway up at left halfback. A spring game knee injury casts some doubt on the status of two-time letterman right halfback Bob Harris, and the backup man to Garnto could be either redshirt sophomore Ronnie Palmer — one of the smallest Gamecocks at 5-5, 157 pounds — or Allen Brown, a non-letterman who played a little in 1966.

Behind Muir, fullback appears adequately stocked with Jimmy Killen, a senior who lettered at fullback in 1965 and tight end in '66, and two sophomores, Don Dunning and Earl Hunter.

DEFENSE

Defensively, the Gamecocks suffered a heavy blow early in spring practice when Lyn Hodge, a starter as a sophomore at right end last year, suffered a compound fracture of his right leg. Hodge will be in a cast until September and won't play this fall.

This leaves junior Gene Schwarting, a starter last year, at left end and redshirt sophomore Ron Zukowski, a former quarterback who looks like a natural at end, on the right side. Dave (The Pencil) Lucas, a 6-5, 184 pounder, will likely be the third end, playing in relief of both Schwarting and Zukowski.

The Gamecocks have two veteran defensive tackles in seniors Joe Komoroski and Don Somma. Reserve strength should come from sophomores Gordon Gibson, Steve Lanford, John Coleman and Ray Edwards.

"PERHAPS OUR FINEST"

The strong side linebacker will be Bob Cole, a senior who has led the Gamecocks in tackles the past two years. Sophomore Billy Tharp should be his relief. At weakside linebacker, Tim Bice is called "perhaps our finest football player" by Coach Dietzel. Bice opened the 1966 season as a safety man and in mid-season became a 176-pound middle guard, making an astounding 17 individual tackles and six assists against Alabama. He's up to 186 pounds now and should team with Cole to give the Gamecocks two of the better linebackers around. Sophomore Fletcher Spigner should back up Bice.

At middle guard, the Gamecocks have Dave (Mudcat) Grant, a 1966 letterman, and Ron Bunch, who saw some action last year but did not letter.

Moving to the secondary, the Gamecocks must replace All-America Bobby Bryant — Atlantic Coast Conference Athlete of the Year — at right halfback, and Stan Juk at rover. Bryant, All-ACC in football and baseball, has signed with the Minnesota Vikings of the NFL, and Juk, drafted by the Miami Dolphins, decided to enter the Duke University medical school instead.

Toy McCord, a sophomore starter, is back at left halfback although he missed virtually all of spring practice to play baseball. Wally Orrel, also a starter, is back at safety, but it remains to be seen if he is fully recovered from a knee operation performed the final week of spring practice.

SOPHS

In any event, it appears there will be at least two sophomores in the defensive secondary — 152-pound Pat Watson at right halfback and Don Buckner at rover. Both are exceptional athletes and could be two Gamecock stars of the future. Jim Mulvihill, a tough senior who lettered twice as an offensive fullback, will challenge Buckner for the rover back job, and sophomore Andy Chavous, a former split end, will compete with Watson.

Besides Orrel at safety, there are Wally Medlin — a non-letterman offensive back in 1966 — and redshirt sophomore Bob White.

Scott Townsend, the regular punter in 1965 who was used in only one game last year, should resume his status as punting specialist, and Jimmy Poole, leading scorer of 1965 and '66 with his extra points and field goals, will do all of the placekicking, including kickoffs.

LOSSES

Besides Bryant and Juk, the Gamecocks lost nine lettermen by graduation. In addition, Hodge was lost due to an injury, promising linebacker Dave Meadow gave up football due to a head injury, and three other lettermen with eligibility remaining — quarterback Ted Wingard, guard Donnie Rose, and defensive back Paul Harman — graduated and will not return.

Graduation losses included offensive tackle Paul Phillips, drafted and signed by the San Diego Chargers; tackle Dave Berry, signed by the Pittsburgh Steelers; guard Billy Nelson, signed by the St. Louis Cardinals; linebacker Bill Dickens, guard Randy Harbour, defensive end Leroy Bailey, tight end Mike Ragin, tackle Jerry Soles, and punter Jeff Jowers.

QUICKER

Coach Paul Dietzel feels the Gamecocks will be better than last year's squad and cites several reasons for his feeling. The coaching staff, which took over midway through spring practice in 1966, has had a full year to install the Dietzel system and acquaint itself with the personnel. The Gamecocks, although smaller in size and number, appear to have considerably more quickness and speed than last year. The addition of Muir adds an explosive, hard-running fullback to the backfield to complement the talents of Galloway, Gornto and Fair.

The defensive system will be virtually the same as last year except for the linebacker positions where Cole will always line up on the strong side and Bice on the weak side. This should better utilize Bice's quickness and agility and Cole's strength. Otherwise, the Gamecocks will usually be in the same 5-4 alignment as last year although there will be variations as down and distance dictates.

OFFENSE SIMPLIFIED

The offense, on the other hand, will be considerably changed from last year when the Gamecocks had a strong side and a weak side, flip-flopping both linemen and backs. Now, there will be left tackles and guards and right tackles and guards rather than strong and weak side linemen, and in the backfield there will be a left halfback and a right halfback rather than the tailback and wingback of last year.

The ends, however, will continue to flip-flop, with the split end lining up on either right or left, depending on the formation, and the tight end on the other side.

The Power-I that was used as the primary formation last year, has been scrapped and the Gamecocks will use multiple sets, including Split-T, Slot-T, and Wing-T. The offense should be considerably simplified from last year, at the same time better utilizing the running abilities of all four members of the backfield. The Gamecocks threw the football 172 times last year, and should also pass quite a bit in 1967, although the basic attack will be the ground game.

The Fighting Gamecock emblem of the University of South Carolina athletic teams emphasizes a "Scholarship-Leadership" theme. The emblem is a registered trademark and may not be copied without permission. The emblem appears on the headgear of members of the Gamecock football squad as well as on the travel blazers worn by Gamecock teams.

Trademark Registered

SCHOLARSHIP · LEADERSHIP

GAMECOCK TRAVEL PLANS

THE DUKE GAME:
Depart Columbia by bus Friday afternoon, Sept. 29. Headquarters, Eden Rock Motel, Durham, N. C. Depart Durham by bus as soon as possible after game, Saturday, Sept. 30, arriving Columbia Saturday evening. Sports Information Director arrives Raleigh-Durham area Wednesday, Sept. 27.

THE GEORGIA GAME:
Depart Columbia by bus Friday afternoon, Oct. 6. Headquarters, Holiday Inn, Athens, Ga. Depart Athens by bus as soon as possible after game, Saturday, Oct. 7, arriving Columbia Saturday evening. Sports Information Director arrives Atlanta Wednesday, Oct. 4; Athens Friday morning, Oct. 6.

THE FLORIDA STATE GAME:
Depart Columbia Metropolitan Airport 11 A.M., EDT, Friday, Oct. 13, aboard chartered United Airlines DC6, arriving Tallahassee, Fla., 12 Noon, EDT. Headquarters Holiday Inn, Tallahassee, Fla. Depart Tallahassee airport 6 P.M., EDT, Saturday, Oct. 14, arriving Columbia Metropolitan Airport, 7:15 P.M., EDT. Sports Information Director arrives Tallahassee Wednesday, Oct. 11.

THE WAKE FOREST GAME:
Depart Columbia by bus Friday afternoon, Nov. 3. Headquarters, Sheraton Motor Inn, Winston-Salem, N. C. Depart Winston-Salem by bus as soon as possible after game, Saturday, Nov. 4, arriving Columbia early Sunday A.M. Sports Information Director arrives Winston-Salem, Greensboro area Wednesday, Nov. 1.

THE ALABAMA GAME:
Depart Columbia Metropolitan Airport 10 A.M., EST, Friday, Nov. 17, aboard chartered United Airlines DC6, arriving Birmingham, Ala., airport 11:15 A.M., CST, departing Birmingham immediately by bus for Tuscaloosa. Headquarters, Stafford Motor Inn, Tuscaloosa, Ala. Depart Tuscaloosa as soon as possible after game by bus for Birmingham airport. Depart Birmingham 6 P.M., CST, arriving Columbia Metropolitan Airport 9:15 P.M., EST. Sports Information Director arrives Birmingham Wednesday, Nov. 15; Tuscaloosa Thursday.

MEET THE GAMECOCKS

THE "B. G." BOYS

South Carolina's football history is dotted with outstanding halfback tandems. Steve Wadiak and Bishop Strickland, who played together in 1948-49-50, and Alex Hawkins and King Dixon, 1956-57-58, are just two examples. The B. G. Boys, Benny Galloway and Ben Garnto, rank with the best and are two reasons for Coach Paul Dietzel saying he wouldn't trade his 1967 offensive backfield for any in the Atlantic Coast Conference. Between them last season, the B. G. Boys rushed for 1,020 yards, caught 35 passes for 453 yards, threw 15 passes, completing 8 for 93 yards, returned kickoffs 252 yards, and scored four touchdowns. The dynamic duo advanced the football offensively 1,818 yards in 1966.

#20 DAVID BENNETT (BENNY) GALLOWAY

187, 5-9, 21, Senior, left halfback, Easley, S. C. . . . Gamecocks' top rusher in '66 with 580 yards and 4.5 average . . . caught 16 passes for 211 yards . . . returned kickoffs 233 yards all despite hobbling injuries. Exclusively on offense last year after soph season when he played mostly defense but was used two-ways enough to rush for 134 yards and 4.0 average. Scored one TD in '66, two in '65 when he was named first team All-ACC defensive back. Led ACC in kickoff returns in '65 with 463 yards and participated in 79 tackles that year. Business Administration major . . . Methodist . . . single . . . high school coach Bill Carr.

#11 BENNIE EDMOND (BEN) GARNTO

195, 5-10, 21, Senior, right halfback, Columbus, Ga. The Gamecocks' "Mr. Versatile," played both halfback positions and quarterback during 1966 when other backs were hurt. Second to Galloway in rushing with 440 yards and 4.4 average after leading in 1965 with 437 yards and 4.9 average . . . two-year rushing total 877 yards . . . caught 19 passes for 242 yards last year to lead team and in two years has 35 receptions to rank seventh among all-time Gamecock receivers. Should move up several notches this fall. Had three TDs last year and one in '65. Had 89-yard run to Wake Forest five-yard line in '65 to set ACC record for non-scoring run from scrimmage . . . Business Administration major . . . Baptist . . . single . . . high school coach Bob Donaldson.

24

#47 TIMOTHY J. (TIM) BICE, 186, 5-10, 21, Junior, weak side linebacker, Dallas, Tex. Quick, tough and aggressive and called "perhaps our finest football player" by Coach Paul Dietzel. Opened 1966 season as safety but switched to middle guard after six games and did great job despite weighing only 176 pounds. Made 17 individual tackles and six assists against Alabama. For season had 44 tackles and 24 assists. Ten pounds heavier and moved to linebacker in spring, and should be a top star this fall. Attended Druid Hills High School in Atlanta but now lives in Dallas, Tex. Business Administration major . . . Baptist . . . single . . . high school coach Sam Edenfield.

#35 HOGAN CANDLER (CANDLER) BOYD, 174, 5-9, 19, Sophomore, defensive halfback, Hinesville, Ga. One of the top defensive backs on 1966 frosh . . . slowed by jaw injury in spring practice, but showed potential and definitely figures in plans. Brother played at Tampa . . . father managers store and Candler's summer job is food service sales clerk. Biology major . . . Methodist . . . single . . . high school coach Hokey Jackson.

#34 JAMES ALLEN (ALLEN) BROWN, 189, 6-0, 20, Junior, right halfback, Hinesville, Ga. Saw some action as soph in 1966 but did not earn a letter. Did not carry the ball last year but caught one pass for seven yards. Moved from fullback to right halfback in spring practice. Pre-law major . . . Methodist . . . single . . . high school coach Hokey Jackson.

#48 DONALD EDWARD (DON) BUCKNER, 180, 6-0, 19, Sophomore, rover back, Cleveland, Tenn. Attended same high school as former Alabama quarterback star Steve Sloan. Linebacker on 1966 frosh team and came along fast in spring to win starting rover back job . . . has potential to be an outstanding football player. Father's occupation welder. Business Administration major . . . single . . . high school coach Harold Henslee.

25

#51 RONALD WAYNE (RON) BUNCH, 199, 5-9, 20, Junior, middle guard, Bamberg, S. C. Played some as linebacker in 1966 but did not letter . . . made four tackles, three assists. One of two top middle guard candidates in spring practice. Father's occupation line superintendent for rural electric co-operative. Business Administration major . . . Baptist . . . single . . . high school coach was present Gamecock backfield mentor Dick Weldon.

#29 ANDREW JULIAN (ANDY) CHAVOUS, 178, 6-2, 19, Sophomore, defensive halfback, Hepzibah, Ga. Regular split end on '66 frosh team where he led in pass receiving with 11 for 164 yards. Shifted to defensive secondary in spring practice and wound up on second team at right halfback. Has moves, quickness, hands to become a star. Father is plant foreman. Pharmacy major . . . Methodist . . . married . . . high school coach Jamie Overton.

#33 ROBERT BURNS (BOB) COLE, 221, 6-3, 22, Senior, strong side linebacker, Columbia, S. C. The Gamecocks' top tackler the past two seasons . . . made 79 individuals and 23 assists last year . . . participated in 77 tackles in '65 although played in only six games due to injuries. A fine football player who has been hampered throughout career by injuries. Was fullback star in high school. Business Administration major . . . married with daughter . . . Presbyterian . . . high school coach Art Baker.

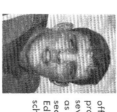

#85 JOHN D. (JOHN) COLEMAN, 209, 6-4, 20, Sophomore, defensive tackle, Latta, S. C. Dislocated elbow spoiled his chance to play in '66 and he became a redshirt. Was an end until late in spring practice when shifted to defensive right tackle. Father's occupation farming. Business Administration major . . . Methodist . . . single . . . high school coach Eddie Rice.

#10 CARL MINER (CARL) COWART, 162, 5-9, 20, Sophomore, defensive halfback, Jesup, Ga. Quarterback on 1965 freshman team and redshirt in '66. Listed on pre-season depth chart as number two defensive right halfback. Small but smart and quick and should help squad. Father is auto parts manager. Banking and Finance major in College of Business Administration. Baptist . . . single . . . high school coach Clint Madrey.

#12 MICHAEL LARRY (MIKE) FAIR, 192, 6-1, 21, Senior, quarterback, Greenville, S. C. A fine athlete who stars in football and baseball. Injuries during '66 cut him to 657 yards total offense after sensational 1,127 yards as sophomore when he set school passing records. All-ACC outfielder last spring when he hit .352 after .309 season in '66. An exciting, scrambling-type player who will be one of the top QBs in the South if he avoids injury. One of organizers of USC chapter of Fellowship of Christian Athletes and considering ministry after graduation. Business Administration major . . . Baptist . . . single . . . high school coach Whitey Kendall.

#65 TONY FUSARO, 230, 6-2, 20, Sophomore, offensive tackle, Huntington, N. Y. One of top line prospects from 1966 frosh team. Experimented at several positions in spring practice and wound up as number two offensive right tackle. Father is security guard. Summer job as golf caddy. Physical Education major . . . Catholic . . . single . . . high school coach J. Lucey.

#75 GORDON L. GIBSON, 203, 6-3, 20, Sophomore, defensive tackle, Greenville, S. C. Played on '65 frosh team and a redshirt in '66. Number two defensive left tackle in spring practice. Brother Tommy was former Gamecock star lineman and co-captain. Father is building contractor. Business Administration major . . . Baptist . . . single . . . high school coach Steve Satterfield.

#68 JOHNNY K. GLASS, 200, 5-11, 21, Senior, offensive guard, Kingsport, Tenn. Lettered as a line-backer in 1965 and played some at defensive end in '66 but did not letter. Made five tackles, three assists last year and blocked punt for a safety in Maryland game . . . in '65, recovered blocked punt for TD against Wake Forest. Management major in College of Business Administration . . . Methodist . . . single . . . high school coach Thomas Brixey.

#50 JAMES CLIFTON (JIMMY) GOBBLE, 232, 6-2, 22, Senior, center, Spartanburg, S. C. The Game-cocks' top center for two years and one of the squad's top leaders as well as a fine blocker. Won tough battle with high blood pressure to become a star. Brother Robert played football at Clemson. Business Administration major . . . Lutheran . . . married with daughter . . . high school coach Bob Bell.

#52 CY DAVID (DAVE, MUD CAT) GRANT, 208, 5-10, 20, Junior, middle guard, Clarkesville, Ga. Lettered in '66 as soph when he made 28 tackles and 20 assists. Was starting middle guard in spring drills. A tough, steady player. Father played foot-ball and baseball at Georgia. Marketing major in College of Business Administration . . . Baptist . . . single . . . high school coach Red Lynch.

#88 JOHN DEMETRIUS (JOHNNY) GREGORY, 172, 5-11, 21, Junior, tight end, Aiken, S. C. A tough little guy who gets the job done despite lack of size. Regular split end in '66 when he caught 17 passes for 299 yards and two TDs. Moved to tight end in spring drills and a starter there. Brother Art was All-America tackle at Duke and now attends USC law school. History major . . . Greek Orthodox . . . single . . . high school coach Jim Fraser.

#42 ROBERT MITCHELL (BOB) HARRIS, JR., 178, 6-0, 21, Senior, right halfback, Point Pleasant Beach, N. J. Two-year letterman whose status for 1966 is clouded by knee injury suffered in spring intra-squad game. Rushed for 34 yards and caught six passes for 68 yards as reserve last year. Sprinter on track team where he also has lettered twice. English major . . . Methodist . . . single . . . high school coach John Kelley.

#24 RUDY PEARSON (RUDY) HOLLOMAN, 173, 5-9, 20, Sophomore, left halfback, McBee, S. C. Rushed for 116 yards with frosh in '66, caught six passes for 53 yards and scored one touchdown. Excellent potential for becoming a future star. Edu-cation major . . . Baptist . . . single . . . high school coach Billy Seigler.

#32 EARL HUNTER III, 195, 6-0, 20, Sophomore, fullback, Greenville, S. C. Broken collar bone in spring of '66 slowed his development and was a redshirt last year. Averaged 4.2 for 162 yards with '65 frosh. Business Administration major . . . Baptist . . . single . . . high school coach Whitey Kendall.

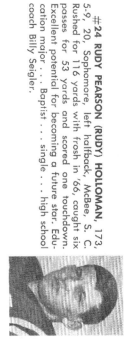

#67 JACK LAMAR (JESSE) JAMES, 198, 5-10, 20, Sophomore, offensive guard, Atlanta, Ga. Red-shirt in 1966 who was second-team offensive left guard in spring practice. Father is an accountant. Had summer job in press room of Atlanta news-paper. Business Administration major . . . Methodist . . . single . . . high school coach Jack Hogg.

#31 JAMES THOMAS (JIMMY) KILLEN, 195, 6-1, 21, Senior, fullback, Georgetown, S. C. Two-year letterman who played fullback in 1965 and opened '66 season at tailback but moved to tight end . . . returns to fullback for '67. Scored first TD of Dietzel era in '66 opener at L. S. U. Caught six passes for 76 yards last year and had 21 rushing yards . . . scored two TDs. Marketing major in College of Business Administration . . . Methodist . . . single . . . high school coach J. C. Hudson.

#77 JOSEPH S. (JOE) KOMOROSKI, 222, 6-2, 22, Senior, defensive tackle, Linden, N. J. Two-year letterman and a starter at left tackle last year when he made 30 tackles and 13 assists. Probably the Gamecocks' strongest physical specimen. Marketing major in College of Business Administration . . . Catholic . . . single . . . high school coach Bob Smith.

#84 DAVID HENRY (DAVE, THE PENCIL) LUCAS, 184, 6-5, 20, Sophomore, defensive end, Bishopville, S. C. Tall, skinny and tough. Redshirt in '66 who came fast in spring practice and should be the "third end" this fall, backing up the starter on both sides. Business Administration major . . . single . . . high school coach W. C. Smith.

#55 GEORGE WALDO McCARTHY, 205, 6-2, 21, Sophomore, center, Washington, D. C. A redshirt in 1966 who should see some action this fall. Brother Brendan is fullback star at Boston College. Father is investigator for Air Force. Arts and Sciences major . . . Catholic . . . single . . . high school coach Morgan Wooten.

30

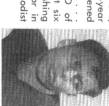

#21 GILBERT TOY (TOY) McCORD, 168, 5-8, 20, Junior, defensive halfback, Manning, S. C. Starter at left halfback in 1966 as soph . . . made 46 tackles, 15 assists, intercepted one pass, returned three punts 24 yards . . . five kickoffs 122 yards. A fine little athlete who was regular shortstop on baseball squad and missed most of spring football practice due to diamond activities. Marketing major in College of Business Administration . . . Presbyterian . . . single . . . high school coach Gus Allen.

#74 ROBERT JOHN (BOB) MAURO, 210, 6-0, 21, Junior, offensive tackle, Madison, N. J. Non-letterman who joined spring drills in final week after baseball season and won left tackle spot in offensive line. Hit .282 as outfielder-catcher-first baseman in baseball, including two home runs. Has won two baseball letters. Physical Education major . . . Catholic . . . single . . . high school coach Ted Monica.

#28 HARRY WALLACE (WALLY) MEDLIN, 183, 5-9, 21, Junior, safety, Ehrhardt, S. C. Saw some action as offensive back in 1966 but did not letter. Rushed for 83 yards, caught three passes for 29 yards. Moved to defense in spring and landed at safety position where he will challenge for the starting job. Business Administration major . . . Baptist . . . single . . . high school coach Glen Varn.

#61 ROBERT ELLINGTON (BOB) MORRIS, 187, 6-0, 19, Sophomore, offensive guard, Virginia Beach, Va. One of top prospects up from 1966 frosh team. Has potential to be a real star . . . small for interior lineman but exceptionally quick and a good blocker. Ended spring practice as starting left guard. Business Administration major . . . Baptist . . . single . . . high school coach Elmer Barbour.

31

282

#36 WARREN H. MUIR, 188, 5-10, 20, Sophomore, fullback, Fitchburg, Mass. Was top back on 1965 Plebe team at U. S. Military Academy, but dropped out of Academy to get married and transferred to Gamecock Roost in September 1966. Number one fullback in spring and expected to be a top star. Civil Engineering major . . . Catholic . . . married with infant daughter . . . high school coach Marco Landon.

#43 JAMES VINCENT (JIM) MULVIHILL, 193, 5-9, 22, Senior, rover back, Atlanta, Ga. Two-year letterman as an offensive fullback who moved to defense in spring drills and did a good job at rover. Rushed for 65 yards and 3.6 average last year and caught one pass for 11 yards. Father played football, basketball, baseball at Catholic U. Physical Education major . . . Catholic . . . single . . . high school coach Fred Keil.

#27 WALTER TERRY (WALLY) ORREL, 185, 5-10, 20, Junior, safety, Savannah, Ga. A starter as a soph and one of top performers in defensive secondary. Made 41 tackles and 31 assists last year, led team in interceptions with three, returning them 61 yards. Knee injury in spring drills clouds his status for '67, but if recovered he'll be number one. Accounting major in College of Business Administration . . . Baptist . . . married . . . high school coach Lamar Leachman.

#30 RONALD OWEN (RONNIE) PALMER, 157, 5-5, 20, Sophomore, right halfback, Morristown, Tenn. A fine little runner who is awfully small. Redshirt in '66 and expected to see some action this fall, possibly as spot player. Business Administration major . . . Presbyterian . . . single . . . high school coach Burleigh Davis.

#63 HYRUM O. PIERCE, JR., 225, 6-2, 22, Senior, offensive tackle, Empire, Ga. A starter at right tackle in 1966 after he was "discovered" following two years on redshirt squad. A steady performer and a team leader who will be one of the Gamecocks' top linemen this fall. Education major . . . Baptist . . . married with small daughter . . . high school coach Bill Screws.

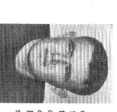

#1 JAMES BERNARD (JIMMY) POOLE, 168, 5-8, 21, Senior, placekicker, Due West, S. C. The Gamecocks' leading scorer the past two seasons as a kicking specialist. Scored 32 points in 1965, 19 last year. His six FGs in '65 is school season record, and 10 for career to date another mark. Father received Ph.D. from South Carolina and now heads history department at Erskine College. Chemical Engineering major . . . Methodist . . . single . . . high school coach Dusty Oates.

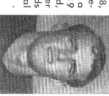

#45 ROY DON REEVES, 178, 5-11, 21, Junior, split end, Americus, Ga. A starting defensive back in 1965 when he participated in 76 tackles. Missed entire '66 season with knee injury. Moved to split end in spring drills and won first team job. Was sensational pass receiver with '64 frosh. Brother Dan was Gamecock quarterback great and last year led NFL in touchdowns as a running back with Dallas Cowboys. Marketing major in College of Business Administration . . . Baptist . . . single . . . high school coach Jimmy Hightower.

#82 GUSTAVUS EUGENE (GENE) SCHWARTING, 196, 6-1, 20, Junior, defensive end, Bamberg, S. C. Starter as a soph and rapidly developing into a fine defensive end. Made 34 tackles and eight assists last year. Should again start at left end. Business Administration major . . . Baptist . . . single . . . high school coach was current Gamecock backfield mentor Dick Weldon.

#66 DONALD THOMAS (DON) SOMMA, 216, 5-11, 21, Senior, defensive tackle, Middlesex, N. J. A starter part of 1966 and a steady, experienced performer. Made 18 tackles and 11 assists last year. Has lettered twice. Pre-season starter at defensive right tackle. Physical Education major . . . Catholic . . . single . . . high school coach Cary Hamrah.

#44 ADOLPHUS FLETCHER (FLETCHER) SPIGNER, 186, 5-11, 19, Sophomore, linebacker, Columbia, S. C. A high school halfback who is a fine athlete. Wound up spring practice as number two weak side linebacker and has a bright collegiate future. Father lettered in football and track at USC. Political Science major . . . Episcopalian . . . single . . . high school coach Charlie Stuart.

#60 GEORGE DEL (BILLY) THARP, 194, 6-2, 19, Sophomore, linebacker, Charleston, S. C. Up from '66 frosh and wound up spring practice as number two strong side linebacker. Father is a highway patrolman. Has good size and potential. Mathematics major . . . Baptist . . . single . . . high school coach Ed Commins.

#4 SCOTT MARK TOWNSEND, 175, 5-9, 21, Senior, punter, Decatur, Ga. Did all the punting in 1965 when he averaged 36.0, but kicked only four times in '66 and did not letter. Back as top punter in spring practice and expected to do the kicking this fall. Two-time baseball letterman as third baseman and outfielder. Marketing major in College of Business Administration . . . member of Christian Church . . . single . . . high school coach Dewey Alverson.

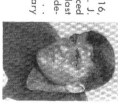

#15 PATRICK EARL (PAT) WATSON, 152, 5-11, 19, Sophomore, defensive halfback, Myrtle Beach, S. C. The smallest Gamecock and one of the squad's best athletes. Regular quarterback on 1966 frosh but moved to defense in spring practice and quickly nailed down the starting right halfback spot despite lack of size. A competitor who is tough and quick. Education major . . . Methodist . . . single . . . high school coach Danny Brabham.

#78 ROBERT PAUL (BOB) WEHMEYER, 225, 6-2, 22, Senior, offensive tackle, Port Murray, N. J. Bounced around as obscure and without earning a letter until moved to offensive tackle last fall. Did a good job there and will challenge for starting left tackle spot this fall. Physical Education major . . . married . . . high school coach C. A. Morrison.

#22 CURTIS EUGENE (COOTER) WILLIAMS, 211, 5-11, 21, Senior, left halfback, Bamberg, S. C. Versatile two-year letterman who has at one time or another played all four offensive backfield spots. Wound up spring drills at left halfback. Knee injuries have reduced his potential but his experience and versatility are extremely valuable. Physical Education major . . . Methodist . . . married with daughter . . . high school coach was current Gamecock backfield mentor Dick Weldon.

#64 THOMAS DAVIS (TOM) WINGARD, 208, 6-1, 20, Junior, offensive guard, Greenwood, S. C. One of the top offensive linemen in the ACC. A fine blocker who was a starter as a sophomore. Supplies ability, leadership and experience at right guard spot. Brother Ted was Gamecock quarterback and will enter medical school this fall. Pharmacy major . . . Lutheran . . . single . . . high school coach Pinky Babb.

#80 FREDERICK (FRED) ZEIGLER, 183, 5-10, 20, Sophomore, split end, Charleston, S. C. A redshirt who impressed coaches in spring practice. Has excellent hands and can catch the football. A leading challenger for the starting job. Attended Carlisle Military Academy and moved to Charleston from Reevesville, S. C. Business Administration major . . . Baptist . . . single . . . high school coach Bob Jenkins.

#86 RONALD THOMAS (RON) ZUKOWSKI, 196, 6-0, 20, Sophomore, defensive end, Trenton, N.J. A former New Jersey high school quarterback great who was a redshirt last year. Moved to defensive secondary in spring drills and then to end when Lyn Hodge broke a leg . . . quickly nailed down starting right end spot. Hard tackler and tough competitor. Business Administration major . . . Catholic . . . single . . . high school coach Walter Porter.

PRONUNCIATION GUIDE

Andy Chavous — CHAY-vuhs

Tony Fusaro — foo-SAR-roh

Ben Garnto — GARN-toh

Jimmy Gobble — GOB-l

Joe Komoroski — kom-Oh-ROS-skee

Bob Mauro — MAW-roh

Warren Muir — MEWR

Jim Mulvihill — MUL-vuh-hill

Wally Orrel — oh-RELL

Don Somma — SOH-muh

Fletcher Spigner — SPY-gner

Bob Wehmeyer — WAY-meyer

Tom Wingard — WING-uhd

Ron Zukowski — zoo-KOW-skee

36

DEPTH CHART

Although some revisions are likely before the Fighting Gamecocks line up for the season opener, a tentative depth chart is listed below, based on the end of spring practice, last season's performance, etc. Lettermen in all caps.

OFFENSE

Split end—
85 *ROY DON REEVES (178)
80 Fred Zeigler (183)
81 Woody Woodside (180)

Left tackle—
74 Bob Mauro (210)
78 BOB WEHMEYER (225)
76 Dennis Frasier (230)

Left guard—
61 Bob Morris (187)
67 Jack J-rnes (198)
72 Frank Tetterton (205)

Center—
50 JIMMY GOBBLE (232)
54 Jim Ross (195)
55 George McCarthy (205)
57 Richard Harrelson (188)

Right guard—
64 TOM WINGARD (208)
68 *JOHNNY GLASS (200)
69 *JOHN DYER (206)

Right tackle—
63 HYRUM PIERCE (225)
65 Tony Fusaro (230)
70 Larry Royal (225)

Tight end—
88 *JOHNNY GREGORY (172)
83 John King (196)

Quarterback—
12 MIKE FAIR (192)
17 Dan Harbison (180)

Left halfback—
20 *BENNY GALLOWAY 192
22 *CURTIS WILLIAMS (211)
24 Rudy Holloman (173)

Right halfback—
21 BEN GARNTO (195)
30 Ronnie Palmer (157)
34 BOB HARRIS (178)
34 Allen Brown (189)

Fullback—
36 Warren Muir (188)
31 *JIMMY KILLEN (195)
46 Don Dunning (196)
32 Earl Hunter (195)

Punter—
4 *SCOTT TOWNSEND (175)

DEFENSE

Left end—
82 GENE SCHWARTING (196)
84 Dave Lucas (184)
87 Don Brant (177)

Left tackle—
77 JOE KOMOROSKI (222)
75 Gordon Gibson (203)
73 Steve Lanford (210)

Strong linebacker—
33 BOB COLE (221)
60 Billy Tharp (194)
59 John Tominack (188)

Middle guard—
52 DAVE GRANT (208)
51 Ron Bunch (199)
62 Clyde Smith (186)

Week linebacker—
47 *TIM BICE (186)
44 Fletcher Spigner (186)
58 Charles Stokes (206)

Right tackle—
66 DON SOMMA (216)
85 John Coleman (209)
79 Ray Edwards (211)

Right end—
86 *Ron Zukowski (196)
25 Allen Owen (174)
26 George Leakes (181)

Left halfback—
21 TOY McCORD (168)
10 Carl Cowart (162)
35 Candler Boyd (174)
49 Pat Caldwell (184)

Right halfback—
15 Pat Watson (152)
29 Andy Chavous (178)

Rover—
48 Don Buckner (180)
43 JIM MULVIHILL (193)

Safety—
27 WALLY ORREL (185)
28 *Wally Medlin (183)
23 Bob White (183)

SPECIALISTS

Placekicker—
1 JIMMY POOLE (168)
2 Martin Becker (155)
14 Richard Genoble (173)

Weights in parentheses are as of the end of 1967 spring practice.

* — Reeves, last lettered in 1965 as a defensive back; Glass last lettered in 1965 as a linebacker; Dyer last lettered in 1966 as a split end; Williams lettered in 1965 and '66 as a fullback; Killen lettered in 1966 as a tailback and a right end, and in 1965 as a fullback; Townsend last lettered in 1966 as a fullback; Bice lettered in 1965 as a defensive back and a middle guard; Mulvihill lettered in 1965

37

285

It isn't often that all eight head football coaches in the Atlantic Coast Conference are together at the same time. Such a rare occurrence happened last May at the annual Atlantic Coast Sportswriters' outing at Linville, N. C., and Hugh Morton, owner of Grandfather Mountain and co-host for the event, had his camera along and snapped the above picture. Standing left to right are Coaches Frank Howard of Clemson, Bill Tate of Wake Forest, Earl Edwards of N. C. State, George Blackburn of Virginia, and Bob Ward of Maryland. Kneeling are Coaches Bill Dooley of North Carolina, Tom Harp of Duke and Paul Dietzel of South Carolina.

1966 SEASON SUPERLATIVES

GAMECOCKS

LONGEST RUN FROM SCRIMMAGE:
Benny Galloway vs. N. C. State, 43 yards (TD).

LONGEST PASS PLAY:
Mike Fair to Benny Galloway vs. Wake Forest, 35 yards.

LONGEST PUNT:
Jeff Jowers vs. N. C. State, 57 yards.

LONGEST KICKOFF RETURN:
Toy McCord vs. Florida State, 50 yards.

LONGEST PUNT RETURN:
Bobby Bryant vs. N. C. State, 98 yards (TD, ACC record).

LONGEST INTERCEPTION RETURN:
Wally Orrel vs. Alabama, 47 yards.

LONGEST FIELD GOAL:
Jimmy Poole vs. N. C. State, 31 yards.

OPPONENTS

LONGEST RUN FROM SCRIMMAGE:
Jacky Jackson, Clemson, 48 yards.

LONGEST PASS PLAY:
Allen Pastrana to Bobby Collins, Maryland, 67 yards (TD).

LONGEST PUNT:
Jim Donnan, N. C. State, Billy van Heusen, Maryland, 60 yards.

LONGEST KICKOFF RETURN:
Jacky Jackson, Clemson, Bill Moreman, Florida State, 28 yards.

LONGEST PUNT RETURN:
Bobby Collins, Maryland, 49 yards.

LONGEST INTERCEPTION RETURN:
Bill Morrow, N. C. State, 32 yards (TD).

LONGEST FIELD GOAL:
Larry Groce, Memphis State, 32 yards.

HAGAN HEADS RICE PROGRAM

A former Gamecock quarterback star is the new head football coach and director of athletics at Rice University. Harold "Bo" Hagan moved up to the dual position last spring at the Southwest Conference school in Houston, Texas upon the retirement of the veteran Jess Neely.

Hagan, a native of Savannah, Ga., was a four-year football letterman under Coach Rex Enright at Carolina. An Army veteran, he came to the University in 1946 and although plagued by knee injuries, he was the Gamecocks' top quarterback for the next four years when healthy.

Perhaps Hagan's finest game was one in which he wasn't scheduled to play, the 1949 Clemson game. A senior, Hagan had been declared out of the Big Thursday classic with two bad knees. However, with Clemson leading 13-0 early in the second period, Bo hobbled off the bench to pull the Gamecocks together.

He passed the Gamecocks to a 13-13 halftime tie, and took complete charge in the second half as South Carolina rolled to a 27-13 victory.

Hagan coached at Georgia Tech and Southern Methodist, and as an assistant for seven years at Rice before moving up to the head job.

Other former Gamecocks in collegiate coaching include Jess Berry at Georgia Tech, Lide Huggins at Texas A. & M., Buddy Bennett at East Tennessee, Gene Alexander at Wofford where he is head basketball coach in addition to being football assistant. In basketball there are Dwane Morrison at Georgia Tech and Bud Cronin at Oklahoma, and in track, Walt Cormack at Virginia Military.

1966 RESULTS AND ATTENDANCE

12	Louisiana State	28	68,547	17	Tennessee	29	44,444
7	Memphis State	16	26,197	14	Maryland	14	35,400
0	Georgia	7	30,141	10	Florida State	32	31,282
31	N. C. State	21	35,200	0	Alabama	24	59,500
6	Wake Forest	10	26,543	10	Clemson	35	47,237

1966 DEFENSIVE STATISTICS

	TACKLES	ASSISTS		TACKLES	ASSISTS
*Cole	79	23	Meadow	25	10
Bryant	54	26	*Somma	18	11
Juk	47	28	*Hodge	17	7
*McCord	46	15	Bailey	10	6
*Bice	44	24	Soles	7	2
*Orrel	41	31	*Glass	5	3
Dickens	36	18	*Bunch	4	3
*Schwarting	34	8	*Medlin	3	0
*Komoroski	30	13	Harman	1	1
*Grant	28	20	*Dyer	0	1

* — Returns for 1967.

SOUTH CAROLINA'S 1967 VARSITY ROSTER

NO.	NAME	Pos.	Hgt.	Wgt.	Age	Class	Home Town	HS Coach
2	Martin Becker	PK	5-7	155	21	Sr.	Orangeburg, S. C.	Jeb Runager
47	*Tim Bice	LB	5-10	186	21	Jr.	Dallas, Tex.	Sam Edenfield
35	Candler Boyd	DB	5-9	174	19	So.	Hinesville, Ga.	Hokey Jackson
87	Don Brant	DE	6-4	177	19	So.	Sycamore, S. C.	Bruce Tate
34	Allen Brown	DB	6-0	189	20	Jr.	Hinesville, Ga.	Hokey Jackson
48	Don Buckner	ROV	6-0	180	19	So.	Cleveland, Tenn.	Harold Henslee
51	Ron Bunch	MG	5-9	199	20	Jr.	Bamberg, S. C.	Dick Weldon
49	Pat Caldwell	DB	6-0	184	19	So.	Anderson, S. C.	Stan Hunnicutt
29	Andy Chavous	DB	6-2	178	19	So.	Hepzibah, Ga.	Jamie Overton
33	*Bob Cole	PK	6-3	221	22	Sr.	Columbia, S. C.	Art Baker
10	John Coleman	DT	6-4	209	20	So.	Columbia, S. C.	Eddie Rice
85	Carl Cowart	DB	5-9	162	20	So.	Florence, S. C.	Clint Madrey
46	Don Dunning	FB	5-10	192	19	So.	Jesup, Ga.	Jim Wall
69	*John Dyer	OG	6-0	206	23	Sr.	Bloomington, Ind.	Walt Gray
79	Roy Edwards	DT	6-0	211	20	Sr.	Chatham, N. J.	Herman Hering
12	*Mike Fair	QB	6-1	192	21	Jr.	Greenville, S. C.	Whitey Kendall
76	Dennis Frasier	OT	6-2	230	19	So.	Walhalla, S. C.	Charlie Johnson
65	Tony Fusaro	OT	6-3	230	19	So.	Huntington, N. Y.	J. Lucey
20	*Benny Galloway	HB	5-9	187	21	Sr.	Easley, S. C.	Bill Carr
11	*Ben Garnto	HB	5-10	195	21	Sr.	Columbus, Ga.	Bob Donaldson
14	Richard Genoble	PK	6-0	173	19	Sr.	Union, S. C.	Bobby Dunlap
75	Gordon Gibson	DT	6-3	203	20	So.	Greenville, S. C.	Steve Satterfield
4	*Johnny Glass	OG	5-11	200	21	So.	Kingsport, Tenn.	Thomas Brixey
50	*Jimmy Gobble	C	5-11	232	22	Sr.	Spartanburg, S. C.	Bob Bell
52	*Dave Grant	MG	5-10	208	20	Jr.	Clarkesville, Ga.	Red Lynch
88	*Johnny Gregory	TE	5-11	172	21	Jr.	Aiken, S. C.	Jim Frasier
17	Dan Harbison	QB	6-0	180	19	So.	Washington, D. C.	Pete Labukas
57	Richard Harrelson	C	6-1	188	20	So.	Barnwell, S. C.	Jim Benson
42	**Bob Harris	HB	5-9	178	21	Sr.	Pt. Pleas. Bch., N. J.	John Kelly
24	Rudy Holloman	HB	6-0	173	20	So.	McBee, S. C.	Billy Seigler
32	Earl Hunter	FB	6-0	195	20	So.	Greenville, S. C.	Whitey Kendall
67	Jack James	OG	5-10	198	20	So.	Atlanta, Ga.	Jack Hogg
31	*Jimmy Killen	FB	6-1	195	21	So.	Georgetown, S. C.	J. C. Hudson
83	John King	TE	6-3	196	19	So.	Lancaster, S. C.	Dalton Rivers
77	*Joe Komoroski	DT	6-2	222	22	So.	Linden, N. J.	Bob Smith
73	Steve Lanford	DT	6-1	210	19	So.	Clinton, S. C.	Claude Howe
26	George Leakes	DE	6-1	181	19	So.	Chappells, S. C.	
84	Dave Lucas	DE	6-5	184	20	So.	Bishopville, S. C.	
55	George McCarthy	C	6-2	205	21	So.	Washington, D. C.	W. C. Smith
21	*Toy McCord	SAF	5-8	168	20	Jr.	Manning, S. C.	Morgan Wooten
74	Bob Mauro	OT	6-2	210	21	Jr.	Madison, N. J.	Gus Allen
28	Wally Medlin	SAF	5-9	183	21	Jr.	Ehrhardt, S. C.	Ted Monica
61	Bob Morris	OG	6-0	187	19	Jr.	Va. Beach, Va.	Glen Varn
36	Warren Muir	FB	5-10	188	20	So.	Fitchburg, Mass.	Elmer Barbour
43	*Jim Mulvihill	ROV	5-9	193	22	Sr.	Atlanta, Ga.	Marco London
27	*Wally Orrel	SAF	5-10	185	20	Sr.	Savannah, Ga.	Fred Keil
25	Allen Owen	DE	6-2	174	19	So.	Columbus, Ga.	Lamar Leachman
30	Ronnie Palmer	HB	5-5	157	20	So.	Morristown, Tenn.	Bill Atkins
63	*Hyrum Pierce	OG	6-0	225	22	Sr.	Empire, Ga.	Burleigh Davis
1	*Jimmy Poole	PK	5-8	168	21	Sr.	Due West, S. C.	Bill Screws
45	*Roy Don Reeves	SE	5-11	178	21	Jr.	Americus, Ga.	J. Hightower

1967 VARSITY ROSTER

NO.	NAME	Pos.	Hgt.	Wgt.	Age	Class	Home Town	HS Coach
54	Jim Ross	C	6-1	195	19	So.	Williamston, S. C.	Donnie Garrison
70	Larry Royal	OT	6-2	225	20	So.	Va. Beach, Va.	Elmer Barbour
82	*Gene Schwarting	DE	6-2	196	20	Jr.	Bamberg, S. C.	Dick Weldon
62	Clyde Smith	MG	5-11	186	19	So.	Church Hill, Tenn.	James Salley
66	*Don Somma	DT	5-11	216	21	Sr.	Middlesex, N. J.	Cary Hamrah
44	Fletcher Spigner	LB	5-11	186	19	So.	Columbia, S. C.	Charlie Stuart
58	Charles Stokes	LB	6-1	206	19	So.	Clover, S. C.	Jerry Frye
72	Frank Tetterton	OT	6-0	205	19	So.	Decatur, Ga.	Dewey Alverson
60	Billy Tharp	LB	6-2	194	19	So.	Charleston, S. C.	Ed Commins
59	John Tominack	LB	5-10	188	20	So.	Triadelphia, W. Va.	Larry Phillips
4	*Scott Townsend	PNTR	5-9	175	21	Sr.	Decatur, Ga.	Dewey Alverson
15	*Pat Watson	DB	5-11	152	19	So.	Myrtle Beach, S. C.	Danny Brabham
78	*Bob Wehmeyer	OT	6-2	225	22	Sr.	Pt. Murray, N. J.	C. A. Morrison
23	Bob White	SAF	5-10	183	20	So.	Sharon, Pa.	
22	*Curtis Williams	HB	5-11	211	21	Sr.	Bamberg, S. C.	Tony Razzano
64	**Tom Wingard	OG	6-1	208	20	Sr.	Greenwood, S. C.	Dick Weldon
81	Woody Woodside	SE	6-1	180	19	Jr.	Charlotte, N. C.	Pinky Babb
80	Fred Zeigler	SE	5-10	183	20	So.	Charleston, S. C.	Gus Purcell
86	Ron Zukowski	DE	6-0	196	20	So.	Trenton, N. J.	Walter Porter

* — Denotes number of letters earned

(SE—Split end; TE—Tight end; OT—Offensive tackle; OG—Offensive guard; C—Offensive center; QB—Quarterback; TB—Tailback; WB—Wingback; FB—Fullback; DE—Defensive end; DT—Defensive tackle; MG—Middle Guard; LB—Linebacker; DB—Defensive back; PK—Placekicker; PNTR—Punter).

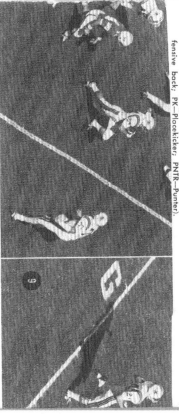

turn ace, set an Atlantic Coast Conference record as well as turning in the d punt back 98 yards in the Gamecocks' 31-21 victory. 1 Bryant fields the field as two members of the Wolfpack close in at the eight; 3 eludes them Cord blocks #68 as Bryant cuts behind Wally Orrel (27) and Bob Cole (33); k (16) arrives to throw block; 7 bursts past #14 into the clear; 8 and heads

REVIEW OF 1966

Based strictly on the 1-9 record, South Carolina's 1966 football season would have to be classified as a disaster.

However, bad as the record was, 1966 was the beginning of an era in the Gamecock Roost; a beginning from which there is no doubt in the minds of everyone close to the organization there will come in the near future not only a strong football machine but an overall athletic program that will rank with the best anywhere. It may be several years away, but it will come!

When Paul Dietzel and his staff moved from the U. S. Military Academy in early April, 1966, spring football practice was more than half completed. Dietzel had nine practices to install his system, familiarize the staff and himself with the personnel, and otherwise organize for the 1966 season.

At the same time, he took over as athletic director of a program that was rocked with turmoil and instability. The job that was done in the year that followed amounted to a minor miracle.

Out of the turmoil has come stability, an ingredient without which no athletic program can ever be successful. True, the Gamecocks did lose two associate coaches, but both moved up to better jobs with more responsibility. Jim Valek became head coach at the University of Illinois and Jimmy Vickers moved from coaching the Gamecock ends to offensive line coach at the University of North Carolina.

Otherwise, the staff remains the same with the shift of Dick Weldon from recruiter to offensive backfield coach replacing Valek, and Don (Scooter) Purvis as coach of the pass receivers replacing Vickers. Lou Holtz, who understudied George Terry last year moved up to defensive secondary coach upon the retirement of Terry from active coaching.

KILLER SCHEDULE

In addition to the above-mentioned problems facing the Gamecocks in Dietzel's inaugural year, there was the matter of the schedule. There's no question that the Gamecocks faced one of the toughest football schedules anywhere in 1966.

There was defending Orange Bowl champion Alabama, the nation's number one team in 1965; defending Cotton Bowl champion Louisiana State University; and defending Bluebonnet Bowl champion Tennessee. In addition there was Georgia, which was destined to tie with Alabama for the Southeastern Conference title and then win the Cotton Bowl game; and strong independent Florida State, which was to earn a Sun Bowl invitation.

There was Memphis State, a traditionally strong independent; Clemson which was enroute to the Atlantic Coast Conference championship; there was also Wake Forest, North Carolina State and Maryland.

HOT NIGHT ON THE BAYOU

It all began on a hot and humid September night in Baton Rouge, where Dietzel had built his coaching reputation and won a national championship, in 1958, in the process. This was the first time that the former L. S. U. coach had returned to Baton Rouge since leaving on Orange Bowl championship team five years earlier to go to Army.

Tiger Stadium was a jam-packed sellout four months before the kickoff. The crowd of 68,547 was the largest to see a college football game in the nation that day. Many L. S. U. fans who refused to forgive Dietzel for leaving after he had built the Bayou Bengals into a power, booed him and the Gamecocks. Many others

44

who remembered that he was the man who gave L. S. U. a winner, cheered him and the Gamecocks as well as their own Bayou Bengals.

A large number of South Carolina fans made the long trip to Baton Rouge. Many others would have if they could have gotten tickets.

The first time the Gamecocks got the football, they began a steady drive that carried to the L. S. U. 27-yard line. It was apparent that the underdog Gamecocks had come to play. Then, frustration—which was to become a steady companion during the next 10 weeks—showed itself.

The Gamecock drive was halted by a fumble and L. S. U. drove to the game's first touchdown. South Carolina came back to score but missed the extra point. Frustration again took over and L. S. U. blocked two punts. Bobby Bryant returned a punt 77 yards to score for South Carolina, but L. S. U. led 21-12 until the last play of the game when the Bengals scored again to make the final tally 28-12.

MANHANDLED

Memphis State come to Columbia for the home opener, and manhandled the Gamecocks. The first of a long series of crippling injuries to the offensive backs occurred when quarterback Mike Fair went down with a hip pointer. The final score was 16-7, but the physical beating the Gamecocks took was much worse.

Georgia brought its finest team in a number of years to Carolina Stadium and the Gamecocks played, defensively, their finest game of the year. Frustration, however, in the form of a fourth-period fumble, gave Georgia the chance it needed and the Bulldogs won 7-0.

Both teams missed field goals when first period drives were halted and when South Carolina stopped Georgia at the Gamecock 36 midway through the fourth period, it looked like a scoreless tie. The Gamecocks fumbled on first down, however, and Georgia drove to score in eight plays.

The Gamecock offense, which had sputtered through three games, found itself the following week as South Carolina dedicated the dedication of North Carolina State's new stadium by whipping the Wolfpack 31-21 for the first Dietzel victory.

BOBBY GOES 98

With the score tied at 7-7, Gamecock All-America Bobby Bryant fielded Jim Donnan's 60-yard punt over his shoulder at the two-yard line and raced 98 yards through the Wolfpack for a touchdown. It was the longest punt return of the year in the nation and an ACC as well as a Gamecock record.

Mike Fair hit Johnny Gregory, who made a sensational catch of a 23 yarder, to make it 21-7, and the Gamecocks went on to win handily. Benny Galloway's 43-yard touchdown run sparked second-half action.

The offense sputtered again as the Gamecocks returned home to lose a 10-6 decision to Wake Forest. Fair passed for 166 yards, including a 34-yard touchdown strike to Ben Garnto, but aside from that score, the Gamecocks couldn't put it all together.

Southeastern Conference power Tennessee was next at Knoxville and the Gamecocks astounded everyone by racing out to an 11-0 lead. Jimmy Poole's 26-yard field goal started it off and Garnto's eight-yard halfback pass to Gregory and Fair's two-point run put the underdogs in command.

Pass interceptions by Bobby Bryant and Bill Dickens kept Tennessee bottled up and Dickens' theft set up the touchdown.

BUGABOO

That old bugaboo, the fumble, cropped up, however, and Tennessee converted

45

it into eight points on Dewey Warren's pass to Richmond Flowers and a two-point conversion to cut South Carolina's lead at halftime to three points.

An interception early in the second half put Tennessee in business and to make matters worse, Fair suffered a knee injury on the play that was to sideline him for a month. Fullback Curtis Williams also went down with a bad knee and the Gamecocks lost the game, 29-17.

With Fair on the shelf, Garnto was shifted to quarterback for the Maryland game, but the Gamecock offense that had moved so well against N. C. State and Tennessee, again misfired continuously. The defense played one of its better games, with Johnny Glass blocking a punt for a safety and South Carolina's only points. There were a couple of pass defense lapses, however, and Maryland won 14-2.

The Gamecocks observed Homecoming against Florida State and with Garnto rushing for 91 yards and Galloway 68, moved the ball well on the ground. Garnto completed four of five passes for 53 yards, but he had one intercepted and the Seminoles picked off four of John Marcotsis' attempts. Florida State also pounded the Gamecock defense for 200 yards rushing and 173 passing and wiped out an early Gamecock lead to win 32-10.

GALLOWAY INJURED

Galloway went down with an injury to make matters worse, and the Gamecocks faced unbeaten Alabama the following week with Garnto the only member of the first-team backfield able to play. The defensive effort was good, but Alabama simply overpowered the Gamecocks to win 24-0. South Carolina's brightest moment came when safety man Wally Orrel intercepted a Crimson Tide pass and returned it 47 yards to the Alabama 18 late in the fourth period.

Fair and Galloway returned to action for the season finale against arch-rival Clemson and it was a real humdinger for nearly three periods when the injury jinx struck again, sending half the Gamecock backfield to the sidelines.

Clemson led 14-10 at halftime but the Gamecocks drove 56 yards with the second-half kickoff to the Tiger 11 before a fumble stopped the drive and also knocked Garnto out of the game with two fractured ribs.

A short time later, Fair was dazed by a blow on the head and the Gamecocks faced the remainder of the day without their quarterback. Clemson scored three times in the final half to win 35-10 and clinch the ACC championship.

Galloway rushed for 105 yards and Garnto for 82 before he was hurt to lead the Gamecock effort.

Thus ended a long and frustrating season that would have to be classified, as far as the won-loss record was concerned, as a disaster. However, there's an old saying that one has to crawl before he can walk, and this is no doubt true also of football programs.

RECORD ATTENDANCE

Attendance-wise, the Gamecocks played before a record 404,491 fans with the 68,547 at L. S. U., 59,500 at Alabama, and 47,235 at Clemson being the three largest crowds. The home opener crowd of 26,197 for Memphis State was the smallest. Financially, the athletic program was in the black—a pleasing statistic for athletic director Dietzel—and all of the Gamecocks' other intercollegiate sports recorded winning seasons, an indication that the overall program is on a solid foundation.

If it was nothing else, the 1966 season was the beginning of an era at the University of South Carolina, and the Gamecocks face the future believing firmly that "The Best is Yet to Come!"

46

"THE FIRST SCORE"

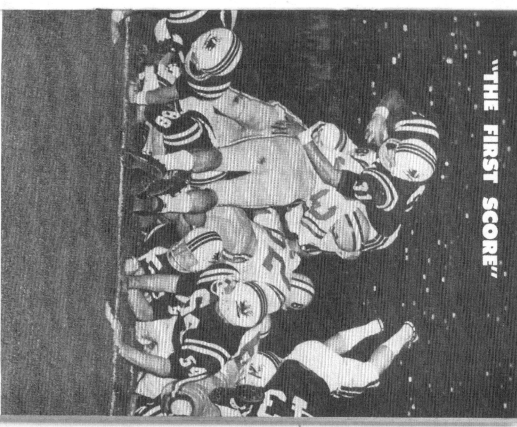

Jimmy Killen (31), who opened the season at tailback and was later shifted to tight end, scored the first touchdown of the Paul Dietzel era at South Carolina when he plunged over in the 1966 season opener at LSU. Killen is scheduled to play at fullback in 1967.

47

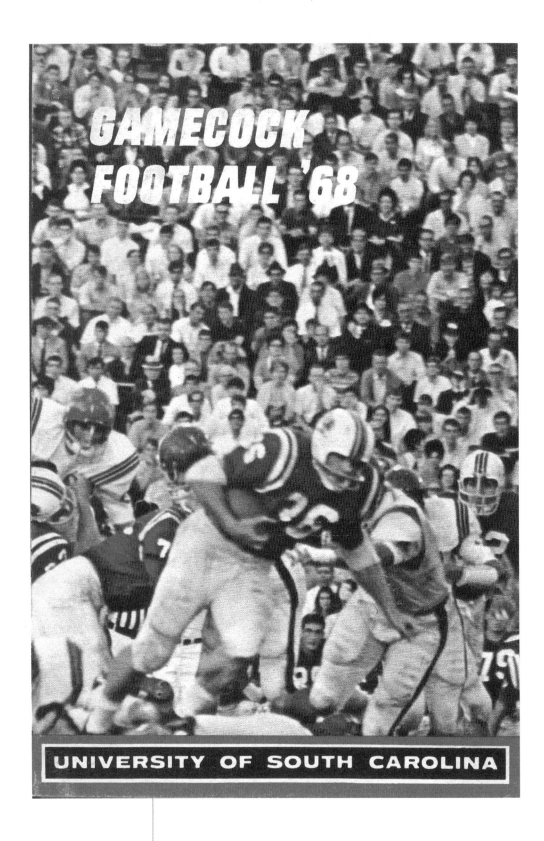

GAMECOCK FOOTBALL '68

UNIVERSITY OF SOUTH CAROLINA

THE LITTLE REDBOOK

Edited by TOM PRICE, Sports Information Director

This brochure of information on the 1968 University of South Carolina football squad is presented as a service to the press, radio and TV with copies also going to members of the Gamecock Club.

Additional information and pictures will be furnished to news media. Working press or scouting tickets to home games should be requested through the Office of Sports Information several days prior to the game date.

MISCELLANEOUS FACTS

Location	Columbia, S. C.
Colors	Garnet & Black
Mascot	Fighting Gamecock
Enrollment (including off campus centers)	15,340
President	Dr. Thomas F. Jones
Faculty Chairman of Athletics	Dr. James A. Morris
Head Football Coach and Athletic Director	Paul F. Dietzel
Football Office	777-4271
Sports Information Office	777-4277
Sports Information Director's Home Phone	787-2395
Ticket Office	777-4274
Gamecock Club	777-4276
Area Code	803
Zip Code	29208

TABLE OF CONTENTS

1968 GAMECOCK SCHEDULE

Sept. 21—DUKE UNIVERSITY AT COLUMBIA—7:30 P.M., EDT—Series record: 6-17-2. Gamecocks won the last game, 21-17, in 1967 at Durham. Tickets $6.00.

Sept. 28—UNIVERSITY OF NORTH CAROLINA AT CHAPEL HILL—1:30 P.M., EDT—Series record: 8-29-4. Gamecocks won the last game, 16-10, in 1967 at Columbia. Tickets $6.00.

Oct. 5—UNIVERSITY OF GEORGIA AT COLUMBIA—7:30 P.M., EDT—Series record: 4-18-2. Georgia won the last game, 21-0, in 1967 at Athens. Tickets $6.00.

Oct. 12—NORTH CAROLINA STATE UNIVERSITY AT RALEIGH—7:30 P.M., EDT—Series record: 15-12-3. Gamecocks won the last game, 31-21, in 1966 at Raleigh. Tickets $6.00.

Oct. 19—UNIVERSITY OF MARYLAND AT COLLEGE PARK—1:30 P.M., EDT—Series record: 9-15-0. Gamecocks won the last game, 31-0, in 1967 at Columbia. Tickets $5.00.

Oct. 26—FLORIDA STATE UNIVERSITY AT COLUMBIA—7:30 P.M., EDT—Series record: 0-2-0. Florida State won the last game, 17-0, in 1967 at Tallahassee. Tickets $6.00. (HOMECOMING, SCOUT DAY.)

Nov. 2—UNIVERSITY OF VIRGINIA AT CHARLOTTESVILLE—1:30 P.M., EST—Series record: 14-9-1. Gamecocks won the last game, 24-23, in 1967 at Columbia. Tickets $5.50.

Nov. 9—WAKE FOREST UNIVERSITY AT WINSTON-SALEM—1:30 P.M., EST—Series record: 19-19-2. Wake Forest won the last game, 35-21, in 1967 at Winston-Salem. Tickets $6.00.

Nov. 16—VIRGINIA POLYTECHNIC INSTITUTE AT COLUMBIA—7:30 P.M., EST—Series record: 4-4-0. Gamecocks won the last game, 14-0, in 1936 at Columbia. Tickets $6.00. (BAND DAY.)

Nov. 23—CLEMSON UNIVERSITY AT CLEMSON—1:30 P.M., EST—Series record: 24-38-3. Clemson won the last game, 23-12, in 1967 at Columbia. Tickets $6.00.

coach of the Gray squad twice in the Blue-Gray classic, head coach of the victorious East team in the Hula Bowl in Hawaii, co-coach of the winning North squad in the 1964 North-South game in Miami, Fla., and on the staff of the victorious East team in the 1966 and 1967 East-West Shrine game in San Francisco, and on the Hula Bowl staff after the 1967 season.

In 1962, Coach Dietzel left LSU to return to West Point as head coach. In four seasons, his teams had a 21-18-1 record. He was named head coach and athletic director at the University of South Carolina in April 1966. His 13-year record as a head coach is 73 wins, 56 losses, and 4 ties.

South Carolina's 43-year-old coach is undoubtedly one of America's most quoted coaches. He is author of the book, "Wing-T and the Chinese Bandits" and co-author more recently of "Go, Shorty, Go." Two of his best known writings are a treatise on "Why Play Football?" and his poem, "Sissy." He is currently writing another book on football.

Coach Dietzel has appeared on many football clinics, including three to our armed forces in Europe. He appeared on bi-weekly television programs while at LSU, and for two years had national weekly radio shows from New York. At South Carolina he has a weekly television program on a statewide network during football season, and a radio program.

Coach Dietzel's great demand as a speaker has taken him throughout the nation. He has served with many civic organizations. He is a former member of the ethics committee of the American Football Coaches Association and at present is the organization's first Vice-President, scheduled for the presidency in 1969, chairman of the National Program Committee and a member of the board of trustees.

Dietzel is an active member and past president of the board of directors of the Fellowship of Christian Athletes. Anne and Paul Dietzel have been happily married for 23 years. They have two children, Steve, 19, and Kathy, 15.

THE DIETZEL YEARS

LOUISIANA STATE UNIVERSITY

Year	Won	Lost	Tied
1955	3	5	2
1956	3	7	0
1957	5	5	0
1958*	11	0	0
1959	9	2	0
1960	5	4	1
1961	10	1	0
TOTALS	46	24	3

*—Won National Championship

U. S. MILITARY ACADEMY

Year	Won	Lost	Tied
1962	6	4	0
1963	7	3	0
1964	4	6	0
1965	4	5	1
TOTALS	21	18	1

UNIVERSITY OF SOUTH CAROLINA

Year	Won	Lost	Tied
1966	1	9	0
1967	5	5	0
TOTALS	6	14	0

ATHLETIC DEPARTMENT SECRETARIES

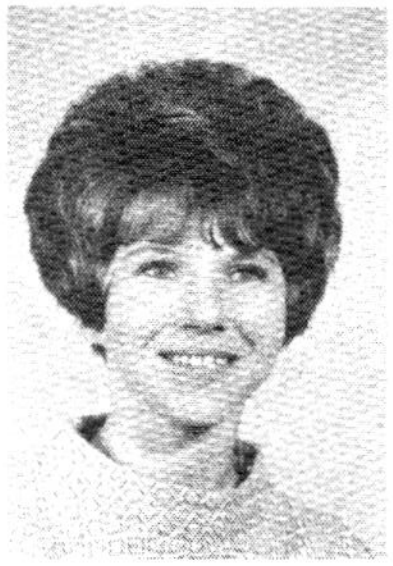

MRS. BETH COOPER
Athletic Director

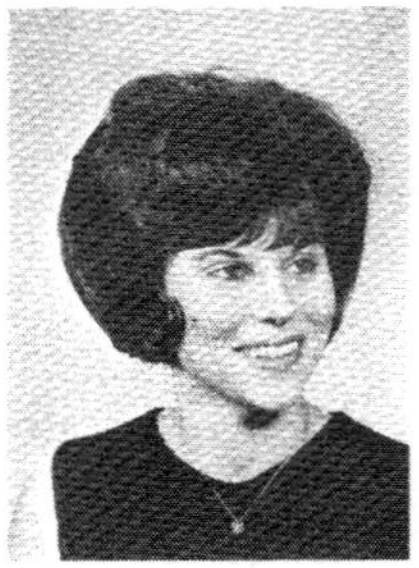

MRS. EMILY WHITE
Football

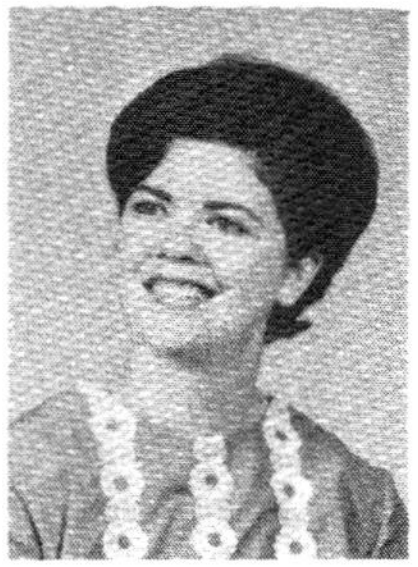

MRS. ANNE AMMA
Gamecock Club

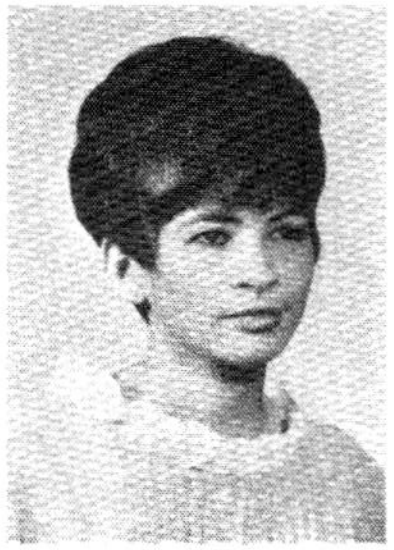

MRS. CHERYL COPE
Business Office

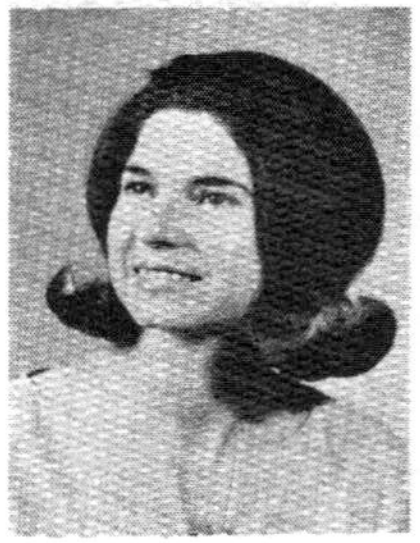

MRS. BARBARA KURTZE
Ticket Office

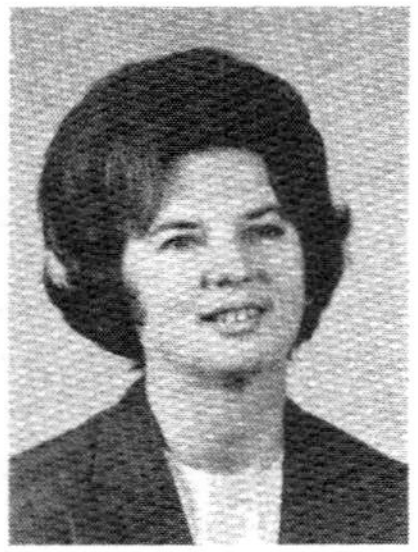

MRS. GINGER RIGDON
Basketball

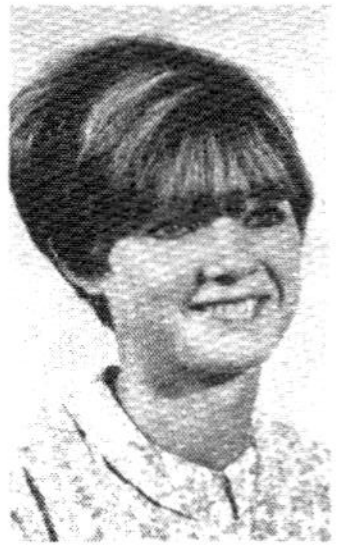

MISS DELORES ANDERSON
Sports Information

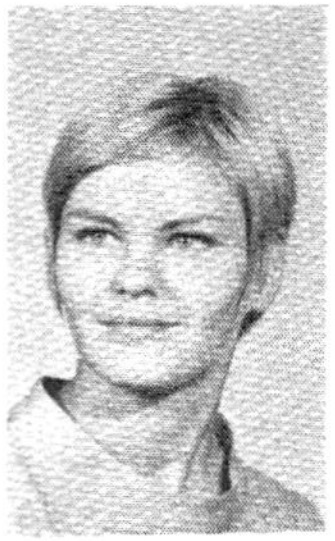

MRS. JON WARD
Ticket Office

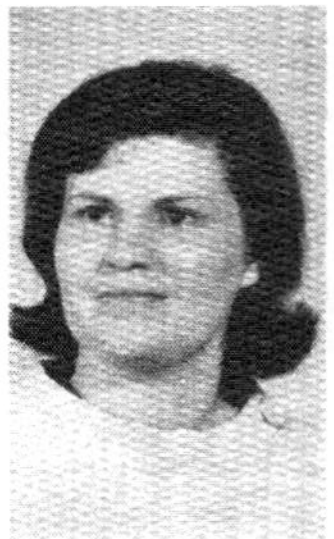

MRS. MARGARET MILLER
Gamecock Club

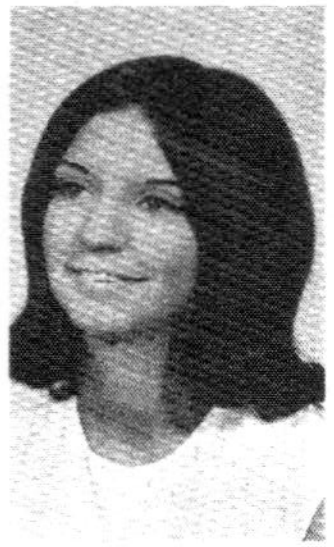

MISS DIANN DENTON
Spring Sports

EVANS BROWN
Graduate Assistant

Evans Brown is in his second season as a graduate assistant coach at the University of South Carolina.

A native of Winnsboro, Brown has lived most of his life in Columbia and Charleston where he graduated from St. Andrews High School. He lettered two years as an end at Mississippi State University and then entered military service. He received the Bachelor of Arts degree in Physical Education from South Carolina in 1967 and then entered graduate school.

While completing requirements for his undergraduate degree, he served as an assistant football coach at Olympia High School in Columbia. Last year, he worked with freshman middle guards and linebackers.

DON SOMMA
Graduate Assistant

Don Somma, All-ACC tackle and captain of last year's Fighting Gamecock squad, joins the staff as a graduate assistant for 1968.

A native of Middlesex, N. J., Somma lettered three seasons with the Gamecocks and was the squad's top tackle last year when he made 62 individual tackles, 26 assists and recovered one fumble.

Somma will work with the freshman defense.

RALPH NIXON FLOYD
Business Manager of Athletics

Ralph Floyd has been a member of the South Carolina Athletic Staff since 1956 and was named business manager of athletics by Paul Dietzel in April 1966. Previously, Floyd served 10 years as an assistant football coach, as well as administrative assistant and chief scout.

Born July 10, 1925 in Washington, D. C., Floyd was graduated in 1949 from the College of William and Mary where he lettered three seasons as a football lineman. He received the Bachelor of Science degree in Physical Education and also attended the U. S. Merchant Marine Academy two years.

Floyd coached one season in high school; one season at Richmond; and two at North Carolina, before coming to South Carolina.

He married the former Susan Sara Trimble of Arlington, Va., and they have two children, Candice, born July 31, 1953, and Nicky, Dec. 31, 1959.

WALTER (CHIEF) MACKOWSKI
Equipment Manager

Chief Mackowski, a retired chief boatswain's mate with 20 years of Naval service, has been South Carolina's equipment manager since February 1956.

Born Aug. 31, 1915 in Syracuse, N. Y., Mackowski married the former Beth Moody of Marshall, Mo., Feb. 8, 1944 and they have a daughter, Donna Mary, 20.

WELDON B. (SARGE) FRYE
Supervisor of Facilities

Sarge Frye, a retired master sergeant with 23 years of Army service, has been supervisor of athletic fields and other facilities since October 1954. His duties in 1964 were expanded to place him in charge of maintaining all campus grounds.

Born May 7, 1913 at Medon, Tenn., Frye married the former Ruby Howard of Anniston, Ala., March 4, 1936, and they have two children, Jerry, 29, and Nancy, 26. Jerry was a star end and co-captain of the Gamecocks and now coaches at Dillon, S. C., High School.

THE 1968 GAMECOCKS

The 1968 Fighting Gamecocks will be a little deeper and the personnel will in general be a little more robust than the skinny, depth-shy 1967 contingent that surprised everyone with a 5-5 record.

To improve on last year's record, however, Coach Paul Dietzel's men will have to duplicate the hustle, desire and drive of 1967, avoid crippling injuries, and have a lot of luck.

"We have more athletes than we did a year ago and we should be a little better," is the way Dietzel summed it up. "We do have some trouble spots that weren't completely solved during spring practice and we appear strong in other areas."

TROUBLE SPOT

The biggest trouble spot appears to be the offensive interior line, where injuries and graduation have thrown a cloud over every position except right tackle, where junior Tony Fusaro returns. Center Jimmy Gobble, a three-year starter, graduated and guard Tom Wingard was forced to give up football due to a head injury. Guard Bob Morris suffered a severe arm fracture in last year's Alabama game and was held out of rough work in the spring. Bob Mauro, starting left tackle last year, fractured a kneecap playing baseball and missed spring practice.

Mauro, a center in high school and as a freshman, is expected to be fully recovered by September and will be moved to the pivot. Steve Vasgaard, up from the frosh and converted from tight end, and Ken Ross — a non-letterman junior — are the other leading center candidates.

Dave DeCamilla, a transfer from Army, is Mauro's likely replacement at left tackle. It's hoped Morris will be fully recovered from his broken arm to take over one guard position and Mack Lee Tharpe — a former fullback who was out of school last year — showed promise during spring drills. Versatile Don Buckner, a junior letterman who has played defensive end, linebacker, rover, fullback and offensive halfback, is a good bet to be a regular at one guard position. He's a hustler who does a good job wherever he's placed. Sophomore Chris Bank, another converted fullback, is another candidate.

So much for the interior line problems. The other big problem facing the Gamecocks in spring practice — quarterback — appears to have worked itself out.

QUARTERBACKS INEXPERIENCED

Mike Fair, second leading ground gainer in Gamecock history, is gone after three years as a starter and the quarterbacks will be inexperienced. However, rising sophomores Tommy Suggs and Randy Yoakum both demonstrated potential during the spring and one of them should wind up with the job. Junior non-letterman Dan Harbison saw some action last year and is in contention.

Getting to the Gamecock strength, there's no better inside runner in collegiate football than junior fullback Warren Muir. He rushed for 805 yards last year — more than any previous sophomore in Atlantic Coast Conference history—and ranks near the top among the great backs in the country.

BEST IN THE LAND

"Warren Muir is the best inside runner in the United States," is the way Coach Dietzel puts it. "He has quickness, strength, balance and football sense; all of the ingredients necessary in an All-America runner. He's the best there is at his position."

Benny Galloway — the oft-injured former high school All-America from Easley — is well again after missing the entire 1967 season with a knee injury. Galloway rushed for 580 yards in 1966 after being named to the All-ACC defensive team as a sophomore. If a season on the sidelines hasn't reduced his effectiveness, he should team with Muir to give the Gamecocks a two-pronged running game equal to any.

A multiple offense team, the Gamecocks will line up in a pro-set with two running backs, flanker and split end much of the time. When in this formation, Muir will be the tailback and Galloway the "Power Back." Rising sophomores Ken Walkup and Tom Trevillian are in line for a lot of action at the running back spots also, especially Walkup, a junior version of Muir, who was the leading rusher on last year's unbeaten frosh team.

RECEIVERS RETURN

All of last year's receivers return, plus a couple of good ones up from the frosh, and — if the young quarterbacks can get them the ball — the passing game should be good.

Fred Zeigler, ACC receiving champion in 1967 with 35 catches, will be at the flanker back position. Johnny Gregory, a 168-pound tight end last year, moves back to split end, a position more suitable to his physique. Gene Schwarting, a two-year defensive end starter, moved to tight end in spring practice and performed well. Junior Rudy Holloman, a letterman, and sophomores Bill Duffie and Eddie Bolton showed promise at the flanker and split end posts, and Doug Hamrick, up from the frosh, will battle Schwarting at tight end.

DEFENSE EXPERIENCED

The defense appears in better shape, experience-wise, than the offense with only the two tackles and one linebacker missing from among last year's starters. Sophomore replacements at these positions have excellent credentials.

All-ACC Don Somma and Joe Komoroski — two excellent performers — are gone at tackle, but sophs Rusty Ganas and Jimmy Poston have outstanding potential and non-letterman junior John Coleman — a converted end — did a fine job in the spring. All three have excellent size with Ganas 6-5, 233; Poston 6-4, 242, and Coleman 6-4, 214.

The defensive ends should be among the Gamecocks' strongest and the depth there made it possible to shift Schwarting to offense. Dave Lucas, the 6-5, 189-pound "Twiggy" who built a reputation as one of the ACC's top pass rushers last year as a soph, will again be among the best in the league. Lynn Hodge, a sophomore starter in 1966 who missed the 1967 season with a broken leg, had an excellent spring and appeared fully recovered. These two veterans will get strong competition from sophomores Joe Wingard and Jimmy Pope, both tall, rangy and with fine potential.

BICE IS BEST

The top individual returnee on the defensive unit is All-ACC Tim Bice, the weakside linebacker last year who moved to middle guard during spring practice. Up to 194 pounds now, this pug-nosed scrapper is one of the top little men — as linemen and linebackers go — in the business. Bice led the Gamecocks in tackles last year with 150 (90 individual and 60 assists), and will again be a candidate for All-ACC honors.

Bob Cole graduated from the strong linebacker spot, but Dave (Mud Cat) Grant, a two-year letterman who has played both linebackers and was last year's middle guard starter, should take over in good style. Al Usher, up from the freshman team with all the credentials of a future star, is counted on at weak linebacker and senior Ron Bunch has good experience at either linebacker or middle guard.

SECONDARY DEEPEST

The defensive secondary shapes up as the Gamecocks' deepest and most experienced department with six lettermen — plus two bright sophomores — vying for the four positions.

Wally Orrel, one of the best safetymen anywhere when in good physical condition, hopes to come back from two knee operations to reclaim the stardom that was his. He'll get a challenge from Tyler Hellams, top defensive back on last year's freshman team with seven interceptions. Candler Boyd, a letterman who played several secondary spots last fall, is also in the picture if he recovers in time from a springtime knee operation. Roy Don Reeves, a two-time letterman who has excelled defen-

sively as well as offensively, is ticketed for the rover position with letterman Wally Medlin — who missed spring practice to pitch for the baseball team — and sophomore Don Montgomery challenging.

Toy McCord, All-ACC shortstop in baseball and a two-year defensive halfback starter, has given up his final season of eligibility to sign a professional baseball contract.

Don Bailey, who approaches Hellams in potential, is up from the frosh and certain to play a lot, as is junior Andy Chavous, who earned a letter as a reserve split end and halfback last fall but switched to defense in the spring.

Junior Pat Watson, a cocky little 157-pounder who started all 10 games last year and led the Gamecocks in time played, is a fixture at right halfback. Watson returned as a punt 67 yards for a touchdown to ignite a comeback against Virginia from a 17-0 halftime deficit to a 24-23 victory.

The kicking game lost Jimmy Poole, regular placekicker for three years, and Scott Townsend, the ACC's leading punter in 1967, but should be at least adequate, perhaps outstanding with sophomores doing the honors. Bill Parker, also a linebacking candidate, is an excellent punter and a two-way battle is brewing between little (5-5, 150) Billy DuPre and Richard Genoble for placekicking duties.

DuPre, a soccer-style kicker, once booted a 51-yard field goal in high school and made good his only try, from 41 yards, in the spring intra-squad game. Genoble, a redshirt sophomore, made two of three field goals in the spring game — from 37 and 44 yards — and the one he missed from 58 yards wasn't short by very much. He's a left-footed kicker and also a reserve quarterback.

Summing up, the Gamecocks have 21 lettermen — 10 on offense and 11 on defense — to form the nucleus of the 1968 squad. Of these, 19 played last year with Galloway and Hodge last year lettering in 1966. About as many from last year's unbeaten freshman squad are expected to make this year's travel team, and several redshirts and non-lettermen veterans are also in the picture.

LETTERMEN LOST

Lettermen lost due to graduation included quarterback Mike Fair, center Jimmy Gobble, halfback Ben Garnto, linebacker Bob Cole, defensive tackles Don Somma and Joe Komoroski, fullback Curtis Williams, offensive tackle Hyrum Pierce, defensive back Jim Mulvihill, placekicker Jimmy Poole and punter Scott Townsend. In addition, offensive guards Tom Wingard and Jack James won't be back. The former was forced to give up football due to a recurring head injury, and the latter dropped off the squad.

Fair holds school records for passes attempted in one season, 175; passes completed, 89; and yards passing, 1,049, all set during among last year's starters. Sophomore replacements at these positions have excellent credentials.

All-ACC Don Somma and Joe Komoroski — two excellent performers — are gone at tackle, but sophs Rusty Ganas and Jimmy Poston have outstanding potential and non-letterman junior John Coleman — a converted end — did a fine job in the spring. All three have excellent size with Ganas 6-5, 233; Poston 6-4, 242, and Coleman 6-4, 214.

The defensive ends should be among the Gamecocks' strongest and the depth there made it possible to shift Schwarting to offense. Dave Lucas, the 6-5, 189-pound "Twiggy" who built a reputation as one of the ACC's top pass rushers last year as a soph, will again be among the best in the league. Lynn Hodge, a sophomore starter in 1966 who missed the 1967 season with a broken leg, had an excellent spring and appeared fully recovered. These two veterans will get strong competition from sophomores Joe Wingard and Jimmy Pope, both tall, rangy and with fine potential.

BICE IS BEST

The top individual returnee on the defensive unit is All-ACC Tim Bice, the weakside linebacker last year who moved to middle guard during spring practice. Up to 194 pounds now, this pug-nosed scrapper is one of the top little men — as linemen and linebackers go — in the business. Bice led the Gamecocks in tackles last year with 150 (90 individual and 60 assists), and will again be a candidate for All-ACC honors.

Bob Cole graduated from the strong linebacker spot, but Dave (Mud Cat) Grant, a two-year letterman who has played both linebackers and was last year's middle guard starter, should take over in good style. Al Usher, up from the freshman team with all the credentials of a future star, is counted on at weak linebacker and senior Ron Bunch has good experience at either linebacker or middle guard.

SECONDARY DEEPEST

The defensive secondary shapes up as the Gamecocks' deepest and most experienced department with six lettermen — plus two bright sophomores — vying for the four positions.

Wally Orrel, one of the best safetymen anywhere when in good physical condition, hopes to come back from two knee operations to reclaim the stardom that was his. He'll get a challenge from Tyler Hellams, top defensive back on last year's freshman team with seven interceptions. Candler Boyd, a letterman who played several secondary spots last fall, is also in the picture if he recovers in time from a springtime knee operation. Roy Don Reeves, a two-time letterman who has excelled defen-

sively as well as offensively, is ticketed for the rover position with letterman Wally Medlin — who missed spring practice to pitch for the baseball team — and sophomore Don Montgomery challenging.

Toy McCord, All-ACC shortstop in baseball and a two-year defensive halfback starter, has given up his final season of eligibility to sign a professional baseball contract.

Don Bailey, who approaches Hellams in potential, is up from the frosh and certain to play a lot, as is junior Andy Chavous, who earned a letter as a reserve split end and halfback last fall but switched to defense in the spring.

Junior Pat Watson, a cocky little 157-pounder who started all 10 games last year and led the Gamecocks in time played, is a fixture at right halfback. Watson returned a punt 67 yards for a touchdown to ignite a comeback against Virginia from a 17-0 halftime deficit to a 24-23 victory.

The kicking game lost Jimmy Poole, regular placekicker for three years, and Scott Townsend, the ACC's leading punter in 1967, but should be at least adequate, perhaps outstanding with sophomores doing the honors. Bill Parker, also a linebacking candidate, is an excellent punter and a two-way battle is brewing between little (5-5, 150) Billy DuPre and Richard Genoble for placekicking duties.

DuPre, a soccer-style kicker, once booted a 51-yard field goal in high school and made good his only try, from 41 yards, in the spring intra-squad game. Genoble, a redshirt sophomore, made two of three field goals in the spring game — from 37 and 44 yards — and the one he missed from 58 yards wasn't short by very much. He's a left-footed kicker and also a reserve quarterback.

Summing up, the Gamecocks have 21 lettermen — 10 on offense and 11 on defense — to form the nucleus of the 1968 squad. Of these, 19 played last year with Galloway and Hodge last lettering in 1966. About as many from last year's unbeaten freshman squad are expected to make this year's travel team, and several redshirts and non-lettermen veterans are also in the picture.

LETTERMEN LOST

Lettermen lost due to graduation included quarterback Mike Fair, center Jimmy Gobble, halfback Ben Garnto, linebacker Bob Cole, defensive tackles Don Somma and Joe Komoroski, fullback Curtis Williams, offensive tackle Hyrum Pierce, defensive back Jim Mulvihill, placekicker Jimmy Poole and punter Scott Townsend. In addition, offensive guards Tom Wingard and Jack James won't be back. The former was forced to give up football due to a recurring head injury, and the latter dropped off the squad.

Fair holds school records for passes attempted in one season, 175; passes completed, 89; and yards passing, 1,049, all set during his sophomore year. In career statistics, he ranks second to Dan Reeves in four categories: total offense, 3,012 yards; passes attempted 422; completed, 199; and yards passing, 2,482. He was named most valuable player on the 1967 squad and signed with the San Diego Chargers of the professional American Football League.

Somma was first team All-ACC last year and he, Komoroski, Cole, Gobble and Garnto were starters for the Gamecocks during most of their three years of eligibility.

Garnto was selected to play in two post-season games after his senior season, the East-West Shrine game in San Francisco in which he threw a pass for the winning touchdown; and the Hula Bowl game in Honolulu. Gobble also played in the East-West game.

Garnto ranks seventh among all-time Gamecock rushers with 1,151 yards, and fifth in pass receiving with 43 for 467 yards. He holds the Atlantic Coast Conference record for a non-scoring run from scrimmage, 89 yards against Wake Forest in 1965.

These standouts will be missed, but the Gamecocks should have the personnel to be slightly stronger overall than last year and — if the 1968 freshmen measure up to expectations — should be even stronger next year because this year's varsity will be a young team with only 12 seniors.

The Gamecocks will continue as a multiple offense team, probably using more of a pro-set with flanker than in the past, and defensively will again use the 5-4 as the basic alignment.

PRONUNCIATION GUIDE

Andy Chavous—CHAY-vuhs
Dave DeCamilla—de-KUH-MIHL-uh
Steve DiCarlo—de-KARR-loh
Danny Dyches—Dikes
Tony Fusaro—foo-SAR-roh
Rusty Ganas—GAY-nus

Richard Genoble—jeh-NOH-bl
Bob Mauro—MAW-roh
Bob Miranda—muh-RAN-dah
Warren Muir—MEWR
Wally Orrel—oh-RELL
Joe Regalis—reh-GAY-liss
Byron Sistare—sis-STAR

24

MEET THE GAMECOCKS

ALL-ACC RETURNEES

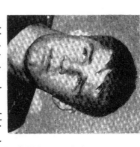

#36 WARREN HOLMES MUIR, 199, 5-10, Junior, one letter, fullback, Fitchburg, Mass. Born 8/16/47, Fitchburg. All-ACC and Detroit Sports Extra All-America in 1967. Prime All-America candidate in '68. Rushed 805 yards, most ever for an ACC sophomore. Set school record with 188 carries for season. Tied one game record with 35 carries against North Carolina. Scored six TDs. Caught four passes for 48 yds. Had 164 yds. rushing against North Carolina. Hip and ankle injuries slowed him in three games or he would probably have topped 1,000 yards. Played 215 minutes. Originally enrolled at U. S. Military Academy, but withdrew to marry his high school sweetheart. Enrolled at Carolina in fall of 1966 as transfer student and became eligible for competition in '67. Called the "best inside runner in collegiate football" by Coach Paul Dietzel who compares him favorably with Jim Taylor whom Coach Dietzel developed at LSU. Stocky, with tremendously powerful legs and exceptional balance, he excels at the tough inside job of running over tacklers, but has enough speed and quickness to go outside. Longest run last year was 42 yards against Duke. Above average blocker. Also lettered in track as shot putter. Attended Fitchburg High where his coach was Marco Landon. Civil Engineering major. Catholic. Married with small son.

#47 TIMOTHY JAMES (TIM) BICE, 194, 5-11, Senior, two letters, middle guard, Atlanta, Ga. Born 10/26/46, Dallas, Tex. All-ACC linebacker in 1967 when he led Gamecocks in tackle participation with 150, including 90 individual tackles and 60 assists. Played 283 minutes. Returns to middle guard for '68 after playing weakside linebacker last year. Quick, tough and aggressive and called "perhaps our finest football player" by coach Paul Dietzel. Opened varsity career in 1966 as 176-pound safetyman but switched to middle guard after six games and did great job despite size. Made 17 individual tackles and six assists against Alabama. Additional weight should help him this fall. Exceptionally quick and likes the rough and tumble of defensive play. Father is Air Force career man. Attended Cross Keys High in Atlanta where he was coached by Sam Edenfield. Accounting major. Baptist and one of leaders in Carolina chapter of Fellowship of Christian Athletes. Single.

#22 DONALD ALSTON (DON) BAILEY, 171, 5-11, Sophomore, defensive back, John's Island, S. C. Born 9/12/48, Charleston, S. C. One of top prospects from 1967 frosh. Intercepted three passes, returned two punts 91 yds., one for TD, and recovered one fumble. Played split end and halfback in high school. Attended St. John's High, where his coach was Robert Biggerstaff. Physical Education major. Methodist. Single.

#66, CHRIS BANK, 220, 6-1, Sophomore, offensive guard, Joliet, Ill. Born 5/23/49, Aurora, Ill. Fullback on 1967 frosh when he rushed 108 yds. in 30 carries for 3.6 avg. and two TDs. Moved to guard in spring and expected to break into first two teams. Attended Joliet Catholic High where his coach was Gordon Gillespie. Physical Education Major. Catholic. Single.

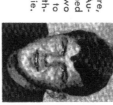

#JAMES EDWARD (EDDIE) BOLTON, 210, 6-4, Sophomore, split end, Greenwood, S. C. Born 2/28/49, Rock Hill, S. C. Caught one pass for 51 yds. and TD in first frosh game, then missed remainder of season with broken collarbone. Showed fine moves and hands in spring game when he caught four passes for 49 yards. Had fine high school and American Legion baseball career as pitcher and performed with frosh last spring. Attended Greenwood High where his coach was Pinky Babb. Physical Education major. Baptist. Single.

#35 HOGAN CANDLER (CANDLER) BOYD, JR., 175, 5-9, Junior, one letter, defensive back, Hinesville, Ga. Born 1/10/48, Brunswick, Ga. Nickname: "Squeaky." Had good soph year, playing several spots in defensive secondary. Had 29 individual tackles, 14 assists and recovered one fumble, played 121 minutes. Knee operation in spring costs some doubt on his condition for '68 season. Brother Bill played at Univ. of Tampa. Attended Broadwell Institute in Hinesville where his coach was Hokey Jackson. Business Administration major. Methodist. Single.

27

298

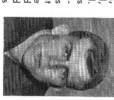

#62 DONALD EDWARD (DON) BUCKNER, 184, 6-0, Junior, one letter, offensive guard, Cleveland, Tenn. Born 12/1/47, Cleveland. Most versatile athlete on Gamecock squad, has played linebacker, rover, defensive end, offensive fullback and halfback, and defensive guard this fall. Played 118 minutes last year. A 100 per center plus no matter where he's playing. Defensive stats last year showed seven individual tackles, nine assists. Attended Bradley Central High in Cleveland where his coach was Harold Henslee. Management major. Baptist. Single.

#51 RONALD WAYNE (RON) BUNCH, 202, 5-9, Senior, one letter, linebacker, Bamberg, S. C. Born 5/25/47, Bamberg. Swing man last year at both linebacker and middle guard spots, logging 121 minutes of playing time. Made 47 individual tackles, 16 assists. Probably used at both linebackers this fall. Played some as soph but didn't letter. Attended Bamberg High where his coach was current Gamecock backfield mentor Dick Weldon. Business Administration major. Baptist. Single.

#29 ANDREW JULIAN (ANDY) CHAVOUS, 180, 6-2, Junior, one letter, defensive back, Hepzibah, Ga. Born 10/13/48, Augusta, Ga. Played split end, halfback, defensive back last year, logging 83 minutes. Caught two passes for 24 yds. Had good spring practice and intercepted two passes in spring game. Attended Butler High in Augusta where his coach was Jamie Overton. Pharmacy major. Methodist. Married.

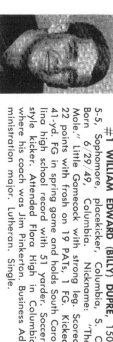

#79 JOHN DOZIER COLEMAN, 214, 6-4, Junior, defensive tackle, Latta, S. C. Born 1/7/47, Dillon, S. C. Redshirt end in '66 and saw few seconds playing time last fall but didn't letter. Moved to tackle and was one of pleasant surprises of spring practice with excellent performance and hustle. Attended Latta High where his coach was Eddie Rice. Banking major. Methodist. Single.

#76 DAVID DANIEL (DAVE) DECAMILLA, 217, 6-2, Sophomore, offensive tackle, Hudson Falls, N. Y. Born 3/18/48, Glens Falls, N. Y. Transfer from U. S. Military Academy and redshirt last year while establishing eligibility. Played well in spring practice and starter on pre-season depth chart. Attended Hudson Falls Central High where his coach was Robert Ryan. Economics major. Catholic. Single.

#81 WILLIAM EDWARD (BILL) DUFFIE, 175, 6-3, Sophomore, flanker, Atlanta, Ga. Born 11/15/48, Atlanta. Leading receiver with 1967 frosh with 18 catches for 248 yards and two TDs. Caught three for 24 yds. in spring game and has bright future. Attended North Springs High in Atlanta where his coach was Leonard Jones. Management major. Christian. Single.

#1 WILLIAM EDWARD (BILLY) DUPRE, 150, 5-5, Sophomore, placekicker, Columbia, S. C. Born 6/29/49, Columbia. Nickname: "The Mole." Little Gamecock with strong leg. Scored 22 points with frosh on 19 PATs, 1 FG. Kicked 41-yd. FG in spring game and holds South Carolina high school record with 51 yarder. Soccer-style kicker. Attended Flora High in Columbia where his coach was Jim Pinkerton. Business Administration major. Lutheran. Single.

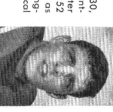

#73 ANTHONY JOHN (TONY) FUSARO, 230, 6-2, Junior, one letter, offensive tackle, Huntington, N. Y. Born 1/23/47, Huntington. Starter second half of season as soph and played 152 minutes. Steady performer and counted on as starting right tackle this fall. Attended Huntington High where his coach was Joe Lucey. Physical Education major. Catholic. Single.

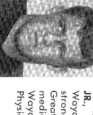

#20 DAVID BENNETT (BENNY) GALLOWAY, 187, 5-9, Senior, two letters, halfback, Easley, S. C. Born 12/28/45, Greenville, S. C. Hard luck star who has had brilliant career clouded by injuries. All-ACC defensive back in '66, led Gamecocks in rushing in '66, missed entire '67 season with knee injury. Sound again and should reclaim stardom this fall. Led ACC in kickoff returns in '65. Career totals 714 yards rushing, 3 TDs, 17 passes caught, 696 yds, KO returns, 79 tackles when playing defense. Attended Easley High where his coach was Bill Carr. Marketing major. Methodist. Single.

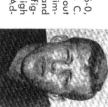

#71 RUSSELL LINDBERG (RUSTY) GANAS, JR., 233, 6-5, Sophomore, defensive tackle, Waycross, Ga. Born 8/12/49, Waycross, Ga. Big, strong, quick, agile prospect from '67 frosh. Great potential and expected to become an intermediate starter. Attended Ware County High at Waycross where his coach was David Shields. Physical Education major. Methodist. Single.

#14 RICHARD ALLEN GENOBLE, 180, 6-0, Sophomore, quarterback-placekicker, Union, S. C. Born 7/1/48, Union. Played with '66 frosh, out of school last fall, returned in spring and impressed as left-footed placekicker. Booted 37 and 42 yd. FGs in spring game and definitely figures in plans as kicker. Attended Union High where his coach was Bob Dunlap. Business Administration major. Baptist. Single.

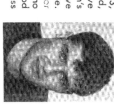

#52 CY DAVID (DAVE) GRANT, 210, 5-10, Senior, two letters, linebacker, Clarkesville, Ga. Born 6/30/47, Atlanta, Ga. Nickname: "Mud Cat." Starting middle guard in '67 when he played 277 minutes, second in tackles with 77 individuals, 38 assists, recovered two fumbles. Moved to strong linebacker in spring and expected to again be starter. Attended North Habersham High in Clarkesville where his coach was Red Lynch. Business Administration major. Baptist. Single.

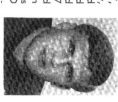

#88 JOHN DEMETRIUS (JOHNNY) GREGORY, 168, 5-11, Senior, split end, two letters, Aiken, S. C. Born 6/14/46, Aiken. Returns to split end after season as the nation's smallest tight end. Two-year regular, played 231 minutes last year, catching 13 passes for 226 yds. In '66, caught 17 for 299 yds. and two TDs. Brother Art was All-America tackle at Duke and now attends USC law school. Attended Aiken High where his coach was Jim Fraser. History major. Greek Orthodox. Single.

#87 LARRY DOUGLAS (DOUG) HAMRICK, 204, 6-2, Sophomore, tight end, Cliffside, N. C. Born 3/11/49, Alexander Mills, N. C. Caught 11 passes for 161 yards with '67 frosh and in spring game caught three for 18 yds. and one TD. Fine prospect who should play a lot as soph. Attended Chase High at Forest City, N. C., where his coach was Bobby Bush. Mechanical Engineering major. Single.

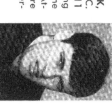

#17 DANIEL KENNETH (DAN) HARBISON, 185, 5-10, Junior, quarterback, Washington, D. C. Born 11/26/46, Washington. Backup quarterback in '67 when he played 36 minutes but did not letter. Completed two of six passes for 27 yds., scored 1 TD. The only '68 QB with any varsity experience. Came to Carolina without scholarship. Attended Woodrow Wilson High in Washington where his coach was Pete Labukas. Marketing major. Catholic. Single.

#11 JOHN TYLER (TYLER) HEILAMS, 163, 5-11, Sophomore, defensive back, Greenwood, S. C. Born 12/7/48, Laurens, S. C. Top defensive secondary prospect from '67 frosh and dean's list student. Intercepted seven passes in five frosh games, led Biddies in punt return yardage. Earned varsity letter in track as frosh hurdler and long jumper. A tremendous athlete who should become a top star. Attended Greenwood High where his coach was Picky Babb. Business Administration major. Presbyterian. Single.

#89 LYNN WARREN HODGE, 202, 6-3,

Junior, one letter, defensive end, Union, S. C. Born 10/1/47, Union. Returns to squad after missing '67 season with broken leg. Had fine spring practice. Started all 10 games as soph in '66 and should take up where he left off. Older brother Wilbur played guard for Gamecocks. Attended Union High where his coach was Bob Dunlap. Management major. Methodist. Single.

#77 RICHARD ALAN (RICK) HIPKINS, 239,

6-4, Sophomore, offensive tackle, Boothwyn, Pa. Born 8/29/46, Chester, Pa. Up from '67 frosh and showed up well in spring practice. Should crack top two units as soph. Attended Chichester High in Boothwyn where his coach was Tony Appichella. Management major. Protestant. Single.

#24 RUDY PEARSON HOLLOMAN, 172, 5-9,

Junior, one letter, flanker, Hartsville, S. C. Born 8/1/47, Hartsville. Played 149 minutes as soph, catching nine passes for 119 yards and rushing 78 yards in 28 carries for 2.8 average. Caught three passes for 55 yards and one TD in spring game. A fine little athlete. Attended Hartsville High where his coach was Billy Seigler. Business Administration major. Baptist. Single.

#84 DAVID HENRY (DAVE) LUCAS, 189, 6-5,

Junior, one letter, defensive end, Bishopville, S. C. Born 5/25/47, Greensboro, N. C. Tall, skinny star whose physique earned him nicknames: "Twiggy," "The Pencil," "The Blade," etc. Led '67 squad in fumble recoveries with four, including one for TD. Participated in 61 tackles, 44 individuals and 17 assists, played 231 minutes. Excells at pass rush and should be one of ACC's top stars this fall. Attended Bishopville High where his coach was W. C. Smith. Arts and Science major. Methodist. Single.

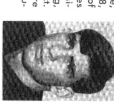

#64 KEVIN MOONEY, 213, 6-4, Sophomore,

middle guard, Bayport, N. Y. Born 7/28/48, Bethlehem, N. Y. One of top defensive stars of unbeaten frosh as defensive end. Resembles former Gamecock great Jim Moss facially, physically. Switched to middle guard in spring. Big, quick, agile and aggressive. A top prospect. Attended West Islip High, West Islip, N. Y., where his coach was Charles Skiptunas. Physical Education major. Catholic. Single.

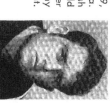

#74 ROBERT JOHN (BOB) MAURO, 215, 6-0,

Senior, one letter, center, Madison, N. J. Born 10/20/46, Summit, N. J. Starting offensive tackle last year when he played 272 minutes and was consistent performer. One of top hustlers on squad. Fractured kneecap playing baseball and missed spring practice. Plans call for moving him to center, his high school position. Attended Madison High where his coach was Ted Monica. Physical Education major. Catholic. Single.

#28 HARRY WALLACE (WALLY) MEDLIN, 183,

5-9, Senior, one letter, defensive back, Ehrhardt, S. C. Born 10/9/46, Ehrhardt. Played 182 minutes in secondary last year, primarily at safety, making 28 individual tackles and 18 assists. Intercepted two passes against Alabama, played as offensive halfback in '66 but didn't letter. Righthanded relief pitcher with baseball Gamecocks. Attended Bells High, Ruffin, S. C., where his coach was Glen Varn. Business Administration major. Baptist. Single.

#31 ROBERT GUY (BOB) MIRANDA, 191,

5-11, Sophomore, fullback, East Haven, Conn. Born 4/12/47, New Haven, Conn. Nickname: "Carmen." Rushed 143 yards in 39 carries for 3.7 average with frosh and scored two TDs. Attended Cheshire Academy at Cheshire, Conn., where his coach was Steve Kuk. History major. Catholic. Single.

32

33

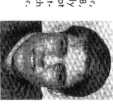

#61 ROBERT ELLINGTON (BOB) MORRIS, 178, 6-0, Junior, one letter, offensive guard, Virginia Beach, Va. Born 6/2/48, Norfolk, Va. Starter as soph in '67 and played 186 minutes until sidelined with compound arm fracture in Alabama game. Missed rough work in spring practice but expected to be ready to play in fall. Small, but quick, and a fine competitor. Attended Cox High in Virginia Beach where his coach was Elmer Barbour. Accounting major. Baptist. Single.

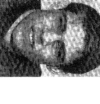

#27 WALTER TERRY (WALLY) ORREL, 182, 5-10, Senior, two letters, defensive back, Savannah, Ga. Born 2/4/47, Savannah. Hard luck Wally has been plagued by injuries, including two knee operations, but has been one of top safetymen in the ACC when well. Played 136 minutes last year before injuries sidelined him. Intercepted three passes, made 15 individual tackles, 26 assists. Skipped rough work in spring practice but counted on this fall. Attended Jenkins High in Savannah where his coach was Lamar Leachman. Economics major. Presbyterian. Married.

#25 ALLEN EARLE OWEN, 181, 6-2, Junior, defensive back, Columbus, Ga. Born 3/19/48, Rome. Played 15 minutes last year, primarily on kickoff and punt coverage teams, but did not earn letter. Should see more action in '68. Attended Jordan High in Columbus where his coach was Bill Atkins. Business Administration major. Methodist. Single.

#53 BENJAMIN (BENNY) PADGETT, 189, 5-10, Sophomore, linebacker, Rome, Ga. Born 3/19/48, Rome. One of top defensive stars on unbeaten frosh team and counted on to become a fine varsity performer. Intercepted three passes, returning 57 yards with frosh. Lots of hustle and desire. Attended West Rome High where his coach was Paul Kennedy. Business Administration major. Baptist. Single.

#19 WILLIAM GLENN (BILL) PARKER, 198, 6-0, Sophomore, punter-linebacker, Kershaw, S. C. Born 8/16/49, Camden, S. C. Pre-season knee injury that required surgery knocked him out of frosh season, but he established himself as top punter on squad in spring practice. Could also break into linebacking picture. Attended Kershaw High where his coach was Bill Few. Business Education major. Baptist. Single.

#86 JAMES KENNETH (JIMMY) POPE, 196, 6-3, Sophomore, defensive end, Rock Hill, S. C. Born 8/20/49, Rock Hill. Pre-season elbow injury knocked him out of frosh participation but he quickly established himself in spring practice as a fine prospect. Figures to break into top two units as soph. Attended Rock Hill High where his coach was Tommy Oates. Physical Education major. Presbyterian. Single.

#75 JIMMY LEE POSTON, 242, 6-4, Sophomore, defensive tackle, Canton, N. C. Born 6/29/49, Waynesville, N. C. Big, strong, tough mountain boy who should develop into a top flight lineman. One of top performers up from unbeaten frosh. Good chance to start for varsity as soph. Attended Pisgah High at Canton where his coach was Boyd Allen. Business Administration major. Baptist. Single.

#45 ROY DON REEVES, 182, 5-11, Senior, two letters, defensive back, Americus, Ga. Born 2/8/46, Americus. Versatile star who has played all secondary positions, split end and offensive halfback with Gamecocks. Counted on to be number one rover in '68. Played 299 minutes in '67, splitting season between offense and defense. Rushed 48 yards in nine carries for 6.9 average, caught nine passes for 119 yards. Defensively, made 17 individual tackles, six assists. Brother of former Gamecock great Dan Reeves, now one of top NFL backs with Dallas Cowboys. Attended Americus High where his coach was Jimmy Hightower. Marketing major. Baptist. Married.

#82 GUSTAVUS EUGENE (GENE) SCHWARTING, 195, 6-1, Senior, two letters, tight end, Bamberg, S. C. Born 2/9/47, Bamberg. Two year starter at defensive end, switched to tight end in spring practice. Impressed with his blocking and caught one pass for 19 yards in spring game. Played 299 minutes last year, making 49 individual tackles, 16 assists, and recovered three fumbles. Attended Bamberg High where his coach was current Gamecock backfield mentor Dick Weldon. Business Administration major. Baptist. Single.

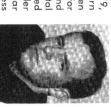

#41 BYRON DALE SISTARE, 210, 6-0, Sophomore, defensive tackle, West Columbia, S. C. Born 2/19/49, Charlotte, N. C. Reserve linebacker with frosh who was switched to tackle in spring and did impressive job, winding up second team on pre-season depth chart. Attended Brookland-Cayce High, Cayce, S. C., where his coach was Bettis Herlong. Business Administration major. Baptist. Single.

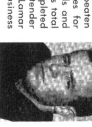

#40 THOMAS RODMAN (TOM) TREVILLIAN, 195, 6-0, Sophomore, halfback, Hampton, Va. Born 6/15/49, Lynchburg, Va. Nickname: "Red." Rushed 185 yards in 54 carries for 3.6 average and one TD with frosh, catching five passes for 47 yards and one TD. Good chance to break into top two units as soph. Attended Hampton High where his coach was Johnny Palmer. Business Administration major. Baptist. Single.

#12 THOMAS ELLISON (TOMMY) SUGGS, 179, 5-9, Sophomore, quarterback, Lamar, S. C. Born 6/9/49, Florence, S. C. Top QB with unbeaten frosh where he completed 41 of 78 passes for 546 yards and six TDs, rushed for 84 yards and three TDs in 57 carries, compiled 630 yards total offense in five games. In spring game, completed six of 10 passes for 69 yards. Strong contender for starting QB job as soph. Attended Lamar High where his coach was John Socha. Business Administration major. Methodist. Single.

#78 LEE McGOWAN (MACK LEE) THARPE, JR., 205, 6-1, Sophomore, offensive guard, Greenwood, S. C. Born 1/3/48, Greenwood. Fullback-linebacker on '66 frosh, but out of school in spring of '67. Returned without scholarship and impressed in spring practice as candidate for offensive guard spot. Attended Greenwood High where his coach was Pinky Babb and Myers Park High, Charlotte, N. C., where his coach was Gus Purcell. Business Administration major. Methodist. Married with small daughter.

36

#33 ALVIN MOORE (AL) USHER, JR., 191, 5-11, Sophomore, linebacker, Pageland, S. C. Born 3/30/49, Lancaster, S. C. Fullback-linebacker with frosh where he rushed 35 times for 138 yards, a 3.9 average, and one TD, catching two passes for 45 yards. Established himself as potential star in spring practice and listed as starting weakside linebacker on pre-season depth chart. Attended Pageland High where he was coached by Ralph Hamm. Physical Education major. Baptist. Single.

#57 STEVEN MILNER (STEVE) VASGAARD, 196, 6-3, Sophomore, center, Winston-Salem, N. C. Born 10/30/48, Natick, Mass. Tight end on frosh squad where he caught seven passes for 89 yards in five games. Moved to center in spring and did a good job. Likely to break into top two units as soph. Attended Reynolds High in Winston-Salem where his coach was Herman Bryson. Business Administration major. Protestant. Single.

#42 KENNETH WALLACE WALKUP, 191, 5-9, Sophomore, fullback, Timmonsville, S. C. Born 7/16/49, Timmonsville. Top running back on '67 frosh with 188 yards in 32 carries for 5.9 average and two touchdowns despite being hampered by broken rib in three games. Caught five passes for 41 yards and two TDs and his 24 points led frosh in scoring. Rushed 40 yards in spring game and counted on to be one of top running backs on squad as a soph. Attended Timmonsville High where his coach was Bill Pate. Arts and Science major. Baptist. Single.

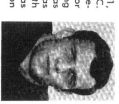

37

303

#15 PATRICK EARL (PAT) WATSON, 157, 5-11, Senior, one letter, defensive back, Myrtle Beach, S. C. Born 8/28/48, Conway, S. C. Cocky little scrapper who led squad in time played last year with 303 minutes. Made 42 individual tackles, 18 assists, recovered two fumbles, returned five kickoffs 99 yards, 11 punts 109 yards, including 67-yard return for TD against Virginia. Campus leader and president of junior class. Attended Myrtle Beach High where his coach was Danny Brabham. Physical Education major. Protestant. Single.

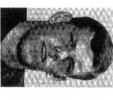

#85 JOSEPH OWEN (JOE) WINGARD III, 203, 6-4, Sophomore, defensive end, Brevard, N. C. Born 4/1/49, Orangeburg, S. C. Big, strong fellow who was one of top performers on unbeaten frosh and certain to crack top two units as soph. Attended Wilson Memorial High at Fishersville, Va., where his coach was Joe Zapotozny. Moved to Brevard from Waynesboro, Va., after high school graduation. Family native South Carolinians. Engineering major. Methodist. Single.

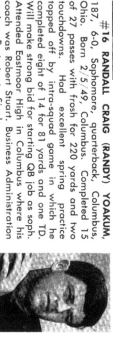

#16 RANDALL CRAIG (RANDY) YOAKUM, 187, 6-0, Sophomore, quarterback, Columbus, Ohio. Born 2/5/49, Columbus. Completed 15 of 27 passes with frosh for 220 yards and two touchdowns. Had excellent spring practice. Topped off by intra-squad game in which he completed eight of 14 for 81 yards and one TD. Will make strong bid for starting QB job as soph. Attended Eastmoor High in Columbus where his coach was Robert Stuart. Business Administration major. Single.

#80 FREDERICK MIDDLETON (FRED) ZEIGLER, 182, 5-10, Junior, one letter, flanker, Reevesville, S. C. Born 5/19/47, Dallas, Tex. Nickname: "Onassis." Came to Carolina without scholarship and after redshirt year led ACC in pass receiving last season with 35 for 370 yards, second highest one-season total in Gamecock history. Played 162 minutes. Moved to flanker in spring from split end and in spring game caught three passes for 55 yards. Has great hands, deceptive moves and speed. One of the ACC's all-time fine receivers. Definite All-ACC candidate. Attended Carlisle Military Academy, Bamberg, S. C., where his coach was Bob Jenkins. Business Administration major. Episcopalian. Single.

DEPTH CHART

Although some revisions are likely before the Fighting Gamecocks line up for the season opener, a tentative depth chart is listed below, based on the end of spring practice, last season's performance, etc. Lettermen in all caps.

OFFENSE

Split end—
88 *JOHNNY GREGORY (168)
90 Eddie Bolton (210)
34 Allen Brown (193)

Left tackle—
76 Dave DeCamilla (217)
77 Rick Hipkins (239)

Left guard—
61 BOB MORRIS (178)
78 Mack Lee Thorpe (205)

Center—
74 *BOB MAURO (215)
57 Steve Vasgaard (196)
54 Ken Ross (191)

Right guard—
62 DON BUCKNER (184)
66 Chris Bank (220)
68 Jimmy Johnson (194)

Right tackle—
73 TONY FUSARO (230)
69 John King (215)
55 George McCarthy (215)

Tight end—
82 GENE SCHWARTING (195)
87 Doug Hamrick (204)

Quarterback—
12 Tommy Suggs (179)
16 Randy Yoakum (187)
17 Dan Harbison (185)

Power back—
20 *BENNY GALLOWAY (187)
40 Tom Trevillion (195)
32 Jimmy Cleckler (170)

Tailback—
36 WARREN MUIR (199)
42 Ken Walkup (191)
31 Bob Miranda (191)

Flankers—
80 *FRED ZEIGLER (182)
24 RUDY HOLLOMAN (172)
81 Bill Duffie (175)

DEFENSE

Left end—
89 **LYNN HODGE (202)
86 Jimmy Pope (196)

Left tackle—
75 Jimmy Poston (242)
79 John Coleman (214)
70 Danny Dyches (258)

Strong linebacker—
52 *DAVE GRANT (210)
51 RON BUNCH (202)
39 Randy Williams (200)

Middle guard—
47 *TIM BICE (194)
64 Kevin Mooney (213)
59 John Tominack (201)

Week linebacker—
33 Al Usher (191)
53 Benny Padgett (189)

Right tackle—
71 Rusty Ganas (233)
41 Byron Sistare (210)
65 Joe Regalis (226)

Right end—
84 DAVE LUCAS (189)
85 Joe Wingard (203)

Left halfback—
22 Don Bailey (171)
29 ANDY CHAVOUS (180)

Rover—
45 *ROY DON REEVES (182)
28 *WALLY MEDLIN (183)
38 Don Montgomery (188)

Safety—
27 WALLY ORREL (182)
11 Tyler Hellams (163)
35 CANDLER BOYD

Right halfback—
15 PAT WATSON (157)
25 Allen Owen (181)
10 Carl Cowart (160)

SPECIALISTS

Placekicker—
1 Billy DuPre (150)
14 Richard Genoble (180)

Punter—
19 Bill Parker (198)

Weights in parentheses are as of the end of the 1968 spring practice.

* — Gregory lettered last year as a tight end; Mauro as an offensive tackle; Buckner as a defensive end, linebacker, rover and fullback; Schwarting as a defensive end; Zeigler as a split end; Grant as a middle guard; Bice as a weak linebacker; Reeves as an offensive and defensive halfback; Medlin as a safety and defensive halfback.
** — Galloway last lettered in 1966; Hodge last lettered in 1966.

GAMECOCKS GO JET IN '68

When the Fighting Gamecocks fly to away games this fall it will be by jet. For the first time, Southern Airways DC-9 jets have been chartered to take the Gamecocks to Maryland and Virginia. In the past, the Gamecocks have chartered propeller-driven aircraft.

For the four shorter trips — North Carolina, N. C. State, Wake Forest and Clemson — the Gamecocks will travel by chartered Greyhound bus as in the past.

TRAVEL PLANS

THE NORTH CAROLINA GAME

Depart Columbia by bus Friday afternoon, Sept. 20. Headquarters, University Motel, Chapel Hill, N. C. Depart Chapel Hill as soon as possible after game, Sept. 21, arriving Columbia Saturday evening. Sports Information Director arrives Raleigh-Durham-Chapel Hill area Wednesday, Sept. 18.

THE N. C. STATE GAME

Depart Columbia by bus Friday afternoon, Oct. 11. Headquarters, College Inn, Raleigh, N. C. Depart Raleigh as soon as possible after game, Oct. 12, arriving Columbia Saturday evening. Sports Information Director arrives Raleigh-Durham area Wednesday, Oct. 9.

THE MARYLAND GAME

Depart Columbia Metropolitan Airport 9:00 A.M., EDT, Friday, Oct. 18 aboard chartered Southern Airways DC-9 Jet. Arrive Washington National Airport 10:15 A.M., EDT. Headquarters, Holiday Inn, College Park, Md. Depart Washington National Airport 5:00 P.M., EDT, Saturday, Oct. 19. Arrive Columbia Metropolitan Airport 6:15 P.M. Sports Information Director arrives Washington-College Park-Baltimore area Wednesday, Oct. 16.

THE VIRGINIA GAME

Depart Columbia Metropolitan Airport 9:00 A.M., EST, Friday, Nov. 1, aboard chartered Southern Airways DC-9 Jet. Arrive Charlottesville, Va., Charlottesville Airport 10:00 A.M., EST. Headquarters, Mount Vernon Motel, Charlottesville, Va. Depart Charlottesville Airport 5:00 P.M., EST, Saturday, Nov. 2. Arrive Columbia Metropolitan Airport 6:00 P.M. EST. Sports Information Director arrives Richmond area Wednesday, Oct. 30; Charlottesville Thursday evening.

THE WAKE FOREST GAME

Depart Columbia by bus Friday afternoon, Nov. 8. Headquarters, Sheraton Motor Inn, Winston-Salem, N. C. Depart Winston-Salem as soon as possible after game, Nov. 9, arriving Columbia Saturday evening. Sports Information Director arrives Winston-Salem-Greensboro area Wednesday, Nov. 6.

THE CLEMSON GAME

Depart Columbia by bus Friday afternoon, Nov. 22. Headquarters, Holiday Inn, Anderson, S. C. Depart Clemson as soon as possible after game, Nov. 23, arriving Columbia Saturday evening. Sports Information Director arrives Anderson-Greenville-Clemson area Thursday, Nov. 21.

40

FINAL 1967 VARSITY FOOTBALL STATISTICS
(Record: 5-5; ACC: 4-2)

TEAM

TEAM	USC	OPP.
First downs rushing	99	109
First downs passing	49	55
First downs penalties	12	7
TOTAL FIRST DOWNS	160	170
Net yards rushing	1601	2156
Number of rushes	489	539
Game rushing avg.	160.1	215.6
Passing yardage	1029	1059
Game passing avg.	102.9	105.9
Passes attempted	181	155
Passes completed	84	86
Intercepted by	7	17
Number of punts	59	54
Yards punted	2318	2067
Punting avg.	39.3	38.3
Return yardage	1074	1073
Fumbles lost	6	15
Yards penalized	430	516

INDIVIDUAL RUSHING

RUSHING	NO.	YDS.	AVG.	TD
*Muir	188	805	4.3	6
Garnto	88	274	3.1	4
Fair	133	258	1.9	7
*Holloman	28	78	2.8	0
Williams	14	54	3.9	2
*Reeves	7	48	6.9	0
*Dunning	9	28	3.1	0
McCord	4	23	5.6	0
Spigner	5	19	3.8	0
*Brown	1	9	9.0	0
*Palmer	2	9	9.0	0
*Harbison	10	—1	—0.1	0
TOTALS	489	1601	3.3	18
OPP.	539	2156	4.0	18

TOTAL OFFENSE

TOTAL OFFENSE	RUSH	PASS	TOTAL
Fair	258	970	1228
Garnto	274	32	306
*Harbison	—1	27	27

(others same as rushing)

PASSING

PASSING	ATT	COMP	INT	PCT	YDS	TD
Fair	165	79	17	.479	970	1
Garnto	8	3	0	.375	32	0
*Harbison	6	2	0	.333	27	0
Williams	2	0	0	.000	0	0
TOTALS	181	84	17	.464	1029	1
OPP.	155	86	7	.555	1059	2

* — Eligible to return in 1968

RECEIVING

RECEIVING	NO.	YDS.	AVG.	TD.
*Zeigler	35	370	10.6	0
*Gregory	13	226	17.4	0
*Reeves	9	125	13.9	0
Holloman	9	119	13.2	0
Garnto	8	70	8.8	1
*Muir	4	48	12.0	0
*Chavous	2	24	12.0	0
Williams	1	15	15.0	0
*King	1	12	12.0	0
Spigner	1	12	12.0	0
Fair	1	10	10.0	0

INTERCEPTIONS

INTCPTS.	NO.	YDS.	AVG.	TD.
Fair	3	32	10.7	0
*Orrel	2	21	10.5	0
*Medlin	1	17	17.0	1
*McCarthy	1	5	5.0	0

SCORING

SCORING	TD	PAT-K	PAT-RP	FG	TP
Fair	7	0-0	0-2	0-0	42
*Muir	6	0-0	0-0	0-0	36
Poole	0	16-18	0-0	3-9	25
Garnto	3	0-0	1-2	0-0	20
Williams	2	0-0	0-2	0-0	12
*Watson	1	0-0	0-0	0-0	6
*Harbison	1	0-0	0-0	0-0	6
*Lucas	1	0-0	0-0	0-0	6
*McCarthy	1	0-0	0-0	0-0	6
TOTALS	22	16-18	1-4	3-9	159
OPP.	21	19-20	0-1	7-13	166

PUNT RETURNS

PUNT RETURNS	NO.	YDS.	AVG.	TD
McCord	15	159	10.6	0
*Watson	11	109	9.9	1
*Holloman	3	27	9.0	0
Garnto	1	3	3.0	0

KICKOFF RETURNS

KICKOFF RETURNS	NO.	YDS.	AVG.	TD
McCord	11	296	26.9	0
*Holloman	8	150	18.8	0
*Watson	5	99	19.8	0
Garnto	3	63	21.0	0
*Palmer	4	62	15.5	0
*Reeves	3	21	21.0	0
Mulvihill	1	6	6.0	0
*Schwarting	1	0	0.0	0

41

305

Punting

PUNTING	NO.	YDS.	BLKD.	AVG.
Townsend	59	2318	—	39.3

Cumulative Score by Periods

GAMECOCKS	21—27—56—55—159		
OPPONENTS	34—58—39—35—166		

RESULTS AND ATTENDANCE

34	Iowa	3	26,443
16	North Carolina	10	39,135
21	Duke	17	25,000
0	Georgia	21	58,182
0	Florida State	17	33,022
24	Virginia	23	34,159
31	Maryland	0	33,247
21	Wake Forest	35	13,000
0	Alabama	35	46,105
12	Clemson	23	43,338

*—Eligible to return in 1968

Defensive Statistics

	TACKLES	ASSISTS	FUMBLE RECOVERIES
*Bice	90	60	0
*Grant	77	38	2
Somma	62	26	1
Cole	61	33	0
Komoroski	48	23	0
*Bunch	47	16	0
*Lucas	44	17	4
*Watson	42	18	2
Schwarting	42	16	3
*Boyd	29	14	1
*Medlin	28	18	1
McCord	19	8	0
*Reeves	17	6	0
*Orrel	15	26	0
Mulvihill	12	5	0
*Buckner	7	9	0
Poole	4	0	0
Gibson	3	3	1
*Cowart	3	0	0
*Owen	2	0	0
Smith	1	1	0
*Thorp	1	0	0

1967 SEASON SUPERLATIVES

GAMECOCKS

LONGEST RUN FROM SCRIMMAGE:
Warren Muir vs. Duke, 42 yards

LONGEST PASS COMPLETION:
Mike Fair-Rudy Holloman vs. Iowa State, 50 yards

LONGEST PUNT:
Scott Townsend vs. Alabama, 60 yards

LONGEST PUNT RETURN:
Pat Watson vs. Virginia, 67 yards (TD)

LONGEST KICKOFF RETURN:
Toy McCord vs. Georgia, 74 yards

LONGEST INTERCEPTION RETURN:
Wally Medlin vs. Alabama, 21 yards

LONGEST FIELD GOAL:
Jimmy Poole vs. Virginia, 45 yards

OPPONENTS

LONGEST RUN FROM SCRIMMAGE:
Kirby Moore, Georgia, 87 yards (TD)

LONGEST PASS COMPLETION:
Chuck Drimal-Rick Carlson, Maryland, 45 yards

LONGEST PUNT:
Spike Jones, Georgia, 65 yards

LONGEST PUNT RETURN:
Bob Haley, Maryland, 28 yards

LONGEST KICKOFF RETURN:
Frank Quayle, Virginia, 90 yards (TD)

LONGEST INTERCEPTION RETURN:
T. K. Weatherell, Florida State, 35 yards

LONGEST FIELD GOAL:
Arthur Craig, Clemson, 39 yards

PLAYING TIME 1967

Defensive halfback Pat Watson topped all Gamecocks in playing time last year with 303 minutes and 35 seconds. Defensive end Gene Schwarting, who has switched to offense for the 1968 season, was close behind with 299:19 and Roy Don Reeves, who began 1967 on offense and wound up on defense, logged an even 299 minutes. The Gamecocks used 52 players over the course of 10 games last year, with playing time for each listed below:

*Watson	303:35	*Zeigler	162:22	*Dunning	18:33
*Schwarting	299:19	*Fusaro	152:51	White	18:19
*Reeves	299:00	*Holloman	149:00	Dyer	16:18
Komoroski	290:14	James	145:36	*Owen	15:32
*Bice	283:21	*King	136:52	*King	15:21
Somma	282:40	*Orrel	136:26	Gibson	13:23
*Grant	277:39	*Boyd	121:38	*Palmer	10:53
*Mauro	272:32	*Bunch	121:02	Wehmeyer	9:43
Gobble	266:38	*Buckner	118:42	*McCarthy	9:06
Fair	245:25	McCord	110:10	*Brown	4:39
*Gregory	231:14	*Chavous	83:41	Sharp	2:42
*Lucas	231:08	Williams	71:39	*Smith	1:13
Garnto	225:46	Mulvihill	71:08	*Tominack	0:41
Cole	225:21	*Ross	39:38	*Coleman	0:19
*Muir	215:03	*Harbison	36:29	Poole	Kicker
*Morris	186:05	*Cowart	26:50	Townsend	Punter
*Medlin	182:10	Glass	23:36		
Wingard	181:20	Spigner	22:47		

*—Expected to return in 1968.

REVIEW OF 1967

Compared with 1966, the Gamecocks were improved 500 per cent in 1967. Following up a disastrous, 1-9 record with the smallest squad, both in numbers and individual size, in many years, Carolina was expected to continue taking its lumps in '67. A scrambling, hustling, fighting style of play, however, captured the fancy of fans everywhere and the Gamecocks won five games and were 4-2 in the Atlantic Coast Conference and in the running for the title up to the final game.

The Gamecocks had turned from the disaster of 1966 with firm resolve that a new era was dawning and the best was yet to come. The best is still yet to come, but the improvement in 1967, along with an unbeaten freshman team, gave promise of greater things on the horizon.

OPENED AT HOME

The Gamecocks had the good fortune of opening at home, and the opposition was a highly respected Iowa State team representing the Big Eight. When Vern Skripsky kicked a first period field goal to put the Cyclones ahead 3-0, things looked bad for the Gamecocks. When Iowa State drove deep in Carolina territory late in the second period, things looked even darker, but two guys named Don — Somma and Buckner—stopped quarterback John Warder short of a first down at the 29 with two minutes left in the half.

The Gamecocks drove 71 yards in 11 plays with quarterback Mike Fair completing four of six passes and running twice for big gains before scoring himself from the one-yard line with seven seconds left in the half.

That drive lit a fire and the Gamecocks engulfed the Cyclones in a sea of second half touchdowns to win, 34-3. Fullback Warren Muir launched what was destined to become a brilliant career by gaining 79 yards and scoring two touchdowns. Reserves Curtis Williams and Dan Harbison scored once each.

North Carolina's Tar Heels came to Columbia a week later and the Gamecocks hadn't had much luck against them in years past. An 80-yard North Carolina drive late in the first period produced a 7-0 Tar Heel lead and the Gamecocks were challenged to come from behind again. They almost duplicated the second period race against the clock of a week before, but had to settle for a 37-yard field goal by Jimmy Poole with 19 seconds left and trailed 7-3 at halftime.

MUIR GAINS 164

With the crowd of 39,135 shouting approval, it was another second half surge as Muir showed the way by plunging for 164 yards and tying a 33-year-old record of 35 carries in one game. He scored to cap a 64-yard drive and put the Gamecocks ahead 9-7, and when Gene Schwarting recovered a North Carolina fumble moments later, the Gamecocks swept 28 yards with Ben Garnto scoring from the one. Although the Tar Heels managed a 24-yard field goal, the final score was South Carolina 16, North Carolina 10 as tall, skinny defensive end Dave (Twiggy) Lucas dumped Tar Heel quarterback Gayle Bomar four straight times for losses in the dying moments.

The first road game was against Duke at Durham and the Gamecocks had never won there. They set out to do something about that right away by scoring seven points the first six seconds of the game. Tim Bice showed why he was to be chosen an All-ACC defensive player when he jarred the kickoff loose from Duke's Bob Hepler at the 13-yard line. The ball skidded back into the end zone and Lucas —last-minute hero a week earlier—became a first-minute hero by covering the fumble for a touchdown.

The second period belonged to the Blue Devils, however, and Duke took a 10-7 halftime lead. Muir, who gained 87 yards for the day, got the Gamecocks untracked with a 42-yard run, and Mike Fair's eight-yard bootleg put Carolina ahead 14-10. Duke, with veteran fullback Jay Calabrese punishing the Gamecocks inside, drove 88 yards for a fourth period TD and the Blue Devils regained the lead with less than six minutes to play.

Ben Garnto, who wasn't usually used on the kickoff return team, raced 52 yards to the Duke 41 with the following kickoff and the Gamecocks appeared on the way back only to have a Mike Fair pass intercepted. The defense held, however, and Toy McCord returned a punt to the Duke 43. Three great catches of Fair passes by Fred Zeigler and one by Johnny Gregory set the stage for Muir's plunge for the winning touchdown from the one with 40 seconds remaining. The Gamecocks won, 21-17, although they still had to withstand a last second Duke surge with Bob Cole intercepting a Devil pass on the game's last play.

UNBEATEN AFTER THREE

After three games, the Gamecocks found themselves undefeated with three times as many wins as they accomplished in all of 1966. Georgia, likewise was unbeaten and a record crowd of 58,182 jammed Sanford Stadium in Athens for the showdown.

The Gamecock defense held Georgia to two first-half first downs, but the first was an 87-yard bootleg by Bulldog quarterback Kirby Moore on a "busted" play and Georgia took a 7-0 lead. An interception stopped a Gamecock drive at the Bulldog five. Georgia drove 76 yards for a third period touchdown and the Gamecocks, trailing 14-0 late in the game, gambled in their own territory and the Bulldogs scored again in the dying moments to win 21-0. Muir rushed for 61 yards but otherwise, Carolina didn't have much offense, netting only 76 yards rushing, and 60 passing. Toy McCord returned a kickoff 74 yards and a punt 28 yards, but the Gamecocks couldn't convert either opportunity and McCord was injured on the punt return and saw little action the remainder of the year.

The Gamecocks traveled to Tallahassee the following week to meet Florida State and the injuries — something the depth-shy Birds couldn't afford—began to mount. Safetyman Wally Orrel twisted his bad knee getting off the bus the night before the game and was out for the remainder of the year. Warren Muir, the man Carolina could least afford to lose, suffered a hip pointer early in the game and the Gamecocks lost much of their offense. A disastrous pass interference penalty on the game's first play set up a Florida State touchdown and the Seminoles won 17-0.

COACH DIETZEL INJURED

The injury jinx hit the head coach the following Wednesday when Coach Dietzel twisted a knee on the practice field and underwent surgery to repair ligament and cartilage damage. He made it to the Homecoming game against Virginia in a golf cart on the sidelines, and witnessed a complete first half mauling of the Gamecocks by the offense-minded Cavaliers, who led 17-0 at halftime and only a goal line fumble kept it from being 24-0.

Pat Watson, the Gamecocks' 152-pound sophomore defensive back, snapped his teammates out of their confusion with a 67-yard scoring punt return, and Gene Schwarting recovered a fumble at the Virginia 21 to set up a Fair to Garnto touchdown pass. Another Fair-Garnto combination for two points narrowed it to 17-15, but the Cavaliers' Frank Quayle promptly returned the kickoff 90 yards to make it 23-15. Virginia elected to go for two points but Candler Boyd intercepted for what proved to be a key play by the Gamecocks.

44

45

307

Muir—whose playing time was limited due to his hip injury—scored from 14 yards out, but Fair's two-point attempt was short and Virginia still led by two points. When Virginia stopped a fourth period drive at the Gamecock 28, all the responsibility was dumped on the shoulders of little Jimmy Poole, Carolina's senior placekicker. He responded with a perfect 45-yarder and, when Virginia missed a field goal of its own, the Gamecocks turned what started out as a fiasco into one of the greatest comebacks of all time and a 24-23 victory.

The Gamecocks had come from behind to win in all of their first four victories, but when Maryland came to Columbia Carolina took charge immediately, driving 63 yards to score in the first five minutes, and went on to win convincingly, 31-0. Warren Muir scored from 11 yards out, and his understudy—Curtis Williams—scored on a one-yard plunge to stoke the Gamecocks to a 14-0 first period lead. Jimmy Poole's 30-yard field goal made it 17-0 at halftime. Second half touchdowns by Mike Fair and reserve tackle George McCarthy, who went 17 yards with an interception, ran up the score. The Gamecocks wound up with 287 yards rushing, 115 of it by the incomparable Muir.

It was Carolina's first shutout in '67 games, since a 26-0 win over Virginia in 1960.

FIRST SHUTOUT SINCE 1960

Things were considerably rougher the next three weekends, however, as the Gamecocks ran into three powerful and red-hot opponents.

Wake Forest, which lost its first six games before living up to its pre-season billing by winning the final four, made the Gamecocks number two with an unstoppable offense. The Gamecocks had little trouble scoring themselves, but couldn't stop the Deacons and lost 35-21. Fair and Gamto scored, but Wake led at halftime 21-14. Fair scored again to tie it up, but Poole missed a field goal that would have put the Gamecocks ahead and Wake Forest surged to the winning touchdown and added another in the closing minutes after Carolina had gambled and lost on fourth down deep in Gamecock territory.

Alabama's Southeastern Conference champions and Cotton Bowl representatives proved too strong for the Gamecocks in the next-to-last game of the season, the Tide winning 17-0 at Tuscaloosa. The Carolina defense stymied the Tide for a period and a half, but a field goal and a sensational 38-yard pass from Ken Stabler to Dennis Homan staked 'Bama to a 10-0 halftime lead. The Tide scored once in the second half while two pass interceptions by Wally Medlin were Carolina's top accomplishments although Muir wound up with 72 yards rushing.

The Gamecocks entered the season finale against arch-rival Clemson with a chance to tie for the ACC championship, but it was not to be. Clemson, winning its second conference title in a row, was just too strong for the Gamecocks. The Tigers mounted a 23-0 lead through three periods as the Gamecocks weren't able to develop much of a running game with Warren Muir hobbling on a sprained ankle suffered in the Alabama game.

Fair scored twice in the fourth period, however, as the Gamecocks recovered a fumble deep in Tiger territory and worked an onside kick successfully. However, the final score before a sellout crowd of 43,338, was 23-12.

Despite loss of the final three games, the season had to be rated as a pleasant surprise. The 5-5 overall record and 4-2 ACC mark were well above what all experts predicted. It can't be said that the Gamecocks were satisfied, however, for nothing short of a perfect season could produce complete satisfaction.

The Gamecocks look to the future still convinced "the best is yet to come."

46

These five Gamecocks were recipients of special awards at the annual football banquet last December. Left to right, Fred Zeigler, letterman with highest scholastic average; Joe Komoroski, alternate captain's cup; Don Somma, captain's cup; Mike Fair, most valuable player; and Don Brant, highest scholastic average for freshman year.

VETS VS. FROSH FEATURE GARNET & BLACK GAME

The Garnet & Black intra-squad game, which annually climaxes spring football practice, took a unique twist in 1968 with the returning veterans matched against last year's unbeaten frosh.

Experience won out, with the Garnet team—comprising the vets—taking a 20-9 decision before 8,000 fans, one of the largest crowds ever for a spring game. The Association of Lettermen held its annual barbecue as a pre-game feature and the game included cheerleaders, pre-game and halftime performances by the Marching Gamecocks band, and all the trappings of a regulation game.

The Gamecock Football Network fed play-by-play to 11 radio stations throughout South Carolina.

The vets, leading 13-9, scored on the last play of the game—a 14 yard pass from quarterback Dan Harbison to flanker Rudy Holloman—for the final margin.

Soccer-style kicker Billy DuPre gave the frosh an early lead with a 41 yard field goal, but Warren Muir's touchdown plunge put the vets ahead to stay. Richard Genoble, a left-footer, kicked field goals of 37 and 42 yards to make it 13-3, before the frosh scored on a three yard pass from Randy Yoakum to tight end Doug Hamrick late in the fourth period.

Muir was the game's leading rusher with 85 yards on 21 carries and Ken Walkup topped the frosh with 40 yards. Yoakum completed eight of 14 passes for 81 yards and Tommy Suggs six of 10 for 69 yards for the frosh. Harbison connected on seven of 17 for 51 yards for the vets.

47

SOUTH CAROLINA'S 1968 VARSITY ROSTER

NO.	NAME	Pos.	Hgt.	Wgt.	Age	Class	Home Town	HS Coach
22	Don Bailey	DB	5-11	171	20	So.	John's Island, S. C.	R. H. Biggerstaff
66	Chris Bank	OG	6-1	220	19	So.	Joliet, Ill.	Gordon Gillespie
63	Tim Beans	OG	6-0	216	20	So.	Silver Spring, Md.	Steve Kuk
47	**Tim Bice	MG	5-11	194	22	Sr.	Atlanta, Ga.	Sam Edenfield
90	Eddie Bolton	SE	6-4	210	19	So.	Greenwood, S. C.	Pinky Babb
35	*Candler Boyd	DB	5-9	175	20	Jr.	Hinesville, Ga.	Hokey Jackson
91	Don Brant	DE	6-4	183	20	So.	Sycamore, S. C.	Bruce Tate
34	Allen Brown	SE	6-0	193	21	Sr.	Hinesville, Ga.	Hokey Jackson
62	*Don Buckner	OG	6-0	184	20	Jr.	Cleveland, Tenn.	Bobby Scott
51	*Ron Bunch	LB	5-9	202	21	Sr.	Bamberg, S. C.	Dick Weldon
18	Buddy Caldwell	DB	5-10	195	20	So.	Davidson, N. C.	Mack Haynes
67	Joe Chandler	OT	6-0	204	19	So.	Spray, N. C.	Bill Kittrell
29	*Andy Chavous	DB	6-2	180	20	Jr.	Hepzibah, Ga.	Jamie Overton
32	Jimmy Cleckler	HB	6-2	170	19	So.	W. Columbia, S. C.	Bettis Herlong
79	John Coleman	DT	6-4	214	21	Jr.	Latta, S. C.	Eddie Rice
10	Carl Cowart	DB	5-9	160	21	Jr.	Jesup, Ga.	Clint Madrey
76	Dave DeCamilla	OT	6-2	217	20	So.	Hudson Falls, N. Y.	Robert Ryan
26	Steve DiCarlo	SE	5-10	166	20	So.	Atlanta, Ga.	Don Shea
81	Bill Duffie	FL	6-3	175	19	Jr.	Jesup, Ga.	Leonard Jones
46	Don Dunning	FB	5-10	204	20	So.	Florence, S. C.	Jim Wall
1	Billy DuPre	PK	5-5	150	19	So.	Columbia, S. C.	Jim Pinkerton
70	Danny Dyches	OT	6-5	258	19	So.	Hanahan, S. C.	Jim Hart
73	*Tony Fusaro	OT	6-2	230	20	Jr.	Huntington, N. Y.	Joe Lucey
20	**Benny Galloway	HB	5-9	187	22	Sr.	Easley, S. C.	Bill Carr
71	Rusty Ganas	OT	6-0	233	19	So.	Waycross, Ga.	David Shields
14	Richard Genoble	QB-PK	6-0	180	20	So.	Union, S. C.	Bobby Dunlap
52	*Dave Grant	LB	6-0	210	21	Sr.	Clarkesville, Ga.	Red Lynch
88	**Johnny Gregory	SE	5-11	168	21	Sr.	Aiken, S. C.	Jim Fraser
87	Doug Hamrick	TE	6-2	204	19	So.	Cliffside, N. C.	Bobby Bush
17	Dan Harbison	QB	5-11	185	20	Jr.	Washington, D. C.	Pete Labukas
11	Tyler Hellams	DB	5-11	163	19	So.	Greenwood, S. C.	Pinky Babb
89	*Lynn Hodge	OT	6-4	239	22	So.	Boothwyn, Pa.	Elmer Davis
24	*Rudy Holloman	FL	5-9	172	20	Jr.	Hartsville, S. C.	Bobby Dunlap
23	Earl Hunter	FB	5-9	197	21	Jr.	Greenville, S. C.	Whitey Kendall
43	Frank Johnson	DT	5-10	204	19	Jr.	Columbia, S. C.	Earl Rankin
68	Jimmy Johnson	OG	5-11	194	19	So.	Jacksonville, Fla.	Howell Boney
69	John King	OT	6-3	215	20	Jr.	Lancaster, S. C.	Dalton Rivers
84	*Dave Lucas	DE	6-5	189	21	Jr.	Bishopville, S. C.	W. C. Smith
	Kevin Malone	OG	6-1	194	19	Jr.	Atlanta, Ga.	Don Monica
74	*Bob Mauro	C	6-2	215	22	Sr.	Madison, N. J.	Ted Monica
55	George McCarthy	OT	6-2	208	22	Jr.	Washington, D. C.	Morgan Wooten
28	*Wally Medlin	DB	5-11	183	22	Sr.	Ehrhardt, S. C.	Glen Varn
31	Bob Miranda	FB	5-11	191	19	So.	E. Haven, Conn.	Steve Kuk
64	Mike Mobley	LB	6-0	191	19	So.	Heath Springs, S. C.	Sidney Cauthen
38	Kevin Mooney	MG	6-4	213	20	So.	Union, S. C.	Charles Skiptunas
61	Don Montgomery	DB	5-10	188	20	So.	Bayport, N. Y.	Lindsey Pierce
36	*Bob Morris	OG	6-0	178	20	Jr.	Kingstree, S. C.	Elmer Barbour
27	**Warren Muir	FB	5-10	199	21	Jr.	Fitchburg, Mass.	Marco Landon
25	*Wally Orrel	DB	6-2	181	21	Sr.	Va. Beach, Va.	Bill Atkins
53	Benny Padgett	C	5-10	189	20	So.	Savannah, Ga.	Lamar Leachman
30	Mike Paine	C	5-10	185	19	So.	Columbus, Ga.	Paul Kenney
19	Ronnie Palmer	HB	5-5	161	21	So.	Rome, Ga.	Wright Bazemore
	Bill Parker	LB-Pntr	6-0	198	19	So.	Valdosta, Ga.	Burleigh Davis
							Kershaw, S. C.	Bill Few

1968 VARSITY ROSTER

NO.	NAME	Pos.	Hgt.	Wgt.	Age	Class	Home Town	HS Coach
86	Jimmy Pope	DE	6-3	196	19	So.	Rock Hill, S. C.	Tommy Oates
75	Jimmy Poston	DT	6-4	242	19	So.	Canton, N. C.	Boyd Allen
45	**Roy Don Reeves	DT	5-11	182	22	So.	Americus, Ga.	Jimmy Hightower
65	Joe Regolis	DT	5-11	226	19	So.	Tamaqua, Pa.	Jack Malarky
54	Ken Ross	C	6-1	191	20	Jr.	Williamston, S. C.	Donnie Garrison
82	*Gene Schwarting	TE	6-1	195	21	Sr.	Bamberg, S. C.	Dick Weldon
92	Gary Scott	DE	6-1	188	19	So.	Moultrie, Ga.	Bud Willis
41	Byron Sistare	DB	6-0	210	19	So.	W. Columbia, S. C.	Bettis Herlong
58	Clyde Smith	MG	5-11	197	20	So.	Columbia, S. C.	Pinky Babb
50	Mike Stirling	FB	6-4	210	19	Jr.	Charlotte, N. C.	James Salley
60	Buzzy Stokes	C	6-0	207	20	Jr.	Clover, S. C.	Jerry Frye
12	Tommy Suggs	QB	5-9	179	19	So.	Lamar, S. C.	John Socha
60	Billy Thorp	DE	6-2	189	20	Jr.	Greenwood, S. C.	Ed Commins
78	Mack Lee Thorpe	OG	6-1	205	20	Jr.	Charleston, S. C.	Pinky Babb
57	John Tominack	LB	5-10	201	21	Jr.	Triadelphia, W. Va.	Larry Phillips
33	Al Usher	C	5-11	191	19	So.	Pageland, S. C.	Ralph Hamm
40	Steve Vasgaard	FB	5-9	196	20	So.	Norfolk, Va.	Pinky Babb
42	Ken Walkup	FB	5-9	191	19	So.	Timmonsville, S. C.	C. Herman Bryson
15	*Pat Watson	DB	5-11	157	20	Jr.	Hampton, Va.	Johnny Palmer
39	Eddie Whittington	OT	6-0	199	20	Jr.	Marion, S. C.	James Neely
85	Randy Williams	LB	5-10	200	20	So.	Marietta, Ga.	French Johnson
16	Joe Wingard	DE	6-4	203	19	So.	Brevard, N. C.	Robert Stuart
80	*Fred Zeigler	FL	5-10	182	21	Jr.	Reevesville, S. C.	Bob Jenkins

NUMERICAL ROSTER

NO.	Name	Pos.
1	Billy DuPre	PK
10	Carl Cowart	DB
11	Tyler Hellams	DB
12	Tommy Suggs	QB
14	Richard Genoble	QB-PK
15	*Pat Watson	DB
16	Joe Wingard	DE
17	Dan Harbison	QB
18	Buddy Caldwell	DB
19	Ronnie Palmer	HB
20	**Benny Galloway	HB
22	Don Bailey	DB
23	Earl Hunter	FB
24	*Rudy Holloman	FL
25	*Wally Orrel	DB
26	Steve DiCarlo	HB
27	**Warren Muir	FB
28	*Wally Medlin	DB
29	*Andy Chavous	DB
30	Mike Paine	C
31	Bob Miranda	FB
32	Jimmy Cleckler	HB
33	Al Usher	LB
34	Allen Brown	SE
35	*Candler Boyd	DB
36	*Bob Morris	OG
38	Kevin Mooney	MG
39	Eddie Whittington	OT
40	Tom Trevillian	HB
41	Byron Sistare	DT
42	Ken Walkup	FB
43	Frank Johnson	DT
45	*Roy Don Reeves	DB
46	Don Dunning	FB
47	*Tim Bice	MG
50	Clyde Smith	MG
51	*Ron Bunch	LB
52	*Dave Grant	LB
53	Benny Padgett	LB
54	Ken Ross	C
55	George McCarthy	OT
57	Steve Vasgaard	C
58	John Tominack	LB
59	Mike Stirling	FB
60	Buzzy Stokes	C
61	Don Montgomery	DB
62	*Don Buckner	OG
63	Tim Beans	DT
64	Bob Morris	OG
65	Joe Regolis	DT
66	Chris Bank	OG
67	Joe Chandler	OG
68	Jimmy Johnson	OG
69	John King	OG
70	Danny Dyches	OG
71	Rusty Ganas	DT
73	*Tony Fusaro	OT
74	*Bob Mauro	C
75	Jimmy Poston	DT
76	Dave DeCamilla	OT
77	Rick Hipkins	OT
78	Mack Lee Thorpe	OG
79	John Coleman	OG
80	*Fred Zeigler	FL
81	Bill Duffie	FL
82	**Gene Schwarting	TE
84	*Dave Lucas	DE
85	Randy Williams	LB
86	Jimmy Pope	DE
87	Doug Hamrick	TE
88	*Johnny Gregory	SE
89	*Lynn Hodge	OT
90	Eddie Bolton	SE
91	Don Brant	DE
92	Gary Scott	SE

*—Denotes number of letters earned.

THE USC ATHLETIC HALL OF FAME

CLARY

DANIEL

TOMPKINS

VON KOLNITZ

WADIAK

Five all-time greats in the athletic history of the University of South Carolina were formally inducted into the University's Athletic Hall of Fame last fall during halftime of the football game with Maryland.

They were the first members elected to the hall of fame begun by the USC Association of Lettermen, an organization of former varsity athletes. Hall of Fame charter members include Earl Clary, Sam Daniel, Freddie Tompkins, Alfred H. (Fritz) Von Kolnitz, and Steve Wadiak.

Clary, the celebrated "Gaffney Ghost," was one of the state's all-time great athletes and was recently also inducted into the South Carolina Hall of Fame sponsored by the state association of sportswriters. Clary carried the football 35 times against Clemson in 1933, a record tied last year by Warren Muir against North Carolina, and is tied with five others for most touchdowns in a season with eight.

Wadiak, the Gamecocks' all-time rushing champion with 2,878 yards, gained 256 yards against Clemson in 1950, 998 for that season, and holds innumerable other school records. He, also, is a member of the state Hall of Fame.

Von Kolnitz was a great Gamecock back in 1911 and '12, and catcher on the baseball team. He later caught for the Cincinnati Reds, and was a veteran of two world wars.

Tompkins was an All-America basketball player for the Gamecocks during the golden years of 1932-34, when South Carolina won 35 games and lost only three.

Daniel was South Carolina Intercollegiate Tennis Champion, 1935-37; number one ranked Carolinas' Junior Davis Cup player, 1934-37; and long one of the top amateur tennis players in the South.

Of the five charter members of the Gamecock Hall of Fame, only Clary and Daniel are still alive.

54

GAMECOCKS IN PROFESSIONAL FOOTBALL

GAMBRELL

REEVES

WILBURN

The names of former Gamecock stars dot the rosters of professional teams in both the National and the American football leagues, and are among the brightest stars among the pros.

Dan Reeves, who holds career total offense and passing records set while a Gamecock quarterback, is now one of the top running backs in the NFL and has helped spark the Dallas Cowboys to division championships the past two years. Beginning his fourth season with the Cowboys, Reeves tied for the NFL lead in touchdowns scored in 1966 and is perhaps the league's best at throwing the halfback running pass. He has been among the league's rushing and receiving leaders the past two seasons.

Alex Hawkins, a former ACC Player of the Year, is beginning his ninth year in the NFL. He spent the first seven with the Baltimore Colts, gaining fame as the Colt's "Captain Who," was traded to the Atlanta Falcons for one season, and returned to the Colts last year. A collegiate halfback, most of his pro career has been spent as a flanker or split end.

Billy Gambrell, also a former ACC Player of the Year, is starting his sixth season as a flanker for the St. Louis Cardinals. One of the smallest players in pro football, Billy is a favorite of fans throughout the NFL.

J. R. Wilburn, holder of Gamecock single season and career passing records, is the top pass receiver for the Pittsburgh Steelers, catching 58 last year in his second season as a pro.

Bobby Bryant, ACC Athlete of the Year in 1966-67 after a brilliant Carolina career in football and baseball, signed with the Minnesota Vikings but spent most of his first year on the injured list. He's expected to break into the Vikings' defensive secondary this fall.

In the AFL, linebacker Tommy Addison recently retired after a long career during which he was defensive captain of the Boston Patriots, president of the AFL Players Association, and a charter member of the league. Sam DeLuca, a Jacobs Blocking Trophy winner at Carolina, is an 11-year veteran offensive guard with the New York Jets. He missed part of last season with a knee injury, but is expected back this fall.

Mike Fair, last year's most valuable player with the Gamecocks, was signed as a quarterback by the San Diego Chargers, and linebacker Bob Cole signed with the Pittsburgh Steelers. Ronnie Lamb, former Gamecock halfback who played the past two seasons with Montreal in the Continental League, was sold at the end of the 1967 season to the Denver Broncos.

Several other former Gamecocks are presently active in the Continental League.

55

310

KING DIXON HEAD COACH AT QUANTICO

GAMECOCK HALFBACK

MARINE MAJOR

Maj. King Dixon, a former Gamecock halfback great and a career officer in the Marine Corps, will serve as head football coach at the Marine base at Quantico, Va., this fall.

Dixon, who last year completed a year's duty as a company commander in Viet Nam, was graduated with honors from the University of South Carolina in 1959. He played three seasons as a Gamecock halfback under Coach Warren. Giese and ranks fifth among all-time Gamecock rushers with 1,250 yards. His 98 yard return of the opening kickoff against Texas in 1957 still stands as a school record and started the Gamecocks toward a 27-21 upset of the Longhorns' Sugar Bowl team.

A native of Laurens, S. C., where he was a high school All-America, Dixon played several years of service football after becoming a Marine officer. In 1959, the Washington Touchdown Club named him Armed Forces Athlete of the Year and the Football Officials' Assn. of Washington named him best service back in the District of Columbia area.

Dixon is married to the former Augusta Mason, also a University of South Carolina graduate, and they have three sons.

Several other former South Carolina players are active in collegiate coaching ranks, the most prominent being Harold (Bo) Hagan, entering his second season as head coach and director of athletics at Rice University. A native of Savannah, Ga., Hagan was a star quarterback under coach Rex Enright, 1947-50.

Former defensive back Lide Huggins is an assistant at Texas A. & M., and was with the Aggies in the Cotton Bowl last season. Former quarterback Buddy Bennett is an assistant at East Tennessee, and Gene Alexander is at Wofford where he is a football assistant and head basketball coach. In basketball, Dwane Morrison is at Georgia Tech and Bud Cronin at Oklahoma, and Walt Cormack is head track coach at Virginia Military Institute.

THE ROOST

Gamecock student-athletes this fall will move into a beautiful new five-building dormitory-dining hall complex at the Rex Enright Athletic Center.

"The Roost," under construction since last winter, is scheduled for completion by fall. It will house 166 student athletes and is being built at a cost of approximately $1 million as the latest addition in the University's rapid expansion.

Located behind and next to the baseball diamond at the north end of the Rex Enright Athletic Center, The Roost will consist of three one-story buildings on the upper level of a terrace, and two buildings of two stories each on a lower level just behind home plate of the baseball field.

The one-story buildings will include a dining hall, reception lobby, game and study rooms, quarters for the building manager, guest rooms and one building of rooms for student-athletes. The two-story buildings will contain bedrooms for student-athletes.

The buildings will be connected by breezeways, and the complex will feature concrete steps from the ground level of the buildings down to the baseball diamond which can be used as stands for spectators during baseball games.

When completed, The Roost will be one of the best equipped and most modern athletic dormitories anywhere.

57

311

FIGHTING GAMECOCKS ON THE AIR

BOB FULTON

WALTER COPELAND

Award winning sportscaster Bob Fulton will be at the play-by-play microphone of the Gamecock Football Network for the 14th season this fall.

Fulton returned to the Gamecock Football Network last year after a two-year absence during which he broadcast Georgia Tech games. Before going to the Yellow Jackets, Fulton broadcast Gamecock football for 12 years. He continued to do Gamecock basketball play-by-play during his two-year absence from football.

Fulton returned to Gamecock football under a long term agreement with the athletic department and the Gamecock Network. Formerly associated with radio station WCOS in Columbia, Fulton now does free lance promotion and broadcast work. He has been voted South Carolina Sportscaster of the Year six of the past seven years.

Fulton did coast-to-coast major league baseball play-by-play on the Mutual Network's "Game of the Day" in 1954, broadcast Southwest Conference games while working out of Little Rock, Ark., for several years, and was play-by-play announcer several times for the Bluebonnet Bowl, Sun Bowl and Gator Bowl football games.

Walter Copeland, network coordinator, will also serve as color announcer for the fourth straight season. Homer Fesperman will continue to handle engineering as technical director of the Gamecock Network.

Copeland is a 1960 graduate of the University of South Carolina's School of Journalism and has been in broadcasting since 1955. He lives in Hartsville, S. C. Fesperman owns and operates Richland Custom Recordings in Columbia and is a veteran in the audio engineering field. He has been technical director of the Gamecock Network for nine years.

The size of the Gamecock Network is expected to range from 25 to 45 radio stations per game this fall and will encompass every area of South Carolina plus markets in North Carolina and Georgia, and in some cases other states.

Radio station executives desiring information on the Gamecock Network may contact Walter Copeland at Box 581, Hartsville, S. C. 29550.

The Fighting Gamecocks are also seen on television throughout South Carolina each Sunday during the fall. Highlights of the previous day's game plus previews of the upcoming opponent with commentary by Coach Paul Dietzel and Russ Benedict, sports director of Columbia's WIS-TV feature "Carolina Football" on a statewide network. Coach Dietzel also has a regular program on WIS Radio.

60

FUTURE GAMECOCK SCHEDULES

Collegiate football schedules must be made many years in advance and South Carolina is no exception to this rule. Most of the scheduling for Fighting Gamecock teams of the future has been done through the 1970's.

Gamecock schedules, traditionally among the toughest anywhere, don't get any easier, as the list of opponents for the next eight years will attest. Looking a little further into the future, the list of opponents includes a three-year series with Texas, scheduled for 1977-78-79, in addition to the below listed dates with Tennessee, Mississippi, Baylor, Houston, Florida State, Georgia and other intersectional opponents in addition to the traditional Atlantic Coast Conference foes.

1969
Sept. 20 — at Duke
Sept. 27 — North Carolina
Oct. 4 — at Georgia
Oct. 11 — N. C. State
Oct. 18 — at Virginia Tech
Oct. 25 — Maryland
Nov. 1 — at Florida State
Nov. 8 — at Tennessee
Nov. 15 — at Wake Forest
Nov. 22 — Clemson

1970
Sept. 19 — Wake Forest
Sept. 26 — at N. C. State
Oct. 3 — Virginia Tech
Oct. 10 — at North Carolina
Oct. 17 — at Maryland
Oct. 24 — Florida State
Oct. 31 — at Georgia
Nov. 7 — Tennessee
Nov. 14 — Duke
Nov. 21 — at Clemson

1971
Sept. 18 — at Duke
Sept. 25 — N. C. State
Oct. 2 — at Memphis State
Oct. 9 — Virginia
Oct. 16 — Maryland
Oct. 23 — at Florida State
Oct. 30 — Georgia
Nov. 6 — at Tennessee
Nov. 20 — at Wake Forest
Nov. 27 — Clemson

1972
Sept. 16 — at Virginia
Sept. 30 — Memphis State
Oct. 7 — North Carolina
Oct. 14 — at Maryland
Oct. 21 — Miami (Ohio)
Oct. 28 — at N. C. State
Nov. 4 — Wake Forest
Nov. 11 — at Virginia Tech
Nov. 18 — Florida State
Nov. 25 — at Clemson

1973
Sept. 22 — at Houston
Sept. 29 — Miami (Ohio)
Oct. 6 — at Virginia Tech
Oct. 13 — at Wake Forest
Oct. 20 — Ohio U.
Oct. 27 — at North Carolina
Nov. 3 — N. C. State
Nov. 10 — Maryland
Nov. 17 — at Florida State

1974
Sept. 21 — Duke
Sept. 28 — at Georgia
Oct. 5 — Houston
Oct. 12 — Virginia Tech
Oct. 19 — at Mississippi
Oct. 26 — North Carolina
Nov. 2 — at N. C. State
Nov. 9 — at Maryland
Nov. 16 — Wake Forest
Nov. 23 — at Clemson

1975
Sept. 20 — at Duke
Sept. 27 — Georgia
Oct. 4 — Baylor
Oct. 11 — Virginia
Oct. 18 — at Mississippi
Oct. 25 — at North Carolina
Nov. 1 — N. C. State
Nov. 8 — Maryland
Nov. 15 — at Wake Forest
Nov. 22 — Clemson

1976
Sept. 18 — Duke
Sept. 25 — at Georgia
Oct. 2 — at Baylor
Oct. 9 — Virginia
Oct. 16 — Mississippi
Oct. 23 — North Carolina
Oct. 30 — at N. C. State
Nov. 6 — at Maryland
Nov. 13 — Wake Forest
Nov. 20 — Clemson

61

A YEAR FOR MATURING

The 1968 football season could be classified as a year of maturing for Carolina's young Gamecocks.

Although the Gamecocks had leaped from a 1-9 record in 1966 to 5-5 in 1967, the 1968 squad was relatively inexperienced with key positions manned by sophomores fresh from the unbeaten 1967 Biddies. It was obvious the Gamecocks would have to grow up in a hurry if they were to equal or improve on the 1967 record.

With no experienced quarterback and a great fullback in junior Warren Muir, Carolina started out as primarily a running team built around Muir's talents for running over enemy tacklers. A severe back injury in the third game of the season sidelined him for a month, however. Meanwhile, Tommy Suggs was emerging as a highly talented scrambler at quarterback who could move the Gamecocks offensively with his rollouts and quick passes to such fine receivers as Fred Zeigler, Johnny Gregory, Rudy Holloman and others.

TRANSITION

Thus, the Gamecocks were transformed into primarily a passing team, winding up with 2,104 yards through the air to only 1,457 on the ground. Suggs virtually rewrote the school passing records while Muir—who regained his earlier form late in the season—saw his rushing total drop from 805 yards in 1967 to 460 in 68. Holloman was the squad's top rusher with 530 yards.

While the transition was underway and the Gamecocks were going through the "growing pains" of gaining experience, the records showed only one win and five defeats after six games. Over the last month of the season, however, the Gamecocks won three of four and—with 30 lettermen, mostly juniors, returning — face 1969 with optimism.

Carolina ran into an ambush in the season opener at Duke. The Blue Devils had lost several players in a cribbing scandal and were generally crying the blues. Prognosticators relegated the Blue Devils to the ACC ash heap in pre-season forecasts. However, a brilliant young

quarterback named Leo Hart who was destined to break ACC total offense records, stung the Gamecocks early with his passing. Duke grabbed a 14-0 first period lead. Although Carolina scored on Muir's touchdown and piled up 410 yards passing and rushing, Duke emerged the winner, 14-7.

MODERN MIRACLE

The next week at Chapel Hill saw one of the modern miracles of football. For three periods the Gamecocks did nothing right. Even when Don Bailey returned a kickoff 90 yards to the Tar Heel 10, Carolina couldn't score and was a badly beaten team, trailing 27-3, as the fourth period began. Suddenly, however, a complete turnabout occurred. Suggs passed to Zeigler for a touchdown and on the following kickoff the Tar Heels fumbled, Pat Watson recovering. Carolina scored in two plays on Muir's run, Suggs went for two and the score suddenly was 27-17. North Carolina had to punt and the Gamecocks stormed 66 yards with Muir smashing over again with Suggs throwing a two-point pass to Holloman and the score changed to 27-25. A poor Tar Heel punt gave Carolina the ball on the Gamecock 39 with eight minutes to play. A 37-yard pass from Randy Yoakum to Eddie Bolton featured a 61-yard drive climaxed when Suggs scored from the four. The Gamecocks scored 29 points in 10 minutes and one second to win 32-27 in what had to be one of the greatest comebacks in history.

DISASTER

Lightning struck the Georgia Bulldogs early in Carolina Stadium the following week but disaster struck the Gamecocks when Muir was injured and Georgia came back to win a thriller 21-20. Lynn Hodge returned an interception for a TD and Roy Don Reeves' interception set up Muir's TD to give the Gamecocks a 14-0 first period lead. Carolina, after Georgia scored, was driving goalward when Muir was injured on a 28-yard run to the Bulldog seven-yard line. Carolina settled for a field goal to lead 20-7 at halftime but without their big fullback, the Gamecocks couldn't move and finally lost by a single point.

TIGERS TAMED

Without Zeigler, coach Paul Dietzel did some personnel switching for the season finale at Clemson. Rudy Holloman moved from tailback to flanker with Muir going to tailback and Benny Galloway the starter at fullback. The strategy worked as Holloman caught seven passes, Muir caught four and rushed 84 yards, Galloway caught two and threw a pass to Suggs. The Gamecocks made 23 first downs to

Perhaps still shaken by the loss of Muir, the Gamecocks were soundly thrashed by N. C. State at Raleigh, 36-12, and lost a heart-brecker in the rain and mud at Maryland, 21-19. The Terrapins' winning touchdown came on a freak interception of a Suggs pass attempt that was deflected into a Maryland linebacker's hand and returned for a TD.

Suggs threw for an ACC record 324 yards in Carolina Stadium against Florida State, but the Gamecocks couldn't do anything with the Seminoles' great receiver, Ron Sellers, who caught 16 passes for three TDs and FSU won a wild 35-28 decision.

Despite playing good football in all but the N. C. State game, the Gamecocks found themselves 1-5 with four games to go.

WORM TURNS

The worm turned at Charlottesville, however, as Suggs threw an ACC record five TD passes, Fred Zeigler caught 12 for 199 yards and three TDs, and the Gamecocks thrashed the Cavaliers 49-28.

Playing in the rain for the third time against Virginia Tech in Carolina Stadium, the Gamecocks were thoroughly manhandled by the Gobblers, losing a 17-6 decision. Muir, back from the injury list, caught a Suggs pass for the only Gamecock TD, and rushed 81 yards but Carolina lost all-time leading pass receiver Zeigler with a broken collarbone.

Playing in the rain for the third time against as he threw four in the first half against Wake Forest in the rain at Winston-Salem. Johnny Gregory caught three of them and Pat Watson intercepted an ACC record four passes as the Gamecocks won, 34-21.

Suggs made it 11 TD passes in three weeks

Clemson's six, gained 400 yards to the Tigers' 156, but it remained for the defense to get the job done as far as winning was concerned. Safetyman Tyler Hellams prevented a 100-yard return of the opening kickoff with a brilliant tackle, deflected a sure TD pass, intercepted two passes and scored the game's only touchdown with a 73-yard punt return as the Gamecocks upset the Tigers 7-3 before the largest crowd ever for an Atlantic Coast Conference game.

A season that was a disaster after six games turned into a respectable showing under the circumstances and laid the groundwork for further improvement in 1969.

FINAL 1968 VARSITY FOOTBALL STATISTICS

(Record: 4-6; ACC: 4-3)

TEAM	USC	OPP.
First downs rushing	65	106
First downs passing	107	70
First downs penalties	14	14
TOTAL FIRST DOWNS	186	190
Net yards rushing	1457	1883
Number of rushes	445	566
Game rushing avg.	145.7	188.3
Passing yardage	2104	1489
Game passing avg.	210.4	148.9
TOTAL OFFENSE	3561	3372
Passes attempted	296	224
Passes completed	150	105
Passes intercepted by	21	19
Number of punts	65	51
Yards punted	2434	2024
Punts had blocked	0	1
Punting avg.	37.4	39.8
Return yardage	456	561
Fumbles lost	11	17
Yards penalized	549	592

SCORING	TD	PAT-K	PAT-RP	FG	SAFETY	TP
*Zeigler	6	0-0	0-0	0-0	0	36
*Muir	6	0-0	0-0	0-0	0	36
*DuPre	0	17-19	0-1	4-11	0	29
Galloway	4	0-0	0-0	0-0	0	24
Gregory	4	0-0	0-0	0-0	0	24
*Suggs	3	0-0	2-4	0-0	0	22
*Hollomon	1	0-0	1-1	0-0	0	8
*Hodge	1	0-0	0-0	0-0	0	6
Bolton	1	0-0	0-0	0-0	0	6
*Yackum	1	0-0	0-0	0-0	0	6
Hamrick	1	0-0	0-0	0-0	0	6
*Hellams	1	0-0	0-0	0-0	0	6
Genoble	0	2-2	0-0	1-3	0	5
TOTALS	29	19-21	3-8	5-14	1	214
OPP.	29	26-28	1-1	6-9	1	223

PUNT RET.	NO.	YDS.	AVG.	TD
*Hellams	24	214	8.9	1
Reeves	2	19	9.5	0
*Watson	2	8	4.0	0

KO RET.	NO.	YDS.	AVG.	TD
*Bailey	18	425	23.6	0
*Watson	11	145	13.2	0
Medlin	4	54	13.5	0
*Hellams	3	43	14.3	0
Reeves	1	23	23.0	0
Orrel	1	21	21.0	0
*Chavous	1	9	9.0	0
Hodge	1	5	5.0	0

RESULTS & ATTENDANCE

Duke	7	14	42,234
North Carolina	32	27	28,000
Georgia	20	21	42,808
N. C. State	12	36	33,400
Maryland	19	21	28,200
Florida State	28	35	42,038
Virginia	49	28	25,600
Wake Forest	21	28	16,000
Virginia Tech	17	21	40,137
Clemson	7	3	53,247

1968 SEASON SUPERLATIVES GAMECOCKS

LONGEST RUN FROM SCRIMMAGE:
Warren Muir vs. Duke, 34 yds.

LONGEST PASS COMPLETION:
Tommy Suggs—Benny Galloway vs. Virginia, 62 yds. (TD).

LONGEST PUNT:
Billy Parker vs. N. C. State, 62 yds.

LONGEST PUNT RETURN:
Tyler Hellams vs. Clemson, 73 yds. (TD).

LONGEST KICKOFF RETURN:
Don Bailey vs. North Carolina, 90 yds.

LONGEST INTERCEPTION RETURN:
Roy Don Reeves vs. Georgia, 54 yds.

LONGEST FIELD GOAL:
Billy DuPre vs. Georgia, 42 yds.

OPPONENTS

LONGEST RUN FROM SCRIMMAGE:
Billy Lovett, Maryland, 62 yds.

LONGEST PASS COMPLETION:
Gene Arnett—Frank Quayle, Virginia, 67 yds.

LONGEST PUNT:
Greg Fries, Maryland, 72 yds.

LONGEST PUNT RETURN:
Jack Whitley, N. C. State, 86 yds. (TD).

LONGEST KICKOFF RETURN:
Jack Anderson, Clemson, 72 yds.

LONGEST INTERCEPTION RETURN:
Steve Gildea, Florida State, 48 yds.

LONGEST FIELD GOAL:
Don Hartig, North Carolina, 45 yds.

OPPONENTS' KICKS BLOCKED (Punts, PATS, FG): *Hel-lams 2; Reeves 1.

RUSHING

	NO.	YDS.	AVG.	TD
*Holloman	111	530	4.8	1
*Muir	112	460	4.1	5
Galloway	76	251	3.3	2
Suggs	71	114	1.6	3
*Walkup	32	94	2.9	0
*Trevillian	12	27	2.3	0
*Hunter	1	10	10.0	0
*Miranda	3	9	3.0	0
*Buckner	6	9	1.5	0
*Yockum	21	—47	—2.2	1
TOTALS	445	1457	3.3	12
OPP.	566	1883	3.3	16

PASSING

	ATT.	COMP.	INT.	PCT.	YDS.	TD
*Suggs	207	110	12	.531	1544	13
*Yockum	88	39	7	.443	540	2
Galloway	1	1	0	1.000	20	0
TOTALS	296	150	19	.507	2104	15
OPP.	224	105	21	.469	1489	11

TOTAL OFFENSE

	RUSH	PASS	TOTAL
*Suggs	114	1544	1658
*Yockum	—47	540	493
Galloway	251	20	271
(Others same as rushing)			

RECEIVING

	NO.	YDS.	AVG.	TD
*Zeigler	59	848	14.2	6
Gregory	20	268	13.4	4
*Holloman	20	238	11.9	0
Galloway	16	266	16.6	2
*Hamrick	11	155	14.1	1
*Muir	11	115	10.5	1
*Bolton	7	165	23.6	1
Schwarting	4	29	7.3	0
*Suggs	1	20	20.0	0
*Trevillian	1	0	0.0	0

INTERCEPTION RETS.

	NO.	YDS.	TD
*Watson	7	63	0
*Hellams	6	11	0
Reeves	3	72	0
*Usher	2	15	0
*Hodge	1	22	0
*Padgett	1	20	0
*Lucas	1	20	0

PUNTING

	NO.	YDS.	AVG.	BLKD.
*Parker	65	2434	37.4	0

DEFENSE

	TACKLES	ASSISTS	FUMBLES CAUSED	FUMBLES RECOVERED
*Usher	86	45	3	0
*Grant	67	33	1	0
*Hellams	62	22	1	0
Bica	56	24	0	1
Orrel	49	23	3	0
*Lucas	42	14	0	0
*Ganas	38	18	1	0
*Padgett	33	15	1	0
*Watson	30	17	4	0
Bunch	27	16	0	0
*Hodge	26	8	2	0
Reeves	22	11	2	0
*Pope	20	10	0	0
*Poston	19	6	0	0
Coleman	15	4	0	0
Medlin	14	2	0	0
*Tharpe	13	9	0	1
*Bailey	7	5	0	0
*McCarthy	3	4	0	0
*Wingard	3	3	0	0
*Chavous	2	0	0	0
Stokes	1	0	1	0
Thomas	0	1	0	0
*Buckner	0	0	0	2

* — Eligible to return in 1969.

Coach Paul Dietzel presents 1968 Most Valuable Player Trophy to Center Bob Mauro at annual Gamecock football banquet.

Senior FRED ZEIGLER

Split End　　　　　　Reevesville
Height: 5-10　Weight: 183　Birth Date: 5/19/47

Full name: Frederick Middleton Zeigler. Two letters. Gamecocks' all-time pass catching champion with one season of eligibility remaining. Caught 59 last year for 848 yards and six TDs. Broke collarbone in ninth game or totals would have been higher. Career totals 94 catches for 1,218 yds. All-ACC in '68. Nickname: "Onassis" and is squad's jokester. Came to Carolina without scholarship and after redshirt year not only made squad but led ACC in receiving. Played split end in 1967, moved to flanker for '68, and back to split end for senior season. Set one game record with 12 catches for 199 yds. against Virginia. Has great hands, deceptive speed and moves. Attended Carlisle Military Academy at Bamberg where his coach was Bob Jenkins. Business Administration major with Law School plans. Born in Dallas, Texas. Episcopalian. Single.

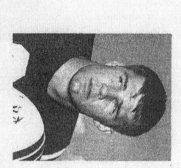

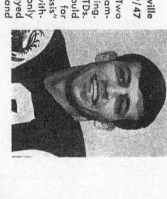

80

36

Senior WARREN MUIR

Fullback　　　　　　Fitchburg, Mass.
Height: 5-10　Weight: 197　Birth Date: 8/16/47

Full name: Warren Holmes Muir. Two letters. All-ACC and Detroit Sports Extra All-America in 1967 when he rushed 805 yds. Back injury in Georgia game sidelined him a month last year but he still managed 460 yards, scored six TDs, caught 11 passes. Already ranks as Gamecocks' fifth best career rusher with one year of eligibility to go. Called "the best inside runner in collegiate football" by Coach Paul Dietzel and a top All-America candidate. Originally enrolled at U. S. Military Academy but withdrew to marry high school sweetheart and transferred to Carolina. The father of two small sons. Injuries limited him to 136 minutes playing time last year compared to 215 in 1967. Stocky with tremendously powerful legs and exceptional balance; quick starter with good speed. Attended Fitchburg High where his coach was Marco Landon. Civil Engineering major. Catholic.

Junior TOMMY SUGGS

Height: 5-9 Weight: 180 Birth Date: 6/9/49 Lamar

Quarterback

Full name: Thomas Ellison Suggs. One letter. Broke virtually all school passing and total offense records as soph. Completed 110 of 207 for 1,544 yds. and 13 TDs, all records. Set ACC record with five TD passes against Virginia. Also rushed 114 yds. for school record total offense of 1,658 yds. Threw 11 TD passes in three-game span. His 324 yds. passing vs. Florida State was another ACC record. Lacks the height desired in QBs but is exceptional scrambler with strong, accurate arm. Scored three TDs and two two-point conversions himself and caught one pass. Born in Florence. Attended Lamar High where his coach was John Socha. Business Administration major. One of leaders in USC FCA chapter. Methodist. Single.

12

24

Senior RUDY HOLLOMAN

Height: 5-10 Weight: 172 Birth Date: 8/1/47 Hartsville

Tailback

Full name: Rudy Pearson Holloman. Two letters. Led Gamecocks in rushing last year with 530 yds. and two-year total is 608 yds. Caught 20 passes last year, nine in '67. Played flanker in Clemson game due to injuries to other personnel and caught seven passes. Had spectacular TD run against Virginia. Played 205 minutes last year, starting every game, and 149 minutes as soph. A fine little athlete who gives Gamecocks a break-away threat. Attended Hartsville High where his coach was Billy Seigler. Business Administration major. Baptist. Married.

Senior TONY FUSARO

Offensive Tackle   Huntington, N. Y.

Height: 6-2   **Weight: 238**   **Birth Date: 1/23/47**

Full name: Anthony John Fusaro (pronounced foo-SAHR-o). Two letters. Starter since midway through sophomore season. Played 257 minutes last year, 152 in 1967. One of the best blocking interior linemen in ACC. One of squad's leaders. Moved to guard for season finale against Clemson last year due to injuries to other personnel and did fine job, contributing to offense that gained 400 yards. Attended Huntington High where his coach was Joe Lucey. Physical Education major with coaching plans . . . but hopes for pro football career first. Catholic. Married.

73

11

Junior TYLER HELLAMS

Defensive Back   Greenwood

Height: 5-11   **Weight: 158**   **Birth Date: 12/7/48**

Full name: John Tyler Hellams. One letter. Starting safety as soph and led squad in time played with 298 minutes. Made 84 tackles—62 individual, 22 assists—caused one fumble, recovered one. Returned 24 punts 214 yds. including 73 yd. scoring return against Clemson in 7-3 victory. Intercepted six passes, prevented 100 yd. KO return in Clemson game with clutch tackle. Considered by Coach Paul Dietzel the best safetyman in ACC. Also a track star who has lettered twice as hurdler, long jumper, triple jumper. Born at Laurens. Attended Greenwood High where his coach was J. W. (Pinky) Babb. Accounting major. Protestant. Single.

21

318

Senior PAT WATSON

Defensive Back

Height: 5-11 Weight: 152 Birth Date: 8/28/48

Myrtle Beach

Full name: Patrick Earl Watson. Two letters. Nickname: "Rat." Cocky little scrapper who has been two-year starter at right halfback in secondary. Led ACC in interceptions last year with seven, including conference record four in Wake Forest game. Played 269 minutes last year, 303 in '67. Made 47 tackles—30 individual, 17 assists—last year caused one fumble, recovered four, including two clutch recoveries in Clemson game. President of senior class and past president of junior class. Had TD on punt return in '67. Born in Conway. Attended Myrtle Beach High where his coach was Danny Brabham. Physical Education major. Protestant. Single.

22

15

33

Junior AL USHER

Linebacker

Height: 5-10 Weight: 211 Birth Date: 3/30/49

Pageland

Full name: Alvin Moore Usher, Jr. One letter. Gamecocks' leading tackler in 1968 with 131, including 86 individuals, 45 assists. Caused three fumbles, recovered one, intercepted two passes. Considered by Coach Paul Dietzel the premier linebacker in ACC. Started all 10 games at weakside linebacker in '68 and played 265 minutes. High school fullback and linebacker with frosh in '67, rushing 138 yds. in 35 carries. Born in Lancaster. Attended Pageland High where his coach was Ralph Hamm. Physical Education major. Baptist. Single.

Senior DAVE LUCAS

Defensive End   Bishopville

Height: 6-5   Weight: 189   Birth Date: 5/25/47

Full name: David Henry Lucas. Two letters. Nicknames: "Twiggy," "The Splinter," "The Pencil," "The Blade." Tall, skinny star whose physique earned him nicknames. Excels at pass rush. Played 206 minutes last year, 231 in '67. Made 56 tackles—42 individual, 14 assists—last year. Led squad in fumble recoveries with four, including one for TD sophomore year. Missed spring practice due to shoulder surgery but ready for good senior season. Born in Greensboro, N. C. Attended Bishopville High where his coach was W. C. Smith. International Studies major. Methodist. Single.

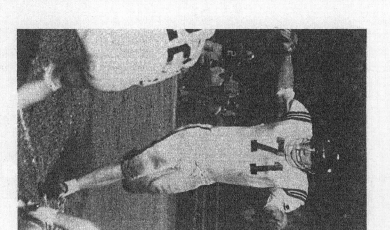

Junior RUSTY GANAS

Defensive Tackle   Waycross, Ga.

Height: 6-5   Weight: 238   Birth Date: 8/12/49

Full name: Russell Lindberg Ganas (pronounced GAY-nus). One letter. Started all 10 games as soph and has size, agility, aggressiveness to rank as one of ACC's top tackles. Second on squad in time played last year with 291 minutes. Made 56 tackles—38 individual, 18 assists—and caused one fumble. Quiet redhead who believes actions speak louder than words. Attended Ware County High at Waycross where his coach was David Shields. Physical Education major. Methodist. Single.

Junior DON BAILEY

Defensive Back   John's Island

Height: 5-11   Weight: 182   Birth Date: 9/12/48

Full name: Donald Alston Bailey. One letter. Played 56 minutes last year as "swing man" at both defensive halfbacks, and kickoff return specialist. His 90-yard return to North Carolina 10 was longest non-scoring kickoff return in ACC history. Returned 18 kickoffs 425 yds., made 12 tackles—seven individual, five assists—recovered one fumble. Starting left halfback in spring drills. Born in Charleston. Attended St. John's High on John's Island where his coach was Robert Biggerstaff. Business Administration major. Methodist. Single.

22

Sophomore BILL BOYTE

Offensive Tackle   Camden

Height: 6-2   Weight: 234   Birth Date: 2/25/50

Full name: William Oscar Boyte III (pronounced BOYT). Defensive tackle with frosh but moved to offense in spring and adjusted well. On second unit pre-season. Was American Legion baseball star. Dad is city policeman. Born in Lancaster. Attended Camden High where his coach was W. L. (Red) Lynch. Business Administration major. Baptist. Single.

60

Split End   EDDIE BOLTON

Junior   Greenwood

Height: 6-3   Weight: 205   Birth Date: 2/28/49

Full name: James Edward Bolton. One letter. Played 85 minutes as soph, caught seven passes for 165 yds., one TD. Also lettered as righthanded pitcher with baseball squad. Big, strong, fast with good hands. Born in Rock Hill. Attended Greenwood High where his coach was J. W. (Pinky) Babb. Physical Education major. Baptist. Married.

90

Offensive Guard   CHRIS BANK

Junior   Joliet, Ill.

Height: 6-1   Weight: 233   Birth Date: 5/23/49

Full name: Christopher Bank. One letter. Starting right guard as soph and played 216 minutes. High school fullback who made transition to interior line in fine fashion. One of squad's better blockers. Born at Aurora, Ill. Attended Joliet Catholic High where his coach was Gordon Gillespie. Physical Education major. Catholic. Single.

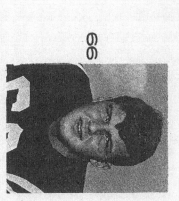

66

24

Senior DON BUCKNER

Offensive Guard   Cleveland, Tenn.
Height: 5-11 Weight: 196 Birth Date: 12/1/47

18

Full name: Donald Edward Buckner. Two letters. Most versatile athlete on Gamecock squad. Has played linebacker, rover, defensive end, offensive halfback, fullback and guard, all well. Played 245 minutes last year as starter, 118 minutes in '67. One of squad's hustlers and leaders. Attended Bradley Central High in Cleveland where his coach was Harold Henslee. Management major. Baptist. Single.

Junior DAVE DeCAMILLA

Offensive Tackle   Hudson Falls, N. Y.
Height: 6-2 Weight: 230 Birth Date: 3/18/48

62

Full name: David Daniel DeCamilla (pronounced de-kuh-MIHL-a). One letter. Starting left tackle last year when he played 262 minutes. Transfer from U. S. Military Academy. Good blocker, steady performer. Born in Glens Falls, N. Y. Attended Hudson Falls Central High where his coach was Robert Ryan. Economics major. Catholic. Single.

Sophomore BO DAVIES

Defensive Back   Gettysburg, Pa.
Height: 6-2 Weight: 181 Birth Date: 2/7/50

29

Full name: Robert Thomas Davies. Star QB in high school, switched to rover back with frosh and made starting varsity in spring practice. Intercepted three passes with frosh, returning one for TD. Was starting guard on frosh basketball team. Dad was Seton Hall basketball star and all-time NBA great. Born in Rochester, N. Y. Attended Gettysburg High where his coach was Don Young. Arts & Sciences major. Lutheran. Single.

Senior ANDY CHAVOUS

Defensive Back   Hepzibah, Ga.
Height: 6-2 Weight: 183 Birth Date: 10/13/48

76

Full name: Andrew Julian Chavous (pronounced CHAY-vuhs). One letter. Earned letter in '67 when he played 83 minutes as split end, halfback and defensive back but saw only nine minutes action in '68. Second team safety on pre-season depth chart. Born in Augusta, Ga., and attended Butler High in Augusta where his coach was Jamie Overton. Pharmacy major. Methodist. Married with one child.

Junior BILLY DuPRE

Placekicker
Columbia
Height: 5-5 Weight: 150 Birth Date: 6/29/49

Full name: William Edward DuPre. One letter. Soccer-style kicker who booted four FGs and 17 of 19 conversion attempts last year to score 29 points. Longest FG was 42 yds., although he booted a 51-yarder in high school. Attended A. C. Flora High where his coach was Jim Pinkerton. Business Administration major. Lutheran. Single.

1

Junior DOUG HAMRICK

Tight End
Cliffside, N. C.
Height: 6-2 Weight: 214 Birth Date: 3/11/49

Full name: Larry Douglas Hamrick. One letter. Played 134 minutes last year, starting about half of season. Caught 11 passes for 155 yds., one TD. Starter in spring practice. Born in Alexander Mills, N. C. Attended Chase High in Forest City, N. C., where his coach was Bobby Bush. Business Management major. Protestant. Single.

87

Junior DANNY DYCHES

Center
Hanahan
Height: 6-5 Weight: 260 Birth Date: 5/5/49

Full name: Daniel Akien Dyches (pronounced DIKES). One letter. Played 65 minutes as offensive tackle as soph. Started Clemson game. Switched to center final week of spring drills and caught on quickly. Biggest Gamecock with exceptional agility and speed for size. Starter on pre-season depth chart. Born in Charleston. Attended Hanahan High where his coach was Jim Hart. Physical Education major. Baptist. Single.

70

Sophomore BILLY FREEMAN

Tight End
Clinton
Height: 6-2 Weight: 198 Birth Date: 5/14/50

Full name: William Troy Freeman. Up from frosh and on second unit after spring drills. Caught four passes with frosh for 88 yards. Born in Laurens. Brother played football at Presbyterian College. Attended Clinton High where his coach was Claude Howe. Physical Education major. Baptist. Single.

83

26

Senior LYNN HODGE

Defensive End   Union

Height: 6-4   Weight: 206   Birth Date: 10/1/47

Full name: Lynn Warren Hodge. Two letters. Starter as soph in '66 but sidelined by broken leg in '67. Came back last year as starter, played 154 minutes. Made 34 tackles—26 individuals, eight assists—recovered two fumbles. Returned interception for TD against Georgia. A fine, veteran football player. Older brother Wilbur played guard for Gamecocks. Attended Union High where his coach was Bob Dunlap. Management major. Methodist. Single.

89

Junior RICK HIPKINS

Offensive Tackle   Boothwyn, Pa.

Height: 6-4   Weight: 254   Birth Date: 8/29/48

Full name: Richard Alan Hipkins. Played 24 minutes as reserve tackle last year but didn't letter. Provides backup experience to make offensive tackle positions strong. One of biggest Gamecocks. Born in Chester, Pa. Attended Chichester High in Boothwyn where his coach was Tony Apichella. Management major. Pentecostal. Single.

77

Sophomore DICK HARRIS

Defensive Back   Pt. Pleasant Beach, N.J.

Height: 6-0   Weight: 156   Birth Date: 5/24/50

Full name: Richard Michael Harris. Speedster up from frosh who dazzled spectators with 227 yds. in kickoff and punt returns in spring game. Also intercepted one pass. Lettered in track as frosh. Brother Bob is former Gamecock football and track letterman. One of brightest sophs. Attended Point Pleasant Beach High where his coach was Al Michigan. Physical Education major. Methodist. Single.

43

Sophomore PAT KOHOUT

Middle Guard   Hampton, Va.

Height: 6-0   Weight: 214   Birth Date: 1/16/50

Full name: Patrick Richard Kohout (pronounced ko-HOOT). Up from frosh where he was starter. Also played fullback in high school. Good prospect. On second unit in spring drills. Born at Pasadena, Texas. Attended Hampton High where his coach was John Palmer. Business Administration major. Catholic. Single.

52

27

Senior GEORGE McCARTHY

Defensive Tackle
Washington, D. C.
Height: 6-2   Weight: 216   Birth Date: 6/8/47

Full name: George Waldo McCarthy. Played briefly in '67 and '68 but has not lettered. Played 32 minutes last year, making seven tackles, three individuals and four assists. Returned interception for TD against Maryland in '67. Brother Brendan starred at Boston College. Born in Needham, Mass. Attended DeMatha High, Hyattsville, Md., where his coach was Morgan Wooten. English major. Catholic. Single.

20

72

Sophomore GLENN MORRIS

Quarterback
Charlotte, N. C.
Height: 6-4   Weight: 193   Birth Date: 6/18/50

Full name: Glenn Franklin Morris. Up from frosh where he was number two QB. Completed 14 of 33 passes for 184 yds., two TDs, rushed impressive 177 yds. for 6.6 avg. and scored one TD. Had fine spring practice and has bright future. Attended North Mecklenburg High, Huntersville, N. C., where his coach was Mack Haynes. Business Administration major. Baptist. Single.

Sophomore JIM MITCHELL

Split End
Greensboro, N. C.
Height: 5-10   Weight: 156   Birth Date: 12/12/49

Full name: James Clayton Mitchell. Mighty mite up from frosh where he caught 23 passes for 339 yds. and five TDs. Also returned 11 punts 152 yds. for one TD to tie for frosh scoring lead with 36 pts. Great moves and hands and expected to be fine receiver. Born in Spartanburg. Attended Grimsley High in Greensboro where his coach was Bob Jamieson. Business Administration major. Baptist. Single.

64

Sophomore KEVIN MOONEY

Middle Guard
Bayport, N. Y.
Height: 6-4   Weight: 218   Birth Date: 7/28/48

Full name: Kevin John Mooney. Knee injury just before season opened made '68 a redshirt year. Big, quick, agile, aggressive and could be a great one. Starter in spring drills. Born in Bethlehem, N. Y. Attended West Islip High at West Islip, N. Y., where his coach was Charles Skipunas. Physical Education major. Catholic. Single.

17

Junior BILL PARKER

Punter   Kershaw
Height: 6-1   Weight: 198   Birth Date: 8/16/49

Full name: William Glenn Parker. One letter. Handled all Gamecock punting as soph, averaging 37.4 on 65 kicks. Should do kicking again and possibly see some action at another position. Born in Camden. Attended Kershaw High where his coach was Bill Few. Education major. Baptist. Single.

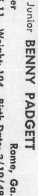

53

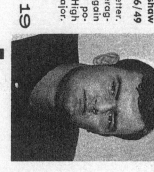

19

Sophomore RICHIE MOYE

Offensive Guard   West Columbia
Height: 6-1   Weight: 200   Birth Date: 11/2/49

Full name: Richard Benjamin Moye. Up from frosh where he was starter. Impressed in spring practice and wound up on second unit. Father played football and participated in track at Presbyterian College. Born in Clinton. Attended Brookland-Cayce High where his coach was Bettis Herlong. History major. Lutheran. Single.

Junior BENNY PADGETT

Linebacker   Rome, Ga.
Height: 5-11   Weight: 194   Birth Date: 3/19/48

Full name: Benjamin Selman Padgett. One letter. Played 153 minutes as soph, starter late in season. Made 48 tackles—33 individual, 15 assists — caused one fumble, intercepted one pass. Starting strong linebacker on pre-season depth chart. Attended West Rome High where his coach was Paul Kennedy. Business Administration major. Baptist. Single.

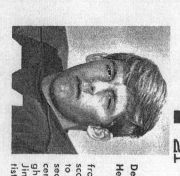

21

Sophomore BOB O'HARRA

Defensive Back   Florence
Height: 6-2   Weight: 182   Birth Date: 8/4/50

Full name: Robert Stone O'Harra. Up from frosh where he played offense, rushing 94 yds., scoring one TD, catching one pass. Switched to defense in spring and listed on pre-season second unit at right halfback. Father starred as center with the Gamecocks. Attended McClenaghan High at Florence where his coach was Jim Wall. Business Administration major. Baptist. Single.

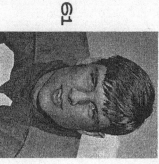

61

29

Junior JIMMY POPE

Defensive End Rock Hill

Height: 6-3 **Weight:** 209 **Birth Date:** 8/20/49

Full name: James Kenneth Pope. One letter. Played 151 minutes as soph and is strong contender at Gamecocks' strongest spot. Made 25 tackles, 19 individuals and six assists. Father is a detective. Attended Rock Hill High where his coach was Tommy Oates. Physical Education major. Presbyterian. Single.

10

86

Junior JIMMY POSTON

Defensive Tackle Canton, N. C.

Height: 6-4 **Weight:** 258 **Birth Date:** 6/2/49

Full name: Jimmy Lee Poston. One letter. Played 159 minutes as soph despite missing couple games with knee injury. Starter last half of season and one of top returnees. Made 30 tackles—20 individual, 10 assists—and recovered one fumble. Born at Waynesville, N. C. Attended Pisgah High at Canton where his coach was Boyd Allen. Physical Education major. Baptist. Single.

Sophomore TOMMY RHODES

Quarterback Chesapeake, Va.

Height: 6-2 **Weight:** 197 **Birth Date:** 12/30/49

Full name: Thomas Wayne Rhodes. Up from frosh where he was top QB with 595 yds. total offense in five games. Rushed 46 yds., completed 33 of 63 passes for 549 yds., five TDs. Good prospect at a position where Gamecocks are strong. Born at Norfolk, Va. Attended Great Bridge High at Chesapeake where his coach was Billy O'Brien. Engineering major. Baptist. Single.

30

75

Sophomore BILLY RAY RICE

Tailback Gaffney

Height: 6-0 **Weight:** 188 **Birth Date:** 11/30/49

Full name: Billy Ray Rice. Up from frosh where he played two games on defense, three on offense, rushing 243 yds. for six TDs, caught one pass. Scored four TDs in one game. Great prospect who should play a great deal as soph. Attended Gaffney High where his coach was Bob Prevatte. Business Administration major. Baptist. Single.

30

Center
Senior   KEN ROSS   Williamston
Height: 6-1   Weight: 200   Birth Date: 1/18/48

26

Full name: James Kenneth Ross. One letter. Played 41 minutes last year, chiefly as specialist snapping ball for punts, FGs and PATs. Only experienced center and will bid for starting job. Born at Pelzer. Attended Palmetto High at Williamston where his coach was Donnie Garrison. Education major. Baptist. Single.

Fullback
Sophomore   TOMMY SIMMONS   Buffalo
Height: 5-10   Weight: 202   Birth Date: 1/16/50

54

Full name: Thomas David Simmons. Leading rusher with unbeaten frosh with 576 yds., 5.4 avg., and four TDs. Caught five passes. Considered a great prospect. Born at Union. Attended Union High where his coach was Bob Dunlap. Physical Education major. Baptist. Married.

Defensive Back
Sophomore   JAKE STONE   Cayce
Height: 6-2   Weight: 178   Birth Date: 2/20/49

55

Full name: James Koy Stone, Jr. Up from frosh where he returned one interception 43 yds. Showed fine progress in spring practice and was second unit rover back at end of drills. Born in Greensboro, N. C. Attended Brookland-Cayce High where his coach was Bettis Herlong. Business Administration major. Lutheran. Single.

Linebacker
Junior   MACK LEE THARPE   Greenwood
Height: 6-1   Weight: 219   Birth Date: 1/3/48

34

Full name: Lee McGowan Tharpe, Jr. One letter. Played 62 minutes last year. Started Clemson game. Gives excellent depth to linebacking spots. Made 22 tackles last year, 13 individual, nine assists. Attended both Greenwood High where his coach was J. W. (Pinky) Babb, and Myers Park High at Charlotte, N. C., where his coach was Gus Purcell. Business Administration major. Methodist. Married with small daughter and son.

31

Junior KEN WALKUP

Flanker
Timmonsville
Height: 5-10   Weight: 189   Birth Date: 7/16/49

Full name: Kenneth Wallace Walkup. One letter. Played 56 minutes as reserve tailback last year, rushing 94 yds. in 32 carries. Switched to flanker in spring and potential starter. Father participated in football and track at Presbyterian College. Attended Timmonsville High where his coach was Bill Pate. Business Administration major. Baptist. Single.

40

Sophomore KEN WHEAT

Offensive Guard
Milledgeville, Ga.
Height: 6-2   Weight: 236   Birth Date: 6/2/50

Full name: Kenneth Ray Wheat. Up from frosh where he played defensive tackle. Shifted to offense in spring drills and showed excellent progress at guard. On second unit at end of spring. Attended Georgia Military College at Milledgeville where his coach was Parnel Rourk. Business Administration major. Christian. Single.

42

Junior TOM TREVILLIAN

Flanker
Hampton, Va.
Height: 6-0   Weight: 196   Birth Date: 6/15/49

Full name: Thomas Rodman Trevillian. Played 26 minutes as reserve fullback last year before being felled by mononucleosis and did not letter. Switched to flanker in spring after brief try at tight end. On second unit at end of spring drills. Born in Lynchburg, Va. Attended Hampton High where his coach was Johnny Palmer. Business Administration major. Baptist. Single.

57

Sophomore STEVE VASGAARD

Center
Winston-Salem, N. C.
Height: 6-3   Weight: 217   Birth Date: 10/30/48

Full name: Steven Milner Vasgaard. Redshirt in '68 while making transition from tight end to center. Was starter in spring drills until knee injury required surgery, casting cloud on '69 status. Born in Natick, Mass. Attended R. J. Reynolds High at Winston-Salem where his coach was Herman Bryson. Business Administration major. Protestant. Single.

78

Junior JOE WINGARD

Brevard, N. C.

Defensive End

Height: 6-4 Weight: 209 Birth Date: 4/1/49

Full name: Joseph Owen Wingard III. One letter. Played 62 minutes as soph, made five tackles, two individual and three assists. Nickname: "Pluto." Big, rawbone, strong boy. Born at Orangeburg, but lived in Waynesboro, Va., during high school and attended Wilson Memorial High at Fishersville, Va., where his coach was Joe Zapotozny. Engineering major. Methodist. Single.

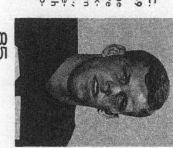

39

85

Junior RANDY YOAKUM

Columbus, O.

Quarterback

Height: 6-1 Weight: 197 Birth Date: 2/5/49

Full name: Randall Craig Yoakum. One letter. Played 60 minutes as soph, completing 39 of 88 passes for 540 yds. and two TDs. Minus 47 yds. rushing gave him 493 yds. total offense. Scored one TD. Attended Eastmoor High in Columbus where his coach was Robert Stuart. History major. Protestant. Single

Sophomore RANDY WILLIAMS

Marietta, Ga.

Linebacker

Height: 5-10 Weight: 205 Birth Date: 2/10/48

Full name: Ransom Eugene Williams. Redshirt in 1968. Made good showing in spring practice and was second unit weakside linebacker at end of spring. Good chance to play some this fall. Born in Rome, Ga. Attended Marietta High where his coach was French Johnson. Education major. Methodist. Single.

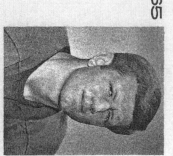

65

16

Sophomore JAKE WRIGHT

Varnville

Defensive Tackle

Height: 6-5 Weight: 219 Birth Date: 10/19/50

Full name: Jacob Maynard Wright. Up from frosh and made good showing in spring practice, winding up on second unit. Was Class A high school lineman of the year. Has put on about 20 pounds and has height to carry much more weight. Born at Fairfax and attended Wade Hampton High at Hampton where his coach was John (Buzzy) McMillan. Business Administration major. Methodist. Single.

33

SOUTH CAROLINA'S 1969 VARSITY ROSTER

No.	NAME	POS.	HGT.	WGT.	AGE	CLASS	HOME TOWN	HIGH SCHOOL COACH
22	*Don Bailey	DB	5-11	182	21	Jr.	Johns Island	R. H. Biggerstaff
45	Lester Ballard	PNT	6-1	188	20	So.	Swannanoa, N. C.	Bill Rucker
66	*Chris Bank	MG	6-1	233	20	Jr.	Joliet, Ill.	Gordon Gillespie
63	Tim Beans	OG	6-0	216	21	So.	Silver Spring, Md.	Steve Kuk
46	Chan Beasley	OG	5-10	175	19	So.	Dublin, Ga.	Don Denning
82	Greg Black	LB	6-4	198	19	So.	Bamberg	Richard Phillips
90	*Eddie Bolton	SE	6-3	205	20	Jr.	Greenwood	Pinky Babb
35	*Candler Boyd	DB	5-9	180	21	Jr.	Hinesville, Ga.	Hokey Jackson
60	Bill Boyte	OT	6-2	234	20	So.	Camden	Red Lynch
91	Don Brant	DE	6-5	190	21	Jr.	Sycamore	Bruce Tate
	Rick Brown	DE	6-3	200	20	So.	Rock Hill	Tommy Oates
62	**Don Buckner	OG	5-11	196	21	Sr.	Cleveland, Tenn.	Harold Henslee
49	Buddy Caldwell	DB	6-0	170	20	So.	Davidson, N. C.	Mack Haynes
27	Gary Campbell	DB	6-0	170	20	So.	Clinton	Claude Howe
29	*Andy Chavous	DB	6-2	183	21	Jr.	Hepzibah, Ga.	Jamie Overton
32	Jimmy Cleckler	FL	6-2	181	20	So.	W. Columbia	Bettis Herlong
47	Greg Crabb	MG	5-11	194	19	So.	Dublin, Ga.	Don Denning
18	Bo Davies	DB	6-2	181	19	So.	Gettysburg, Pa.	Don Young
76	*Dave DeCamilla	OT	6-2	230	20	So.	Hudson Falls, N. Y.	Robert Ryan
81	Bill Duffie	FL	6-4	183	20	Jr.	Columbia	Leonard Jones
1	*Billy DuPre	PK	5-5	150	20	Jr.	Hanahan	Jim Hart
70	*Danny Dyches	C	6-5	260	20	Jr.	Clinton	Claude Howe
83	Billy Freeman	TE	6-2	198	19	So.	Huntington, N. Y.	Joe Lucey
73	*Tony Fusaro	OT	6-2	238	21	Sr.	Waycross, Ga.	David Shields
71	*Rusty Ganas	DT	6-5	230	20	Jr.	Elkin, N. C.	John Charles
88	Deane Hall	DE	6-1	206	19	So.	Cliffside, N. C.	Bobby Bush
87	*Doug Hamrick	TE	6-2	214	20	Jr.	Pt. Pleas. Bch., N. J.	John Kelly
43	Dick Harris	DB	6-0	156	19	Jr.	Greenwood	Pinky Babb
11	*Tyler Hellams	DB	5-10	158	20	Jr.	Boothwyn, Pa.	Elmer Davis
77	Rick Hipkins	OT	6-4	254	20	Jr.	Union	Bobby Dunlap
89	**Lynn Hodge	DE	6-4	205	22	Sr.	Hartsville	Billy Seigler
24	**Rudy Holloman	TB	5-10	172	21	Sr.	Orangeburg	Jack Miller
58	Steve Holstad	OG	5-10	205	20	So.	Myrtle Beach	Charlie Floyd
59	Phil Hudson	OG	6-0	195	19	So.	Charlotte, N. C.	Robert Cummings
23	Charlie Jetton	TB	5-9	177	19	So.	Jacksonville, Fla.	Howell Boney
67	Jimmy Johnson	OG	6-0	190	20	So.	Canton, N. C.	Boyd Allen
28	Carroll Jones	DB	5-11	170	19	So.	Bamberg	Richard Phillips
14	Butch Jones	FL	6-2	179	19	So.	Winston-Salem, N. C.	Herman Bryson
74	Terry Key	DT	6-3	250	19	So.	Lancaster	Dalton Rivers
69	John King	OT	6-4	220	21	Sr.	Hampton, Va.	Johnny Palmer
52	Pat Kohout	MG	6-0	214	19	So.	Atlanta, Ga.	Leonard Jones
	Gary Latham	OG	5-10	190	19	So.	Gaffney	Bob Prevatte
84	**Dave Lucas	DE	6-5	189	22	Sr.	Bishopville	W. C. Smith
68	Kevin Malone	MG	6-0	217	20	So.	Atlanta, Ga.	Don Shea
72	George McCarthy	DT	6-2	216	23	Sr.	Washington, D. C.	Morgan Wooten
31	Bob Miranda	TB	5-11	191	22	Sr.	E. Haven, Conn.	Steve Kuk
20	Jim Mitchell	SE	5-10	156	19	So.	Greensboro, N. C.	Bob Jamieson
	Mike Mobley	LB	6-0	199	20	So.	Heath Springs	Sidney Cauthen
38	Don Montgomery	DB	5-9	181	20	So.	Kingstree	Lindsey Pierce
64	Kevin Mooney	MG	6-4	218	21	So.	Bayport, N. Y.	Charles Skipjuncas
17	Glenn Morris	QB	6-4	193	19	So.	Charlotte, N. C.	Mack Haynes
61	Richie Moye	OG	6-1	200	20	So.	W. Columbia	Bettis Herlong
36	**Warren Muir	FB	5-10	197	22	Sr.	Fitchburg, Mass.	Marco Landon
3	Jimmy Nash	DB	5-11	168	19	So.	Charlotte, N. C.	Robert Cummings
21	Bob O'Hara	DB	6-2	181	19	So.	Florence	Jim Wall
53	*Benny Padgett	LB	5-11	194	21	Jr.	Rome, Ga.	Paul Kenney

Alphabetical Roster (continued)

No.	Name	Pos.	Ht.	Wt.	Age	Class	Hometown
	*Mike Paine	C	5-10	199	20	So.	Valdosta, Ga.
19	*Bill Parker	PNT	6-1	198	20	Jr.	Kershaw
86	*Jimmy Pope	DE	6-3	209	20	Jr.	Rock Hill
75	*Jimmy Poston	DT	6-4	258	20	Jr.	Canton, N. C.
	Joe Regalis	DT	6-1	233	20	Jr.	Tomaqua, Pa.
10	Tommy Rhodes	QB	6-2	197	19	So.	Chesapeake, Va.
30	Billy Ray Rice	TB	6-0	188	19	Sr.	Gaffney
54	*Ken Ross	C	6-1	200	21	So.	Williamston
	Tim Russell	DE	6-2	200	19	So.	Thomasville, N. C.
34	Tommy Simmons	FB	6-1	202	19	So.	Buffalo
41	Byron Sistare	FB	5-11	213	20	So.	W. Columbia
	Clyde Smith	MG	6-0	192	21	Sr.	Church Hill, Tenn.
48	Mike Stirling	TE	5-10	216	20	So.	Charlotte, N. C.
26	Jake Stone	DB	5-9	178	20	Sr.	Coyce
50	Mack Stone	C	6-2	200	19	So.	Greenwood
12	*Tommy Suggs	QB	5-9	180	20	Jr.	Lamar
	Jeff Tape	OT	5-10	219	20	Jr.	Greenwood
55	*Mack Lee Thorpe	LB	6-5	250	19	So.	Aiken
40	Tom Trevillian	FL	6-0	196	20	Jr.	Hampton, Va.
	Pete Unsworth	DT	6-1	230	20	So.	Norfolk, Va.
33	*Al Usher	LB	5-10	211	20	Jr.	Pageland
57	Steve Vasgaard	C	6-3	217	21	So.	Winston-Salem, N. C.
	*Steve Wade	TE	6-3	198	20	So.	Greer
42	*Ken Walkup	FL	5-10	189	20	Jr.	Timmonsville
15	**Pat Watson	DB	5-11	152	21	Sr.	Myrtle Beach
78	Ken Wheat	OG	6-2	236	19	So.	Milledgeville, Ga.
	Eddie Whittington	DT	6-0	208	21	Sr.	Marion
39	Randy Williams	LB	5-10	205	20	So.	Marietta, Ga.
85	*Joe Wingard	DE	6-4	209	20	Jr.	Brevard, N. C.
65	Jake Wright	DT	6-5	219	20	So.	Varnville
16	*Randy Yockum	QB	6-1	197	19	So.	Columbus, Ohio
80	**Fred Zeigler	SE	5-10	183	22	Sr.	Reevesville

* — Denotes number of letters earned. Ages are to nearest birthday prior to end of 1969 season.

NUMERICAL ROSTER

No.	Name
1	*Billy DuPre, PK
3	Jimmy Nash, DB
10	Tommy Rhodes, QB
11	*Tyler Hellams, DB
12	*Tommy Suggs, QB
14	Butch Jones, FL
15	**Pat Watson, DB
16	*Randy Yockum, QB
17	Glenn Morris, QB
18	Bo Davies, DB
19	*Bill Parker, PNT
20	Jim Mitchell, SE
21	*Bob O'Harra, DB
22	*Don Bailey, DB
23	Charlie Jetton, TB
24	**Rudy Holloman, TB
26	Jake Stone, DB
27	Gary Campbell, DB
28	*Carroll Jones, DB
29	*Andy Chavous, DB
30	Billy Ray Rice, TB
31	Bob Miranda, TB
32	*Jimmy Cleckler, FL
33	*Al Usher, LB
34	Tommy Simmons, FB
35	*Candler Boyd, DB
36	**Warren Muir, FB
38	Don Montgomery, DB
39	Randy Williams, LB
40	Tom Trevillian, FL
41	Byron Sistare, FB
42	*Ken Walkup, FL
43	Dick Harris, DB
45	Lester Ballard, PNT
46	Chan Beasley, LB
47	Greg Crabb, MG
48	Mike Stirling, TE
49	Buddy Caldwell, DB
50	Mack Stone, C
52	Pat Kohout, MG
53	*Benny Padgett, MG
54	*Ken Ross, C
55	*Mack Lee Thorpe, LB
57	Steve Vasgaard, C
58	Steve Holstad, OG
59	Phil Hudson, OG
60	Bill Boyte, OT
61	Richie Moye, OG
62	*Don Buckner, OG
63	Tim Beans, OG
64	Kevin Mooney, MG
65	Jake Wright, DT
66	Chris Bank, OG
67	Jimmy Johnson, OG
68	Kevin Malone, MG
69	John King, OT
70	*Danny Dyches, C
71	*Rusty Ganas, DT
72	George McCarthy, DT
73	**Tony Fusaro, OT
74	Terry Key, DT
75	*Jimmy Poston, DT
76	*Dave DeCamilla, OT
77	Rick Hipkins, OT
78	Ken Wheat, OG
80	**Fred Zeigler, SE
81	Bill Duffie, FL
82	Greg Black, SE
83	Billy Freeman, TE
84	**Dave Lucas, DE
85	*Joe Wingard, DE
86	*Jimmy Pope, DE
87	*Doug Hamrick, DE
88	Deane Hall, DE
89	**Lynn Hodge, DE
90	*Eddie Bolton, SE
91	Don Brant, DE

Clyde Smith, MG
Mike Mobley, LB
Mike Paine, C
Pete Unsworth, DT
Eddie Whittington, DT
Rick Brown, DE
Gary Latham, OG
Tim Russell, DE
Jeff Tape, OT
Steve Wade, TE
Steve Lipscomb, OG
Joe Regalis, DT

THE ROOST

"The Roost," a beautiful new five-building dormitory-dining hall complex at the Rex Enright Athletic Center, houses 166 student athletes. It was built at a cost of approximately $1 million and occupied for the first time during the 1968-69 fall semester.

Located adjacent to the USC baseball diamond, The Roost consists of three one-story buildings on the upper level of a terrace, and two buildings of two stories each on a lower level just behind home plate of the baseball field.

The one-story buildings include a dining hall, reception lobby, game and study rooms, quarters for the building manager, guest rooms and one building of rooms for student athletes. The two-story buildings contain bedrooms for student-athletes.

The five buildings are connected by breezeways, and the complex features concrete steps down to the baseball diamond which are utilized as stands for spectators when the Gamecock baseball team is in action.

Mrs. Sue Kurpiewski, affectionately known as "Mrs. K" to all the boys living in The Roost, is dietician in charge of the dining hall and she carefully plans the delicious meals served the Gamecock athletes.

Bob Jubenville, a graduate student, and his wife Karen, are resident managers of The Roost. They maintain an apartment in the complex and are in immediate charge of the facility.

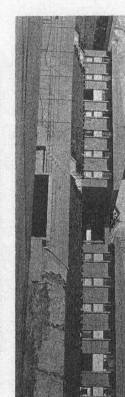

Mrs. Sue Kurpiewski

Bob Jubenville

41

CAROLINA COLISEUM

Carolina Coliseum is not only the largest facility of its kind in the Southeast, but is probably the most versatile building of this type in the United States.

Accommodating 13,500 people for many functions and 12,133 for basketball in the arena area, the Coliseum serves many purposes.

On one day it could be the site of a circus, housing a convention on the next, and being converted into a theater for a broadway musical on the next, concerts, trade shows, ice shows, student assemblies, dances . . . there's no limit to the use of the huge arena section of the giant Coliseum.

By far the most popular use of the arena, however, is for athletic events, particularly basketball, and the Fighting Gamecocks drew 119,999 spectators for 10 home games their first season in the Coliseum. The first event in the huge structure was the Carolina-Auburn basketball game Nov. 30, 1968. Construction was completed during the 1968-69 academic year.

Within the same walls of the multi-million dollar structure are housed the School of Journalism and the College of General Studies, along with faculty and administrative offices. Outside of the arena there is 145,000 square feet of office space in Carolina Coliseum, comparable to that of a 15-story building.

A dozen 10-story buildings could be fitted into the space occupied by the Coliseum. Planners utilized the most modern equipment and features and acoustics and lighting are designed to be ideal for any of the many uses of the facility. Upholstered arm-chair seats afford maximum c o m f o r t for spectators.

The arena floor is made of Tartan, a new synthetic court. Tartan is also easier on the legs of basketball players and reduces the chance of injury, because of its resiliency.

A n u m b e r of a w a y games—both football and basketball—will be piped into the Coliseum via closed c i r c u i t television and projected onto giant screens for the entertainment of Carolina students and fans. Sellout home events, such as this year's football game with Clemson, also will be piped into the Coliseum.

Carolina Coliseum will be the site of the 1970 NCAA Eastern Regional B a s k e t b a l l Tournament next March.

The arena floor is made of Tartan, a new synthetic court. Tartan is also easier on the legs of basketball players and reduces the chance of injury, because of its resiliency.

necessary firmness but is far tougher and longer lasting than wood and requires less maintenance. Circus elephants can tramp on the Tartan floor and hours later a basketball game can be played there without the expense and time involved in moving and assembling a wooden court.

42

334

FIGHTING GAMECOCKS
ON THE AIR

Award-winning sportscaster Bob Fulton will be at the play-by-play microphone of the Gamecock Football Network this fall for the 15th season

Fulton, a native of Philadelphia, has broadcast Carolina football since 1952 except for a two-year absence when he handled play-by-play for Georgia Tech. He did major league baseball on the Mutual Network's "Game of the Day" in 1954, broadcast Southwest Conference games while working out of Little Rock, Ark., and was play-by-play announcer several times for the Bluebonnet Bowl, Sun Bowl, and Gator Bowl games. Fulton has been voted South Carolina Sportscaster of the Year seven times.

He also does Gamecock basketball and when basketball games are televised, handles the audio portion of those telecasts, usually as a "simulcast" with radio.

Homer Fesperman continues to handle engineering as technical director, a position he has held with the network for 10 years. The network will again have its veteran spotters, John and Cliff Terry.

Fesperman owns and operates Richland Custom Recordings in Columbia and is a veteran in the audio engineering field.

The network ranges from 25 to 45 stations, depending upon the opponent and kickoff time, and encompasses every area of South Carolina plus markets in North Carolina, Georgia and other states.

The Fighting Gamecocks are also seen on television throughout South Carolina each Sunday during the fall. Highlights of the previous day's game plus previews of the upcoming opponent with commentary by Coach Paul Dietzel and Russ Benedict, sports director of WIS-TV feature. "Carolina Football," on a statewide network. "Carolina Football" is followed on the same stations by the "Quarterback Show" on which Coach Dietzel answers live questions telephoned in by fans throughout the state. Fulton and Benedict also appear on the "Quarterback Show."

Coach Dietzel also has a regular program on WIS Radio during the season and "Gamecock Report," with sports information director Tom Price is heard five days each week on WIS Radio.

BOB FULTON

CAROLINA STADIUM

Carolina Stadium, where the Fighting Gamecocks play, is located adjacent to the South Carolina state fairgrounds, approximately one mile south of the University's main campus. When built, in 1937, its seating capacity was 17,600. Carolina Stadium has been enlarged several times, the last time in 1959 when it was made into a bowl to raise the seating capacity to 43,212. However, in 1966 field level seats on either side were replaced with armchair type game box seats and this reduced the overall capacity to 42,338.

GAMECOCK TRAVEL PLANS

THE GEORGIA GAME

Depart Columbia Metropolitan Airport Saturday, Oct. 4, 8:30 A.M., aboard two chartered Southern Airways Martin 404s. Arrive Athens, Ga., airport 9:15 A.M. Headquarters, Holiday Inn of Athens. Depart from stadium immediately after game Saturday, Oct. 4, for airport. Depart Athens 5 P.M., arrive Columbia Metropolitan Airport 5:45 P.M.

THE VIRGINIA TECH GAME

Depart Columbia Metropolitan Airport Friday, Oct. 17, 1 P.M., aboard chartered Southern Airways DC-9 Jet. Arrive Roanoke, Va., airport 1:45 P.M. Headquarters, Holiday Inn of Salem, Va. Depart from stadium, Blacksburg, Va., immediately after game Saturday, Oct. 18, for Roanoke airport. Depart Roanoke 5 P.M., arrive Columbia Metropolitan Airport 5:45 P.M.

THE FLORIDA STATE GAME

Depart Columbia Metropolitan Airport Friday, Oct. 31, 1 P.M., aboard chartered Southern Airways DC-9 Jet. Arrive Tallahassee, Fla., airport 1:50 P.M. Headquarters, Holiday Inn of Tallahassee. Depart from stadium immediately after game Saturday, Nov. 1, for airport. Depart Tallahassee 5 P.M., arrive Columbia Metropolitan Airport 5:50 P.M.

THE TENNESSEE GAME

Depart Columbia Metropolitan Airport Friday, Nov. 7, 1 P.M., aboard chartered Southern Airways DC-9 Jet. Arrive Knoxville, Tenn., airport 1:50 P.M. Headquarters, Esquire Inn, Alcoa, Tenn. Depart from stadium immediately after game Saturday, Nov. 8, for airport. Depart Knoxville 5 P.M., arrive Columbia Metropolitan Airport 5:45 P.M.

THE WAKE FOREST GAME

Depart Columbia Metropolitan Airport Saturday, Nov. 15, 8:30 A.M., aboard chartered Southern Airways DC-9 Jet. Arrive Smith Reynolds Airport, Winston-Salem, N. C., 9:05 A.M. Headquarters, Sheraton Motor Inn, Winston-Salem. Depart from stadium immediately after game, Saturday, Nov. 15, for airport. Depart Winston-Salem 5 P.M., arrive Columbia Metropolitan Airport 5:35 P.M.

From The
Gamecock Roost

VOL. 4, No. 5   COLUMBIA, S. C.   SEPTEMBER 25, 1969

TOMMY DOES HIS THING

Quarterback Tommy Suggs cuts between Duke defenders Ernie Jackson (43) and Rich Searl (12) and breaks into the clear on a 48-yard touchdown run, one of many big plays by Suggs in Carolina's 27-20 opening victory. (Photo by Ed Tilley, courtesy The State Record.)

FROM COACH PAUL DIETZEL

CAROLINA 27 — DUKE 20

Game Captain
WARREN MUIR

One Game A Season Does Not Make! But it certainly does help to win that first one. It was really a great victory with lots of heroes. It had many anxious moments for us all. Duke is a fine team with an excellent set of receivers and a superior quarterback, Leo Hart. He really has great poise and talent.

Defensively, we were pleased with our end play. Our two seniors, **Lynn Hodge** of Union and **Dave Lucas** of Bishopville played well with a couple of big plays each, but

we also had good play from **Joe Wingard** of Brevard, N. C., and excellent play by **Jimmy Pope** of Rock Hill. It was that extra effort at crucial times that saved the day. Jimmy Pope threw Hart for three long losses himself. **Rusty Ganas** of Waycross, Ga., played a real good, steady game at right tackle. Senior Co-Captain **Pat Watson** did a great job with our secondary. He was the old man back there. Pat graded 96% which is great, but it is his leadership

Continued on Page Two

Game Captain
PAT WATSON

ONE GAME VARSITY STATISTICS
(Record: 1-0; ACC: 1-0; Home: 1-0; Away: 0-0)

TEAM	USC	OPP
First downs rushing	15	7
First downs passing	6	13
First downs penalties	0	1
TOTAL FIRST DOWNS	21	21
Net yards rushing	339	112
Number of rushes	55	44
Game rushing avg.	339.0	112.0
Passing yardage	107	194
Game passing avg.	107	194
TOTAL OFFENSE	446	306
Passes attempted	16	35
Passes completed	10	20
Intercepted by	0	0
Number of punts	4	5
Yards punted	141	168
Punts had blocked	0	0
Punting avg.	35.3	33.6
Return yardage	9	21
Fumbles lost	1	0
Yards penalized	71	20

RUSHING	NO	YDS	AVG	TD
Holloman	16	113	7.1	1
Suggs	15	98	6.3	1
Rice	6	65	10.8	0
Muir	12	47	3.9	1
Simmons	4	11	2.8	0
Walkup	2	5	2.5	0
TOTALS	55	339	6.2	3
OPPONENTS	44	112	2.5	0

PASSING	ATT	COMP	INT	PCT	YDS	TD
Suggs	16	10	0	.625	107	0
OPPONENTS	35	20	0	.571	194	2

RECEIVING	NO	YDS	AVG	TD
Zeigler	6	73	12.2	0
Muir	2	23	11.5	0
Hamrick	1	7	7.0	0
Holloman	1	4	4.0	0

INTERCEPTION RETURNS
None

PUNT RETURNS	NO	YDS	AVG	TD
Harris	3	9	3.0	0

KICKOFF RETURNS	NO	YDS	AVG	TD
Harris	2	45	22.5	0
Hellams	1	18	18.0	0
Davies	1	8	8.0	0
Bailey	1	4	4.0	0

SCORING	TD	PAT-K	PAT-RP	FG	TP
DuPre	0	3-3	0-0	2-2	9
Holloman	1	0-0	0-0	0-0	6
Suggs	1	0-0	0-0	0-0	6
Muir	1	0-0	0-0	0-0	6
TOTALS	3	3-3	0-0	2-2	27
OPPONENTS	2	2-2	0-0	2-2	20

DEFENSIVE STATISTICS

	TACKLES	ASSISTS	FUMBLES CAUSED	FUMBLES RECOV.
Usher	8	2	0	0
Harris	8	1	0	0
Nash	8	0	0	0
Padgett	6	0	0	0
Davies	4	3	0	0
Ganas	4	2	0	0
Poston	3	2	0	0
Pope	3	0	0	0
Lucas	3	0	0	0
Wingard	3	0	0	0
Kohout	2	0	0	0
Hellams	2	0	0	0
Watson	2	0	0	0
Hodge	1	4	0	0
Tharpe	1	0	0	0
Wright	0	1	0	0

THREE FORMER GREATS ENTER HALL OF FAME

HAMBRIGHT   RUCKS   ROGERS

Three of Carolina's all-time great athletes were inducted into the USC Athletic Hall of Fame during halftime ceremonies at the football season opener with Duke.

Enshrined in the ceremonies co-sponsored by the University administration and the USC Association of Lettermen were former football star Fred Hambright, the late Bill Rogers, a football great, and the late Norman (Scooter) Rucks, a track star.

They join seven other former Gamecock stars and the late coach Rex Enright as members of the Hall of Fame which was begun in 1967.

Rogers played mostly quarterback during one of the most successful eras enjoyed by the Gamecocks against archrival Clemson. His freshman team in 1923 beat the Cubs 34-0, and in Rogers' three varsity seasons, Carolina outscored Clemson 60-0.

Hambright also played on Carolina teams that beat Clemson three straight years, 1931-33. He was a crushing blocking back in Coach Billy Laval's "Crazy Quilt" formation. Hambright, now an official with the state highway department, was present for the induction ceremonies while the two deceased inductees were represented by relatives.

Rucks won the NCAA 400-meter championship in 1948 with a time of 47.2 and is the only Carolina track man ever to win a national championship. He set a school 440-yard record of 47.4 which still stands although it has been tied.

ATTENTION, ALL FORMER CAROLINA ATHLETES

If you earned a varsity letter in any of the recognized sports at Carolina you are eligible for membership in the USC Association of Lettermen.

You are invited to come by the Lettermen's Lounge under section 47 at Carolina Stadium before any home football game. The lounge opens at 6 P.M., prior to each night game.

ATTENTION, ALL GAMECOCK CLUBBERS

If you are planning to attend any future home football games on a bus and you have in your possession $1,000 worth of parking permits, excluding permits for personalized parking, you may call Ed Pitts at (803) 777-4276 in Columbia for details on special parking for buses. If you do not call in advance, please do not expect special consideration.

CAROLINA 27, DUKE 20

that you cannot measure. When **Tyler Hellams** broke his leg in the first five minutes of the game, the safety duties fell to rising sophomore **Jimmy Nash** of Charlotte, N. C. What a

| Lucas | Hodge | Pope | Wingard |

shame to have an injury so early in the season. Tyler has great value to our team. But with Nash in the game, we had three true sophomores in our secondary.

And, against one of the fine passers in the country today!

Bo Davies	Jimmy Nash	Dick Harris
Gettysburg, Pa.	Charlotte, N. C.	Pt. Pleasant, N. J.
6'2", 175	5'11", 168	6'0", 156
4 Tackles, 3 assists	graded 96%	Graded 93%
tredendous job	8 Tackles	8 Tackles

Offensively

It's hard to say just who stole the show. We had some top performances. **Dave DeCamilla**, from Hudson Falls, N. Y., is certainly one of our top offensive linemen. Blocks well over 80% pretty consistently. He engulfed the Duke tackle!

Junior Letterman	Senior two-year	Senior letterman	Junior letterman
LT Dave DeCamilla	letterman	Center Ken Ross	RG Chris Banks
Hudson Falls, N. Y.	LG Tony Fusaro	Williamston	Joliet, Ill.
6'2", 234	Huntington, N. Y.	6'1", 200, 78%	6'2", 235, 82%
	6'2", 240. 84%		

And, we are going to get some fine help for our starting backs from **Tommy Simmons** of Union and **Billy Ray Rice** of Gaffney. They are good prospects and graded at 89% and 90%, respectively. Very good for sophomores. Senior two-year letterman tailback **Rudy Holloman** of Hartsville really turned in a spectacular performance (83%) with many excellent runs including a 60-yard burst for a score. He really does the job for us. The passing combo of **Tommy Suggs** of Lamar to **Freddie Zeigler** of Reevesville was on target. Freddie caught six for 73 yards and made his 100th career catch—right in the clutch. In addition, Zeig graded at 80%, as he usually does. Tommy had one of his finest nights as a quarterback. He made

Holloman

From The
Gamecock Roost

Published weekly during football season and periodically throughout the year by the University of South Carolina GAMECOCK CLUB. Sent to members of the GAMECOCK CLUB in the interest of better education through athletics at Carolina. Republication of any of the contents is invited.

PAUL F. DIETZEL
Head Football Coach & Athletic Director
ED PITTS
Director, The Gamecock Club
Edited by TOM PRICE, Sports Information Director

very few errors and graded at 89%. And his clutch fourth and one carry for a touchdown was really an unbelievable one. Senior two-year letterman **Warren Muir** of Fitchburg, Mass., turned in an 85% performance including some fine receptions and a tremendous night blocking. Warren has really become a complete football player.

But the thing that pleased us most was that even though we made some big errors, we were able to come back and do something about them. The final drive for the "go-ahead" score was really fine football.

Well, that is all past history now! We are in for a real battle again this week. North Carolina, smarting from a 10-3 loss to N. C. State are as mad as Tarheels can be. They are extremely well-coached and very tough. Luckily, we play them here and it'll be another complete sellout. We are really pleased with the crowd and delighted with our new band. They are sharp! And we have to be sharper! We need to replace middle guard **Don Buckner** whose leg is in a cast for two weeks, and **Tyler Hellams** who is out for probably six weeks. We'll have a real battle against a potent ground and air attack.

Hope to see you

in the COCKPIT!

NOTES FROM THE GAMECOCK ROOST:

When Fred Zeigler caught a Tommy Suggs fourth down pass to set up the winning touchdown late in the fourth period of Carolina's opening 27-20 victory over Duke, it was the Gamecock All-America split end's 100th career reception. The Atlantic Coast Conference career record is 102 pass receptions set by North Carolina's Bob Lacey, 1961-63.

— o —

Zeigler needs 71 yards on pass receptions to match the ACC career pass receiving yardage record. Lacey caught passes for 1,362 yards, 1961-63. Zeigler has caught 100 passes for 1,291 yards so far.

— o —

The 47 rushing yards gained by fullback Warren Muir in the win over Duke moved the Fitchburg, Mass., senior up a notch to fourth place among all-time Carolina career rushers. Muir's 1,312 yards so far moved him ahead of Mike Caskey, who gained 1,276 yards, 1952-55. Muir's next target is the 1,490 yards rushed by Alex Hawkins, 1956-58.

— o —

Quarterback Tommy Suggs, just beginning his junior season, already ranks seventh among all-time Gamecocks in total offense. Suggs passed and ran for 205 yards in the opening win over Duke to move ahead of Mackie Prickett, 1954-56, with 1,863 yards total offense . . . and the stocky little quarterback from Lamar, has played only 11 varsity football games so far.

From The
Gamecock Roost

VOL. 4, No. 6 COLUMBIA, S. C. OCTOBER 2, 1969

FROM COACH PAUL DIETZEL

CAROLINA 14, NORTH CAROLINA 6

Good or Bad, It Still Counts!

If we ever needed proof of whether it is better to have a beautifully played, spectacular loss or a poorly played dull victory, Saturday night established it very readily.

That is not to say that we thought North Carolina's  Tar Heels played anything but real, real fine football. They did. They deserved a far better fate, probably. In addition, they are an especially tough, rugged defensive team. They will be a fine team **this** year.

The thing that really disturbed me, I guess, is that, except for the **third** quarter, we just **didn't get after it!** We

Game Captain DAVE LUCAS

Game Captain RUDY HOLLOMAN

were really not a cranked-up football team, and it nearly cost us a victory. It is true that it is impossible to be at your peak every week, but you just can't have a let-down either. **Very good** teams are always good.

With every good intention you people probably help in this attitude. You are all very appreciative and tell the squad. That's great right after the game, but when Monday comes let's forget last week and get ready for next Saturday. Of course, flattery is somewhat like poison—it won't hurt you unless you swallow it.

Some of you wondered why we didn't throw more—for the second straight week, we were victims of poor field position. We put the ball into play 13 times in the game and 10 times behind the 50-yard line. Of the 10, seven times were inside our own 30-yard line. In the first half, seven times we put the ball in play, and six were behind our own 30; the seventh from our own 40.

The catch by Fred Zeigler for the second touchdown was **really** a spectacular one—and has tied the all-time ACC record at 102 catches. It came at a most opportune time.

And the final play by North Carolina —a pass by Miller, batted by **Bo Davies** and intercepted by **Dick Harris**, was a most welcome sight.

But, so much for Bill Dooley's bunch. We have his brother Vince to contend with now. And a great football team

ZEIGLER

Georgia is. Last year here at Carolina we had a very shaky start. We lost to Duke in the opener and then made an impossible come-from-behind conquest of North Carolina. We had definitely not been very impressive to Georgia or anyone. We had a couple of early breaks and jumped out in front. But they did what very good teams generally do—they bounced back and beat us. They did it with a sophomore quarterback named Mike Cavan.

HARRIS THE HERO

Sophomore halfback Dick Harris leaps high to intercept pass intended for North Carolina split end Ricky Lanier at the Gamecock seven-yard line with 22 seconds to play. The ball was deflected by Gamecock rover Bo Davies and the interception preserved Carolina's 14-6 victory. (Photo by Ed Tilley, courtesy The State-Record).

We saw them in their spring game and they really had a **great** one. Our scouts said they had the two best teams they had ever seen in a spring game. They are very deep, experienced, aggressive, quick and mean.

They opened with Tulane and Tulane felt that they had a good chance to beat Georgia. They were quite confident.

Georgia - 35   Tulane - 0

Then came Clemson, right off a fine season opening win over Virginia in Charlottesville, 21 to 14. And, Georgia had to play Clemson on Clemson's home grounds. Clemson—big, very strong, good offense, etc.

Georgia - 30   Clemson - 0

And now, it's time for us to travel to Athens to take on the Bulldogs.

Continued on Page Two

TWO-GAME VARSITY STATISTICS
(Record: 2-0; ACC: 2-0; Home: 2-0; Away: 0-0)

TEAM	USC	OPP.
First downs rushing	20	21
First downs passing	10	17
First downs penalties	0	1
TOTAL FIRST DOWNS	30	39
Net yards rushing	469	363
Number of rushes	99	105
Game rushing average	234.5	181.5
Passing yardage	212	279
Game passing average	106.0	139.5
TOTAL OFFENSE	681	642
Passes attempted	32	51
Passes completed	17	28
Intercepted by	3	0
Number of punts	11	11
Yards punted	442	392
Punts had blocked	0	0
Punting average	40.2	35.6
Return yardage	76	45
Fumbles lost	2	0
Yards penalized	141	97

RUSHING

	NO.	YDS.	AVG.	TD
Holloman	29	149	5.1	1
Muir	28	121	4.3	2
Suggs	22	100	4.5	1
Rice	10	72	7.2	0
Simmons	6	18	3.0	0
Walkup	4	9	2.3	0
TOTALS	99	469	4.7	4
OPPONENTS	105	363	3.5	0

PASSING

	NO.	COMP.	INT.	PCT.	YDS.	TD
Suggs	32	17	0	.531	212	1
OPPONENTS	51	28	3	.549	279	2

RECEIVING

	NO.	YDS.	AVG.	TD
Zeigler	8	119	14.9	1
Hamrick	3	34	11.3	0
Muir	3	28	9.3	0
Holloman	2	23	11.5	0
Simmons	1	8	8.0	0

INTERCEPTION RETURNS

	NO.	YDS.	AVG.	TD
Davies	1	5	5.0	0
Nash	1	5	5.0	0
Harris	1	2	2.0	0

PUNT RETURNS

	NO.	YDS.	AVG.	TD
Harris	7	64	9.1	0

KICKOFF RETURNS

	NO.	YDS.	AVG.	TD
Harris	4	85	21.3	0
Hellams	1	18	18.0	0
Davies	1	8	8.0	0
Wingard	1	7	7.0	0
Bailey	1	4	4.0	0

SCORING

	TD	PAT-K	PAT-RP	FG	TP
Muir	2	0-0	0-0	0-0	12
DuPre	0	5-5	0-0	2-3	11
Zeigler	1	0-0	0-0	0-0	6
Holloman	1	0-0	0-0	0-0	6
Suggs	1	0-0	0-0	0-0	6
TOTALS	5	5-5	0-0	2-3	41
OPPONENTS	2	2-2	0-0	4-6	26

CUMULATIVE SCORE BY PERIODS:

GAMECOCKS	0 — 10 — 14 — 17 — 41
OPPONENTS	3 — 6 — 7 — 10 — 26

DEFENSIVE STATISTICS

	Tackles	Assists	Fumbles Caused	Fumbles Rec.
Usher	17	5	0	0
Nash	16	0	0	0
Harris	13	2	0	0
Padgett	11	3	0	0
Davies	9	6	0	0
Kohout	8	6	0	0
Ganas	7	4	0	0
Watson	7	2	0	0
Poston	6	6	0	0
Hodge	5	6	0	0
Pope	5	2	0	0
Lucas	5	2	0	0
Wingard	4	0	0	0
Tharpe	3	1	0	0
Hellams	2	0	0	0
Crabb	1	0	0	0
Bailey	1	0	0	0
Parker	1	0	0	0
Wright	0	1	0	0

FROM COACH PAUL DIETZEL
Continued from Page One

They have not been scored upon this season. They average scoring over 30 points a game. They are the leading contender for the Southeastern Conference crown. They are also ranked anywhere from 6th to 2nd in the nation. WOW!

Enough said, right?

Hope to see you in Athens.

From The
Gamecock Roost

Published weekly during football season and periodically throughout the year by the University of South Carolina GAMECOCK CLUB. Sent to members of the GAMECOCK CLUB in the interest of better education through athletics at Carolina. Republication of any of the contents is invited.

PAUL F. DIETZEL
Head Football Coach & Athletic Director

ED PITTS
Director, The Gamecock Club

Edited by TOM PRICE, Sports Information Director

ED SAYS
By ED PITTS

Basketball ticket applications have been mailed to all 1969 Gamecock Club contributors who purchased season tickets last season.

Reorder priority expired October 1. If you purchased tickets last year and would like to retain them, we hope you have returned your application. If you did not have tickets last year, it is doubtful that there will be anything available this year.

N. C. STATE

All of the tickets available for public sale for the Carolina-North Carolina State football game have been sold. There is a possibility that our students will not pick up all of the tickets we are required to hold for them. If you will mail your check to the ticket office and ask them to hold it until they have finished issuing the student tickets on October 9, any tickets left will be distributed to the people whose checks have already been received, giving priority to Gamecock Club contributors. You may call the ticket office at 777-4274 on Friday, October 10, to see if they are able to take care of you, and then arrange to pick up your tickets. Please do not telephone your order or ask us to hold tickets unless you send payment in advance. There are still approximately 500 tickets available for the Carolina-Maryland game.

PARKING

Anyone who plans to bring a bus to any of our home games may park in the reserved parking area in the fairgrounds if you have in your possession $1,000 worth of parking permits, excluding permits for personal parking spaces. However, you must notify us in advance before each game; otherwise, we will not have room for you in the area.

Overall, our parking has worked out very satisfactorily. We realize that only a very limited number of our Century Club members are able to park in the area around the stadium, and we certainly appreciate your cooperation.

We would like to ask the people driving automobiles with low tag numbers to cooperate with us and abide by our policies. You certainly put the Highway Patrol and the University in a very embarrassing position. Please consider contributing according to your needs.

The All-Time Gamecock Squad:

	FIRST TEAM	SECOND TEAM
E	—J. R. Wilburn	Clyde Bennett
E	—Fred Zeigler	Larry Craig
T	—Ed Pitts	Jim Moss
T	—Sam DeLuca	Dom Fusci
G	—Frank Mincevich	Dave Sparks
G	—Jake Bodkin	Ernie Bauer
C	—Lou Sossamon	Leon Cunningham
QB	—Dan Reeves	Johnny Gramling
HB	—Steve Wadiak	Alex Hawkins
HB	—Earl Clary	Billy Gambrell
FB	—Warren Muir	Bill Wohrman

CAROLINA'S ALL-TIME TEAM

Halfback Steve Wadiak and center Lou Sossamon have been named the greatest Carolina back and lineman of all time and two current Gamecock stars are on the all-time USC football eleven picked by Gamecock fans and alumni.

The all-time team and outstanding back and lineman were selected in commemoration of college football's Centennial Year. More than 9,000 ballots were sent to all

Outstanding Back
STEVE WADIAK

Outstanding Lineman
LOU SOSSAMON

members of the University's Gamecock Club and Alumni Association.

Fullback Warren Muir and end Fred Zeigler, now playing for the USC varsity, were selected for the all-time eleven at their respective positions. The only repeat selection from a similar all-time Gamecock team picked in 1935 was halfback Earl Clary, although many members of that team received votes.

Linemen selected were ends J. R. Wilburn and Zeigler, tackles Ed Pitts and Sam DeLuca, guards Frank Mincevich and Jake Bodkin, and Sossamon at center. The all-time USC backfield included Dan Reeves at quarterback, Wadiak and Clary at halfbacks and fullback Muir.

Modern players dominated the team selections, with all but two of the all-timers having played during either the 50's or 60's. Only Clary, who starred for the Gamecocks in the early 1930's and Sossamon, a line bulwark for USC during the pre-war years of the 40's, did not play during the last two decades.

Wadiak, who led the all vote getters both for halfback and outstanding back, was killed in an automobile accident in 1952 after his senior season. He still holds USC career records for points scored, touchdowns, yards rushing (over 900 ahead of the next player), and rushing attempts, as well as the single game record for rushing, 256 yards against Clemson in 1950.

Sossamon, who beat out Leon Cunningham at the

J. R. WILBURN   **FRED ZEIGLER**   **ED PITTS**

center spot, won the outstanding lineman honor by edging guard Frank Mincevich in the voting. He anchored the Gamecock line for three years, being selected second Associated Press All-America in 1942.

Wilburn, currently starring for the Pittsburgh Steelers of the National Football League, led the vote getting at the end position by a large margin.

Zeigler beat out Clyde Bennett for the other end spot in the closest race among the selections. He already ranks as the Gamecock receiving leader with 100 catches for 1,291 yards and is only two catches and 71 yards short of breaking Atlantic Coast Conference records in these categories.

At tackle, Ed Pitts, an All-ACC choice in both 1958 and '59, and an All-America selection the latter year, led the balloting. He was co-captain of the Gamecocks, and played in the North-South Shrine game.

At the other tackle, DeLuca starred for the San Diego Chargers and the New York Jets of the American Football League as a guard for 10 years after graduation. While

SAM DeLUCA   **FRANK MINCEVICH**   **JAKE BODKIN**

playing for the Gamecocks in 1954-56, DeLuca, who earned his spot by edging Jim Moss in the voting, won the Jacobs Blocking Trophy while at USC and made third team All-America in 1956.

Guard Frank Mincevich, known as the "Friendly Bear" (6-2, 243 pounds) during his playing days, garnered more votes than any other interior lineman at the guard spot and was a close runnerup for the Gamecocks' all-time outstanding lineman honor. He made All-America his senior year, as well as earning All-ACC honors in both 1953 and '54. Jake Bodkin, who handily won the other guard spot from the late Gamecock star Dave Sparks, won All-ACC honors in 1960.

At the quarterback spot, Reeves was an overwhelming choice, outpolling all others combined at the position. He has been a star halfback with Dallas Cowboys of the National Football League since leaving USC. Reeves holds Gamecock career records for passing and total offense and set many other school records, since broken by current Gamecock quarterback Tommy Suggs.

Lined up with Wadiak at halfback is Earl Clary, known during his playing days in 1931-33 as the "Gaffney

DAN REEVES   **EARL CLARY**   **WARREN MUIR**

Ghost." He made All-State for three years, and after his senior season, was selected first team All-Southern, second team All-South, and honorable mention All-America.

At fullback, Muir ranks as the fourth leading rusher in Gamecock annals with the remainder of his senior year remaining. He has picked up 1,312 yards, and set a USC sophomore rushing record with 805 yards his first year on the varsity, when he made All-ACC.

From The
Gamecock Roost

Vol. 4, No. 7   Columbia, S. C.   October 9, 1969

FROM COACH PAUL DIETZEL

GEORGIA 41 – CAROLINA 16

That doesn't tell the tale, but it tells enough!

It's really hard to find yourself speechless, but that is the way I felt in Athens after the game. We were so certain we were going to win. We showed real fine poise to come

Game Captain
WARREN MUIR

back from a 14-0 deficit to score a touchdown and then a field goal to go out at the half 14-10. And then at the half we were more convinced than ever that we would win.

Man, but we had pulled the boners! We did so very many dumb things that you cannot do against a good foot-

Game Captain
ANDY CHAVOUS

ball team. We hadn't had an interception this season, but we had three in this one game. Of course, Georgia is an alert defensive team. And then, those fumbles. One fumble for a touchdown. And the others were costly. We really kept ourselves in serious trouble.

Georgia does such a fine job with their kicking game that they kept us in the hole the entire fourth quarter. And that is a tough place to have to start a drive—your own 20-yard line.

BILLY PARKER

Our team gave us great effort. They worked hard all week and were ready to play. Our kicking was good, too. Billy Parker has been kicking well all of this year. And Billy Du-Pre has also been kicking extremely well. Both Georgia and Carolina were kicking off very

BILLY DuPRE

deep into the end zone. But I hate to receive that many kick offs.

Warren Muir played as well as he has in his career. He ran the ball 21 times for 136 yards, but that just doesn't tell the tale of his leadership for the game and his great effort throughout the game. Warren is a real all-around football player.

One of the things that didn't help our cause was the loss of Al Usher at linebacker. He had injured his ankle against North Carolina and then Wednesday he went into the hospital with the flu. He played a couple of plays, but he was so gimpy that he couldn't help, so we took him out. He was the third defensive starter that we have lost since our opener. And all three—Buckner, Hellams, and Usher are probably as valuable as any men we have. We have had some tough moments in the middle of our defense.

THE "RAT" IN ACTION

Halfback Pat "The Rat" Watson leaps high to intercept a Bulldog pass during action in Carolina's 41-16 loss to Georgia at Athens. Other Gamecock defenders are game captain Andy Chavous (29) and Bo Davies (18). (Photo by Vic Tutte, courtesy The State-Record.)

And Georgia's idea is to just line up and run right over you. They did just that.

Georgia just has more good football players than we do at the moment. And they are well-coached and disciplined. As I said last year, Mike Cavan, the Georgia quarterback, is really a good one. He was probably the best we played against last year. He's just one of those guys who can beat you. And he has lots of good help.

But it's all over and we get back into our all-important conference wars. This week we have North Carolina State. N. C. State had an experience similar to ours Friday night against Miami. They have had a disappointing season (for them)!

N. C. STATE 21 – WAKE 22
N. C. STATE 10 – N. CAROLINA 3
N. C. STATE 24 – MARYLAND 7
N. C. STATE 13 – MIAMI 23

Continued on Page 3

343

THREE-GAME VARSITY STATISTICS
(Record: 2-1; ACC: 2-0; Home: 2-0; Away: 0-1)

TEAM	USC	OPP.
First downs rushing	24	44
First downs passing	16	21
First downs penalties	1	1
TOTAL FIRST DOWNS	41	66
Net yards rushing	594	740
Number of rushes	143	186
Game rushing average	198.0	246.7
Passing yardage	315	390
Game passing average	105.0	130.0
TOTAL OFFENSE	909	1130
Passes attempted	54	65
Passes completed	24	32
Intercepted by	5	3
Number of punts	21	15
Yards punted	851	575
Punts had blocked	0	0
Punting average	40.5	38.3
Return yardage	93	89
Fumbles lost	4	4
Yards penalized	171	129

RUSHING

	NO.	YDS.	AVG.	TD
Muir	49	257	4.9	3
Holloman	33	161	5.2	1
Rice	15	86	5.7	0
Suggs	28	49	1.8	1
Simmons	10	24	2.4	0
Walkup	4	9	2.3	0
Yoakum	1	8	8.0	0
Miranda	3	0	0.0	0
TOTALS	143	594	4.2	5
OPPONENTS	186	740	4.0	6

PASSING

	NO.	COMP.	INT.	PCT.	YDS.	TD
Suggs	47	21	3	.447	261	1
Yoakum	7	3	0	.429	54	1
TOTALS	54	24	3	.444	315	2
OPPONENTS	65	32	5	.492	390	2

RECEIVING

	NO.	YDS.	AVG.	TD
Zeigler	11	153	13.9	1
Muir	4	43	10.8	0
Hamrick	3	34	11.3	0
Freeman	2	29	14.5	1
Holloman	2	23	11.5	0
Rice	1	25	25.0	0
Simmons	1	8	8.0	0

INTERCEPTION RETURNS

	NO.	YDS.	AVG.	TD
Harris	2	2	1.0	0
Davies	1	5	5.0	0
Nash	1	5	5.0	0
Watson	1	0	0.0	0

PUNT RETURNS

	NO.	YDS.	AVG.	TD
Harris	7	64	9.1	0
Bailey	1	2	2.0	0
Mitchell	1	2	2.0	0

KICKOFF RETURNS

	NO.	YDS.	AVG.	TD
Harris	4	85	21.3	0
Bailey	3	41	13.7	0
Hellams	1	18	18.0	0
Davies	1	8	8.0	0
Wingard	1	7	7.0	0

PUNTING

	NO.	YDS.	BLKD.	AVG.
Parker	21	851	0	40.5

SCORING

	TD	PAT-K	PAT-RP	FG	TP
Muir	3	0-0	0-0	0-0	18
DuPre	0	6-6	0-0	3-4	15
Zeigler	1	0-0	0-0	0-0	6
Holloman	1	0-0	0-0	0-0	6
Suggs	1	0-0	0-0	0-0	6
Freeman	1	0-0	0-0	0-0	6
Yoakum	0	0-0	0-1	0-0	0
TOTALS	7	6-6	0-1	3-4	57
OPPONENTS	8	7-8	0-0	4-8	67

CUMULATIVE SCORE BY PERIODS:

GAMECOCKS	0 —	20 —	14 —	23 —	57
OPPONENTS	10 —	13 —	7 —	37 —	67

DEFENSIVE STATISTICS

	Tackles	Assists	Fumbles Caused	Fumbles Rec.
Harris	21	3	0	1
Usher	18	6	0	0
Nash	18	3	0	0
Padgett	15	6	0	0
Davies	14	8	2	1
Kohout	13	6	0	1
Tharpe	12	5	0	0
Ganas	10	5	0	0
Wingard	9	1	0	0
Watson	8	4	0	1
Hodge	7	6	0	0
Pope	7	4	0	0
Poston	6	7	0	0
Crabb	6	2	0	0
Lucas	5	3	0	0
Bailey	5	1	0	0
Parker	4	0	0	0
Chavous	3	0	0	0
Hellams	2	0	0	0
McCarthy	1	0	0	0
Wright	0	1	0	0

From The
Gamecock Roost

Published weekly during football season and periodically throughout the year by the University of South Carolina **GAMECOCK CLUB**. Sent to members of the **GAMECOCK CLUB** in the interest of better education through athletics at Carolina. Republication of any of the contents is invited.

PAUL F. DIETZEL
Head Football Coach & Athletic Director
ED PITTS
Director, The Gamecock Club
Edited by TOM PRICE, Sports Information Director

ED SAYS
By ED PITTS

If you have not purchased your official Carolina Blazer, there is a good chance our supplier has your size in stock. Just send your jacket size along with your check for $65.00 to the Gamecock Club. This includes jacket, Carolina buttons, Gamecock patch, handling charges and sales tax.

PARKING

Anyone who plans to bring a bus to any of our home games may park in the reserved parking area in the fairgrounds if you have in your possession $1,000 worth of parking permits, excluding permits for personal parking spaces. However, you must notify us in advance before each game; otherwise, we will not have room for you in the area.

N. C. STATE

All of the tickets available for public sale for the Carolina-North Carolina State football game have been sold. There is a possibility that our students will not pick up all of the tickets we are required to hold for them. If you will mail your check to the ticket office and ask them to hold it until they have finished issuing the student tickets on October 9, any tickets left will be distributed to the people whose checks have already been received, giving priority to Gamecock Club contributors. You may call the ticket office at 777-4274 on Friday, October 10, to see if they are able to take care of you, and then arrange to pick up your tickets. Please do not telephone your order or ask us to hold tickets unless you send payment in advance. There are still approximately 500 tickets available for the Carolina-Maryland game.

NOTES FROM THE GAMECOCK ROOST:

Split end Fred Zeigler tied the listed record for Atlantic Coast Conference pass receptions against North Carolina and surpassed it against Georgia, but he still doesn't actually hold the record. Research following Zeigler's 102nd career reception revealed that North Carolina's Bob Lacey, listed as the record holder in the ACC brochure, actually was second to 106 passes caught by Clemson's Phil Rogers, 1965-67. Zeigler caught three passes against Georgia to give him 105 for his career, and he still needs one to tie the record held by Rogers, two to surpass it.

When Carolina entertains North Carolina State in Carolina Stadium Saturday night, one of the closest football rivalries in the Atlantic Coast Conference will be renewed. The Gamecocks have won 15 games in the series which began in 1900, the Wolfpack has won 13 and there have been three ties. Although South Carolina has a two-game lead in the series, N. C. State has scored the most points, 389-350. The series in recent years has generally featured close games although last year was an exception as N. C. State routed the Gamecocks, 36-12, at Raleigh.

ONE-GAME FRESHMAN STATISTICS

(Record: 1-0; ACC: 0-0; Home: 1-0; Away: 0-0)

TEAM	USC	OPP.
First Downs Rushing	16	5
First Downs Passing	1	2
First Downs Penalties	1	0
TOTAL FIRST DOWNS	18	7
Net Yards Rushing	248	44
Number of Rushes	68	34
Game Rushing Average	248.0	44.0
Passing Yardage	21	75
Game Passing Average	21.0	75.0
TOTAL OFFENSE	269	119
Passes Attempted	7	16
Passes Completed	2	4
Intercepted by	0	0
Number of Punts	7	9
Yards Punted	263	306
Punts Had Blocked	0	0
Punting average	37.6	34.0
Return yardage	64	66
Fumbles lost	1	2
Yards Penalized	60	20

RUSHING	NO.	YDS.	AVG.	TD
Kuritz	23	101	4.4	1
Mimms	15	79	5.3	0
Files	8	41	5.1	1
Kooker	5	30	6.0	0
Haywood	5	19	3.8	0
Young	6	-9	-1.5	0
Rushing	6	-13	-2.2	0
TOTALS	68	248	3.6	2
OPPONENTS	34	44	1.3	0

PASSING	NO.	COMP.	INT.	PCT.	YDS.	TD
Rushing	3	2	0	.667	21	0
Young	4	0	0	.000	0	0
TOTALS	7	2	0	.286	21	0
OPPONENTS	16	4	0	.250	75	0

RECEIVING	NO.	YDS.	AVG.	TD
Barfield	1	14	14.0	0
Kuritz	1	7	7.0	0

PUNT RETURNS	NO.	YDS.	AVG.	TD
Haggard	4	26	6.5	0
Williams	1	3	3.0	0

KICKOFF RETURNS	NO.	YDS.	AVG.	TD
Mimms	2	35	17.5	0

SCORING	TD	PAT-K	PAT-RP	FG	TP
Files	1	0-0	0-0	0-0	6
Kuritz	1	0-0	0-0	0-0	6
Cline	0	1-2	0-0	0-1	1
TOTALS	2	1-2	0-0	0-1	13
OPPONENTS	1	1-1	0-0	0-0	7

CUMULATIVE SCORE BY PERIODS:

BIDDIES	7	— 0	— 6	— 0	— 13
OPPONENTS	0	— 0	— 0	— 7	— 7

FUMBLES RECOVERED	NO.	YDS. RTN.
Privette	1	0
Kuritz	1	0

RESULTS, ATTENDANCE & REMAINING GAMES

SOUTH CAROLINA 13, The Citadel 7 — Attendance 2,768
Oct. 10—At Clemson, 1:30 P.M.
Oct. 16—At N. C. State, 3 P.M.
Oct. 23—WAKE FOREST, 7:30 P.M.
Nov. 17—At Georgia, 2 P.M.

FROM COACH PAUL DIETZEL

Continued from Page One

Two wins and two losses. Their record in the ACC is 2 and 1. After playing us, they have only Virginia and Duke in our league. On paper, at least, you would have to say that that would add up to about 4 and 1 in the ACC (plus our game). So this game of ours has great significance in the ACC race for this year.

Last year we had N. C. State right after our Georgia game and we played them in Raleigh. We were battered up and they literally beat us to death. They dominated the game completely, and we played poorly. We need to get regrouped and get ready to play. N. C. State is one of the toughest and most well-drilled teams in the South. Earle Edwards is a fine football coach. We will have our hands full.

Hope to see you in the COCKPIT!

BIDDIES MEET CUBS; BEAT BULLPUPS

Carolina's freshman football team, sporting a tough defense, a powerful running attack, and an 11-game undefeated streak, takes on Clemson's Cubs at Tiger Stadium Friday. Game time is 1:30 P.M., a change from the previously announced 2 P.M. starting time.

Both squads are coming off wins in their opening games, the Biddies defeating The Citadel frosh 13-7, and

RUSS KURITZ   NEVILLE FILES

the Cubs rallying from a halftime deficit to upset the Georgia freshmen 27-21.

The win was the ninth in a row for the USC freshmen, dating back to the third game of the 1967 season. Only a 14-14 tie with The Citadel marred the slate that year, and last season the Biddies posted a 5-0-0 record and have not been defeated since their last game in 1966 against Wake Forest.

Against the Bullpups, the Biddies were sporadic on attack, racking up 248 yards rushing, but managing only 21 yards in the passing department. It was the first time in nine games that the Carolina frosh had been held under 21 points.

Defensively, the first-year-men were extremely tough, limiting the Bullpups to only 44 yards rushing and 75 yards through the air. Only a 41-yard aerial strike late in the game got The Citadel on the scoreboard after the Biddies had held them to one first down and nine yards total offense in the opening half.

Tailback Russ Kuritz of Charleston was the workhorse of the ground attack, carrying 23 times for 101 yards and bursting 24 yards for a touchdown. Fullback Chuck Mimms of Bishopville cracked up the middle for 79 yards, while halfback Neville Files of Greenwood scooted five yards for the other score and picked up 41 yards.

Leading the defensive charge were tackle Sal Pecoraro, who smothered the Bullpup quarterback for three long losses, and middle guard John Le Heup, who closed off the center against Bullpup charges.

The Cubs demonstrated a balanced and versatile attack in their first game as they came from the short end of a 14-3 halftime score to win against the strong Georgia first-year men.

The 136 yards that fullback Warren Muir gained against Georgia moved the Fitchburg, Mass., senior into third place among all-time Gamecock rushers with 1,522 yards. Muir, who last week was named to Carolina's all-time team, passed Alex Hawkins (1,490 yards, 1956-58) and his next goal is the 1,965 yards rushed by Bishop Strickland, 1947-50.

From The
Gamecock Roost

Vol. 4, No. 8 — Columbia, S. C. — October 16, 1969

FROM COACH PAUL DIETZEL

CAROLINA 21 - N. C. STATE 16

When you go after a game as hard as we did for the State game and then you win, it's hard not to be very, very proud. We are most pleased with the outcome of the game and there were many heroes, not the least of which was a

Game Captain
LYNN HODGE
70%, 3 Ind. Tackles

fine group of associate coaches who have really "hung in there" trying to get our train back on the track. They get very little credit much of the time and yet they deserve so very much.

These a r e really six great young men. They a r e all talented a n d dedicated coaches and I am proud to be associated with them.

Game Captain
FRED ZEIGLER

Coach Billy Rowe was the man who kept insisting all week that we work on the particular punt return that we finally put in for State (and I'm glad that Bill Shalosky recruited **Jim Mitchell** from Greensboro, too!!).

LARRY JONES
Defensive Coordinator

BILL ROWE
Linebackers—Mike

JOHNNY MENGER
Defensive Perimeter

But we can only tell them what to do. The players are the ones who have to do it. And they **DID** do it.

Our four defensive ends really played fine football. All

DICK WELDON
Offensive Running

DON PURVIS
Offensive Passing

BILL SHALOSKY
Offensive Coordinator

of them came up with some big plays and were fine as a group. **Dave Lucas** set a fine block on the punt return that put down two men.

It was great to have **Buckner** back in action, and our

SWING ALONG WITH MITCH

Jim Mitchell outruns N. C. State's Leon Mason (25) to light the Gamecocks' fire with a 72-yard punt return in last Saturday night's action at Carolina Stadium. The run by the 156-pound sophomore from Greensboro, N. C., brought Carolina from behind and sparked a 21-16 victory that cements the Gamecocks' hold on first place in ACC standings. (Photo by Ed Tilley, courtesy The State-Record.)

secondary played extremely well. The "save" made by **Watson** on the long run was really remarkable. He's a real **Gamecock!**

And we will not soon forget **Dickie Harris'** fine kick-off return to put us in business in the third quarter. It gave us excellent field position. The punt return by Jim Mitchell really doesn't need any comment because it was just great. Mitchell forgot and threw the ball down and I was afraid we would get a penalty, but we didn't. Mitchell also graded at 83% when he substituted for Zeigler.

These four offensive linemen played well against State. We feel that we have gotten consistently good football from **David DeCamilla**. He's done a heck of a good job for us. On **Warren Muir's** touchdown run "Deac" knocked Carpenter back three yards into the end zone—and Carpenter is a **good** man. And Co-Captain Fred has now officially

Continued on Page 3

346

FROM COACH PAUL DIETZEL
Continued from Page One

broken the ACC receiving record.

These four backs played super football. **Tommy Suggs** has not played better football for us at any time. Had we not dropped four passes right in our hands, we would have had a **fabulous** night. **Tom Trevillian** improves every week. **Rudy Holloman** caught the ball and ran like a jack rabbit. He did a fine job. And I don't know how to describe **Warren Muir's** value to our team. The complete football player—blocker, pass receiver, faker, leader, and runner superb.

The ACC to date (only Conference Games)!

	WON	LOST	
CAROLINA	3	0	
*CLEMSON	1	0	Nov. 22 (PIT)
N. C. STATE	2	1	
*MARYLAND	1	1	Oct. 25 (PIT)
VIRGINIA	1	1	
DUKE	1	2	
*WAKE FOREST	1	2	Nov. 15 (there)
NORTH CAROLINA	0	2	

A fine **START!** We still have to play **three*** of these. And **EACH** one counts just as much as any other in the standings.

FINIS 1969 N. C. STATE GAME
VPI @ BLACKSBURG, VIRGINIA

Before the year the people in Virginia felt that this was going to be Jerry Claiborne's best football team ever at VPI. He has **had** some good ones. They felt that if they

Continued on Page 4

POPE 72%
3 Ind. Tackles

LUCAS 85%
2 Ind., 2 Assts.

WINGARD 83%
3 Ind. Tackles

TWO-GAME FRESHMAN STATISTICS
(Record: 1-1; ACC: 0-1; Home: 1-0; Away: 0-1)

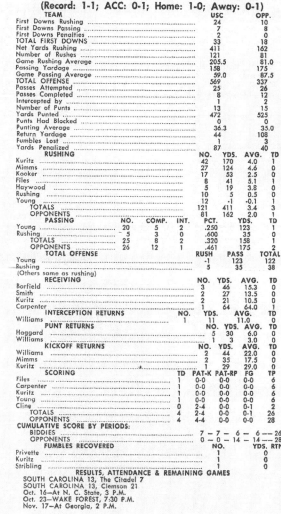

TEAM	USC	OPP.
First Downs Rushing	24	10
First Downs Passing	7	8
First Downs Penalties	2	0
TOTAL FIRST DOWNS	33	18
Net Yards Rushing	411	162
Number of Rushes	121	81
Game Rushing Average	205.5	81.0
Passing Yardage	158	175
Game Passing Average	59.0	87.5
TOTAL OFFENSE	569	337
Passes Attempted	25	26
Passes Completed	8	12
Intercepted by	1	2
Number of Punts	13	15
Yards Punted	472	525
Punts Had Blocked	0	0
Punting Average	36.3	35.0
Return Yardage	44	108
Fumbles Lost	1	3
Yards Penalized	87	40

RUSHING	NO.	YDS.	AVG.	TD
Kuritz	42	170	4.0	1
Mimms	27	124	4.6	0
Kooker	17	53	2.5	0
Files	8	41	5.1	1
Haywood	5	19	3.8	0
Rushing	10	5	0.5	0
Young	12	-1	-0.1	1
TOTALS	121	411	3.4	3
OPPONENTS	81	162	2.0	1

PASSING	NO.	COMP.	INT.	PCT.	YDS.	TD
Young	20	5	2	.250	123	1
Rushing	5	3	0	.600	35	0
TOTALS	25	8	2	.320	158	1
OPPONENTS	26	12	1	.461	175	2

TOTAL OFFENSE	RUSH	PASS	TOTAL
Young	-1	123	122
Rushing	5	35	38
(Others same as rushing)			

RECEIVING	NO.	YDS.	AVG.	TD
Barfield	3	46	15.3	0
Smith	2	27	13.5	0
Kuritz	2	21	10.5	0
Carpenter	1	64	64.0	1

INTERCEPTION RETURNS	NO.	YDS.	AVG.	TD
Williams	1	11	11.0	0

PUNT RETURNS	NO.	YDS.	AVG.	TD
Haggard	5	30	6.0	0
Williams	1	3	3.0	0

KICKOFF RETURNS	NO.	YDS.	AVG.	TD
Williams	2	44	22.0	0
Mimms	2	35	17.5	0
Kuritz	1	29	29.0	0

SCORING	TD	PAT-K	PAT-RP	FG	TP
Files	1	0-0	0-0	0-0	6
Carpenter	1	0-0	0-0	0-0	6
Kuritz	1	0-0	0-0	0-0	6
Young	1	0-0	0-0	0-0	6
Cline	0	2-4	0-0	0-1	2
TOTALS	4	2-4	0-0	0-1	26
OPPONENTS	4	4-4	0-0	0-0	28

CUMULATIVE SCORE BY PERIODS:

BIDDIES	7 —	7 —	6 —	6 —	26
OPPONENTS	0 —	0 —	14 —	14 —	28

FUMBLES RECOVERED	NO.	YDS. RTN.
Privette	1	0
Kuritz	1	0
Stribling	1	0

RESULTS, ATTENDANCE & REMAINING GAMES
SOUTH CAROLINA 13, The Citadel 7
SOUTH CAROLINA 13, Clemson 21
Oct. 16—At N. C. State, 3 P.M.
Oct. 23—WAKE FOREST, 7:30 P.M.
Nov. 17—At Georgia, 2 P.M.

BUCKNER 70%
6 Ind., 2 Assts.

DAVIES 90%
5 Ind., 5 Assts.

HARRIS 90%
5 Ind. Tackles

WATSON 85%
2 Ind. Tackles

MITCHELL
72 Yd. Return

DeCAMILLA 75%

FUSARO 76%

HIPKINS 83%

SUGGS 92%

TREVILLIAN 93%

HOLLOMAN 84%

MUIR 85%

347

FOUR-GAME VARSITY STATISTICS
(Record: 3-1; ACC: 3-0; Home: 3-0; Away: 1-0)

TEAM				USC	OPP.
First downs rushing				29	55
First downs passing				28	26
First downs penalties				1	3
TOTAL FIRST DOWNS				58	84
Net yards rushing				751	887
Number of rushes				187	239
Game rushing average				187.8	209.3
Passing yardage				496	521
Game passing average				128.0	130.3
TOTAL OFFENSE				1247	1408
Passes attempted				75	79
Passes completed				38	42
Intercepted by				5	3
Number of punts				26	23
Yards punted				1027	901
Punts had blocked				0	0
Punting average				39.5	39.2
Return yardage				213	101
Fumbles lost				4	4
Yards penalized				202	134

RUSHING	NO.	YDS.	AVG.	TD
Muir	65	311	4.8	4
Holloman	42	195	4.6	1
Rice	18	94	5.2	1
Suggs	33	74	2.2	1
Simmons	11	28	2.5	0
Miranda	7	24	3.4	0
Walkup	6	13	2.2	0
Yoakum	2	6	3.0	0
Trevillian	2	4	2.0	0
Sistare	1	2	2.0	0
TOTALS	187	751	4.0	7
OPPONENTS	239	887	3.7	7

PASSING	NO.	COMP.	INT.	PCT.	YDS.	TD
Suggs	68	35	3	.545	442	1
Yoakum	7	3	0	.429	54	1
TOTALS	75	38	3	.507	496	2
OPPONENTS	79	42	5	.532	521	3

TOTAL OFFENSE	RUSH	PASS	TOTAL
Suggs	74	442	516
Yoakum	6	54	60
(Others same as rushing)			

RECEIVING	NO.	YDS.	AVG.	TD
Zeigler	15	199	13.3	1
Holloman	7	96	13.7	0
Muir	6	69	11.5	0
Hamrick	4	46	11.5	0
Rice	2	33	15.5	0
Freeman	2	29	14.5	1
Trevillian	1	16	16.0	0
Simmons	1	8	8.0	0

INTERCEPTION RETURNS	NO.	YDS.	AVG.	TD
Harris	2	2	1.0	0
Davies	1	5	5.0	0
Nash	1	5	5.0	0
Watson	1	0	0.0	0

PUNT RETURNS	NO.	YDS.	AVG.	TD
Mitchell	4	106	26.5	1
Harris	10	77	7.7	0
Watson	1	3	3.0	0
Bailey	1	2	2.0	0

KICKOFF RETURNS	NO.	YDS.	AVG.	TD
Harris	5	129	25.8	0
Bailey	5	68	13.6	0
Hellams	1	18	18.0	0
Davies	1	8	8.0	0
Wingard	1	7	7.0	0

PUNTING	NO.	YDS.	BLKD.	AVG.
Parker	26	1027	0	39.5

SCORING	TD	PAT-K	PAT-RP	FG	TP
Muir	4	0-0	0-0	0-0	24
DuPre	0	9-9	0-0	3-6	18
Zeigler	1	0-0	0-0	0-0	6
Holloman	1	0-0	0-0	0-0	6
Suggs	1	0-0	0-0	0-0	6
Freeman	1	0-0	0-0	0-0	6
Rice	1	0-0	0-0	0-0	6
Mitchell	1	0-0	0-0	0-0	6
Yoakum	0	0-0	0-1	0-0	0
TOTALS	10	9-9	0-1	3-6	78
OPPONENTS	10	8-9	0-1	5-9	83

CUMULATIVE SCORE BY PERIODS:

GAMECOCKS	0	20	28	30	78
OPPONENTS	13	13	14	43	83

DEFENSIVE STATISTICS

	Tackles	Assists	Fumbles Caused	Fumbles Rec.
Harris	26	3	0	1
Nash	20	5	0	0
Davies	19	13	2	1
Usher	18	6	0	0
Tharpe	17	9	0	0
Padgett	15	6	0	0
Kohout	15	6	0	1
Wingard	12	1	0	0
Hodge	10	6	0	0
Ganas	10	5	0	0
Watson	10	4	0	1
Pope	10	4	0	0
Crabb	10	3	0	0
Poston	9	8	0	0
Lucas	7	5	0	0
Bailey	7	2	0	0
Parker	7	1	0	0
Buckner	6	2	0	0
Chavous	3	0	0	0
Hellams	2	0	0	0
McCarthy	2	0	0	0
Wright	0	1	0	0

From The
Gamecock Roost

Published weekly during football season and periodically throughout the year by the University of South Carolina GAMECOCK CLUB. Sent to members of the GAMECOCK CLUB in the interest of better education through athletics at Carolina. Republication of any of the contents is invited.

PAUL F. DIETZEL
Head Football Coach & Athletic Director

ED PITTS
Director, The Gamecock Club

Edited by TOM PRICE, Sports Information Director

ED SAYS
By ED PITTS

Basketball season ticket reorder priority has expired. It is very doubtful that we will be able to improve the location of anyone's seats or increase the number of season tickets purchased last year even though a considerable increase in contributions over last year's was made.

All of our seats were committed to Gamecock Club contributors last year and we just don't have anything else available.

At the beginning of this week there were less than 400 tickets remaining for our Oct. 25 Homecoming football game with Maryland. When these are sold, Carolina Stadium will be a complete sellout for the 1969 season. However, there are still tickets available for the closed circuit telecast of the Nov. 22 game with Clemson in Carolina Coliseum. These tickets are $6 each.

We still have a very limited number of tickets available for our game Nov. 8 at Tennessee. If you are planning to attend our game at Florida State Nov. 1 and Wake Forest Nov. 15, please order tickets now.

Anyone bringing his automobile to Carolina Stadium early and parking it in the reserved parking area must park in a proper parking space.

If you park before the highway patrol checks you in, you must leave your parking permit where it can be seen. Automobiles left in the reserved parking area without a visible parking permit will be towed away at the owner's expense.

Anyone who plans to bring a bus to any of our home games may park in the reserved parking area in the fairgrounds if you have in your possession $1,000 worth of parking permits, excluding permits for personal parking spaces. However, you must notify us in advance before each game; otherwise, we will not have room for you in the area.

Upset BY Cubs; Biddies Tackle State

Carolina's freshman footballers, their nine game winning streak derailed by Clemson's Cubs, 21-13, seek to get back on the winning track against an always tough N. C. State Wolflet outfit in Raleigh Thursday at 3 P.M.

The Biddies, now 1-1 for the year, will face an improving Wolflet squad. After an opening game loss to the potent North Carolina frosh, the State first-year men have defeated Wake Forest and East Carolina freshman teams, for a 2-1 record.

After two games, leading rusher for the USC frosh is Tailback Russ Kuritz, with 170 yards and a 4.0 average. Fullback Chuck Mimms has a 4.6 average in gaining 124 yards. Quarterback Jackie Young has completed 5 of 20 passes for 123 yards and one touchdown.

The game with the N. C. State freshmen will be originated by the Gamecock Radio Network with Bob Fulton doing the play-by-play, and will be carried by many of the Gamecock Network stations.

FROM COACH PAUL DIETZEL

CAROLINA 17 - VIRGINIA TECH 16

BEAUTIFUL!

It was quite a ball game. You just can't have a real good year if you don't win the close ones. Frankly, we should have put the game away earlier, but we didn't. We had some very costly penalties at most inopportune times.

Right before the half, we threw for a first down at the VPI six-yard line and had a 15-yard holding penalty. That really cost us a touchdown, and we would have gone at the half 21 to 7.

One of the biggest penalties, which could have cost us the game, was on a punt. We were leading in the game 14

Game Captain GEORGE McCARTHY

Game Captain KEN ROSS 81%

to 7 and punted the ball which we downed on the VPI four—but we were penalized 15 yards for illegal use of the hands and had to punt again. This time they took over on their 40-yard line. That field position led to their field goal.

Man, but that Simcsak can put the foot to the ball. He averaged 45 yards a kick against us. He can really keep you backed up.

But the little man who came through when he had to come through—**Billy DuPre**. In addition to the usual

pressure, we had to call a time out to insure that the clock did not run out—and to be sure we were all set. Therefore, he had time to stand there and contemplate the situation—the goal post was 47 yards away. The snap was a little high and they put on a real tough rush. But it was perfect—right

BILLY DUPRE

FUSARO 81%

thru the middle!! It was really unbelievable—and a good test of **GUTS!** He has 11 straight PATs and four of nine field goal attempts. And, we did appreciate the crowd of folks who were on hand at the airport to welcome us back to Columbia. It was a short flight!!

After grading the film, we are now convinced that this was our best game to date. The VPI coaches told us after the game that our game was the best game they played this year. They said they were really fired up for the game and felt that they would win. We were really proud of the comeback. Perhaps my memory is short, but I can't remember a drive any better in a shorter period of

time. **97 yards in 1:06 for three points and a VICTORY for CAROLINA.**

The offensive stick-outs for the Gamecocks were:

HAMRICK 80%
4 great catches
for 53 yds.

ZEIGLER 96%
6 great catches
for 49 yds.
1 TD

SUGGS 88%
13 of 21 for 127 yds.
1 TD

The Fitchburg, Mass. senior carried for 29 times and 95 yards but had 35 yards taken away by penalties. Warren has been consistently a **great** performer and is a great team man!

Defensively, we really popped! There were some great moments by quite a few of our people.

MUIR 80%

BUCKNER 70%
4 Tackles
2 Ass'ts.

KOHOUT 72%
4 Tackles
1 Ass't.
1 Fumble Recovery

This is the best job we have had in the middle of our line. These men have really adjusted well to a **tough** situation, and we are really proud of them. They have had to come through in the absence of USHER and PADGETT and they really have.

The secondary played real well again:

Davies	89%	7 tackles 3 assists 1 interception
Harris	82%	3 tackles 2 assists
Nash	88%	4 tackles
Senior Andy Chavous	100%	2 tackles (and a fine leader!)

But I have to single out **Pat Watson**—our Myrtle Beach Senior who was remarkable. With 1:06 on the clock, he was running up and down the sideline yelling "We're

(Continued on Page 3)

FIVE-GAME VARSITY STATISTICS
(Record: 4-1; ACC: 3-0; Home: 3-0; Away: 1-1)

TEAM	USC	OPP.
First downs rushing	33	67
First downs passing	37	28
First downs penalties	2	3
TOTAL FIRST DOWNS	72	98
Net yards rushing	898	1083
Number of rushes	243	298
Game rushing average	179.6	216.6
Passing yardage	623	563
Game passing average	124.6	112.4
TOTAL OFFENSE	1521	1646
Passes attempted	96	91
Passes completed	51	43
Intercepted by	6	4
Number of punts	36	28
Yards punted	1367	1126
Punts had blocked	0	0
Punting average	38.0	40.0
Return yardage	228	164
Fumbles lost	4	8
Yards penalized	247	159

RUSHING

	NO.	YDS.	AVG.	TD
Muir	94	406	4.3	5
Holloman	56	224	4.0	1
Rice	21	97	4.6	1
Suggs	38	76	2.0	1
Simmons	16	46	2.9	0
Miranda	7	24	3.4	0
Walkup	6	13	2.2	0
Yoakum	2	6	3.0	0
Trevillian	2	4	2.0	0
Sistore	1	2	2.0	0
TOTALS	243	898	3.7	8
OPPONENTS	298	1083	3.6	8

PASSING

	ATT.	COMP.	INT.	PCT.	YDS.	TD
Suggs	89	48	4	.539	569	2
Yoakum	7	3	0	.429	54	1
TOTALS	96	51	4	.531	623	3
OPPONENTS	91	45	6	.495	563	4

TOTAL OFFENSE

	RUSH	PASS	TOTAL
Suggs	76	569	645
Yoakum	6	54	60
(Others same as rushing)			

RECEIVING

	NO.	YDS.	AVG.	TD
Zeigler	21	248	11.8	2
Holloman	9	105	11.7	0
Hamrick	8	99	12.4	0
Muir	6	69	11.5	0
Freeman	3	45	15.0	1
Rice	2	33	16.5	0
Trevillian	1	16	16.0	0
Simmons	1	8	8.0	0

INTERCEPTION RETURNS

	NO.	YDS.	AVG.	TD
Davies	2	5	2.5	0
Harris	2	2	1.0	0
Nash	1	5	5.0	0
Watson	1	0	0.0	0

PUNT RETURNS

	NO.	YDS.	AVG.	TD
Mitchell	5	121	24.2	1
Harris	10	77	7.7	0
Watson	1	3	3.0	0
Bailey	1	2	2.0	0

KICKOFF RETURNS

	NO.	YDS.	AVG.	TD
Harris	7	206	29.4	0
Bailey	5	68	13.6	0
Hellams	1	18	18.0	0
Davies	1	8	8.0	0
Wingard	1	7	7.0	0

PUNTING

	NO.	YDS.	BLKD.	AVG.
Parker	36	1367	0	38.0

SCORING

	TD	PAT-K	PAT-RP	FG	TP
Muir	5	0-0	0-0	0-0	30
DuPre	0	11-11	0-0	4-9	23
Zeigler	2	0-0	0-0	0-0	12
Holloman	1	0-0	0-0	0-0	6
Suggs	1	0-0	0-0	0-0	6
Freeman	1	0-0	0-0	0-0	6
Rice	1	0-0	0-0	0-0	6
Mitchell	1	0-0	0-0	0-0	6
Yoakum	0	0-0	0-1	0-0	0
TOTALS	12	11-11	0-1	4-9	95
OPPONENTS	12	9-11	0-1	6-12	99

CUMULATIVE SCORE BY PERIODS:

GAMECOCKS	0	34	28	33	95
OPPONENTS	20	13	17	49	99

DEFENSIVE STATISTICS

	Tackles	Assists	Fumbles Caused	Fumbles Rec.
Harris	29	4	0	1
Davies	26	16	2	1
Tharpe	24	10	0	0
Nash	24	5	0	0
Kohout	19	7	0	2
Usher	18	6	0	0
Poston	15	9	2	0
Padgett	15	6	0	0
Ganas	15	5	0	0
Watson	15	4	0	2
Crabb	14	8	0	0
Hodge	14	6	0	0
Wingard	13	1	0	0
Pope	11	4	0	0
Lucas	10	5	0	0
Buckner	10	4	0	0
Bailey	9	2	0	0
Parker	8	1	0	1
Chavous	5	0	0	0
McCarthy	2	0	0	0
Hellams	2	0	0	0
Wright	0	1	0	0
Fusaro				1

From The
Gamecock Roost

Published weekly during football season and periodically throughout the year by the University of South Carolina GAMECOCK CLUB. Sent to members of the GAMECOCK CLUB in the interest of better education through athletics at Carolina. Republication of any of the contents is invited.

PAUL F. DIETZEL
Head Football Coach & Athletic Director
ED PITTS
Director, The Gamecock Club
Edited by TOM PRICE, Sports Information Director

ED SAYS
By ED PITTS
FOOTBALL TICKET SITUATION

There are no tickets remaining for our game with Maryland October 25 and Tennessee November 8. The USC ticket office still has a limited number of tickets available for our games at Florida State November 1 and at Wake Forest November 15. Tickets can still be purchased for the Carolina-Clemson game in Carolina Coliseum.

STATE FAIR

This is State Fair week and Homecoming. Please plan to come to the game early Saturday. Traffic and parking will be a much bigger problem this week than at any of our earlier games this season.

Anyone bringing his automobile to Carolina Stadium early and parking it in the reserved parking area must park in a proper parking space.

If you park before the highway patrol checks you in, you must leave your parking permit where it can be seen. Automobiles left in the reserved parking area without a visible parking permit will be towed away at the owner's expense.

Anyone who plans to bring a bus to any of our home games may park in the reserved parking area in the fairgrounds if you have in your possession $1,000 worth of parking permits, excluding permits for personal parking spaces. However, you must notify us in advance before each game; otherwise, we will not have room for you in the area.

BASKETBALL

Basketball season ticket reorder priority has expired. It is very doubtful that we will be able to improve the location of anyone's seats or increase the number of season tickets purchased last year even though a considerable increase in contributions over last year's was made.

All of our seats were committed to Gamecock Club contributors last year and we just don't have anything else available.

NOTES FROM THE GAMECOCK ROOST:

Freshman tight end Billy Carpenter might be described as a touchdown pass receiving specialist. The 6-2, 198-pounder from Greenville, caught only two passes in Carolina's first three freshman football games, but both of them went for touchdowns. Carpenter caught a 64-yard scoring pass from quarterback Jackie Young against the Clemson frosh and a 49-yard TD pass from Young against the N. C. State frosh.

Carolina, 4-1 at the halfway point in the 1969 football season, is off to its finest start in 13 years. The last time the Gamecocks won four of their first five games was 1956 when they posted a final mark of 7-3.

BIDDIES MEET WAKE FOREST FROSH IN CAROLINA STADIUM; BEAT N. C. STATE FROSH 22-16 AT RALEIGH

Carolina's freshmen, seeking to add to the new win streak they started with an up and down 22-16 win over N. C. State last week, tackle the Deaclets of Wake Forest Thursday at 7:30 P.M. in Carolina Stadium.

The Biddies, now 2-1 for the year, will be trying to end the season unbeaten at home for the third straight year. They close their season with a road game against Georgia Nov. 17. The USC freshmen's last defeat by a Wake Forest frosh outfit was in 1966 and last year the Biddies swamped the Deaclets, 35-3.

Against N. C. State, the Biddie defense played superbly for almost three quarters, limiting the Wolflets to only nine yards rushing. But the State frosh sprang a halfback loose for a long gain, got their offense going, and the Biddies had to withstand a 16-point last quarter barrage to win.

The USC freshmen completely dominated the first half and capitalized on N. C. State miscues for a 15-0 lead. They led in total offense at the half, 158-37, but the last quarter Wolflet heroics closed the final gap to 251-181.

The State frosh scoring drives were aided by the fact that four Biddie defensive starters were hindered by slight injuries sustained during the contest, thus curtailing the Baby Birds' earlier fierce line play and pass rushing.

Tailback Russ Kuritz lugged the ball 23 times for 75 yards, bringing his team leading season total to 245 yards. Fullback Chuck Mimms added 43 yards rushing and also caught two passes.

The Biddie touchdowns were scored by Kuritz on a one-yard plunge, halfback Neville Files on an 11-yard burst up the middle and end Billy Carpenter on a 49-yard pass from quarterback Jackie Young that proved to be the margin of victory. The Biddies improved the passing part of their offense, with Young and Lynn Rushing connecting on six of seven attempts.

FROM COACH PAUL DIETZEL
Continued from Page One

still going to WIN!" And he contributes so greatly on the field and off. He's a **WINNER!** He had 96%—5 tackles—and a fumble recovery!!!

Our ends played their usual good game

Hodge	70%	4 Tackles
Pope	77%	1 Tackle
Lucas	73%	3 Tackles
Wingard	86%	

But the men who really did the job were our two junior tackles:

Continued on Page 4

THREE-GAME FRESHMAN STATISTICS
(Record: 2-1; ACC: 1-1; Home: 1-0; Away: 1-1)

TEAM	USC	OPP.
First Downs Rushing	32	15
First Downs Passing	12	11
First Downs Penalties	2	1
TOTAL FIRST DOWNS	46	27
Net Yards Rushing	546	263
Number of Rushes	174	127
Game Rushing Average	182.0	87.7
Passing Yardage	274	255
Game Passing Average	91.3	85.0
TOTAL OFFENSE	820	518
Passes Attempted	32	41
Passes Completed	14	19
Intercepted by	2	2
Number of Punts	19	21
Yards Punted	667	753
Punts Had Blocked	0	0
Punting Average	35.1	35.9
Return Yardage	72	113
Fumbles Lost	1	5
Yards Penalized	132	111

RUSHING	NO.	YDS.	AVG.	TD
Kuritz	65	245	3.8	2
Mimms	39	167	4.3	0
Files	14	62	4.4	2
Kooker	20	60	3.0	0
Haywood	5	19	3.8	0
Rushing	17	4	0.2	0
Young	14	-11	-0.8	1
TOTALS	174	546	3.1	5
OPPONENTS	127	263	2.1	2

PASSING	NO.	COMP.	INT.	PCT.	YDS.	TD
Young	23	7	2	.304	202	2
Rushing	9	7	0	.778	72	0
TOTALS	32	14	2	.438	274	2
OPPONENTS	41	19	2	.463	255	3

TOTAL OFFENSE	RUSH	PASS	TOTAL
Young	-11	202	191
Rushing	4	72	76
(Others same as rushing)			

RECEIVING	NO.	YDS.	AVG.	TD
Barfield	4	55	13.8	0
Smith	3	57	19.0	0
Kuritz	3	24	8.0	0
Carpenter	2	113	56.5	2
Mimms	2	25	12.5	0

INTERCEPTION RETURNS	NO.	YDS.	AVG.	TD
Williams	1	11	11.0	0
Robinson	1	0	0.0	0

PUNT RETURNS	NO.	YDS.	AVG.	TD
Haggard	10	58	5.8	0
Williams	1	3	3.0	0

KICKOFF RETURNS	NO.	YDS.	AVG.	TD
Haggard	2	65	32.5	0
Williams	2	44	22.0	0
Mimms	2	35	17.5	0
Kuritz	1	29	29.0	0
Barfield	1	0	0.0	0

PUNTING	NO.	YDS.	BLKD.	AVG.
Barfield	19	667	0	35.1

SCORING	TD	PAT-K	PAT-RP	FG	TP
Files	2	0-0	0-0	0-0	12
Carpenter	2	0-0	0-0	0-0	12
Kuritz	2	0-0	0-0	0-0	12
Young	1	0-0	0-1	0-0	6
Cline	0	3-6	0-0	0-1	3
Cash	0	0-0	0-0	1-1	3
TOTALS	7	3-6	0-1	1-2	48
OPPONENTS	6	4-4	2-2	0-0	44

CUMULATIVE SCORE BY PERIODS:

BIDDIES	16	13	6	13	48
OPPONENTS	0	0	14	30	44

FUMBLES RECOVERED	NO.	YDS. RTN.
Privette	1	0
Kuritz	1	0
Stribling	1	0
Haggard	1	0
Gillis	1	0

RESULTS, ATTENDANCE & REMAINING GAMES
SOUTH CAROLINA 13, The Citadel 7 — 2,768
SOUTH CAROLINA 13, Clemson 21 — 3,000
SOUTH CAROLINA 22, N. C. State 16 — 1,000
Oct. 23—WAKE FOREST, 7:30 P.M.
Nov. 17—At Georgia, 2 P.M.

THARPE 71%
7 Tackles

CRABB 71%
4 Tackles
5 Ass'ts.

PARKER 100%
1 Tackle
1 Fumble Recovery

WATSON

GANAS 73%
5 Tackles

POSTON 70%
6 Tackles
1 Assist
Caused two fumbles

351

From The
Gamecock Roost

FROM COACH PAUL DIETZEL

WOULD YOU BELIEVE? CAROLINA 17 - MARYLAND 0!

GAME CAPTAIN TONY FUSARO
83%

We had a couple of people here who had told us before the game that they would have to leave at half-time to catch the last flight home. At the half, we were ahead 3-0 and were not playing too well. They missed the game!

We found out that Maryland is a rugged, hard-nosed team. They have a couple of real tough running backs in Thomas and Miller. Thomas is as good a runner as we have faced this year. He is really tough to bring down.

Offensively, we were especially pleased with the performance of several

the ACC. **Warren Muir** of Massachusetts really is in a class by himself at fullback. A tremendous team man and leader, Warren is a real threat when he has the ball under his arm and is averaging 4.2 yards per carry. Consider that this is the fella you can count on when it's 3rd and one or 4th and one and he is always getting you that real **tough** yardage. **Tom Trevillian** of Virginia at flanker ends up being our tight end on many formations and what tremendous effort and hustle he gives us. **Tommy Suggs,** the remarkable little Lamar scrambler, is now

GAME CAPTAIN DON BUCKNER
71% 3 Tackles 1 Assist

by far the most accurate passer in Gamecock football history. At the moment he has a completion percentage of 55.7% for this season and a career record of 170/313 for 2,303 yards and 16 touchdowns—a career percentage of 54.3%. The funny thing about it is that Tommy is at his best when he is scrambling.

In the Maryland game one wag in the stands yelled—"Go ahead and score, Maryland, so Carolina can get started!" When we went ahead 3 to 0, it was the first time this season, I believe, that we were ahead first!

Although our defense started off slow it gained momentum the second half. We were especially pleased with our defensive ends.

Continued on Page 4

HOLLOMAN 80%
Tailback
Hartsville

TREVILLIAN 80%
Flanker
Hampton, Va.

ZEIGLER 88%
Split End
7 passes for 107 yds.
Reevesville

SUGGS 91%
Quarterback
Lamar

Gamecocks.

Actually, the rest of the line graded well, too. Only one position was under 70%. **Rudy Holloman** now ranks seventh in all-time Gamecock receivers. He made some clutch catches and runs in the Maryland game. **Fred Zeigler** of Reevesville now has caught 122 for 1,573 yards and leads

MUIR 84%
Fullback
Fitchburg, Mass.

HODGE 80%
8 Tackles
4 Assists

LUCAS 79%
3 Tackles

POPE 79%
1 Tackle
1 Assist

SIX-GAME VARSITY STATISTICS
(Record: 5-1; ACC: 4-0; Home: 4-0; Away: 1-1)

TEAM	USC	OPP.
First downs rushing	35	80
First downs passing	46	30
First downs penalties	3	5
TOTAL FIRST DOWNS	84	115
Net yards rushing	988	1288
Number of rushes	281	362
Game rushing average	164.7	214.7
Passing yardage	821	625
Game passing average	136.8	104.3
TOTAL OFFENSE	1809	1913
Passes attempted	115	112
Passes completed	64	52
Intercepted by	7	4
Number of punts	45	35
Yards punted	1737	1430
Punts had blocked	0	0
Punting average	38.6	40.9
Return yardage	240	160
Fumbles lost	6	10
Yards penalized	313	232

RUSHING

	NO.	YDS.	AVG.	TD
Muir	113	475	4.2	6
Holloman	65	253	3.9	1
Rice	23	102	4.4	1
Suggs	42	64	1.5	1
Simmons	18	51	2.8	0
Miranda	7	24	3.4	0
Walkup	6	13	2.2	0
Trevillian	3	5	1.7	0
Sistare	1	2	2.0	0
Yoakum	3	1	0.3	0
TOTALS	281	988	3.5	9
OPPONENTS	362	1288	3.6	8

PASSING

	ATT.	COMP.	INT.	PCT.	YDS.	TD
Suggs	106	60	4	.566	759	3
Yoakum	9	4	0	.444	62	1
TOTALS	115	64	4	.557	821	4
OPPONENTS	112	52	7	.464	625	4

TOTAL OFFENSE

	RUSH	PASS	TOTAL
Suggs	64	759	823
Yoakum	-1	62	61
(Others same as rushing)			

RECEIVING

	NO.	YDS.	AVG.	TD
Zeigler	28	355	12.7	2
Holloman	12	174	14.5	1
Hamrick	8	99	12.4	0
Muir	6	69	11.5	0
Freeman	3	45	15.0	1
Rice	2	33	16.5	0
Mitchell	2	14	7.0	0
Trevillian	1	16	16.0	0
Simmons	1	8	8.0	0
Miranda	1	8	8.0	0

INTERCEPTION RETURNS

	NO.	YDS.	AVG.	TD
Watson	2	5	2.5	0
Davies	2	5	2.5	0
Harris	2	2	1.0	0
Nash	1	5	5.0	0

PUNT RETURNS

	NO.	YDS.	AVG.	TD
Mitchell	8	128	16.0	1
Harris	10	77	7.7	0
Watson	1	3	3.0	0
Bailey	1	2	2.0	0

KICKOFF RETURNS

	NO.	YDS.	AVG.	TD
Harris	8	236	29.5	0
Bailey	5	68	13.6	0
Hellams	1	18	18.0	0
Davies	1	8	8.0	0
Wingard	1	7	7.0	0

PUNTING

	NO.	YDS.	BLKD.	AVG.
Parker	45	1737	0	38.6

SCORING

	TD	PAT-K	PAT-RP	FG	TP
Muir	6	0-0	0-0	0-0	36
DuPre	0	13-13	0-0	5-10	28
Zeigler	2	0-0	0-0	0-0	12
Holloman	2	0-0	0-0	0-0	12
Suggs	1	0-0	0-0	0-0	6
Freeman	1	0-0	0-0	0-0	6
Rice	1	0-0	0-0	0-0	6
Mitchell	1	0-0	0-0	0-0	6
Yoakum	0	0-0	0-1	0-0	0
TOTALS	14	13-13	0-1	5-10	112
OPPONENTS	12	9-11	0-1	6-14	99

CUMULATIVE SCORE BY PERIODS:

GAMECOCKS	0 —	37 —	35 —	40 —	112
OPPONENTS	20 —	13 —	17 —	49 —	99

DEFENSIVE STATISTICS

	Tackles	Assists	Fumbles Caused	Fumbles Rec.
Harris	31	4	0	1
Davies	30	16	2	1
Tharpe	30	13	0	0
Nash	28	7	0	0
Hodge	22	10	0	0
Kohout	22	7	0	2
Crabb	21	12	0	0
Poston	20	11	2	0
Padgett	18	6	0	0
Usher	18	6	0	0
Watson	18	5	0	2
Ganas	17	7	0	0
Wingard	16	3	0	0
Buckner	13	5	0	0
Lucas	13	5	0	0
Bailey	14	2	0	0
Pope	12	5	0	0
Parker	10	1	0	1
Chavous	5	1	0	0
McCarthy	3	4	0	0
Wright	3	3	0	0
Hellams	2	0	0	0
Boyd	1	1	0	0
Fusaro				1
Ross				1

From The
Gamecock Roost

Published weekly during football season and periodically throughout the year by the University of South Carolina GAMECOCK CLUB. Sent to members of the GAMECOCK CLUB in the interest of better education through athletics at Carolina. Republication of any of the contents is invited.

PAUL F. DIETZEL
Head Football Coach & Athletic Director
ED PITTS
Director, The Gamecock Club
Edited by TOM PRICE, Sports Information Director

ED SAYS
By ED PITTS

When this newsletter went to press, the Ticket Office had tickets available for all of our remaining football games including University of Tennessee at Knoxville, November 8. We were able to get a few more tickets from Tennessee since our last newsletter was published.

PARKING

Anyone bringing his automobile to Carolina Stadium early and parking it in the reserved parking area must park in a proper parking space.

If you park before the highway patrol checks you in, you must leave your parking permit where it can be seen. Automobiles left in the reserved parking area without a visible parking permit will be towed away at the owner's expense.

Anyone who plans to bring a bus to the Clemson game may park in the reserved parking area in the fairgrounds if you have in your possession $1,000 worth of parking permits, excluding permits for personal parking spaces. However, you must notify us in advance, otherwise, we will not have room for you in the area.

BASKETBALL

If you purchased basketball season tickets last year and have reordered your same seats this year, but had not renewed your Gamecock Club membership when basketball ticket priority expired October 1, do not expect to receive basketball tickets for the coming season.

DIETZEL HEADS SOUTH STAFF FOR LIONS AMERICAN BOWL

Coach Paul Dietzel has been named head coach of the South squad for the second annual Lions American Bowl football game in Tampa, Fla., next Jan. 3.

The game, sponsored by the Lions Club, was inaugurated last year and Gamecock defensive back Roy Don Reeves played in the first contest.

Dietzel's assistants with the South squad will be coaches Darrell Royal of Texas, Charlie Tate of Miami (Fla.), and Fran Curci of Tampa. Notre Dame head coach Ara Parseghian will serve as head coach of the North and he will be assisted by Joe Paterno of Penn State, Bob Devaney of Nebraska and Walt Corey of Utah State.

OPPONENTS FACE FOUR GOOD ONES WHEN THEY ATTACK GAMECOCK ENDS

At the outset of the 1969 football season, Coach Paul Dietzel said the defensive ends were the Gamecocks' strongest positions from a standpoint of depth.

This statement has been borne out repeatedly through the first six games—five of them Gamecock victories—and was never more evident than in Saturday night's 17-0 Atlantic Coast Conference win over Maryland.

Senior Lynn Hodge, 6-4, 202, especially, was outstanding, playing what Dietzel described as "the finest game of Lynn's career." Hodge made eight individual tackles, assisted on four others and graded 80 per cent on techniques, a "Championship" rating in the Carolina coaching staff's

Gamecock defensive end Lynn Hodge (89) fends off a Maryland blocker before making the tackle on a Terp ball carrier in Carolina's 17-0 ACC win. Hodge, playing what Coach Paul Dietzel described as "his finest game," made eight individual tackles, had four assists and graded 80 percent to lead the Gamecock defense in the shutout. (Photo by Vic Tutte courtesy The State-Record.)

grading system.

Close behind were senior Dave Lucas, 6-5, 189, and junior Jimmy Pope, 6-4, 207, both at 79 per cent; and junior Joe Wingard, 6-4, 206, at 76 per cent. Wingard made three tackles and two assists, Lucas three tackles, and Pope one tackle and one assist.

With four lettermen defensive ends, the Gamecocks have been alternating them throughout the season with each playing about as much as the others. Hodge and Lucas, perhaps because they are seniors, are the starters but Pope and Wingard command equal status as regulars.

All four of them are tall, but weight-wise they aren't exceptionally big as major college defensive ends go. All are native South Carolinians although Wingard—who was born in Orangeburg—went to high school in Virginia and now lives in Brevard, N. C. Hodge is from Union, Lucas from Bishopville and Pope from Rock Hill.

Hodge is a five-year man who made a miraculous recovery from a compound fracture of one of his legs to play football again. A starter as a sophomore in 1966, he spent the 1967 season as team manager while recovering from the broken leg suffered in spring practice. He was a regular again in 1968 and against Georgia returned an intercepted pass for a touchdown.

Lucas also is a five-year man but he was redshirted in 1966 and has been a starter the past three seasons. He is generally regarded as the finest pass rusher in the Atlantic Coast Conference. In 1967 he recovered a Duke fumble on the opening kickoff in the end zone for a touchdown.

Pope and Wingard are both true sophomores. Pope missed his freshman season with a dislocated elbow but Wingard was a regular on that freshman team, in 1967.

FOUR-GAME FRESHMAN STATISTICS

(Record: 2-2; ACC: 1-2; Home: 1-1; Away: 1-1)

TEAM	USC	OPP.
First Downs Rushing	38	28
First Downs Passing	22	13
First Downs Penalties	3	4
TOTAL FIRST DOWNS	63	45
Net Yards Rushing	681	491
Number of Rushes	212	197
Game Rushing Average	170.3	122.8
Passing Yardage	503	374
Game Passing Average	125.8	93.5
TOTAL OFFENSE	1184	865
Passes Attempted	60	50
Passes Completed	30	23
Intercepted by	2	6
Number of Punts	23	26
Yards Punted	774	922
Punts Had Blocked	0	0
Punting Average	33.7	35.4
Return Yardage	112	120
Fumbles Lost	1	6
Yards Penalized	181	137

RUSHING

	NO.	YDS.	AVG.	TD
Kuritz	79	297	3.8	2
Mimms	50	233	4.7	0
Files	17	65	3.8	2
Kooker	21	58	2.8	0
Haywood	5	19	3.8	0
Young	21	8	0.4	2
Rushing	19	1	0.1	0
TOTALS	212	681	3.2	6
OPPONENTS	197	491	2.5	5

PASSING

	NO.	COMP.	INT.	PCT.	YDS.	TD
Young	39	17	4	.438	356	4
Rushing	21	13	2	.619	147	0
TOTALS	60	30	6	.500	503	4
OPPONENTS	50	23	2	.460	374	5

TOTAL OFFENSE

	RUSH	PASS	TOTAL
Young	8	356	364
Rushing	1	147	148

RECEIVING

	NO.	YDS.	AVG.	TD
Barfield	7	116	16.6	0
Kuritz	6	39	6.5	0
Carpenter	5	162	32.4	0
Mimms	4	62	15.5	0
Haggard	4	61	15.3	0
Smith	3	57	19.0	0
Kooker	1	6	6.0	0

INTERCEPTION RETURNS

	NO.	YDS.	AVG.	TD
Williams	1	11	11.0	0
Robinson	1	0	0.0	0

PUNT RETURNS

	NO.	YDS.	AVG.	TD
Haggard	13	98	7.5	0
Williams	1	0	0.0	0

KICKOFF RETURNS

	NO.	YDS.	AVG.	TD
Haggard	7	130	18.5	0
Williams	2	44	22.0	0
Mimms	2	35	17.5	0
Kuritz	2	35	17.5	0
Barfield	1	0	0.0	0

PUNTING

	NO.	YDS.	BLKD.	AVG.
Barfield	23	774	0	33.7

SCORING

	TD	PAT-K	PAT-RP	FG	TP
Carpenter	4	0-0	0-0	0-0	24
Files	2	0-0	0-0	0-0	12
Kuritz	2	0-0	0-0	0-0	12
Young	1	0-0	0-1	0-0	12
Cline	0	6-9	0-0	0-1	6
Cash	0	0-0	0-0	1-1	3
TOTALS	10	6-9	0-1	1-2	69
OPPONENTS	11	9-9	2-2	0-0	79

CUMULATIVE SCORE BY PERIODS:

BIDDIES	16	27	6	20	69
OPPONENTS	0	7	35	37	79

FUMBLES RECOVERED

	NO.	YDS. RTN.
Haggard	2	0
Privette	1	0
Kuritz	1	0
Stribling	1	0
Gillis	1	0

RESULTS, ATTENDANCE & REMAINING GAMES

SOUTH CAROLINA 13, The Citadel 7 — 2,500
SOUTH CAROLINA 13, Clemson 21 — 3,000
SOUTH CAROLINA 22, N. C. State 16 — 1,000
SOUTH CAROLINA 21, Wake Forest 35 — 1,000
Nov. 17—At Georgia, 2 P.M.

354

FROM COACH PAUL DIETZEL

FLORIDA STATE 34 - CAROLINA 9

GAME CAPTAIN RUDY HOLLOMAN

GAME CAPTAIN PAT WATSON

It's very difficult to find anything good to say after a loss such as we suffered at Tallahassee.

It was really a catastrophe for us to lose that one, and we really knew what it meant before the game, too! Although I've seen it happen many times before, darned if it didn't happen to us.

Prematurely, along a young season, after a few successes, the talk begins about bowls and such. All of a sudden, the team starts thinking about the bowl possibility a little too much, and not enough about next week's opponent. Otherwise, I cannot for the life of me explain why we played so poorly at Florida State. We really made them look like a great team — they are pretty darn good anyway. There is just not that much difference in our two teams.

One of the principal things I had tried very hard to bear down on during the week was the kicking game because this was a phase that I figured would have a large bearing on the game. It did!! And I'll be darned if we didn't have four huge breakdowns on the kicking game:

1. Fake field goal pass completed for big yardage—lineman down field!

2. Fumbled and lost ball on a kick-off return—their ball on the 20.

3. An on-side kick and we look like "little sisters of the poor"—it wasn't even an attempt—he missed the ball.

4. Covering a punt—have them really backed up—and tackle the safety before the ball gets there—give them the ball on the 30 instead!

Things like that make you feel so darn stupid—like it is your first night of practice! You ask yourself how many times you have covered that exact situation and the answer is "one less than you should have!"

Another key to the game was missed tackles and not being alert. There is no excuse for missing tackles unless you are not ready to play. And apparently we were just not ready to play. It was d bitter, galling experience.

But we have yet another game this week. And it is the University of Tennessee, and it is in Knoxville. Tennessee is ranked number three in the nation and unbeaten. They

TENNESSEE	31	Chattanooga	0
TENNESSEE	45	Auburn	19
TENNESSEE	35	Memphis State	16
TENNESSEE	26	Georgia Tech	8
TENNESSEE	41	Alabama	14
TENNESSEE	17	Georgia	3

Before the season began, Tennessee was to have an excellent defense but their offense was questionable. They have really fooled the "experts" on the offense because it has been great — and their defense has lived up to all of its predictions. They are a going concern. It's quite a challenge!!

Shall we see you there?

New Office Building At Athletic Center Open

Four offices of the athletic department that have been occupying temporary quarters at 503 Main Street in Columbia since last May have moved into enlarged and renovated offices at the Rex Enright Athletic Center.

The athletic annex adjacent to the "Roundhouse" on Rosewood Drive has been enlarged and remodeled to house the ticket office, business office, Gamecock Club, and sports information office.

Head football recruiter Jesse Berry and head track coach John West also have offices in the new building.

Telephone numbers remain 777-4274 and 777-4275 for the ticket office and business office; 777-4276 for the Gamecock Club; and 777-4277 for the sports information office.

Berry and West, who also assists Berry in recruiting, have a new telephone number, 777-5204.

The ticket office still has tickets available for the Nov. 15 football game against Wake Forest at Winston-Salem, N. C., and tickets are available in Carolina Coliseum for the closed circuit telecast of the Nov. 22 football game with Clemson.

SEVEN-GAME VARSITY STATISTICS

(Record: 5-2; ACC: 4-0; Home: 4-0; Away: 1-2)

TEAM	USC	OPP.
First downs rushing	41	94
First downs passing	54	40
First downs penalties	3	6
TOTAL FIRST DOWNS	98	140
Net yards rushing	1072	1546
Number of rushes	317	415
Game rushing average	153.1	220.9
Passing yardage	1024	844
Game passing average	146.3	120.6
TOTAL OFFENSE	2096	2390
Passes attempted	146	143
Passes completed	81	70
Intercepted by	8	7
Number of punts	49	38
Yards punted	1884	1529
Punts had blocked	0	0
Punting average	38.4	40.2
Return yardage	253	195
Fumbles lost	7	10
Yards penalized	353	292

RUSHING

	NO.	YDS.	AVG.	TD
Muir	126	538	4.3	6
Holloman	71	266	3.7	1
Rice	23	102	4.4	1
Simmons	24	60	2.5	0
Suggs	46	42	0.9	1
Miranda	9	25	2.8	0
Walkup	7	16	2.3	0
Yoakum	7	16	2.3	0
Trevillian	3	5	1.7	0
Sistare	1	2	2.0	0
TOTALS	317	1072	3.4	9
OPPONENTS	415	1546	3.7	10

PASSING

	ATT.	COMP.	INT.	PCT.	YDS.	TD
Suggs	120	67	6	.558	836	3
Yoakum	26	14	1	.538	188	2
TOTALS	146	81	7	.555	1024	5
OPPONENTS	143	70	8	.490	844	5

TOTAL OFFENSE

	RUSH	PASS	TOTAL
Suggs	42	836	878
Yoakum	16	188	204
(Others same as rushing)			

RECEIVING

	NO.	YDS.	AVG.	TD
Zeigler	30	425	14.2	2
Holloman	13	176	13.5	1
Hamrick	13	146	11.2	1
Muir	8	111	13.9	0
Freeman	3	45	15.0	1
Trevillian	3	37	12.3	0
Walkup	3	15	5.0	0
Rice	2	33	16.5	0
Simmons	2	20	10.0	0
Mitchell	2	14	7.0	0
Miranda	2	2	1.0	0

INTERCEPTION RETURNS

	NO.	YDS.	AVG.	TD
Harris	3	2	0.7	0
Watson	2	5	2.5	0
Davies	2	5	2.5	0
Nash	1	5	5.0	0

PUNT RETURNS

	NO.	YDS.	AVG.	TD
Mitchell	9	141	15.7	1
Harris	10	77	7.7	0
Watson	1	3	3.0	0
Bailey	1	2	2.0	0

KICKOFF RETURNS

	NO.	YDS.	AVG.	TD
Harris	12	335	27.9	0
Bailey	5	68	13.6	0
Davies	2	20	10.0	0
Hellams	1	18	18.0	0
Wingard	1	7	7.0	0

PUNTING

	NO.	YDS.	BLKD.	AVG.
Parker	49	1884	0	38.4

SCORING

	TD	PAT-K	PAT-RP	FG	TP
Muir	6	0-0	0-0	0-0	36
DuPre	0	13-13	0-0	6-12	31
Zeigler	2	0-0	0-0	0-0	12
Holloman	2	0-0	0-0	0-0	12
Suggs	1	0-0	0-0	0-0	6
Freeman	1	0-0	0-0	0-0	6
Rice	1	0-0	0-0	0-0	6
Mitchell	1	0-0	0-0	0-0	6
Hamrick	1	0-0	0-0	0-0	6
Yoakum	0	0-0	0-2	0-0	0
TOTALS	15	13-13	0-2	6-12	121
OPPONENTS	16	13-15	0-1	8-19	133

CUMULATIVE SCORE BY PERIODS:

GAMECOCKS	3 — 37 — 41 — 40 —	121
OPPONENTS	20 — 33 — 24 — 56 —	133

DEFENSIVE STATISTICS

	Tackles	Assists	Fumbles Caused	Fumbles Rec.
Davies	37	16	2	1
Tharpe	36	14	0	0
Harris	33	5	0	1
Nash	31	8	0	0
Crabb	26	13	0	0
Padgett	25	9	0	0
Hodge	24	11	0	0
Kohout	24	8	0	2
Watson	22	8	0	2
Poston	21	14	2	1
Buckner	19	8	0	0
Ganas	19	7	0	0
Usher	18	6	0	0
Lucas	18	5	0	0
Bailey	18	2	0	0
Wingard	16	3	0	0
Pope	14	5	0	0
Parker	11	2	0	1
Chavous	8	1	0	0
McCarthy	5	4	0	0
Wright	4	3	0	0
Hellams	2	0	0	0
Boyd	1	0	0	0
Fusaro				1
Ross				1

From The
Gamecock Roost

Published weekly during football season and periodically throughout the year by the University of South Carolina GAMECOCK CLUB. Sent to members of the GAMECOCK CLUB in the interest of better education through athletics at Carolina. Republication of any of the contents is invited.

PAUL F. DIETZEL
Head Football Coach & Athletic Director

ED PITTS
Director, The Gamecock Club

Edited by TOM PRICE, Sports Information Director

ED SAYS
By ED PITTS

The USC Ticket Office has tickets available for our game with Wake Forest. Ticket sales for the Carolina-Clemson game on closed circuit TV in the Coliseum have really picked up. If you do not have tickets for our game with Clemson, let us encourage you to go ahead and purchase them before all of the desirable seats are gone. These tickets are $6 each.

BASKETBALL

Basketball season tickets will be mailed around November 15, 1969.

GAMECOCK COUNTRY

All Gamecock Club members were mailed **Gamecock Country** window decals last week. Our only request is that you put it somewhere that it can be seen. Additional window decals are available at the Gamecock Club and Ticket Office for 25¢ each.

NOTES FROM THE GAMECOCK ROOST:

More than half the 1,072 yards gained rushing by Carolina during the first seven games of the 1969 football season was picked up by fullback Warren Muir. The 195 pound senior from Fitchburg, Mass., has rushed 538 yards. All other Gamecock backs combined have totaled 536 yards.

* * * * *

Carolina and Tennessee, Saturday's opponents at Knoxville, have met only seven times previously in football, with the Vols holding a 4-1-2 edge, but the series dates back 66 years. The Gamecocks won the first meeting, 24-0, in 1903, but haven't bested Tennessee since. There was a 6-6 tie in 1919 and a scoreless deadlock in 1942. The Volunteers won in 1916, 1929, 1965 and 1966. The Vols won the last game 27-19.

* * * * *

Carolina placekicker Billy DuPre tied a school record for most field goals in a season when he booted a 32-yarder against Florida State. The three pointer was DuPre's sixth of the season, tying the school mark set in 1965 by Jimmy Poole. Earlier this season, DuPre tied a 43-year-old school record for longest field goal when he kicked a 47-yarder against Virginia Tech.

1969 FOOTBALL SEASON SUPERLATIVES

GAMECOCKS

LONGEST RUN FROM SCRIMMAGE
Rudy Holloman vs. Duke, 60 yds. (TD)

LONGEST PASS COMPLETION
Tommy Suggs to Fred Zeigler vs. Maryland, 51 yds.

LONGEST PUNT
Billy Parker vs. Georgia, 56 yds.

FOUR-GAME FRESHMAN STATISTICS
(Record: 2-2; ACC: 1-2; Home: 1-1; Away: 1-1)

TEAM	USC	OPP.
First Downs Rushing	38	28
First Downs Passing	22	13
First Downs Penalties	3	4
TOTAL FIRST DOWNS	63	45
Net Yards Rushing	681	491
Number of Rushes	212	197
Game Rushing Average	170.3	122.8
Passing Yardage	503	374
Game Passing Average	125.8	93.5
TOTAL OFFENSE	1184	865
Passes Attempted	60	50
Passes Completed	30	23
Intercepted by	2	6
Number of Punts	23	26
Yards Punted	774	922
Punts Had Blocked	0	0
Punting Average	33.7	35.4
Return Yardage	112	120
Fumbles Lost	1	6
Yards Penalized	181	137

RUSHING	NO.	YDS.	AVG.	TD
Kuritz	79	297	3.8	2
Mimms	50	233	4.7	0
Files	17	65	3.8	2
Kooker	21	58	2.8	0
Haywood	5	19	3.8	0
Young	21	8	0.4	2
Rushing	19	1	0.1	0
TOTALS	212	681	3.2	6
OPPONENTS	197	491	2.5	5

PASSING	NO.	COMP.	INT.	PCT.	YDS.	TD
Young	39	17	4	.438	356	4
Rushing	21	13	2	.619	147	0
TOTALS	60	30	6	.500	503	4
OPPONENTS	50	23	2	.460	374	5

TOTAL OFFENSE	RUSH	PASS	TOTAL
Young	8	356	364
Rushing	1	147	148

RECEIVING	NO.	YDS.	AVG.	TD
Barfield	7	116	16.6	0
Kuritz	6	39	6.5	0
Carpenter	5	162	32.4	4
Mimms	4	62	15.5	0
Haggard	4	61	15.3	0
Smith	3	57	19.0	0
Kooker	1	6	6.0	0

INTERCEPTION RETURNS	NO.	YDS.	AVG.	TD
Williams	1	11	11.0	0
Robinson	1	0	0.0	0

PUNT RETURNS	NO.	YDS.	AVG.	TD
Haggard	13	98	7.5	0
Williams	1	0	0.0	0

KICKOFF RETURNS	NO.	YDS.	AVG.	TD
Haggard	7	130	18.5	0
Williams	2	44	22.0	0
Mimms	2	35	17.5	0
Kuritz	2	35	17.5	0
Barfield	1	0	0.0	0

PUNTING	NO.	YDS.	BLKD.	AVG.
Barfield	23	774	0	33.7

SCORING	TD	PAT-K	PAT-RP	FG	TP
Carpenter	4	0-0	0-0	0-0	24
Files	2	0-0	0-0	0-0	12
Kuritz	2	0-0	0-0	0-0	12
Young	1	0-0	0-1	0-0	12
Cline	0	6-9	0-0	0-1	6
Cash	0	0-0	0-0	1-1	3
TOTALS	10	6-9	0-1	1-2	69
OPPONENTS	11	9-9	2-2	0-0	79

CUMULATIVE SCORE BY PERIODS:

BIDDIES	16 — 27 — 6 — 20 —— 69
OPPONENTS	0 — 7 — 35 — 37 —— 79

FUMBLES RECOVERED	NO.	YDS. RTN.
Haggard	2	0
Privette	1	0
Kuritz	1	0
Stribling	1	0
Gillis	1	0

RESULTS, ATTENDANCE & REMAINING GAMES
SOUTH CAROLINA 13, The Citadel 7 — 2,500
SOUTH CAROLINA 13, Clemson 21 — 3,000
SOUTH CAROLINA 22, N. C. State 16 — 1,000
SOUTH CAROLINA 21, Wake Forest 35 — 1,000
Nov. 17—At Georgia, 2 P.M.

LONGEST PUNT RETURN
Jimmy Mitchell vs. N. C. State, 72 yds. (TD)

LONGEST KICKOFF RETURN
Dick Harris vs. Virginia Tech, 48 yds.

LONGEST INTERCEPTION RETURN
Jimmy Nash vs. North Carolina, 5 yds.
Bo Davies vs. North Carolina, 5 yds.
Pat Watson vs. Maryland, 5 yds.

LONGEST FIELD GOAL
Billy DuPre vs. Virginia Tech, 47 yds.

MOST RUSHES
Warren Muir vs. Virginia Tech, 29

MOST YARDS RUSHING
Warren Muir vs. Georgia, 136 yds.

MOST PASSES ATTEMPTED
Tommy Suggs vs. N. C. State, 21

MOST PASSES COMPLETED
Tommy Suggs vs. N. C. State, 14

MOST YARDS PASSING
Tommy Suggs vs. Maryland, 190 yds.

MOST TOTAL OFFENSE
Tommy Suggs vs. N. C. State, 206 yds.

MOST PASSES CAUGHT
Fred Zeigler vs. Maryland, 7

MOST YARDS ON PASS RECEPTIONS
Fred Zeigler vs. Maryland, 107 yds.

OPPONENTS

LONGEST RUN FROM SCRIMMAGE
Paul Magalski, Florida State, 33 yds. (TD)

LONGEST PASS COMPLETION
Darrell Moody to Leon Mason, N. C. State, 54 yds.

LONGEST PUNT
Greg Fries, Maryland, 59 yds.

LONGEST PUNT RETURN
Buck Swindle, Georgia, 23 yds.

LONGEST KICKOFF RETURN
Jack Whitley, N. C. State, 29 yds.

LONGEST INTERCEPTION RETURN
John Montgomery, Florida State, 27 yds. (TD)

LONGEST FIELD GOAL
Dave Pugh, Duke, 43 yds.
Jack Simscak, Virginia Tech, 43 yds.

MOST RUSHES
Bruce Kemp, Georgia, 31

MOST YARDS RUSHING
Bruce Kemp, Georgia, 142 yds.

MOST PASSES ATTEMPTED
Leo Hart, Duke, 34

MOST PASSES COMPLETED
Leo Hart, Duke, 20

MOST YARDS PASSING
Bill Cappleman, Florida State, 203 yds.

MOST TOTAL OFFENSE
Bill Cappleman, Florida State, 207 yds.

MOST PASSES CAUGHT
Marcel Courtillet, Duke, 8

MOST YARDS ON PASS RECEPTIONS
Marcel Courtillet, Duke, 91 yds.

From The
Gamecock Roost

Vol. 4, No. 12   Columbia, S. C.   November 13, 1969

FROM COACH PAUL DIETZEL

TENNESSEE 29 - CAROLINA 14

GAME CAPTAIN DON BUCKNER

WARREN MUIR

GAME CAPTAIN FRED ZEIGLER

What small consolation there is when you look good losing. It's really hard to reconcile yourself to anything being good when you have gotten beat. However, honesty compels us to look a few facts in the face. That is a fine Tennessee team—observers on the spot told us they were the best Tennessee team since 1951. And they are ranked number 3 in the nation. And they now are 7 and 0 on the year.

After the game, it took a while to get our squad settled down because they had really planned to win it. It was close to a huge upset—with five minutes remaining, we were 14-16 and in real good shape. But after our kick-off to Tennessee, we didn't hold them. We made them fumble and option pitch on second down and darned if they didn't come up with the ball, and then it was third and 14. We should have been in great shape, but they threw a bomb and kept it going until they scored.

Warren Muir really had himself a day of football. He was really the best football player on the field. His statistics were really impressive: 31 attempts for 159 yards and caught 2 passes for 32 yards. But they do not begin to tell the tale of his value to the team. He was sick at the half and on the sideline, but you would never know it based on his performance. He is the best inside runner in college football! And what a fierce competitor. Every soul at Shields-Watkins field realized who the best athlete on the field was.

But we had other fine performances, even in defeat.

On defense we were hurting all week because of injuries to our secondary down at Florida State. As it turned out, we had to use **Jimmy Nash** sparingly and **Bo Davies** could not play. **Andy Chavous** and **Candler Boyd** played most of the game at these positions, and we were most

ANDY CHAVOUS
82%
4 Tackles, 1 Assist

CANDLER BOYD
91%
3 Tackles

MACK THARPE
84%
2 Tackles, 1 Assist

impressed with their fine efforts. **Mack Tharpe** had a fine game at linebacker and our best linemen were our two senior ends, who gave us excellent leadership and hustle. **Don Buckner** really played as well as he could have played, I believe. He was a fine leader all week.

Offensively, our line played quite well against a real top-notch defensive team. **Zeigler** played extremely well as

(Continued on Page 3)

EIGHT-GAME VARSITY STATISTICS
(Record: 5-3; ACC: 4-0; Home: 4-0; Away: 1-3)

TEAM	USC	OPP.
First downs rushing	51	100
First downs passing	63	47
First downs penalties	4	7
TOTAL FIRST DOWNS	118	154
Net yards rushing	1276	1647
Number of rushes	369	458
Game rushing average	159.5	205.9
Passing yardage	1166	1058
Game passing average	145.8	132.3
TOTAL OFFENSE	2442	2705
Passes attempted	180	166
Passes completed	97	80
Intercepted by	8	10
Number of punts	56	46
Yards punted	2176	1893
Punts had blocked	0	0
Punting average	38.9	41.2
Return yardage	260	317
Fumbles lost	8	11
Yards penalized	432	349

RUSHING

	NO.	YDS.	AVG.	TD
Muir	157	697	4.4	7
Holloman	81	302	3.7	1
Rice	26	108	4.2	1
Simmons	26	72	2.8	0
Miranda	11	32	2.9	0
Suggs	50	26	0.5	1
Walkup	7	16	2.3	0
Yoakum	7	16	2.3	0
Trevillian	3	5	1.7	0
Sistare	1	2	2.0	0
TOTALS	369	1276	3.5	10
OPPONENTS	458	1647	3.6	10

PASSING

	ATT.	COMP.	INT.	PCT.	YDS.	TD
Suggs	141	77	8	.546	937	3
Yoakum	39	20	2	.513	229	3
TOTALS	180	97	10	.539	1166	6
OPPONENTS	166	80	8	.482	1058	8

TOTAL OFFENSE

	RUSH	PASS	TOTAL
Suggs	26	937	966
Yoakum	16	229	245

(Others same as rushing)

RECEIVING

	NO.	YDS.	AVG.	TD
Zeigler	38	485	12.8	2
Holloman	16	217	13.6	2
Hamrick	14	160	11.4	0
Muir	10	143	14.3	0
Trevillian	4	38	9.5	0
Freeman	3	45	15.0	1
Walkup	3	15	5.0	0
Simmons	3	14	4.7	0
Rice	2	33	16.5	0
Mitchell	2	14	7.0	0
Miranda	2	2	1.0	0

INTERCEPTION RETURNS

	NO.	YDS.	AVG.	TD
Harris	3	2	0.7	0
Watson	2	5	2.5	0
Davies	2	5	2.5	0
Nash	1	5	5.0	0

PUNT RETURNS

	NO.	YDS.	AVG.	TD
Mitchell	11	148	13.5	1
Harris	10	77	7.7	0
Watson	1	3	3.0	0
Bailey	1	2	2.0	0

KICKOFF RETURNS

	NO.	YDS.	AVG.	TD
Harris	16	431	26.9	0
Bailey	6	89	14.8	0
Davies	2	20	10.0	0
Hellams	1	18	18.0	0
Pope	0	14	......	0
Wingard	2	7	3.5	0

PUNTING

	NO.	YDS.	BLKD.	AVG.
Parker	56	2176	0	38.9

SCORING

	TD	PAT-K	PAT-RP	FG	TP
Muir	7	0-0	0-0	0-0	42
DuPre	0	15-15	0-0	6-14	33
Holloman	3	0-0	0-0	0-0	18
Zeigler	2	0-0	0-0	0-0	12
Suggs	1	0-0	0-0	0-0	6
Freeman	1	0-0	0-0	0-0	6
Rice	1	0-0	0-0	0-0	6
Mitchell	1	0-0	0-0	0-0	6
Hamrick	1	0-0	0-0	0-0	6
Yoakum	0	0-0	0-2	0-0	0
TOTALS	17	15-15	0-2	6-14	135
OPPONENTS	19	15-18	0-1	11-22	162

CUMULATIVE SCORE BY PERIODS:

GAMECOCKS	3	44	41	47	135
OPPONENTS	20	43	27	72	162

DEFENSIVE STATISTICS

	Tackles	Assists	Fumbles Caused	Fumbles Rec.
Tharpe	38	15	0	0
Davies	37	16	2	1
Nash	36	8	0	0
Harris	33	6	0	1
Hodge	30	12	0	1
Crabb	28	14	0	0
Padgett	28	9	0	0
Poston	25	17	2	1
Kohout	24	9	0	2
Buckner	23	9	0	0
Watson	23	8	0	2
Ganas	22	9	0	0
Lucas	21	6	0	0
Bailey	19	3	0	0
Usher	18	6	0	0
Wingard	17	3	0	0
Pope	16	5	0	0
Chavous	12	2	0	0
Parker	11	2	0	1
McCarthy	5	4	0	0
Wright	4	3	0	0
Hellams	2	0	0	0
Boyd	4	0	0	0
Fusaro				1
Ross				1

From The Gamecock Roost

Published weekly during football season and periodically throughout the year by the University of South Carolina GAMECOCK CLUB. Sent to members of the GAMECOCK CLUB in the interest of better education through athletics at Carolina. Republication of any of the contents is invited.

PAUL F. DIETZEL
Head Football Coach & Athletic Director
ED PITTS
Director, The Gamecock Club
Edited by TOM PRICE, Sports Information Director

ED SAYS
By ED PITTS

Tickets are still available for the Carolina-Clemson game on closed circuit TV in Carolina Coliseum. These tickets are $6.00 each.

Basketball season tickets will be mailed around November 15, 1969. There will be no tickets available for any of Carolina's out-of-town basketball games through the Gamecock Club. In most cases we receive only the limited number of complimentary tickets allotted in the contracts. We suggest that you write our opponents if you would like tickets for any of the away games.

Anything concerning our away basketball games is handled by Mr. Ralph Floyd in the Athletic Business Office.

GAMECOCK COUNTRY

We would like to encourage all Gamecock Club members to put a Gamecock Country decal on your auto window. Additional decals are available at the Gamecock Club and Ticket Office for 25¢ each.

PARKING

Anyone who plans to bring a bus to the Clemson game may park in the reserved parking area in the fairgrounds if you have in your possession $1,000 worth of parking permits, excluding permits for personal parking spaces. However, you must notify us in advance, otherwise, we will not have room for you in the area.

New Office Building At Athletic Center Open

Four offices of the athletic department that have been occupying temporary quarters at 503 Main Street in Columbia since last May have moved into enlarged and renovated offices at the Rex Enright Athletic Center.

The athletic annex adjacent to the "Roundhouse" on Rosewood Drive has been enlarged and remodeled to house the ticket office, business office, Gamecock Club, and sports information office.

Head football recruiter Jesse Berry and head track coach John West also have offices in the new building.

Telephone numbers remain 777-4274 and 777-4275 for the ticket office and business office; 777-4276 for the Gamecock Club; and 777-4277 for the sports information office.

Berry and West, who also assists Berry in recruiting, have a new telephone number, 777-5204.

1969 FOOTBALL SEASON SUPERLATIVES

GAMECOCKS

LONGEST RUN FROM SCRIMMAGE
Rudy Holloman vs. Duke, 60 yds. (TD)

LONGEST PASS COMPLETION
Tommy Suggs to Fred Zeigler vs. Maryland, 51 yds.

LONGEST PUNT
Billy Parker vs. Georgia, 56 yds.

FROM COACH PAUL DIETZEL
Continued from Page One

TOMMY SUGGS
91%

RANDY YOAKUM
91%

RUDY HOLLOMAN
83%

FRED ZEIGLER
86%
8/60

did our quarterbacks and **Holloman** — and, of course, Muir. We moved the ball on Tennessee as no one else has been able to this year. The Tennessee folks (coaching staff and players) said that we were the best team they had met this year and that Muir was far and away the best back they had played against. But there is **no way** to rationalize a great losing effort into a victory, and I do not mean to do that in any way.

But now it's the whole s e a s o n wrapped up in two conference games. And we can only play one at a time.

WAKE FOREST!

The Deacons are not in the running for the conference title, but they really figure very heavily in our conference plans. It has settled down even more into strictly a two-team battle. Since we are one of those two, we look upon the Wake Forest game as one of the real big games of the year. For the third straight year we play it at Winston-Salem. Before the year began I told our squad that one of our toughest games would be the Wake game—because I felt it would be one we had to have for the championship. And we do!

Hope that you all will be there because we'll need you. We had great support at Tennessee—just great. Our band really stayed with us, too. And we appreciate all of the fine support we received all week long from so many of you people. Thank you all.

See you in Winston!

NOTES FROM THE GAMECOCK ROOST:

The 159 yards gained by Warren Muir against Tennessee raised the All-America candidate to within three yards of second place among all-time Gamecock rushers. Muir has 697 yards through eight games this season and 1,962 for his three-year career. Bishop Strickland, who played four varsity seasons (1947-50), gained 1,965. The record is 2,878, set 1948-51 by Steve Wadiak who also played four years.

LONGEST PUNT RETURN
Jimmy Mitchell vs. N. C. State, 72 yds. (TD)

LONGEST KICKOFF RETURN
Dick Harris vs. Virginia Tech, 48 yds.

LONGEST INTERCEPTION RETURN
Jimmy Nash vs. North Carolina, 5 yds.
Bo Davies vs. North Carolina, 5 yds.
Pat Watson vs. Maryland, 5 yds.

LONGEST FIELD GOAL
Billy DuPre vs. Virginia Tech, 47 yds.

MOST RUSHES
Warren Muir vs. Tennessee, 31

MOST YARDS RUSHING
Warren Muir vs. Tennessee, 159 yds.

MOST PASSES ATTEMPTED
Tommy Suggs vs. N. C. State, 21

MOST PASSES COMPLETED
Tommy Suggs vs. N. C. State, 14

MOST YARDS PASSING
Tommy Suggs vs. Maryland, 190 yds.

MOST TOTAL OFFENSE
Tommy Suggs vs. N. C. State, 206 yds.

MOST PASSES CAUGHT
Fred Zeigler vs. Tennessee, 8

MOST YARDS ON PASS RECEPTIONS
Fred Zeigler vs. Maryland, 107 yds.

OPPONENTS

LONGEST RUN FROM SCRIMMAGE
Paul Magalski, Florida State, 33 yds. (TD)

LONGEST PASS COMPLETION
Darrell Moody to Leon Mason, N. C. State, 54 yds.

LONGEST PUNT
Greg Fries, Maryland, 59 yds.

LONGEST PUNT RETURN
Bobby Majors, Tennessee, 28 yds.

LONGEST KICKOFF RETURN
Jack Whitley, N. C. State, 29 yds.

LONGEST INTERCEPTION RETURN
Tim Priest, Tennessee, 33 yds.

LONGEST FIELD GOAL
Dave Pugh, Duke, 43 yds.
Jack Simscak, Virginia Tech, 43 yds.

MOST RUSHES
Bruce Kemp, Georgia, 31

MOST YARDS RUSHING
Bruce Kemp, Georgia, 142 yds.

MOST PASSES ATTEMPTED
Leo Hart, Duke, 34

MOST PASSES COMPLETED
Leo Hart, Duke, 20

MOST YARDS PASSING
Bobby Scott, Tennessee, 214 yds.

MOST TOTAL OFFENSE
Bill Cappleman, Florida State, 207 yds.

MOST PASSES CAUGHT
Marcel Courtillet, Duke, 8

MOST YARDS ON PASS RECEPTIONS
Gary Kreis, Tennessee, 151 yds.

FROM COACH PAUL DIETZEL

CAROLINA 24 - WAKE FOREST 6

GAME CAPTAIN TONY FUSARO   GAME CAPTAIN DAVE LUCAS   GAME CAPTAIN LYNN HODGE

THE FIRST USC CHAMPIONSHIP IN ANY SPORT
The First Time in History For a Clean Sweep
of the Four North Carolina Teams in One Year

It was really almost impossible to expect that we would be fortunate enough to win the title before the Clemson game. In order to do this we had to beat WAKE FOREST and Clemson had to lose to North Carolina. Frankly, I had convinced myself that we would be playing the final game of the year to determine the championship. That was some of that "Expect the toughest possible situation, and then anything less than that will be real welcome."

Our game with Wake was a great victory for us in many, many ways. It put us 6-3 for the year and 5-0 in the ACC. We weren't at our best, perhaps, but it certainly was a good example of taking quick advantage of breaks. We did a fine job of that. Wake Forest really came after us and their sophomore quarterback Russell really did an

excellent job of scrambling. He really ran well against us and impressed our whole squad.

There was one particular group of Gamecocks who were the happiest bunch you have ever seen. Those were our 11 "Black Hats" (seniors). Our seniors have always been called "Black Hats" since they have always worn headgears in practice that were painted black. And they are very proud of their championship.

George McCarthy has really done a great job here at Carolina. He has been an excellent leader and invaluable on all of our kicking teams and as an alternate defensive tackle. He is also one of the four members of the "Campus Bowl" Champions from the Roost. **Andy Chavous** has really done a fine job in our secondary and I am particularly pleased with the fine attitude he has always displayed. He has played an excellent game at safety the past two weeks

(Continued on Page 3)

GEORGE McCARTHY   ANDY CHAVOUS   KEN ROSS   FRED ZEIGLER   WARREN MUIR   RUDY HOLLOMAN

NINE-GAME VARSITY STATISTICS
(Record: 6-3; ACC: 5-0; Home: 4-0; Away: 2-3)

TEAM	USC	OPP.
First downs rushing	58	121
First downs passing	68	52
First downs penalties	4	7
TOTAL FIRST DOWNS	130	180
Net yards rushing	1445	1887
Number of rushes	410	534
Game rushing average	160.6	209.7
Passing yardage	1269	1161
Game passing average	141.0	129.0
TOTAL OFFENSE	2714	3048
Passes attempted	198	180
Passes completed	106	87
Intercepted by	12	11
Number of punts	62	48
Yards punted	2417	1954
Punts had blocked	0	0
Punting average	39.0	40.7
Return yardage	320	327
Fumbles lost	9	16
Yards penalized	482	415

RUSHING	NO.	YDS.	AVG.	TD
Muir	179	790	4.4	7
Holloman	87	321	3.7	1
Rice	29	117	4.0	1
Simmons	26	72	2.8	0
Suggs	54	62	1.1	1
Miranda	15	50	3.3	0
Walkup	7	16	2.3	0
Yoakum	8	9	1.1	0
Trevillian	3	5	1.7	0
Sistare	2	3	1.5	0
TOTALS	410	1445	3.5	10
OPPONENTS	534	1887	3.5	10

PASSING	ATT.	COMP.	INT.	PCT.	YDS.	TD
Suggs	156	85	9	.545	1033	6
Yoakum	42	21	2	.500	236	3
TOTALS	198	106	11	.535	1269	9
OPPONENTS	180	87	12	.484	1161	8

TOTAL OFFENSE	RUSH	PASS	TOTAL
Suggs	62	1033	1095
Yoakum	9	236	245
(Others same as rushing)			

RECEIVING	NO.	YDS.	AVG.	TD
Zeigler	43	536	12.5	3
Holloman	18	246	13.7	4
Hamrick	15	176	11.7	1
Muir	10	143	14.3	0
Trevillian	4	38	9.5	0
Freeman	3	45	15.0	1
Rice	3	40	13.3	0
Walkup	3	15	5.0	0
Simmons	3	14	4.7	0
Mitchell	2	14	7.0	0
Miranda	2	2	1.0	0

INTERCEPTION RETURNS	NO.	YDS.	AVG.	TD
Watson	3	15	5.0	0
Harris	3	2	0.7	0
Nash	2	21	11.5	0
Davies	2	5	2.5	0
Boyd	1	22	22.0	0
Chavous	1	7	7.0	0

PUNT RETURNS	NO.	YDS.	AVG.	TD
Mitchell	11	148	13.5	1
Harris	10	77	7.7	0
Watson	1	3	3.0	0
Bailey	1	2	2.0	0

KICKOFF RETURNS	NO.	YDS.	AVG.	TD
Harris	16	431	26.9	0
Bailey	9	145	16.1	0
Davies	2	20	10.0	0
Hellams	1	18	18.0	0
Pope	0	14		0
Wingard	2	7	3.5	0

PUNTING	NO.	YDS.	BLKD.	AVG.
Parker	62	2417	0	39.0

SCORING	TD	PAT-K	PAT-RP	FG	TP
Muir	7	0-0	0-0	0-0	42
DuPre	0	18-18	0-0	7-16	39
Holloman	5	0-0	0-0	0-0	30
Zeigler	3	0-0	0-0	0-0	18
Suggs	1	0-0	0-0	0-0	6
Freeman	1	0-0	0-0	0-0	6
Rice	1	0-0	0-0	0-0	6
Mitchell	1	0-0	0-0	0-0	6
Hamrick	1	0-0	0-0	0-0	6
Yoakum	0	0-0	0-2	0-0	0
TOTALS	20	18-18	0-2	7-16	159
OPPONENTS	20	15-19	0-1	11-23	168

CUMULATIVE SCORE BY PERIODS:

GAMECOCKS	3 —	58 —	44 —	54 —	159
OPPONENTS	20 — 49 — 27 — 72 — 168				

DEFENSIVE STATISTICS

	Tackles	Assists	Fumbles Caused	Fumbles Rec.
Tharpe	45	18	0	0
Padgett	39	12	0	0
Davies	37	16	2	1
Nash	36	9	0	0
Harris	36	8	0	1
Crabb	35	19	0	0
Kohout	31	10	0	2
Hodge	30	12	0	2
Poston	29	18	2	1
Ganas	26	10	1	0
Watson	25	9	0	2
Lucas	25	8	0	0
Bailey	24	5	0	0
Buckner	23	9	0	0
Wingard	21	6	0	0
Pope	18	6	0	1
Usher	18	6	0	0
Chavous	16	3	0	1
Boyd	16	3	0	1
Parker	12	3	0	1
McCarthy	5	4	0	0
Wright	5	3	0	0
Hellams	2	0	0	0
Fusaro				1
Ross				1
Bank				1

From The
Gamecock Roost

Published weekly during football season and periodically throughout the year by the University of South Carolina GAMECOCK CLUB. Sent to members of the GAMECOCK CLUB in the interest of better education through athletics at Carolina. Republication of any of the contents is invited.

PAUL F. DIETZEL
Head Football Coach & Athletic Director
ED PITTS
Director, The Gamecock Club
Edited by TOM PRICE, Sports Information Director

Senior class president Pat Watson, who also performs as "Mister Hustle" in the Gamecock secondary, sells "Beat Clemson" buttons to head football coach Paul Dietzel and University president, Dr. Thomas F. Jones. The senior class had the buttons manufactured and has been selling them for 50 cents each as a boost for school spirit.

ED SAYS
By ED PITTS
SUGAR BOWL BASKETBALL TOURNAMENT

The University Ticket Office has received 250 tickets for the Sugar Bowl Basketball Tournament in New Orleans, December 29 and 30. Tickets are $10 each. This includes one ticket for each night. Please order your tickets now if you plan to attend.

SUGAR BOWL BASKETBALL TOURNAMENT

Name _____

1969 Contribution _____

Address _____

City _____ State _____ Zip Code _____

_____ Tickets @ $10.00 each _____

postage and insurance _____ .50

TOTAL _____

1969 FOOTBALL SEASON SUPERLATIVES

GAMECOCKS

LONGEST RUN FROM SCRIMMAGE
Rudy Holloman vs. Duke, 60 yds. (TD)
LONGEST PASS COMPLETION
Tommy Suggs to Fred Zeigler vs. Maryland, 51 yds.
LONGEST PUNT
Billy Parker vs. Georgia, 56 yds.
LONGEST PUNT RETURN
Jimmy Mitchell vs. N. C. State, 72 yds. (TD)
LONGEST KICKOFF RETURN
Dick Harris vs. Virginia Tech, 48 yds.
LONGEST INTERCEPTION RETURN
Candler Boyd vs. Wake Forest, 22 yds.
LONGEST FIELD GOAL
Billy DuPre vs. Virginia Tech, 47 yds.
MOST RUSHES
Warren Muir vs. Tennessee, 31
MOST YARDS RUSHING
Warren Muir vs. Tennessee, 159 yds.
MOST PASSES ATTEMPTED
Tommy Suggs vs. N. C. State, 21
MOST PASSES COMPLETED
Tommy Suggs vs. N. C. State, 14
MOST YARDS PASSING
Tommy Suggs vs. Maryland, 190 yds.

MOST TOTAL OFFENSE
Tommy Suggs vs. N. C. State, 206 yds.
MOST PASSES CAUGHT
Fred Zeigler vs. Tennessee, 8
MOST YARDS ON PASS RECEPTIONS
Fred Zeigler vs. Maryland, 107 yds.

OPPONENTS

LONGEST RUN FROM SCRIMMAGE
Paul Magalski, Florida State, 33 yds. (TD)
LONGEST PASS COMPLETION
Darrell Moody to Leon Mason, N. C. State, 54 yds.
LONGEST PUNT
Greg Fries, Maryland, 59 yds.
LONGEST PUNT RETURN
Bobby Majors, Tennessee, 28 yds.
LONGEST KICKOFF RETURN
Jack Whitley, N. C. State, 29 yds.
LONGEST INTERCEPTION RETURN
Tim Priest, Tennessee, 33 yds.
LONGEST FIELD GOAL
Dave Pugh, Duke, 43 yds.
Jack Simscak, Virginia Tech, 43 yds.
MOST RUSHES
Bruce Kemp, Georgia, 31
MOST YARDS RUSHING
Bruce Kemp, Georgia, 142 yds.
MOST PASSES ATTEMPTED
Leo Hart, Duke, 34
MOST PASSES COMPLETED
Leo Hart, Duke, 20
MOST YARDS PASSING
Bobby Scott, Tennessee, 214 yds.
MOST TOTAL OFFENSE
Bill Cappleman, Florida State, 207 yds.
MOST PASSES CAUGHT
Marcel Courtillet, Duke, 8
MOST YARDS ON PASS RECEPTIONS
Gary Kreis, Tennessee, 151 yds.

FROM COACH PAUL DIETZEL Continued from Page One
—against Tennessee and against Wake Forest. **Ken Ross** has been absolutely invaluable to the 'Cocks for the past two years. He has snapped every ball for punts and place kicks and done a great job in coverage, too. We would have been in real trouble if we had lost him at any time. **Tony Fusaro,** the unofficial leader of the offensive line, has really done an outstanding job for us for three straight years. And Tony is a real Horatio Alger story because he came to Carolina without a scholarship and made it. So we are a little more proud of him. **Fred Zeigler** is really something. He's out of a special "one-of-a-kind" mold that will never be duplicated. He sets a new record every time he catches a pass, and he has been the best receiver I've ever had. He keeps the whole team loose. **Warren Muir** is really one of the best athletes I've had in the last ten years. He is a dead ringer for Jimmy Taylor in every way and just as good. We certainly believe that Warren should make All-America and he deserves it in every way. **Rudy Holloman** has really been something for us. He has come in for so very many **big** plays in the past three years. A fine receiver and runner—he has come up with some tremendous plays and has been invaluable to us. **Lynn Hodge** has been one of our most consistent performers for three years. He has made many big plays, but we have been most proud of the tremendous consistency and leadership he has given the 'Cocks. And his counterpart Dave Lucas probably has

DON BUCKNER

come up with as many big plays as anyone on our squad. Luke has the knack of coming through with a huge play right in the biggest possible clutch situation. **Don Buckner** has been one of the great 100%'ers on our squad for three years. It's hard to believe how many different places Buck has

PAT WATSON

played for the 'Cocks. He has **started** at both linebackers,

middle guard, end, offensive guard and fullback—and has done a darn good job at each spot. **Pat Watson** is hard to describe because almost no one would believe you. He's 151 lbs. and a three-year regular at defensive right halfback for the 'Cocks. He's really a fiesty one and one of the great leaders on our squad. What a warm place we have in our hearts for Pat! What a scrapper he has been.

And these 11 seniors have one more VICTORY to go after against arch rival Clemson. This is really a big one for those 11—and for all of us. Clemson is a good team and will be really cranked up for the game. They need to win it for a break-even season. They have lost to some excellent football teams. And they have had some fine victories, too. The records:

CLEMSON		CAROLINA	
21	VIRGINIA 14	27	DUKE 20
0	GEORGIA 30	14	NC 6
21	GEORGIA TECH 10	16	GEORGIA 41
0	AUBURN 51	21	NC STATE 16
28	WAKE 14	17	VPI 16
13	ALABAMA 38	17	MARYLAND 0
40	MARYLAND 0	9	FSU 34
27	DUKE 34	14	TENN 29
15	NC 32	24	WAKE 6
4	5	6	3

And so, we have finished the first half of the season. And now for the last half.

Hope to see you there!

From The
Gamecock Roost

Vol. 4, No. 14   Columbia, S. C.   December, 1969

THE ELEVEN BLACK HATS

WARREN MUIR
Fullback
Civil Engineering
Fitchburg, Mass.

FRED ZEIGLER
Split End
Business Administration
Reevesville

TONY FUSARO
Offensive Guard
Physical Education
Huntington, N. Y.

CO-CAPT. PAT WATSON
Defensive Halfback
Physical Education
Myrtle Beach

LYNN HODGE
Defensive End
Management
Union

DAVE LUCAS
Defensive End
International Studies
Bishopville

CAROLINA 27
CLEMSON 13

ANDY CHAVOUS
Safety
Pharmacy
Hepzibah, Ga.

RUDY HOLLOMAN
Tailback
Business Administration
Hartsville

KEN ROSS
Center
Education
Williamston

GEORGE McCARTHY
Defensive Tackle
English
Washington, D. C.

CO-CAPT. DON BUCKNER
Middle Guard
Management
Cleveland, Tenn.

TEN-GAME VARSITY STATISTICS
(Record: 7-3; ACC: 6-0; Home: 5-0; Away: 2-3)

TEAM	USC	OPP.
First downs rushing	73	126
First downs passing	80	60
First downs penalties	4	7
TOTAL FIRST DOWNS	157	193
Net yards rushing	1732	2005
Number of rushes	482	568
Game rushing average	173.2	200.5
Passing yardage	1499	1345
Game passing average	149.9	134.5
TOTAL OFFENSE	3231	3350
Passes attempted	222	208
Passes completed	122	102
Intercepted by	13	12
Number of punts	67	55
Yards punted	2568	2253
Punts had blocked	1	0
Punting average	38.3	41.0
Return yardage	379	371
Fumbles lost	9	17
Yards penalized	527	420

RUSHING	NO.	YDS.	AVG.	TD
Muir	205	917	4.5	8
Holloman	109	384	3.5	2
Rice	31	130	4.2	1
Simmons	33	107	3.2	0
Suggs	63	93	1.5	1
Miranda	20	66	3.3	0
Walkup	7	16	2.3	0
Yoakum	9	11	1.2	0
Trevillian	3	5	1.7	0
Sistare	2	3	1.5	0
TOTALS	482	1732	3.6	12
OPPONENTS	568	2005	3.5	11

PASSING	ATT.	COMP.	INT.	PCT.	YDS.	TD
Suggs	179	100	10	.559	1244	7
Yoakum	42	21	2	.500	236	3
Parker	1	1	0	1.000	19	0
TOTALS	222	122	12	.550	1499	10
OPPONENTS	208	102	13	.490	1345	9

TOTAL OFFENSE	RUSH	PASS	TOTAL
Suggs	93	1244	1337
Yoakum	11	236	247
Parker	0	19	19
(Others same as rushing)			

RECEIVING	NO.	YDS.	AVG.	TD
Zeigler	52	658	12.6	3
Holloman	21	317	15.1	5
Hamrick	15	176	11.7	1
Muir	11	157	14.3	0
Trevillian	5	47	9.4	0
Rice	4	52	13.0	0
Freeman	3	45	15.0	1
Walkup	3	15	5.0	0
Simmons	3	14	4.7	0
Miranda	3	4	1.3	0
Mitchell	2	14	7.0	0

INTERCEPTION RETURNS	NO.	YDS.	AVG.	TD
Watson	3	15	5.0	0
Harris	3	2	0.7	0
Chavous	2	24	12.0	0
Nash	2	21	11.5	0
Davies	2	5	2.5	0
Boyd	1	22	22.0	0

PUNT RETURNS	NO.	YDS.	AVG.	TD
Mitchell	15	186	12.4	1
Harris	10	77	7.7	0
Watson	2	7	3.5	0
Bailey	1	2	2.0	0

KICKOFF RETURNS	NO.	YDS.	AVG.	TD
Harris	18	467	25.5	0
Bailey	9	145	16.1	0
Davies	2	20	10.0	0
Hellams#	1	18	18.0	0
Pope	0	14	......	0
Wingard	2	7	3.5	0

PUNTING	NO.	YDS.	BLKD.	AVG.
Parker	66	2568		38.9
Team	----		1	----

SCORING	TD	PAT-K	PAT-RP	FG	TP
Muir	8	0-0	0-0	0-0	48
DuPre	0	21-21	0-0	9-19	48
Holloman	7	0-0	0-0	0-0	42
Zeigler	3	0-0	0-0	0-0	18
Suggs	1	0-0	0-0	0-0	6
Freeman	1	0-0	0-0	0-0	6
Rice	1	0-0	0-0	0-0	6
Mitchell	1	0-0	0-0	0-0	6
Hamrick	1	0-0	0-0	0-0	6
Yoakum	0	0-0	0-2	0-0	0
TOTALS	23	21-21	0-2	9-19	186
OPPONENTS	22	16-21	0-2	11-23	181

CUMULATIVE SCORE BY PERIODS:
GAMECOCKS	17	61	51	57	186
OPPONENTS	20	62	27	72	181

DEFENSIVE STATISTICS

	Tackles	Assists	Fumbles Caused	Fumbles Rec.
Tharpe	48	18	0	0
Padgett	43	14	0	0
Davies	42	16	2	1
Crabb	41	19	0	0
Harris	38	8	0	2
Nash	36	10	0	0
Poston	33	20	3	1
Hodge	33	12	1	2

From The
Gamecock Roost

Published weekly during football season and periodically throughout the year by the University of South Carolina GAMECOCK CLUB. Sent to members of the GAMECOCK CLUB in the interest of better education through athletics at Carolina. Republication of any of the contents is invited.

PAUL F. DIETZEL
Head Football Coach & Athletic Director

ED PITTS
Director, The Gamecock Club

Edited by TOM PRICE, Sports Information Director

ED SAYS
By ED PITTS

Ticket applications for Peach Bowl tickets were mailed to all 1969 Gamecock Club contributors November 20th. Tickets are $6.50 each. Please return your application and payment to the Ticket Office before December 3. We have held what we consider our better seats, which includes a good number of end zone seats, for our Gamecock Club contributors.

Gamecock Club members, Carolina Alumni, guests and friends of Carolina, are invited to stay and join in on all the festivities at Gamecock Headquarters, Calloway Gardens, at Pine Mountain, Georgia, on South Carolina Day Monday, December 29, 1969. The University of South Carolina Band and cheerleaders and many others are staying at Calloway for all Peach Bowl events. There will be a band concert at 8 p.m. on Monday, December 29 and a Carolina party afterward. Come and join in on the fun!

Calloway is easy to reach by car, bus, train, and air and is located on U. S. Highway 27, 80 miles southwest of Atlanta. For further information and reservations, write to Calloway Gardens, U. S. Highway 27, Pine Mountain, Georgia 31822, or call 404-663-2281.

BASKETBALL

Basketball Red Books are being mailed to all 1969 Gamecock Club contributors as fast as possible. Even though your neighbor may have received his Red Book, please wait until December 8 before you notify us that you have not received yours.

GAMECOCK BLAZERS

If you have not purchased your official Gamecock Blazer, there is a good chance our supplier has your size in stock if it is not larger than a 48 long. Gamecock blazers, including Carolina buttons, Gamecock Club patch, tax and handling are $65 each. You may send your jacket size and check to the Gamecock Club.

Kohout	32	10	0	2
Ganas	30	12	1	0
Watson	30	10	0	2
Lucas	28	8	0	2
Bailey	26	5	0	1
Wingard	24	6	0	0
Buckner	23	9	0	0
Pope	19	8	0	1
Boyd	19	4	0	0
Usher#	18	6	0	0
Chavous	17	3	0	1
Parker	13	3	0	1
McCarthy	5	4	0	0
Wright	5	3	0	0
Hellams#	2	0	0	0
Fusaro				1
Ross				1
Bank				1

(#—Injured and unavailable for Peach Bowl)

GREAT! JUST GREAT!

What a tremendous finish to our regular season! And better yet, what a fine "get-ready" for the PEACH BOWL!

In complete honesty for our first bowl we could not have picked a better one. WHY? Because all of our fans can attend the game. If it were farther away some of the loyal followers would have to miss it — and after their patient wait they certainly deserved to be able to see the game in person. Amazing but we sold nearly 5000 tickets the first couple of days we had them. (We will have told the Peach Bowlers a fib if we don't take a real **mob** of people to Atlanta.)

We had the most total offense against Clemson that has ever been mustered in a single game in South Carolina history — 517 yards. And our first touchdown in the first quarter this year. Would you believe — two touchdowns.

RECRUITING WARS

The game is really history and you know what it was like. Our entire team played real well. We are now off into the rough, tough recruiting wars. The signing date is December 13th at high noon. That is still a few weeks off, but it'll be a real busy time. This coming Saturday, I'm off to New York City for the All-American team weekend. As the President of the Coaches Association, I am sort of presiding over the weekend. Of course, Tuesday night we have our football banquet and that should be great.

OPEN PRACTICE

Our team will take a week or so off and then back to work. We will hold open practice sessions getting ready for the Bowl so you will be welcome to watch at any time that you like. We'll let you know our practice times.

And during this lay-off time, our fine basketball team will get under way. Frank and his whole gang have given us great support all year and we plan to repay the favor. We know that you all will give him the same splendid spirit you gave to the Gamecock Football team all fall.

Yep!

It's the Year of the Rooster!

44 Gamecocks Receive Letters; Muir MVP

Block C letters were awarded to 44 members of the 1969 Atlantic Coast Conference championship football squad November 26 at the fourth annual banquet sponsored by the USC Association of Lettermen, and fullback Warren Muir was named the Gamecocks' most valuable player.

Muir, who two days later was named to the American Football Coaches Association All-America football team, received the Steve Wadiak award as MVP.

Letters went to 11 seniors, 19 juniors and 14 sophomores who sparked the Gamecocks to a 7-3 overall record, a 6-0 ACC mark and a berth against West Virginia December 30 in the Peach Bowl game in Atlanta.

Defensive halfback Pat Watson of Myrtle Beach and middle guard Don Buckner of Cleveland, Tenn., received the co-captains awards and academic awards went to offensive guard Tony Fusaro of Huntington, N. Y., for the best academic average last year by a varsity player and to Jeff Tope of Aiken for best average last year by a freshman.

A new award, the George J. Terry award to a member of the scout squad who most unselfishly gave of himself to the Gamecock football program was presented to Eddie Whittington of Marion.

Senior letter winners included: Watson, Buckner, Muir, Fusaro, split end Fred Zeigler of Reevesville; tailback Rudy Holloman, Hartsville; defensive end Dave Lucas, Bishopville; defensive end Lynn Hodge, Union; center Ken Ross, Williamston; defensive back Andy Chavous, Hepzibah, Ga.; and defensive tackle George McCarthy, Washington, D. C.

Juniors: tight end Doug Hamrick, Cliffside, N. C.; offensive tackles Dave DeCamilla, Hudson Falls, N. Y., and Rick Hipkins, Boothwyn, Pa.; offensive guard Chris Bank, Joliet, Ill.; center Danny Dyches, Hanahan; quarterbacks Tommy Suggs, Lamar, and Randy Yoakum, Columbus, Ohio; flankers Tom Trevillian, Hampton, Va., and Ken Walkup, Timmonsville; defensive tackles Jimmy Poston, Canton, N. C., and Rusty Ganas, Waycross, Ga.; linebackers Mack Lee Tharpe, Greenwood, Benny Padgett, Rome, Ga., and Bill Parker, Kershaw; defensive ends Joe Wingard, Brevard, N. C., and Jimmy Pope, Rock Hill; defensive backs Don Bailey, John's Island, and Candler Boyd, Hinesville, Ga.; and kicking specialist Billy DuPre, Columbia.

Sophomores: tight end Billy Freeman, Clinton; split end Jim Mitchell, Greensboro, N. C.; offensive tackles Joe Regalis, Tomaqua, Pa., and Bill Boyte, Camden; offensive guards Richie Moye, West Columbia, and Ken Wheat, Milledgeville, Ga.; fullback Tommy Simmons, Buffalo; tailback Billy Ray Rice, Gaffney; defensive backs Dick Harris, Point Pleasant Beach, N. J., Bo Davies, Gettysburg, Pa., and Jimmy Nash, Charlotte, N. C.; defensive tackle Jake Wright, Varnville; middle guard Pat Kohout, Hampton, Va.; and linebacker Greg Crabb of Dublin, Ga.

The list of lettermen includes 22 offensive players, 21 defensive players and one specialist.

From The
Gamecock Roost

Vol. 5, No. 1   Columbia, S. C.   January, 1970

FROM COACH PAUL DIETZEL

PEACH BOWL REPORT

Coach Jim Carlen of West Virginia on Saturday before the Tuesday game said, "We want every advantage we can get! We've played and won in the rain or snow six times this year. I hope we have sleet and rain, at the least!"

The day before the game we worked out briefly in Grant Field, and it was obvious that there was precious little turf on the field. At the time I said to our coaches privately, "I'd hate to have to play here if we had any rain. It wouldn't take much!"

CLOUDBURST

It was great weather up until about six o'clock the night of the game. Had we played in the afternoon, there would have been no problem. The tarpaulin was removed early so that the TV cameras could get focused; at about 6:45 p.m. the roof really caved in! **What a cloudburst!!** That's the first time I can ever remember getting absolutely soaked running 75 yards from our bus to the dressing room before a game. The field became an absolute quagmire. Can't remember ever walking on a field before a game and being ankle-deep in water—in the **middle** of the field. Then seven bands sloshed around and eliminated any semblance of turf that there might have been.

After the game was over, I really had to bite my tongue to keep from saying anything about the weather, but I felt that it was really very obvious to anyone who was interested anyway. And then lots of folks would have had comments about our "making excuses for the loss." We needed to make no excuses—our team played their guts out. And that bunch of seniors were something else again. Pat Watson—what a **Fighting Cock!!!**

The rain actually eliminated every asset we had going for us. The plusses we have on defense are our quickness, our team hustle, and our desire and pursuit. The mud really eradicated everything except the desire and hustle. And our 150-pound deep backs really had a time getting those big backs of W. Virginia's down. They were good ones!! After the game, several members of the press asked me if Williams had really surprised me or hurt us? I told them that it was so muddy that I had no idea who it was, but someone out there was doing some real damage.

As to our offense, it has been no secret that our offense

has been going on the scrambling and passing of Tommy Suggs to Zeigler and Holloman, and the running of Warren Muir. When we played in that quagmire, we utterly lost the effectiveness of our air arm, and that was a devastating blow.

Perhaps we would have been beaten by the Mountaineers on a beautiful, dry night. We'll never know. But I am convinced of two things:

1. If we played that same West Virginia team in the same quagmire, under the same conditions, we would lose to them four out of five times.

2. If we played them on a dry field, with normally good playing conditions, we would beat them four out of five times.

As I said, I am completely convinced of those two facts and I do have a right to my opinion.

A GOOD BOWL

As to the Peach Bowl: A famous poet once said, "It is far better to have loved and lost than never to have loved at all."

As much as I abhorred losing that game, I'm still happy that we were invited, accepted, and played in Atlanta. It is a good Bowl and a start in the proper direction. And I am proud of the 1969 Atlantic Coast Conference Champions. We wanted to be **sure** to win the ACC Crown **THIS YEAR**—the Year of the Rooster!

BASKETBALL

And now to Basketball. What a real pleasure it is for us to enjoy Coach Frank McGuire and his men. They are a fine bunch and we are mighty proud of them. We hope for them the greatest of success, but we're 100% for them regardless of the outcome. They have pulled for football all through the year and we have appreciated them immensely. And we hope that you will give them the same great enthusiasm and support that you gave to the football Gamecocks.

A Most Happy and Blessed New Year to You.

Special Offer to GAMECOCK CLUB MEMBERS:

The album TOTAL EXCITEMENT featuring Bob Fulton's

(Continued on Page Two)

367

ED SAYS

By ED PITTS

PEACH BOWL TICKETS

We have heard from many good Carolina supporters who were unhappy with the location of their seats for the Peach Bowl, and I am sure that many of you were dissatisfied with the location of your seats even though you did not inform us. I can certainly understand your feelings and really don't blame you for being dissatisfied. We were very disappointed when we did not receive tickets for more desirable seats from the Peach Bowl Office.

We took this up with the Peach Bowl officials, and they informed us that the Peach Bowl is sponsored by the Lions Club of Georgia and receives financial backing from Davison's and other large companies in Georgia. They also informed us that the above mentioned had an opportunity to purchase as many tickets as they would like in a desirable location before either of the teams had been given an invitation to play in the game. The Peach Bowl also mails ticket applications to a large number of people and fills their ticket orders before the bids are actually given to the teams. Last year the two teams that played in the Peach Bowl sold an average of 2,000 tickets each. We feel sure that this was in the minds of the Peach Bowl officials when they sent University of South Carolina and West Virginia their allotment of tickets this year.

The University of South Carolina originally received a total of 15,000 tickets. These tickets were for seats located in the lower parts of Sections one through six, 120 tickets for seats in the upper part of Section one, and 500 tickets in the upper part of Section two. USC also received tickets for seats in Sections 33, 34, 35, 36, 37, 39, 40, 51, 52, 53, 57 and 58. At our request for additional tickets the Peach Bowl officials sent us 4,800 tickets for seats in Sections 11 through 16.

We were advised by the Peach Bowl officials that for a night game in December the upper deck would be the least desirable seats in the stadium, so we sold Sections 51, 52, 53, 57 and 58 along with Sections 39 and 40, which are temporary bleacher seats, to the general public.

The Athletic Department used all of the tickets we received in Section six and some in Sections four and five for our athletes, coaches, University President, Trustees and Press. Requests from Full Scholarship Donors took the remainder of seats in Section five, Half Scholarship Donors were assigned seats in Sections four and three, Roundhouse contributors received tickets for the remainder of Section three, Section two, part of Section one and part of Section 11. Century Club contributors received tickets for the remainder of Sections one and 11 with the majority of Century Club members receiving tickets for seats located in the end zone. Gamecock Club members were assigned seats in the end zone. Orders for additional tickets were also filled in the end zone.

EASTERN REGIONALS

The University Ticket Office began accepting orders after midnight, Tuesday, December 9, for tickets to the

From The
Gamecock Roost

Published weekly during football season and periodically throughout the year by the University of South Carolina GAMECOCK CLUB. Sent to members of the GAMECOCK CLUB in the interest of better education through athletics at Carolina. Republication of any of the contents is invited.

PAUL F. DIETZEL
Head Football Coach & Athletic Director
ED PITTS
Director, The Gamecock Club
Edited by TOM PRICE, Sports Information Director

1970 Eastern Regional Basketball Tournament scheduled for March 12-14 in Carolina Coliseum. On December 13 the Ticket Office declared a sellout. The Regional Tournament is controlled by the NCAA. The policy for the distribution of tickets was set by the NCAA. Only mail orders could be accepted. Each purchaser could order no more than two tickets per mail order. All orders will be filled by the University Ticket Office on a first received basis.

The Gamecock Club has nothing to do with the distribution of these tickets.

BLAZERS

If you do not have your Gamecock blazer, there is a good chance our supplier has your size in stock. The official blazer, including Carolina buttons and Gamecock Club patch, are $65.00. Please send your check and jacket size to the Gamecock Club, University of South Carolina, Columbia, S. C. 29208

RENEWALS

Gamecock Club membership renewal applications will be mailed around February 1.

FROM COACH PAUL DIETZEL
(Continued From Page One)

play-by-play of the recorded highlights of Carolina's championship football season is now available through the Gamecock Club at the special price of $4.50, which includes tax and mailing costs. Profits from sale of this album will go to the Gamecock Club.

If you wish to order five albums or more, the cost per album would be $4.00.

Coach Paul Dietzel said, "This is a super album capturing all the highlights of our championship season. It would be a nice thing for all Gamecock fans to save as a memento of this season."

Fill out your order blank below:

I want_____(no.) albums

Mail to:_____

Address_____

City_____State_____Zip Code_____

Enclose check made payable to
RICHLAND CUSTOM RECORDING.

Mail order to: GAMECOCK CLUB,
University of South Carolina,
Columbia, S. C. 29208

Contract Let For Spring Sports Center

The University has awarded a contract for construction of the George J. Terry Memorial Spring Sports Center at the Rex Enright Athletic Center to Charles J. Craig Construction Co., of Columbia.

The $375,000 project—to be financed entirely with athletic department funds, primarily football gate receipts—is expected to be completed by Oct. 15. Architect for the project is James Lupton of Columbia.

The new spring sports center will be named in memory of George J. Terry, Assistant Director of Athletics, who died last summer. The project includes a three-story building of approximately 11,000 square feet of floor space, four outdoor handball courts and an outdoor basketball court.

It will be located just West of The Roost, the University's residence-dining facility for student athletes, at the North end of the 22-acre complex known as the Rex Enright Athletic Center.

The lowest floor of the building will be used for storage of equipment and supplies necessary to maintain the athletic fields at the athletic center and to house mechanical equipment required for heating and air conditioning the building.

The middle floor will provide varsity and freshman dressing rooms, showers, etc., for spring sports, a training room, an athletic equipment storage room and two coaches' offices.

The top floor will contain two visiting team dressing rooms, showers, etc., a visitor's training room, an officials' room, visiting coaches' room, public rest rooms, concession area and extra space which may be used for additional sports. Provision has been made for a large sun bathing area on the roof.

The spring sports center will be close to and easily accessible to the residential elements of The Roost and will, in addition to providing needed space for spring sports, will provide all students on athletic scholarship with a place for recreational exercise.

Director of Athletics Paul Dietzel hailed the new spring sports center as another big step toward the ultimate goal of providing the University with athletic facilities in all sports unsurpassed in collegiate athletics.

"This spring sports center was the dream of George Terry and he worked very hard to make it a reality," Dietzel said. "It is very fitting that the trustees have honored his memory by naming this new facility the George J. Terry Memorial Spring Sports Center."

Basketball Gamecocks 12-1; Turn To Exams

Carolina's Atlantic Coast Conference leading basketball Gamecocks turned their attention to fall semester final examinations after surviving a series of slowdown tactics by opponents that resulted in low scoring games but failed to prevent Gamecock victories.

Carolina reached the halfway point in its regular season with a 12-1 overall record, including 11 wins in a row. Only a one-point loss to Tennessee in the second game of the season mars the record. In the Atlantic Coast Conference the Gamecocks are 5-0. All other teams have lost at least one ACC game.

The next action for Coach Frank McGuire's Gamecocks is Jan. 26 at Clemson with the next Carolina Coliseum game scheduled for Jan. 28 against non-conference opponent Virginia Tech.

The Gamecocks won their fourth low scoring game in a row at Furman although the Paladins did not resort to the outright stall that North Carolina, Maryland and Duke had tried in futile attempts to upset South Carolina in the three previous games.

Coach Frank Selvy had his big men set high post screens with guards Charles Selvy (the coach's brother) and Jerry Martin attempting to pick off the Gamecock guarding them for open jump shots. Selvy, who had been averaging less than 11 points per game, had 15 at the half and 22 for the night. Martin—a 36 per cent shooter for the season—hit 10 of 20 from the outside to score 21 points.

The strategy worked so well that Furman led 33-31 at halftime, but All-America John Roche took personal charge of the game to shoot the Gamecocks to a nine-point lead in the second half. Furman scored eight straight points to cut it to one but the Gamecocks held on to win by three, 59-56. Roche scored 23 points.

At the semester break Roche is averaging 20.4 points per game while Tom Owens is averaging 18.1 and an ACC-leading 14.8 rebounds. Overall scoring and rebounding totals have taken a tumble in the face of the slowdown tactics. Sophomore center Tom Piker is averaging 14.2 points and nine rebounds per game. Sophomore Rick Aydlett is scoring at a 5.8 pace as the Gamecocks' sixth man while starters Bobby Cremins and John Ribock are averaging 5.5 points each.

While the slowdowns have hurt the individual and team scoring averages, they have bolstered the Gamecocks defensively. Among the top three teams in the nation all season in defense against scoring, Carolina saw its defensive average drop to 55.5 points per game after holding Maryland to 44 points, Virginia to 42, North Carolina to 52 and Furman to 56.

Through the first half of the season the Gamecocks are outscoring their opponents an average of 18.8 points per game.

Colophon

This book has been designed for an 8 x 10" format with a basic two column grid with 6 master pages in InDesign CS6. Running copy typesetting is 9.85/11.5pt Bertold Garamond Regular.

Günter Gerhard Lange studied the original Claude Garamond *(ca. 1490 – 1561, was a French publisher from Paris and was one of the leading type designers of his time)* prints extensively before adapting his own interpretation, released by Berthold in 1972.

Title and chapter heads are set in Athletic, while chapter subheads are 9.5/11.5 Frutiger 65 Bold.

Frutiger is a sans-serif typeface by the Swiss type designer Adrian Frutiger. It was commissioned in 1968 by the newly built Charles de Gaulle International Airport at Roissy, France. Originally called *Roissy*, was completed in 1975 and installed at the airport the same year. Frutiger's goal was to create a sans-serif typeface with the rationality and cleanliness of Univers, but the organic and proportional aspects of Gill Sans.

Cover photographs are made with a Nikon D800 using a AF-S 70-200 f/2.8 ED VR II lens at f/8 @ 1/3 sec. and f/10 @ 1/2 sec.

20687700R00209

Made in the USA
San Bernardino, CA
20 April 2015